AMERICAN POLITICS

AMERICAN POLITICS

THE PEOPLE
AND THE POLITY

SECOND EDITION

Peter K. Eisinger
UNIVERSITY OF WISCONSIN, MADISON

Dennis L. Dresang
UNIVERSITY OF WISCONSIN, MADISON

Robert Booth Fowler
UNIVERSITY OF WISCONSIN, MADISON

Joel B. Grossman
UNIVERSITY OF WISCONSIN, MADISON

Burdett A. Loomis
UNIVERSITY OF KANSAS

Richard M. Merelman
UNIVERSITY OF WISCONSIN, MADISON

Little, Brown and Company
BOSTON   TORONTO

Library of Congress Catalog Card No. 81–84228
ISBN 0-316-22564-9

9 8 7 6 5 4 3

BP
Published simultaneously in Canada
by Little, Brown & Company (Canada) Limited
Printed in the United States of America

PHOTOGRAPH CREDITS

p. 4 United Press International (top and bottom right); © Dennis Brack/ Black Star (bottom left). p. 7 Joe Peirotti, reprinted by permission of the New York Post © 1974, New York Post Corp. (top left); Library of Congress (bottom left); © 1980 Ed Gamble/ Nashville Banner (right). p. 14 The Bettmann Archive (top left); New York State Historical Association, Cooperstown (bottom right). p. 27 Independence National Historical Park Collection (left); The Bettmann Archive (center); Charles Wilson Peale, courtesy of The Thomas Gilcrease Institute of American History and Art, Tulsa, Oklahoma (right). p. 18 The Library of Congress. p. 58 © Ivan Massar/ Black Star. p. 59 United Press International (top); © John Lemois/ Black Star (bottom left); © Anthony Korody/ Black Star (bottom right). p. 75 United Press International (bottom left); Photo Trends (top); Michael Abramson/ Liason Agency (bottom right). p. 69 The Granger Collection. p. 88 © Bern Keating/ Black Star (top left); United Press International (top right and bottom). p. 89 United Press International. p. 98 © Gil Kenny/ Black Star (top right); © Cary Wolinsky/ Stock, Boston (bottom right); Marilyn K. Yee/ New York Times Pictures (top left); © Doug Wilson/ Black Star (bottom left). p. 113 Wide World Photos (top); Arthur Grace/ Sygma (center); United Press International (bottom). p. 133 © Dennis Brack/ Black Star (top right); Owen Franklin/ Sygma (top left); White House Photo/ United Press International (center right); United Press International (bottom right). p. 164 Arthur Grace/ Sygma (top right); Tom Zimberoff/ Sygma (bottom right). p. 165 Black Star (top left); © Dennis Brack/ Black Star (bottom left); © 1933 New York News, Inc. (top right); Courtesy of the Franklin D. Roosevelt Library, Hyde Park, N.Y. (bottom right). p. 169 Historical Pictures Service, Chicago (top and center right); The Granger Collection (bottom right). p. 200 © 1975 The Chicago Tribune/ Historical Pictures Service, Chicago (top); Neal Boenzi/ New York Times Pictures (bottom left). p. 214 © Marc PoKempner/ Black Star. p. 246 United Press International; p. 247 Wide World Photos (top left); United Press International (center left); Wide World Photos (top left). p. 254 From *Herblock on All Fronts* (New American Library, 1980) © 1977 by Herblock in *The Washington Post* (top right);

Continued on p. 556

THE AUTHORS

Peter K. Eisinger (Ph.D., Yale University), Professor of Political Science at the University of Wisconsin-Madison, specializes in ethnic group and urban politics. He wrote Chapters 4 and 6, and was the coordinator of *American Politics,* second edition.

Dennis L. Dresang (Ph.D., University of California, Los Angeles) is Professor of Political Science at the University of Wisconsin-Madison. His fields of specialty are comparative politics and public administration. He wrote Chapters 7 and 13.

Robert Booth Fowler (Ph.D., Harvard University) is Professor of Political Science at the University of Wisconsin-Madison. His area of concentration is contemporary American political thought. He is responsible for Chapters 15 and 16.

Joel B. Grossman (Ph.D., University of Iowa) is Professor of Political Science at the University of Wisconsin-Madison. He specializes in judicial politics and Constitutional law. He contributed Chapters 8, 9, and 14.

Burdett A. Loomis (Ph.D., University of Wisconsin) is Associate Professor of Political Science at the University of Kansas. A Congressional Fellow, his area of concentration is Congress. He wrote Chapters 5, 11, and 12.

Richard M. Merelman (Ph.D., Yale University) is Professor of Political Science at the University of Wisconsin-Madison. He specializes in political socialization and political culture. His contributions to the text are Chapters 2, 3, and 10.

PREFACE

This is a book about how Americans have tried to reconcile two political values often in conflict with one another: democracy and authority. Over the course of our history the American people have sought with varying degrees of success to make the nation more democratic; that is, to create greater possibilities and more opportunities for rule by the people. The expansion of the franchise, the direct election of senators, the opening up of party conventions, the extension of primary elections, the growth of citizen participation requirements in public policy-making, the development of investigative journalism, and the challenge to seniority norms in Congress are some examples of efforts to make the ideal of rule by the people a more genuine possibility.

Yet democratic politics — a politics of participation, of open debate, of compromise — can be terribly slow in getting things done. Furthermore, democracy assumes a certain degree of equality among citizens, but if anything is to get done, a few people must have authority over the many. The critical question is: How can the desire for democratic rule by the many be balanced against the need for effective authority by the few?

The problem is clearly vexing from the citizens' point of view. How can they make sure that the few in authority will do what the people want? How can citizens check the power of those in high office, at least enough to prevent abuses of authority? For those in positions of power — our political leaders — the problem of democracy and authority is equally troubling. It is not that leaders all have antidemocratic tendencies; but how do they figure out what the people want? The people do not speak with one voice. And how are leaders to act confidently and decisively amidst the clamor of public debate or in the face of popular suspicion of power?

The tension that develops in a democratic society between the ideal of citizen rule and the need for leaders to exercise authority cannot explain all of American politics. Often authority is exercised to expand or protect popular influence, as when the franchise is extended or when the courts rule to protect the civil liberties of unpopular groups. Then, too, there are some facets of American politics that are best understood as a competition among more or less equal interest groups, in which questions of authority and democracy are not paramount.

We believe, nevertheless, that the tension between leaders and the led, between those in government trying to exercise authority and a citizenry wishing to have its say, offers a rich focal point for exploring the dynamics of politics in the United States. Such a perspective helps us to understand our historical obsession with the power of the presidency as well as our growing lack of confidence of Congress. It sheds light on our resistance to strong centralized parties and our enduring commitment to some notion of state power in the federal system. And it helps to explain our tolerance for a strong, policy-oriented judiciary while at the same time extolling the benefits and virtues of majority rule. The political stage crowded with interest groups and the American attraction to elections can best be understood as products of our democratic impulses, and so can our concern for the quality of our civil liberties. "Don't Tread on Me" was our first motto, the tax revolt, its modern progeny.

The organizing perspective of this book is a flexible one. It allows the instructor to treat most aspects of American government and politics without forcing the material into a set of ideological pigeonholes or into a particular disciplinary approach. It raises questions broad enough to permit the comprehensive treatment of the subject necessary to a basic college course. Yet the theme of democracy and authority is developed and pervasive enough to provide a coherence to the book and a sense of the institutional and cultural connections among the elements of American politics.

We have changed much of the book for this second edition. Naturally the material has been updated. Our efforts have involved more than keeping abreast of the current news, however; a number of key chapters have been entirely rethought to take account of changing patterns in American politics. The resurgence of the presidency under Ronald Reagan, the contraction of federal intergovernmental aid, the Democratic retreat from convention reform, the supine Congress — all could not easily have been anticipated when we published the first edition. Fortunately, in textbook writing there is generally a second chance.

We have also added some new material. Our treatment of the Constitution is far more extensive than in the first edition of the book, and we have added a substantial chapter on individual rights. Our chapter on policy-making includes a case study of the budget process during Reagan's first year in office; and new material on the president's role in economic policy-making has been incorporated into Chapter 6.

We have always felt that the special strength of this book lay in our diverse skills and interests. Each of the authors was responsible for certain chapters, but, as with the first edition, the entire manuscript was read by each of us and one person took responsibility for editing. The book is, then, a collective product, the beneficiary (or victim) of many shared discussions in the corridors of North Hall and its environs. We were, it is good to report, friends when this enterprise began in the mid-1970s, and we still are.

Two editors at Little, Brown have played shepherd to this second edition, Greg Franklin and Will Ethridge. We are grateful for their support and (we admit) for their occasional sensible guidance. Jane Muse, our book editor, saw the book through from typescript to bound version, and Mary Grossman (with Alison and Joanna) again prepared the index. The secretarial staff at the University of Wisconsin — Judy Lerdahl, Betsy Johnson, Renee Gibson, and Norma Lynch — provided helpful assistance, for which we thank them.

We thank the following people for reviewing the manuscript: Lawrence Baum, Ohio State University; John Bibby, University of Wisconsin; Charles Bullock, University of Georgia; Bradley Canon, University of Kentucky; Eric Davis, Middlebury College; Lawrence Dodd, Indiana University; George Edwards, Texas A & M University; Charles Elder, Wayne State University; Richard Elling, Wayne State University; Jeff Fishel, American University; John Harrigan, Hamline University; Robert Huckshorn, Florida Atlantic University; Herbert Jacob, Northwestern University; Michael Maggiotto, University of Florida; Francis Rourke, Johns Hopkins University; Allan Sindler, University of California-Berkeley; Jack Walker, University of Michigan; and John Hendry.

CONTENTS

Chapter 1 Introduction

For many years the United States has been among the leading countries in the world in the faithful payment of taxes by citizens. Over three-quarters of American taxpayers regularly pay all their legally obligated taxes, with the remaining quarter evading at least some portion of their taxes. This rate of compliance is a considerable achievement; other western societies have not been so lucky.

Why do so many Americans pay all their taxes? True, the penalties for proven tax evasion are unpleasant, but it is hard to catch most evaders. The Internal Revenue Service maintains only a handful of auditors, who check less than 2 percent of all tax returns. Most tax cheaters, therefore, go undetected. And certainly most Americans would love to use their tax money on a new house or a second car. Thus, Americans have both the motive and the opportunity to evade. Why have they not done so in greater numbers?

One reason is that for most Americans paying taxes constitutes a vote of confidence in our government. Americans believe in the argument that taxes are an important obligation they owe to the country as a whole. Fewer people pay taxes out of fear of being caught for noncompliance than out of a positive feeling of political obligation.

It is therefore significant that the "underground economy" in the United States (income received, say, from garage sales or for various services that are not reported for tax purposes) has grown markedly in recent years. Some estimates now place the unrecorded sector of the economy at as much as 20 percent of the gross national product (the total amount of goods and services Americans produce); the underground economy is growing twice as fast as the rest of our economy. Thus, tax evasion and tax cheating appear increasingly acceptable to many Americans. Why? Possibly because many Americans believe that taxes are spent inefficiently or for the wrong purposes.

Tax cheating has important economic and social consequences, but its real significance may lie in what it tells us about the relationship between our government and its citizens — our polity and our people. A large increase in tax cheating is evidence of citizens' increasing unhappiness with the American political process. It is an illustration of a growing tension between government, which is seen as too expensive, inefficient, and corrupt, and the ordinary citizen, who must contend with the harsh and often inequitable impact of inflation.

THE TENSION BETWEEN GOVERNED AND GOVERNORS IN AMERICA

The inevitable discrepancy in power between government and the people — the leaders and the led — creates tension in any society. Power may be used to good ends, and every society requires some decisions to be made that affect all. But power may also do harm. The concentrated power of government may send one's children to die in a war, empty cities of their people (as recently occurred in Cambodia), misuse public resources, or enforce total racial segregation (as in contemporary South Africa). Thus it is not surprising that people in all political systems fear government even as they need it; for the people are usually weak, and government is usually strong.

Yet in most countries people accept the discrepancy in power between themselves and their leaders as inevitable. They have no voice in government, and they have little recourse against the abuse of power. Perhaps their leaders emerge from ancient aristocracies, or from the only political party, or from a small body of wealthy landowners. In such cases people have a limited choice among leaders, if they have any choice at all. To bring about political change they must act forcefully — often violently. They lack the power either to bring about peaceful change or the peaceful reduction of tension between themselves and their leaders.

In a system that aspires to be democratic, the inevitable tension between leaders and led is especially poignant. In the United States we have tried to manufacture traditions, institutions, and practices that will allow for peaceful change in the balance of tension between leaders and led. Unlike people in less democratic systems, we firmly espouse the belief that people should control their own destinies. Our democratic tradition makes the continued tension between leaders and led a central aspect of our political life. We invite people to suspect and challenge authority. But the cost of this is that we are faced constantly with the contrast between our ideal of peaceful popular control of government and the reality of unequal power.

Consider, for example, expectations about the conduct of our leaders. Writing over 150 years ago about life in the United States, the Frenchman Alexis de Toqueville was greatly impressed that public officials in America seemed in appearance to be indistinguishable from ordinary citizens. Simple in manners, American officials had neither palaces nor guards; more noteworthy still, they did not wear ceremonial costumes. Toqueville considered all this a telling characteristic of democratic government: in his view, here was visible evidence that the American people were governing themselves.

Americans have always chosen leaders from a diversity of backgrounds, elevating to the highest offices ordinary people who were once actors, peanut farmers, lawyers, men's clothing salesmen, and college professors. We do not call on a hereditary aristocracy or a royal family to perform our governing chores. But if our public officials do not look or act in essential ways differently from the rest of us, there is nevertheless an important difference: Public officials are distinguished by the fact that they possess formal authority to make enforceable decisions that affect us all.

American democracy is not limited to the comparatively ordinary origins of our leaders. It also embraces three basic ideals, from which much else of importance flows. These ideals are *political equality, popular sovereignty,* and *individual liberty.*

Political equality is the belief that people ought to have equal power over government decisions and ought to be treated equally by government. In practice, political equality means that there should be no privileged group of people able to shape power exclusively to their own selfish ends. Each person is equally worthy of respect; therefore, each person should have the same right to share in the common task of governance.

Popular sovereignty is the belief that the people should rule. This ideal is essential to any system that calls itself democratic; it goes back to the first democracy, fifth century Athens. Popular sovereignty rests on the proposition that the ordinary person knows what is best for himself or herself. No one else, no matter how intelligent or compassionate, can say what is best for that particular person. Therefore, if government is to work for the good of society, it can do so only by heeding the expressed desires of the people. If people cannot make crucial governmental decisions themselves, then they should at least make sure that their leaders make the decisions the people themselves prefer.

Individual liberty is the belief that each person should retain some area of private control over his or her life, an area free from the intrusions of other people or of government. Decisions about where to live, whom or whether to marry, whether to have children, what job to seek, what career to pursue — these are decisions that fall within the individual's private domain of liberty. The line between the individual's rightful sphere of liberty and the public's rightful domain of decisions is not clear. Quarrels about where to draw the line contribute to the tension between citizens and their leaders.

Today the United States is a nation of more than 225 million people who

"Just Folks" at the Top

Presidents often make conscious efforts to appear ordinary: pictures of Reagan relaxing after chopping wood at his ranch, Carter carrying his own clothes bag, and Ford toasting his own English muffin all project images of presidents as "just folks." These moments of informality may be understood as deliberate appeals to the public for support for a fellow citizen thrust into a demanding and complex office.

come from a remarkable variety of ethnic, religious, and racial backgrounds. We inhabit a vast and diverse landscape, cherish varied aspirations, possess different needs, and depend for our livelihoods on very different occupations. Governing ourselves is a complex business.

Because of our size and complexity we have created an elaborate set of local, state, and national governmental institutions to make and carry out the processes of government. We have staffed these with nearly 520,000 elected officials and about 16 million civilian public servants ranging from file clerks and janitors to engineers, budget analysts, research scientists, and high-level administrators. It is between these comparatively "few" decision makers and the citizenry that the tension we speak of develops. This tension raises some fundamental questions about the processes of democratic government in America:

If all are to be equal politically, what is the best way to give a few unequal authority over others?

How can liberty be enjoyed by the many when authority is in the hands of the few?

How can the people rule when all the people are not organized politically?

Once the few gain authority, is there a way to limit that authority? And how much should it be limited?

If all are politically equal, whose interests and desires are the few to heed when there are disagreements?

It is evident from these questions that the tension between citizens and leaders in America may be understood as (1) a struggle over the limits of governmental authority and (2) a struggle over the degree to which popular desires are to influence the decisions of leaders. As for the first, citizens must maintain constant vigilance against possible abuses of authority, while at the same time leaders must seek to amass enough authority to govern effectively. As for the second, the question is whether popular desires will prevail in every case or whether the "inside" knowledge and experience of those in leadership positions will always play the decisive role.

AMERICAN POLITICAL TRADITIONS AND INSTITUTIONS Americans have tried to manage these struggles by employing democratic principles and constitutional checks to distribute and limit authority and to provide a delicate balance in decision making between popular influence and the great influence of leaders. Here are some of the institutions and principles we employ.

Elections Because Americans are too numerous to have a *direct* say in the policies of government, we understand political equality to imply that each person should at least have an equal say in who shall have the authority to make those policies. We choose leaders to represent us through free, competitive elections.

The unequal distribution of authority, then, is accomplished by the more or less equal choice of the people themselves.

Democracy requires, however, that those who achieve positions of authority must be checked, and that they must be accountable for their actions. There are several ways in which this is accomplished in the United States. For example, our Constitution requires *periodic* elections as a way of allowing citizens regularly to review and pass judgment on the record of incumbents. Elections are also occasions for new leaders to gain positions of authority. The need to account to the people and the threat of electoral challenge is not only an important check on the exercise of authority, but is also a way of encouraging responsiveness by leaders to popular desires.

The Tradition of Rights We also limit authority by protecting certain rights and liberties: Freedom of speech and religious belief, the freedom to organize groups, the freedom to write and publish are examples of rights we guarantee to all people. By protecting these civil liberties, American democracy not only limits the scope of authority, but also seeks to make sure that those in positions of authority will be open to constant public scrutiny and criticism. It is harder to abuse authority under the watchful eye of a free press and a political opposition than to do so where the press is controlled and a political opposition nonexistent.

Checks and Balances Americans designed a constitutional framework for our democratic processes in which authority, although held by the few, is divided. This is known as the theory of checks and balances. As James Madison argued in *The Federalist Papers*, the separate and distinct exercise of power by an executive, a legislature, and a judiciary "is essential to the preservation of liberty." Each branch of government can in some way check the others, as, for example, when the president vetoes a bill passed by Congress or when the Supreme Court declares an action of the president unconstitutional. This system of checks and balances among the three branches of the national government is known as the theory of *separation of powers*. But there is another set of checks and balances — that between the nation and the states. Under our Constitution, the national government has only those powers delegated to it (or fairly implied from those delegated powers) by the Constitution. All other powers not specifically prohibited by the Constitution are reserved by it to the states, or to the people. This vertical division of authority is known as *federalism*.

Majority Rule The authority of leaders may be limited, but those leaders must still make decisions, often of a momentous nature. What criteria are they to use in making these decisions, in choosing between various policy alternatives? How are they to act in the face of honest disagreements? The answer that democracy provides is that the will of the majority prevails. In practice this democratic rule is not easy to follow, nor may it always be desirable to do so. It is difficult to ascertain the will of the majority with respect to many issues; even when preferences can be ascertained, they cannot (or should not) be followed if they

Abusing the Authority of Government

   Corruption in government, even at the highest levels, has not been uncommon in American politics. Ulysses S. Grant's administration was afflicted by several financial scandals (none actually involving the president himself), and Warren Harding's presidency is best remembered for the Teapot Dome affair. Harding's Interior Secretary connived to turn over the Teapot Dome oil deposits, which had been set aside for the Navy, to private oil companies, all at great profit to himself. The Watergate revelations during the Nixon presidency were unique, however, for these abuses of power in the Oval Office itself threatened the basic fabric of constitutional government.

threaten minority rights. Nevertheless, the will of the majority offers a standard against which the legitimacy of decisions may be judged.

MANAGING THE TENSION IN PRACTICE Democracy is a way of managing the tension between a free citizenry and its leaders. The principles and practices of democracy and constitutionalism that we have just discussed — popular elections, civil liberties, checks and balances, majority rule — are attempts to keep this tension from getting out of hand. In the chapters that follow in this book, we ask over and over again the following questions: To what extent do American political institutions operate in ways consistent with democratic principles? How well do the processes and safeguards of American politics work to manage the tension between leaders and citizens? If democracy is to work, what are the responsibilities of the citizenry?

Democracy is an elusive ideal. In the 1970s we worried that the institutions we had nurtured over our two-hundred-year history were no longer working very well. Americans clearly suffered a crisis of confidence in government. The power of the presidency, particularly in the early part of the decade, seemed unchecked. Political parties, which Americans counted on to organize opinion and contest elections, seemed in disarray. Political leaders, especially those in Congress, commanded scant respect from the citizenry they were supposed to represent. Indictments of public officials for corruption rose annually in the years following the Watergate scandals of the Nixon administration. Citizens and leaders seemed to be talking past one another. Government was widely perceived as ineffective in the face of challenges both in the international sphere and on the domestic economic front.

Technological innovation and industrial development have presented Americans with special difficulties in managing the tension between leaders and the led. Great centers of private power have grown up to threaten both the power of the people and that of government itself. Consider the massive corporations that have dominated markets for oil, automobiles, and other important economic goods. These corporations are private, and are therefore not formally accountable to the public. Yet they wield tremendous power over the lives of all Americans. Should government attempt to control them? Can the people control them?

Of course, the government itself has taken an active role in trying to control the economy, through a bewildering variety of regulatory agencies, financial subsidies, tax policies, and direct assistance to corporations and individuals. The government has been a builder of homes, a provider of hot lunches for school children, an underwriter of cheap mortgage loans, and a producer of cheap electric energy. Is the government too big and cumbersome as a regulatory force? Does government stifle initiative among private business people? Is government insensitive either to public wants or to the needs of business?

The primary areas in which government in the twentieth century has grown are defense and social services. We retain a large standing army. We constantly design new weapons of war, which are costly to the taxpayers while providing large profits to arms manufacturers. Can we support a massive military establishment without effectively removing government from the hands of the people? Can we maintain our international position while shrinking the size of the defense sector to manageable proportions? At the same time, since the New Deal of the 1930s, government has provided an increasing array of services and funds to public education; to medical care for the elderly and the poor; and, through the welfare system, to the unemployed and the chronically poor.

The growth of government, particularly in the domestic sphere, has created many new expectations of what government should provide. Inevitably, these expectations fail to be met. And there is constant competition between groups and interests for a larger share of this governmental largesse. As a result, some writers believe, our society has become "balkanized," that is, split into warring ethnic, racial, and class groups. As people feel more pressure from government, they come to believe that they have little in common with people unlike themselves; they retreat into selfish enclaves, seeking favors only for themselves. Has the public become nothing more than a ravenous collection of self-interested groups? Does there even exist any longer a public capable of holding its own against government? Is there such a thing as "the public interest"?

In the best of times the tension between leaders and the citizenry animates the American political system. Leaders stay attentive to the demands of citizens; citizens become energetic in their vigilance against abuse and in their efforts to influence the political system. Unresponsive leaders are replaced; the society is a marketplace of political ideas. At other times, however, the level of tension becomes threatening. Many citizens refuse to trust leaders and withdraw from politics. Others seek political solutions outside the rules of democratic procedures. Leaders, becoming isolated, abuse their power partly out of fear.

In recent years the United States has hovered between these two poles. It is important to ask whether our democratic system has the resilience to channel the tension between leaders and citizens productively, in order to produce a balanced pattern of popular control and political responsiveness. We now embark upon that task.

Chapter 2   The American Political Tradition

In every political system, some people have more power than others. By power, we mean the capacity to get things accomplished by governmental action. Regardless of who actually holds most power — an elite of rich men, a particular social class, a military-industrial complex, even the elected representatives of the people — the problem remains: How can those who have the most power be made to use it for the good of all the people? A more complex form of the same question is: How can the positive goals of government be secured without simultaneously empowering potential oppressors? To work efficiently *for* people, government must have some concentrated power — yet the more power government concentrates, the greater its capacity to work *against* people. A government without power cannot do its job. A government with too much power is dangerous. The first problem of politics, then, is to reduce the risks associated with an effective government.

As we noted in Chapter 1, the tension between the government and the governed is the organizing theme of this book. Whatever their differences, all political systems, ancient and modern, share this problem. Therefore, studying the tension between government and the governed will take us to the very heart of the political experience.

ROOTS OF AMERICAN DEMOCRACY

Studying American politics in this way has a special significance, because it was Americans who, in the eighteenth century, initially popularized the belief that the people as a whole possess the historic right and responsibility to control government for their own purposes. This idea, which we take for granted today, was revolutionary two hundred years ago.

Not only has this belief shaped American political thought and practice, but it has also been America's legacy to political systems around the globe. The American Revolution helped trigger the great age of democratic expansion throughout the world. The American experience inspired democrats everywhere — first in France, then throughout Europe, then beyond. Today, despite democracy's many reverses, democratic ideals remain strong among the world's peoples. As evidence of that strength, even transparently despotic regimes find it convenient to call themselves "democracies." Our present task is to describe the roots of the American democratic tradition.

America: The Promised Land?

American views of nature contributed much to the American political experience. To seventeenth-century Europeans and Americans both, America appeared as a truly "promised land." The Old World pictured the New as a half-primitive, half-civilized "garden," blessed by a temperate climate and filled with the promise of abundance. Here true harmony between people and nature, as well as among people themselves, could finally exist.[1]

Several aspects of this view had political significance. For one thing, any intrusions on the right of people to cultivate the American "garden" as they saw fit became immediately suspect. People could attain harmony with nature only by their own doing; intrusions by external forces, such as government, would therefore upset the delicate balance between humans and nature. To Thomas Jefferson, one of the greatest exponents of America as a Garden of Eden, dangers came from every side — not only from despotic government, but even from cities, which he characterized as "sores on the body politic." Later, as the Industrial Revolution took hold, many Americans came to see technology and the machine as serpents in the American Eden.[2] Arguments about the role of technology and urbanism in American life contributed much to the early formation of political parties in America. Alexander Hamilton and his supporters pressed the case for technology, commerce, urbanism, and a strong central government. The Jeffersonians defended the cause of the yeoman farmer — independent, close to nature, and free from governmental restrictions.

The American Religious Tradition

The belief that Americans were destined to live in pastoral harmony with nature was not the only aspect of American culture that affected the relationship between the governed and their governors. There was also the American reli-

---

[1] This argument relies heavily on Leo Marx's brilliant *The Machine in the Garden* (New York: Oxford University Press, 1964).
[2] Ibid., chaps. 4–5.

gious tradition. Many of the colonists had sought refuge in America from religious persecution elsewhere. Most of these fugitives had fled the Anglican church establishment in Great Britain. This was true of the Puritans and Congregationalists of New England and the Quakers of Pennsylvania. Other Americans, such as the Germans of the middle colonies, had fled religious persecution on the European continent.

Still other colonists, such as those who populated Connecticut, were dissenters from dominant *American* religions. Ironically, the New England Presbyterians and Baptists found themselves forced to protest alliances between colonial governors and the dominant Anglicans and Congregationalists in much the same terms that Americans of all religions later used against the British.[3] The separation between church and state that ultimately became part of the American political creed originated in this purely American religious struggle. How, argued the Presbyterians and Baptists, could Americans in good conscience struggle against the British while some Americans persecuted other Americans on religious grounds? Only religious freedom — including the freedom *not* to be religious — would guarantee freedom for any one religion.

But this was not the only spur to the American conception of religious freedom. Another was the influence of Calvinism on colonial American Protestantism. John Calvin (1509–64) was a French theologian who made Geneva, Switzerland the seat of his activities. Calvin had preached that people owed allegiance only to God and conscience, not to religious authorities or institutions and certainly not to any political authority. Calvinism infused American Protestantism — from Congregationalists in the North to Presbyterians and Baptists in the South. One major effect of Calvinist dominance was the fragmentation and decentralization of the American religious community. Particularly in New England, religious jealousies and doctrinal differences helped decentralize religious life and bred hatred of ecclesiastical authorities. Later the Revolution would reformulate these antiestablishment habits into political terms.

The so-called Great Awakening of the 1740s crystallized many of these ideas. The Great Awakening was an evangelical religious movement spearheaded by radical Calvinist preachers such as Jonathan Edwards. The movement not only democratized religious authority by redistributing power from pastors to parishioners, but also produced a generation of American clergymen schooled in dissent and willing to translate their beliefs into political terms when necessary.

The Great Awakening also brought religious questions into the arena of American politics by implying that the pursuit of such political liberties as the right to free worship was simultaneously a quest for religious salvation. The marriage of politics and religion created a formidable force against the British.

---

[3] Bernard Bailyn, *The Ideological Origins of the American Revolution* (Cambridge, Mass.: Belknap Press, 1967), pp. 257–71.

Moreover, as an evangelical movement, the Great Awakening preached that God's heaven on earth was imminent. Some colonists believed that God had chosen America as the particular instrument of his desires, and that the Revolution itself was a political prelude to the Second Coming of Christ as foretold in the Bible.[4]

All these currents of thought came to a head in 1765, when the Anglican church attempted to install a bishop of the American colonies. To the colonists, many of whom had fled Anglican authority in Britain, this proposal was a clear signal that American religious freedoms were in danger. Not surprisingly, therefore, to many an American the independence movement was a religious as well as a secular struggle.

Religion has continued to spawn important political movements throughout American history. For example, fundamentalist Protestant groups led the drive for the prohibition of alcoholic beverages, a movement that culminated in the Eighteenth Amendment to the Constitution, which in 1919 outlawed the sale of liquor. But Prohibition proved unenforceable and was repealed in 1933. Between World War I and World War II fundamentalist Protestant ministers, such as Gerald L. K. Smith, played leading roles in the powerful Ku Klux Klan, which advocated "white supremacy" in much of the South and some border states. A Catholic priest, Father Charles Coughlin, used his popular radio program to attack Franklin Roosevelt's New Deal and its "socialist, Jewish" supporters. Following World War II, black ministers, such as Martin Luther King, Jr., spearheaded the early drive for racial equality in the South, slowly gathering support from such liberal religious organizations as the National Conference of Christians and Jews.

In our own time fundamentalist Protestantism has again become an important political force, as manifested in such organizations as Gerald Falwell's "Moral Majority." The new Protestant evangelism opposes "permissive" books in school libraries, sex education, divorce, and homosexual rights. Most important, it advocates an end to legalized abortion, through constitutional amendment if necessary. Today's politics of religion reflect the continuing vitality of the colonial vision of America as God's peculiar instrument for stamping out vice and implanting virtue.

AMERICAN SCIENTIFIC THOUGHT   American revolutionary thought was also grounded in a view of scientific laws of nature. American thinkers were impressed by Sir Isaac Newton's (1642–1727) formulation of physical laws in nature. They believed that, "The political and social world is governed by laws as certain and universal as those which govern the physical world."[5] One such law, Jefferson thought, was that revo-

---

[4] Alan Heimert, *Religion and the American Mind* (Cambridge, Mass.: Harvard University Press, 1966), p. 409.
[5] Clinton Rossiter, *1787: The Grand Convention* (New York: Macmillan, 1966), p. 60.

The Hamilton-Jefferson Dialogue

The Hamilton-Jefferson dialogue about the future of American politics was a great divide in American history. As his words suggest, Hamilton believed that by encouraging industry, manufacturing, and commerce the well-being of all would be sustained, not only because of the growth of national wealth, but also because industrial activity would liberate people to use the whole range of their talents. But to Jefferson Hamilton's "solution" was a formula for slavery, not liberation. The "diversity" of which Hamilton speaks was for Jefferson inequality, dependence, and corruption—as citizens became slaves to employers.

Hamilton and Jefferson disagreed about more than politics. They disagreed about the "good life." And, like most people deeply committed to a particular view, they often deceived themselves. After all, the farmer is dependent, because he must sell his produce on the market. And won't importing manufactured goods, as advocated by Jefferson, make Americans dependent on foreigners? And isn't it blind of Hamilton simply to assume that wealth and effort equal happiness? Arguments about politics often are really concealed arguments about the ideal of the "good life," and about the ways in which the tension between the governors and the governed can best be moderated so as to attain this ideal.

lutions were necessary periodically in society. By "necessary" Jefferson meant that they were determined by laws of nature that could not be revoked.[6] Many of the important revolutionary thinkers, especially Jefferson and Franklin, were either scientists themselves or conversant with the scientific break-throughs of their time. They reasoned that in carrying through a revolution they were doing not just God's will or the people's will, but the will of nature itself.

WAS THE AMERICAN REVOLUTION REALLY REVO-LUTIONARY? The American Revolution has always occupied an uncertain position in the study of American politics. Certainly as a military operation it was modest enough. The casualties of the war — about 7,000 battle deaths and 18,000 other fatalities — were minimal compared with those of other wars.

Moreover, as a political upheaval the Revolution suffers by comparison with its French counterpart, which erupted thirteen years later. Whereas the French Revolution seemed to turn the European world upside down, the American Revolution left much in its own world apparently untouched. Whereas the French Revolution spurred an expansionist French nationalism that culminated in the Napoleonic wars, the American Revolution turned America inward, not outward. Washington announced this inward-looking turn of mind when he argued in his Farewell Address that Americans should avoid "entangling alliances" with foreign governments. Most important, whereas the French Revolution was heated and bloody, the American Revolution was more sober.

Some writers have even argued that the American Revolution was a revolution in name only. They contend that since Americans were merely asserting their rights as British subjects against the British crown, the political ideas of the American Revolution were neither innovative nor important.[7] Certainly it is true that many American demands were no more than assertions of rights guaranteed to them as Englishmen but denied by colonial practices. A real revolution must introduce *new* political values and practices; it cannot be just a provincial rebellion.

Even the Declaration of Independence itself can be seen as something less than a truly revolutionary document. The Declaration merely stated the reasons that Americans fought the British. It did not state clearly any governmental course that Americans should follow after the Revolution. Even Jefferson himself — the author of the Declaration — felt that its final form was not sufficiently revolutionary. Many of his most revolutionary arguments for independence were not permitted to appear in the Declaration's final draft, a circumstance that embittered him until the end of his life.[8]

[6] Garry Wills, *Inventing America: Jefferson's Declaration of Independence* (Garden City, N.Y.: Doubleday, 1978), chap. 7.

[7] For a reconsideration, see Gordon S. Wood, "Rhetoric and Reality in the American Revolution," *William and Mary Quarterly* 23 (1966): 3–32.

[8] Wills, *Inventing America*.

Another argument is that the Revolution was simply an attempt by American merchants to liberate themselves from the commercial restrictions of British colonialism.[9] It is true that New England merchants were hamstrung by British regulations of trade and that such measures as the Stamp Act enraged them. Was the American Revolution then merely an economic skirmish, rather than a noteworthy social or political phenomenon?

Debates about the origins and significance of the American Revolution seem certain to continue, but we believe that the "nonrevolution" position is both historically and politically inaccurate. The American Revolution was a genuine revolution, sufficient to set the example for the French revolutionaries who soon after demolished the French feudal order. Certainly the American revolutionaries themselves believed in their revolutionary role. Indeed, they claimed to be ushering in a new age for the world as a whole, not just for themselves.

Certainly no other generation ever had such a grand opportunity to act as both political theorists and practical politicians, to formulate new political theories and then actually to construct new governments to test them. And the American revolutionaries took advantage of their opportunity. This is not to say that the political ideas of the Revolution were tidy and intellectually consistent. Instead, the American Revolution began a vast social and political experiment, with laboratories in every state legislature and in the national government itself. The flood of journals, letters, and pamphlets turned out by the leading politicians of the era — Madison, Jefferson, Franklin, Paine, Hamilton, John Adams, John Dickinson, Jonathan Witherspoon — shows clearly that American leaders believed they were making a real revolution, a decisive break with past political history.

Still, beliefs are one thing; reality may be another. What actually was novel about the political theory and practice of the American Revolution? American political ideas around the time of the Revolution broke with English tradition on two major concepts: political power and rights.

THE AMERICAN IDEA OF POLITICAL POWER To the American revolutionary mind, political power — especially the power exercised by monarchs and the executive branch of government — tended to become conspiratorial and concentrated, to expand, and ultimately to engulf the rights of citizens. Americans had seen the colonial governors, most of them appointed by the English crown and wholly unrepresentative of the colonists themselves, turn into petty tyrants. They also believed that unscrupulous British political leaders were gradually suppressing the political rights of the Brit-

---

[9] This argument is perhaps most completely associated with the American revisionist historian, Charles Beard. For a contemporary interpretation, see E. James Ferguson, "The Nationalists of 1781–1783 and the Economic Interpretation of the Constitution," in Stanley Katz and Stanley Kutler, eds., *New Perspectives on the American Past*, vol. 1: *1606–1877*, 2nd ed. (Boston: Little Brown, 1972), pp. 83–101.

ish themselves. These conclusions led them to argue that the power of the executive must be curtailed.

Most Americans believed that only popularly elected legislatures could rightfully lay claim to power because only elections expressed the popular will. Thus, when the executive and judiciary gained power, it was at the expense of the legislature's legitimate power. And because of the executive's power over appointments, finances, and — most important — military force, in the contest between the executive and the legislature, the executive had the advantage. Therefore, legislative supremacy had to be secured. This, in its simplest form, was the American conception of political power at the time of the Revolution.

It should be pointed out, however, that the expansion of the executive branch or of the power of the king was only a symptom of a larger problem: the tendency of any group or individual to abuse power. The American suspicion of the executive could therefore be transferred to other agencies of government as well, should they also concentrate and abuse power. Americans considered legislatures less likely to become tyrannical, but they did not rule out such a possibility entirely.

The British View of Power British political thought was less suspicious of executive power for several reasons. First, the British believed that theirs was a *mixed* government in which the various parts of government — like parts of a human body — cooperated for the benefit of the people as a whole. Consequently, just as it would be foolish to imagine the head "usurping" the power of the heart, so would it be absurd to imagine the king usurping the power of Parliament. If an occasional monarchical abuse occurred, it was the exception, not the rule. Second, the British believed that Parliament represented distinct *orders* of society — the aristocrats in the House of Lords, commoners in the House of Commons. Each person therefore had a place in the larger society, a society notable for the continuity of its social classes throughout history. Third, the British held that their government itself — as embodied by Parliament and the king — was the constitution of its society; therefore, Britain needed no written constitution. As a result, the government could rule legitimately in any respect it pleased. To the British, "unconstitutional" rule was literal nonsense, and the American argument that executive power inherently tended toward tyranny was absurd — how could the people become tyrants over themselves?[10]

Britons did not fear the abuse of power because they believed that the British social order and governmental institutions were joined together in an *organic* whole. In this organic theory of government, already connected parts merely required proper regulation. By contrast, Americans believed that the groups and institutions that made up their society were related not organically,

[10] See Gordon S. Wood, *The Creation of the American Republic, 1776–1787* (Chapel Hill: University of North Carolina Press, 1969), pp. 260–61.

While the English force tea and taxes down the throat of an American (represented by an Indian maiden), the guardian of liberty shields her eyes from the horrible sight. This 1774 engraving by Paul Revere indicates that the art of political propaganda was well-developed in the colonies.

but *mechanically*. Government was like a large machine rather than a human body. The parts of society and the parts of government were interrelated not *naturally*, but only by deliberate human effort. Thus, it could not be assumed that the institutions of government were sympathetic with each other: Sympathy is a human quality, not a mechanical one. The problem of government, therefore, was to make potentially unchecked, uncontrolled, unbalanced institutions and groups cooperate — a more difficult problem than the British, with their organic theory, realized.

The American Response Americans therefore found the British concepts of executive power and constitutional rule inapplicable to their own experience. They argued that the British king and his representatives in America, the colonial governors, had little rightful place in American history or society. America had been made not by them but by its diverse settlers. Indeed, Jefferson even argued that, merely by colonizing America, English settlers had dissolved their ties with the king.

Moreover, Americans looking at Britain in the late eighteenth century thought they could detect royal authority subverting parliamentary power through bribery and corruption. Surely, they reasoned, a truly mixed, cooperative government could not have permitted such corruption and imbalance.

Some Americans went so far as to argue that in fighting against the crown they were actually fighting for the British people as well as themselves.

Most important, Americans denied that their own society was composed of distinct social orders. America lacked an aristocracy based on inherited titles. In America, firstborn sons did not automatically inherit their fathers' property, as they did in Britain. Property did not pass from generation to generation protected from the competitive pressures of the market. Americans had no long-established institutions of higher learning that could transmit a distinctive culture to an aristocracy. For all these reasons, Americans were convinced that theirs was a society of individuals, not distinct social groups. Americans could find their own places within the class and status groupings of their society; they were not fixed in place, as were the British.

Nevertheless, there *were* distinct social classes in revolutionary America. Particularly in the eastern regions of most colonies, remnants of English traditions joined with a newly bustling commercial economy to produce a stratified social system. However, as opposed to the situation in England, "From the bottom of society to the top was a short step; from top to bottom was not much longer a slide. Top and bottom nevertheless existed. . . ."[11] In addition, society appeared to permit more rapid movement across class lines than one encountered in England. In America there were social classes made up of individuals; in Britain there were social orders made up of groups. America was the New World, Britain the Old.

Of course, this argument overlooked the presence of slaves as well as that of indentured servants and apprentices bound by contract to their masters. Clearly, elements of a more traditional society could still be found in America, political rhetoric notwithstanding.

Nevertheless, Americans found themselves thinking about power in a very different way from their British counterparts. After all, if government represents dynamic individuals rather than static social orders, then the link between government and the governed poses a thorny problem, for individuals are surely more vulnerable to domination than are traditional, recognized social orders. It seemed to follow, therefore, that whereas a mixed constitution of the English sort could perhaps prevent tyranny in Britain, only the people as a whole could prevent tyranny in America. And the only agencies of American government that spoke for the people as a whole were the popularly chosen colonial legislatures. Naturally enough, therefore, American revolutionary thought made the legislature the centerpiece of government.

Guarding Against Executive Power To the American Revolutionary mind, then, the immediate problem was to check the power of an unrepresentative and abusive minority — as embodied in the executive — by transferring power to the legislative representatives of the majority. Not surprisingly, the first thing the revolutionaries did when war

[11] Rossiter, *1787*, p. 30.

broke out with England was to remove the colonial executives and empower the colonial legislatures to make laws virtually unhindered by other institutions. Each state accomplished this task in its own way. Pennsylvania's solution was the most radical and thoroughgoing. Pennsylvania's new constitution, adopted in the summer of 1776, gave the vote to all male taxpayers who had lived there for at least one year. It did away with imprisonment for debt, and authorized free schools. It also eliminated property qualifications for holding public office, and so reduced religious qualifications for office that one critic lamented: "Farewell Christianity when Turks, Jews, Infidels, and what is worse Deists and Atheists are to make laws for our State."[12] The net result everywhere was to concentrate power in the hands of an elected legislature. This deliberate effort to being power closer to the people represented a new direction in the political thought of the time.

This shift of political power was necessary because, in the American view, unrepresentative minorities — centered in the executive — continually usurped the people's power. Americans cited four examples of executive usurpation that played crucial roles immediately before the Revolution and left their imprint on the American political tradition thereafter. These examples involved the role of the military in civil life, the system of trial by jury, the method of appointing public officials, and the power to tax.

The Military Threat. As Americans saw it, one of the chief ways executives and monarchs gradually subverted legislatures, and thus society as a whole, was by controlling the military. Inevitably, it seemed, executives recruited and paid professional mercenaries loyal only to themselves.[13] Executive control of a standing, professional army — often a private army — took the power of legitimate coercion away from the people as a whole and gave it to a group whose interests were purely selfish. When the crown imported large numbers of regular British Army officers and men into the colonies in the early 1770s, Americans became incensed. To the Americans this action was a signal that the colonial governors intended to buttress their own power by relying on outside force.

Yet every society needs an army. The American solution was to create a military force that could not pose a threat to popular liberties, one composed of local militiamen recruited voluntarily for short periods at low pay. The army must be a *citizen* army that could not develop into an oppressive arm of the state, but would remain close to the people.[14] The army and the people must stand for the same, not different, things.

[12]Norman A. Graebner, Gilbert C. Fite, and Philip L. White, *History of the American People*, vol. 1 (New York: McGraw-Hill, 1970), pp. 222–23.

[13]Bailyn, *Ideological Origins*, pp. 61–63. Discussion of the comparative merits of a national as opposed to a mercenary army goes back beyond this period. It may be found prominently in Machiavelli. See Niccolo Machiavelli, *The Discourses* (New York: Modern Library, 1940), chap. 20.

[14]Bailyn, *Ideological Origins*, pp. 112–19, traces the historical events that supported this colonial view.

Overriding the Juries.   British executive power had also expanded into the judicial arena. By the time of the Revolution most Americans viewed the jury trial as a means of checking arbitrary executive power in a particularly crucial area. Americans believed that juries composed of ordinary citizens helped to prevent executives from stilling political dissent by prosecuting dissenters as if they were criminals. Before the Revolution, the crown had made several attempts to extend the power of the colonial governors over trials. In some colonies, the crown had succeeded in broadening the range of judicial decisions that could be appealed only to the governor and his council rather than to a higher court. The colonists saw this maneuver to avoid jury trials as just another attempt by the executive to infringe on the power of the people.

Abusing the Power of Appointment.   A third example of executive expansion lay in the power of appointment. The Revolutionary generation was angered by the colonial governors' practice of appointing officials to newly created offices that performed no useful functions. This practice was objectionable on several counts. First, the power of appointment was used simply to reward friends of the crown and thereby to prop up an increasingly unpopular royal authority. Second, the crown was using the appointment power to create an artificial aristocratic order on American soil. Third, Americans were required to tax themselves to pay for governmental officials they did not want. Fourth, and most important, the power of appointment was being used to restrict the people's power over their leaders. After all, appointees enjoyed power without being subject to popular controls. Americans therefore concluded that unless the appointment power of executives was curtailed, executive power would expand uncontrollably. The sole purpose of royal appointments was to forestall political dissent by creating a class of wealthy Americans dependent for status and position on the British crown. In very large measure, the Revolution was directed against this class.

Unjust Taxation.   The most famous example of the American distrust of executives emerged from the argument over "taxation without representation." Although the pre-revolutionary arguments about taxation were complex, the chief question was simple enough. Was the British Parliament, three thousand miles away, capable of representing American financial interests properly? The rebels argued that it was not. Parliament could not appreciate the novelty of American life and therefore did not know how to use American taxes for American interests.[15] It was not the Parliament in England that was primarily at fault, however, but to a large extent the king and his court, who wished to use American tax money to support adventures of their own over which the Americans had absolutely no control.

---

[15] This argument was, however, linked closely to a more serious source of difference with the British, namely, differences about the problem of representation. See Wood, *Creation of the American Republic,* chap. 5.

Legislative Tyranny? American fear of executive power was only symptomatic of the American fear of power in general. Many Americans found any concentration of power obnoxious because power, no matter what its form, tended to become oppressive.

Once the Revolution had begun and the royal governors and most of their supporters had been forcibly ejected from the colonies, power switched to the newly liberated state legislatures. Because these were representative, elected bodies, an unrepresentative minority no longer tyrannized the majority. But this was not the end of the American debate about power. Throughout the Revolutionary War, people in western Pennsylvania, western Massachusetts, and western North Carolina found their own state legislatures almost as obnoxious as their former British masters.[16] In 1786 a rebellion broke out in western Massachusetts when the state legislature rejected farmers' appeals to grant them financial relief by issuing paper money to prohibit mortgage foreclosures on their land, and to halt their imprisonment for indebtedness. The insurrection, known as Shays's Rebellion, was quelled by force of arms.

Meanwhile, eastern merchants worried that the state legislatures were being *too* kind to poor farmers and those who owed money to banks and businessmen. Many state legislatures, controlled by the "debtor class," erased all debts. Merchants, businessmen, and bankers considered this action as tyrannical as any of the British acts that preceded the Revolution. Slowly the idea grew that legislatures could be as tyrannical as executives, states as tyrannical as national governments, majorities as tyrannical as minorities.

From these experiences a few people drew the most radical conclusion of all: Only the people themselves could be trusted to legislate in their own behalf. The people should act whenever and however they chose. No artificial body of representatives should ever be permitted to speak in their name. The people should rule directly, through seizure of power if necessary.[17]

Other Americans were far more cautious. Some reasoned that the solution to the problem of tyranny lay in a reevaluation of executive power and in a "balance of power" among the branches of government. And others were unwilling to give up on genuine popular control through the legislature.

The debate between advocates of legislative power, advocates of direct popular control, and advocates of a balance of power gradually led to a peculiarly American conception of the relationship between leaders and led. Again, the contrast with Britain is instructive. We have said that Parliament represented a small number of established social groups that were fixed in place by custom and tradition. Theoretically, Parliament and society were one. Americans rejected this vision because their own society consisted of dynamic individuals, not social orders. Therefore, representation of the people must be different in America. In the American scheme all branches of government were artificial creations, useful only for certain limited, practical purposes.

Thus, when the Americans created their governments, both state and na-

[16] Ibid., part 3.
[17] Ibid., pp. 319–28.

tional, they envisioned a much sharper distinction between the people and their governors than existed in England. For example, they empowered the legislature to make decisions only within the narrow compass of authority expressly delegated to it. Further, legislatures themselves were never permitted to determine their own powers. That right was reserved to the people, and was to be exercised in an entirely separate governing process: the making and remaking of their constitution in special conventions. The Americans' experience led them to try to separate the constitution, the people, and the government from each other, and thus to reconstruct their polity according to an entirely new theory of politics.

THE AMERICAN CONCEPTION OF RIGHTS

The Founding Fathers developed a new conception of human rights to fit their new analysis of power. One of the more interesting ways to illustrate the newly developed American conception of rights is by examining a famous political document that was *not* instrumental in shaping that conception. The Magna Carta, essentially a list of rights granted a group of English barons by King John in 1215, is generally considered one of the great milestones in the history of rights. Yet the Magna Carta played no role in the American debate about rights. Why? The answer, although simple, is far reaching: Americans believed that the Magna Carta was based on a false premise. Rights are not the *possession* of a king or of any other political body. Instead, rights are embodied in the whole people. Therefore, in the language of the Declaration of Independence, rights are "unalienable": They can neither be given nor taken away.[18] The problem with the Magna Carta was that the king gave the people what was already theirs by right.

It follows from this new conception that whenever a political system begins to infringe on popular rights, the people should change it. Coupled with the view that governments were inherently prone to tyranny, this abstraction led some to conclude that political change would be necessary often if rights were to be protected. Jefferson himself believed this. But this view bypasses important questions: What particular rights did the Founding Fathers have in mind? What specifically did people deserve as a matter of right?

The American Bill of Rights — the first ten amendments to the Constitution — was not adopted until 1791, eight years after the Revolutionary War ended and some time after the body of the Constitution was written. The Bill is a fair sample of American thinking about rights. It specifically mentions, among other rights, freedom of speech, of the press, and of religion; freedom from self-incrimination in trial proceedings; freedom of assembly; freedom from unreasonable search and seizure; freedom from military authorities; and freedom to bear arms. Virtually all these freedoms had been practiced in America before the Revolution, and most had become objects of contention in

---

[18] The key phrase is "all men are created equal, that they are endowed by their Creator with certain unalienable Rights."

the growing friction with the British. Most of the Founders believed these rights to be implied by the original Constitution, but some felt that unless they were explicitly spelled out, the Constitution would not receive crucial political support. The actual meaning in practice of these rights remained to be worked out long after 1791. Many still remain objects of contention. We therefore postpone their detailed discussion until Chapter 14.

The Bill of Rights gives us an idea how the Founders fleshed out the abstract concept of rights. But it does not tell us where Americans got their ideas about the origins of these rights, or about their inalienable character.

Origins of the People's Rights   The origins of the American conception of rights are ambiguous. It would be naive to assume that most Americans of the time delved deeply into political philosophy, or that they considered philosophical issues any more seriously than most people do today. The generation of the Revolution was, above all, a generation of politicians, not philosophers. They ironed out their differences as much by pragmatic compromise as by philosophical discourse. Nevertheless, we can trace the American notion of rights back to a well-developed intellectual tradition that had begun to pervade American thought at the time of the Revolution. This was the tradition of "natural rights."

Several political philosophers since Aristotle had argued that nature conveyed certain "rights" and "freedoms" to people generally. The strongest intellectual influence on Americans at the time of the Revolution was that of John Locke, the seventeenth-century British philosopher. Locke divided human history into two periods: people in the state of nature and people in society. People in the state of nature lived in relative harmony with their fellows. Because of differences of temperament and ability, however, some chose to infringe on the natural rights of others to achieve their own selfish ends. To protect themselves against these violators of "natural law," people found it necessary to move from the state of nature to the state of society and governance. Nevertheless, government had only one legitimate purpose: to prevent persons from infringing on the rights of others.[19] Government could not define, expand, or restrict rights. People enjoyed all rights directly as a creation of nature — not as subjects of government.[20]

Again, these conceptions of rights may be contrasted with the British view. The British too had been influenced by the natural-rights tradition, but they had taken as much from Thomas Hobbes as from Locke. Hobbes considered people in the state of nature to be pitiful, totally insecure, and unable to fend off the attacks of their enemies. Therefore, when people took part in establishing a government for their own protection, they gave up what little freedom they had in order to empower a sovereign powerful enough to save them from

---

[19] John Locke, *Second Treatise of Civil Government* (Chicago: Regency, 1955).

[20] The consequences of this primarily negative, highly restrictive sense of government are spelled out provocatively in Louis Hartz, *The Liberal Tradition in America* (New York: Harcourt, Brace and World, 1955).

the attacks of their enemies. Consequently, once a part of society, a person no longer possessed the rights that had been his or hers in the state of nature but, rather, only those rights that the state chose to extend.[21]

Americans rejected the British view. They considered the state of nature far more benign than had Hobbes. They also argued that before any government could be established, there must exist a social agreement or *contract* among free individuals to form a government in the first place. Because this social compact *preceded* any political arrangement, government could not have been a party to the compact and therefore could never properly abridge or alter it. Thus, government was the creation of the people acting as free individuals in concert; it possessed no rights other than those the people specifically granted it.[22]

Rights in the New Country

To most Americans of the Revolutionary generation, then, there seemed to be no contradiction between political liberty and social equality. After all, the natural rights they possessed ensured that Americans were at least born equal.[23]

Nevertheless, as we have seen, there were social and economic inequalities in American life at the time of the Revolution, inequalities that affected political thinking and political motives. Merchants and farmers had different, and often conflicting, interests; large property owners and tenants were often at odds; rich townspeople and poorer country folk did not always see eye to eye. But most Americans believed that by securing political liberty through the Revolution they would be able to prevent social inequalities from becoming too severe. They also believed that the absence of a hereditary aristocracy, a state bureaucracy, guilds, and the other paraphernalia of the Old World would open up society to men of genuine merit — in Jefferson's phrase, an "aristocracy of talent." In short, as long as opportunity and *freedom* could be secured, all would go well. A proper government would ensure opportunity, which in turn would erode any potentially dangerous social inequalities that might arise.[24]

American political thought was not entirely consistent. People differed about many things, in particular about slavery, a legally recognized deprivation of liberty that already divided northerners from southerners. Jefferson himself admitted that there was an obvious inconsistency between a belief in natural rights and the practice of slavery. Moreover, many people realized that a belief in the unqualified right of the people to rule is inconsistent with a

[21] Thomas Hobbes, *Leviathan* (New York: Collier, 1962).

[22] Wood, *Creation of the American Republic*, p. 290.

[23] The consequences of the American attitude toward equality were traced most completely by Alexis de Tocqueville, *Democracy in America*, vol. 1 (New York: Schocken Books, 1961), chaps. 3, 13–15.

[24] Rush Welter, *The Mind of America, 1820–1860* (New York: Columbia University Press, 1975), chap. 4. For a critique of the American conception of equal opportunity, see John D. Schaar, "Equality of Opportunity, and Beyond," in J. Roland Pennock and John W. Chapman, eds., *Equality*, Nomos IX (New York: Atherton, 1967), pp. 228–50.

belief that individual rights must be protected from government.[25] And where did the rights of legislatures to carry on the day-to-day operations of government unhindered begin, and the rights of the people as a whole to make changes in government end? These questions were constant sources of debate and division throughout the Revolutionary era.

Nevertheless, a revolution need be neither intellectually consistent nor complete to qualify as a true revolution. The important thing is that the American Revolution ushered in a new way of thinking about the tension between governed and governors. And the Revolution itself began a utopian experiment to manage that tension.

FRUIT OF THE REVOLUTION: THE CONSTITUTION

The period between 1776 and 1787 was a time of continuous political experimentation in America. When war broke out in 1775, each colony suddenly found itself virtually on its own. Each therefore proceeded to set up its own constitution and to regulate most of its own affairs. Hence, during the next eleven years most of the political action that really mattered took place at the state level. As we noted earlier, each state in effect became a laboratory for constitution making and political innovation.

Independence and Impotence

The American Revolution had been conducted under an unratified draft of the Articles of Confederation. This document had been hammered out by a committee of the Continental Congress in 1776, but its ratification, which required unanimous approval by the states, was not achieved until 1781, the year the war ended. The Articles created a league of independent states; no strong national government presided over the fledgling confederation. Article II stated the matter clearly: "Each state retains its sovereignty, freedom and independence, and every power, jurisdiction and right which is not by this Confederation expressly delegated to the United States, in Congress assembled." The Americans' deeply held suspicions of government power, then, extended to this confederation of their own making. Moreover, Americans made certain that the national government they set up under the Articles would be no threat. By denying it the authority to raise money with which to pay for law enforcement, they withheld from the new government any real power to enforce the laws it passed. Although the Articles permitted Congress to determine how much tax money each state should pay, it did not empower the central government to force states actually to collect and deliver the money. The collection of taxes was the state's job; understandably, states differed in the zeal with which they chose to collect taxes for a distant government.

The weaknesses of the confederal arrangement quickly became apparent as the war with England came to an end. The new nation seemed especially vul-

---

[25] The best critique of this problem (and many of the other logical problems in the Constitution) is Robert A. Dahl, *A Preface to Democratic Theory* (Chicago: University of Chicago Press, 1956).

Three Framers of the Constitution

If the careers of the framers of the Constitution are at all indicative, changing positions on the part of politicians is no recent phenomenon. John Dickinson (left) represented a small state —Delaware—at the Convention, but nevertheless supported a strong national government and was an effective advocate of the "Great Compromise." This agreement, by representing the states according to population in the House of Representatives and as equal units in the Senate, made the Constitution a reality. Dickinson signed the Constitution and campaigned strongly for its ratification. He had come a long way from his states' rights position as supporter of the Articles of Confederation a scant four years earlier in 1783.

Edmund Randolph of Virginia (center) came to the Convention as a firm advocate of a strong national government. He presented James Madison's Virginia Plan, which formed the working basis of the Convention, but saw this plan repeatedly compromised during the deliber-

ations. He refused to sign the finished Constitution. Later he explained, "I am not really an American, I am a Virginian." Yet as a Virginian, Randolph spoke for the Constitution in his state's ratifying convention.

Few were as consistent as James Madison (right), one of the most scholarly of the delegates. Based on his study of old and new governmental arrangements, Madison was convinced that only a federal republic with a strong national component could preserve both individual liberty and national security. His steady, moderate, incisive voice cleared away many obstacles at the Convention. Madison threw all his energies into the campaign to ratify the Constitution, taking to his bed for three days after one impassioned debate at the Virginia ratifying convention. His position prevailed ultimately and his proratification essays in The Federalist *remain classics of political theory.*

nerable to foreign military and diplomatic aggression as long as Congress lacked the power to collect taxes, borrow money, or maintain an armed force. The British, who still controlled several forts on American territory, refused to send a diplomatic representative to the new nation. Adding insult to injury, they asked the American envoy to London, John Adams, whether he represented one nation — or thirteen. It might be thought, given America's distance from Europe, that Americans had little to fear from foreigners. But many states had made extensive land claims on the western frontier. The lack of a centralized armed force put all those claims at risk to hostile Indians, to European powers who retained their own ambitions along the frontier, and even to separatist elements among Americans themselves who wished to seize land from the western claims.

There were other difficulties as well. The Articles made no provision for a court system to settle disputes between states; Congress was not granted the authority to regulate interstate commerce; and, perhaps worst, all important legislation required the consent of nine of the thirteen states. Each state had one vote. Because delegations from several states were often absent from the unicameral (one-house) Congress, absolute veto power could be held by any one or two states in any given situation. As one congressional delegate glumly put it, Congress "was responsible for everything and unable to do anything."

The financial situation of the new country was especially disconcerting. Many of those who had spent their money on bonds issued to finance the Revolutionary War now discovered that no government could or would repay them for their efforts. In addition, manufacturers in New England found that the central government could not erect a protective tariff to support their industries. Meanwhile, state governments regularly passed laws postponing or reducing payment of debts to creditors, or making cheap paper money legal for the payment of debts. And Congress's inability to regulate interstate commerce prevented much assistance to either creditors or debtors. Not surprisingly, perhaps, the economic situation of the new country suffered, making recovery from the damage of the war itself slow and uncertain.

As time went on, commercial chaos and domestic turmoil threatened the new confederation. In 1787, on receiving word of Shays's Rebellion in Massachusetts, Washington pronounced himself "mortified beyond all expression." He feared the worst: "There are combustibles in every state which a spark might set fire to. . . . Good God!" By contrast, Jefferson's reaction to the uprising seemed almost approving: "I hold that a little rebellion now and then, is a good thing, and as necessary in the political world as storms in the physical."[26] But Alexander Hamilton probably spoke for more of his American contemporaries when he found "something . . . contemptible in the prospect of a number of petty states, with the appearance only of union, jar-

---

[26] Based on T. Harry Williams, Richard N. Current, and Frank Friedel, *A History of the United States*, vol. 1 (New York: Knopf, 1965), p. 18.

ring, jealous and perverse . . . weak and insignificant in the eyes of other nations."[27]

By 1787 many Americans had come around to Washington's view that under the Articles, the Confederation was "little more than the shadow without the substance," and that a remedy must be found. Thus it was that in May of that year, fifty-five delegates met in Philadelphia to revise this unwieldy blueprint of American government. There were some notable absences, however. Rhode Island, protective of its independence and fearful that it would lose its lucrative port revenues to a national government, refused to send representatives. A few delegates elected from other states likewise refused to attend, one of them the staunch states' righter, Patrick Henry of Virginia, who said he "smelt a rat."

Indeed, even some of the delegates who did attend found themselves unable to accept the new Constitution the delegates hammered out. Thus, two of the three New York delegates — Robert Yates and John Lansing, Jr. — attended only long enough to discover that they could not accept the Constitution, and then simply went home, leaving only one delegate — Alexander Hamilton — to sign the finished Constitution for the populous state of New York. Even Hamilton was not entirely happy with the result. It is clear that the Constitutional Convention and its product — the Constitution itself — was a contentious and vexing moment in American history.

The Constitutional Convention The debates that eventually produced the Constitution have been interpreted in a variety of ways. Some historians believe that the Constitution represented a repudiation of the revolutionary hopes and goals of 1776, and a desperate bid to conceal the return of a potentially tyrannical central government. A more moderate interpretation sees the Constitution as a fresh look at the tension between the people and the government. American experience between 1776 and 1787 provided new ideas and concerns for American statesmen; it was only natural that they should attempt to alter the governing structure that had emerged with the Revolution. It is for this reason that Martin Diamond sees the Constitution as a *completion* rather than a repudiation of the Revolution.[28]

All we know for certain is that the delegates agreed on the need to replace the Articles of Confederation, a decision that already exceeded their state-mandated authority simply to *revise* the Articles. As they began to explore their task, however, they quickly discovered that they could agree on little else. Most of the writers of the Constitution believed that their job was to wipe the political slate clean, to seek a new and acceptable balance between the governed and the governors. But what would be acceptable to all the diverse in-

[27] Graebner, et al., *History of the American People*, vol. 1, p. 264.
[28] Martin Diamond, *The Revolution of Sober Expectations*, (Washington, D.C.: American Enterprise Institute, 1974).

terests represented by these fifty-five delegates from the twelve attending states? The smaller states in particular were anxious to protect their newly won independence. Not surprisingly, the delegates soon found themselves grappling with the familiar problem of power. They now had to admit — reluctantly in most cases — that some form of centralized national authority was necessary if the United States was to be in fact united. But the form such an authority would take — its relation to the states, the extent of its power, and its internal organization — was barely visible in the political haze that hung over Philadelphia that fateful summer of 1787.

Power Reconsidered As we have seen, the makers of the Revolution thought the first problem of politics was to keep government from oppressing the people. They believed this could be accomplished in two ways. First, all power should be vested in popularly elected legislatures representative of the people. Second, "interests" or "factions" should be prevented from developing. The Revolutionaries argued that, once formed, powerful interest groups would surely repress the people sooner or later. Hence, each state should be limited in size and homogeneous in population, to prevent tyrannical factions from developing.

But these ideas failed in practice. Small governments — those of the states — appeared to be as given to tyranny as large governments. Moreover, popularly elected legislatures did not appear to protect the people as well as the Revolutionaries had hoped. Even in small governmental units, groups with conflicting interests formed; Americans came to politics as farmers, merchants, lawyers — not as like-minded individuals. And the competing needs and desires of these "interest groups" or "factions" formed a constant danger to popular government. Given these realities, the Constitution's framers finally agreed that factions could not be prevented from forming.

Moreover, Americans feared tyranny in any form, whether that which oppresses a majority or that which oppresses a minority. Even a legislature that did represent a majority could become tyrannical if it suppressed people's rights. Thus, the problem was as much a matter of protecting minorities from majorities as of protecting the rights of the latter.

The real difficulty, therefore, was to reconcile "republicanism"— the principle that governments depend for their rightful powers on popular election — with the existence of "factions" created by such elections. After all, factions that got out of control could become tyrannical, not only suppressing each other but also destroying republicanism itself.

It was James Madison, a young delegate from Virginia, who formulated this problem most clearly and made it the foundation of the Constitution. Even before the Constitution began, Madison had set himself the task of finding a new solution to the problem of tyranny. Part of Madison's argument is contained in *The Federalist Papers*, a series of newspaper articles he wrote with Alexander Hamilton and John Jay as part of the campaign to win the holdout states' approval of the new Constitution. In *The Federalist* (No. 10), Madison addresses the relationship between the size of a political unit, the appearance of tyranny, and the emergence of factions. He first argues that it is fruitless to try to prevent the emergence of interest groups: Their causes are part of human nature. Rather, the problem is to find an acceptable way of coping with factions. Perhaps, says Madison, factions will be less dangerous in a large state than in a small state:

> The smaller the society, the fewer probably will be the distinct parties and interests composing it; the fewer the distinct parties and interests, the more frequently will a majority be found of the same party; and the smaller the compass within which they are placed, the more easily will they concert and execute their plans of oppression. Extend the sphere, and you take in a greater variety of parties and interests; you make it less probable that a majority of the whole will have a common motive to invade the rights of other citizens; or if such a common motive exists, it will be more difficult for all who feel it to discover their own strength, and to act in unison with each other.[29]

In short, in a large enough state one could continue to have a republican government while, at the same time, controlling factions and preventing tyranny. It would be hard to imagine a more clever argument for the superiority of a national government over state governments!

Balancing Power in the Constitution Whereas the makers of the Revolution had placed their faith in sovereign state legislatures, the framers of the Constitution placed theirs in a national government with built-in checks and balances between its partially independent branches. That is, each branch would have its own considerable — and competing — powers. The makers of the Revolution believed in a decentralized government of limited powers with legislative predominance. The makers of the Constitution settled on a truly national government divided within.

Above all, the framers were anxious to establish the principle of supremacy of the national government over that of the states. The Constitution establishes the principle of national supremacy in several ways. Article VI, Section 2 of the Constitution provides specifically that laws made pursuant to the Constitution, as well as the Constitution itself, should be "the supreme Law of the Land." This phrase makes the national government predominant *only* in the areas of legislation specifically given to it by the Constitution; these, however, were extensive. For example, the Constitution gave the sole power of treaty making to the president with the "advice and consent" of two-thirds of the senators present and voting. The Constitution gives Congress the right to raise armies and the taxes to pay for them. These are just some of the powers that the "supremacy" provision gave to the central government over the states.

The Constitution provided in many other ways for the supremacy of the national government over the states. For example, after prolonged discussion at the Constitutional Convention, it was agreed that the salaries of senators and congressmen should be paid out of the national treasury. John Dickinson

---

[29] *The Federalist* No. 10 (New York: Modern Library, 1937), pp. 60–61.

argued for this provision on grounds of "the necessity of making the general government independent of the prejudices, passions, and improper views of the state legislatures." Indeed, no longer would the states be able to hamstring the operations of the national government merely by withdrawing the payment of salaries to their representatives in Congress.

Equally indicative of the Founders' determination to establish a national government not dependent on the states was the long debate over election of the president. The complicated process of presidential election — to be described later — was agreed to very late in the convention, after many different ideas were proposed, some of which now seem almost astounding in their ingenuity. At one point, James Wilson proposed the election of the executive by a tiny group of national legislators chosen by lot. More important for our purposes, however, was the decision on three separate occasions to prevent the state legislatures from having any direct role in presidential elections. Thus, in ways both great and small, the Founders moved toward establishing a national power able to counter the power of the states.

But the framers of the Constitution could not be content merely to set up a large centralized government to offset the power of the state legislatures; they also had to worry about the potential oppressiveness of their own creation. They therefore constructed the presidency, the two houses of Congress, and even the judiciary in such a way that these branches would be in almost continual conflict with each other. The Senate represented each state equally. The House of Representatives spoke for the people as a whole organized into small electoral constituencies within states. The president represented the people as a whole organized into state constituencies. Finally, the Supreme Court, with life tenure for justices, embodied an impartial sense of right and wrong. These conditions would seem to fulfill Madison's prescription in *The Federalist* (No. 51) for the management of power: "Ambition must be made to counteract ambition." By this, Madison meant that conflict among leaders and factions was the only way of securing the people's rights. And because each part of the national government was based on different constituencies or principles of selection, each could be assumed to be responsive to different people or groups. In this way, continuous and beneficial conflict would be assured.

Each of the institutions of our government — the restructured legislative power, the independent judiciary, the remodeled executive, and the states — reflects Madison's vision. Let us look at each in turn.

The Legislature. We have said that the makers of the Revolution did not believe in social orders. Therefore, they could find no justification for legislatures with two houses — bicameral legislatures. The upper house of bicameral legislatures in other countries invariably represented the rich or the aristocracy; in America there was no aristocracy, and the rich were not entitled to special treatment.

But the Madisonian synthesis changed things. If the upper house was viewed as a way of dividing the legislative power and checking popular majorities that might otherwise become dangerous in the lower house, it once more became useful. Thus, the new constitutional system reinvigorated the bicameral notion of legislation by giving it a new theoretical basis.

But how to put such a bicameral legislature together? That was the question that almost tore the Constitutional Convention asunder. Under Madison's original plan, introduced by his fellow Virginian, Edmund Randolph, each state's representation in both houses of the national legislature would be proportional to its population. This plan would give the more populous states — like Virginia — great power. Naturally enough, the smaller states feared that such a scheme of representation eventually would crush them. John Dickinson, who represented tiny Delaware and championed the small states' position, warned: "We . . . would sooner submit to a foreign power than be deprived of equality of suffrage in both branches of the legislature, and thereby thrown under the domination of the larger states." James Wilson of populous Pennsylvania thundered back, "if the small states will not confederate on this plan, Pennsylvania and I presume some other states, will not confederate on any other." Nevertheless, Wilson and the other large staters soon faced a counterproposal to their own. Paterson of New Jersey proposed a unicameral legislature representing states, not individuals, with each state, no matter how small, having one vote.

And so matters stood until the solution arose in the "Great Compromise." The idea of a bicameral legislature with equal state representation in the Senate and proportional representation based on population in the House of Representatives had been around from the beginning of the convention. But only when large staters and small staters realized that neither could win did they finally forge a compromise. Even at the last, the vote for this scheme was close, with Virginia, South Carolina, Georgia, and Pennsylvania resisting to the very end. But eventually the wisdom of Oliver Ellsworth of Connecticut, an advocate of the compromise, prevailed. Ellsworth stated that, although "He was not in general a halfway man . . . he preferred doing half the good we could, rather than do nothing at all."

Nevertheless, the Great Compromise involved some compensation to the large states for agreeing to equal representation in the Senate. In return, the large states won the right to have all bills raising revenue originate in the House of Representatives. This provision of the Constitution gave the large states, which would presumably control the House, initiative over matters of spending and taxation. The role of the Senate was limited to either approving or rejecting such bills, with no power of initiation. Thus, the large states could set the agenda of legislative policymaking.

Other Founders had different ideas about the Senate. Some of the more conservative defenders of the Constitution, such as Alexander Hamilton, hoped that the Senate could function as a sieve of virtue. By sifting the nation's men, discarding the mediocre and corrupt and rewarding the competent and viruous, the Senate would develop the nation's leaders. Of course, this would be true only if the Senate provided ample time for each of its members to learn about politics and to make a name for himself. Partly for this reason, the tenure of senators was put at six years, with one-third of the body elected every two years. In addition, unlike the House of Representatives, whose members all came up for reelection every two years, the Senate had a membership that would change only gradually. Therefore, the Senate would resist the sudden changes in course almost certain to be advocated by a popularly chosen House newly elected at brief two-year intervals.

Although states were equally represented in the Senate, there was no reason to expect similar stability in House representation. Changes in population from year to year could affect representation of various states in the House of Representatives. To handle this problem, the Constitution provides for a census every ten years in order to ascertain the number of representatives to which each state is entitled. Originally, the Constitution provided for an average of one representative for every 30,000 population; today, however, the average constituency is slightly over half a million. Every state, no matter how small, is to have at least one representative in the House.

The Constitution gave each state the right to decide for itself who could vote for Senate and House. It only hinted at a generous electorate by specifically declining to require the ownership of property as a qualification to vote. Nevertheless, most states held onto property qualifications for voting until the nineteenth century. The Constitution did not discriminate against the poor in voting, but neither did it extend the franchise to the poor. This delicate matter was left to the states, and it was not until the 1960s that the federal government finally completed its democratization of voting by making certain that blacks in the South were registered to vote if they chose to be.

One reason that the large states wanted representation according to population is that many such states, particularly South Carolina and Virginia, had large slave populations that they wanted to count for voting purposes. Other southern states, particularly Georgia, anticipated the growth of a large slave population. This time the northern states objected, and the three-fifths rule was adopted. The Constitution provides in Article I, Section 2 that each slave will count as three-fifths of a person for electoral purposes. This compromise was in fact no more than the continuation of a practice that had been followed under the Articles. It is noteworthy that almost no one at the convention envisaged the Constitution as outlawing slavery, although a number of delegates had strong personal reservations about the practice. But all knew that an attack on slavery would end the convention immediately.

Congress was given extensive powers by the Constitution. It was given the power to raise taxes and to outfit armies. It was also given the power to regulate the money supply, an important means of centralizing economic development in the new country. This power was a significant new addition to the national arsenal against the states. Congress alone could declare war and could impeach or accuse and convict the president of "high crimes and midemeanors." The House was given the power to impeach and the Senate the power to convict the president (by a two-thirds vote of the senators present). In addition, Congress has the power to set up federal courts but not to interfere with the operations of the Supreme Court, although it can — and has — altered the size of the Supreme Court.

Two provisions of the Constitution in particular paved the way for congressional expansion of national power. The "commerce clause" (Article I, Section 8) gives Congress the right to regulate interstate commerce, a power that, as interpreted by the Supreme Court, gave the federal government much latitude in regulating economic development in the country and in reducing state power in the economic area. In addition, Article I gives the legislature the right to enact any laws "necessary and proper" to effect the specifically enumerated powers given to Congress. This broad grant of power has permitted Congress to set up, for example, a Federal Reserve System, despite the fact that the Constitution never mentions the Federal Reserve.

Finally, the Constitution gives Congress the power to override presidential vetoes of legislation by a two-thirds vote in each house. Thus, although the framers had been troubled by legislative power under the Articles of Confederation, in the last analysis they trusted the legislature to make laws more than they did any other governmental organ.

The Judiciary. Under the Articles of Confederation there had been no national court system. The framers of the Constitution agreed that a national judiciary was needed — but what should its role be? The Revolution had freed the court system from royal control, but the Revolutionaries had not intended the courts to be independent of the legislative power since, after all, the legislature spoke for the people as a whole. But now, of course, the court system had to be viewed as part of an intricate system of checks and balances. It had to contribute its part to the division of powers. In order to accomplish this, the framers specified that judges in the new national court system should neither be elected nor be appointed for limited terms. Judges hold their offices "during good behavior," which in practice means for life. Also, judges' salaries are protected because the Constitution prevents the reduction of salary during the tenure of office. In these ways the new court system was given some independence from legislative interference.

At the same time, this independence is not complete. Presidents appoint federal judges, but only with the consent of the Senate. And Congress can create or abolish courts, other than the Supreme Court, as it sees fit. Finally, either through constitutional amendment or congressional action, decisions of the Supreme Court can be overturned or significantly modified.

The Constitution enumerates few specific powers of the Supreme Court. The Court has "original jurisdiction" (immediate control) over domestic cases involving the new nation's foreign affairs. This provision removes from state courts the capacity to interfere legally in the conduct of American foreign policy. In addition, the Supreme Court has jurisdiction over cases between states and over land-grant disputes among citizens of the same state. Further, the Court exercises power over all cases arising under the Constitution itself or under any federal law. The Court also enjoys appellate jurisdiction — that is, jurisdiction in other sorts of cases from lower courts of either state or nation — but only as Congress specifically permits. But the Constitution specifically limits Court power by guaranteeing to every person accused of a crime before a federal court the right to a trial by jury. The new court system was not to repeat the arbitrary punishments practiced by the old royal courts.

But the Supreme Court's power grew most dramatically because of the institution of "judicial review," the right to declare federal and state laws "unconstitutional." Nowhere in the Constitution is such a right specifically granted, and scholars still debate whether the framers intended the Court to perform this function. The practice grew under the first Chief Justice of the Court, John Marshall, and some have argued that Marshall was unjustified in introducing the practice into American politics. This reading of the situation seems misguided. During the debates in Philadelphia a number of delegates spoke as if they expected the Court to play a role in what Eldridge Gerry called the "exposition of the laws, which involves a power of deciding on their constitutionality." Indeed, some delegates went further, arguing that the Court should actually exercise a veto power over *any* new legislation without waiting for such legislation to reach the courts through litigation. Thus, it seems clear that Marshall did not invent the practice of "judicial review" out of whole cloth, although he was the instrument by which the practice was actually first applied.

The Executive. Because the executive had been the enemy to the Revolutionary generation, it was natural for the new state governments to limit executive power. The Articles of Confederation did not even provide for a separate executive branch in the national government. However, the makers of the Constitution wished to increase the number of agencies that played a role in legislation, while reducing the power of the legislature itself. The new executive — the president — was therefore accorded two important legislative powers. The first of these was a negative power: the power of veto. The president could block any piece of legislation simply by refusing to sign it, provided that his veto was not overridden by a two-thirds vote of Congress. Second, the president received an implied positive power: He could propose legislation to Congress.

The president's legislative role was expanded further by the fact that he became the only American politician to be selected by a national constituency. This gave him a broad base, even though he was not chosen directly by the people as a whole, but rather by a special temporary body, the electoral college, composed of representatives chosen by each state legislature. Many proposals were offered at the convention for selecting the president. Everything from direct election by the people (an astounding thought in 1787) to complicated schemes by which each state would choose "its best citizen" for nomination, followed by selection of one of these worthies by Congress — schemes of enormous complexity were envisaged. Means for selecting the president proved to be the last important hurdle before the convention adjourned. The delegates faced the problem of ensuring that the other branches of government, the states, and the people should all play some role in the election of the president, but that the president himself should have an autonomous role to play in the balancing of powers.

It was not until the very end of the convention that a "committee on postponed matters," working mainly under the spur of Gouverneur Morris of Pennsylvania, proposed the scheme that was finally adopted. The president was to be elected for a four-year term and to be eligible for reelection. The electoral college was to make the choice. The college was composed of electors from each state equal in number to each state's total representation in Congress. Thus, the large states would enjoy the advantage in electing a president. The legislatures of each state were empowered to choose the members of the electoral college. The people were given no role in this process. Each member of the electoral college voted for two candidates, of whom no more than one could be a citizen of the state from which the elector came. The president was required to win a majority of electoral votes, and vice-president was the person winning the next largest number of votes. If no candidate received a majority, election of the president fell to the House of Representatives voting as state units on the top five candidates, with a majority of votes being sufficient to elect the president.

However, this system did not take into account the rise of political parties. By the election of 1800, electors, instead of being independent, distinguished citizens appointed by the state legislatures as autonomous agents, had simply become pledged to one or another candidate for the presidency. The unworkability of the original constitutional procedure became apparent under these new conditions when, in the election of 1800, Aaron Burr and Thomas Jefferson, bitterly opposed candidates of the same party, each received the same number of electoral votes. This threw the final decision into the House of Representatives, where Jefferson finally won but was forced to serve with Burr as his bitterly hostile vice-president. The Twelfth Amendment to the Constitution, adopted in 1804, repaired this situation by mandating separate elections for president and vice-president. Gradually, the states passed the power to choose electors from the state legislatures to the people.

The president's positive role in legislation was expanded by the fact that he became the only American politician to be selected by a national constituency, the general public voting for president. Domestically, the president is enjoined to provide information to Congress on "the state of the Union" and to recommend useful legislation. The State of the Union message has since become a traditional place for presidents to propose legislation and their own program. The Constitution enumerates certain specific powers the president enjoys. The president is commander-in-chief of the armed forces, which gives him specific warmaking powers. He is given the power to make treaties with the advice and consent of two-thirds of the senators. In a world in which foreign affairs are major elements of American politics, these powers gave the president enormous influence. In addition, the Constitution gives the president power to appoint department heads and to require in writing from them reports on their activities, thus giving him the power to run a coordinated domestic administration.

Some have argued that the president's powers are more implied than explicit. The argument for "inherent powers" of the president concludes that, by the very fact of being responsible for executing the laws, presidents have far-reaching, if unstated, powers, often being able to override Congress and the Supreme Court. The "inherent powers" doctrine was President Nixon's ground for claiming "executive privilege" in not making public information he claimed to be vital to national security. The Court in 1974 rejected this claim to inherent power. The balance-of-power doctrine thus remains vital, despite the growth of the presidency.

The States.   Finally, the Constitution provided a new role for the states. Ours was to be a *federal system,* with the states playing an important role. The Revolutionaries had left the states with ample powers, powers the framers neither wanted to nor could remove. But now, in keeping with the balance-of-power approach of the Constitution, state power had an additional justification: The states became important as a check on federal power.

Unlike the Articles of Confederation, however, the Constitution provided loopholes through which, in later years, the power of national government over the states would slowly expand. As we have seen, three new national powers turned out to be particularly important: the power of the federal government to conduct foreign affairs and make war, to raise and spend its own money, and to regulate interstate commerce. In particular, this last power eventually allowed the federal government to begin its attempt to regulate the economy.

Nevertheless, the Constitution protected the states in several ways. The states retained their own court systems, power over their own elections, and their own taxing powers. The Constitution set up a system of concurrent powers between national and state governments with points of intersection in the concept of federalism, although a system of divided powers between states and national government remained to be worked out. The Tenth Amendment to the Constitution, part of the original Bill of Rights adopted in 1791, specifically reserves all nonenumerated governmental powers in the Constitution to the states. This became a foundation for "states' rights" arguments in the South against national encroachments on slavery. Finally, the Constitution provided methods to bring new states into the union, but also required that there be no alterations in the boundaries of existing states. Thus, the physical integrity of states was secure.

What Powers to the People?   Yet we should not exaggerate the changes wrought by the Constitution. As we have noted, the Tenth Amendment, the last article of the Bill of Rights, states: "The powers not delegated to the

United States by the Constitution, nor prohibited by it to the States, are reserved to the States respectively, or to the people." Amendments to the Constitution required indirect popular assent. Senators were chosen by state legislatures, which were in turn chosen by the people. Members of the electoral college, which chose the president, also were chosen by the state legislatures. And the people themselves elected the House of Representatives, where all appropriations of money were required to originate. The Constitution was a reconsideration and modification of the work of the Revolutionary generation; it was not a counterrevolution in itself.

But there was one important theoretical difference between the Constitution makers and the Revolutionary generation. The Revolutionaries believed that the public should speak directly through its agents in the legislature — that its agents would faithfully enact laws that mirrored popular sentiment. Most of the framers, however, believed this alternative to be unworkable because of factional conflicts that naturally arose among the people. Therefore, the public as a whole would be served best if it spoke indirectly through the bargains struck by partly autonomous elected leaders.

The complicated handiwork the framers produced did not win easy acceptance. The framers knew that many state legislatures would balk at the new Constitution. The campaign for ratification was long and hard. The Constitution provided that ratification would require the assent of only nine of the thirteen states through special conventions chosen for this purpose. The supporters of the Constitution — Federalists, as they came to be called — thus avoided having to submit the Constitution to the state legislatures, where they could expect it to run into opposition. Moreover, they controlled election to the ratifying conventions, and arranged to underrepresent the backcountry and frontier regions in each state, those areas in which people would most object to a centralized government protective of creditors against debtors. Even so, ratification was impossible without appending to the Constitution specific protections of individual rights. The Bill of Rights, the first ten amendments to the Constitution, was thus the price of ratification.

The Notion of Rights Reconsidered The Revolutionary generation believed that persons possessed natural rights, but that majorities possessed legitimate power. This formulation raised a serious problem: In the absence of any clear or enforceable definition of precisely what rights were inalienable, there was always the possibility that majority power could abridge individual rights. The makers of the Constitution believed that several cases of such abridgment had already occurred. In some states legitimate debts had been wiped out, worthless money issued, trial by jury abrogated. Meanwhile, opponents of the Constitution were worried about *their* rights. Therefore, it became important to enumerate the rights individuals possessed and to develop a method for protecting those rights.

As we have seen, the most significant way in which the framers defined rights was by adding a bill of rights to the Constitution. The Bill of Rights states specifically what rights the individual possesses as a matter of law. This group of ten constitutional amendments was a concession to those who, like Patrick Henry, had opposed the Constitution in its original form because, in their view, it lacked sufficient guarantees of individual rights. Others, including Alexander Hamilton, argued that adding a bill of rights would actually be a bad thing: People would erroneously believe that it contained the only rights to which they were entitled.

Still others simply doubted the usefulness of such a bill. Jefferson, for example, argued that statements of rights were mere scraps of paper, and that the people themselves had to protect their own rights. Madison ultimately supported such a bill of rights — "not," as he said, "because they are necessary, but because they can produce no possible danger, and may gratify some gentlemen's wishes." Necessary or not, the Bill of Rights was finally ratified in 1791 and eventually became, along with the Fourteenth Amendment, the main focal point of debates about rights in America.

The Bill of Rights built on statements of traditional individual liberties already contained in most state constitutions from the Revolutionary period.[30] However, the federal Bill of Rights specified more narrowly the rights possessed by people and, therefore, gave the tradition of natural rights the most complete form it had ever had. We will discuss these rights — and the protection of them — in detail in Chapter 14.

The framers also separated ordinary legislation from constitutional reform. The legislative branch of the government was confined to making laws within the provisions of the Constitution; the power to amend the Constitution itself was reserved to special conventions appointed for the purpose, or to Congress and the electorates of the several states. The hope was that this arrangement would not only allow the people periodically to reconsider the health of individual rights but would also make it suitably difficult for any part of government — or the people themselves — to alter the scope of those rights (see Figure 2.1).

The makers of the Constitution also provided for periodic reaffirmations of rights by creating the opportunity for the judicial branch to review legislation. Even without the process of judicial review in the Supreme Court, conflicts about how one law or another should be applied would have forced judges and juries to make decisions about the powers of the state versus the rights of individuals. This slow evolution of rights out of particular cases and through experience was, in fact, a heritage from the British that the Americans preserved after independence.

Finally, of course, the framers hoped that the constitutional provisions for checking power with power, as Madison proposed, would work to protect the people's rights. They realized that those rights could not be entrusted solely to the people's good faith because good faith alone was an insufficient guarantee against a tyranny of the majority. Madison had put the problem succinctly in *The Federalist* (No. 51): "If a majority be united by a common in-

[30] Lawrence J. Friedman, *A History of American Law* (New York: Simon and Schuster, 1973).

Figure 2.1 The Process of Constitutional Amendment

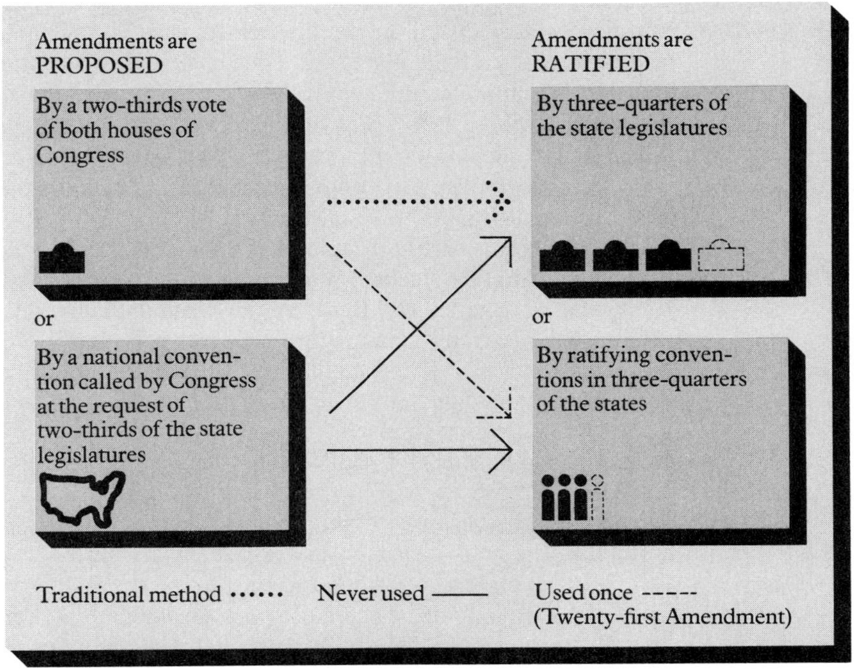

Amendments are
PROPOSED

By a two-thirds vote
of both houses of
Congress

or

By a national conven-
tion called by Congress
at the request of
two-thirds of the state
legislatures

Amendments are
RATIFIED

By three-quarters of
the state legislatures

or

By ratifying conven-
tions in three-quarters
of the states

Traditional method ······ Never used ——— Used once - - - - -
(Twenty-first Amendment)

Source: Gary Wasserman, *The Basics of American Politics* (Boston: Little, Brown, 1976), p. 41.

terest, the rights of the minority will be insecure." Nor could the people's rights be entrusted to the good faith of the people's elected leaders: As Madison so prophetically observed in the same installment of *The Federalist*, "Enlightened statesmen will not always be at the helm."

Rather, the framers reasoned with Madison that the very pervasiveness of conflict, rather than its absence, would help safeguard individual liberties. Thus, they saw to it that the Constitution institutionalized this conflict. Potential tyrants would be checked and controlled by other potential tyrants; ambition would be counteracted by ambition.

However, even the most ardent defenders of the Constitution admitted that neither carefully worded constitutional statements of rights nor carefully conceived political processes could be counted on to protect individual freedoms. The people must protect their own rights, and opinions varied about their ability to do so. The framers of the Constitution realized that the tension between the governed and the governors could never be eliminated, but they hoped that it could at least be controlled in the interest of the people. Ultimately, however, it was the people's job to control themselves and their leaders.

POWER AND RIGHTS: THE TENSION CONTINUES

The framers of the Constitution must have found it immensely frustrating never to know how their careful plans worked out in practice. Would later generations continue to be suspicious of governmental power? Would the Constitution rearrange power in America so as to reconcile a strong national government with individual rights? Today, almost two centuries later, we can see what the framers could not foresee: how the gap between the governed and the governors has fared. The answer, of course, is that the framers were right. Fear and suspicion of governmental power have shaped American political history ever since the constitutional period, as a few examples will show. But the constitutional framework has survived.

An important early example of tension was the so-called Bank War during President Andrew Jackson's administration. Jackson's congressional opponents had chartered the Bank of the United States with extensive power to bankroll large transportation projects and commercial ventures. But to Jacksonian Democrats of the 1830s, the bank represented an attempt by eastern financiers to take power away from the people and to monopolize it themselves. Jackson saw himself very much as a defender of the "people"— the workers and farmers of the West — against the corrupt and moneyed East. Advocates of the bank argued that its growth would hasten the internal development of American commerce and industry. But the Jacksonians had their way, and the bank's charter was eventually terminated.

The fear of power emerged again during the industrial expansion that followed the Civil War. To finance that expansion, as well as to enrich themselves, large corporations built trusts and holding companies (special agencies for business investment), manipulated banks and stockholding ventures, and systematically corrupted public officials. Slowly, opposition gathered. In the West and the South, the Populist party developed as an instrument of reform. Gradually, antitrust and regulatory legislation was passed, and other attempts were made to control industrial expansion. Meanwhile, journalists and writers were busy exposing the sordid working conditions and corrupt practices of many American industries. These writers, known as the muckrakers, attempted to stir up public opinion against the trusts by arguing that industrial power had usurped the power of the people. These developments came to a head in 1896, when William Jennings Bryan, the Populist-Democrat, ran for president. But Bryan and Populism alienated many conservative Democrats as well as most Republicans, and Bryan suffered a crushing defeat. Nevertheless, despite his loss, Bryan managed to highlight the tension between the governed and the governors, a tension that was perhaps as great in the period from 1880 to 1896 as at any other time in American history. And subsequently the Supreme Court began slowly to interpret the Constitution so as to bring trusts and large corporations under some slight control.

Finally, the gap between those who rule and those who do not has reappeared dramatically in our own time. In 1960, in his most famous speech, President Eisenhower warned against the emergence of what he called "the military-industrial complex" in America. Eisenhower argued that a combination of defense industries, bureaucrats, and military professionals could well come to dominate American politics. Eisenhower's fears were anticipated earlier in academic writing, particularly that of the sociologist C. Wright Mills, who argued that military leaders, the political elite, and the controllers of large corporations constituted a "power elite" that was both wholly unresponsive to the public and thoroughly in control of the major decisions in American life. We will examine Mills's ideas more closely in Chapter 15.

These fears were revived in the mid-1970s by revelations that our national government itself for years had engaged in massive, systematic violations of the people's rights. Knowledgeable critics of our government's intelligence operations had long been aware that the Federal Bureau of Investigation (FBI), the Central Intelligence Agency (CIA), the Internal Revenue Service (IRS), Army Intelligence, and other government agencies infringed on American citizens' rights at home and abroad. But not until April 1976, when the Senate Select Committee on Intelligence issued its two-volume report on these activities, did the extraordinary — and appalling — record of abuses become public.

The opening words of the committee's final report, entitled "Intelligence Activities and the Rights of Americans," put the matter starkly: "The constitutional system of checks and balances has not adequately controlled intelligence activities." The report of the committee, also called the Church committee after its chairman, Senator Frank Church of Idaho, catalogued dozens of abuses. Here are a few excerpts from that report:

> United States intelligence agencies have investigated a vast number of American citizens and domestic organizations. F.B.I. headquarters alone has developed over 500,000 domestic intelligence files.

> At least 26,000 individuals were at one point catalogued on an F.B.I. list of persons to be rounded up in the event of a "national emergency."

> From "late 1963" until his death in 1968, Martin Luther King, Jr. was the target of an intensive campaign by the Federal Bureau of Investigation to "neutralize" him as an effective civil rights leader. In the words of the man in charge of the F.B.I.'s "war" against Dr. King, "No holds were barred."

> During the 1960s alone, the F.B.I. and C.I.A. conducted hundreds of [illegal] break-ins, many against American citizens and domestic organizations.

> Officials of the intelligence agencies [frequently testified] that the law and the Constitution were simply ignored. [31]

In the 1980s we enter a period of new challenge to the constitutional framework. The energy crisis and the falterings of a poorly functioning economy offer many opportunities for the abuse of power. One can foresee the possibility of conflict between governed and governors over how to manage these problems and over whether government should assert itself more forcefully in

---

[31] *The New York Times,* April 29, 1976.

these areas. At the same time we see the rise of right-wing groups (the so-called New Right) who argue that "governmental interference" in the lives of individuals should be removed, yet in the same breath demand that government require prayer in schools and prevent women from having abortions, as if these did not constitute forms of governmental interference. It seems clear that in the 1980s, as before, there will be no cessation of tensions between governed and governors and no lack of debate about how the constitutional framework of divided powers should operate.

CONCLUSION The difference in perspective between those in power and those out of power lies at the heart of the American political experience. It had its beginnings in the philosophical traditions the colonists brought with them from England, and was nurtured by the unique combination of geography and religion in colonial America. However, a peculiarly American response to the tensions between leaders and led did not appear until the Revolution. By that time, Americans had developed a theory of popular sovereignty that vested total power in legislatures. These were considered to represent free individuals, rather than social groups as the English Parliament did.

The colonies' political problems during and after the Revolution convinced many Americans that this theory was inadequate. The Constitution, then, emerged as a reconsideration and modification of American political beliefs. The Constitution prescribes a government in which separate executive, legislative, and judicial branches check and balance each other. This arrangement was intended to ensure specific individual rights while providing for considerable centralized decision making.

The Constitution has proved to be the foundation of American politics. It has provided the framework within which American politics has operated, and it has also provided the reference point for judging American political innovations. Its fundamental job — to hold a union of states together — has been challenged several times, once by force of arms in the Civil War. Yet the document has expanded through interpretation and amendment to absorb conflicts, rather than to break under them.

On the other hand, *how* the Constitution has accomplished its unifying task is a matter of debate. Is the Constitution no more than a symbolic mask behind which plays naked self-interest? Is the Constitution a legal formula providing judicial mechanisms for regulating society according to natural law? Is the Constitution a cleverly construed outline for an eighteenth-century government that somehow, in defiance of historical forces, has proved politically effective in the twentieth century? Or, finally, is the Constitution a set of mythic aspirations the ideals of which are so grand that they hold Americans together even as they reveal the gap between aspiration and attainment? These are questions the reader may be better able to answer at the end of this book.

Of course, the Constitution has not eliminated the struggle between those who govern and those who do not. Indeed, its basic premise is that such a struggle cannot be eliminated but must instead be contained. Ever since 1787, Americans have striven to keep a proper balance of power between the governors and the governed. Major conflict over this question occurred in Jacksonian America, again in the late nineteenth century, and yet again in our own time.

Today we confront an American government that is much more powerful and complex than anything the Founding Fathers could have foreseen. For example, to the makers of the Revolution, the mere presence of a standing army guaranteed governmental tyranny. Now we have so many other potential sources of tyranny to occupy us that we seldom think twice about a standing army. As our government has expanded in size and function, the opportunities for it to alienate its citizens or to become internally divided and inefficient have multiplied. Indeed, it was precisely such a view that impelled President Reagan, in his presidential campaign, to argue that it was "time to get the American government off the backs of the American people." Yet can we do without a powerful national government capable of playing a major domestic role? These questions will once again test the political theory of the Constitution.

SUGGESTIONS FOR FURTHER READING

Bailyn, Bernard. *The Ideological Origins of the American Revolution.* Cambridge, Mass.: Belknap Press, 1967. A pathbreaking study of the origins of the political ideas of the Revolution.

Boorstin, Daniel. *The Genius of American Politics.* Chicago: University of Chicago Press, 1953. A controversial account of continuity in American politics.

The Federalist. New York: Modern Library, 1937. The political theory of the Constitution in the words of Alexander Hamilton, James Madison, and John Jay.

Hartz, Louis. *The Liberal Tradition in America.* New York: Harcourt, Brace and World, 1955. A classic argument about the intellectual "blinders" imposed on Americans by their political origins.

Rossiter, Clinton. *1787: The Grand Convention.* New York: Macmillan, 1966. A lively account of the making of the Constitution.

Wood, Gordon S. *The Creation of the American Republic, 1776–1787.* Chapel Hill: University of North Carolina Press, 1969. A painstaking and precise account of shifts in the character of American political thought from the Revolution to the Constitution.

Chapter 3 Political Culture and Socialization

Imagine a ten-year-old American boy visiting Italy for the first time. What will impress him? He will probably be struck by several things. For example, he may be surprised at how much attention strangers pay to him. In restaurants other patrons may openly stare at him, talk to each other about him, smile at him, and even wave at him, all the while ignoring his little sister. He may also notice that Italian men spend a good deal of time together drinking coffee in cafes, with women nowhere in sight. He may put these two obervations together and conclude that, in Italy, being a male means something different than it does in America.

The complicated feelings a person experiences in a new country have been called *culture shock*. As our example suggests, "culture" is something we become most conscious of when we find ourselves in a novel setting; as long as we stay within our own culture, we rarely see it as distinctive. Culture, therefore, encompasses those things we take for granted, the aspects of our lives as Americans — or as midwestern whites or southern blacks — that are so fully shared by those around us that we are not even aware of them.

Although we can take it apart for analysis, in real life culture is always unified. One aspect of culture is the *habits* shared by a people — for example, the tendency of Italian males to congregate in cafes, or the tendency of salespersons in American stores to be friendly and informal to customers. These cultural habits express a people's characteristic *assumptions* about life and how it ought to be lived — for example, the American assumption that all of us, salespersons and customers alike, are fundamentally equal.

Cultural assumptions are usually unspoken and unexamined. Only when they are challenged by those who do not share them do they become explicit and overt, at which point they reveal themselves as *beliefs* widely shared by people, such as the Italian belief that males should play the leading role in society. In turn, Americans believe in being "plain folks" and not "putting on airs."

Beliefs often express the deepest *values* that unite a people. Values are statements of our most important aims in life; they represent the goals toward which we strive, and they usually include the ethical code that makes us, in our own eyes, worthy persons. Values are the things we live for and, if necessary, stand ready to die for.

Each culture expresses its particular blend of habits, assumptions, beliefs, and values through *symbols*. Symbols are specific things or events that stand for the ties that bind a people together. In England the coronation of a king or queen symbolizes much that is "truly" English. In America, cultural symbols range from the American eagle to the Thanksgiving turkey, from a Fourth of July parade to the funeral of a president. Our political institutions — most particularly the president — have considerable influence as symbols in addition to their official functions. This makes them an important part of our political culture.

THE SUBSTANCE OF AMERICAN POLITICAL CULTURE

Much that is distinctive about American character and American culture emerges from our confrontation with two ideas that moved the Founding Fathers: the tension between those who govern and those who do not, and the promise of democracy. American *political culture* may be defined as the bundle of habits, assumptions, beliefs, values, and symbols that refer to the tension between those who govern and those who do not, and to the possibility that democracy might help reduce this tension.

Still, to talk about "American political culture" is to assume a great deal. For the United States, although not really a "melting pot" where diverse peoples blend into one, is nevertheless the home of people who immigrated from many different countries. Is there only one American political culture? Are there several? Or is there one American political culture with many subcultural variations?

And to exactly what aspects of life does American political culture extend? It includes democracy; but is democracy best understood narrowly as an arrangement between government and the citizenry? Or should we see democracy broadly in the relationship of ordinary people to each other as they go about their everyday lives? If American political culture embraces this latter conception of democracy, there must exist subtle connections between personal democracy and political democracy in American politics. Identifying these connections may be a difficult task.

Still, despite these problems, political culture is too important to bypass, for it may greatly influence a society's politics. We are all — leaders and followers alike — products of our culture, and we are influenced continuously by it. Therefore, we cannot fully understand politics in America without understanding American political culture.

Has Political Culture Changed since 1776? A good way to start our examination of present-day American political culture is to see how some of its prominent elements have changed (or not) over time. The founders' attitudes toward power, the role of government, popular participation, and government officials were described in Chapter 2. What are Americans' attitudes on these topics today?

Attitudes toward Power. As we have seen, the Founding Fathers made the problem of controlling power a focal point of American constitutional thought. What is the status of power today in American political culture? Do modern Americans agree with the Founding Fathers about the dangers of power, or has our experience with power made us somewhat less cynical about its uses?

The answer seems to be that, in most respects, Americans today agree with the founders. For example, only 59 percent of those sampled in a recent study of American beliefs about power described the distribution of power along the lines laid out in the Constitution — that is, as fragmented and available to many different groups in America. A substantial minority, 41 percent, believed power to be concentrated among the rich or the politically well connected.[1] Despite the founders' attempts to divide power, many Americans remain skeptical about the power structure of their society.

Not all Americans agree on this point, however. Unsurprisingly, the poorer the person, the more likely he or she is to feel that the distribution of political power in American society is neither equal nor fair. Of the wealthy in the study already cited, 65 percent thought power was distributed fairly equally among groups, as compared with 55 percent of the less well off. Poorer people are also less likely to feel that people who hold power deserve to do so, and they also doubt that they themselves are treated fairly in confrontations with political and legal authorities.[2] Thus, the founders' suspicions about power still prevail in much of American life.

And Americans have become increasingly concerned about their access to those with power. In a recent investigation, 41 percent doubted that their views had much impact on their political leaders. This finding suggests a widespread view that government has divorced itself from the people, a view that the founders would have recognized very easily.[3]

[1] Joan Huber and William Form, *Income and Ideology* (New York: Free Press, 1973), p. 135.
[2] Ibid., p. 93.
[3] See Samuel Barnes, et al; *Political Action* (Beverly Hills, Calif.: Sage, 1979), p. 489.

Attitudes toward Government's Role. Compared with people in other countries, however, Americans in general are probably *less* suspicious about the distribution of political power than one might expect. This is partly because the government the founders created has been able to some extent to vindicate their hopes, thereby moderating their successors' tendencies toward suspicion and hostility. Over the years, Americans have come to accept the idea that government can be useful as well as dangerous. The result is that although we are still quick to criticize government, we also have grown to depend on it.

Paradoxically, however, the acceptance of a positive role for government has not made people content. More and more, Americans object to the cost of government, and the majority complain that the tax burden they must bear is more than they can stand.[4] Americans appear to want government to continue providing services, but they increasingly resent having to pay for those services, especially when they suspect that some of their tax money is "wasted" by "inefficient bureaucrats." The conjunction of these attitudes is proof that widely held political attitudes need not be entirely logical.

Political Participation. The Founding Fathers also stressed the importance to Americans of protecting themselves, through periodic political action, from the abuses of power to which political leaders were prone. With the expansion of governmental services in the United States, political participation has become even more important than it was in the 1780s. Have Americans responded to government's expanded powers by increasing their participation in politics?

In general, the answer is "no." Most Americans have not developed a habit of political participation. Even national elections leave many potential voters at home. Of the roughly half of adult Americans who report belonging to at least one politically relevant community group, the majority belong only to a church organization. Very few Americans report continued membership in political organizations, and only a small percentage belong to more than one political interest group.[5] Nor are other kinds of political participation common. For example, no more than 29 percent of American college students during the 1960s ever took part in campus protests over the Vietnam War, the Cambodia invasion, or the way their university or college was run.[6] And only a fraction of those students were members of specific protest organizations. Thus, despite the Founders' warnings, political culture in America has not become a habitually participatory culture.

Attitudes toward Politicians. Our culture's suspicions about power focus particularly on perceptions of politicians. As many as half of adult Americans

---

[4] See Everett Ladd, "The Polls: Taxing and Spending," *Public Opinion Quarterly* 43, no. 1 (Spring 1979): 126–36, 127.

[5] Sidney Verba and Norman Nie, *Participation in America* (New York: Harper and Row, 1972), p. 42.

[6] This estimate is consistent with Philip G. Altbach, *Student Politics in America* (New York: McGraw-Hill, 1974), chaps. 3, 7.

feel that politicians cannot be trusted and are only self-interested, that many are incompetent, and that political parties are no more than vehicles of self-interest.[7] Even the chief symbol of authority, the president, is not immune to these criticisms. Watergate dealt a considerable blow to our views of politicians generally, but this is only part of the story. Judging by decreases in voter turnout, public confidence in American leaders was on the decline even before Watergate.

Yet again we confront an apparent contradiction in American political culture: Our negative disposition toward politicians rarely moves us to action. Instead, Americans continue to return incumbent officeholders to power. Even when a scandal touches an officeholder, there is no certainty that he or she will meet political defeat. Robert Sikes, a Democratic congressman from Florida, was stripped in 1976 of his committee chairmanships by fellow Democrats reacting to charges of corrupt practices. Yet his constituents returned him to office. Might it be that, although we distrust "politicians," we have positive feelings toward those officeholders whom we know most about because we are aware of the services they perform for us?

Recently, however, Americans may have become less tolerant of the misdeeds of their leaders. The ABSCAM investigation of purported efforts by Arab businessmen to gain congressional favors presented videotape evidence of congressmen accepting bribes. Acutally seeing congressmen accept bribes apparently reduced the willingness of Americans to forgive and forget. Most of the congressmen who chose to run for reelection despite their ABSCAM involvement were defeated.

A Political Culture of Inertia? What explains the fact that, despite our national suspicion of power, politics, and politicians, most Americans do not make a more serious effort to change things? Why are we willing to depend heavily on government even as we criticize it? Why do we not take a more active part in our political system?

There are several reasons for the inertia of American political culture. For one thing, dissatisfaction flourishes most at the bottom of the social class system. But the poor and the ill educated lack the time, the energy, and the organizational skills for effective political action. They are therefore prone to accept their political lot as inevitable in some respects.

A second factor is the widespread feeling that the frustrations of politics are counterbalanced by hope in other areas of American life. Most Americans of all classes still feel generally optimistic about the future; they contrast their own economic progress with that of their parents or that of people in other countries, and they feel well off.[8] Although most will agree that there are

---

[7] James D. Wright, *The Dissent of the Governed* (New York: Academic Press, 1976), part II; Jack Dennis, "Trends in Support for the American Party System," *British Journal of Political Science* 5 (April 1975): 187–230.

[8] For a general consideration, see Angus Campbell, "Aspiration, Satisfaction, and Fulfillment," in Angus Campbell and Philip Converse, eds., *The Human Meaning of Social Change* (New York: Sage, 1972), pp. 441–67; Angus Campbell, *The Sense of Well-Being in America* (New York: McGraw-Hill, 1981).

serious economic inequalities in American life, individuals rarely expect to be prevented from improving their lot.[9] American society appears to many still to be an open system that recognizes individual merit. And when people feel themselves justly treated, whatever their reservations about the system as a whole, they are unlikely to demand major social and political changes.

Our culture also retains a tradition of trust in other people. Even though the government itself may not deliver on all its promises, and even though politicians do act corruptly sometimes, at least ordinary people can continue to rely on each other. Besides, people realize that "politicians" are not responsible for *all* that goes wrong in government. Hence, trust in others remains, despite growing fear of crime and violence in our cities as well as substantial changes in family and friendship patterns. Americans continue to see their neighbors and friends as sources of comfort and aid.

Another factor that prevents people from translating their discontent into political action is their difficulty in generalizing from the behavior of an individual politician to his or her office. If an individual congressman is exposed for abusing the power of his office, his acts may not be seen as typical of members of Congress. Or, if a person believes that members of Congress *generally* are corrupt, he or she may still have faith in his or her own senators and representatives. It may often be difficult to decide where to place the blame, and what to do about it.

Besides, it would be a misunderstanding of culture to expect people's beliefs to be translated automatically into action. In the United States the disaffected and the supportive alike are expected to abide by norms of civility in their political conduct. Most Americans believe in at least listening to both sides of a question, and are put off by groups that refuse to "give and take." Bargaining and compromise are staples of American political culture, just as they were two hundred years ago. A group that gets a reputation for uncompromising positions — as the Black Panthers did in the 1960s — usually finds itself at a political disadvantage.

But again we confront an ambiguity in American political culture. Reaching a compromise requires that all parties be flexible and willing to yield even on deeply felt principles. But Americans who favor and expect compromise are often the same people who criticize politicians for not taking stronger stands, and who complain about "political expediency" and manipulation. It would therefore be wrong to label groups that will not compromise as "un-American." We believe in both principles *and* expediency.

However, American tolerance does not extend to groups that take to the streets in forceful protest. Americans often approve of the political goals of such groups, but they reject protests outside accepted legal channels.[10] Indeed, groups that feel themselves so thoroughly excluded from power that they

---

[9] This is a view that extends even to children. See Alan J. Stern and Donald Searing, "The Stratification Beliefs of British and American Adolescents," *British Journal of Political Science* 6 (April 1976): 177–203.

[10] A case in point is response to protests at the Democratic convention in 1968. See John P. Robinson, "Public Reaction to Political Protest," *Public Opinion Quarterly* 34 (Spring 1970): 1–9.

must resort to protest at all usually explain that their tactics are regrettable and temporary, and will be abandoned as soon as they receive fair treatment.

The rejection of protest as a political strategy in America owes much to the widespread belief that ultimately most people are responsible for their own success or failure. People must learn to "cope."[11] They should not ask for "special favors" even when they have been subjected to generations of wrongdoing. People should work for what they receive; even the poor are not owed a living, only aid *toward* a living. Not surprisingly, therefore, policies that are aimed at redistributing income are not very popular in American politics.

TWO SIDES OF AMERICAN POLITICAL CULTURE   As we have seen, American political culture is a collection of contradictions. Can we reconcile conflicts between belief in principle and acceptance of compromise, between a heritage of limited government and present demands for large social programs, between a suspicion of politicians and reluctance to replace them? How should we interpret the diversity of our political culture?

The best answer seems to be that there is more than one side to political culture. Much of our political culture consists of formal beliefs — political principles taught to us in school, repeated by our political leaders, and invoked symbolically on special occasions. These *formal* aspects of political culture are what all of us share as Americans; therefore, when we act as a united people they become central. But this formal culture exists alongside an *informal culture* that expresses the reality of our everyday lives. The informal culture is composed of the truths bequeathed to us by our families, our religion, the street language of our communities. These two aspects — the one formal and symbolic, the other informal and pragmatic — are equal partners in American political culture.[12]

The Formal Political Culture   The core of American formal culture is our commitment to liberty, equality, and private property. These values help make up the liberal tradition in American politics, the tradition we inherit from the Founding Fathers.

Of these three values, individual freedom is especially important to Americans. In a 1973 study, Americans ranked freedom first among eighteen values — ahead of such strong competitors as happiness, family security, and even equality (which was rated thirteenth).[13] The question, of course, is what Americans mean by freedom. Although there are some practical conflicts on this point, as we will see in Chapter 15 on liberty and justice, on a formal level the answer is unequivocal. Most Americans agree with the Founding Fathers, who construed freedom as the absence of control over the citizen, whether by government or by other people.

Most Americans also share the faith of the Founders in the virtues of private

[11] Paul Sniderman and Richard Brody, "Coping: The Ethic of Self-Reliance," *American Journal of Political Science* 21 (1977): 501–21.

[12] We borrow some of this conceptualization from Frank Parkin, *Class Inequality and Political Order* (New York: Praeger, 1971), chap. 3.

[13] Milton Rokeach, *The Nature of Human Values* (New York: Free Press, 1973), p. 89.

property. A higher proportion of Americans own their own homes than do people in other countries. Americans also continue to support private enterprise, a system in which private owners control their own firms, with as little governmental interference as possible. Even during the worst of the depression years of the 1930s, when bank failures cost many ordinary depositors their life savings, few people favored having the government take control of the banks (see Table 3.1).[14] Today, governmental regulation of the private economy remains a policy Americans grudgingly accept as an unfortunate necessity, rather than one eagerly embraced as efficient or just. And many think that there is "too much regulation."

Finally, Americans continue to value equality, although we value liberty and private property more. But our commitment to equality is narrow and specialized, as we shall see in Chapter 15. We feel little commitment to social and economic equality. One indication of this is the fact that the progressive income tax, which has the effect of redistributing a very small proportion of people's incomes, came to the United States later than to most other western industrialized countries — in 1913, and then only after a prolonged debate. Americans favor political equality: People are supposed to have an equal chance to compete against each other politically, and all people should be able to vote and to participate freely in politics.

The Informal Political Culture When we turn from formal culture to the informal, pragmatic culture that guides Americans' daily lives, we find ourselves on very different ground. The informal culture is worked out in response to the actual living circumstances of particular groups and persons, not as a set of political ideals. And because everyday life is often ambiguous and contradictory, so is the informal political culture.

One example of ambiguity and contradiction involves our informal ideas about government's role as service provider. In their everyday lives people confront numerous problems of education, transportation, discrimination, housing, health, and so on. Although in the abstract Americans agree that government should be limited, we nevertheless expect and demand assistance for ourselves. And we expect civil servants to treat us as people, not as "cases," and to bend the rules in the interest of compassion. Yet we also want competent civil servants, fair and impartial procedures, and just decisions. We respect the need for a rational, expert bureaucracy; but, paradoxically, we also want the bureaucracy staffed by "folks" who will understand and sympathize with our own special problems.

Much of the informal culture revolves around group stereotypes. Children learn group stereotypes quite early in life; once learned, such perceptions are not easily changed.[15] One recent study of American teenagers reported strong

[14] Donald J. Devine, *The Political Culture of the United States* (Boston: Little, Brown, 1972), p. 213.
[15] For an examination, see Judith J. R. Porter, *Black Child, White Child* (Cambridge, Mass.: Harvard University Press, 1971), esp. p. 85.

Table 3.1 Attitudes Toward Redistributive Politics in the 1930s

	Total	Upper White Collar	Lower White Collar	Wage Worker	Unemployed
Welfare Programs					
Percent saying:					
The government should see that everyone is above subsistence	73%	59%	73%	82%	86%
The government should provide relief for those in need	66	56	65	73	83
The government should guarantee job opportunities	61	46	60	73	76
Government Control of Economy					
Percent wanting:					
The government to regulate utilities	55%	47%	57%	58%	62%
Some government ownership of railroads	38	27	39	42	54
Some government ownership of telephone & telegraph system	33	23	34	38	42
Percent saying:					
The government should redistribute wealth through high taxes on the rich	35%	24%	32%	44%	54%
There should be a law limiting income	24	13	22	32	42
The government should confiscate wealth beyond what people need	15	6	12	24	28
End of "Free Enterprise"					
Percent wanting relief even if it means:					
The end of capitalism	16%	7%	16%	20%	32%
Government assignment of jobs	12	5	12	16	26

	Total	Upper White Collar	Lower White Collar	Wage Worker	Unem- ployed
Change in the Constitution					
Percent wanting:					
Some changes in the Constitution	30%	22%	31%	36%	31%
Complete change in the Constitution	6	3	6	10	7
March	(2102)	(563)	(803)	(539)	(197)
December	(2048)	(530)	(818)	(508)	(192)

Source: Sidney Verba and Kay Lehman Schlosman, "Unemployment, Class Consciousness, and Radical Politics: What Didn't Happen in the Thirties," *Journal of Politics* 39, no. 2 (May 1977): 302.

anti-Semitic and antiblack stereotypes even among the wealthy and well educated, those who had been most thoroughly exposed to arguments designed to break down prejudice.[16] Nonetheless, group images do change in American life. When people of different races or religions are forced to work together, they usually can do so efficiently despite their private views. Partly, this is because they are aware that the *formal* culture condemns outright prejudice and promotes tolerance.

The informal culture also extends to the central formal concepts of American political life, such as equality. Although equal treatment is an important formal aspect of American political culture, not everyone truly expects equality in dealing with authorities. Many blacks complain that police treat them with unjustified hostility and suspicion. Many whites resist "unfair" encroachments on their neighborhoods by programs like school busing and government subsidies for low-cost housing in affluent suburbs. Many whites protest "reverse discrimination" in affirmative-action programs designed to aid blacks. Thus we see constant tension between the formal and informal aspects of American political culture.

AMERICAN POLITICAL SUBCULTURES   Americans come in many varieties. We are divided by social and economic histories, religious differences, and racial and ethnic heritages. It would be astonishing, then, if each group of Americans did not develop its own subcultural variations on American political culture, reflecting its own particular experience in America. Although we cannot chronicle these variations in detail, we can at least offer some sense of their range.

[16] Charles Glock, et al., *Adolescent Prejudice* (New York: Harper and Row, 1975).

Black Americans Three related facts have shaped black American political culture. The first is the experience of *racial discrimination.* Whites' discrimination against and mistreatment of blacks began during the period of slavery; but discrimination in education, employment, and politics continued after emancipation. This sad historical legacy has inevitably been reflected in the political culture of American blacks.

The second important factor is *poverty.* Blacks as a group have always been poorer than whites, and the poverty gap between blacks and whites has not closed in recent years. Poverty affects the political culture of any group; poverty combined with a perception of white hostility gives poor blacks a grim conception of their situation. The legacy of discrimination and poverty is reflected in a widespread belief among blacks that as individuals they have little control over their own futures or over the things that affect them most. This perception of personal weakness, in turn, reduces satisfaction with life and weakens action to improve one's own situation.

The third important factor is *migration.* Before World War II, most blacks lived in the rural South. Today they are predominantly urban. The migration from country to city and from South to North occurred at a time when American cities were already beginning to decay, a fact that exaggerated the natural strains associated with urbanization.

Racial discrimination, both as present reality and as historical legacy, pervades blacks' assumptions about American politics. For example, what most whites called "criminal activities"— the urban riots of the 1960s — most blacks saw as "revolutionary expressions." [17] Because blacks see American politics as less open to them by conventional means than do whites, they are more prone to turn to unconventional tactics.

The legacy of discrimination also affects images of political authorities. For example, fewer blacks than whites feel that their contacts with political authorities proceed fairly, and fewer blacks expect the courts to treat them impartially. [18] This skeptical attitude toward political authorities has to do with poverty as well as discrimination. Because so many blacks are poor, they often find themselves in contact with governmental authorities on whom they must depend for needed services. The negative conception blacks have about their treatment is based on two aspects of these contacts. First, as beneficiaries of government services, blacks are inevitably reminded of their dependent, subservient status. Therefore, contacts with officials often are humiliating and demeaning. In addition, our history demonstrates that government has yet to find a system for aiding the poor efficiently and effectively. The inadequacies of governmental and welfare programs are naturally most visible to the recipients, especially the black poor. Perhaps it should come as no surprise, then,

[17] Angus Campbell, *White Attitudes Towards Black People* (Ann Arbor, Mich.: Institute for Social Research, 1971).
[18] Huber and Form, *Income and Ideology,* p. 93.

that over twice as many blacks as whites believe that they have had less than the share of happiness out of life they should reasonably expect.[19]

Nevertheless, it would be wrong to conclude that black political culture represents a wholesale rejection of American politics. Instead, two factors, the urbanization of blacks and the civil rights movement of recent decades, have served to link the black subculture with the larger American culture. Blacks now demand entry to American politics, as evidenced by the fact that the political activity of blacks now resembles that of whites at comparable income levels. In some cities, black political organizations have become extremely effective in electing black public officials. The situation is similar in rural areas. Since the passage of the Voting Rights Act of 1965, which ensured the right of qualified blacks to vote, registration of blacks in the rural South has accelerated rapidly. In sum, the legacy of discrimination, poverty, and migration has not entirely alienated blacks from the main themes of American political culture. Indeed, some sociolgists and historians argue that racial politics is now more a matter of social *class* than of race.

But the politicization of blacks does not necessarily signal an end to racial awareness as a stimulant of black political action. On the contrary, as one study of black rioters showed, greater political awareness among blacks must be accompanied by changes in the way white Americans absorb blacks into the political culture if the legacy of black awareness is not to be alienation rather than support. Indeed, in an unresponsive political environment, protest and riot serve to increase black pride and self-awareness. In a time of reduced attention to the political problems and progress of blacks, we should not forget how narrow is the line between activism that *affirms* the political system and activism that *rejects it.*[20]

American Jews Unlike blacks, Jews came to America deliberately, with the goal of realizing the American dream of freedom and prosperity. In this country they have no history of slavery, nor are they set apart from other Americans by skin color. The factors that have particularly affected the political culture of American Jews, then, are quite different from those that have influenced black culture.

First, although history bears on American Jews as it does on black Americans, it is largely a European rather than an American experience. Most American Jews are descended from immigrants who came to America to escape persecution in Europe. For many, their lingering sense of persecution was stimulated by the virtual destruction of European Jewry during World War II.

---

[19] Angus Campbell, *The Sense of Well-Being in America* (New York: McGraw-Hill, 1981), p. 233.

[20] David O. Sears and John B. McConahay, *The Politics of Violence: The New Urban Blacks and the Watts Riot* (Boston: Houghton Mifflin, 1973), chap. 13.

The Emergence of Black Political Leaders

If the quest for equality and justice has been trying for the mass of black Americans, it has been equally difficult for their leaders to find an accepted place in the larger structure of American politics. Until recent years most black leaders could emerge only by standing at the periphery of American leadership. Some, such as the Reverend Adam Clayton Powell (top right), could survive only by a combination of the support of a massive church membership, a strategic position in Congress, and a charismatic personality appreciated among his Harlem constituents. But Powell was never able to find the center of American politics in such a way as to have a major positive impact on black people nationally. Others, such as Martin Luther King Jr. (top), eschewed the traditional paths to political power pursued by Powell, in favor of nonviolent demonstrations which, though leading to racial equality for

blacks, earned him the enmity of many whites, including many white leaders; ultimately, his leadership cost him his life. Still others, such as Malcom X (near right), found American life so alienating for blacks that they advocated an ambiguous separatism in the form of the Black Moslem movement, a minority among a beleaguered minority.

It is only in our time that black leaders have been able to emerge within the traditional framework of American politics. A leading figure among this group is Mayor Thomas Bradley of Los Angeles, a major force for black people within the mainstream of the Democratic party. Black leaders no longer stand at the periphery of American politics: they are merging into the traditional channels where the main currents of American political power flow.

Not surprisingly, therefore, the political culture of American Jews is pervaded by fears of intolerance and political oppression. Politically, these fears have usually driven Jews toward the left, where they hope to find reforms that will rid societies of race and class prejudice.

A second important factor is that, on the whole, America has been good to Jews. From humble economic beginnings, many Jews have overcome their handicaps and have prospered. Today, in terms of education and professional success, Jews rank near the top of American ethnic groups.

The combination of a history of political persecution and one of economic success has produced a mixture of political loyalties. Although in educational and occupational terms Jews would seem best served by political programs that would protect their gains, elevate private property, and promote individual initiative, Jews are predisposed by their history to policies of government intervention to help those in need and to protect the weak. As a result, Jews remain considerably to the left of other groups that are comparably situated economically.

A third factor that shapes American Jewish political culture is an uncertain sense of acceptance in American life. Although overt discrimination against Jews is now rare, discrimination in hiring and "restrictive covenants"— informal exclusion of Jews from certain choice residential areas — plagued Jews in the recent past. This legacy of discrimination has made Jews hesitant to translate their educational and economic advantages into political action. One finds relatively few major Jewish political leaders — certainly fewer proportionately than the percentage of Jews in other important professions. Jews as a group do vote more often than other ethnic groups, and they also engage in much voluntary participation in election campaigns, but they have not yet entirely broken through the psychological barriers created by a legacy of discrimination.

Yet Jewish political culture now appears to be moving away from its primarily liberal bent. As Jews have become more accepted in America, their sense of estrangement may have slightly moderated, moving them away from their peripheral position on the left. In addition, the commitment of American Jews to the state of Israel puts them into conflict with left-wing groups, whose members look favorably on the aspirations of Palestinian Arabs. American Jews are suspicious of any apparent moves by American leaders, such as Jimmy Carter, away from commitment to Israel and toward a compromise solution of Arab-Jewish tensions. Finally, the New Deal, which Jews firmly supported, is now a remnant of the past; many elderly Jews feel themselves vulnerable to street crime and high taxes, factors that estrange them from their former allies on the left — blacks and other minority groups. The strains on the commitment to the left of American Jews was expressed in 1980, when many Jews found themselves voting for a conservative Republican — Ronald Reagan — for President.

LEARNING POLITICAL CULTURE: POLITICAL SOCIALIZATION AND VALUES

Over the years, then, the political culture that grew out of the founders' theories and plans has been passed down from one generation to the next. Some of this culture remains distinctly recognizable; other elements, particularly in our informal culture, have changed. Still other elements have been created by events in other spheres of American life. Yet somehow there remains a connection between the ideas expressed in the Declaration of Independence and the Constitution and those espoused by Americans today. How has this come about? Or, to put it another way, how is political culture transmitted?

Political culture does not just appear in each new generation; it must be learned. The process by which a society's culture is taught is called *socialization*. In many societies, especially the more primitive ones, political socialization is a fairly narrow, one-way process: The adults of the community, most notably the parents, convey the elements of political culture to their children, who are expected to learn and abide by them. However, American children have a much greater opportunity to reject or modify the political culture of their society than do most of their contemporaries in other countries. The result is a dynamic political culture in America.

Essentially, there are three reasons that the process of political socialization provides room for American political culutre to change. First, Americans give their children a freer rein than do people in most other societies. American children often take an active role in family decision making and planning. In addition, American children are encouraged to think independently fairly early in life.[21] Second, Americans distinguish sharply between the public and the private sides of childrearing. Parents feel that they personally should have control over their children, and they resist attempts by politicians and educators to control the process of socialization directly. Third, the American economic system relies heavily on scientific expertise, which helps explain the scientific emphasis in most public schools. Training in science helps develop a taste for rational, detached, even skeptical thought, a quality of mind that is ill suited to automatic acceptance of a static political culture.

The Role of the Family

The family is a living embodiment of the past impressing itself on the child's present. As such, it cannot help transmitting the political values of the past. But families change; and as they do, they both register and create changes in political culture.

How the Family Socializes.   Few families are deliberate political socializers. Most Americans are not regularly interested in politics, and few American parents spend much time discussing politics in detail with their children. Indeed, one recent study reported that a full 56 percent of American parents say

---

[21] Wayne Holtzman, et al., *Personality Development in Two Cultures* (Austin: University of Texas Press, 1975), p. 304.

they *never* discuss politics with their children.[22] Family commitments to particular parties, ideologies, or leaders therefore emerge as byproducts of family discussions about other things. Only with adulthood does the individual become fully conscious of the political world of his or her childhood, and able to reevaluate what formerly appeared self-evident.

But children's relationships with their parents do seem to set a pattern for attitudes about political leadership. For example, young children who admire and feel protected by their fathers often react the same way to the president.[23] Only in late childhood do children begin to differentiate between the presidency and the role of the father.[24] By contrast, in families where the father's position has been undermined — as, for example, among poor families in Appalachia — children may not develop a clear idea of political authority.[25]

The Family's Lasting Influence. Evidence about the family's lasting influence on children's later political behavior is surprisingly limited. However, studies suggest that there is a childrearing pattern that most encourages later political involvement: a blend of relaxed discipline, frequent political communication, nonphysical punishment, emotional demonstrativeness, high standards for the child's contribution to the family, and the encouragement of independence.[26] There is some evidence that people who become continually active in politics most often emerge from this type of family.[27] Professional politicians generally report that they began to learn about politics quite early from their parents, partly because their parents were themselves involved politically, partly because their parents encouraged them to take an active part in politics (see Figure 3.1).

The student protesters of the late 1960s also emerged from families that were politically involved.[28] Their parents treated them in an egalitarian, affectionate, but demanding fashion. Contrary to the popular stereotype, such children *were* disciplined and were expected to follow certain standards of behavior; but their standards were meant to be self-imposed and self-policed. The

---

[22] Annick Percheron and M. Kent Jennings, "Political Continuities in French Families: A New Perspective on an Old Controversy," Unpublished paper, Center for Political Studies, University of Michigan, 1980, pp. 6–8, 13–14.

[23] For a balanced discussion, see Richard Dawson, Kenneth Prewitt, and Karen Dawson, *Political Socialization,* 2nd ed. (Boston: Little, Brown, 1977), pp. 99–100.

[24] David Easton and Jack Dennis, *Children in the Political System* (Chicago: McGraw-Hill, 1969), part I.

[25] Dean Jaros, Herbert Hirsch, and Frederic J. Fleron, Jr., "The Malevolent Leader: Political Socialization in an American Sub-Culture," *American Political Science Review* 62 (1968): 564–75.

[26] Richard M. Merelman, "The Development of Political Ideology: A Framework for the Analysis of Political Socialization," *American Political Science Review* 63 (September 1969): 750–67; for a critique, see John L. Sullivan, George E. Marcus, and Daniel Richard Minns, "The Development of Political Ideology: Some Empirical Findings," *Youth and Society* 7, no. 3 (December 1975): 148–70.

[27] Kenneth Prewitt, *The Recruitment of Politicians* (Indianapolis: Bobbs-Merrill, 1970), chap. 3.

[28] Kenneth Keniston, *Young Radicals* (New York: Harcourt, Brace and World, 1968).

children's own feelings of guilt and responsibility guided them, rather than parental controls such as physical punishment or verbal abuse. And, perhaps significantly, the political reforms the protesters advocated — more frequent communication between those with power and those without, more egalitarian political relationships — resembled their own relationships with their parents.

For most Americans — those who are not highly involved politically or especially radical in orientation — the impact of the family is primarily confined to identification with political parties. But American children seem to slip away to the political left of their parents in fairly substantial numbers, although surely not enough to represent a "generation gap." And when it comes to more "conceptual" elements of politics, such as the differences between liberals and conservatives in politics, parental influence seems to be comparatively low.[29]

The Role of the School Like families, schools are important forces in the transmission of political culture. From civics class to student council, the schools attempt to diffuse their particular brand of political values. Several characteristics of this transmission process are particularly important.

The Emphasis on Consensus. Most American schools are supported by public funds and serve children of all groups and classes. Therefore, political education in schools naturally steers away from controversy. This position of "neutrality" is congenial to teachers, many of whom believe that controversy might compromise their position of authority or alienate some of their students. But as a result, children of the poor and of ethnic-minority backgrounds often find that political education in the schools has an air of unreality, for political issues of importance to these groups are often "too controversial" for teachers to handle.

Still, today's teachers are less likely to avoid controversial political issues than teachers once were. For one thing, the violent protest among blacks in the 1960s, coupled with campus protests against the Vietman War, injected political issues directly into many classrooms. Teachers found it impossible to ignore such issues because pupils themselves raised them in social studies classes. In addition, innovative classroom curricula have emerged slowly, helping teachers to debate controversial issues without turning the classroom into a forum for any single view. Finally, teachers themselves became more involved in political action as traditional norms against teacher political involvement began to break down, and as the teacher unionization movement spread.

Textbook content, however, changes more slowly than teaching techniques. The recent openness to controversy in the classroom has yet to be fully reflected in textbooks and curricula.

[29] Samuel Barnes, et al, *Political Action: Mass Participation in Five Western Democracies* (Beverly Hills, Calif.: Sage, 1979), chaps. 15 and 16.

Figure 3.1   American Political Families

ADAMS
Massachusetts

Samuel (1722-1803)
Signer of the Declaration of Independence
Member of Congress (to 1781)
Governor of Massachusetts (1794-1797)

John (1735-1826) — second cousin of Sam
Signer of the Declaration of Independence
Second President of the United States
(1797-1801)

John Quincy (1767-1848) — son of John
Sixth President of the United States
(1825-29)
U.S. Representative from Massachusetts
(1831-48)

Charles Francis 1807-1886 — son of John Quincy
U.S. Ambassador to Great Britain
(1861-68)

ROOSEVELT
(Republican, Democrat)
New York

Theodore (1858-1919) "Oyster Bay
Roosevelts"
Governor of New York (1899-1900)
26th President of the United States
(1901-1909)

Franklin Delano (1882-1945) "Hyde Park
Roosevelts" — distant cousin of
Theodore
Governor of New York (1929-32)
32nd President of the United States
(1933-45)

James (1907-1981) — son of Franklin
Congressman from California (1954-64)

TAFT
(Republican)
Ohio

Alphonso (1810-1891)
Attorney-General of the United States
(1876-77)

William Howard (1857-1930) — son of
Alphonso
27th President of the United States
(1909-13)
Chief Justice, U.S. Supreme Court
(1921-30)

Robert A. (1889-1953) — son of William
U.S. Senator (1939-1953)

Robert, Jr. (1917-) — son of Robert
U.S. Senator (1970-1976)

The family may play an important role in socializing its offspring toward involvement in politics.
This role is illustrated by the significant number of American families, past and present, known for

STEVENSON
(Democrat)
Illinois

Adlai E. (1835-1914)
  Vice-President of the United States
  (1893-97)
Adlai E. (1900-1965) — grandson of Adlai E.
  Governor of Illinois (1949-1953)
  Democratic presidential candidate (1952, 1956)
  U.S. Ambassador to the United Nations (1961-65)
Adlai E., III (1930-   ) — son of Gov. Adlai E.
  U.S. Senator (1970-80)

KENNEDY
(Democrat)
Massachusetts

Joseph P. Kennedy (1888-1969)
  U.S. Ambassador to Great Britain (1936-37)
John F. (1917-63) — son of Joseph
  U.S. Senator (1953-60)
  35th President of the United States (1961-63)
Robert F. (1925-68) — brother of John
  U.S. Attorney General (1961-64)
  U.S. Senator (N.Y.) (1965-68)
Edward M. (1932-   ) — brother of John
  U.S. Senator (1962-   )

ROCKEFELLER
(Republican)
New York

Nelson A. (1908-   )
  Governor of New York (1958-74)
  Vice-President of the United States (1974-76)
Winthrop (1912-73) — brother of Nelson
  Governor of Arkansas (1966-70)
John D. (Jay) (1937-   ) — nephew of Nelson
  Governor of West Virginia (1976-   )

their tradition of political activity. Other politically notable families include the LaFolletes of Wisconsin, the Byrds of Virginia, the Longs of Louisiana, and the Talmadges of Georgia.

Overt Political Education. American schools give a number of required courses in political affairs. Most American high school students take courses in state and national history, and in "current problems." In some places, courses in particular social sciences, such as economics or sociology, are also available. American history, of course, remains a staple of the curriculum. The comprehensiveness of such offerings testifies to the importance Americans attach to the school's role in transmitting political culture.

Political education in American public schools usually covers mainly institutions and history. That is, it emphasizes how American governmental institutions work, and focuses on important personages and events. Moreover, teachers and textbooks tend to glorify the American system, glossing over its weaknesses. Each of these emphases deserves special mention.

Social studies teaching in the United States emphasizes the close tie between our governmental institutions and law. This is partly because our government is based on a written constitution, which is constantly being interpreted by judges and legislators. One important consequence of this emphasis in political education is that it creates an image of continuity. Legal precedents, the slow evolution of constitutional interpretation, and the gradual development of American politics show that our society is stable, yet able to adapt to change. Whether this sort of interpretation fits all the facts is another matter, which we will consider shortly.

As for American history, it is commonly taught as a progression of great men and great events: Washington leading the Revolutionary army, Lincoln giving the Gettysburg Address.[30] Interestingly, such teaching is to some degree at odds with the legalistic-institutional approach to American politics. After all, if great men create great events, then how can we claim to have "a government of laws, *not* of men"? Moreover, teaching of this sort is inaccurate: Rarely can one provide an adequate explanation of a complicated political event by focusing on a single individual. The person-event emphasis ignores the complex interplay of groups, individuals, and situations that make up the politics of any society.

A final characteristic of much grade school teaching about American politics is its stress on national pride and patriotism. Most textbooks emphasize that "we are the greatest."[31] There is much discussion of the way America has united races and religious groups that have historically been at odds in other parts of the world. Perhaps the greatest emphasis of all is on the American concept of individual freedom from the intrusions of the outside world. This American conception of freedom is probably the single major element underlying patriotic themes in American textbooks.

Given this kind of teaching, we should hardly be surprised to discover that

[30] See, in particular, Frances FitzGerald, *America Revised: History Schoolbooks in the Twentieth Century* (Boston: Little, Brown, 1979).

[31] Byron G. Massialas, "American Government: We are the Greatest," in C. Benjamin Cox and Byron Massialas, eds., *Social Studies in the United States* (New York: Harcourt, Brace and World, 1967), pp. 167–95.

when American schoolchildren are asked what they most like about their country, they mention its governmental institutions and its heritage of freedom. Schoolchildren in other countries less often focus on their governmental heritage. Indeed, French schoolchildren almost entirely ignore their government, turning instead to the great landmarks of French literature and cultural history. To American schoolchildren, the United States is above all a *manufactured* society, a society consciously constructed by its founders to realize values of freedom and equality.

The Effects of Education. The effects of education on political socialization are difficult to trace. Herbert Hyman and his associates show quite conclusively that Americans who have completed college are 30 to 40 percent more tolerant, democratic, and confident of their own political power than those who have only completed the sixth grade.[32] And better-educated Americans are significantly more informed about politics and more likely to have a firm conceptual grasp of political issues than are less well educated Americans. At the same time, however, it is unclear to what extent these differences can be attributed solely to the school as a political socialization agency, and to what extent they must be attributed to the ability of a college education to place people into positions of power in American society where political action and democratic values become expedient. It is also uncertain how fully the professed democratic values of the better educated are actually translated into democratic behavior.

The Role of the Mass Media The most modern institutions for transmitting political learning to children are the mass media — television, newspapers, books, magazines, and radio. Television, in particular, plays an important role in transmitting political information. Television cuts across all ages and intellectual levels; even very young children may be influenced by what they see of politics on television. Today, in fact, the average American child spends far more time in front of a television set than with his or her parents or teachers.[33] Children of all ages are exposed to television news and public affairs programs, and substantial numbers of young people choose to watch such programs, although perhaps not as systematically or attentively as their parents do. In any case, children agree that they learn more facts about politics from television than they do from either their parents or their schools.[34]

Political learning through television is not limited to news and public affairs programs. Many types of television programs present political themes, albeit

[32] Herbert Hyman, Charles R. Wright, and John Shelton Reed, *The Enduring Effects of Education* (Chicago: University of Chicago Press, 1975).

[33] The recourse to television is common among all age groups. See Angus Campbell and Michael Robinson, "Social Change Reflected in the Use of Time," in Campbell and Converse, eds. *Human Meaning of Social Change*, pp. 17–87.

[34] Lee Becker, et al., "The Development of Political Cognitions," in Steven Chaffee, ed., *Political Communication* (Beverly Hills, Calif.: Sage, 1975), pp. 21–64, 36.

fictional ones. Consider the prevalence of violence on television. The control of violence is a crucial political issue for any society. Therefore, the handling of televised violence may be a matter of great political consequence. If police heroes on TV meet all violence with even more violence of their own, it is hard to imagine that children will get the idea that violence can be handled peacefully or constructively in the real world. The popularity of police shows testifies to the enduring interest of people of all ages in law and order, individualism, and community. These, too, are important political themes.

Finally, television depicts the peculiarities, uniqueness, and foibles of important social groups. It may also stereotype these same groups, often as much by omission as by inclusion. For example, there used to be a notable absence of working-class and black characters on television programs and in commercials. When such characters *did* appear, they were usually in demeaning positions. Subtly, television suggested that such people were not really part of the respectable mainstream of American life. Women, too, were (and still are) often depicted in unflattering ways, confined to the demonstration of kitchen aids and the salving of male egos. Indeed, recent evidence suggests that, despite apparent political changes in the status of women and minorities, on television these groups continue to play subsidiary and occasionally demeaning roles. We shall have more to say about the media's impact on culture, socialization, public opinion, and elections in Chapter 10.

RESULTS OF SOCIALIZATION: CHILDREN'S ATTITUDES Directly or indirectly, children learn about the political culture from adults — parents, teachers, and the adults who control the media. We might expect, then, that children's political attitudes would amount to a simplified version of those of adults. But such an expectation would fail to take account of the psychological differences between children and adults. Children do not reason as adults do; they do not evaluate ideas in the same way adults do, nor do they see each aspect of the political culture as part of a larger whole. As a result, children grasp certain elements of political culture before others; and their idea of each element is colored by their level of maturity.

Moreover, each new generation differs somewhat from its predecessors. The period in which a child grows up may have an impact on the child's attitudes. Generations themselves differ in their internal characteristics — their cohesion, their sense of collective purpose or identity. And long-term changes in adult society may affect the way succeeding generations learn about politics. For these reasons, political socialization must not be assumed automatically to reproduce adult patterns.

Attitudes toward the President The first political concept American children form is usually an image of the president. Some years ago researchers discovered that children as young as six already possessed a well-formed view of the president as a benevolent, responsive, powerful leader anxious to do all he could for the country.[35] Importantly,

---

[35] Fred Greenstein, *Children and Politics* (New Haven: Yale University Press, 1965), chap. 3.

A happy, self-confident president, flanked by Abraham Lincoln, George Washington, and an American flag, smiles benignly from his desk. To the child who drew this picture, the president is formidable but friendly, a typically American conception.

most children saw the president not as an occupant of an enduring political role, but rather as a particularly powerful *person.*

By contrast, only in late childhood and early adolescence do children evidently become aware of Congress, the Supreme Court, and other American political institutions. Not until late childhood, for example, do children begin to realize that Congress, not the president, has primary responsibility for making laws in the United States. Older children also can distinguish between the president as a person and the presidency as an office. Still, their positive feelings toward the president seem to rub off on the presidency. Thus, their progressive political socialization appears usually to support American political institutions.

Persistence and Variation. How significant are youthful attitudes toward the political system? Do these attitudes persist into adulthood?

This is a hard question to answer with certainty, for the evidence is mixed. We know, for example, that adolescents are normally more skeptical about political authority than children are. Whether this skepticism represents a lasting change or merely a temporary lapse is still uncertain, however. Most researchers sidestep the issue by simply assuming that, as with so many things, what the child learns earliest has a lasting effect throughout life. Lately, however, evidence suggests that late childhood and adolescence may be the times when the individual's political views become more stable.[36]

[36] Neal Cutler, "Generational Approaches to Political Socialization," *Youth and Society* 8, no. 2 (December 1976): 175–207.

A second question is how widely children's attitudes toward authority vary. Not surprisingly, the most supportive children are those from white, middle-class Protestant homes. Among ethnic minorities and the deprived, the findings change. Children of the Appalachian poor see the president as considerably less powerful and benevolent than do middle-class whites. Poor blacks have an even more negative picture of political authority, and Chicanos apparently fall between the supportive patterns of middle-class whites and the hostile patterns of poor blacks.[37] Within these groups there are further variations. For example, Chicano children from homes where Spanish is the predominant language are considerably more skeptical of political authority than are Chicano children from English-speaking homes.[38] Thus, the cleavage between the political system and the young is great in some groups, virtually absent in others.

Universality. Finally, how widely can these findings be generalized? We know that the transmission of political culture is not independent of political events and personalities. Conceivably, children's supportiveness toward presidential authority could decline with political events and with the character of individual presidents. Children studied in the 1950s could well have been influenced both by the comparative political quiet of those years and by the popular personality of President Eisenhower.

Vietnam and Watergate did take their toll on the presidential image; children certainly found President Nixon less trustworthy and benevolent than Eisenhower.[39] After this period of decline, children's images of the presidency apparently "bottomed out," and tended toward recovery of a more positive quality.[40] More recently, however, children seem to have returned to some of the skepticism engendered in the Watergate and Vietnam eras. Although they are not thoroughly disillusioned with the presidency, they are markedly less supportive than children were during the 1950s.

Attitudes toward Parties and Voting   As we will see in Chapter 10, partisan identification is one of the major links between the individual and the political system. It is probably the earliest specifically *political* connection that children make between themselves and their leaders. Children may pick up a party label as early as the fourth or fifth grade. In the vast majority of cases, they simply take this label from their parents.

[37] Jaros, Hirsch, and Fieron, "The Malevolent Leader"; Charles S. Bullock III and Harrell R. Rodgers, Jr., eds., *Black Political Attitudes* (Chicago: Markham, 1972), part I; F. Chris Garcia, *Political Socialization of Chicano Children* (New York: Praeger, 1973).

[38] James W. Lamare, "Language Environment and Political Socialization among Mexican-American Children," in Richard G. Niemi et al., *The Politics of Future Citizens* (San Francisco: Jossey-Bass, 1974), pp. 63–83.

[39] Howard Tolley, Jr., *Socialization to War* (New York: Teachers' College Press, 1973), pp. 129–31.

[40] For contrasting views, see Fred I. Greenstein, "The Benevolent Leader Revisited: Children's Images of Political Leaders in Three Democracies," *American Political Science Review* 69 (December 1975): 1371–99; and F. Christopher Arterton, "The Impact of Watergate on Children's Attitudes Towards Political Authority," *Political Science Quarterly* 89 (June 1974): 269–324.

Again, however, times may be changing. Although American high school students continue to believe that the political system will respond to their actions, they no longer rely exclusively on partisanship or voting to accomplish their aims. More are willing to practice and tolerate unconventional participation than perhaps ever before. For example, in a recent study of high schoolers, 48 percent claimed to have signed petitions relevant to politics; 13 percent claimed to have acted in protest demonstrations; and 15 percent claimed to have engaged in boycotts.[41] Thus, voting and partisan identification are now only parts of a larger youthful repertoire of political action.

Still, voting remains an important aspect of political socialization. Early on, voting becomes an important symbol of American democracy for children.[42] Although we cannot be sure where this idea comes from, it seems a fair guess that school is mainly responsible. As early as elementary school, children vote for their favorite activities or to elect class or club officers. In addition, voting is the only real political activity most children see their parents perform. Further, voting and the hoopla surrounding it have a dramatic quality capable of vividly impressing even quite young children. This dramatic quality also suggests that children may see voting not as a means for the citizenry to control its leaders but, rather, as a tangible way for people to take part in and thus affirm their loyalty to the system.

Limitations on Childhood Socialization It would be wrong to conclude that the school, the home, and the mass media are entirely successful at transmitting American political culture to children. This is partly because effective socialization is not simply a matter of presenting information. It depends also on the receptiveness of the receiver. For various reasons, young people sometimes reject the image of political culture they receive through socialization.

All the evidence shows that adolescents usually back away somewhat from their positive childhood commitment to the political system. Their earlier belief in the benevolence and knowledge of the president turns to skepticism and, especially for youths from minority groups, to outright rejection.[43] In addition, adolescents often cast off their earlier identification with their parents' political party. In 1975 surveys of eighteen-year-olds indicated that 38 percent of them consider themselves "independents."[44] A more recent study of adolescents between sixteen and twenty, however, reported only 23 percent who avowed no attachment to a political party.[45] Thus it may be that the tendency toward independence during adolescence varies over historical time periods.

One reason for adolescent hesitancy is simply maturation, as we have noted.

[41] Barnes et al., *Political Action*, pp. 505–6.

[42] Richard M. Merelman, *Political Socialization and Educational Climates* (New York: Holt, Rinehart, and Winston, 1971), chap. 3.

[43] Dean Jaros, *Socialization to Politics* (New York: Praeger, 1973), pp. 68–78.

[44] Paul Abramson, *Generational Change in American Politics* (Lexington, Mass.: Lexington Books, 1975), p. 53.

[45] Barnes et al., *Political Action*, p. 459.

Children form their earliest political attitudes before they are able to reason and to comprehend complex and abstract ideas. A child's attachment to the presidency and to the party system is almost never based on a firm understanding of how these institutions operate, or on a clear set of political principles. Not until early adolescence do we see young people acquiring a sense of liberal-conservative differences in politics, and large numbers of young people cannot relate politics to such principles as equality, fairness, and reciprocity. For many, well into adolescence, the political system simply lacks clear intellectual definition.

When understanding does come, full approval may not follow. In modern industralized societies most young people between the ages of thirteen and twenty-one are eager but unable to put their skills to productive use. Instead, they generally stay in school, competing with each other for further education and good jobs. During these adolescent years, naturally enough, young people experience a growing drive toward self-assertion and independence, a drive that their dependent status frustrates. They sometimes respond by rebelling in those ways they can, sometimes by rejecting the democratic values of the larger society. Thus, in the 1950s studies indicated that many young people were uncertain about and even hostile to such democratic ideas as free speech and a free press.[46] There is little reason to believe that the situation is fundamentally different now.

THE DYNAMICS OF POLITICAL CULTURE

As our discussion of childhood socialization should have made clear, people do not enter adulthood with their political ideas firmly implanted. There is ample room for each person to move away from the beliefs of parents, teachers, and friends. Therefore, political culture inevitably changes somewhat from generation to generation. This is particularly true in an industrialized, highly educated society, which prizes such qualities as adaptability, flexibility, and openness to change. Let us look, then, at the major forces that change American political culture over time.

Population Movement and Social Mobility

Every political culture responds to underlying social patterns. For example, people who live in large metropolitan areas are exposed to a very different set of political and social influences than are people who grow up on farms or in small towns. Therefore, changes in the residential distribution of our population are bound to change aspects of our political culture.

Urbanization has affected nearly the entire United States over the past century. Americans in large cities, particularly those on the east and west coasts, always have come into contact with cultural influences from abroad, thereby developing a sense of America's links with the rest of the world. Indeed,

[46] H. H. Remmers and Richard D. Franklin, "Sweet Land of Liberty," in H. H. Remmers, ed., *Anti-Democratic Attitudes in American Schools* (Evanston, Ill.: Northwestern University Press, 1963).

American urbanization in the twentieth century helped erode "isolationism" both in our foreign policy and in our political culture.

Social mobility — an individual's movement from one occupational status to another — may have similar dynamic effects. Americans today are constantly changing jobs, usually in the hope of "getting ahead." As they move up (or down) in occupational status, they must confront new situations, new norms, and new people. As a result, many of their attitudes, expectations, beliefs, and habits may change. By and large, social mobility is a moderating influence on political culture. Most socially mobile people adopt political positions that fall between those of the group they have left and those of the group they are joining.[47] Generally, therefore, high rates of social mobility reduce cleavages in American political culture, binding it together even while changing its contours.

Changes in Education Education is related to a host of political attitudes and behaviors. Higher education in particular promotes political participation and increases political knowledge, encourages self-confidence in dealing with politics, and stimulates verbal support for liberal ideals such as civil liberties.[48] Therefore, the changing distribution of education in America can alter important aspects of American political culture.

One place in which the power of education has been felt is in the broadened range of life-styles considered acceptable in our political culture. The educated young have been in the forefront of reform movements designed to protect the rights of homosexuals, women, and drug users, among others. In so doing, they have broadened the scope of American political culture by raising questions about the applicability of American political ideas to stigmatized groups, questions we will consider further in Chapter 14 on liberty and justice.

Perhaps more important, however, has been the apparent tendency of higher education to produce shifts in political values. Many college graduates wish for more than economic well-being from the efforts of government and the private sector; they desire also that the government implement ideals of justice, equality, and fraternity. But college-educated young people are especially skeptical about the likelihood that government can meet their desires, and thus higher education appears to add somewhat to a more or less permanent reservoir of dissatisfaction with the performance of government in America.[49]

Changes in the Distribution of Occupations A person's job usually exposes him or her to special influences on political attitudes. Thus, a construction worker will be expected to support the union's position on business-related legislation, whereas a junior executive may be ex-

[47] James A. Barber, *Social Mobility and Voting Behavior* (Chicago: Rand McNally, 1970).
[48] Robert Jackman, "Political Elites, Mass Publics, and Support for Democratic Principles," *Journal of Politics*, August 1972, pp. 753–74; Mary Jackman, "General and Applied Tolerance: Does Education Increase Commitment to Racial Integration?" *American Journal of Political Science* 22 (1978): 303–25.
[49] Barnes et al., *Political Action*.

pected to echo his or her colleagues' complaints about government interference with business. In fact, members of some professions begin learning appropriate political attitudes and become enmeshed in a network of cultural influences while still in school. A medical or law student joins a professional organization, works with senior colleagues, and inevitably gains an appreciation of the particular political issues that will affect his or her future practice.

From what we have said, it follows that changes in the distribution of particular occupations in a society may alter the distribution of political attitudes, habits, and beliefs. And it is characteristic of our society that new occupations can quickly come into existence. Thirty years ago, for example, there were no computer programmers; today, there are very many. Forty years ago many poor women were loyal, politically conservative domestic servants in the houses of the rich; today, few are.

Changes in Family Patterns Both family life and methods of childrearing change over time in most societies, with results that are potentially important politically. Although specific relationships between the family and the political culture are hard to document, we can present two illustrations of how changes in the family may have political effects.

Many contemporary observers argue that the traditional nuclear family structure in America has been put under great strain as a result of rising levels of divorce and trends toward fewer children per family and toward more women entering the work force. Contemporary children often face quite different family problems than did earlier generations, and some of those problems may have political consequences. For example, children raised in mother-only homes seem to become less interested and involved in politics than children from two-parent homes.[50] By contrast, working wives usually become more involved in politics and more committed to political views than do nonworking wives.[51]

The Effect of the Mass Media The mass media play an important role in changing the shape of American political culture. Television in particular has the capacity to convey instantaneously to viewers the drama and excitement of fastbreaking political stories. Newspapers can conduct in-depth investigations of politics, including aspects of political corruption. And as the focus of media attention shifts, so also may important aspects of political culture.

Consider the way television portrays political events. First of all, it is the newscaster, not the public, who decides just what *is* the news of the day. Many events may be newsworthy, but the news has to fit in a half-hour slot, which it shares with features like sports, the weather, and perhaps the commentator's editorial message. The result is that "the news" tends to consist of those

[50] Kenneth Langton, *Political Socialization* (New York: Oxford University Press, 1969), chap. 2.

[51] Kristi Andersen, "Working Women and Political Participation, 1952–1972," *American Journal of Political Science* 19 (August 1975): 439–55.

Politics as Glamor

The emergence of leading sport, television, and movie personalities in American politics raises some important questions. Could the fusion of entertainment and politics have occurred without the spread of the mass media? Why are entertainers able to enter the political arena with apparent ease? How successful are celebrities in political activities? Perhaps doors open because entertainers and athletes have instantly recognizable names yet have not had the experience in which they might have made political enemies. Or perhaps we are looking for heroes and we don't find them in ordinary politicians.

What media celebrities symbolize for the public in the way of heroism may be quite diverse. Some, like one-time child star Shirley Temple Black (above right), may stand for a certain innocence that has ripened into a stable — but still innocent — middle age. Some, like Ronald Reagan (above), may symbolize the nice balance of toughness and friendliness said to characterize that classic figure of American folklore — the frontiersman. And some, like Jane Fonda (right), may stand for the New American Woman, confident, unafraid, and progressive, a spokesperson for the downtrodden.

The success of glamour as politics prompts a question: Do politicians like Tom Hayden (right) get more from their associations with celebrities than celebrities like Frank Sinatra (above) get from their associations with politicians? Perhaps the balance of power between the politician and the celebrity will tell us much about the American politics of the 1980s.

events that are most dramatic, or that show up best on television: airplane crashes, earthquakes, summit meetings between heads of state, presidential trips. Legislation passed by Congress is featured less often; the same is true of Supreme Court decisions. Some call this selective aspect of the mass media *agenda setting*, a process whereby the media help determine the focus of the public's political attention.

Another result of the television news format is that the news is presented as a series of headlines. Three minutes on a presidential speech — two minutes on a flood in Pennsylvania — three minutes on an airplane hijacking in which a terrorist group is holding hostages — one minute on a scientific report that yet another common food additive has been found to cause cancer in mice. No event, however important, can be covered in depth. Even during a presidential compaign, when political happenings receive more news time than usual, the focus is on dramatic highlights rather than candidates' thoughtful analysis of issues. The audience thus is tacitly encouraged to believe that any event or issue can be examined adequately in a few moments. Indeed, one rule of thumb for political candidates is that Americans will not watch a TV spot that runs over three minutes. In reality, of course, there has probably not been a single political event or issue in history that could be fairly portrayed to a diverse audience in three minutes.

The Effect of Political Events   Major political events also play a role in altering political culture. Some would say that America has never been the same since the assassination of John Kennedy — that some intangible element of innocence, political trust, hope, and optimism vanished with his death. For an earlier generation, World War I was a similar event, thrusting the United States from naive isolationism to the center of the world's political stage and thereby reshaping American attitudes toward the world.

More recently, the generation of the 1960s may remain a distinctive element in American political life. These were the young people who experienced most vividly the cumulative effects of Vietnam and Watergate and who were the campus protesters of those years. Political culture often changes most dramatically when a set of traumatic political events — war, revolution, economic depression — strikes especially hard at the generation of young people just entering active political life. As the youthful generation takes its place in the political system, it carries with it the scars of its earlier years, its own unique "generational consciousness."

In our own time persistent economic problems — especially chronic inflation — may well be undercutting public confidence in the American political system. Economic problems create political dissatisfaction, and the persistence of such problems over a long period may well challenge the very structure of our political system, making the gap between leaders and led harder to bridge. Historical examples — especially the experience of Germany in the 1930s — show us that economic difficulties may be the prelude to political disasters. It is noteworthy, however, that Americans weathered the Great Depression of the 1930s without seriously challenging the legitimacy of the political system.

CONCLUSION   American political culture comprises the beliefs, habits, attitudes, symbols, and values that help Americans define their political system. Its foundations are the twin American problems of political power and democracy. That is, our political culture has to do mainly with how power should be distributed and controlled, and how democratic institutions should be balanced against the rights of individuals. Political culture has two sides: the formal culture, consisting of the traditional principles all Americans share; and the informal culture, which is the application and modification of these principles by various groups in their daily life.

American political culture is transmitted from generation to generation through childhood socialization. The family, the school, friends, and the mass media all play major roles in socializing children. Nevertheless, political culture in America is constantly changing with changes in the population: social mobility, shifting family structures, increased education, and new occupational patterns. Moreover, the mass media (especially television) are novel influences on our political culture.

Clearly, the specific features of the political culture suggested to us in the writings and doings of the Founding Fathers have changed. Americans now accept "big government," habitually acquiesce to concentrated power, and participate only casually in the politics of our society. True, many citizens feel a residual hostility toward power and politicians that is consistent with the Founders' views. But, despite this fact, many new structures of concentrated economic and political power have grown up: a huge defense establishment dependent on the government; mass media perhaps capable of manipulating millions; corporate conglomerates that control vast markets; and political leaders and institutions that dispense great sums for public services, but are poorly controlled by a weak party system and an often noncompetitive electoral process.

Still, although our society has changed, the patterns of political culture and political socialization we have surveyed in this chapter continue in the main to sustain the founders' vision of politics. The ideal of American democracy has survived; so has the gap between those who govern and those who do not. In fact, the tension between leaders and followers in the United States may be wider now than at any other time since the Civil War. This tension certainly cannot be appreciably reduced by rhetoric, such as former President Carter's promise of "a government as good as the American people." Yet Carter's promise, along with our continuing search for a way to manage our affairs democratically, is a reminder that the struggle between the people and the polity is still alive. And in this struggle, political culture and political socialization will continue to play an important role.

SUGGESTIONS FOR FURTHER READING   Almond, Gabriel, and Verba, Sidney. *The Civil Culture.* Boston: Little, Brown, 1965. The "granddaddy" of political-culture studies. Almond and Verba argue that American political culture is characterized by a unique blending of participatory and deferential elements that underlie democratic politics.

Barnes, Samuel; Kaase, Max; et al. *Political Action*. Beverly Hills, Calif.: Sage, 1979. An important comparative study of political culture and political socialization in several industrialized societies.

Easton, David, and Dennis, Jack. *Children in the Political System*. New York: McGraw-Hill, 1969. A theory of the role of childhood socialization in American politics and a set of findings about children's favorable attitudes toward political authority.

Greenstein, Fred I. *Children and Politics*. New Haven: Yale University Press, 1965. Greenstein's is the pathbreaking study of children's political attitudes. It departs from a psychological framework and presents useful findings on partisan identification and attitudes toward authority.

Jennings, M. Kent, and Niemi, Richard. *The Political Character of Adolescence*. Princeton, N.J.: Princeton University Press, 1974. The best recent study of political socialization. It stresses the necessity to study adolescence as a distinct socialization period, and presents useful information on the effect of socialization agencies, like the family and the school.

Lane, Robert E. *Political Ideology*. New York: Free Press, 1962. A unique investigation of the political beliefs of average Americans, based on a small number of intensive interviews. The basic outlines of American political beliefs come through boldly in this analysis.

Wright, James. *The Dissent of the Governed*. New York: Academic Press, 1976. Wright's is the first major work to reconsider American political culture in light of recent evidence of alienation. To deal with recent changes, Wright puts forth an unusual theory about how a political system can survive without a supportive political culture.

Chapter 4 Federalism

Toward the close of the nineteenth century, white supremacists in the American South were determined to codify in law a comprehensive system of racial separation. Their first efforts focused on state legislation to segregate the races on railroad cars. A South Carolina newspaper, the *Charleston News and Courier*, argued against such "extreme" measures — first by reminding its readers that the South had managed to get along quite well since the end of the Civil War without legal segregation, and second by drawing out to the point of absurdity the practical consequences of such a plan. "If there must be Jim Crow cars on the railroads," wrote the editor,

> there should be Jim Crow cars on street railways. . . . If there are to be Jim Crow cars, moreover, there should be Jim Crow waiting saloons at all stations, and Jim Crow eating houses. . . . There should be Jim Crow sections of the jury box, and a separate Jim Crow dock and witness stand in every court — and a Jim Crow Bible for colored witnesses to kiss.[1]

What the author of this editorial thought was an ironic attack on legal segregation was in fact a remarkably accurate prediction of what was soon to be.

[1] C. Vann Woodward, *The Strange Career of Jim Crow*, 2nd ed. (New York: Oxford University Press, 1966), p. 68.

"Jim Crow laws" separating blacks from whites in railroad cars were passed by most southern states prior to 1900. In the next decade the states of the old Confederacy passed laws establishing separate waiting rooms in railway stations, separate seating in streetcars, and separate decks on steamboats. Most southern states prohibited interracial marriage, and South Carolina prohibited blacks and whites from working together in the same room and from using the same entrances, exits, toilets, drinking buckets, and even pay windows.[2] Until the mid-1960s arrangements such as these, required by state law and elaborated on by local ordinances, were virtually unquestioned policies in the South.

THE DILEMMA OF FEDERALISM This oppressive practice of racial separation was the product of a strong regional culture, distinctive historical experiences, and the compliance of the national government in Washington. But it is important to understand that it was made possible by the American system of federalism. In a federal system, one central or general government rules over a territory divided into a number of smaller units, each with its own government. The central government, which we will call the *national* or *federal government,* has sovereign power, but the smaller governments retain a certain degree of autonomy. The example of legally enforced racial segregation in the South dramatizes a fundamental dilemma of American federalism: the difficulty of reconciling generally held standards of justice with state claims of autonomy.

Federal organization has made it possible for the different states to deal with the same problems in many different ways. One consequence of federalism, then, has been that people are treated differently, by law, from state to state. The great strength of this system is that differences from state to state in cultural preferences, moral standards, and levels of wealth can be accommodated. In contrast to a unitary system in which the central government makes all important decisions (as in France), federalism is a powerful arrangement for maximizing regional freedom and autonomy. The great weakness of our federal system, however, is that people in some states receive less than the best or the most advanced or the least expensive services and policies that government can offer. The federal dilemma does not invite easy solutions, for the costs and benefits of the arrangement have tended to balance out.

Let us look at some contemporary examples of how Americans are treated differently from state to state.

Most states require their residents to pay an income tax. But several states, among them the wealthy state of Connecticut, have refused again and again to levy such a tax. Instead they rely on sales taxes (usually regarded as regressive — *that is, bearing disproportionately on people with lower incomes) and on so-called nuisance taxes on such things as hotel rooms, stock transfers, and entertainment. Among those states that do have an income tax, the rate and progressiveness vary widely. Not only do income*

[2] Ibid., p. 98.

taxes differ from state to state, but so do sales tax rates and excise taxes (levies on commodities like cigarettes and liquor). The point is, of course, that residents of different states bear very different tax burdens.

State penalties for the possession of marijuana range from modest fines to stiff jail sentences. Some states have "decriminalized" marijuana, treating its possession as a misdemeanor, which does not go on an individual's police record.

In 1981 thirty-eight states permitted the death penalty; the rest forbade it.

Some states — notably New York, California, and Wisconsin — finance huge and complex public university systems. Other states, such as New Jersey and the New England states, run less elaborate systems of higher education, which means that many residents must go outside their state to go to college.

Several states provide welfare assistance that exceeds the federally established guideline considered to be the "poverty line." Other states provide assistance substantially below that line.

This brief list, which could be greatly extended, makes the point that states treat people differently. Such differential treatment can be extremely costly to the individual. The northern black who went south and was denied a meal in a Howard Johnson's restaurant in the early 1960s was paying one of the costs of federalism. The welfare mother in South Carolina is paying another when she receives a monthly welfare check that is a fraction of what she would get if she lived in New York.

The federal arrangement, then, allows states to maintain policies that may be unjust or regressive or simply outmoded. But it also allows states to set higher standards than the national average and to devise innovative policy solutions to public problems. Thus there are two sides of the coin of federalism: The backwardness of some states is matched by the progressivism of others. Consider the situation in which a progressive state policy serves as a standard for other states and the nation. The first governmental efforts to combat housing discrimination, for example, came not from the United States Congress but from the New York state legislature in 1955. By 1958 another dozen states had followed New York's lead and passed open housing laws, but the federal government did not ban housing discrimination until 1968.[3]

THE ORIGINS OF AMERICAN FEDERALISM   To understand the federal dilemma more fully we must go back to the beginnings of the federal system. That system was, like so much in politics, a product of compromise. As we saw in Chapter 2, the American Revolution had been conducted under the Articles of Confederation, which created a league of independent states. No strong national government presided over this confederation. Indeed, the confederal government was powerless to levy taxes, regu-

---

[3] David McKay, *Housing and Race in Industrial Society* (Totowa, N.J.: Rowman and Littlefield, 1977), p. 59.

late interstate commerce, or adjudicate interstate disputes (there was no national court system). Nor did it have any direct authority over individual citizens of the several states. These domestic weaknesses were crippling diplomatic weaknesses as well. Because it had virtually no power over its member states, the confederal government was in no position to negotiate binding, advantageous agreements with other nations. As Alexander Hamilton wrote of the Confederation in *The Federalist* No. 22, "It is a system so radically vicious and unsound as to admit not of amendment but by an entire change in its leading features and characters." [4]

The deficiencies of the Articles of Confederation eventually led to the calling of the Constitutional Convention in 1787, the formation of a strong national government, and the creation of our federal system.

The central cleavage at the Constitutional Convention was between the big and wealthy states on the one hand and the smaller states on the other. The fundamental problem facing the framers was how to establish a national government strong enough to avoid the difficulties caused by the fragmentation of authority under the Articles, while preserving the integrity of the individual states. It is important for contemporary Americans to remember that state loyalties in the post-Revolutionary period were much stronger than any sense of national identity. In those days people thought in terms of rivalry and conflict among the states more readily than in terms of competition among parties, classes, races, and economic interests, as we do now. The desire to preserve state integrity — indeed, to preserve state parity in the Congress, as under the Articles — was particularly strong among the small states, which feared domination by the large states.

The "Great Compromise" We saw in Chapter 2 that the solution to this problem was the Great Compromise, which established a bicameral legislature with equal state representation in the Senate and proportional representation based on population in the House of Representatives. This arrangement guaranteed the survival of the small states. Thus reassured, they agreed to the formation of a stronger union, opening the way for the National Federalists, such as Madison, Hamilton, Robert Morris, and James Wilson, to establish provisions for a strong national government. The essence of the federal arrangement was, and still is, a strong national government with supreme powers arching umbrella-like over a number of state governments whose powers and integrity are constitutionally guaranteed.

The Constitutional Basis of Federalism National constitutions do not tell us a great deal about how governments really work, for as William Penn, the founder of Philadelphia, once observed, "Governments, like clocks, go from the motion men give them." [5] Constitutions do,

---

[4] *The Federalist Papers* (New York: New American Library ed., 1961), p. 151.

[5] Quoted in Alpheus T. Mason, *The States' Rights Debates*, 2nd ed. (New York: Oxford University Press, 1972), p. 189.

however, provide us with a blueprint for tracing the governmental framework, which sets constraints on government and defines the powers and relationships of government's various parts. Thus the American Constitution establishes the structure of federalism, although it tells us little of how its parts interact with one another.

The words *federal* and *federalism* are not mentioned in the Constitution. But the federal principle was in effect established and guaranteed by the Great Compromise of the Constitutional Convention. Federalism, of course, involves a good deal more than the two different forms of representation in the bicameral Congress. The Constitution treats the federal arrangement at some length (see Figure 4.1), although it is extremely vague on some crucial points, such as the limits of state powers.

It establishes national supremacy in Article VI, which states that "This Constitution, and the Laws of the United States which shall be made in Pursuance thereof . . . shall be the supreme Law of the Land . . . the Constitution or Laws of any State to the Contrary notwithstanding."

It ensures the integrity of the states, however, in Article IV, by promising that state boundaries and territory will be inviolate and by guaranteeing each state "a Republican Form of Government."

It further bolsters national supremacy by establishing in Article III a Supreme Court to decide, among other things, controversies between two or more states.

It creates a division of powers between the national and state governments by granting certain exclusive powers to the national government, by prohibiting certain powers to the states, and by reserving other powers to the states. Article I, Section 8 empowers the Congress to coin money, regulate interstate commerce, and declare war. Article II, Section 2 authorizes the president to conduct foreign affairs, occasionally with the "advice and consent" of the Senate. Powers expressly prohibited to the states but lodged in the national government include coining money, entering into foreign alliances, and laying duties on imports and exports. Finally, the Tenth Amendment reserves to the states, or to the people, "powers not delegated to the United States by the Constitution nor prohibited by it to the States."

It further strengthens the hand of the states by leaving to them the election of the president through the electoral college created in Article II, and by giving them a central role in the amending process in Article V.

The most crucial of the ambiguities in the constitutional blueprint for federal — that is, for state-national — relations lay in the Tenth Amendment. As soon as the completed draft of the Constitution (without the Tenth or any other amendment, at that point) was sent to the states for ratification, antifederalist politicians vehemently criticized the so-called supremacy clause of Article VI. They feared that it was designed to create a "consolidated government," and that it would deprive the states of their independent existence. The Tenth Amendment, proposed by the First Congress and ratified by the states in 1791 along with the preceding nine amendments of the Bill of Rights,

Figure 4.1   The Constitutional Allocation of Powers
to Federal and State Government Provides a Framework
for the Operation of Federalism

**Delegated to
Federal Government**

1. To tax.
2. To borrow and coin money.
3. To conduct foreign relations.
4. To regulate interstate and foreign commerce.
5. To provide an army and navy.
6. To declare war.
7. To establish inferior courts.
8. To establish post offices.

**Implied to
Federal Government**

1. To establish banks, corporations — from powers to tax, borrow, regulate commerce.
2. To spend money for roads, schools, health insurance — from powers to establish post roads, provide for general welfare, regulate commerce.
3. Establish army, navy, air force academies — from power to raise and support army and navy.

Powers

**Reserved to
States**

1. To establish local governments.
2. To protect life, property, health, safety, and morals.
3. To regulate intrastate commerce.
4. To conduct elections.
5. To change state governments and constitutions.
6. To ratify amendments to the federal constitution.

**Concurrent to Both Federal
and State Governments**

1. To tax.
2. To borrow money.
3. To establish courts.
4. To make and enforce laws.
5. To charter banks, corporations.
6. To spend money for the general welfare.
7. To take private property for public purposes.

Constitution
of the
United States

On Congress

1. May not abridge Bill of Rights.
2. May not unilaterally change state boundaries.
3. May not tax exports.
4. May not impose direct taxes disproportionate to state population.
5. May not favor one state over another in matters of commerce.
6. May not permit slavery nor grant titles of nobility.

Prohibitions

On States

1. May not deny equal protection of laws.
2. May not violate federal constitution.
3. May not obstruct federal laws.
4. May not enter into treaties.
5. May not tax imports or exports.
6. May not deny voting rights because of sex or race.
7. May not coin money.
8. May not permit slavery nor grant titles of nobility.

Source: Adapted from John H. Ferguson and Dean E. McHenry, *The American System of Government,* 12th
ed. (New York: McGraw-Hill, 1973), p. 95. Reprinted by permission.

was a promise to the states that they would play an important role in governing the United States.

The degree to which the Tenth Amendment was meant to limit the power of the national government has been a matter of debate from the beginning of the nation to the present. For John Marshall, the Chief Justice of the Supreme Court from 1801 to 1835, the Tenth Amendment was no limitation at all but merely restated the content of the supremacy clause of Article VI. Marshall's successor, Roger Taney, sought to redefine federalism in terms far more favorable to the states. Taney held, for example, in the famous *Dred Scott* case (1857) that Congress could not abolish slavery: It was purely a state matter. Within the domain of reserved powers, the states were sovereign, in Taney's view. The issue of states' rights lay at the heart of the Civil War. If the states were sovereign and the Union a mere loose compact among the states, then any state had the right to secede. The states of the Confederacy tested this idea unsuccessfully in armed conflict with the North. Neither Lincoln's insistence on the preservation of the Union nor the military victory of the North put an end to the issue, however. /States' rights arguments came to the fore again in the 1950s and 1960s as southern states fought federal attempts to integrate schools and public accommodations and to guarantee blacks the right to vote.

THE CASE FOR FEDERALISM The federal method of organizing government in America has at least five major advantages.[6]

1. *The federal arrangement allows government to accommodate diversity.* Different parts of the country are peopled by different ethnic, racial, and religious groups. These groups have differing standards of morality, varying sorts of needs, conflicting ideas about the proper role of government, and different notions about the nature of one's obligations to the greater community in which we live (that is, to the "public good").[7] Some parts of the nation are highly urbanized, with economies based on heavy industry; others are rural and agricultural. States are thought to be able to deal with these specialized cultural and regional outlooks, needs, and demands more efficiently and more responsively than can the government in Washington.

Although it is true that state governments can be responsive to local needs (for example, the needs of tobacco farmers in North Carolina or the timber industry in Maine), it is also true that a chief source of diversity among states is their degree of wealth. Thus the states differ in their abilities to meet local needs. Poor states must impose heavier tax burdens on their residents to meet spending needs than do the wealthier states, which can meet their needs better with less tax effort. One of the drawbacks of a system designed to maximize

[6] Arthur W. MacMahon, *Administering Federalism in a Democracy* (New York: Oxford University Press, 1972), pp. 5–6.

[7] See Daniel J. Elazar, *American Federalism: A View from the States* (New York: Thomas Crowell, 1966).

responsiveness to local demands and needs, then, is that its member units are not equally able to meet those needs.

2. *Federal organization allows flexibility in the administration of large areas.* Most of the largest nations in the world — Brazil, Canada, India, the Soviet Union, and Australia, as well as the United States — have federal systems. Partially autonomous provincial or state policymakers can be more sympathetic, more responsive, and more knowledgeable about specific problems than policymakers in the national capital can be. They can also establish shorter communication channels between citizen and polity. In contrast, regional administrative units that are directly responsible to the national government, such as France's *départements*, are less satisfactory on the aforementioned counts because their first loyalty is to the national government and not to the areas they serve.

3. *Federalism makes experimentation and policy innovation more likely.* No state must wait for any other state, or the national government, to design and implement services and social policy. Some states have a reputation for being innovative; some seldom innovate and are slow to copy the innovations of others. New York, Massachusetts, California, New Jersey, and Michigan are leaders in the development of new programs and services.[8] Other states have made their mark in particular areas of public policy: Wisconsin developed the first state income tax in 1911; Mississippi pioneered the sales tax in 1933; Indiana and Maine developed model pollution control and environmental-protection legislation in the 1960s; Washington has led other states in penal reform.

The federal principle puts into practice the idea that innovative solutions to a given problem are more likely to emerge when several independent centers of power and resources are working on the problem. New solutions frequently diffuse throughout the nation, although the time lag between innovation and emulation by other states may amount to as much as twenty-five years.[9]

4. *Federalism widens opportunities for political participation.* With more independent units of government, people have more opportunities to compete for political office. This in turn makes it possible for more interests and more groups to be represented in government. Over the course of American history, for example, ethnic and racial minorities have been able to capture significant numbers of seats in state legislatures long before they have won positions in the U.S. Congress. More levels of government also mean more points at which pressure for government action can be applied by letter writing, lobbying, testifying, demonstrating — or even suing.

5. *Federalism serves to counteract high concentration of power.* As we saw in Chapter 2, decentralized power was seen by the authors of *The Federalist Papers* as a bulwark against tyranny. The federal system has been given partial

---

[8] Jack L. Walker, "The Diffusion of Innovations among the American States," *American Political Science Review* 63 (September 1969): 880–99.
[9] Ibid., p. 895.

credit for the highly decentralized nature of the American party system. Federalism also increases the chances for the less populous national party (in recent years, the Republican party) to gain pockets of control. The dispersion of power characteristic of a federal system, then, has long been viewed as a safeguard against excessive concentration of power.

But this same dispersion of power permits a minority to veto policies widely deemed desirable. As William Riker puts it:

> Losers at the national level may reverse the decision at the constituent level. Thus, the losers nationally may become the winners locally which of course negates the national decision in at least portions of the federal nation. Thereby, of course, the freedom of the national majority is infringed upon by local majorities.[10]

Thanks to the dispersion of political power in our federal system, elites in the South were able to maintain a system of legal segregation even though such policies were generally rejected elsewhere in the nation. Such a problem is the essence of the federal dilemma: Which values should prevail — those of the national majority or those of the local or regional majority?

THE ROLE OF THE STATES Even though the responsibilities of the national government have increased since the 1930s in areas once left pretty much to state and local government, such as education and health, state governments are alive, well, and busy. States perform such august functions as ratifying constitutional amendments and running elections for national offices. They are also responsible for "matters of homely concern": regulating marriage, divorce, and inheritance; enforcing business contracts and chartering corporations; licensing occupations; and developing and enforcing criminal laws. This is "workaday" government. Washington alone would find it difficult to handle these functions efficiently or in accord with such different regional cultures.

States are also the federal system's major contributors to higher public education, and they regulate and heavily support elementary and secondary education. They run massive highway programs. The welfare system is financed and administered to a large extent by the state and its subdivisions, the counties. States also manage vast forest resources and recreation lands, run agricultural experimentation laboratories, maintain large public-health programs, and regulate public utilities.

Despite the general homogenization of American society, state boundaries are still important in the 1980s. States routinely engage in conflict and competition with one another, most of it designed to protect and enhance their respective environments and economies. The western states, for example, have a long history of struggle over the use of Colorado River water for agricultural

---

[10]William H. Riker, *Federalism* (Boston: Little, Brown, 1964), p. 142.

The Struggle from Segregation to Civil Rights

Southern segregation in particular gave rise to the Civil Rights movement of the late 1950s and 1960s. Beginning with the Montgomery bus boycott (a response to the arrest of Rosa Parks for sitting in bus seat reserved for whites), the movement soon took on other targets such as segregated lunch counters and parks. The March on Washington in 1963, punctuated by Martin Luther King's "I have a dream" speech, was followed by the 1964 Civil Rights Act and the 1965 Voting Rights Act. Although much discrimination remained in American life, these two pieces of Congressional legislation — one banning discrimination in public accommodations and in programs funded by federal money, the other guaranteeing the right of blacks to vote — ended legal segregation for all intents and purposes.

purposes, and interstate agreements and court decisions have had to establish the exact number of gallons of water to which each state is entitled.

Many such conflicts end up in the courts. New Jersey, Pennsylvania, and New York recently resolved the "Great Garbage War" in the United States Supreme Court, which ruled that New Jersey could not keep cities in the other two states from dumping garbage in landfill sites in New Jersey. And Connecticut plaintiffs recently sued New York and New Jersey because the lower air pollution standards in those states allowed noxious industrial fumes to drift on the wind into Connecticut, which maintains more stringent laws.

The states are also fast becoming the main battleground in what some commentators have called America's "regional wars." Over the last two decades population and industry have moved in increasing numbers from the aging cities of the so-called Frostbelt — the Northeast and Midwest — to the cities of the South and Southwest. They have gone in search of warmer climates, cheaper energy, more jobs, and lower tax rates. Industry has also been attracted by the weakness or absence of the labor union movement in the South.

This great migration has meant a decline in jobs and industry in the Frostbelt states, which in turn has meant lower tax revenues for them and their cities. To counter the loss of people and jobs, state legislatures have begun to experiment with a variety of inducements to retain existing industry and to attract new industry. The most common state programs allow local governments to offer industries tax credits, low-interest loans, or tax abatements in return for making new investments. The hope is that a firm contemplating a move will find that these new economic-development incentives make expansion rather than departure the more attractive option. States also hope to lure industry away from other states by the use of such inducements.[11]

In the early 1980s several states also considered legislation that would make departing industries pay some of the costs borne by the communities they leave behind. When a major employer closes down its plant — as the Chrysler Corporation did in Hamtramck, Michigan in the late 1970s, for example —not only are people thrown out of work, but also a major property is removed from the city's tax rolls. City revenues shrink, and the capacity to offer high-quality services declines. In Maine the loss of shoe factories and paper mills recently prompted the legislature to pass a bill requiring companies that close plants to pay workers one week's severance pay for each year of service.

Most observers agree that state government has a new vitality in the 1980s. Once the domain of corrupt political dynasties, "good ole boys," antiquated bureaucracies, and amateur legislatures, state governments have been modernized in the last fifteen years and their tax systems made more equitable and productive. With the Supreme Court decision of *Baker* v. *Carr* (1962) — the so-called one man, one vote ruling — state legislatures were forced to create legislative districts more or less equal in population. Rural domination of state

[11] Advisory Commission on Intergovernmental Relations (ACIR), *State Community Assistance Initiatives* (Washington, D.C.: U.S. Government Printing Office, May 1979), p. 7.

legislatures, heretofore maintained even in states with large urban populations by the underrepresentation of city and suburban dwellers, was undercut. Legislatures in most states have begun to meet annually instead of every two years, and other reforms — higher legislator salaries, professional staff assistance — have attracted better-qualified people to office. Increasing numbers of professionals, graduates of burgeoning public-administration programs in state universities, have come to work for state government bureaucracies.

In most states the office of the governor has been strengthened by making the term of office four years rather than two and by allowing incumbents to succeed themselves. Tax systems also have been revamped: In 1981, thirty-seven states had both income and sales taxes, compared with only nineteen states in 1960. These improved tax systems proved so productive before the recession at the end of the 1970s that many states built up large surpluses in their treasuries. In that period many states began major programs of financial aid to towns and cities.

During the 1960s, when a number of new federal programs bypassed the states to provide aid directly to local governments, pronouncements that state government was obsolete and on the way out were common. But with modernization, expanded revenues, and the stimulus of interstate economic competition, states have assumed a much more important role in the federal system than at any time in the post–World War II period.

THE DYNAMICS OF AMERICAN FEDERALISM

Throughout its history the American political system has dealt with the federal dilemma by steadily increasing the scope of the national government's power and responsibility. Although state governments have also become stronger, the national government has sought to guide the states' use of their power by providing them with money, skills, and technical assistance. This effort to *share* power over functions previously left up to the states has been an attempt to establish the validity and universality of many national standards. It has also been designed to increase the capacity of the states and cities to deal with the problems for which they have primary responsibility.

But the increase in national power has not been accomplished without problems and conflicts. Governments receiving financial aid from Washington complain of excessive paperwork, intrusive regulations, insensitive federal administrators unfamiliar with local conditions, and the high cost of administering federal grants. One indication of what city hall and statehouse officials are talking about is that the number of regulations imposed by Washington on state and local governments as a condition of receiving federal aid has grown from virtually none in 1960 to over 1,200 in 1981. The number of court cases involving state and local challenges to federal regulations has increased sharply since 1975, and the cost of federal paperwork imposed on state and local governments and private businesses was more than $100 billion annually by the end of the 1970s. A good example of what some analysts call this federal pleasure/pain syndrome is the growth of federal aid to higher education. In 1960 colleges and universities received about $1.7 billion from Washington; by 1980 federal aid had grown to more than $12 billion. But this growth in aid, although welcomed by the academic institutions, was accompanied by an increasing number of regulations. Many of these are worthy in themselves — guaranteeing access to the handicapped, establishing affirmative-action hiring goals, protecting human subjects in scientific experiments, disposing safely of radioactive wastes — but in combination they are costly and often troublesome to administer.

Occasionally, a state or city will simply refuse federal aid in order to avoid the regulations that go with it. Not long ago New Mexico refused federal aid for the education of handicapped children because, as a state education official explained, "We didn't need the strings and headaches for just $4.5 million." Georgia recently turned down $1.5 million in federal aid for coastal-zone planning, citing excessive interference by officials far away in Washington.[12]

To understand how increased sharing of powers among governmental levels has come about, we must examine the accompanying changes in the nature of the federal relationship as well as changes in ways of thinking about federalism. In practice, the states and the national government established cooperative relationships from the very beginning. The two levels of government shared in the financing and sometimes the planning of canals, roads, and harbors. They cooperated in establishing a sound national fiscal system — in part through the national government's creation of the Bank of the United States, which, among other things, supplied capital and credit to state banks.[13] And they worked jointly to establish public schools — in some states through direct federal grants, in others through land grants.[14]

National Supremacy versus Dual Federalism While this pattern of shared functions between the two levels of government was developing, two opposing theories of federalism were emerging. One, more or less compatible with the practice of shared functions, involved the doctrine of *national supremacy*. Developed most explicitly in the opinions of Supreme Court Chief Justice John Marshall, this theory stressed national supremacy and the so-called implied powers of Congress inherent in Article I, Section 8 (that Congress shall have the power "to make all Laws which shall be necessary and proper for carrying into Execution the foregoing Powers"), This theory was important because it provided a basis for extending the power of national government.

The other theory, which had become dominant by the 1820s and held sway until the years of the Great Depression, was that of *dual federalism*. This theory held that there was a sharp division between national and state powers and

[12] R. Stanfield, "What Has 500 Parts, Costs $83 Billion, and Is Condemned by Almost Everybody?" *National Journal*, January 3, 1981, p. 6.

[13] President Andrew Jackson and his supporters, however, saw the bank as a creature of the eastern financiers and an instrument that worked against the interests of "the people." Jackson refused to renew its federal charter, and it went out of existence in 1837.

[14] See Daniel J. Elazar, *The American Partnership* (Chicago: University of Chicago Press, 1962).

functions. As President James Monroe, himself a proponent of dual federalism, wrote in 1822:

> There were two separate and independent governments established over our Union, one for local purposes over each state by the people of the state, the other for national purposes over all the states by the people of the United States. . . . The National government begins where the state governments terminate, except in some instances where there is concurrent jurisdiction between them.[15]

The idea of dual federalism, then, entailed the notion of two domains of exclusive powers. Lord Bryce, the great English commentator on American government, likened the two levels of government in the federal system to two sets of factory machines, "each set doing its own work without touching or hampering the other."[16] In an 1871 decision (*Tarble's Case*) the Supreme Court held that "Neither government can intrude within the jurisdiction [of the other] or authorize any interference therein by its judicial officers with the action of the other." In this view, federalism was a conflict-ridden relationship between two levels of government, each jealously guarding its preserves of power. Morton Grodzins has suggested that this notion of federalism can be likened to a layer cake, its two layers neatly separated by a thin cement of jam.[17]

The classic Supreme Court statement of the doctrine of dual federalism came in the case of *Hammer* v. *Dagenhart* (1918). The Congress in 1916 had sought to regulate child labor by prohibiting — through its authority to regulate interstate commerce — the transportation across state lines of goods produced in places where children worked more than an eight-hour day. The Court ruled the act unconstitutional by arguing that the Congress had attempted to regulate *production,* which is a state matter, through its constitutional power to regulate *distribution.* In other words, in the Court's view the national government had intruded on powers reserved to the states.

The Marble Cake of Federalism Dual federalism was in many respects a view that the Court and others sought to force on a system that was in fact working very differently. As Grodzins argued in his famous description of the federal arrangement:

> the American system of government as it operates is not a layer cake at all. . . . Operationally, it is a marble cake. . . . No important activity of government in the United States is the exclusive province of one of the levels, not even what may be regarded as the most national of national functions, such as foreign relations; not even the most local of functions, such as police protection and park maintenance.[18]

[15] Ibid., p. 19.
[16] Morton Grodzins, ed. Daniel J. Elazar, *The American System* (Chicago: Rand McNally, 1966), p. 7.
[17] Ibid., p. 8.
[18] Grodzins, *American System*, p. 8.

Not only has the federal system in practice always involved sharing functions among levels (the mix that gives rise to the marble-cake metaphor), but it has also involved a *triadic* rather than a dual relationship. Proponents of the doctrine of dual federalism saw the system as composed of two tiers, the states and the national government, in a *competitive* relationship. In fact, however, such relations have largely been *cooperative,* and local governments have always been distinct third partners in the federal arrangement. Although neither cities nor municipal governments are mentioned in the national Constitution, local jurisdictions as more or less independent units nevertheless established a variety of cooperative relationships with the national government from the beginning.

The nineteenth century abounds with examples of cooperation among all three levels of government. The Army Corps of Engineers, for example, shared in the construction, financing, and maintenance of river and harbor projects with state and local governments beginning in 1826. The national government also made cash grants, land grants, and grants of materials to state and local governments in the areas of education, land reclamation, roads, canals, defense (state militias), veterans' homes, and agriculture.

FEDERALISM TODAY: INCREASED SHARING Although the sharing of functions among levels of government in the federal system has been a feature of the American experience from the beginning, the scope and number of such arrangements have increased sharply since the 1930s. In the three decades after the beginning of the Great Depression, Congress passed laws providing federal assistance to state and local governments for public housing, welfare, hospital construction, urban renewal, highways, poverty programs, and education, to name only a few examples. Today even the most local of government functions exemplify the pattern of sharing. Since 1960, for example, Congress has passed or seriously considered bills involving such apparently local responsibilities as home insulation, jellyfish control, urban gardening, snow removal, pothole repair, rural fire protection, and the development of bikeways.

Factors in Federal Sharing There are several reasons for the widened scope and accelerating pace of federal sharing. One has to do with the very different fiscal capacities of the different levels of government. Both cities and states labor under strict debt and borrowing limitations imposed by state constitutions. The national government, however, has constitutionally unlimited borrowing power. Federal revenues are also better able to grow with the economy, in part because the national government relies on the progressive individual and corporate income tax. ("Progressive" here means that the tax *rate* is progressively higher as income goes up.) Whereas the national tax take increases approximately 1.5 percent for every 1 percent increase in the gross national product, state revenues increase only slightly less than 1 percent and local revenues increase only about 0.5 percent. Despite recent reforms, state tax structures, including the sales tax — the major revenue producer for states — as well as as state income taxes, are much more regressive (that is, more burdensome to those with lower incomes) than the progressive federal income tax. Local revenues are tied mainly to property taxes, which are slower to change and are often unfairly administered.

The capacity of the national government to raise money is also less sensitive than that of the states and localities to fluctuations in the economic fortunes of geographic regions or particular industries. The severe depression suffered by the automobile industry in recent years, for example, has sharply reduced state and local revenues in Michigan, but has had only modest effects on national revenues.

Thus the national government has had to come to the financial rescue of other governments in the federal system. This rescue role grew to truly major proportions during the Great Depression as many states and cities neared bankruptcy. Some, like Detroit, actually did go bankrupt. The national government stepped into the breach to help pick up welfare, housing, and un-employment-insurance costs with the passage of the Social Security Act (1935) and the Housing Act of 1937.

Technological developments have also contributed to the need for increased federal sharing. As more and more automobiles and trucks took to the road, demands for highways outstripped state and local capacities to build them. As air transportation grew, so did demands for more and better airports, and national safety standards. As the harmful effects of air pollution came to light, so did the fact that this problem spilled over the boundaries of local and state governments. In short, the growth of modern technology produced problems of financing, control, safety, and coordination that local and state governments could not handle alone.

In addition, enormous political pressures for increased involvement by Washington in social-welfare programs were generated in the 1960s and 1970s by the emergence of the black-power movement and a host of student, con-sumer, environmental, and welfare rights groups. Many citizens also came to believe in the years before the Reagan presidency that housing, welfare, pov-erty programs, urban renewal, hospital construction, and education were not simply local responsibilities to be financed entirely by local resources. The costs of social problems in the cities and of poverty were seen to affect the national economy, the nature and the strength of the work force, and national morale.

To leave all responsibility for such problems in the hands of state and local governments meant that solutions would vary widely according to the eco-nomic resources of the particular state and its own distinctive political culture. The question Americans increasingly asked themselves in the decades after the depression was whether high standards of social justice and a strong national economy could be achieved if the nation depended on varying state capacities and political desires. All this is to say, of course, that Americans were coming to recognize at last the nature of the federal dilemma. *Cooperative federalism,* meaning increased involvement by the national government in areas once left largely to the states and localities, is the principal response we worked out to that dilemma.

Cooperative Federalism: Mostly a Matter of Money Intergovernmental relationships in the federal system are largely fiscal relationships. The transfer of money from the national government to states and localities, or "fiscal federalism," as it is often called, has been the major force in shaping the cooperative federal system.

Since 1955, the growth of federal aid to state and local governments has been awesome (see Table 4.1). By 1981 Washington was sending more than $91 billion back to state and local governments, twenty-eight times the amount in 1955. Taking inflation into account, the 1981 figure still represented more than a sixfold increase in the real value of federal aid.

The prime vehicle for such transfers, accounting for about 75 percent of all federal intergovernmental aid, is the categorical grant-in-aid, by which Congress makes funds available to a state or locality for specified purposes. Although a few such programs were established in the nineteenth century, their numbers have swelled only in this century. Most of the growth took place during the New Frontier administration of John F. Kennedy and the Great Society years of Lyndon Johnson; the number of federal categorical grant-in-aid programs went from 150 in 1960 to nearly 400 by 1968. In 1981 the number had increased to nearly 500.

Before 1960 the typical categorical grant-in-aid program was designed to help state and local governments meet *their* responsibilities and accomplish *their* objectives. Federal controls were instituted primarily to ensure efficient use of funds. During the Kennedy and Johnson years, however, federal assistance programs were designed to foster specific *national* purposes whereby

Table 4.1 The Growth of Federal Aid to States and Localities, 1955–81 (in Billions of Dollars)

Fiscal Year	Amount in Billions of Dollars	As a Percentage of Total Federal Expenditures	As a Percentage of Gross National Product
1955	3.2	4.7	0.8
1960	7.0	7.6	1.4
1965	10.9	9.2	1.7
1970	24.0	12.2	2.5
1975	49.8	15.3	3.4
1980	89.8	15.8	3.5
1981 (est.)	91.1	14.9	3.2

Source: Advisory Commission on Intergovernmental Relations, Intergovernmental Perspective 6 (Summer 1980): 19.

"The federal government executes the program through state or local governments. . . . The motive force is federal, with the states and communities assisting — rather than the other way around."[19] These so-called national-objective programs, most common during the mid-1960s, included the Economic Opportunity Act of 1964, the Area Redevelopment Act of 1961, and the Demonstration Cities and Metropolitan Development Act of 1966. In the preambles of each of these acts, as well as in others, Congress stated the national concerns and objectives of the legislation. "It is in the national interest," Congress wrote in the Manpower Development and Training Act of 1962, "that current and prospective manpower shortages be identified and that persons who can be qualified for these positions through education and training be sought out and trained, in order that the nation may meet the staffing requirements of the struggle for freedom."

There are two major types of categorical grants: *project grants* and *formula grants*. Project grants, which make up about two-thirds of all categorical programs, represent an attempt to establish a mix of local initiative and national standards. Such grants are awarded only on application by the recipient government. The proposed use of the grant money must meet the standards and purposes of the program as spelled out by the Congress. The state or local government must also provide some matching funds, usually about 15 percent of the cost of the project. The need to submit impressive applications, to develop the comprehensive planning documents that must usually accompany the application, and to enhance the state's or city's visibility in Washington gave rise to the art of "grantsmanship." Mayor Richard Lee of New Haven, who rebuilt his city with urban-renewal funds in the 1950s and 1960s, was perhaps the most accomplished master of the art of urban grantsmanship.

A second type of federal categorical aid, namely, *formula grants*, is allocated to all eligible governments for a specific purpose as a matter of *entitlement*. The amount each recipient gets is determined not by the nature of the project in mind to be funded but rather by a formula that may take into account such factors as population, the number of poor people in the recipient government's jurisdiction, per capita income, housing quality, and so on. Matching funds are usually required.

The increasing use of formula grants in recent years has understandably raised the stakes in the outcomes of the decennial census. With an estimated $500 billion in federal aid to be allocated in the 1980s according to formulas that take population into account, it is clear that the loss of population from the Frostbelt states, from older central cities, and from metropolitan counties will be extremely costly to those jurisdictions.[20] Compounding these population losses is the tendency of the Census Bureau to undercount the urban poor and minorities. After the 1980 census, some mayors claimed that the undercount amounted to as much as 10 percent of their cities' population. Detroit

[19] James L. Sundquist, *Making Federalism Work* (Washington, D.C.: Brookings, 1969), pp. 3–4.

[20] *The New York Times*, August 24, 1980.

What Government Buys

Nearly one-quarter of the roughly $700 billion spent by the federal government in the 1981 fiscal year went for defense appropriations. The largest item, however, was for a category called income security, which includes Social Security, public assistance, and other fiscal transfers to individuals. More than a third of the budget went for this purpose. Interest on the public debt consumed about 10 percent of federal expenditures.
The rest went for services as diverse as Meals on Wheels for the elderly to superhighways, from meat inspection to national parks, from scientific research to mortgage insurance.

actually sued the Census Bureau, contending that nearly 70,000 Detroit residents were not tallied in the census, costing the city millions of dollars in federal aid.

Within the framework of a grant-in-aid program's national objectives and implementation standards, recipient governments can spend the money pretty much as they choose. They must, of course, adhere to the various federal regulations pertaining to particular programs. In addition, there are certain federal controls, such as occasional national inspections of local or state administered projects, periodic reports to the granting agency, and federal audits. Failure to comply with federal standards can mean withdrawal of federal funds, although in fact Washington rarely uses this sanction.

Coordinating Federal Programs As grant-in-aid programs proliferated in the mid-1960s, governors, mayors, and federal officials began to complain that no one in the federal government had a comprehensive plan for coordinating the administration and planning of the various programs. In 1966 Senator Edmund Muskie of Maine, chairman of the Senate Subcommittee on Intergovernmental Relations, pointed out that there was substantial duplication and overlapping of federal programs, sometimes as a direct result of empire building. Mayor Henry Maier of Milwaukee complained in 1968 that "a whole maze of from thirty possible agencies involving the city, the county, the state, and the federal government, and, yes, the private sector" could be simultaneously involved in dealing with the welfare problems of a single family.[21] Both major political parties pledged in their platforms that year to overhaul the administration of federal programs by improving coordination and eliminating duplication and delay.

One of the first congressional efforts to confront the problem of coordination was the Demonstration Cities and Metropolitan Development Act of 1966. Among other things, this act required each applicant for federal aid to submit its proposals for review and comment to a local metropolitan-wide planning agency in its area. The act also required cities to establish a single coordinating agency that would draw on and seek to mesh in a comprehensive program "the complete array of all available grants and urban aids in the fields of housing, renewal, transportation, education, welfare, economic opportunity, and related programs."[22] But this effort, which came to be called the Model Cities Program, failed to live up to initial hopes. Not only were its resources spread thin among too many cities, but the programs that Model Cities agencies were to draw on languished for lack of adequate funding. The Model Cities Program expired in 1974.

From Grants-in-Aid to Revenue Sharing While the national government was trying to streamline its growing grant-in-aid program by improving coordination and planning, other forces were at work to pass federal funds back to state and local governments without any federal requirements. This was the movement for *revenue sharing*.

[21] Sundquist, *Making Federalism Work*, pp. 16–17.
[22] Ibid., p. 82.

Revenue sharing is a device whereby a specified portion of federal tax revenues are automatically returned each year to lower-level governments. Recipient governments may spend the money virtually as they wish. The antecedents of revenue sharing go back as far as 1836, when, under Andrew Jackson, surplus revenues from the sale of federal lands were apportioned back to the states for unrestricted use. In this century serious efforts to establish such a program did not begin until the administration of John F. Kennedy, whose economic advisors endorsed and promoted the idea. Soon revenue sharing was being hailed by liberals and conservatives alike. Liberals saw it as a vehicle for more public spending, which they favored. Conservatives liked the idea of fewer federal controls over states' and localities' uses of federal funds.

The idea of revenue sharing was debated throughout the 1960s. In 1969 Richard Nixon made it a major feature of his call for a "new federalism," and in 1972 the Congress passed a general revenue-sharing bill entitled the State and Local Fiscal Assistance Act. Revenue sharing has been renewed twice, first in 1976 and again in 1980. The last time Congress refused to renew the program for the states in fiscal year 1981 but authorized the resumption of state revenue sharing for later fiscal years subject to appropriations action. Washington attaches only minimal strings to the money it sends back. Local governments have used most of their revenue-sharing money to combat crime (although some small towns have used their grants to build swimming pools or youth recreation centers). State governments spent a large portion of their money for property-tax relief for local taxpayers. No matching funds by recipient governments are required, and neither is the approval of a plan or proposal, although the law requires that recipient governments publish planned-use reports.

President Nixon envisioned this *general revenue sharing* as only one part of a larger system of fiscal transfers. The other part was to be composed of *special revenue sharing* programs, in which money would be passed back to the states and localities to replace specialized, or categorical, grant-in-aid programs for law enforcement, manpower training, urban community development, rural community development, transportation, and education. The only special revenue sharing program passed during Nixon's presidency was for manpower training. The first piece of legislation signed by President Gerald Ford, however, was the Housing and Community Development (HCD) Act of 1974, which eliminated such categorical-aid programs as Model Cities and urban renewal. Instead, local governments could apply for and receive "block" grants to pay for a wide variety of housing, renewal, and public-works projects. Unlike the old "national-objective" acts, the HCD Act allows local governments themselves to establish priority programs and goals, with almost complete freedom from federal guidelines.

Revenue sharing quickly gained wide support among state and local officials. Not only did it lessen the massive burden of writing grant applications, but it also allowed states and localities to hold down taxes in an inflationary period without forcing cuts in services. As the recession of the early 1970s deepened, revenue-sharing money became, in some places, such as Detroit, virtually the only barrier between bankruptcy and solvency. Yet for all the flexibility and support that revenue sharing provides, it aggravates the dilemma of federalism. With the diminished commitment to grant-in-aid programs, the whole idea of national objectives and priorities goes by the board. It is impossible for the national government to finance uniform and universal programs through revenue sharing. A national effort to end poverty or to build low-income housing funded through revenue sharing money would require local initiatives in thousands of towns and cities rather than the one federal initiative required in the old grant-in-aid programs.

Furthermore, many people were worried that local majorities, mostly white and middle class, would ignore the preferences and desires of special constituencies created and protected by the old grant-in-aid programs. The poor, the unemployed, the poorly housed, and minority groups had a formal role to play in the Community Action and Model Cities programs, which were specifically geared to their needs. But revenue sharing does not guarantee attention to the needs of the deprived. One critic of this open-ended federal aid program complained that it "plays to the tyranny of the local majority. And the minority is subject to their whims and there is no redress. It's very hard to guard poor people's rights in these circumstances."[23]

Some of the same criticisms of revenue sharing have been directed at block grants. Indeed, a great deal of the money spent under the manpower block grant called CETA (Comprehensive Employment and Training Act of 1973) went to hire relatively well off, more highly skilled, and better-educated workers rather than to hire the hard-core unemployed. In contrast, however, studies of the community-development block grant program show that much of the money is spent in low- and moderate-income neighborhoods rather than in middle-class areas.[24] There is, therefore, evidence on both sides of the debate.

A strong case for block grants can be made on the grounds of sheer efficiency. Many federal categorical grants are very small. In fact, about 420 of the 500 grant programs account for only 10 percent of the total aid passed down from Washington. Block grants typically consolidate several categorical programs dealing with the same general type of problem. Thus proponents of reform have argued that a block grant for education programs would be more efficient than the current system of more than 70 different categorical programs aiding elementary and secondary schools. Similarly, it would be more efficient to consolidate the 78 different programs relating to health in a single health block grant.

---

[23] *The New York Times,* March 8, 1976.
[24] U.S. Department of Housing and Urban Development, *Fifth Annual Community Development Block Grant Report* (Washington, D.C.: U.S. Government Printing Office, 1980).

**CITIZEN
PERSPECTIVES
ON THE
FEDERAL
SYSTEM**

Popular sentiment about the federal government has shifted several times in this century. Before the Great Depression, people trusted their economic well-being to private enterprise rather than government. The private sector, or non-governmental sphere of activity, appeared more than adequate to meet a limited range of social needs. But the depression prostrated much of private enterprise, threw millions out of work, and virtually bankrupted local and state governments. By the time of Lyndon Johnson's presidency three decades later, most people had come around to the view that the federal government should play a strong role in ensuring the well-being of Americans.

Since the late 1960s, sentiment about the federal government has changed again, taking on a complex and deeply ambivalent character. Many people see the federal government's participation — or "intervention"— in our daily lives as simultaneously reassuring and threatening. To give one example, local school officials have become dependent on federal grants and subsidies for school lunch programs, school construction, and other activities. But at the same time most of these local officials deeply resent federal efforts to integrate the schools through court orders to bus children. To give another example, citizens in most American cities live in fear of crime and applaud federal efforts to bolster local police capabilities. Yet at the same time many of these same citizens fear that such efforts could lead to an erosion of their civil liberties. They point, for example, to the proposals for federally financed national data banks that could make information about people instantly accessible to local police departments everywhere. The danger of such a national information system, they say, lies in its potential for abuse by unscrupulous or over-zealous police and other government officials.

**A Loss
of Faith**

During the 1970s there was a clear loss of faith in the effectiveness of the federal government, particularly in relation to other levels of government (see Table 4.2). In the face of the Watergate scandals (1974), double-digit inflation (1979), and the highest unemployment levels since the Great Depression (1980), Washington seemed helpless.

The sense that government is ineffective has potentially grave implications: In such a situation government begins to lose its credibility when it asks citizens to make sacrifices. If government cannot do its part, if it cannot use effectively the resources it commands, then why should citizens comply with burdensome rules, taxes, and regulations? The public response to the energy crisis provides an apt example. Many Americans do not believe that a crisis — an imminent shortage of fossil fuels — exists at all. Many others believe that the government response to high energy costs and the disappearance of fuels is misguided, uncoordinated, and geared to the interests of the big oil companies. It is little wonder, then, that noncompliance with the 55-mile-per-hour speed limit, designed to save gasoline, runs as high as two-thirds of all drivers.[25]

[25] *The New York Times*, August 24, 1980.

Table 4.2 Some Indicators of Confidence
in the Federal Government
Compared with Other Levels of Government

1. From which level of government do you feel you get the most for your money?

	Percentage of U.S. Public		
	1980	1976	1972
Federal	33	36	39
Local	26	25	26
State	22	20	18
Don't know	19	19	17

Source: Advisory Commission on Intergovernmental Relations, *Changing Public Attitudes on Governments and Taxes* (Washington, D.C.: 1980), p. 2.

2. Which level of government do you think wastes the biggest part of its budget?

	Percentage Answering
Federal	62
State	12
Local	5
None	13
Don't know	8

Source: CBS News/*New York Times* poll, June 1978. Reprinted by permission.

To some extent this general loss of faith must be attributed to a sense of lost control, a feeling that the arena in which important decisions are made is increasingly distant and too complex to understand. Hence a central theme in the political rhetoric of the 1970s and 1980s has been the "return" of government to the people.

What accounts for this sense of lost control?

Let us begin by understanding that when pollsters ask Americans how the federal government affects them personally, the most frequently given answer is that it taxes them, not that it provides them with services or benefits. Americans view governments at all levels as takers first; and of all the governments the federal government is certainly the biggest taker. Apparently it does not occur to most people that much of this money is redistributed directly to individuals (through transfer payments like social security or veterans' benefits) or indirectly (through state and local grants-in-aid).

Coupled with the image of the national government as a taker is its image as a profligate spender on "minority groups" and as a generous benefactor of "big business." Programs like "welfare" (Aid to Families with Dependent Children), food stamps, and public housing have achieved a level of visibility completely out of proportion to what the government spends on them. At the other extreme, government subsidies to "big agriculture," the oil industry, and the Chrysler Corporation strike many citizens as being patently unfair. Where, they ask, are the programs that meet the needs of the great middle class? To many Americans, then, the whole pattern of federal development — the increased scope of national concerns and the increased commitment to federal sharing — seems to bypass the interests of the ordinary taxpayer.

Closely related to these resentments are others that have arisen from the federal dilemma in the area of race relations, especially school desegregation. The 1964 Civil Rights Act, for example, empowered the federal government to withhold funds from school districts that did not work out school-desegregation plans. This authority has seldom been exercised, but it spurred local efforts to bring black and white children together in the public schools. After much experimenting, school officials concluded that busing offered the only practical solution. Busing was upheld as a means of desegregation by the Supreme Court in 1971 (*Swann* v. *Charlotte-Mecklenburg*), and state and lower federal courts began ordering segregated school districts to develop and implement busing plans. Such a court order in Boston in 1974 led to several years of bitterness, defiance, and violence as the predominantly Irish community of South Boston fought to resist a busing program.

Public opinion in the busing controversy has tended to view the federal government as an unwelcome, even tyrannical, meddler in local affairs. But some parts of the federal government itself have encouraged public opposition, including the Congress (which forbade the use of federal funds for busing) and, during the Nixon years, the president himself.

The National Government: How "Close" to the People? This widely felt sense that the people have lost control over big government has renewed an old debate about which level of government is really closest to the people. Many simply assume that the answer is local government, and this assumption underlies much of the current movement in the Reagan administration to "return power to the states and localities," where officials presumably best know local conditions and desires. This assumption requires careful examination, however. "Closeness to the people" has a variety of meanings.

Certainly, local government provides more direct services to citizens than does any other level, although the financing of nearly all these services — roads, schools, police, mass transit, sewage treatment — is shared with state and national government.

Table 4.3 Washington Is Just Around the Corner:
Selected Federal Agencies in Madison, Wisconsin
(Population 170,000)

Agricultural Research Service	Food and Nutrition Service
Air Force	Forest Service Products Laboratory
Animal Eradication Division	Game Management Agent
Animal and Plant Health Inspection	Geological Survey, Water Resources
Service	Internal Revenue Service
Army	Interstate Commerce Commission
Bureau of Alcohol, Tobacco, and	Marine Corps
Firearms	Marshal
Bureau of Prisons	Passport Office
Consumer and Marketing Service	Peace Corps
Defense Investigation Service	Selective Service System
Federal Aviation Administration,	Small Business Administration
Department of Transportation	Social Security Administration
Federal Bureau of Investigation	Soil Conservation Service
Federal Deposit Insurance	United Migrant Opportunity Services
Corporation	United States District Court
Federal Energy Administration	Veterans Administration
Federal Job Information Center	Wage and Hour Division, Department
Food and Drug Administration	of Labor

"Closeness" can also mean geographical proximity: Washington is distant, whereas city hall is close. But in fact 90 percent of national-government employees work not in Washington, but in thousands of towns, cities, and counties around the country. Federal agencies maintain thousands of local offices, as Table 4.3, compiled from telephone listings, shows. In truth, the national government is no farther away geographically than city hall.

"Closeness of the government to the people" might also imply a special familiarity. We might expect that people feel closer to a government when they are familiar with its ongoing activities — with what it is doing. We might also expect that such familiarity would make them more willing to take part in its affairs. True, the chances of knowing one's city council member or the cop on the beat are better than those of knowing one's United States senator or local Internal Revenue Service agent. But if we examine data on how up to date people feel about what is going on at the different levels of government, we find that they are scarcely more familiar with local government than they are with the affairs of the federal government (see Table 4.4).

And if we compare people's participation rates — say, the frequency and scope of voting activity or giving money to a campaign or letter writing to public officials — we find that most people are far more active at the national level. Local voting turnouts often hover around 20 or 25 percent of the eligible

Table 4.4   Keeping Up with Government: Citizens' Estimates of
Their Familiarity with Happenings at Different Levels of
Government

	Excellent	Good	Fair	Poor
Local	8%	35%	38%	19%
State	3%	24%	49%	24%
National	6%	34%	42%	18%

Source: *Confidence and Concern: Citizens View American Government*, A Survey of Public Attitudes by the Subcommittee on Intergovernmental Relations of the Committee on Government Operations (Washington, D.C.: U.S. Government Printing Office, December 1973), pp. 238–40.

electorate, whereas recent presidential elections have drawn from about 61 percent (1968) to a modern low of 52 percent (1980). Such data suggest that even if people do feel a closer affinity with local government, this feeling may have little practical effect.

Now it is true that local government is closer to the people in terms of what we might call its *penetrability*. That is, it is certainly easier for ordinary citizens to get elected to local government positions than it is to penetrate the state or national governments through the electoral process. But opportunities for citizen participation in federal activities are widespread. Some 155 federal grant programs, from general revenue sharing to community development to coastal-zone management, require citizen participation. Citizen advisory and policy-making boards that develop or review plans and open hearings are the most common vehicles for such participation.[26]

It is clear that glib assumptions about the relative closeness of local government to the people in relation to that of the federal government are open to question. We may conclude with Morton Grodzins that closeness is in no sense "exclusively or principally the attribute of local (as opposed to state or federal) governments. . . . Closeness to the citizen is an attribute of all American governments."[27]

THE FUTURE OF THE FEDERAL SYSTEM   Many analysts believe that the gargantuan system of federal relationships is in bad trouble and in need of reform. The Advisory Commission on Intergovernmental Relations (ACIR), a nonpartisan public body that monitors the federal system, asserts that the government in Washington has become "more pervasive, more intrusive, more unmanageable, more ineffective, more costly, and

[26] Advisory Commission on Intergovernmental Relations, *Citizen Participation in the Federal System* (Washington, D.C.: 1979), p. 5.
[27] Grodzins, *The American System*, p. 211.

above all unaccountable."[28] The remedy, many believe, including President Reagan, is to diminish Washington's power by consolidating overlapping categorical grants in some areas and eliminating other grant programs entirely. A major consequence of both strategies would be to place much greater responsibility for the administration and financing of public programs on the shoulders of the states.

If, however, the growth of national power can be understood historically as the way in which we have tried to counteract inequalities in the treatment of people from state to state and to establish national programs and priorities, then how will passing power back to states and localities affect us as a society committed to some ideal of equality?

This is not an easy question to answer, but in principle it should be possible to strike a balance between a more efficient, more accountable federal system and equality of treatment in areas of national concern. For example, at the same time that the ACIR recommends reducing the number of categorical grant programs, creating more block grants, and easing the burden of federal regulations, it has also called for the national assumption of responsibility for welfare, nutrition, housing, employment, and medical care. "Only national financing can assure that an adequate standard of benefits exists throughout the nation," the ACIR contends.[29] Other areas, however, such as arson control, police pensions, firefighting, libraries, and pothole repair, all of which received federal aid in the 1970s and early 1980s, could be turned back to the states and localities without causing serious inequities from state to state. Unlike basic welfare needs, these need not be areas of national concern.

Even if political reform does not succeed in cutting down the size or rate of growth of the federal system in the 1980s, economic forces are likely to do so. One of the dominant forces affecting the shape of the federal system in the future is likely to be the persistent high rate of inflation, which economists now believe is a long-term phenomenon built into our society. The impact of this inflation on federal aid to state and local governments will undoubtedly be to slow down its growth. By the end of the 1970s, the rate of increase in such federal aid was already beginning to slow down after years of rapid growth. Annual increases in amount of financial aid in the first years of the 1980s actually represented a *decline* in the amount of assistance when adjusted to real dollars. Federal aid as a percentage of state and local expenditures declined from 25.4 percent in 1979 to 23.6 percent in 1980.[30]

Inflation works to contract federal intergovernmental aid in several related ways. Federal spending itself — for new or expanded social programs, for public works, for new weapons — is seen by many economists as one of the sources of inflation. Curbing federal spending, including the spending of fed-

[28] Advisory Commission on Intergovernmental Relations, *In Brief* (Washington, D.C.. December 1980), p. 1.

[29] Ibid., p. 28.

[30] Advisory Commission on Intergovernmental Relations, *Intergovernmental Perspective* (Washington, D.C.: Spring 1980), p. 6.

eral money by other levels of government, is one way to stop pumping money into an overheated economy.

Inflation has also worked to "hobble" the federal income tax. A source of expanding revenues in a growing economy, the income tax has been cut in recent years to offset inflationary losses in individual purchasing power and to encourage saving and investment of personal and corporate income. Taxes have also been cut to compensate for increases in social security. In short, the income tax, which had served so well as a device for expanding federal spending, has been sharply constrained.

Finally, taxpayer resistance in an era of sharply rising consumer prices has put a damper on congressional willingness to spend more, at least for innovative social programs.

For reasons of both political reform and economics, then, it is unlikely that the United States will experience in the 1980s the same magnitude of federal expansion as in the 1960s and 1970s.

CONCLUSION We have suggested that American federalism, with its blend of national supremacy and state independence, facilitates experimentation and accommodation of diversity. At the same time, it allows the existence of certain inequalities. Although an Oregon can lead the nation in banning disposable cans, the other side of the coin is that an Arkansas cannot maintain a modern prison system. Poor states simply cannot offer the same range and quality of services that wealthy states can afford.

If national power and responsibility truly cease to grow, more and more of the burden for providing public services will fall on state and local governments. Unequal economic resources and unequal problems mean that inequalities among citizens of different states and localities will persist. When such inequalities come to be sharply felt, one response is to call for a reinvigoration of the federal system by increasing national power. How we balance the desire for national priorities and resources to prevail in certain areas of public policy against the belief in the virtues of local and regional independence and diversity — in short, the federal dilemma — is clearly an abiding problem in the politics of American federalism.

SUGGESTIONS FOR FURTHER READING

Gelfand, Mark. *A Nation of Cities.* New York: Oxford University Press, 1975. A rich account of the growth of federal aid to cities from the Great Depression through the Great Society.

Grodzins, Morton. *The American System.* Chicago: Rand McNally, 1966. The classic discussion of the structure and dynamics of American federalism.

Listokin, D., and Burchell, R., eds. *Cities under Stress.* Rutgers, N.J.: Center for Urban Policy Research, Rutgers University, 1981. A thorough examination of federal aid patterns and effects in American cities.

Reagan, M. *The New Federalism,* 2nd ed. New York: Oxford University Press, 1980. A discussion and critique of various aspects of fiscal federalism.

Riker, William. *Federalism: Origin, Operation, Significance.* Boston: Little, Brown, 1964. One of the most critical views of the operation of American federalism, concentrating on its impact on racial inequality.

Sundquist, James. *Making Federalism Work.* Washington, D.C.: Brookings, 1969. An account of the Great Society programs — how they were formulated and how they were implemented.

Wright, Deil. *Understanding Intergovernmental Relations.* North Scituate, Mass.: Duxbury, 1978. A general introduction to a wide range of issues in American federalism.

Chapter 5 Congress

In creating our three-part national government, the framers of the Constitution assigned to Congress primary responsibility for representing the people. The president would provide unified leadership and direction; the Supreme Court would ensure that law, not individual whim, resolved conflicts; and Congress would serve as the vital main bridge between citizens and their government.

Logically, then, Congress was also the branch in which most powers were vested, for the framers intended government to be an instrument of the people. All laws must come from Congress, as well as all funds for the federal government's activities, and all declarations of war against other nations.

A closer look at the Congress shows, however, that the Founding Fathers were cautious about how the Congress would represent the citizenry. Their first crucial decision was to make the Congress *bicameral;* that is, they created two legislative chambers, which they felt would represent different interests among the people at large.

All eligible voters — adult white male property owners — could cast ballots every two years for members of the House of Representatives. The framers intended the House to be the legislative body in which a democratic majority could work its will. Representation in the House was based solely on total state population, and the House grew from 59 members in 1789 to 435 in 1920 by adding seats after each decade's census. In 1920, however, the House was

110

becoming unwieldy, and it voted to stabilize its number of members, necessitating automatic reapportionment of the 435 seats among the states every ten years.

The Senate, on the other hand, was designed explicitly to minimize the power of the people as a whole. Each state, regardless of population, was served by two senators, who were appointed by their state legislature. The framers intended the Senate to represent the more "aristocratic" interests — the propertied and well-to-do — and protect them against what Madison, in No. 62 of *The Federalist*, called "the propensity of all single and numerous assemblies to yield to the impulse of sudden and violent passions and to be seduced by factious leaders into intemperate and pernicious resolutions." Indirect election would insulate senators against public pressure for hasty and ill-conceived legislation. And six-year terms would also make them less vulnerable to such pressure than their colleagues in the House, who must renew their contract with their constituents every two years.

The two houses of Congress would therefore represent different interests. Congress as a whole would balance the interests of the propertied classes and the common folk, of trade and agriculture, of minorities and majorities.

Our representative scheme has changed over the years. The Seventeenth Amendment, ratified in 1913, provided for the direct, popular election of each state's two senators. The average number of constituents for each House member has grown from 30,000 in 1789 to slightly more than 500,000 today. And the Supreme Court ruled in the 1960s that state legislatures can no longer draw congressional district boundaries in ways that systematically underrepresent certain population groups. This means that each House member now represents approximately the same number of people. Such equity, of course, does not hold for the Senate, where all states, regardless of population, are served by two senators.

The problems of representation are difficult, and we will consider them later at some length. First, however, let us fix our sights on the congressional political setting and the ways the House and Senate operate.

CONGRESS AS A POLITICAL INSTITUTION   Congress is a large, complex, and fragmented institution. Power is widely dispersed within it, and congressional organization is extremely decentralized. Congress is bicameral, as specified by the Constitution, and the House and Senate must reach accord on issues in order to pass legislation. Agreement within each chamber is necessary, too, and it often comes hard. One hundred senators and 435 representatives, all elected on their own, are difficult to move in any direction.

Compounding the problems posed by bicameralism and numbers is the massive and complex congressional work load. As one first-term member of Congress noted,

> I am appalled at how much congressmen are expected to do for the nation. We have to know too much. We have to make too many decisions. There is a

tremendous problem in international relations and congressmen are constantly involved in this. But in addition we are supposed to know all about domestic activities — about education, water pollution, small business problems, dams, etc. No matter how hardworking and conscientious a congressman is, no matter how much homework he does, he just can't master these problems. We just don't have the time to keep informed properly.[1]

Time is indeed a problem. According to a 1978 congressional committee report, the average representative puts in an eleven-hour work day, allowing himself twelve minutes for reading; "for more than one-third of that day, the Representative is scheduled to be at least two places at once."[2]

Still, Congress gets things done. Like any complex organization, it relies on certain formal and informal working arrangements to order its operation. *Committees* and *parties* provide formal organization for the House and Senate, and informal "rules of the game" encourage cooperation and generally make the legislative process go more smoothly.

Committees: The "Little Legislatures"

"Congress in session is Congress on exhibition, whilst Congress in its Committee rooms is Congress at work." Thus wrote Woodrow Wilson in 1883,[3] and thus it remains today. Most of the business of Congress is accomplished in committees. By dividing up the legislative labor, individual committees can scrutinize, hold hearings on, and revise several times as many bills as either chamber acting as a whole could manage. The House and Senate Agriculture committees, for example, consider possible changes in crop support prices and family-farm legislation. Neither house, acting as a whole, could devote much time to such detailed and often highly technical problems. Indeed, much of the actual work is performed by subcommittees. Currently the 24 House committees have 138 subcommittees; the Senate has 20 committees with 112 subcommittees. In addition, there are four joint Senate-House committees.

This division of labor helps Congress to deal with some 20,000 legislative proposals yearly. (The majority are sent to committees, never to be returned for action on the House or Senate floor.) However, it can also fragment responsibility and lead to struggles over jurisdiction. Consider the differences between the House and Senate in their treatment of energy policy.

The Senate, operating under 1977 reforms, established a single committee, Energy and Natural Resources, to deal with most energy matters. This consolidation meant that several other committees — including Armed Forces and Public Works — lost much of their say in energy policy. The House, on the other hand, has allowed energy politics to become snarled in the fragmentation the committee system encourages. No fewer than 83 House subcommittees

[1] Charles Clapp, Jr., *The Congressman: His Work as He Sees It* (Washington, D.C.: Brookings, 1963), p. 118.

[2] *The New York Times*, March 27, 1978.

[3] Woodrow Wilson, *Congressional Government*, 15th ed. (Boston: Houghton Mifflin, 1900), p. 79.

Congressional Committee Hearings

As might be expected, committee hearings help inform Congress about complex policy issues, but they also provide opportunities for members to obtain publicity, often by questioning top-level bureaucrats about Administration policy. Although dozens of hearings are conducted each week, in both the Senate and the House, only a few attract much media coverage. The presence of a Cabinet officer, like Carter's Health, Education, and Welfare Secretary Califano or Reagan's Secretary of State Haig (pictured here) assures substantial attention from the press. Most hearings, however, go virtually unnoticed beyond Capitol Hill; their major purpose is to build a record on behalf of proposed legislation.

On occasion, Congress will generate truly dramatic committee hearings, which the entire nation watches. The Watergate hearings of the 1970s and the Army-McCarthy hearings of the 1950s were such events, and they led eventually to the resignation of President Nixon and the discrediting of Sen. McCarthy. This infrequent, but powerful, publicity is a powerful congressional weapon, and could easily be misused by careless or overly ambitious members.

claim some jurisdiction over energy policy.[4] In 1977 the House used an Ad Hoc Energy Committee to serve as a clearinghouse for the individual committees' proposals, but the problem of divided control over energy policy remains acute.

Because committee and subcommittee chairmen are often extremely jealous of their policy "fiefdoms," House committees have resisted reorganization like that of the Senate. Such reluctance may seem irrational, but we must remember that Congress is a representative as well as a legislative body. By maintaining many committees with jurisdiction over energy, the House is maximizing public and special interest access to its decision making (see Chapter 14). In Congress, as elsewhere, the price of democracy is often inefficiency.

Congressional committees continue to be important, but the contemporary Congress has given increasing weight to its subcommittees. This makes sense, in that as legislation becomes more complex, a number of subcommittees can consider policy specifics more carefully than can a few committees. Such a division of labor may not, however, lead to better policy results. There is a great potential for fragmentation of authority. As Dodd and Oppenheimer report, in the House, "Basic legislative responsibility has shifted from approximately 20 standing committees to more than 160 committees and subcommittees."[5] Further, lobbyists often outnumber the subcommittee members actually present at any given meeting; in general, subcommittee government appears to benefit well-organized special interests who can focus their attention on the narrow concerns of particular subcommittees.[6]

Subcommittee chairs have become important positions; chairpersons usually hire their own staff, schedule their own hearings, and manage their own legislation on the floor of the chamber. In other words, they do almost everything within their jurisdiction that committee chairmen used to do.

Senate subcommittees are less dominant than their House counterparts, in that the Senate, with only a hundred members, relies less heavily on a formal division of labor than does the larger House. Nevertheless, Senate subcommittees do play important roles in the legislative process. This means that majority-party senators all hold at least one subcommittee chair and thus control some part of the legislative agenda. Early in the 97th Congress, President Reagan and Majority Leader Howard Baker learned that the new Republican Senate committee and subcommittee chairs understood the strength of their formal positions. Baker and other Republican leaders devised a tentative plan to slide through the Senate a lid on total federal spending. There was to be almost no committee consideration of this legislation.

[4]*Congressional Quarterly Weekly Report*, November 3, 1979, p. 2486.

[5] Lawrence Dodd and Bruce Oppenheimer, "The House in Transition," in Dodd and Oppenheimer, *Congress Reconsidered*, 2nd ed. (Washington, D.C.: CQ Press, 1981), p. 43.

[6] The subcommittee–interest group relationship represents one leg of an "iron triangle" that often develops among bureaucratic offices, interest groups, and congressional subcommittees dealing with the same issue — such as tobacco subsidies or airline regulation.

But the plan . . . ran into instant resistance from some of their new Republican chairmen, who had waited up to a quarter century for a taste of power. "They're talking about turf, said one [chairman] indispensible to Reagan. "We might just tell him to shove it."[7]

Appropriations and Authorizations. Although in general congressional sub-committees have become more important in recent years, there are a number of subcommittees that have always been taken very seriously — those of the Appropriations committees in both chambers, and especially in the House. The most basic congressional power is the control of federal spending — the power of the purse. Congress has taken its role here so seriously that proposed spending must pass twice through the legislative process. Congress first *authorizes* a program and spending levels and only then passes legislation *appropriating* money to pay for the program. Authorization levels are almost always higher than the actual amounts appropriated, and on some occasions no money at all is appropriated. Many water projects (dams, dikes, locks, etc.) that won authorization in the 1950s and 1960s have yet to receive any appropriations at all. Even some ongoing projects, such as the B-1 bomber or Tennessee's Clinch River Breeder Reactor, which produces nuclear fuel, lost their appropriations during the Carter administration.

The Constitution dictates that all "money bills" originate in the House of Representatives. The Framers thought that the House members, with their two-year terms, would be less likely to tax too severely or spend too rashly. This constitutional requirement remains significant, in that the House sets the basic appropriations levels to which the Senate must react. Losers in the House often regard the Senate Appropriations Committee as a "Court of Appeals."[8] Although the reformed congressional budget process (discussed later on) has slightly reduced the importance of the Appropriations committees, they remain very attractive bodies for senators and representatives who wish to affect policy as specifically as possible.

Committee Membership. For many members, committee (and subcommittee) service is the heart of congressional life. Committees provide opportunities to gain (and use) expertise; to mold public policy; and to reward particular interests, including one's constituents. Membership on some committees, like Appropriations; on the taxing bodies (Ways and Means in the House, Finance in the Senate); and, currently, the Budget committees, is highly valued. Members of these units have a say over a wide range of policies while simultaneously being able to affect very specific parts of programs. For reasons peculiar to each chamber, the House Rules Committee and the Senate Foreign Rela-

[7]*Newsweek*, March 2, 1981, p. 24.
[8]See Richard F. Fenno, Jr., *The Power of the Purse* (Boston: Little, Brown, 1966); and Stephen Horn, *Unused Power* (Washington, D.C.: Brookings, 1970).

tions Committee also attract great attention. The Rules Committee controls the flow of legislation in the House; the Foreign Relations panel not only is the chief overseer of administration foreign policy but also acts on ratification of treaties and confirmation of ambassadorial appointments.

Other committees frequently provide specific benefits to their members. Farm-state members of Congress crowd the Agriculture committees; western members seek assignments on Interior, which controls policy over federal lands. Liberals have traditionally sought Education and Labor positions in the House, whereas more conservative members have populated the Armed Services committees of both chambers. Some important committees attract relatively little interest. The House Judiciary Committee, for instance, handles many controversial subjects, ranging from abortion to free speech issues to criminal-code reform. Whatever proposals emerge from this committee, they are sure to anger many important interests and to produce few political benefits for the members. In the 97th Congress, no House Democrats, aside from those already on the committee, sought a Judiciary assignment, and Speaker O'Neill was forced to offer incentives (additional positions on other committees) to attract members to serve on the committee.

In sum, if Woodrow Wilson were to return to the Congress of the 1980s, he would easily recognize the institutional arrangements of committees and subcommittees. The congressional fragmentation of power and division of labor remain key characteristics. But there has been some genuine change over the years. In the 1970s, congressional leaders found themselves confronted with over a hundred legislative "cooks" rather than being able to negotiate with a few dozen committee-based "chefs," as was the case in the 1950s and 1960s. As Representative Morris Udall (D-Arizona) put it, "Before we had [committee] tyrants who had to be dealt with. Now there's an obscure congressman from Iowa who runs a key subcommittee that can foul up a President."[9] Subcommittee government, featuring unclear and overlapping jurisdictions and an abundance of eager young legislators, renders ordered and coherent policymaking increasingly unlikely.

Parties and Party Leadership in Congress Political parties are said to "organize" the House and the Senate. Because virtually all representatives and senators are either Democrats or Republicans, this means:

1. The majority party in each chamber selects the body's leadership —Speaker and Majority Leader in the House, Majority Leader and (an assistant leader) in the Senate. The minority party provides a Minority Leader and a Whip in each chamber.
2. Every committee and subcommittee chairman is a majority-party member; the minority provides a "ranking member" for its delegation on each com-

---

[9]*Newsweek,* January 26, 1981, p. 41.

mittee and subcommittee. This person has few formal responsibilities but would chair the committee should his or her party become the majority.

3. The majority party of each house controls the flow of legislative business. It also controls an assortment of patronage positions (for example, clerk and doorkeeper of the House) and the appointment of most committee staff members.

The Speaker of the House. Although the Speaker of the House and the Senate Majority Leader hold the top party positions in their respective chambers, the Speaker has considerably greater formal power. This power derives from the greater importance of organization to the larger body: It must conduct more of its business according to strict and formal rules of procedure, and it needs a strong leader to apply, interpret, and enforce those rules. The Speaker, then, has several important powers. He schedules legislation, presides over the House, decides points of order, refers bills to appropriate House committees, and appoints certain committee members. Although a Speaker can act with some discretion, he usually works closely with committee chairmen and sponsors of legislation.

Around the turn of the century, Speakers such as Thomas ("Czar") Reed and "Uncle Joe" Cannon enjoyed nearly dictatorial powers in appointing committee members and chairmen and regulating the flow of House business. The members of the House revolted against such treatment, stripping the Speaker of many of his formal powers. Nevertheless, the speakership retained a great potential for power, as Sam Rayburn illustrated in the 1950s. As the current Speaker, Thomas P. (Tip) O'Neill, has noted,

> Old Sam Rayburn couldn't name 12 new members of Congress, and he was an institution that awed people. . . . Only on the rarest of occasions could a Congressman get an appointment to see him. And when he called the Attorney General and said, "You be in my office at 3 in the afternoon," that Cabinet officer was there at 3 in the afternoon.[10]

Coordinating party actions in today's decentralized House strains the capabilities of leaders past the breaking point. Although Speaker O'Neill's formal powers are greater than were Sam Rayburn's twenty years ago, his ability to lead is dramatically less. Despite some success, notably in energy legislation, O'Neill — even before the 1980 Democratic losses — generally saw his party as fragmented:

> We're five parties in one. We've got about 25 really strong liberals, 110 progressive liberals, maybe 60 moderates, about 45 people just to the right of moderate and 35 conservatives.[11]

[10] O'Neill, quoted in *The New York Times*, April 5, 1977.
[11] *Congressional Quarterly Weekly Report*, September 13, 1980, p. 2696.

O'Neill has made some adjustments designed to broaden the base of the House leadership team. He has appointed many junior Democrats to serve as: (1) assistant Whips; (2) members of issue-oriented task forces, designed to push through a specific bill; or (3) members of the leadership's Steering and Policy Committee (discussed later on). The fact remains, however, that members of Congress win their seats independent of most party or presidential efforts. As a result, the party leaders, whether from the executive or legislative branch, have little control over the rank-and-file legislator. United party effort continues to be an occasional thing. As Finance Committee Chair Robert Dole (R-Kansas) observed in the early days of the 97th Congress, "The last time I counted, there were a hundred prima donnas in the Senate."

The Democratic Caucus.   In recent years the House Democratic caucus (all Democrats serving in the House) has become increasingly important both as a forum for policy discussions and, especially, as a body capable of making decisions altering the basic balance of power in the House. Although the airing of policy alternatives has been useful, the real effect of the caucus has been its rewriting of party rules in selecting committee (and appropriations subcommittee) chairmen. The caucus can now decide, by secret ballot, whether a chairperson should be retained or not. In addition, the caucus has established a strong Steering and Policy Committee, which sets party strategy on upcoming legislation in concert with the leadership. Because the Democrats controlled both House and Senate from 1955 through 1980, their party decisions have had a great effect on the way the Congress as a whole has operated.

The Power of Party.   A single party's control of the presidency and the Congress can reduce some of the effects of congressional fragmentation. A president's power to bestow numerous favors and to command public attention can induce members of Congress to minimize their institutional squabbling.

Consider the passage of President Johnson's Model Cities program and the subsequent competition for federal funds. As John Harrigan observes,

> In order to get the bill through Congress, administrative supporters tacitly promised over 100 congressmen and senators that their cities would be chosen for model cities sites. In order to get Senator Muskie to be floor manager of the bill in the Senate, he was informally promised that three cities from his home state of Maine would qualify for the program. . . . Smithfield, Tennessee, was an appropriate winning city, since it was the home town of the chairman of the House Appropriations Subcommittee that dealt with HUD's [Housing and Urban Development] budget. Another appropriate winner was Pikesville, Kentucky, which was the home town of another key subcommittee chairman. Montana, the home state of Senate Majority Leader Mike Mansfield, had two cities among the winners. And Maine, floor leader Muskie's home state, got the three winners Muskie had been promised.[12]

[12] John J. Harrigan, *Political Change in the Metropolis* (Boston: Little, Brown, 1976), p. 306.

Although Jimmy Carter bestowed his share of favors to individual congressmen, he did not succeed in articulating and enacting a party-oriented legislative agenda. His most important proposals often met defeat or legislative indifference. Carter did not use the Democratic congressional majorities effectively; in fact, he frequently made little effort to lobby on behalf of his legislation. As Senator Robert Byrd, the majority leader in the Carter years, observed: "At the [congressional-executive] leadership meetings, he urges certain actions. . . . But he can't force it."[13] In short, to return to an old refrain, the president proposes, but the Congress disposes.

Even with a Democratic president in the White House and large Democratic majorities in the House and Senate, Congress did not grant the chief executive a free rein. In the wake of Vietnam and Watergate, Congress has reemphasized the notion of separation of powers — perhaps to an extreme. As congressional veteran Robert Giaimo noted, "In the post-Watergate years, I doubt that the Congress would have listened to any President."[14] The Congress that President Reagan faces, although divided on party lines (a Democratic House and a Republican Senate), has been more ready to respond to presidential leadership, as the era of executive-legislative confrontation draws to a close. President Reagan effectively courted the Congress in winning sweeping budget reallocations and tax cuts in 1981. While holding his Republican troops almost unanimously on all key tax and budget votes, Reagan attracted the support of enough conservative House Democrats (often by making individual deals) to overcome the real possibility of partisan stalemate.

Informal Rules of the Congressional Game Any large and complex organization has unwritten "rules of the game," or norms, as well as formal procedures for doing business. The Congress is no exception. Congressional norms are neither unchanging nor inviolate, but they do provide some basic guidelines for much of the interaction between members. At present the most important rules of the congressional game are:[15]

1. Be sure you have something to say before saying it, but do not let junior status inhibit you from contributing to the legislative process (*expertise* and *restraint*).
2. Specialize in a few substantive areas and work hard in those areas (*specialization* and *hard work*).
3. Respect your fellow members — both as individuals and as experts in specific areas. Deal with them openly and courteously in ways that will lead to the maximum achievement of their goals and your own. Do not let party or ideological stances get in the way of making mutually agreeable and profitable bargains (*courtesy, reciprocity, muted partisanship, compromise*).
4. Keep your word (*trust*).

[13]*Congressional Quarterly Weekly Report*, September 13, 1980, p. 2700.
[14]*Newsweek*, January 26, 1981, p. 41.
[15] Adapted from Randall B. Ripley, *Congress: Process and Policy*, 2nd ed. (New York: Norton, 1978).

These rules can change over time. In the 1950s, one important rule was "apprenticeship." New members of Congress were to watch and listen, not speak — observing the gospel according to Speaker Sam Rayburn, "If you want to get along, go along." Beginning with such "mavericks" (nonconformists) as Senator William Proxmire (D-Wisconsin) in the late 1950s, many new senators immediately became active in all phases of Senate business. Today, there is simply no expectation that a senator will serve any apprenticeship period. First-term House members likewise participate fully in all House business.

The seniority norm has also changed, although it has not been eliminated. Seniority (years of consecutive service) was, in both chambers, an ironclad determinant of advancement within all committees. Other minor benefits, like more spacious offices and better parking places, came with seniority in the Congress, but naming chairmen based on years of consecutive committee service was the heart of seniority. With the adoption of Democratic caucus reforms on the selection of House committee chairmen, and with their proliferation of subcommittee chairmanships, which give many members their bit of power, seniority has become much less important in determining who has power on Capitol Hill.

One folkway that is threatened, if not completely defunct, is "institutional loyalty." In the past, members shied away from criticizing the Congress, believing that such attacks would injure their standing within the House or Senate. But today, an unpopular Congress has become an inviting target for incumbents, as well as challengers. As Fenno discovered, members almost universally run *for* the Congress by campaigning *against* it — as a wasteful, slow, and sometimes corrupt institution.[16] Such campaign tactics have helped weaken any remaining sense of institutional loyalty. Congress may be all the less effective as a result, in that its own members often prompt increases in citizen skepticism.[17]

A New Order:
Congress
Today

In the old days when a committee chairman would meet
some junior members in a House corridor, they would bow
deferentially as he passed. Nowadays the same thing
happens — only it's the chairman who bows.
Congressional anecdote, c. 1975

The halls of the Congress have yet to fill with bowing committee chairmen, but such individuals are a more deferential and responsive lot than were chair-

---

[16] Richard F. Fenno, Jr., *Home Style* (Boston: Little, Brown, 1978).

[17] See for instance, Morris Fiorina, *Congress: Keystone of the Washington Establishment* (New Haven: Yale University Press, 1977). Glenn Parker and Roger Davidson suggest that the public gets service-oriented members who respond to its desires on constituency matters, while simultaneously denigrating the Congress as a whole as inefficient and ineffective. See Parker and Davidson, "Why Do Americans Love Their Congressmen So Much More than Their Congress," *Legislative Studies Quarterly*, February 1979, pp. 53–62.

men of the past. Indeed, many profound changes have occurred since the mid-1960s, making the contemporary Congress a different institution than it was as recently as ten or fifteen years ago. Some changes have taken place dramatically, such as the Democratic caucus' revolt against the seniority system in 1975. Other changes have been more subtle and slower in coming, such as the increasing volume of congressional work — a trend that makes the job of being a representative or senator more demanding and time-consuming than ever before. We will briefly describe five major recent changes in the way Congress goes about its business.

Democratization. More individual House and Senate members have a "piece of the action" today than at any time in the past century. Such a change is especially important in the House, where a majority of representatives are currently either committee or subcommittee chairmen (or ranking members, for Republicans) or members of an "elite" committee (Appropriations, Ways and Means, Rules, Budget). This means that in the congressional game, where bargaining is crucial, almost every player holds at least a small stack of chips. In addition, the entire Democratic membership of the House and the Senate each elects its committee chairmen by secret ballot, and House Democrats elect Appropriations Subcommittee chairmen and Ways and Means members. These individuals must be generally responsive to their fellow members or risk losing their positions — the fate of four chairmen in 1975. (Three were actually voted out; a fourth resigned rather than face sure defeat in a vote.)

Openness. The Congress of the 1950s was a private, even a secretive, place. Committees closed their doors when making important decisions; many floor votes went unrecorded; the proceedings of House-Senate conference committees were a mystery even to younger members of Congress, because their senior colleagues were always the conferees. Things are very different today. Virtually all committee and subcommittee sessions not involving national security matters are open to the public, as are most conference-committee meetings. Legislation is written (*marked up*, in congressional language) in public. Democratic caucuses are often open to the public and frequently provide some of the liveliest and most dramatic action on the Hill, as when Representative James Jones (D-Oklahoma) won his 1980 runoff for Budget Committee chairman over David Obey (D-Wisconsin) after the two members had tied on an initial ballot. Regardless of the democratic virtues of such open elections, the very fact that they are so well publicized may increase intraparty divisions in the wake of emotional and hard-fought contests.

More visibility arrived with the 1979 commencement of live television coverage of House floor proceedings. (The Senate may soon follow, if Majority Leader Howard Baker has his way.) Relatively little obvious showboating has occurred in response to the televising of debates, but many members have taken to giving short (one-minute) speeches, to be videotaped and distributed to district television outlets. In addition, the members' increased visibility places one more obstacle before the party leaders, who occasionally request their colleagues to act in ways that might not play so well at home. Gone are the days of completely anonymous House members, who could assume that their constituents would know little, if anything of their Capitol Hill activity.

Related to the reforms that led to procedural openness are the campaign-finance disclosure provisions of the 1974 Campaign Reform Act. Congressional candidates must report all major campaign contributions and expenditures, thus giving citizens, journalists, and potential opponents much information about the members' political bases of support. Increasingly, such finance data concerning the amounts contributed by political-action committees have become issues in congressional campaigns.

Workload. The work we expect our representatives and senators to perform has grown tremendously in recent years. This does not mean that Congress is passing more legislation; it is not (see Table 5.1). But its responsibilities have grown dramatically. When Congress expanded many federal social programs during the 1960s (in education, welfare, and transportation, for example), it also ensured that more and more of its members' time would be taken up in *legislative oversight* (overseeing the federal bureaucracy's administration of these programs) and *casework* (helping constituents in their efforts to benefit from these programs). We shall say more about these two legislative functions later.

Staffing and Other Resources. To contend with a heavier legislative workload, more oversight responsibilities, and larger caseloads, the Congress has generously increased its staff and technical assistance. Staff size has grown about fourfold from the mid-1950s — to over 20,000 in the 97th Congress. Today's congressional staffers are better educated and more professional than their predecessors. Such changes go hand in hand with a rising quality (and volume) of research performed by the Congressional Research Service (an arm of the Library of Congress), the Congressional Budget Office, and the Office

Table 5.1 Congressional Work:
A Winnowing Process (1959–80)

Number of Measures Introduced	Number of Laws Enacted
86th Congress (1959–60) 20,164	800
88th Congress (1963–64) 19,236	666
90th Congress (1967–68) 29,083	640
92nd Congress (1971–72) 25,354	707
94th Congress (1974–75) 26,219	588
96th Congress (1979–80) 14,594	613

of Technology Assessment. Although some observers worry that the glut of information available to the Congress will increase its indecisiveness, one congressional veteran sees the younger members as able to take advantage of the situation. Such members are "better educated. They're inclined to seek good advice and have the ability to use it, skills that many older members haven't had." Still, he continues, the question remains, "do we threaten to overwhelm ourselves with our own bureaucracy?"[18]

Some critics argue that another consequence of legislators' dependence on staff is that all too often it is not our elected representatives but their staffs who actually formulate legislation and achieve the consensus needed for its passage. In 1978, for example, Senators Edward M. Kennedy and Herman Talmadge, each of whom chaired a subcommittee concerned with a bill to control hospital costs, favored different approaches to the problem. At one point Kennedy told his staff: "Work something out with Jay." Talmadge's main interest was agriculture rather than health, and he left the details of a compromise health bill to Jay Constantine, his staff expert in that policy area. As one Senate aide put it, "The staff tends to frame the options, and if you frame the options you can often frame the outcome."[19]

Because a senator sits on more committees and must contend with more issues than does a representative, Senate staffers probably have more influence than their counterparts in the House. But representatives also rely heavily on their staff assistants. As Representative Michael L. Synar (D-Oklahoma) observed to a reporter, "We're supposed to be experts on everything, and making intelligent decisions is a very difficult task. . . . I've learned that staffers are everything. We are stretched so thin that a lot of the bargaining goes along at the staff level."[20]

Along with the growing importance of staff has come a virtual explosion in the use of sophisticated information-processing technology. In 1970 computers were nonexistent on Capitol Hill; by the 1980s they were integral parts of almost every House and Senate office — providing links to central data banks that allowed both members and staff to become reasonably well informed on a wide range of policies and proposals. Ironically, although this can be a great asset to the individual member, such a capacity may actually reduce the legislature's ability to reach thoughtful decisions. Widespread information dissemination reduces the power of actual congressional experts, who specialize in given subjects and who traditionally have been deferred to by other members. Again, the democratizing tendencies of the Congress may work against efficiency and coherent policymaking.

Aside from assisting in legislative research, computers also provide members an opportunity to communicate personally (or apparently so) with a great number of constituents. When coupled with the congressional franking privi-

---

[18] Former representative Charles Mosher, quoted in *Science*, January 19, 1979, p. 245.
[19] The Kennedy-Talmadge example was reported by Steven V. Roberts in "The Making of A Congressional Bill: Aides," *The New York Times*, May 26, 1979.
[20] Quoted in *The New York Times*, May 26, 1979.

lege (free mail for official business), computer-based files of letters are powerful weapons in the hands of incumbents and their press secretaries. Some representatives and senators, however, abuse this tool, prompting Representative Pat Schroeder's complaint that:

> It is an incumbent's dream. It has enabled all Congressmen to write their constituents and tell them exactly what they want to hear. The frank and the technology together have turned most congressional offices into full-time public-relations firms rather than offices that spend at least part of each day thinking seriously about issues.[21]

In any event, the technological and staff-related changes have dramatically affected both the Congress and the individual member. Each House office, with up to twenty-two staffers (earning a total of $300,000 per year), has the potential to perform research, serve constituents, and advertise its member — and to do these jobs independently of either committee or party channels; Senate offices have even more resources. It is no surprise that Speaker O'Neill somewhat regretfully observed:

> The congressman of today is a different breed. There are no political organizations, no leaders out there any more. You've got these young, talented, able people — with great media presence — who are pretty much on their own. They have their newsletters, TV broadcasts and newspaper columns. They give better public service than ever before. People in their districts say, "What a beautiful congressman I have. I don't agree with him on philosophy, but he works so hard for the economy of the area, and he is so erudite and so learned."[22]

Such is the image developed by clever members and professional staff, using the technology afforded all members of Congress.

The Budget. Congressional power ultimately lies in the so-called power of the purse. Only Congress can appropriate money — a power it derives from the constitutional provision (in Article I, Section 9) that "No Money shall be drawn from the Treasury, but in Consequence of Appropriations made by Law." After Lyndon Johnson, with congressional approval, diverted much spending from his Great Society domestic programs to the Vietnam War effort, and after Richard Nixon illegally impounded (refused to spend) billions of dollars on congressional measures he disapproved of, Congress in the early 1970s reasserted its power of the purse. Its chief instrument in doing so has been the Congressional Budget and Impoundment Control Act of 1974. This law places severe limitations on the presidential impoundment of funds. Even more important, it has given Congress a real measure of control over expenditures, revenues, and budget priorities.

[21] Quoted in David Burnham, "Congress's Computer Subsidy," *New York Times Magazine,* November 2, 1980, p. 98.

[22] Interview, *U.S. News and World Report,* August 11, 1980, p. 24.

To achieve this control, the Congress established House and Senate budget committees and, in the 1974 act, created the Congressional Budget Office (CBO), a professional research and information agency. The CBO provides Congress with information it needs to evaluate presidential legislative proposals — and to originate its own bills — in every policy area (health, housing, transportation, defense, etc.). It also provides Congress with facts, figures, and advice on such broader problems as inflation and unemployment.

The first fiscal year under the new act began on October 1, 1977, and since then Congress has generally held to the target figures for spending and revenue raising set by the Budget committees. For the first time the Congress has stated, through the budget process, that it is willing to set firm policy priorities and budget ceilings — and stick to them. This gives the Congress a much greater ability to set its own agenda rather than relying solely on the president's budget proposals, and to bring "runaway spending" under control.

Although the budget process has worked passably well, there remain great tensions between the perceived needs for, on the one hand, expanding or maintaining certain specific programs and, on the other, keeping total budget outlays as low as possible. As John McEvoy, a top Senate Budget Committee aide, concluded:

> In the end, I am convinced from five and one-half years in the vineyard of the budget process that Congress will do what the people want them to do. Controlling the budget is not a process question. It is really an ethical question. It's a question of whether we are prepared . . . to succeed politically with reductions in the federal budget. . . . Virtually every one of the 600 billion dollars in the federal budget reaches the hand of somebody in the United States. And when the federal government begins to pull back on that dollar, somebody is out there at the other end holding on.[23]

The Congress has given itself the resources and the formal process to deal with complex budgetary issues, but it must still make the tough political choices. At President Reagan's behest, the Congress aggressively employed the budget process to hold down spending in the 1982 budget. Over the course of a few months, Republicans and conservative Democrats consistently used budget mechanisms to redirect many spending priorities. Such swift, wholesale action raised questions of whether the budget process was being abused, in that important spending decisions were made outside the normal appropriations process. The ultimate role of the new budget process remains unclear, but the 1982 results illustrate that the Congress has produced a device that can, given a tough-minded majority, work to hold down overall spending levels and to rearrange policy priorities.

In sum, Congress has created a mechanism to cope with the expanding federal budget; it has also become more democratic, more open to the public,

---

[23] Quoted in *The Congressional Budget Process: Some Views from Inside* (St. Louis: Center for the Study of American Business), p. 18.

more professional, and better staffed. Things have definitely changed, but how much? The House and Senate remain large and unwieldy policymaking bodies, which the public continues to label unresponsive and ineffective. The Congress must still fulfill its constitutional responsibilities — legislation and representation. But these responsibilities become ever greater as American society becomes more complex: All the reforms imaginable cannot ease the burdens of legislating solutions to complicated problems and representing hard-to-please constituents, and these tasks remain the heart and soul of the congressional job.

ENACTING LEGISLATION

Although the Congress performs many tasks, citizens are probably most concerned with its job of enacting legislation. Indeed, people often look to Congress, along with the president, for clear-cut solutions to pressing national problems. The legislative process can work smoothly and swiftly, but on major legislation it rarely does so. The passage of most bills is a tortuous and lengthy process. Congressional responsibility is fragmented among many committees and individuals, and its independently elected members often have very different legislative goals. So it is hard to push Congress into any action, much less swift action.

Legislation usually passes through six distinct stages in each house of Congress. Opponents of the legislation can attack, modify, and delay it at each stage along what has been aptly called the "obstacle course on Capitol Hill."[24] Only when the supporters of a major bill can muster majorities at each of several key points and skillfully "manage" the bill to hold these majorities together, can the bill become law (see Figure 5.1).

The Agenda Stage

At any given moment, thousands of problems are important to different groups of citizens. Members of Congress learn of these problems through their contacts with constituents, lobbyists, staff members, officials in administrative departments and agencies, reporters, the news media, or other members of Congress. Often at the specific request of a constituent, a senator or representative will introduce a bill intended to solve one of these problems. Other legislative proposals come from private interest groups and, of course, from the executive branch of government. The bill is drafted, placed in a hopper for new bills, referred to a committee — usually, that is all. Most bills never even receive a hearing in committee; fewer than one in ten are ever reported out of committee for a decision by the full House.

The literal authoring of legislation is ordinarily of little importance. The Office of Legislative Counsel will make sure that the bill is in proper form. More interesting are the roles of staff, interest groups, and, often, the executive branch, all of whom may have a stake in the form a bill takes. T. R. Reid depicts a single instance of drafting, which began when Senator Pete Domenici

[24] Robert Bendiner, *Obstacle Course on Capitol Hill* (New York: McGraw-Hill, 1966).

Figure 5.1 The Path from Bill to Law

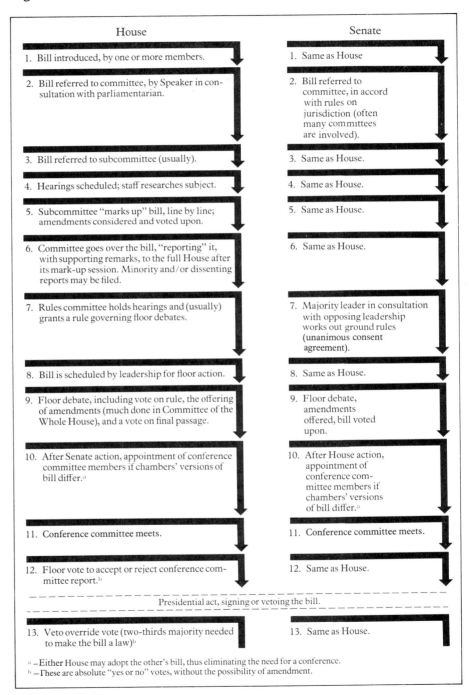

House	Senate
1. Bill introduced, by one or more members.	1. Same as House
2. Bill referred to committee, by Speaker in consultation with parliamentarian.	2. Bill referred to committee, in accord with rules on jurisdiction (often many committees are involved).
3. Bill referred to subcommittee (usually).	3. Same as House.
4. Hearings scheduled; staff researches subject.	4. Same as House.
5. Subcommittee "marks up" bill, line by line; amendments considered and voted upon.	5. Same as House.
6. Committee goes over the bill, "reporting" it, with supporting remarks, to the full House after its mark-up session. Minority and/or dissenting reports may be filed.	6. Same as House.
7. Rules committee holds hearings and (usually) grants a rule governing floor debates.	7. Majority leader in consultation with opposing leadership works out ground rules (unanimous consent agreement).
8. Bill is scheduled by leadership for floor action.	8. Same as House.
9. Floor debate, including vote on rule, the offering of amendments (much done in Committee of the Whole House), and a vote on final passage.	9. Floor debate, amendments offered, bill voted upon.
10. After Senate action, appointment of conference committee members if chambers' versions of bill differ.[a]	10. After House action, appointment of conference committee members if chambers' versions of bill differ.[a]
11. Conference committee meets.	11. Conference committee meets.
12. Floor vote to accept or reject conference committee report.[b]	12. Same as House.

Presidential act, signing or vetoing the bill.

House	Senate
13. Veto override vote (two-thirds majority needed to make the bill a law)[b]	13. Same as House.

[a] —Either House may adopt the other's bill, thus eliminating the need for a conference.
[b] —These are absolute "yes or no" votes, without the possibility of amendment.

(R-New Mexico) decided to introduce a proposal to charge fees for using federal waterways.

> . . . it was the staff's job to write a bill for him to introduce. This task was relatively easy; like most experienced Congressional aides, Rawls and Brayman could dash off legislative language with the skill of a French chef whipping up a silky meringue. Moreover, once word got around that they were working up a bill, the Domenici team had numerous offers of help. Railroad-industry lobbyists were more than happy to contribute to a bill that would increase costs for a competing mode of transit, and various "public interest groups," including the major environmental lobbies, sent their experts around to lend a hand.[25]

However well written, a bill will become part of the actual congressional agenda only under certain favorable circumstances. These include:

1. Recognition of the problem by the public or by a vocal special interest.
2. A decision by the president to make the bill part of his legislative program.
3. A decision by the majority congressional party to push the legislation.
4. A special interest in the bill on the part of an important member of the committee that considers it.

Without the support of the committee and subcommittee chairmen to whom it is referred, a bill has little chance of success. If one of these individuals opposes the bill, even if it is a part of the presidential or party program, he or she may delay action and sometimes kill the bill altogether. The chances for the success of such negative tactics depend directly on a committee's support for its chairman. Before the 1970s, a committee or subcommittee chairman could bottle up a bill he or she opposed even if a majority of committee members favored it. But since the Democratic caucus reforms of the early 1970s, one of which empowers caucus members to oust committee and subcommittee chairmen by a majority vote, few Democratic chairmen have opposed the wishes of a majority of their committee members.

After a bill becomes part of the committee or subcommittee agenda, the chairman schedules hearings on it. Often several competing bills will be offered as solutions to a single problem. Offering testimony at the hearings are representatives of various interested parties — government officials, academic experts, and lobbyists (representatives of interest groups that support or oppose the bill). Bills that have little or no chance of passage can still serve important purposes. Hearings on them bring issues to the attention of other members of Congress and the public. Even a bill that never reaches the hearing stage can be useful to a member of Congress. He or she can say "I tried" to constituents who proposed or supported it, and thereby build goodwill that might produce votes or campaign contributions in the future.

[25] T. R. Reid, *Congressional Odyssey* (San Francisco: Freeman, 1980), p. 14.

The Committee Stage Congressional committees have a unique, important role in the legislative process. They sift the information from hearings and develop the principal elements of the legislation. Decisions made at this stage are difficult to alter later in the process, because the House and Senate tend to ratify most work done by their subunits.

The committee (or subcommittee) determines the specific language of a bill at a markup session, in which the committee members go over the bill line by line. Using opinions and data from the hearings, along with other information gathered by its staff, the committee may ratify the proposal, change it slightly, or virtually rewrite the entire bill. Sometimes only full committees mark up a bill, but usually they follow their subcommittees through the process, thus providing two successive internal committee reviews of pending legislation.

When the bill is in final form, it is *reported* to the full House. That is, the committee sends the bill to the House along with its report on the measure. This report explains the bill's provisions and indicates whether the committee favors passage. It may also include dissenting statements by a minority group on the committee. The bill is then ready to be brought before the full House or Senate for discussion and a vote.

The Scheduling Stage In the Senate, on most occasions the majority leader decides when to bring up a bill for consideration. He ordinarily consults first with the minority leader and the senators most interested in the legislation. In the resulting arrangement, called a *unanimous consent agreement,* key senators agree to abide by a set of ground rules in considering the legislation. A single senator, on the chamber floor, can object to the entire package, so these agreements are generally fair in allocating debate time and scheduling votes on the proposed legislation. On some occasions the majority leader may manipulate the timing of the legislative process. For example, he might postpone a vote on a bill if a favorable majority could not be gathered or, under opposite circumstances, might rush to a vote.

Bringing a bill to the House floor is more complicated. With some exceptions, such as appropriations measures, it must be granted a special *rule,* or set of ground rules, from the House Rules Committee. The rule specifies the length of debate, the division of debate time between supporters and opponents, and the number and type of amendments to be permitted.

The House Rules Committee is conventionally likened to a "traffic cop" that directs the flow of pending legislation. But it is far more than a scheduling device; it also shapes the substance of legislation.[26] Before granting a rule, the committee holds hearings at which congressional supporters and opponents of the bill testify. Those who support the bill in its current form seek a rule

---

[26] See James A. Robinson, *The House Rules Committee* (Indianapolis: Bobbs-Merrill, 1963); and Bruce I. Oppenheimer, "The Rules Committee: New Arm of Leadership in Decentralized House," in Lawrence C. Dodd and Oppenheimer, eds., *Congress Reconsidered* (New York: Praeger, 1977), pp. 96–116.

strictly limiting amendments that would weaken it. The Rules Committee members look into the substantive aspects of the bill, and they may require certain amendments before granting a rule. The committee also may protect House members by bottling up a bill on which most representatives do not wish to take a position. For example, the Rules Committee might refuse to grant a rule on a measure dealing with school busing or congressional pay increases. Because this refusal kills the bill, members are spared the need to take a position on a roll-call vote.

In the past the Rules Committee was dominated by southern conservatives who opposed much social and civil rights legislation. They prevented many bills from reaching the floor simply by refusing to grant a rule at all. In 1975 the Democratic majority gave the Speaker the power to appoint Rules Committee members, thus increasing the responsiveness of the committee to the House leadership. As a result, the Rules Committee is far from the obstructionist force it was twenty years ago. In fact, one close observer notes that "It is a committee whose majority party membership works in such close harmony with the party leadership as to be considered almost part of the leadership itself."[27]

The Decision Stage If a bill has mustered enough support to get through the committee and scheduling stages, it comes up for a vote by the full House or Senate. Many bills are backed by enough members of the majority party for passage to be almost automatic. But voting alignments do not follow strict party lines. Particularly on social-welfare measures, a group of Republicans and southern Democrats known as the *conservative coalition* sometimes defeats liberal proposals. Northern and southern Democrats differ on 20 to 40 percent of all legislation, making the conservative coalition an important voting bloc. The coalition was especially effective in the 1950s, usually revolving around the leadership of conservative southern Democrats such as Virginia's Howard ("Judge") Smith, long-time chairman of the House Rules Committee. Over the past two decades the conservative coalition has remained a force to be reckoned with in congressional decision making (see Table 5.2), coming together on about one-quarter of all votes and winning about six times in every ten appearances.

At present, conservative southern Democrats in the House have gone a step further, organizing themselves into a group called the Conservative Forum. They seek to gain a stronger say in Democratic party affairs as well as to maintain their option of joining the Republicans in voting alignments.[28] To date, these members have been more successful in helping reforge old conservative coalition ties than in influencing their fellow Democrats.

There are voting alignments with bases other than party, and these align-

---

[27] Bruce I. Oppenheimer, "The Changing Relationships between House Leadership and the Committee on Rules" (Paper presented at Dirksen Center Conference on Understanding Congressional Leadership, Washington, D.C., June 10–11, 1980).

[28] Richard E. Cohen, "They're Still a Majority, but Are the Democrats Really in Control?" *National Journal*, January 31, 1981, p. 189.

Table 5.2 Conservative Coalition Appearances and
Victories, 1961–1980.

Congress	Appearance (Percentage of Roll-Call Votes Both Houses)	Victories (Percentage of appearances Both Houses)
87th (1961–62)	21	59
88th	16	51
89th (1965–66)	25	38
90th	22	68
91st	24	67
92nd (1971–72)	28	76
93rd	24	60
94th (1975–76)	26	54
95th	23	60
96th (1979–80)	19	71

Source: *Congressional Quarterly Weekly Report*, January 10, 1981, p. 85. Coalition appearances occur when a majority of southern Democrats vote in agreement with a majority of Republicans. By permission.

ments can be important too. Especially in the areas of foreign policy and defense, the president influences the votes of many members of his own party — and a significant number in the opposing party. Furthermore, some influential members, particularly certain committee chairmen, often can sway many votes on the strength of their expertise in a policy area, their legislative craftsmanship, and their ability to strike harmonious compromises among diverse factions. In the past, various Budget Committee chairs (currently Representative James Jones, D-Oklahoma, and Senator Pete Domenici, R-New Mexico) have frequently won unpopular fights to hold the line on spending.

House Floor Action. In the House, *floor action* — the debating and amending process — usually takes place in the *Committee of the Whole House* rather than in *regular session*. The membership of this committee is identical to that of the House of Representatives. Its advantage is that its procedures are more flexible, and the *quorum* (the number of members that must be present for a vote to be taken) is only 100, rather than a majority (218). Activity in the Committee of the Whole, as it is normally called, is governed by the party leaders and the floor manager of the bill, a member of the committee reporting the bill who is assigned to coordinate debate.

Assisting each party's leader is a Whip and a number of deputy and regional Whips. Their main duty, as their title suggests, is to round up party members for a vote when the party leadership needs them. Most members of Congress spend little time on the floor; they may be in their offices meeting with constituents, conferring with staff, attending committee hearings, or catching up on their mail. The press of business draws members of Congress away from the floor because there is little to keep them there. Most floor debate is routine, and a member's presence makes little difference. When the bells sound indicating a roll call, the member may not respond. If his or her vote is urgently needed, the Whip follows up with a call "from the Speaker."

The Whips also provide a great deal of information to their party leaders because they are well informed about the positions and intentions of the membership on important upcoming votes. This information is extremely important, especially when the leadership doubts its ability to command enough votes to pass a given bill and needs an accurate "head count" of members against a bill.

Senate Floor Action. In the Senate, floor action follows much the same pattern as in the House. The focus of activity in the Senate is the majority leader, whose personal style governs the course of activity. When Lyndon Johnson was majority leader, he bargained vigorously, anticipated his opposition, cajoled reluctant party members, "twisted arms," and kept careful count of available votes. Johnson's most important resource was his wealth of information about each senator, his state, and his problems — information that could often be translated into votes. The most recent Democratic majority leader, Robert Byrd of West Virginia, operated in somewhat the same fashion, using his central position to build support for legislation that could be passed. But Byrd was rarely willing to try to twist other senators' arms, given the independence of contemporary senators. Observed Byrd, "I talk to senators, have meetings with senators, I try to stimulate a party position. . . . I don't think there has ever been an era in the Senate in which there has been a party 'boss' except for Lyndon Johnson. But Lyndon Johnson could not operate in that fashion now."[29] The current Republican majority leader, Howard Baker, faces similar difficulties in seeking to bring together moderate and conservative Senate Republicans. This is especially true for such noneconomic subjects in the Reagan agenda as abortion, busing, and school prayer.

The Filibuster. Although the length of time a member can speak in floor debate is strictly regulated in the House, the Senate permits unlimited debate. Unlimited debate in turn permits the *filibuster* — a tactic whereby a small group of senators who oppose a bill can prevent it from coming to a vote by prolonging debate. Filibustering senators seek to talk a bill to death, speaking for hours on end, often on topics not relevant to the issue at hand. As one speaker tires, he simply recognizes another opponent of the bill, who talks until *he* grows tired.

A filibuster can be stopped only by a *cloture,* or a vote of at least sixty senators to end debate. Because some senators are usually absent from the floor and others are reluctant to vote for cloture in deference to the Senate

[29]*Congressional Quarterly Weekly Report,* September 13, 1980, p. 2699.

Divided Control of Congress

Since 1955, the President's party has controlled both Houses of Congress in only twelve years — less than half the time. And no Republican President since Dwight Eisenhower, in his first term (1953–1954) has enjoyed a GOP edge in either House, until the 1980 elections produced a Republican Senate to go along with the Reagan Presidency. Most presidents, of either party, need some support from the opposing party to win adoption of their policies in the Congress. Ronald Reagan has demonstrated a considerable talent for encouraging coalitions that bring together Republicans with conservative Democrats. Thus, Democratic leaders, like Speaker Tip O'Neill and Majority Leader Jim Wright (bottom right), are often not in control of the House that they nominally lead.

More generally, parties can provide some links between the separate branches of government. Presidents confer frequently with their party's leadership in Congress, and Senate Majority Leader Howard Baker (top right) therefore becomes a central figure in guiding the President's program through the Congress.

tradition of unlimited debate, the votes required to stop a filibuster are difficult to muster.

The success of a filibuster usually depends on which side is more determined. Supporters of the blocked measure may attempt to break the filibuster by scheduling round-the-clock sessions to wear out the opposition. Those attempting the filibuster must be hardy indeed. They must stand while speaking, without leaning on their desks, and may not consume solid food. Speakers may pause and rest if a quorum is not present. To prevent this, supporters of the bill must remain in or near the chamber. Some senators may take naps on cots set up in nearby hallways. Sooner or later one side will tire; either the Senate will move on to new business, or a cloture vote will finally succeed.

Filibusters often occur in the waning days of a congressional session, when the senators' desire to adjourn is great and a bill's delay may well mean its defeat. For example, in December 1980, near the end of the 96th Congress, opponents of a strengthened federal fair housing proposal used a filibuster to postpone and ultimately to defeat the measure. This probably meant the shelving of any such legislation for the foreseeable future, given the more conservative nature of the 97th Congress and the Reagan administration. As Senator Orrin Hatch (R-Utah), a leading opponent of the bill, concluded, this was "one of the last-gasp ultraliberal [efforts]" before the Republicans assumed control of the Senate.[30] As is often the case, to put off the legislation was to kill it, even though advocates of a strong federal antidiscrimination policy might have been able to muster majority support, had the bill come to a vote.

In the past, the filibuster was infrequently used; cloture was voted even more infrequently. More recently, however, senators have become less reluctant to employ filibusters, and cloture has been voted with increasing frequency. In fact, the greatest problems at present have arisen *after* cloture has been voted. As the *Congressional Quarterly* reported,

> An unwritten rule binds senators to abide by cloture and stop talking when the Senate votes to proceed.
>
> In 1976, however, Senator James B. Allen, D-Alabama, began to violate these rules. He used parliamentary delaying tactics [i.e., large numbers of amendments] even after cloture had been voted.
>
> In 1979 the Senate imposed a new limit on the post-cloture filibuster. . . . [A] final vote on that bill had to occur after no more than 100 hours of debate.
>
> "[Allen] taught every senator how to bring the policy-making branch of the government to a halt," said Senator Adlai E. Stevenson, D-Illinois. . . . [and] according to [Acting] Senate Minority Leader Ted Stevens, R-Alaska, the [100-hour] rule is just a psychological barrier waiting to be broken.[31]

Although the Senate remains something of a club, the ties that bind its members are not as strong as they were in an earlier era.

---

[30] *Congressional Quarterly Weekly Report*, December 13, 1980, p. 3545.
[31] *Congressional Quarterly Weekly Report*, September 13, 1980, p. 2699.

Individual Voting Decisions. Despite the importance of agenda setting and committee maneuvering, it is the votes of the 535 senators and representatives that ultimately determine the fate of a legislative proposal. When a bill deals with important or controversial measures, a member of Congress usually studies the issue, weighs its merits, considers the views of constituents, and solicits the advice of experts in his or her party. Most bills, however, do not receive such careful examination. It is impossible for any legislator to devote much time to each of the thousands of votes he or she is called on to make in each session. And on most bills, constituents express little opinion, either for or against. The result is that on many bills, even important and controversial ones, a senator or representative defers to the judgment of others (usually fellow party members) who are more familiar with the issue.

Even without carefully studying each bill, a legislator's voting decisions, taken as a whole, can accurately reflect the interests of his or her constituency. John Kingdon studied House voting decisions and found that many forces seem to influence the decisions reached.[32] These include interest groups in the legislator's district, constituency opinion, the president's position, the party leadership position, the legislator's own attitude, the position of respected fellow members of Congress, and the views of the legislator's staff. Even on the most controversial issues, there is often remarkable consistency; all forces point in the same direction nearly half of the time. When one or two elements are at odds with the rest, the member almost always votes with the larger number of factors.

On most votes, a senator or representative finds little conflict among the influential forces. Constituents, staff, friends, and expert consultants all offer similar "cues," making the task of voting much easier. On such bills, a member can represent his or her constituents adequately without having to scrutinize the bill's provisions or keep continually abreast of the ongoing floor strategy.

With a single notable exception, for example, the entire Michigan congressional delegation voted in favor of the 1980 Chrysler loan guarantee legislation.[33] Even the most conservative members saw an overwhelming need to keep Chrysler in business, regardless of philosophical niceties. Their political cue was clear.

The Conference Committee Stage For a bill to become law, it must be passed in identical form by both houses of Congress. Senators and representatives often introduce identical measures, but these bills are usually altered in committee or on the floor. The House and

[32] John Kingdon, *Congressmen's Voting Decisions,* 2nd ed. (New York: Harper and Row, 1980), chap. 10.

[33] The one maverick was conservative Republican David Stockman, who saw the Chrysler loan as another unwarranted governmental intrusion into the private sector. Stockman subsequently joined the Reagan administration as director of the Office of Management and Budget and has served as Reagan's chief budget cutter.

Senate versions of a bill must thus go through another stage — the conference committee — to resolve their differences.

A conference committee is, in the words of one Washington observer, "the essence of the Congressional process. It is where, after all the demogoguery and the political posturing take place on the floor of the House and the Senate, the laws of the land are finally written." [34] Because of their crucial role in the legislative process, conference committees are often called "the third house of Congress." [35]

Each house is represented on a conference committee, usually by senior members of the committees that worked on the bill. In theory, members of each house are supposed to defend the provisions that were adopted in their own house's version of the bill. On occasion, the House or Senate even "instructs" its conferees to resist certain compromises. However, conferees sometimes find the other chamber's version of the bill more appealing. The bill approved in conference can include any provision that was part of either chamber's version of the legislation, and a skillful legislator can exploit this opportunity. If he desires a provision that faces strong opposition in his own house, a legislator may not include it in the original version of the bill, but will instead encourage the other House to adopt the provision. The legislator can then "accept" this provision in the conference committee.

Once the conferees agree on identical language for the legislation, each house must accept or reject the entire bill; no new amendments are allowed. The controversial provision may survive this final vote simply because most members approve of the rest of the bill.

The Presidential Stage When a bill has passed both houses of Congress in identical form, it is sent to the president for his signature. The president has three choices. (1) He can sign the bill within ten days, whereupon it becomes law. (2) He can veto the bill and return it to the originating house for reconsideration. Overriding a presidential veto is quite difficult because it requires a two-thirds majority vote in both houses. (3) He can refuse to sign the bill. If Congress remains in session for ten days, the bill becomes law without the president's signature. By refusing to sign the bill, the president expresses mild disapproval of it: He does not like it, but neither is he so opposed to it that he will veto it (and risk seeing his veto overridden). If Congress adjourns before the ten days expire, the bill does not become law, but fails by a "pocket veto," which Congress has no opportunity to override. Although the pocket veto can occur only at the end of the congressional session, it is an important presidential weapon, because many bills are passed just before adjournment.

Implications of the Legislative Process The legislative process, as we have seen, resembles an obstacle course. If a bill stumbles at even one hurdle, it dies. A "money bill" (one involving expenditures) must pass through the congressional part of this process twice — once

[34] *The New York Times*, November 23, 1975.
[35] David J. Vogler, *The Third House* (Evanston, Ill.: Northwestern University Press, 1971).

to *authorize* spending money on the project and once to *appropriate* a specific amount of funds to it.

Although the legislative process is time-consuming and strewn with obstacles, it does have at least two major redeeming qualities. First, the necessary bargaining and compromise of the legislative process usually provide some tangible benefits for everybody. To succeed, a measure must be acceptable to majorities at each step in the process. A committee may write a bill in such a way as to ensure support of a majority on the floor. The president, by merely threatening to veto a measure, can often prompt compromises that make the bill more acceptable to him.[36]

Second, the interests of minorities are protected. Determined opponents of a proposal can fight and delay it in a number of forums. Ultimately, such a bill must have strong majority support or must be modified to make it less objectionable to minorities who vigorously oppose it. Indeed, Congress is especially good at reaching "consensus-type decisions," which in the words of Richard Fenno, "are likely to be regarded as fair decisions."[37]

Other Congressional Functions. Legislation is the main job of Congress. But, as we noted earlier, legislators spend much of their time and effort on other tasks. Members of Congress engage in *legislative oversight* — reviewing the federal bureaucracy's administration of previously enacted legislation. They perform *casework* for their constituents — helping them in their dealings with the federal bureaucracy. And they *legitimate* government policy by enacting it in the name of the people, whose elected representatives they are.

Legislative Oversight Congress makes policy by passing laws. It does not enforce them, however: Most of the policies Congress legislates must be implemented by the bureaucracy of the executive branch. Congress cannot write legislation specific enough to deal with all possible cases. Usually it must be content to specify the basic provisions of the law and set out its general objectives. Federal bureaucrats then must translate those general objectives into procedures and decisions that specify how congressional policy will be carried out.[38] Bureaucrats have considerable influence, then, in deciding what congressional policy "means." This freedom is often referred to as *executive discretion.*

Congress has, for example, enacted legislation calling for national safety standards in certain occupations. But this legislation is necessarily very general; even legislators who are well informed about industrial safety problems would find it impossible to draft detailed regulations and standards for the nation's hundreds of different industries to follow. Instead, they must leave it

---

[36] Jimmy Carter acted in such a manner to ensure that the Congress would consider both a fee for barge operators and improvements on an important Mississippi River lock, which the operators wanted badly. Carter threatened to veto any bill not containing both measures. See Reid, *Congressional Odyssey.*

[37] Richard F. Fenno, Jr., "Strengthening a Congressional Strength," in Dodd and Oppenheimer, *Congress Reconsidered,* p. 263.

[38] See Lawrence C. Dodd and Richard L. Schott, *Congress and the Administrative State* (New York: Wiley, 1979).

to an executive agency, the Occupational Safety and Health Administration (OSHA), to formulate specific safety standards. OSHA, like many other agencies, is charged with writing regulations that carry the force of law. On occasion, however, affected groups (such as farmers) or industries (such as auto manufacturers) may put pressure on the Congress to restrain an agency like OSHA or the Federal Trade Commision (FTC). The Congress retains the ultimate responsibility for policymaking and thus serves as the eventual target for interests that have lost their cases within the regulatory process. In recent years, for instance, funeral home operators successfully appealed FTC rulings to the Congress, much as they would have appealed an unfavorable local zoning board decision to a city council.

Congress maintains its control over the legislative function by overseeing the executive departments and agencies that implement its policies, a procedure called *legislative oversight*. If an agency is especially stubborn or the original legislation is unclear, Congress may pass correcting or "perfecting" legislation. Usually, however, it exercises oversight through other means: the appropriations process, the audit, the legislative veto, or congressional investigation.

Appropriations.   The appropriations process, by which Congress approves funds for executive agencies' activities, is probably the most frequently used and most important means of congressional oversight. Because an agency's programs depend on its budget, Congress' power of the purse can influence agency policy. Each year, before funds are appropriated for an agency and its programs, the relevant subcommittee of the House Appropriations Committee calls the agency head, other bureaucrats, and interested groups to testify. These appropriations hearings give members of Congress the opportunity to discuss past policy decisions, question present policies, and offer suggestions regarding future policy.

Audit.   Congress can also oversee executive agencies through the use of the audit, a thorough accounting procedure designed to ensure that funds have been properly spent. In 1921, Congress passed legislation transferring all aduit control to the General Accounting Office (GAO), a nonpartisan agency for financial analysis, which is directly accountable to Congress. Gradually, the GAO has broadened its work, providing information and evaluations dealing with program content as well as straight financial audits.

In addition, the Congressional Budget Office (CBO), established in 1974, compares the effectiveness of various agencies' programs and helps Congress determine budget priorities. The CBO complements the GAO by offering cost projections for future programs, thus providing guidelines for subsequent oversight efforts.

The Legislative Veto.   A powerful and increasingly used technique of legislative oversight is the *legislative veto*, which reverses the normal roles of the executive and legislative branches. Using this procedure Congress authorizes an executive agency to take certain specified actions, but retains the power to "veto" these actions by resolution of *either* house within a specified time, usually thirty to ninety days. For example, in 1977, Jimmy Carter asked Congress for legislation that would give him sweeping authority to reorganize the federal bureaucracy by creating, merging, or shifting agencies around within the existing executive departments. Congress agreed but reserved the right to block part or all of the reorganization plan within sixty days after the president proposed it.

Critics of the legislative veto make two major criticisms of this oversight technique. One is that it may be unconstitutional because it permits Congress to participate in the *execution* of the laws (a job the Constitution assigns to the president).[39] Under the guise of oversight, so this argument goes, Congress can intimidate executive personnel and hobble the president's ability to act swiftly and decisively. The legislative veto has more than once been challenged in the courts, but the question of its constitutionality has never been resolved there.

A second, more general, objection to the legislative veto lies in its capacity to delay and confuse the policymaking process. Responsibility for policies is difficult to assign if both Congress and the administrative agencies claim ultimate authority. A bill calling for congressional review of all administrative regulations was narrowly defeated in the 94th Congress; opponents argued that Congress would have to look over 10,000 regulations annually, in addition to its current workload. Table 5.3 shows the extent of use of the legislative veto for various periods between 1932 and 1980.

Table 5.3 Use of Legislative Vetoes, 1932–80

Time Period	Number of Acts Including Legislative Veto Decisions Per Year
1932–40	0.7
1941–50	1.8
1951–60	3.7
1961–70	5.8
1971–75	15.6
1976–80	10 (estimate)

Source: Lawrence C. Dodd and Richard L. Schott, *Congress and the Administrative State* (New York: Wiley, 1979), pp. 221–22. Reprinted by permission.

[39] *Inside Congress* (Washington, D.C.: Congressional Quarterly Press, 1979), p. 89 ff. In 1981 a Court of Appeals ruled unanimously that the legislative veto was unconstitutional — a result that would probably be appealed to the Supreme Court.

Investigations. The congressional investigation is still another means by which Congress may oversee executive agencies. Technically, committees hold investigations to provide Congress with information relevant to new or revised legislation. In fact, investigations have also been used to publicize particular problems, to reassure the public, and to advance personal or partisan interests. Investigations may be carried out either by a standing (permanent) congressional committee or by a special ("select") committee established for the purpose. Whichever body (Senate or House) sponsors an investigation may grant the designated committee the power to subpoena witnesses and documents.

One recent special investigation looked into Billy Carter's dealings with the Libyan government and the possible misuse of executive power. A special Senate Judiciary subcommittee, although it found no criminal actions, did roundly criticize the president's brother and many executive officials. In addition, select committees have also pursued alleged illegal activities by the CIA and FBI and have inquired into the assassinations of Martin Luther King and John F. Kennedy. Although congressional investigations such as these rarely lead directly to new laws, they can dramatize issues, bring them to the public's attention, and place the problems on some future legislative agenda.

Casework:
The Ombudsman
Function

Some Scandinavian countries have established the position of *ombudsman* — a local governmental official who hears and investigates citizens' complaints about public officials. Citizens can appeal to the ombudsman if they feel they have been teated unfairly by an executive agency. The idea is simple and natural, given citizens' low confidence in the bureaucracy and the popular belief that bureaucrats, because they are not elected officials, are not responsive to popular pressure.

There is no official ombudsman in the United States government. Rather, each member of Congress fills that role for his or her own constituents. Legislators refer to these efforts as *casework*, and they treat it as very important business. Although casework falls under a broader heading of constituency service, its essence is, in the words of one scholar, "the role of the congressional office as an intermediary between the needy or aggrieved constituent and the government's executive bureaucracy, programs, and operations."[40] Casework occupies a great deal of members' time and energy and consumes the efforts of several staff assistants in virtually every office. These are the individuals who must deal with the hundreds of problems a typical senator or representative receives each week.[41]

Casework is important to most legislators because of its alleged vote-getting potential. It enables the legislator to be a benefactor, helping people regardless

[40] John R. Johannes, "The Distribution of Casework in the U.S. Congress During the 95th Congress: An Uneven Burden" (Paper presented at 1980 Western Political Science Association meetings), p. 2.

[41] Johannes, in "The Distribution of Casework," estimates that about 100 cases that fall under his strict definition come into a House office in an average week, in addition to many other requests for information.

of party affiliation or seniority. Unlike voting for a controversial bill or serving on an unpopular committee (like Ethics), casework does not offend anyone. There is, rather, a possible payoff in votes with no risk of losing any.

Recently elected House members have been especially aggressive in soliciting casework and creating routines to handle it effectively. More and more members handle most of their casework, initially at least, in their districts. This increases their visibility as well as reassuring the constituents that their member, in the person of his or her staff aide, is accessible and on the job.

Types of Casework. Casework is not easy to handle; constituents ask for help on a wide range of problems. Many people ask where they should go for help in the government bureaucracy. Often, however, constituents ask their senator or representative to intervene for them with the bureaucracy — to assist in getting a passport processed more quickly, in having a decision on veterans' benefits reconsidered, or in straightening out a foul-up in Social Security payments. Most of this help is provided by the legislator's staff. But the inquiries to bureaucratic personnel are usually made in the name of the legislator. And although almost all the replies to constituents are drafted by the staff, the legislator usually signs them. If the constituent has already applied to an executive agency for help and is awaiting action, a call from the representative's office to the agency may speed things up. Sometimes several citizens complain about the same problem; this may spur the representative to propose corrective legislation. Of course, there is often nothing a legislator can do to help: The constituent has been treated fairly and is merely unhappy with the result. Even so, the office staff may contact the executive agency and report back to the constituent, who at least has the satisfaction of getting apparently personal attention from the legislator.

Pros and Cons of Casework. How useful is casework? This is a difficult question to answer. On the one hand, casework benefits relatively few citizens. A Gallup poll, for example, found that only 4 percent of the citizens surveyed said that their congressman had "definitely done something for them" that they knew of.[42] Furthermore, casework consumes immense amounts of governmental time and effort, not only by legislators and their staffs but by the bureaucracy as well. Executive agencies must maintain large staffs just for legislative liaison — checking on and processing inquiries from congressional offices. When a congressional staffer calls an agency about a particular case, all the other cases may have to be dealt with more slowly. Given the number of citizens it helps, casework is not a very efficient system.

On the other hand, efficiency is not everything, and casework serves at least three very useful purposes. First, it does help a certain number of people, many of whom might not get that help otherwise. Second, it affords legislators

---

[42] George H. Gallup, *The Gallup Poll: Public Opinion 1935–1971,* vol. 3 (New York: Random House, 1971), p. 2264.

one more useful means of legislative oversight — as, for instance, when several people complain about the same thing, and investigation shows that a change in bureaucratic policy or procedure may be called for. Third, it can reduce the gap between citizens and their government. Many people who hold Congress as an institution in low esteem are nevertheless confident that they can call on their own representative or senator. One study concludes, for instance, that although

> citizens' expectations for Congress are vague and anchored to generalized policy and stylistic concerns, [t]heir expectations for their own representatives are unmistakable. Legislators are judged very largely on the way they serve their districts and communicate with them. . . . Legislators who lose touch or who seem preoccupied with national issues may be disciplined with declining support or even defeat.[43]

Citizens know that they cast their ballots for a single representative or senator, not an entire institution. And members react by doing what they can to win those votes — giving constituents casework and a broad range of constituency service.

The Legitimating Function Because Congress makes the laws, and because laws are popularly regarded as the appropriate source of new national policy, Congress has an important role in giving legitimacy to controversial decisions. Th average citizen is not even aware of this congressional function; yet it is extremely important. A policy is said to be *legitimate* if most of the people believe that it is reasonable (even if they do not personally agree wth it) and that the policymakers acted within the proper scope of their authority. A policy is most likely to be accepted as legitimate if the policymakers appear to consider the matter carefully and completely, allowing all interested groups and individuals to speak their piece.

Both Lyndon Johnson and Richard Nixon fought ultimately losing battles against the congressional power to legitimate governmental actions. In justifying his conduct of the United States involvement in Vietnam, President Johnson relied heavily on the 1964 Gulf of Tonkin Resolution. The Congress, almost unanimously, had passed this resolution after receiving extremely misleading information about North Vietnamese aggression. With no formal declaration of war passed by the Congress, and with relatively little legislative debate during the first years of the conflict, President Johnson's actions in Vietnam became increasingly suspect by the American people.

Richard Nixon acted in a similarly "imperial" manner by impounding (refusing to spend) billions of dollars in congressional appropriations. Federal courts ruled that he had exceeded his legitimate authority by not carrying out the intent of the congressional spending legislation — that he had, in fact, usurped the congressional power of the purse.

[43] Parker and Davidson, "Why Do Americans . . . ," p. 60.

Congressional actions are less likely to provoke this type of reaction. Why? First, Congress is regarded as the appropriate constitutional body for determining the fate of controversial issues. Second, congressional processes involve minorities in the business of policy formation. Through public hearings, debate, and extensive coverage in the press and on TV, congressional leaders create the impression that all viewpoints have received a fair hearing.

Although many citizens and commentators complain about the slowness of the legislative process, perhaps this very slowness is the most important reason that people see congressional actions as legitimate. Congress often creates a climate of public acceptance before acting, generating publicity and educating the public, as it did in the Nixon impeachment controversy. If the legislators feel that this climate of acceptance is lacking and that they cannot develop it, they may postpone legislative action until events themselves create it. For example, in the early 1970s Congress did not develop a comprehensive energy policy, despite many proposals; the American people had come to no agreement about the need for strict energy measures. Such a lack of consensus continues as illustrated by the dual 1980 Republican platform promises to foster energy self-sufficiency and to remove the 55-mile-per-hour speed limit, which conserves fuel. If the people or their political parties cannot agree on how to deal with the energy crisis, it is no surprise that their representatives in Congress have similar difficulties.

The essence of legitimacy is people's willingness to comply with a decision simply because they respect the authority of the decision-making institution. At present, however, Congress is somewhat short on popular support, as we shall see in a moment. Just how seriously a decline in public confidence may undermine future congressional performance depends on the reactions of Congress and its leaders.

HOW CITIZENS VIEW CONGRESS Public approval of Congress has declined in recent years. Although 64 percent of the people rated Congress as "excellent" or "pretty good" during President Johnson's administration, a series of events has caused a great decline in public confidence.[44] First, Republican presidents Nixon and Ford confronted a succession of Democratically controlled Congresses. Legislation would not satisfy the president; he would veto it, and Democratic majorities were usually not strong enough to override these vetoes. This created the impression in the mind of Amerians that Congress was divided and was unable to act effectively on major problems. Second, during the months when the entire nation watched the events of the Vietnam War and Watergate unfold, public approval of Congress fell even lower, to below 40 percent. Watergate in particular apparently reinforced a general citizen mistrust of government; Congress, as well as the president, was a victim. Although the Congress reasserted itself strongly in foreign, domestic, and budgetary matters during the 1970–80 period, citi-

[44] Louis Harris poll release, August 5, 1974.

zens continued to lose confidence in Congress, even after Watergate. In fact, this can be attributed to congressional lethargy, bickering, and fragmentation; but citizens also could view a steady stream of unethical and often criminal behavior flowing from Capitol Hill. With their transgressions ranging from salary kickbacks (Representative Charles Diggs, D-Michigan) to sexual exploitation (Representative Wayne Hays, D-Ohio) to shady, if not illegal, personal financial arrangements (Senators Brooke, R-Mass., and Talmadge, D-Georgia) to accepting bribes (six representatives, including two committee chairmen, and one senator, Harrison Willimas, D-New Jersey) in the so-called ABSCAM scandal, many members of Congress acted as if the law did not apply to those who write it. The continuing lack of public confidence is understandable.

In short, these conflict of interest and sexual exploitation accusations seriously and somewhat unfairly hurt the image of Congress. Most representatives and senators work long hours, and many find it a money-losing proposition to serve in the Congress. Yet the spectacular scandal, be it financial or sexual, makes much more sensational news (and is easier to report) than the grinding process of enacting legislation or overseeing the bureaucracy.

Ideas about the Institution

What determines how citizens view the Congress?

First, people want Congress to pass legislation and to do so without delay. Yet Congress only rarely fulfills this expectation. Television commentator David Brinkley once cynically noted, "It takes Congress 30 days to make instant coffee," reflecting the public's perception of Congress as a glacially slow-moving body. As long as representatives and senators must respond to their diverse constituencies and engage in extended bargaining in order to pass legislation, citizens are likely to be disappointed in their legislators' performance.

Second, people are very much concerned with the character and behavior of individual members of Congress. Although the public response to the 1980 congressional scandals was particularly strong, public displeasure attends all such cases. Even before the ABSCAM incident, a Harris survey reported that 84 percent of the population rejected the notion that "we have a government almost wholly free of corruption and payoffs." [45] And incidents of improper or scandalous behavior occur often enough in the Congress to reinforce this view.

Third, people tend to be indignant and resentful about the salary, privileges, and fringe benefits accorded members of Congress. People are understandably upset when they hear or read about congressional "junkets" (overseas "fact-finding" trips that are often little more than paid vacations) and "slush funds" (unofficial office accounts fattened by secret political contributions). In 1977, many people were outraged when senators and representatives got a salary raise from $44,600 to $57,500 without having to vote on it. An independent commission had recommended the raise, and — as we noted earlier — the

[45] This November 13, 1978, poll was cited by James L. Sundquist in "Congress, the President, and the Crisis of Competence in Government," in Dodd and Oppenheimer, *Congress Reconsidered,* 2nd ed., p. 354.

president was empowered by law to grant it. Subsequently, members gave themselves an additional increase (to more than $60,000, but in this instance they voted on the raise and limited it to 5 percent rather than accepting the commission's figure of 8 percent. Republican legislators were especially energetic in holding the majority-party Democrats' feet to the fire on this emotional issue, although President Reagan and the majority Senate Republicans had to confront the salary problem in the 97th Congress.

In the aftermath of the public outcry against the salary increase (the first major raise since 1969) and the sex and financial scandals of the preceding two years, both houses adopted ethics codes prohibiting slush funds, restricting travel privileges, limiting outside earnings, and instituting various other reforms. Many members of Congress were unhappy with these self-imposed restrictions, but they felt that the reputation of Congress — and perhaps their own political futures — depended on them. In 1980, acting on its Ethics Committee's recommendations, the House expelled Representative Michael O. Myers (D-Pennsylvania) in the wake of his felony conviction in the ABSCAM bribery case. In addition, Representatives Raymond Lederer (D-Pennsylvania) and John Jenrette (D-South Carolina) resigned rather than face almost certain expulsion under similar circumstances. The Myers expulsion was the first such action since three admitted Confederates were ousted in 1861. Nevertheless, Congress has a long way to go before restoring public confidence in its ability to act effectively and, to an extent, honestly.

An important characteristic of citizens' evaluation of Congress is that it is often based on what is most obvious, rather than what is most important. It is much easier for people to see how slowly Congress generally moves than to evaluate the specific provisions of each bill it does pass. A legislator's salary is more comprehensible to the average citizen than departmental budgets measured in billions of dollars. Sexual shenanigans and official misconduct involve straightforward questions of values, problems that the average person can relate to.

At the same time, congressional service has become more visible. Rank-and-file members do an increasingly good job of "advertising" themselves, with the help of the tremendous resources available to them (cut-rate recording facilities, newsletters, mobile office vans in their districts, to name but three). In addition, many congressional leaders gain additional visibility by virtue of their positions. This is not necessarily an unmixed blessing. Representative Al Ullman (D-Oregon), chair of the Ways and Means Committee, and Whip John Brademas (D-Indiana) lost their 1980 reelection bids. Much of their trouble may have stemmed from their reputations as national leaders, on whom constituents could vent their anger.

The ultimate test of how constituents feel about a representative comes when he or she is up for reelection. If each member were held responsible for the performance of Congress, one would expect more incumbents than usual to be defeated at times when the institution is rated poorly. But this has not been the pattern. People may reason that their own representative differs from

Table 5.4 House and Senate Turnover, 1952–80

	Number of Retirees	Number of Members Defeated (Primary and General Elections)	Percentage of Members Seeking Reelection Successfully
House			
1952–60	29	25	94
1962–70	26	26	94
1972–80	43	30	92
Senate			
1952–60	5	7	74
1962–70	4	5	81
1972–80	7	9	68

Source: Table figures (numbers are averages) based on data in John Bibby, Thomas E. Mann, and Norman J. Ornstein, *Vital Statistics on Congress: 1980* (Washington, D.C.: American Enterprise Institute, 1980), and *Congressional Quarterly Weekly Reports*, November 11, 1980.

the rest, that the challenger would be no better, or that it is unfair to hold one person responsible for the actions of such a large body. Whatever the explanation, incumbents have generally enjoyed great success in remaining in office.

Although House members ordinarily win reelection with little difficulty, Senate incumbents encountered rough going in the 1970s. Their greater visibility, more diverse constituencies, and longer terms have attracted stronger challenges than is common for House members (see Table 5.4). Senators seeking reelection were especially vulnerable in the 1976, 1978, and 1980 elections, when over 40 percent lost their bids to return to Capitol Hill. Many of the defeats were suffered by liberal Democrats, and the resulting Republican victories dramatically changed the congressional balance of power.

Low public confidence in Congress has contributed to some turnover, perhaps not so much directly as indirectly. The public mood has signaled an opportunity to many challengers who mounted vigorous campaigns, although relatively few House incumbents have lost their seats. Of greater significance is the marked surge in congressional retirements (see Table 5.4). Many representatives and senators have found that the increased workload, the heightened visibility, the various financial sacrifices, and the overall legislative fragmentation have come to outweigh the positive aspects of the congressional job. Some members have found the costs too great in terms of time and misplaced priorities. Representative Gary Myers (R-Pennsylvania), who retired while still in his thirties, observed,

What it takes to get the job done is 80 hours a week. That's not compatible with how much time I'd like to spend with my family. I just wanted to get to know my kids before it was too late.[46]

For others, the job becomes tiresome and even boring. Otis Pike explained that

Being expected to put in a full day's work at the office and a full night's appearance on the banquet circuit can get to be and has become a bore. . . . People bug me more than they used to. They are asking their government to do more for them and are willing to do less and less for themselves. . . . So much of the work is nit-picking trivia.

For still others, the economic and policy rewards do not measure up. As one retiree put it, "I want to practice law while I'm still young enough to pursue another career. I'm going to triple my income." Another, Representative Lee Alexander, saw the Congress itself as much of the problem.

Congress is a disappointment. I don't see movement or progress. . . . The legislative process here is cumbersome; the system isn't designed to take on major reforms. I ran because I was unhappy with the political scene. I'm still unhappy.
You want to have pride in what you're doing, but it is hard — very hard — when you see Congress continually cast in a bad light. Lately it's assumed that we're both undisciplined and immoral. That isn't true, but increasingly that's the perception.

The large number of House retirements and the increasing vulnerability of incumbent senators has produced a Congress that is younger, more energetic, but less experienced than its predecessors. The results of such personal changes have yet to be sorted out, but the Congress is a much less predictable place than it was a generation ago. As Speaker Tip O'Neill observed to a House visitor:

Look out there [the House floor]. So many members have never served in public office before, they never came up through the ranks. They have no sense of party discipline; they run more as individuals.[47]

THE PROBLEM OF REPRESENTATION For the legislative process to work effectively, the attitudes, values, and decisions of a representative must correspond in some fashion to the values, preferences, and interests of his or her constituents. Elections provide a mechanism that helps to achieve this correspondence in two ways. First, people can

---

[46] Joseph Cooper and William West, "The Congressional Career in the 1970s," in Dodd and Oppenheimer, *Congress Reconsidered*, pp. 90–91.
[47] *The New York Times*, June 4, 1979.

choose representatives who are like themselves in important ways, for example, who share their ideas and views of public policy. Second, elections exist as incentives to representatives to take their duty seriously and as a means for replacing them if they do not.

Taking the process seriously, however, is not enough. The individual representative must somehow embody the aspirations, values, beliefs, and attitudes of hundreds of thousands of people. Naturally enough, there are few issues on which so large a group of people can agree. A legislator cannot, therefore, simply be a passive recorder of public opinion; the representative process is much more complicated.[48] This complexity is captured in four basic questions about representation:

1. Which characteristics of the constituency should be represented?
2. Should the representative consider not just the number of constituents who feel a certain way about an issue, but also how strongly they feel about it?
3. Which segments of the constituency should be represented?
4. Should the representative attempt to change his or her constituents' political opinions?

Let us consider each of these questions in turn.

Types of Representation The 225,000,000 people in the United States vary widely in nearly every respect, including their opinions on many important public policy questions. The first essential question in establishing a representative legislature is to determine *which characteristics* of the population should be reflected in its representatives. There are many ways to resolve this problem, but the two principal ones involve quite different types of representation.

Demographic Representation. The objective of demographic representation is to create a legislative body that reflects the distribution of demographic characteristics — age, race, occupation, sex, religion, and so forth — in the population represented.[49] The assumption here is that legislators who share various groups' characteristics are best able to reflect those groups' values and preferences. The Democratic party, for example, has worked toward demographic representation in its last two national conventions by writing rules that increase the number of delegates from formerly underrepresented groups — young people, blacks, and women.

The framers of the Constitution, however, explicitly rejected the demographic approach to representation. Voting rights were extended only to white males. Young people were not represented, for the Constitution required that House members be at least twenty-five years of age and senators at least thirty.

---

[48] The seminal work here is Hannah F. Pitkin, *The Concept of Representation* (Berkeley: University of California Press, 1967).
[49] Ibid., pp. 60 ff.

(Given the shorter life span of that era, these requirements represented a relatively later period in life then than now.) Perhaps the most serious bias came from the kind of people who were chosen. The framers thought — and hoped — that senators would be drawn from the wealthy, propertied classes, because they would be chosen by members of state legislatures, who were themselves well-to-do. Members of the House of Representatives would be similarly biased because most candidates would be wealthy and prominent local leaders.

Several changes in the Constitution brought a broader range of Americans into the electorate. The Fifteenth Amendment (adopted in 1870) established the right of people to vote regardless of race; the Nineteenth Amendment (1920) extended suffrage to women; the Twenty-fourth Amendment (1964) prohibited poll taxes (which discouraged poor people and blacks from voting); and the Twenty-sixth Amendment (1971) lowered the voting age to eighteen. These measures, however, have had little impact on the makeup of Congress. In the Ninety-seventh Congress (1981–82) the Senate's 100 members included no blacks and just two women; of the 435 House members, only 16 were black and 17 were women. No poor people and few blue-collar workers were elected to the Ninety-seventh Congress. But professional people, especially lawyers (253 of 535 members of Congress in 1981), are tremendously overrepresented. In short, the white, male, professional membership of Congress does not come close to demographically representing the American people.

Agency Representation. Must members of all the different population groups actually serve in the legislature for it to be representative? Those who support the concept of *agency representation* argue that constituents will be adequately represented if legislators act as their "agents" — that is, if legislators faithfully reflect the views and values of the various groups in their constituencies.[50] According to this view, Senator Edward Kennedy of Massachusetts successfully represents poor people and minorities through his support for social-welfare measures even though he is neither poor nor a minority group member himself.

Advocates of agency representation argue that national policy should be made by those who are most intelligent, informed, and capable. Because these people are often well educated and gravitate toward professions rather than blue-collar occupations, it is no surprise that these occupations are overrepresented numerically in the Congress.

Agency representation is closer than demographic representation to the Founding Fathers' views. By arranging for members of the House of Representatives to be selected by popular elections every two years, the framers of the Constitution ensured that unresponsive "agents" could be removed. They expected that this arrangement would eliminate representatives whose views

---

[50] Pitkin, *The Concept of Representation,* pp. 112 ff.

differed greatly from their constituents', but not that it would produce a legislature demographically similar to the nation as a whole.

In fact, elections often do produce legislators who share some important personal characteristics with their constituents. An ethnic or religious group that is a minority in national politics is often a majority in one or more congressional districts; and to be elected to Congress from that district, one may have to be a group member. Black districts often select black representatives. Polish-American districts may choose Polish-Americans. Utah nearly always elects a Mormon. This does not, however, occur on a wide enough scale to provide more than local pockets of demographic representation.

Judging how well a legislature meets the standard of agency representation is more difficult. But if the low public esteem for it is any guide, Congress does not meet this standard either.

Representation of Strong Preferences
The second essential question about representation is whether the representative should consider the strength of feeling on an issue as well as how many people support it. Most people do not hold very strong opinions about most issues the Congress considers. But when a given piece of legislation promises to have a considerable effect on a particular group, members of that group are likely to feel strongly about it. For example, President Carter placed an embargo on grain shipments to the Soviet Union in the wake of the 1980 Soviet invasion of Afghanistan. This decision barely touched the average American; but farmers, who saw their grain market collapsing, were outraged. Farm-state congresspersons reacted strongly against the embargo, which the Senate attempted to end by cutting off funds to enforce it. In this case, the Senate action had no immediate impact, but it did symbolize to farmers the legislators' commitments to their interests (in an election year).

A representative may be willing to disagree with the majority of his or her constituents on an issue of little importance to them, if a significant minority holds very strong views on the issue. As a result, many policies that have the lukewarm support of majorities can be delayed indefinitely by strong and active minority opposition. Some form of federal gun control legislation, for example, is favored by more than 70 percent of the American people. Despite this large supporting majority, however, the very active and intense opponents of gun control have prevented the passage of even the most watered-down handgun registration laws.

Such a situation may seem unfair to most people. However, if the supporters of gun control were as active as the opponents, guns would probably be controlled. It is the majority's willingness to *accept* the outcome, even if they do not like it, that encourages their representatives to weigh more heavily the minority's intense preferences. Only when a majority comes to feel strongly about an issue is it likely to back up its view with its votes as a minority does.

As we saw in Chapter 2, the Founding Fathers realized that the strongly felt interests of minority groups needed representation, and they structured the legislative process to give such groups an advantage in blocking offensive legislation. They particularly wanted to protect the property rights of land-holders and the wealthy, but the devices they created protect many other minorities as well. Because both houses of Congress must approve all legislation, an active minority has two opportunities to block an unfavorable bill. A third chance comes with the need for presidential approval of legislation. If the president vetoes a bill, it can become law only if two-thirds of both houses vote to override the veto; a minority thus can block legislation with only the support of the president and one vote over one-third of the members of one house.

Clever interest groups take advantage of the multiple veto points in the legislative process. Consider the fate of the "common situs" picketing bill, which would have enabled a single construction union to shut down an entire construction project. In 1976, with Republican Gerald Ford in the White House, the business community directed its attention at him, eventually winning a presidential veto of the legislation. A year later, after the new Democratic president Jimmy Carter promised to sign a common situs bill, business lobbied hard against the bill in Congress and eventually defeated it in the House by a vote of 217 to 205. The business community thus twice converted its intense feelings about common situs picketing into policy victories, at two separate stages of the legislative process.

Intensity of preference is also accommodated in ways not formally established by the Constitution. The most important of these is the give-and-take process called *logrolling:* A representative whose constituency is significantly affected by an issue seeks out members whose districts are not affected and attempts to gain their support. In exchange, the legislator offers them support on other matters that concern his or her district less and theirs more. In this way, legislators can often build majority backing for a minority position by offering future support on other issues.

These formal and informal mechanisms of the legislative process, then, have built-in biases that favor politically well-organized minorities, especially those that seek to protect existing advantages. The legislative process is much less helpful to groups that seek change, even if their views are intensely held (as we will see in Chapter 12 on interest groups).

Who Should Be Represented? Merely possessing the right to vote, to speak, and to petition the government does not guarantee representation for any group or individual. The third essential question of representation, then, concerns *who* should be represented. Legislators can, and in some instances must, choose which parts of their constituency they will represent once they are elected.

Each member of Congress must maintain a supporting coalition of interest groups that embrace enough of the district's voters to get him reelected. When faced with a difficult decision, a legislator usually considers how the issue affects one or more groups he depends on for reelection. Take, for example, the two senators from California in the 97th Congress, Alan Cranston and S. I. Hayakawa. Although both technically represented the same citizens, they often cast opposing votes. Their electoral bases were in fact quite different.

Cranston, a liberal Democrat, usually stood behind social programs and increased federal spending, whereas Hayakawa, a Republican, was consistently more conservative and supported aggressive American foreign and military policies. Each senator obtained the support of a different segment of the California electorate, but no single interest was likely to win control over either man. Rather, each chose policy stances compatible with his personal views and developed support from certain voting groups. In a very real sense, each senator has chosen which constituency he wants to represent. Such a choice is common and, indeed, is almost unavoidable in states like California whose populations are heterogeneous.

The constituency a member of Congress chooses often extends far beyond his or her own district. The representative who becomes identified with a national issue will receive letters, support, and even campaign contributions from all over the country. In such a case the legislator's chosen constituency may be different from his or her *formal constituency* (those citizens actually eligible to vote for the legislator's reelection). For example, Representative John Brademas of Indiana, a former Rhodes scholar, chose to develop a national "higher education" constituency.[51] With a seat on the House Education and Labor Committee and a district that includes Notre Dame University, he made a choice that meshed his own interests with those of his committee and his district. Ironically, after Brademas won a position within the Democratic leadership, as House Whip, his electoral vulnerability increased. His 1980 opponent successfully linked him to an entire array of alleged Democratic policy failures, and no specific constituency effectively rallied to Brademas' support. As we saw before, one's visibility may increase one's vulnerability. In Brademas's case, it may have cost him his House seat.

Even within a member's district, several different (and different kinds of) constituencies can be identified.[52] Beyond the formal, *geographic* boundaries of the district, the member also must contend with his *reelection* constituency, his *primary* constituency (of core supporters), and his *personal* constituency (of friends and key political allies). Even the apparently straightforward notion of constituency may have multiple layers and interpretations — all of which affect *whom* the legislator chooses to represent and *how* he or she does so.

Changing Constituents' Opinions The fourth and final essential question of representation is whether the legislator must accept and abide by constituents' opinions, or whether he should sometimes try to change people's views. Often the representative faces a dilemma. He may believe that legislation on some policy question — say, energy — is urgently needed. He may feel that such legislation is in the interests of his own district, or perhaps of the nation as a whole. Yet his constituents may feel quite differently. Possibly they are ill informed, possibly they do not

[51] Jack H. Schuster, "An 'Education Congressman' Fights for Survival: Congressman John Brademas' Bid for Re-election, 1968," in Allan P. Sindler, ed., *Policy and Politics in America* (Boston: Little, Brown, 1973), pp. 200–42.
[52] Richard F. Fenno, Jr., *Home Style* (Boston: Little, Brown, 1978).

realize the urgency of the problem, or perhaps they are merely unwilling to make the sacrifices the legislation would entail.

In such a situation the representative may take the safe course and vote in accordance with his constituents' views. Many legislators feel uneasy with such a decision and prefer to follow their own interpretation of the national interest. On most issues, when a legislator's actions are not well publicized, he or she may escape active opposition. But if the issue is important and has the voters' attention, the legislator's dilemma becomes more severe. Legislators often try to change their constituents' minds by increasing public awareness of the problem's urgency. In fact, members sometimes act a lot like teachers, trying to explain complex national issues in district-related terms. Not all members feel comfortable in this role, but many find such activities extremely rewarding. As one congressman exclaimed:

> That's why I ran — to have a chance to talk to a quarter-million people. And the opportunities have far exceeded my expectations. You can say just about anything . . . , although you don't know who is listening. I haven't been disappointed at all.

If these efforts fail, the representative who wants to be reelected may decide to wait until events bring the problem home to the average citizen. This is precisely what happened in the slowly developing energy crisis of the 1970s. Public acceptance of the Alaskan Oil pipeline, the 55-mile-per-hour speed limit, and higher gasoline prices could not really be expected until the problem reached crisis proportions. Only then could average citizens understand the need for national sacrifices they would be expected to share.

The representative who persists in following his or her personal views on highly visible issues must be prepared to face the consequences. A classic illustration occurred in 1957–58, when Representative Brooks Hays of Arkansas tried to help settle the Little Rock school-integration controversy without violence.[53] He was widely accused by whites of being "soft on integration," a charge that encouraged his opponent, a segregationist, to embark on a write-in campaign that unseated Hays in the next election. In a survey taken in the district after the election, every voter polled had read about both candidates before the election — a stunning contrast to the usual low levels of voter information. Such occasional electoral retribution reminds member of Congress of the potential peril awaiting those who follow their own views rather than their constituents'.

Representation: Two Case Studies It is clear that representation is a complex process. Even though the basic elements — the constituents' views, the representatives' views, and the electoral mechanism — are not complicated, the links among them are often dif-

---

[53] Warren E. Miller and Donald E. Stokes, "Constituency Influence in Congress," *American Political Science Review* 57 (March 1963). Also see Thomas E. Mann, *Unsafe at any Margin* (Washington, D.C.: American Enterprise Institute, 1978).

ficult to disentangle. Not everyone's opinion counts equally, and most opinions are subject to change.

Sometimes all the elements of the representative function weave together on a single issue. Two recent examples of representation are (1) the House Judiciary Committee's 1974 decision to bring impeachment charges against President Nixon and (2) the full Congress' 1977 decision to modify the Clean Air Act. In both instances, members answered the questions of representation in different ways, depending on their own views, those of their constituents, and their choice of electoral coalition.

Impeachment: Agency Representation. For some Judiciary Committee members, the impeachment issue involved very simple agency representation. John Conyers (D-Michigan), for instance, acted in accord with his liberal and partisan district in becoming an active advocate of impeachment. Republican Charles Wiggins (California) also faced an easy choice of agency representation. His district consisted largely of conservative, partisan supporters of President Nixon. Since their sentiments meshed with Wiggins's personal position, it was natural for him to take a leading role in the president's defense.

Impeachment: Intensity of Preferences. Of all the committee members, Chairman Peter Rodino (D-New Jersey) was probably most concerned with the nationwide intensity of public opinion. By a small majority, Americans favored impeachment in the House, followed by a Senate trial. Many of those who backed the president, however, did so very strongly. If the Congress were to act only on majority opinion, many citizens might think that President Nixon had been treated unfairly. The legitimacy of his impeachment would thus be in question.

Rodino attempted to reduce the intensity of minority opinion in several ways. First, he strove to create an image of impartiality, procedural correctness, and moderation. He restrained the committee's aggressive liberal members. Second, he sought to fashion a bipartisan majority in favor of impeachment, which might illustrate the strength of the evidence to Republicans in the electorate. Such a strategy required some moderation in phrasing the Articles of Impeachment, in order to make them acceptable to committee Republicans. Finally, Rodino orchestrated the televised, prime-time presentation of evidence. Although the array of evidence might have completely changed some people's minds, it was also intended to foster doubts among those who still defended the president.

Impeachment: Choice of Constituency. Given the importance of the issue, each committee member represented both a national and a single-district constituency. Yet some members had to choose between constituencies within their districts. Representatives Tom Railsback of Illinois and William Cohen of Maine, both Republicans, had the most difficulty, because their electoral coalitions included both supporters and opponents of impeachment. Their dilemma was severe, for the issue was important and their actions were highly visible. They could support the president and lose much-needed votes among Democrats, independents, and moderate Republicans; or they could support impeachment and alienate their hard-core Republican support. In short, although these legislators could choose which elements of their constituency to represent, they really had no completely satisfactory alternative choice.

Impeachment: Changing Constituents' Opinions. One way a legislator can deal with the dilemma of a divided constituency is by trying to restructure the opinions of key supporters. Republicans Cohen and Railsback took this risky strategy, assuming the role of educator rather than agent. Personally convinced of the merits of at least one article of impeachment, they returned to their districts during the hearings to meet with citizen groups, speak on television and radio, and convince their supporters that the evidence for impeachment was strong.

Representative Walter Flowers (D-Alabama) faced a similar situation because his district contained a large number of Democratic opponents of impeachment. Before casting his vote in favor of the first impeachment article, Flowers spoke eloquently and persuasively on prime-time national television. His remarks, although heard by the entire country, were really directed at his own constituents. To judge by his sincere and moving speech, Flowers clearly found it difficult to oppose his country's president, a sentiment his district undoubtedly shared. His conversion to the proimpeachment view unquestionably influenced the views of many of his constituents.

Representative David Dennis (R-Indiana) was less fortunate. He faithfully supported President Nixon throughout the hearings, even though he held a "marginal" (very competitive) congressional seat. Dennis acted on his conscience and sought, often effectively, to poke holes in the Democrats' positions. Nevertheless, his lack of skepticism toward Nixon's assertions finally placed him in the untenable position of defending a man who was seen by most citizens, including Dennis's constituents, to have violated his oath of office. Dennis suffered a convincing defeat in his 1974 reelection attempt.

Because the impeachment controversy was so dramatic and important, the dilemmas over representation that the Judiciary Committee members faced were more public than usual. The problems raised, however, are similar to those that arise almost daily in the Congress.

Clean Air: Agency Representation. In 1970 the Congress overwhelmingly passed revolutionary environmental legislation that required automobile manufacturers, among others, to meet increasingly strict emission standards. The Clean Air Act evoked sharp responses from the auto industry, which mounted a continuing campaign through the 1970s to have the standards modified. The issue came to a head in 1977, when both auto-industry management and labor rallied behind the position that the industry could not meet the clean air standards for 1978-model cars, which were about to go into production. Their key "agent" in the Congress was Democratic Representative John Dingell, a Detroit congressman who sat on the House Commerce Committee. Dingell, a long-time liberal and conservationist, in this case served the interests of his auto-industry constituents.

Although many members of congress rallied to represent environmental interests, the most important force was then-Senator Edmund Muskie (D-Maine), who had played a central role in the passage of the original 1970 act. With little industry and much natural beauty, Maine provided Muskie with a strong environmental constituency. In addition, Muskie's chairmanship of the relevant Senate subcommittee on environmental pollution gave him great leverage over the legislation.

Clean Air: Intensity of Preferences. In 1976 over half (52 percent) of a sample of Americans thought that pollution standards should not be relaxed in order to increase the availability of fuel.[54] Only one-third of the sample expressed support for such a change. Although such survey results did not express the intensity of citizens' preferences, there is little doubt that a Michigan auto worker who believed in relaxing standards would have stronger preferences than most "proenvironment" respondents. Thus, Representative Phil Sharp, from an industrial Indiana district that is heavily dependent on the auto industry, heard a great deal about air quality standards from his constituents. Although Sharp had a good environmental record, he cast a key committee vote in favor of relaxing the pollution standards. He had heeded his constituents' strongly held and well-articulated attitudes.

Clean Air: Choice of Constituencies and Constituent Education. The Clean Air amendments posed difficult choices for many members, but perhaps none were tested more severely than Representative Tim Lee Carter (R-Kentucky), a medical doctor and a political conservative. Whereas almost all his Republican colleagues came down on the side of the auto industry, Representative Carter turned to a broader constituency in voting to maintain strict standards. "Our actions here . . . will impact on each and every individual in this nation, and it is exactly the decisions we make on these issues which decide the extent to which our constituents feel the pinch."[55] Carter opted to represent a national "clean-air" constituency, but he could sympathize with those who had strong local interests to protect.

Other members on both sides of the pollution-standard issue sought to educate their constituents through the presentation of various scientific evidence, which was frequently open to serious challenge. Democrat Harry Waxman of California observed that "the cost of air pollution in health and material dam-

[54]"Opinion Roundup," *Public Opinion*, August–September 1979, pp. 21–23.
[55]*Congressional Quarterly Weekly Report*, May 28, 1977, p. 1023. In addition, an enlightening and entertaining film, *HR6161: An Act of Congress*, covers this controversy and the various actors involved. It is an excellent introduction to the pulls and tugs of the legislative process.

age exceeds $25 billion annually," and Republican James Broyhill of North Carolina speculated that "decreased auto sales due to overstrict standards would have resulted in shutting down a large segment of the auto industry."[56]

Unlike the Nixon impeachment hearings, but more typical of most legislative action, the Clean Air controversy ended in compromise. Strict standards were deferred, but retained. No single set of constituents won a clear-cut victory, and both sides knew that they would continue this legislative struggle throughout the 1980s. Acting for many diverse and powerful interests within the society, legislators will seek to reconcile economics and environmentalism. This promises to be a long-running show.

Congressional Caucuses: A New Form of Representation? In the past decade almost fifty groupings of congresspersons have sprung up, mostly within the House. Each represents some particular interest, ranging from an economic force (the Congressional Steel Caucus) to an ethnic group (the Hispanic Caucus) to a region (the New England Caucus). These groups are frequently bipartisan and are formed to offer members an additional avenue of representation. The Congressional Black Caucus, for example, has a paid staff of ten, an annual budget of over $200,000, and the attention of the press when its members, the sixteen black members of the House, want to make a statement.

Increasingly, the newer caucuses tend to represent narrow economic interests such as tourism, coal, shipyards, or textiles. There is nothing new about these interests being represented vigorously in the legislative process. Members whose states or districts include such interests have often fought diligently on their behalf. What is new is the formal organization of these groups — within the Congress and populated by its members. It is as if the Congress opened its doors to special interests and allowed them to set up shop within the institution. Indeed, many caucuses have received free space within congressional office buildings. And as the Reagan administration's budget cuts prompt reactions from particular interests, more caucuses are likely to form. This was the strategy adopted by Representative Fred Richmond (D-New York), who organized a 130-member Congressional Arts Caucus after the 1981 Reagan budget cut 50 percent of the proposed spending for the National Endowment for the Arts. Speaking for many caucus advocates, Richmond noted that in Congress "the best lobbyist is a congressman."[57]

Richmond's statement was proved true, and it demonstrates the extent to which particular interests have penetrated the Congress. Many members are leery of this trend. Some simply join caucuses, and others decry their development. As Representative Pat Schroeder (D-Colorado) observed, in explaining why she, as a supporter of the arts, was not joining the Arts Caucus. "We shouldn't call them caucuses. We should call them what they are — special interests." Nevertheless, caucuses proliferate. As usual, members of con-

---

[56] Ibid., pp. 1024, 1026.
[57] "CBS Evening News," February 27, 1981.

gress find it easier to represent constituents and interests than to make the legislative process work smoothly.

CONCLUSION Try as we may, our understanding of the Congress can never be complete. The dual tasks of making laws and representing citizens produce surprises and incongruities that defy easy explanation. In theory, the public should feel closer to the Congress than to either the president, in his splendid isolation, or the Supreme Court, so distant from the popular will. But the complexity of the legislative process raises barriers to popular understanding and approval that are not easily overcome.

Can the Congress do anything to lower these barriers? Again, the dual congressional responsibilities of legislation and representation work against any easy answer. To the extent that members of Congress actively represent their constituents' interests, perform casework, and visit their home districts or states, they may reduce their ability to work as effective policymakers, shepherding bills through the legislative process or overseeing current laws in operation.

In recent years the public has, to a great extent, separated Congress' lawmaking and representational functions. It has reacted negatively to the institution, which is slow to make decisions and apparently unresponsive to public opinion; at the same time, citizens have reelected almost all their individual representatives and most senators. A recent Gallup poll reported that only 18 percent of those interviewed felt "a great deal of confidence" in the Congress;[58] yet, in 1980 Americans voted to return 372 of the 399 members of the House who sought reelection, a success rate of over 92 percent. As Richard Fenno notes, "We do, it appears, love our Congressmen. . . . On the other hand, it seems equally true that we do not love our Congress."[59]

The gap between citizens and leaders is wide when we consider legislative performance, but it narrows dramatically when we look at representation. Here citizens seem satisfied. Although Congress has done much in recent years to strengthen its policymaking abilities, its greater strength lies in representing its constituents' many, widely diverse interests. To expect efficiency and speed from such a body may be to ask too much. It may not even be an appropriate request.

SUGGESTIONS FOR FURTHER READING Dodd, Lawrence, and Oppenheimer, Bruce, eds. *Congress Reconsidered*, 2nd ed. Washington: CQ Press, 1981. An excellent and recently revised reader covering many, if not all, aspects of the changing Congress.

---

[58]*Public Opinion*, October–November 1979.

[59]"If, As Ralph Nader says, Congress is 'The Broken Branch' How Come We Love Our Congressmen So Much?" in Norman J. Ornstein, ed., *Congress in Change* (New York: Praeger, 1975), p. 278.

Fenno, Richard F., Jr. *Home Style.* Boston: Little, Brown, 1978. First-rate congressional research on members in their districts, and an entertaining piece of work.

Mann, Thomas E. *Unsafe at Any Margin.* Washington, D.C.: American Enterprise Institute, 1978. An overview of how incumbents ought to get reelected — but sometimes don't.

Mann, Thomas E., and Ornstein, Norman, eds. *The New Congress.* Washington, D.C.: American Enterprise Institute, 1981. Another first-rate reader on congressional changes.

Peabody, Robert. *Leadership in Congress.* Boston: Little, Brown, 1976. The most comprehensive work on party leaders and how they win their positions.

Reid, T. R. *Congressional Odyssey: Saga of a Senate Bill.* San Francisco: Freeman, 1980. A solid case study of the contemporary legislative process.

Vogler, David. *The Politics of Congress*, 3rd ed. Boston: Allyn and Bacon, 1981. An excellent and lively text on the Congress.

Chapter 6 The Presidency

What is the proper scope of presidential power? This question has always posed a problem for Americans. From the president's perspective, the problem is the inadequacy of his power to achieve his legislative objectives and to deal flexibly but decisively with events in a fast-changing and complex world. An independent-minded Congress, a vast federal bureaucracy, and the other nations of the world are just some of the forces that can frustrate presidential visions of a "New Frontier" at home or a "World Safe for Democracy" abroad.

From the people's vantage point, the problem has a different cast. On the one hand the public worries about the problem of *too much* presidential power — the power to do harm, say, by making unpopular wars or by ordering the intelligence services to spy on United States citizens. On the other hand the public often finds that the president has *too little* power to achieve what it wishes — often unrealistically — presidents could do in a positive way: sweep away inflation, put people back to work, solve the energy crisis, make America "respected" in the world. The ordinary mortals who inhabit the White House usually fail to meet these expectations. Thus from either perspective, the president's or the people's, the modern presidency seems almost destined to fail.

The powerlessness of the president is a persistent complaint from the White

House. Harry Truman, a man we usually think of as a strong president, once complained: "I thought I was the President, but when it comes to these bureaucracies, I can't make 'em do a damn thing." [1] In a similar vein, Lyndon Johnson grumbled, "Power? The only power I've got is nuclear — and I can't use that." [2] Jimmy Carter's experience with the frustrations of the presidency was equally discouraging. Determined at the beginning to use his office for everything from preaching the morality of global human rights to effecting sweeping governmental reorganization, he became resigned by midterm to far less ambitious goals: "There are so many things I would like to do instantly," he once commented wistfully. "The most difficult thing is to recognize the limitations of a President's power." [3]

Such presidential laments are common. From the president's perspective, the powers that come with the office are often inadequate to surmount the multitude of obstacles lying in wait for him. Yet for a press and public that still remember the depths of presidential deceit during Vietnam and Watergate, the issue is often not whether presidents have enough power to meet public expectations, but whether the people and their representatives can control the president. Can presidents be made to accept responsibility for their failures and mistakes — and be prevented from repeating them? Can presidential behavior be kept within constitutional bounds? Can presidential secretiveness be restricted to matters whose public revelation would constitute a real threat to national security? These are all open questions. We now know that every president from Franklin Roosevelt to Richard Nixon used the government's intelligence organizations against American citizens. Presidential staffs have "protected" their employer so well that they have shielded him from reality. And presidents caught in bald lies have had their press secretaries blandly inform us that they "misspoke." A responsive and controllable presidency has been an elusive ideal.

These problems of power — too little or too much — converge, of course. The key question is: Can we retain a strong presidency, capable of leadership and action, yet at the same time "make the president safe for democracy," as Thomas Cronin puts it? [4]

THE PRESIDENTIAL JOB The presidency is a big and complex job. Clinton Rossiter likens the American president to a Gilbert and Sullivan character in *The Mikado*, a "particularly haughty and exclusive person" who fills every office from First Lord of the Treasury to Master of the Buckhounds to Groom of the Backstairs. [5] Presidents, however, really seem to play twice as many roles. In Rossiter's terms,

[1] According to David Brinkley, quoted in Thomas E. Cronin, *The State of the Presidency* (Boston: Little, Brown, 1975), p. 19.
[2] Quoted in Congressional Quarterly Service, *Congressional Quarterly Guide to Current American Government*, August 1969, p. 25.
[3] *The New York Times*, May 21, 1978.
[4] Cronin, *State of the Presidency*, p. 289.
[5] Clinton Rossiter, *The American Presidency* (New York: Mentor, 1960), p. 14.

a president fills not only the obvious constitutional roles of chief executive and commander-in-chief of the armed forces, but also the roles of head of state in relations with foreign governments, chief legislator, head of his political party, voice of the people, manager of the economy, and several more.

The presidency is also a grueling job. Looking back at his first hectic days in office after the death of Franklin Roosevelt, Harry Truman recalled, "I always thought . . . all the time I was President it would let up, but it never did. It never got any easier."[6] Presidential memoirs are full of references to sleepless nights and endless days. "During my first thirty days in office," Lyndon Johnson wrote, "I believe I averaged no more than four or five hours' sleep a night. If I had a single moment when I could go off alone, relax, forget the pressures of business, I don't recall it."[7] The rigors of the presidency are nowhere more graphically illustrated than in photographs of presidents at the beginning and end of their terms: The aging process that occurs is cruel and extraordinary.

The Constitutional Framework Reading the Constitution hardly gives one a clue to the complexity or tensions of the presidential job. The Constitution is curiously vague and brief about the nature and powers of the office. As one astute student of the presidency, Edwin S. Corwin, has noted:

> Article II [which deals with the presidency] is the most loosely drawn chapter of the Constitution. To those who think that a constitution ought to settle everything beforehand, it should be a nightmare; by the same token, to those who think that constitution makers ought to leave considerable leeway for the future play of political forces, it should be a vision realized.[8]

The vagueness and brevity of Article II scarcely reflects the concern with which the framers approached the problem of executive power. As we saw in Chapter 2, Americans had grown suspicious and fearful of executive power under the British crown. After independence, under the Articles of Confederation, they had sought to resolve the problem of executive power by simply doing without an executive branch. But by the time the framers met in 1787 to draft a new constitution, they knew that an effective national government required an executive — and thus executive power — in some form.

The framers argued at length over whether there should be a plural or a single executive. James Wilson of Pennsylvania and Gouverneur Morris of New York wanted a single strong figure at the head of government. Edmund Randolph of Virginia, however, feared a single president as "the foetus of monarchy" and so argued for several executives. The framers also struggled

[6] In Merle Miller, *Plain Speaking: An Oral Biography of Harry S. Truman* (New York: Berkeley, 1974), p. 206.

[7] Lyndon Baines Johnson, *The Vantage Point: Perspectives of the Presidency, 1963–1969* (New York: Holt, Rinehart, and Winston, 1971), p. 21.

[8] Edward S. Corwin, *The President: Office and Powers, 1787–1957* (New York: New York University Press, 1957), pp. 3–4.

over the question of whether the president should be independent of the legislature or part of it, as in a parliamentary system. They debated at least four different proposals for selecting the president, ranging from election by Congress to direct popular election to Hamilton's plan for indirect election by electors.

The final product of these deliberations, Article II, seems to reflect a greater concern with the mechanics of the presidency than with its powers and character. Most of the article is devoted to a description of how the electoral college should work. Very little attention is given to the powers a president may exercise. Section 1 of Article II vests "the executive power" in a president, but it does not go on to elaborate or illustrate that power. Section 2 designates the president commander-in-chief of the armed forces, and Section 3 enjoins him to "take Care that the Laws be faithfully executed." These are the principal constitutional bases of presidential power.

Other powers are given equally brief treatment. There is no difference in emphasis between major and minor powers. For example, the same sentence that names the president commander-in-chief also empowers him to grant pardons for offenses against the United States and to grant reprieves. Although Gerald Ford's controversial pardon of Richard Nixon may have loomed large to Americans at the time, pardoning cannot be thought of as a major presidential power. The president may also require the opinion in writing of the principal officers of the executive departments (which themselves are not mentioned in the Constitution); make treaties and appoint ambassadors and other officials, in each case with the advice and consent of the Senate; receive ambassadors; and give Congress information on the state of the union "from time to time," recommending to that body measures he deems necessary. In addition, Article I, Section 7 grants the president veto power over congressional action. Very little more is said about presidential powers. It is on this slim base that one of the most powerful offices in the world is built. As Grant McConnell has observed, "For the rest, the presidency is the work of presidents."[9]

The Expanding Presidency Clearly, "the work of presidents" has involved defining and elaborating on the nature of the office while filling it. The Constitution, by its deliberate vagueness, has made possible this development of the office through continual interpretation and reinterpretation to accommodate changing circumstances and to meet unexpected needs. Woodrow Wilson, who was well aware of this, once observed that "The President is at liberty, both in law and in conscience, to be as big a man as he can." The presidency, then, is defined as much — or even more — by practice as by constitutional law. How does this "work of presidents" proceed? What are the circumstances and factors that make the ongoing development of the office possible?

[9] Grant McConnell, *The Modern Presidency*, 2nd ed. (New York: St. Martin's Press, 1976), p. 9.

The Cost of Being President

The presidency tends to wear men out, physically and emotionally. The toll is etched in the faces of these recent incumbents.

Support from the People.   One factor certainly has been popular attitudes toward presidents and the presidency. From George Washington on, the American people have generally invested the presidency with a heroic quality that has transformed many otherwise ordinary politicians into transcendent figures in the popular imagination. Not every president has enlarged the presidential myth, nor has every one of them benefited from it. But it has grown, especially in the twentieth century, to such proportions that Camelot seemed the only appropriate metaphor for John F. Kennedy's Washington.

This is not to say that presidents are invariably popular or that they are immune to criticism, as we shall see later in this chapter. Rather, it suggests that presidents as *symbolic figures* representing the nation, not presidents as *politicians,* are generally accorded great legitimacy and support.

Along with such generally supportive public attitudes, two other factors seem to have been especially important in enabling the president to define and expand his job. They are (1) his perceived need to respond to various international and domestic crises and (2) his personality.

Responding to Crises.   The presidential office is characterized by unity (a single person is ultimately in charge), considerable independence from the other branches of government, the ability to act secretly, and the ability to act swiftly. Thus it is uniquely suited in the American national system to respond to crises. Congress, in contrast, is a slow and fractious debating society. Extraordinary circumstances — the Civil War, international war, the Cold War, economic depression — have seemed to require extraordinary presidential responses.

Often this has meant taking actions that are, by normal standards, dictatorial or illegal. During the Civil War, Abraham Lincoln authorized the Army to arrest, imprison, and try in military courts northerners who criticized the war effort or who were suspected of being disloyal to the Union cause. Thousands of citizens were arrested under this authorization. Lincoln also permitted the Army to suspend the writ of *habeas corpus* — that is, to suspend the right of an imprisoned citizen to obtain a court order directing his jailer to show in court why he should be held. After Pearl Harbor, Franklin Roosevelt was able, by executive order, to put 112,000 Japanese-Americans behind barbed wire in "relocation centers" and keep them there for most of the war. Roosevelt's slim justification for this massive violation of civil liberties was that as commander-in-chief he had to guard against espionage and sabotage. In 1969 Richard Nixon authorized various wiretaps without court orders. When the Senate Select Committee on Intelligence queried him about this in 1976, he claimed in written testimony that such actions are lawful "if undertaken because of a Presidential determination that it was in the interest of national security." [10]

Actions like these have not established for all time the president's right to

[10] *The New York Times,* March 14, 1976.

intern civilians, spy on citizens at will, or suspend other civil liberties. Rather, they have established the president's power, in a crisis, to take quick actions that have no clear constitutional basis and no congressional authorization.

Presidential Personality.   Although circumstances create opportunities for presidential leadership and initiative, it is the personality — the psychological makeup — of the president that determines how he will seek to use the power of the office. Some presidents are activists; others are not. Some want power and seek it; others do not. As Richard Pious has commented, "The presidents who go down in the history books as 'great' are those who reach for power, who assert their authority to the limit."[11]

Some presidents seek single-handedly to take Washington by storm and to lead by force of personal will. They define the job of the president as that of an idea broker and as the major source of energy in the system. Other presidents have been ambivalent about the use of power and about their role as leaders. They have done little to mark out new ground for presidential action or to lead the nation to new policy commitments.

Franklin Roosevelt and Dwight Eisenhower illustrate these two very different personality types. FDR brought to the job an immense self-confidence and a great desire for mastery. To achieve his goals, he employed an array of political strategies ranging from flattery to diplomacy to threat. His first hundred days in office, during which he launched the New Deal programs aimed at economic recovery, are legendary.

FDR was not a great thinker, nor was he an originator of ideas. He was interested in action and results. He listened to people and took from them the ideas that fitted his grand schemes. Often he would assign two or more people to perform the same task so that he could maximize his choices of action. In contrast, Eisenhower was reluctant to assume the presidency and was relatively inactive in office. "I don't know why people are always nagging me to run for president," Eisenhower complained in 1950. "I think I've gotten too old."[12] He accepted the Republican nomination for president in 1952, not because he wanted to wield power or to shape policy but because he felt a sense of duty to the Republican party and to the nation, in whose name he wished to repudiate what many Republicans saw as the cronyism and backroom style of the Truman administration.

Although Fred Greenstein has recently argued that Eisenhower was a much more astute politician and manager than he is given credit for,[13] the fact is that he did little to exploit his immense popularity. He was driven neither by a desire to enhance his own reputation nor by a set of policy goals. He was,

---

[11] Richard Pious, *The American Presidency* (New York: Basic Books, 1979), p. 11.

[12] In James D. Barber, *The Presidential Character* (Englewood Cliffs, N.J.: Prentice-Hall, 1972), p. 159.

[13] Fred Greenstein, "Eisenhower as an Activist President," *Political Science Quarterly* 94 (Winter 1979–80): 575–600.

for example, virtually unaware of domestic poverty, urban blight, and the growing discontent of black people.

Roosevelt's presidency, like those of Lincoln and Wilson before him and of Johnson after him, had an immense impact on both the nation and the office. His New Deal legislation transformed the basic relationships among the domestic economy, the federal government, and public welfare; his wartime leadership placed the office of the president at the head of the western alliance. Eisenhower's less active presidency maintained — perhaps reestablished —the dignity of the office, but it did little to enlarge presidential power or change the character of American society.

To summarize, the job definition of the presidency contained in the Constitution is terse and vague. It has remained for the presidents themselves to define the job, to chart new courses and areas of presidential action, to bring the nation to new commitments. Presidents have defined their task not so much by looking to the Constitution as by looking to events — and the need to respond to them — and by looking within themselves. From the president's point of view, as well as from the citizen's perspective, such a system has both advantages and disadvantages. Although it allows flexibility in responding to needs and crises, it has also permitted the abuse of presidential power.

PRESIDENTIAL POWER: SCOPE AND LIMITS By exploring several areas in which presidents are active, we can gain some sense of how presidents go about defining a course of action and justifying what they have done. This should help us to understand both the power and the occasional weakness of the presidency from the vantage point of the White House.

International Relations The presidential job can be divided roughly into two components: international and domestic. The president has emerged as the dominant actor in foreign affairs, although the Constitution assigns to the whole Congress the power to declare war and raise armies, to the Senate the power to approve treaties and ambassadorial appointments, and to the House control over the purse strings of the Treasury. Nevertheless, supported principally by the commander-in-chief clause (Article II, Section 2) of the Constitution and by the visibility and unity of the presidential office, presidents have tended since early in the nineteenth century to take the lead in foreign policy.

Presidents do, of course, have a great deal of help in the executive branch in making and carrying out foreign policy. Much presidential energy, however, is taken up by the need to coordinate, mollify, prod, and direct the numerous institutional participants and advisors. Henry Kissinger, who was successively national security advisor and secretary of state under President Nixon, once noted that "the outsider believes a presidential order is consistently followed out. Nonsense. I have to spend considerable time seeing that it is carried out and in the spirit the President intended."[14] Frequent struggles

[14] Pious, *The American Presidency*, p. 363.

Presidential Activism: A Threat to the Constitution?

"Can executive efficiency be maintained amid a crisis and constitutional government be still preserved? This, as I see it, was the central problem of Lincoln's administration," wrote historian James Randall.*

Many of Lincoln's actions during the Civil War either stretched or directly contravened the Constitution. The president increased the army and issued the Emancipation Proclamation without congressional authorization. He also suspended the writ of habeas corpus, a legal notice justifying the lawfulness of an arrest.

On the night of May 25, 1861, shortly after the fall of Fort Sumter, General George Cadwalader of the U.S. Army dispatched a squad of soldiers to arrest one John Merryman, suspected of treason. Merryman was taken from his bed to Fort McHenry in Baltimore, where he was kept in "close custody." Lawyers for the imprisoned man denied his guilt and asked for a writ of habeas corpus. Chief Justice Roger Taney promptly issued a writ for General Cadwalader to answer. The general refused, maintaining that he had been authorized by the president to suspend habeas corpus proceedings in the interest of public safety. "It is a plain case, gentlemen,"

Taney wrote, admonishing Lincoln. "The President, under the Constitution and laws of the United States, cannot suspend the privilege of the writ of habeas corpus, nor authorize any military officer to do so."

Lincoln's defense of his position was simple: "Are all the laws but one to go unexecuted," he asked, "and the Government itself go to pieces, lest that one be violated?"

*James G. Randall, *Constitutional Problems under Lincoln* (New York: Appleton, 1926), p. vii.

for power within the foreign policy establishment are not uncommon. President Nixon, Carter, and Reagan for example, all had to deal with conflicts between their national security advisors and their secretaries of state over their respective responsibilities. Another constant source of tension for presidents concerns disagreements between the professional foreign service and the intelligence community over when and how to use covert operations. Yet another problem that commands presidential energies is how to integrate and use the National Security Council, which includes, among others, the director of the CIA, the head of the Joint Chiefs of Staff, the vice-president, and the secretaries of defense and state.

Along with the task of managing the foreign policy apparatus at home, the president has a diverse array of responsibilities in the international arena. These range from serving as spokesman for the noncommunist nations to making formal alliances and commitments; from making peace to making war.

Leadership of the "Free World." Perhaps the most difficult responsibility of modern presidents in foreign affairs is that of leadership of the western alliance. Striking a balance between restraint and toughness, between conciliation and determination — and getting America's allies to follow — has been especially problematic in the postwar era. Since the end of World War II the nations of western Europe have looked to the American president for leadership in the struggle with the Soviet Union and its allies. It has fallen to presidents to enunciate the posture and determination of the noncommunist nations and to use American power to protect our mutual interests. In the more innocent years before the Vietnam War, President Kennedy declared, "We will pay any price, support any friend, oppose any foe, to assure the survival of liberty."

Ironically, the Europeans, despite their dependence on America's nuclear shield against the Russians, are not always willing to follow the American leadership that they want and expect. President Carter discovered this when he called for a boycott of the 1980 Olympic Games to protest the Soviet invasion of Afghanistan. Few allies heeded his call. And President Reagan won little European support for his policy of sending arms to El Salvador, although he argued that his purpose was to "stop Soviet expansionism."

Presidential Diplomacy. Presidents not only seek to provide leadership for the nations of the western alliance, but they also take part in diplomacy — the forging and maintaining of relationships among nations. One of President Carter's major achievements in this respect was his personal role in bringing Israel and Egypt to the peace table. Presidents can also recognize nations — either formally, as when Truman recognized Israel in 1948, or when Carter established diplomatic relations with China in 1978; or in a de facto sense, as when George Washington in 1793 received "Citizen" Genêt, the representative of the new French Republic. Richard Nixon, by traveling to the People's Republic of China, provided de facto recognition of that country.

If presidents can recognize nations, so too can they break diplomatic relations. Perhaps the most controversial recent instance of the exercise of this power came in conjunction with the recognition of the People's Republic of China. President Carter decided at the same time to end formal relations with Taiwan. The Congress, ever vigilant for opportunities to play a role in foreign affairs, insisted that the president formally assure Taiwan that the United States would continue to be concerned with that island's security.

Presidents can also establish mutual agreements and commitments with allies through *executive agreements* — a wide variety of binding accords made by the president with one or more foreign governments. Executive agreements have the effect of treaties but do not require the approval of the Senate. Prior to 1972 the president did not even have to inform the Congress of such agreements, but legislation introduced in 1971 now requires that Congress be informed. The president may make executive agreements in the course of carrying out the provisions of a treaty. He may also make them to carry out the intent of Congress, or simply to fulfill his role of executive. Theodore Roosevelt's "Gentleman's Agreement" of 1907, limiting Japanese immigration to the United States, is an example; so is Franklin Roosevelt's agreement with Britain in 1940 to exchange American destroyers for the lease of British bases. A more recent example is Jimmy Carter's promise in 1979 to guarantee Israel's oil supply until 1994 to compensate Israel for returning oil lands to Egypt.

Presidential War Powers. The president also can make war. Nowhere else has the expansion of presidential power been so apparent. Lincoln is generally seen as the first president to seek unprecedented and extraordinary powers in wartime. He did so — successfully — by arguing that he had certain "war powers" that derived from his role as commander-in-chief and from his constitutional duty "to take care that the laws be faithfully executed." Lincoln employed his "war powers" to do things that constitutionally only Congress could do: He raised an army, paid out unappropriated funds from the Treasury, and proclaimed a blockade of southern ports (an act of war). The effect of Lincoln's actions, many of which he eventually asked Congress to ratify or authorize, was to claim for the president virtually unlimited control over domestic life during wartime.[15]

During World War I, Woodrow Wilson responded to the requirements of massive warfare not by acting independently of Congress, as Lincoln had done, but rather by seeking in advance vast grants of delegated power. Thus the Lever Food and Fuel Control Act of 1917 allowed the president to regulate the importation, manufacture, storage, mining, and distribution of necessaries; to requisition food and fuels; to purchase, sell, and store certain foods; to take over and operate factories, mines, and pipelines; and to regulate coal and coke prices. Wilson was empowered by other legislation to take over and operate the railroads, to regulate the foreign-language press, and to censor all mail and

[15] Corwin, *The President*, p. 232.

other communications going abroad. Eventually (mostly after the war) these delegations of extraordinary power were upheld by the Supreme Court.

Wilson also invoked the commander-in-chief clause to create several regulatory boards (the War Industries Board, the Committee on Public Information), which coordinated private industry during the war years, censored the press through so-called voluntary methods, and performed other mobilization and domestic control functions. During World War II, Franklin Roosevelt used similar authority to create at least thirty-five war-related commissions and boards whose functions ranged from censorship to price controls.

During the war in Korea, President Truman ordered his secretary of commerce to seize the nation's steel mills in the face of a threatened strike so that the flow of war materiel would not be interrupted. "The President of the United States," Truman declared, "has very great inherent powers to meet great national emergencies."[16] The Supreme Court declared the steel seizure unconstitutional, however, and restored the mills to their owners.[17]

Presidents, of course, employ extraordinary "war powers" abroad as well as at home. Every president from Truman through Reagan has sent American military forces to foreign lands without congressional authorization. When North Korea invaded South Korea in 1950, Truman sent American troops into combat there. Congress could ratify his actions only after the fact. On the advice of Dean Acheson, then secretary of state, Truman justified his action by citing his power as commander-in-chief. The State Department, supporting Truman, argued that there was "a traditional power of the President to use armed forces of the United States without consulting Congress."[18]

Presidential dispatch of troops abroad has been frequent since Korea. Eisenhower sent 14,000 marines to Lebanon (although, as it turned out, there was no fighting); John Kennedy sent 16,000 military "advisors" to Vietnam; Lyndon Johnson poured another half-million soldiers into Vietnam and also dispatched a force to the Dominican Republic; Richard Nixon ordered a massive invasion of Cambodia in 1970; Gerald Ford sent marines to an island off Cambodia in an attempt to rescue the crew of the United States merchant ship *Mayaguez*, which had been seized by the Cambodians; Jimmy Carter secretly dispatched a small military force to Iran in a futile attempt to rescue American hostages held in Teheran; and Ronald Reagan sent noncombat military advisors to El Salvador.

Congress and the courts usually have responded to such presidential initiatives by accepting and supporting them after the fact. But the other branches of government have not been wholly supine in the fact of what Arthur Schlesinger has called an "imperial" presidency. They have resisted presidents, occasionally in ways that seriously hindered the president's ability to act.

In *Ex parte Milligan*, a case decided by the Supreme Court in 1866 concern-

---

[16] In Arthur Schlesinger, Jr., *The Imperial Presidency* (Boston: Houghton Mifflin, 1973), p. 142.

[17] *Youngstown Sheet and Tube Co.* v. *Sawyer*, 343 U.S. 579 (1952).

[18] Schlesinger, *Imperial Presidency*, p. 133.

ing Lincoln's imposition of martial law and the suspension of habeas corpus during the Civil War, the decision read in part: "No doctrine involving more pernicious consequences was ever invented by the wit of man than that any of [the Constitution's] provisions can be suspended during any of the great exigencies of government. Such a doctrine leads directly to anarchy or despotism. . . ." [19] The importance of this judicial rebuke of Lincoln (who was dead by this time) was that it led the reaction to the wartime expansion of the presidency. Efforts to constrain the presidency after wartime were to become a general pattern. As Schlesinger has observed, "Nearly every president who extended the reach of the White House provoked a reaction toward a more restrictive theory of the presidency, even if the reaction never quite cut presidential power back to its earlier level." [20]

But Congress, not the Court, has made the most persistent efforts to restrain presidential power in foreign affairs. It responded to Wilson's wartime leadership by refusing to support American participation in the League of Nations. Still moving on an isolationist current two decades after World War I, the Congress during Franklin Roosevelt's first and second terms restricted the president's ability to send arms to allies facing German aggression. After World War II, Congress obstructed Truman's efforts to persuade the Chinese to accept Mao Tse-tung into a coalition government as a way out of their civil war. Congress also bound Truman's hands in foreign policy development by seeking to cut Marshall Plan aid to postwar Europe and by forcing American loans to the Franco government in Spain over the president's objections.

In response to the presidential rampage in Vietnam, the Congress debated at length various means by which it could constrain a president's war-making powers yet leave him free to respond to crises. The result was the War Powers Act of 1973, enacted over President Nixon's veto. According to this law, a president may send American troops into combat for no more than sixty days, unless a joint resolution of Congress during that period demands an immediate end to the engagement. After sixty days Congress must explicitly approve all further military involvement. This act seemed to end unilateral war making by presidents, although it was also the first time that Congress had explicitly acknowledged that a president may dispatch troops without authorization.

Some observers believe that congressional constraint of presidential freedom in foreign policy simply shows the American system of checks and balances at work. Presidents, however, have worried since the passage of the War Powers Act about their ability to respond to crises: As Gerald Ford noted, "There can be only one commander-in-chief."

President Carter's record with Congress in foreign affairs, however, suggests that presidential concerns may be exaggerated. Presidents are still the preeminent force in international matters. Carter, despite a chronically shaky relationship with Congress, was nevertheless able to win a two-thirds Senate

[19] *Ex parte Milligan,* 4 Wall 2, 125 (1866).
[20] Schlesinger, *Imperial Presidency,* p. 68.

majority for the Panama Canal treaty; he also won tests with Congress over the sale of nuclear fuel to India, the sale of jets to Saudi Arabia, lifting the embargo on weapons to Turkey, lifting the Rhodesian sanctions, and rejecting the B-1 bomber (in each case he favored the action). The SALT II treaty with the Soviet Union was his only major foreign policy initiative that failed.

Domestic Affairs The tale of the presidency in foreign affairs is, on balance, one of gradually expanding executive power punctuated by resistance — often short lived — from Congress and the Court. The president is still far and away the most influential shaper of our country's international relations. Whether through personal summitry, the decision to threaten or employ armed force, or the use of a spectacular envoy like Henry Kissinger to intercede in conflicts around the world, the president can perform on the world stage in ways that Congress simply cannot.

On the domestic side of the presidential job, matters are somewhat different. Here the president is often one in a cast of thousands, rising only occasionally above the clamor on the national stage to steal a scene with a few arresting lines. For this reason, perhaps, domestic policy has generally held less allure than foreign affairs for modern presidents and has commanded less of their energy. There is no better way to understand the frustration and sense of powerlessness presidents face in their role in this area than to examine the domestic record with respect to two major presidential functions: legislative leadership and economic policymaking.

Legislative Leadership. The president is often called the "chief legislator" of the nation. The title derives mainly from the constitutional requirement in Article II, Section 3 that the president give Congress "Information of the State of the Union, and recommend to their Consideration such Measures as he shall judge necessary and expedient." The annual State of the Union message has become an occasion for presidents to make major policy statements and to urge Congress to consider their programs. The notion of chief legislator also stems from the fact that the president has run on a party platform that lays out policy priorities and program promises.

Congress has seldom been eager to accommodate presidents, however. George Washington himself had to endure a month-long delay in his election because the required number of legislators took their time in getting to Philadelphia to witness the electoral count. The legislative box score of recent presidents suggests that Congress is still as uncooperative as it was when it kept George Washington waiting: John Kennedy, for example, saw only about 40 percent of his programs passed by Congress. Kennedy had campaigned hard in 1960 on domestic issues that seemed to command wide public interest, including medical care for the aged and federal aid to education. But once in the White House, Kennedy felt reluctant to push for his New Frontier program as hard as he could. For one thing, he had won the presidency by the narrowest of margins and was wary about pushing his program on a divided country.

A bigger obstacle was the coalition in Congress between Republicans and conservative southern Democrats. Together they blocked most of JFK's legislative proposals. One piece of domestic legislation after another failed during the Kennedy administration: federal aid for elementary, secondary, and college education; Medicare; wilderness preservation; a Youth Conservation Corps measure. His notable domestic successes, which came early in his presidency, were the passage of an area-redevelopment bill, aimed mainly at Appalachia (which had been on the congressional agenda since the Eisenhower years), and a manpower training bill. The record is a slim one. The New Frontier was more a state of mind than a successful legislative program.

In a similar fashion, Richard Nixon watched about two-thirds of his major domestic proposals fall victim to lack of congressional interest, including government reorganization, welfare reform (the Family Assistance Plan), and special revenue sharing. His successor, Gerald Ford, made few major domestic proposals during his twenty-nine months in the White House, except for a campaign-inspired suggestion for a massive increase in the national park system. It was duly ignored by Congress.

Jimmy Carter's legislative success record was comparable to Kennedy's. Congress scuttled many of his major domestic proposals, including tax reform, an urban-development bank, a consumer-affairs agency, and hospital cost containment.

Of course, not all presidents have such unhappy experiences with Congress. Franklin Roosevelt and Lyndon Johnson compiled impressive domestic records, as did Woodrow Wilson and Theodore Roosevelt. What explains the different capacities of presidents to get their programs through Congress?

Lyndon Johnson and Woodrow Wilson each had a large party majority in Congress; but, then, so did Kennedy and Carter. Clearly, belonging to the same party as the congressional majority is not sufficient to win passage of presidential proposals. FDR and Lyndon Johnson were both aided by their accession to power in times of great crisis — Roosevelt in the depths of the Depression and LBJ in the wake of Kennedy's assassination. Congress in both cases was receptive to vigorous leadership. But a president must seek to lead the nation in noncrisis times as well.

Although such situational factors are clearly important, a number of observers believe that presidential-congressional relations are shaped by the more enduring ways in which presidents use their resources to bargain with and influence Congress. Presidents vary in their political skills: Some are good at politics, others are not.

What kinds of resources do presidents have in their dealings with Congress? First of all, they have *time* and *attentiveness*. Some presidents remain aloof from the legislative process; others are in constant contact with their party leadership in Congress, on the phone with wavering legislators, or otherwise trying to maintain a close involvement in the workings of Congress. No president was better at this than Lyndon Johnson: "There is but one way for a President to deal with Congress," he once commented, "and that is continuously, incessantly, and without interruption."[21] Aside from personal involvement in the legislative process, presidents also rely to varying degrees on the White House Office of Congressional Relations. Created under President Eisenhower, the OCR keeps track of the progress of administration bills in Congress and lobbies legislators.

Presidents also have *favors* to hold out in return for congressional support; they can apply *muscle;* and they can *mobilize public opinion and interest groups* to put pressure on Congress. *Favors* can range from making sure that a senator's friend is appointed to the federal judiciary to posing for a photograph with an important constituent of a congresswoman to making sure that certain districts get approval for water projects. Such favors are usually employed as rewards for loyalty, but occasionally a president may hope to induce future support by distributing patronage.

Muscle refers to putting very heavy pressure on members of Congress. Sometimes this involves explicit presidential threats. President Kennedy occasionally used such "hardball" tactics, once ordering the Bureau of the Budget (now the Office of Management and Budget) to drop funding for a project sponsored by a senator who had voted against an administration measure. President Nixon was no stranger to the use of muscle tactics either: He once threatened several senators opposed to his Supreme Court nominations of Clement Haynesworth and G. Harrold Carswell with the cutoff of national campaign funds, elimination of public works projects in their states, an end to access to the White House, and even an Internal Revenue Service audit of their tax returns.[22] As one presidential aide in another administration described muscle to an interviewer, "You insist, as much as you can with these people. And you can be pretty insistent."[23]

Some rough tactics have a way of backfiring, of course, especially when threatened legislators defiantly harden their positions. Perhaps a more effective way to bring presidential pressure to bear on Congress is by mobilizing outside interest groups to lobby legislators on behalf of an administration bill. Lyndon Johnson's aides drummed up support for an aid-to-education bill from religious groups and teachers' organizations in a classic illustration of successful politicking.

Carter's domestic failures probably could be attributed in large part to his aloofness from the world of Congress. Never a member of Congress himself, Carter campaigned in 1976 as an outsider, without a political base in Washington, against the federal "establishment." Once in office, he often displayed a pious style that angered many members of Congress. Carter was never eager to consult regularly with legislators, and some believed that he preferred a "government by surprise." Making deals, as one student of the presidency has pointed out, seemed alien to Carter. "Thus he gladly sold the presidential

[21] John Manley, "Presidential Power and White House Lobbying," *Political Science Quarterly* 93 (Summer 1978): 265.
[22] Pious, *The American Presidency,* p. 193.
[23] Quoted in Manley, "Presidential Power," p. 268.

yacht, the *Sequoia*, an action many congressmen say, in retrospect, was a big mistake. It was on that pleasure boat that Lyndon Johnson and his cabinet did some of their most effective congressional relations lobbying."[24] In short, Carter was less successful with Congress than some other recent presidents in part because he would not or could not use the resources he had at hand.

Presidential Vetoes.   Sometimes the president's problem is not how to get Congress to act on something but rather how to stop it from doing so. Faced with this problem, presidents may rely on their constitutional veto power (Article I, Section 7), a weapon of last resort. Congress still may, of course, override a veto by a two-thirds vote of each house; but such overrides are rare, as Table 6.1 shows. Carter, incidentally, was the first president since Harry Truman to have vetoes overridden by a Congress controlled by his own party.

Table 6.1   Presidential Vetoes and Congressional Overrides, Washington through Carter

President	Total Vetoes	Overridden	President	Total Vetoes	Overridden
Washington	2	—	Arthur	12	1
Adams	—	—	Cleveland	413	2
Jefferson	—	—	Harrison	44	1
Madison	7	—	Cleveland	170	5
Monroe	1	—	McKinley	42	—
Adams	—	—	Roosevelt	82	1
Jackson	12	—	Taft	39	1
Van Buren	—	—	Wilson	44	6
Harrison	—	—	Harding	6	—
Tyler	10	1	Coolidge	50	4
Polk	3	—	Hoover	37	3
Taylor	—	—	Roosevelt	635	9
Fillmore	—	—	Truman	250	12
Pierce	9	5	Eisenhower	181	2
Buchanan	7	—	Kennedy	21	—
Lincoln	6	—	Johnson	30	—
Johnson	29	15	Nixon	43	6
Grant	93	4	Ford	66	12
Hayes	13	1	Carter	31	2
Garfield	—	—			

Source: *Presidential Vetoes: 1789–1961* (Washington, D.C.: U.S. Government Printing Office, 1961), p. iv.; *Congressional Quarterly Almanac*, 1976, p. 28.
Carter information supplied by the White House.

[24] Thomas E. Cronin, "A Resurgent Congress and the Imperial Presidency," *Political Science Quarterly* 95 (Summer 1980): 228–29.

Historically, presidents used their veto power mostly against so-called private bills, that is, legislation designed to aid particular individuals or private businesses. Presidents Nixon and Ford, however, facing overwhelmingly Democratic Congresses, used their veto power as a negative device for shaping social policy. Both sought to curb public spending and slow the expansion of government by vetoing a wide range of social programs passed by Congress. Ford, for example, vetoed a public-employment bill, a housing assistance bill, a school lunch program, a veterans' benefits aid bill, aid to the handicapped, a tax cut, oil price controls, strip mining regulation, and air pollution controls, to name only a few. Ford's veto strategy, however, so broad in scope, produced a rate of congressional overrides exceeded only during the Andrew Johnson administration after the Civil War.

Whether the task is getting a program through Congress or sustaining a veto, it is clear that the presidential role of chief legislator, especially in domestic affairs, is not an easy one. Congress is not awed by presidents, and it seldom does their bidding without a fight. High rates of presidential success in achieving the passage of domestic legislation are rare and almost always come in times of crisis or during the "honeymoon" period, the first few months of a new president's administration. Understanding this, Reagan advisor David Stockman and others constantly stressed the need for speed in getting the president's economic program to Congress as soon as possible after the inauguration. And the extraordinary record of domestic legislation under Franklin Roosevelt and Lyndon Johnson, it is important to remember, came in brief spurts followed by long periods of congressional inaction and resistance. All this is, of course, the working out of the system of checks and balances envisioned by the Founding Fathers. But it makes for frequent presidential frustration, for a sense of the president's powerlessness, for public impatience, and for an impression of White House failure.

Economic Policymaking.   The economic responsibilities now vested in the president are far beyond the powers and capabilities of any single public official. Like King Canute before the tides, presidents are relatively powerless before the fluctuations of a complex world economy. Cheap labor in Korea, OPEC's oil cartel, the rise of gold prices on the London money markets, and the production of efficient Japanese automobiles are all examples of forces that shape the American economy but over which presidents have only the most tangential influence. To make matters even more difficult, economists who advise the president seem neither able to agree on the nature of the dynamics of the modern world economy nor even to understand it very well.

Yet by law the president is the guardian and manager of American prosperity and productivity. The Employment Act of 1946 singles out the president as the official who is "to foster and promote free competitive enterprise, to avoid economic fluctuations or to diminish the effects thereof, and to maintain employment, production, and purchasing power." Few presidential tasks are so complex and so likely to be unfulfilled.

For purposes of analysis we may usefully divide the president's economic responsibilities into two parts: foreign trade and domestic fiscal policy. In an effort to strengthen the national economy, presidents must monitor the balance of trade between the United States and its trading partners, protect the integrity of the dollar on the world market, and attempt to protect United States industry from foreign competition. In addition, the president is always on the lookout to serve as chief salesman for American goods, particularly farm products, arms, and high technology.

Formal presidential authority in the area of foreign trade is not extensive: Presidents may on occasion strike a trade deal with another nation, and some congressional acts delegate to the chief executive the responsibility of imposing or raising tariffs on particular goods. But presidents also use their obligation to monitor foreign trade as a way of gaining influence and taking initiatives in the domestic economy. Take the case of the ailing United States steel industry, for example. American steel producers, working in aging plants with outmoded technology, are no longer competitive with Japanese and European mills. With cheaper foreign steel entering the American market, domestic steel production in 1978 fell to its lowest level since 1962. Many United States companies, unable to sell their steel, closed plants around the country, bringing hardship to steel towns and steelworkers.

In 1978 President Carter appointed a Steel Tripartite Advisory Committee, composed of business, government, and labor representatives, to make recommendations. The committee's report, released just before the 1980 election, recommended government support of modernization of American mills and equipment, programs to help communities where steel plants have closed down, and a variety of mechanisms to protect domestic producers from foreign steelmakers whose cheaper product is subsidized by their own governments. Carter adopted many of the specific suggestions as part of a package of economic policy recommendations to Congress. To revive and protect the steel industry, the president argued, would be to produce "more secure jobs and more prosperous communities."[25]

The president's major economic responsibility revolves mainly about the establishment of *fiscal policy*, that is, the coordinated use of taxes and expenditures to affect the nation's economy. To perform this policy task, presidents command a substantial army of data gatherers and interpreters in the Departments of Labor, Commerce, and the Treasury; a Council of Economic Advisors (established in 1946); the Office of Management and Budget; and private analysts and advisors. Through continual review of figures on productivity; interest rates (influenced by the Federal Reserve Board, which controls the money supply); personal earnings and savings; the gross national product; unemployment; the Consumer Price Index; and other indicators, presidents gain information that helps to shape their tax policy and budget plans.

[25] Steel Tripartite Advisory Commission, *Report to the President on the United States Steel Industry*, September 25, 1980.

It is evident that the sheer number of economic variables that go into the making of fiscal policy, as well as their interpretation, make this job extremely complex. Sometimes presidents are faced with seemingly impossible choices. For example, orthodox economic doctrines call for deficit government spending or tax cuts in times of high unemployment; but many think that this only fuels inflation. Either raising taxes or decreasing government expenditures has been the traditional remedy for inflation since the period just after World War II, since these strategies lessen consumer demand and decrease private-sector production. In recent years, however, the economy has been plagued by both sharply rising prices and ever increasing numbers of jobless workers. Since the remedy for the one situation is thought to worsen the other, presidents have believed that they simply had to establish priorities. In 1978, for example, President Carter decided that job creation was more important than addressing inflation; hence, he expanded federally financed public-employment programs and business tax incentives designed to stimulate investment and create jobs. As the 1980 election approached, however, inflation became the president's chief concern. As pundits were quick to note, the jobless are less likely than consumers to go to the polls.

President Reagan entered office promising to fight inflation and unemployment simultaneously through the application of new "supply-side" economic theories. Rather than trying to change consumption patterns, supply-side economists seek to increase investment. They call for cutting government expenditures while at the same time cutting taxes. Supply-side economists believe that the added money in people's pockets will be saved or invested rather than spent for consumer goods (the latter would fuel inflation), thus upgrading and expanding industry's productive capacity, creating jobs, and promoting real growth. As economic growth occurs, inflation is supposed to moderate.

Although presidents may send periodic messages to Congress calling for specific fiscal measures — tax cuts or investment tax credits for business, for example — the annual culmination of their fiscal thinking is contained in the budget, the plan for raising and spending the money it takes to run the nation's government and programs. Although Congress is constitutionally empowered to raise and spend money, drawing up the overall national budget has been considered a major executive function for more than half a century. Up until the Civil War the budget process was controlled largely by two congressional committees. Then these committees began to delegate their powers and responsibilities to other committees, and control over the budget became highly fragmented. In 1921 Congress passed the Budget and Accounting Act. This act created the Bureau of the Budget, located in the Treasury Department. It also commanded the president to submit an executive budget to the Congress each January. This massive plan for raising and allocating the government's money quickly became the base from which the Congress worked. Congress reacted to presidential budget initiatives; although modifying priorities and expenditure levels here and there, it generally accepted the basic structure of national expenditures he outlined. In 1939 Congress allowed

Franklin Roosevelt to establish the Executive Office of the President — that is, the professional staff that advises and serves the chief executive — and the Bureau of the Budget became one of its first components. This brought the office with major responsibility for developing the budget under the president's direct control and further strengthened his influence in the budget-making process.

As noted in Chapter 5, in recent years Congress has challenged presidential domination of the budget process, in large part as a reaction to Richard Nixon's abuses of the president's *impoundment powers*. Impoundment involves the president's refusal to allow the expenditure of money authorized and appropriated by Congress for a specific purpose. In the past, presidents used this power sparingly, mostly for the purposes of economizing by deferring expenditures temporarily. But Nixon's impoundments far exceeded those of his predecessors and extended to major programs with which the president disagreed. By 1973 Nixon's impoundments amounted to $15 billion and affected more than 100 federal programs.

These unprecedented impoundments, which had the effect of nullifying the congressional will (Nixon even impounded funds for programs passed over his veto), led Congress to pass the Congressional Budget and Control Act of 1974. Not only did the act greatly curb the president's freedom to impound money; but it also, through the creation of the Congressional Budget Office, substantially bolstered the ability of Congress to participate in the budget process. This gave Congress its own staff of economic experts and researchers, reducing its dependence on the OMB for its economic information. Furthermore, the act mandates that Congress establish spending targets each year to serve as an alternative to the executive budget.

It is clear that economic policymaking is one of the most difficult of all presidential responsibilities. President Reagan discovered this early on. As a candidate, Reagan had readily blamed Jimmy Carter for the nation's economic condition. Once in office, however, he came face to face with the limits of his power. Committed to drastic spending cuts, he discovered that more than three-quarters of the federal budget consists of expenditures that the Office of Management and Budget told him were "relatively uncontrollable under current law." Some of these items consist of interest on the federal debt and prior contracts and are immune to the budget cutter's axe. The largest segment of "uncontrollable expenditures" are *entitlement transfers* — benefits to which eligible people are entitled by law, such as Social Security, federal pensions, food stamps, Medicare, and veterans' benefits. To make matters even more difficult for a president, many of these expenditures are *indexed* — they increase with the cost of living. Thus, each percentage-point rise in inflation automatically lifts spending on indexed entitlements by about $2.5 billion.[26] Although President Reagan did manage to persuade Congress to cut food stamp outlays in his first budget and to move toward eliminating or reducing certain Social Security

[26] *The New York Times*, July 23, 1981.

benefits, the political costs of entitlement cuts are very high and therefore very constraining. President Reagan had pledged to increase not to cut defense expenditures, which account for nearly one fifth of the federal budget. This left less than 10 percent of the budget available for cutting, and Reagan was quick to caution the American people not to expect economic miracles.

Since the end of the 1960s Americans' purchasing power has eroded severely, interest rates have soared, and economic growth has come to a virtual standstill. Presidents are expected to deal with these problems. But it is clear that the complexity of poorly understood economic processes, the large number of official actors in economic policymaking, the disagreement among economists regarding remedies, the unwieldy nature of the national budget, and foreign economic trends all converge to make the president's efforts to master the nation's economic fortunes a task with a high risk of failure.

THE PRESIDENTIAL ESTABLISHMENT

The burdens and frustrations of presidential leadership do not end with the struggle to shape foreign policy and pass a domestic program. The president is also the manager of the government's vast executive branch. He must keep abreast of the operations of the various agencies and cabinet-level departments, occasionally seek to reorganize them, appoint their top executives as well as a host of second-rank officials, coordinate the budget demands of the various agencies, and oversee or participate in their major policy decisions. This is, of course, an impossible task for a single individual. There are approximately 3 million civilian employees in the executive branch, organized into some 1,800 agencies, offices, bureaus, and departments. Most of them are civil servants with well-established routines, who came to their jobs long before the president came to his job and who may look forward to remaining in government service long after the president has left office.

To manage the executive branch the president needs a great deal of help. We may speak of the president's help as the *presidential establishment*. Like the other facets of presidential power, all the help that surrounds the president both increases his resources and constrains him seriously in certain ways. We usually think of the presidential establishment as consisting of two major components: the cabinet and the Executive Office. To these we will add the vice-president.

The Cabinet

The cabinet is a small body of councillors who advise the president and participate in policymaking. It is composed of the heads of the thirteen major executive departments, ranging from State and Defense to Transportation and Agriculture (see Chapter 7, The Federal Bureaucracy), as well as other assorted officials who have been accorded cabinet rank (such as the United Nations ambassador). Cabinet officers are appointed by the president, subject to Senate confirmation, and serve at his pleasure. The Constitution makes no mention of a cabinet, so it is an extralegal body with no formal authority or function.

George Washington, however, established the practice of meeting with his secretaries of state, war, and treasury as a group, and the custom has persisted to this day.

Few presidents have relied heavily on their cabinets. Lincoln regarded the cabinet as an unnecessary nuisance. Teddy Roosevelt believed that vigorous presidential leadership precluded consultation with a cabinet. John F. Kennedy believed that the cabinet was an unwieldy body and that the best advice came from smaller and more specialized groups of people. And Richard Nixon, perhaps to a greater degree than most presidents, ignored his cabinet in favor of personal aides and advisors.

One exception to this pattern was Dwight Eisenhower, who placed heavy emphasis on what he called "the team." The contrast is striking between this unusually cohesive and integrated cabinet and the cabinets of Kennedy, Johnson, and Nixon, whose domestic department secretaries felt isolated and barred from the inner circle around the president. President Reagan has taken the Eisenhower pattern as his model.

Often the members of the cabinet are relegated to second rank in favor of advisors without formal cabinet status. These figures frequently have direct access to the president and serve as leading policy shapers, eclipsing and bypassing the cabinet secretary responsible for the area. Henry Kissinger, who dominated foreign policymaking as a White House advisor even before Richard Nixon appointed him secretary of State, is a good example. Harry Hopkins, who coordinated domestic policy for FDR, is another.

The Executive Office Most presidents are more likely to rely on advisors in the Executive Office than on the cabinet as a body. The Executive Office consists of a number of staff aides, referred to collectively as the White House Office, and a variety of formal commissions and agencies (see Figure 7.1). The Executive Office was established in 1939, first by executive order and then by the Reorganization Act of that year, chiefly to institutionalize staff assistance for the president. The various units of the Executive Office develop policy, take on administrative responsibilities, gather information, and advise the president. Presidents create and abolish units in the Executive Office according to their particular interests, the problems they believe deserve priority, and their ideological bent. Lyndon Johnson, for example, created the Office of Economic Opportunity to guide his War on Poverty, but it was later eliminated by President Nixon. President Reagan abolished the Council on Wage and Price Stability soon after taking office.

The major units of the Executive Office include the Office of Management and Budget (OMB), the National Security Council, and the Council of Economic Advisors. The OMB is responsible not only for helping the president put together the national budget, but also for managing the operations of the federal bureaucracy. Since Nixon established this successor to the Bureau of the Budget, the agency has been a major political tool in the partisan struggle to fashion a national budget. David Stockman, President Reagan's head of the

OMB, became one of the most prominent figures in the new administration as he led the fight for the first Republican budget.

The National Security Council, which brings together high-ranking military and diplomatic officials, advises the president on defense and security matters, while the Council of Economic Advisors, often composed of academic economists, participates in economic policymaking.

In addition to the formal agencies of the Executive Office, the president commands a large White House staff. This includes a wide range of personal aides and assistants, ranging from the press secretary to the chief White House counsel to the president's personal secretary and his chief of staff.

The number of people on the White House staff has increased substantially since the establishment of the Executive Office in 1939 (see Table 6.2). Such growth, of course, reflects the widening scope of governmental activities; nevertheless, many observers speak of a "bloated" or "swollen" presidential establishment. After the staff reached a peak in the Nixon White House, Jimmy Carter found it politically advantageous to promise drastic reductions, which he carried out successfully.

The growth of the presidential establishment, and in particular of the White House staff, has been a mixed blessing for the president. The major liability has been the isolation of the president, who is all too often shielded from alternative viewpoints and sources of information by a staff whose loyalties are fiercely personal. The president operates in an "environment of deference"; no staff member has the courage to tell the president "go soak your head," as George Reedy, a White House press secretary under Johnson, put it.[27] A presi-

Table 6.2   Growth of the White House Staff, from Roosevelt to Carter

President	Year	Number of Staff Members
Franklin Roosevelt	1940	177
Harry Truman	1948	268
Dwight Eisenhower	1956	392
John F. Kennedy	1962	432
Lyndon Johnson	1966	497
Richard Nixon	1970	632
Gerald Ford	1975	560
Jimmy Carter	1980	339

Source: Carter figures are from the White House. All others are from Hugh Heclo, *Studying the Presidency*, a report to the Ford Foundation, 1977, pp. 36–37.

[27] George Reedy, *The Twilight of the Presidency* (New York: World, 1970), p. 10.

dent can become shut off from his critics by a staff determined to protect him at all costs. Surrounded by "yes men" who are determined not to cross the president and who have no independent bases in politics or the civil service, the president can easily pursue a course of action whose alternatives have not been adequately and honestly debated or challenged in the inner sanctum. The country's abortive Vietnam policy and the Watergate scandal both flourished in this environment of isolation and deference.

The Vice-President

The vice-presidency of the United States is perhaps the most paradoxical job in Washington. Powerful men, like Hubert Humphrey, have been known to fade away in the obscurity of the office; yet thirteen vice-presidents have become president. In the period since 1945, Presidents Truman, Johnson, Nixon, and Ford all served in the second spot before attaining the White House.

Presidential candidates normally do not choose their running mates for the quality of the help they might offer or their potential performance as president. Rather they seek to strengthen their ticket by adding regional, ethnic, or ideological balance. John F. Kennedy, a Catholic eastern liberal, chose Lyndon Johnson, a Protestant Texas moderate. When it was Johnson's turn to run, he chose Humphrey, a northern liberal. Many observers believe that Gerald Ford's choice of Senator Robert Dole, a conservative midwesterner like himself, contributed heavily to the Republicans' loss in 1976 by failing to provide a sufficiently balanced ticket. President Reagan's choice of George Bush as a running mate conforms to the general pattern: Bush, with ties in Texas and Connecticut, brought a moderate image and eastern establishment connections to a ticket headed by a California conservative.

The formal and informal roles of the vice-president are not impressive. Mostly the job is a matter of waiting in the wings. The vice-president must succeed the president in case of the latter's death, and, according to the Twenty-fifth Amendment, becomes acting president if the president is for any other reason "unable to discharge the powers and duties of his office." In addition, the vice-president presides over the Senate (few make it their full-time occupation), sits on the National Security Council, attends cabinet meetings, and heads various special boards and task forces as the president sees fit.

Presidents invariably promise a large role for their vice-presidents in making policy and running the country. But more often vice-presidents are employed for ceremonial duties. Eisenhower sent Vice-President Nixon on numerous goodwill trips around the world. Carter sent Walter Mondale to Europe with greetings from the new administration. Presidents may also use their understudies to play the hatchet man, that is, to take highly aggressive or extremely partisan positions in situations where the president prefers to remain above the fray. Spiro Agnew's assaults on the press served to convey the Nixon administration's displeasure with the nation's journalists without directly involving the president in the attack.

For the most part, vice-presidents are not included in the inner circle of policymakers in the White House, although Mondale was something of an exception to the rule. Vice-presidential advice, if it is asked for, is often taken lightly and given little publicity. A story from the Eisenhower years suggests the limits of vice-presidential help. Ike was asked at the end of his two terms if he could give an example of a major idea of Vice-President Nixon's that had been adopted by the White House. The president replied: "If you give me a week, I might think of one."

THE PRESIDENT AND THE NEWS MEDIA For the president of the United States, privacy is a rare commodity. Wherever he goes, a cameraman or reporter follows, observing not only the historic moment of the attempted assassination of Ronald Reagan but also the tiny embarrassment of Ford bumping his head on a helicopter door or Carter slipping on the ice. The press can be intrusive and sometimes tasteless, as when it presses the First Lady to consider, on national television, the possibility that her children have used drugs, or prints a photograph of the surgery scar on Lyndon Johnson's belly. But the news media — the newspapers, magazines, radio, and TV — cannot be viewed merely as purveyors of gossip, human interest, or sensationalism. In the modern era, the mass media are the principal link between the people and the president. Through the press, presidents inform the public and seek to mold its attitudes. The public in turn relies on the media for its knowledge and image of the president.

If the news media were wholly passive, neutral conduits of information and image, the relationship between them and the president would scarcely merit attention. But in fact the president and practicing journalists tend to view the purposes of the media somewhat differently. The consequence of these different perspectives is to build into the relationship between the president and the press a considerable degree of conflict.

Presidents generally wish to use the news media for three basic purposes: *agenda setting*, in which the president seeks to use the media to establish the issues he believes the nation must address; *reporting*, in which the president uses the media to pass on information about what his administration is doing; and *appealing*, in which the president seeks support for his proposals.

Presidents carry out these tasks in a variety of ways. Daily briefings of journalists are offered by the president's press secretary, and periodically presidents themselves answer questions in the unrehearsed setting of the press conference. Although most presidents pledge initially to meet often with journalists, the frequency of press conferences typically declines as press scrutiny becomes sharper over the course of an administration. Woodrow Wilson, the first president to hold formal press conferences, discontinued the practice al-

[28] R. Locander, "Carter and the Press: The First Two Years," *Presidential Studies Quarterly*, vol. X (Winter 1980), p. 109.

together because of what he considered to be the "impertinence and stupidity of reporters."[28]

With the advent of radio and television, presidents discovered that they could communicate directly with the American people (an estimated 60 million people will watch a major presidential address today) without undergoing the potential embarrassment of sharp questions or mistakes inherent in the rough-and-tumble press conference. The major TV networks, however, have recently become less willing to put free air time at the disposal of presidents when a proposed appearance seems more to serve political rather than public interest purposes. Today, television executives make their own judgments as to the newsworthiness of what presidents have to say on prime time TV.

The news media, then, are not always willing to be used as the president wishes. As journalists see it, the functions of the news media are to report "the facts" and at the same time to provide a kind of independent check on government. Because the press cannot report *all* the facts, reporters and editors must be selective. One source of conflict between press and presidents is the way the press chooses which news to report. For example, the press often focuses on a presidential blunder as being particularly newsworthy. During the Ford-Carter television debates in the 1976 campaign, Gerald Ford's remark that Poland was free of Russian influence received far more media attention than most of his policy pronouncements.

A second source of conflict arises from the media's conviction that a free press can help check abuses or unwise use of government power. "Investigative reporting" — that is, in-depth efforts by the press to explore possible misdeeds and shady doings — may embarrass the president or frustrate his plans. To the press, this is a valuable function; to the president, it is often a great nuisance, for the publicity goes on whether or not any misdeeds actually have occurred. In the case of Richard Nixon, reporting on the Watergate affair set the stage for his downfall. Press investigation of Abe Fortas' questionable financial dealings made it impossible for Lyndon Johnson to name Fortas chief justice of the Supreme Court, and the revelations in the press of G. Harrold Carswell's antiblack actions led to the Senate's refusal to confirm this Nixon nominee to the Supreme Court. During the Carter administration the press embarrassed the president by revealing his brother's dealings with the Libyans and by exploring the unusual financial dealings of the director of the Office of Management and Budget, Bert Lance, an old friend of Carter's.

In general, the tension between the media and the president is healthy for the country. Although the press is not always unbiased in its reporting (most newspapers and TV stations are editorially Republican; a few, particularly the major newspapers like *The New York Times* and *The Washington Post*, are Democratic), it still serves as a major limit on the abuse of power. Knowing their actions may be publicized, presidents are more careful about what they do than they might be if secrecy were easier. If the press is occasionally myopic or vindictive, it may nevertheless take much credit for guaranteeing the people's right to know what their government is doing and plans to do.

HOW CITIZENS VIEW THE PRESIDENCY

Public attitudes toward the presidency and presidents are exceedingly complex. Occasionally they exhibit sharp reversals; always they embrace certain contradictions. In this last section we shall offer a variety of generalizations about public thinking on presidents and the office itself.

Public attitudes toward the president are viewed in Washington, and especially in the White House, as crucial. (Lyndon Johnson found the polls so compelling that he carried the weekly Gallup data around in his pocket and waved favorable results in front of his visitors.) Popular criticism in particular can be a powerful and damaging force. For example, in response to widespread public complaint that his campaign remarks about Ronald Reagan were "mean," Jimmy Carter felt obliged to apologize on national television. And Richard Nixon released damaging tape recordings of his own conversations during the Watergate affair when public anger and impatience reached a peak. But reading the shifts and complexities of public attitudes toward the presidency can be as tricky as reading tea leaves. The following generalizations, which summarize much of what we seem to know about citizen perspectives on presidents and the presidency, show why this is so.

Attitudes Toward Presidential Power

Even as Americans have respected the presidential office, distrust of presidential power has run like a thread through American history. During the Constitutional Convention, suspicion of executive authority was evident in the debates over how to fashion the presidency so that its powers would be both significant and limited. In the modern era a variety of poll data shows this distrust expressed in several ways.

For example, since the 1930s major polling organizations have been asking Americans whether "the president should have more or less power than he now has." Until the Carter presidency, the number of people who answered "less" was twice that of those who said "more." By the end of the Carter administration, however, people were ready to blame everything from rising meat prices to gasoline shortages to America's diminished power in world affairs on weak presidential leadership. When the Gallup poll asked the public in 1979 whether it favored really strong leadership "without worrying about how Congress or the Supreme Court might feel," 63 percent said yes.[29]

But this yearning for a powerful leader was perhaps a temporary response by a frustrated citizenry: In general, the level of confidence in the presidency has been comparatively low all during the 1970s, as we can see in Table 6.3. Compared with those of the 1960s, contemporary attitudes are characterized by acute distrust.

Declines in the Incumbent's Popularity

Every president from Truman to Carter, with the exception of Eisenhower, experienced a fairly steady decline in popularity over each of his terms. The Gallup poll has been asking a national sample of Americans the same question about a dozen times each year since the beginning of Franklin Roosevelt's

[29] Cronin, "A Resurgent Congress," p. 230.

Table 6.3 Confidence in Selected Institutions

"As far as people in charge of running (READ EACH ITEM) are concerned, would you say you have a great deal of confidence, only some confidence, or hardly any confidence at all in them?"

	Percentage Responding "Great Deal"					
	1980	1979	1977	1976	1973	1966
The Military	28	29	27	23	40	61
Television news	29	37	28	28	41	X
The Press	19	28	18	20	30	29
Major companies	16	18	20	16	29	55
The White House	18	15	31	11	18	X
Congress	18	18	17	9	X	42

X = not asked.
*In 1966 the Harris survey asked whether the public had confidence in the people in charge of running "the executive branch."
Source: ABC News — Harris Survey, November 24, 1980. Reprinted by permission of Louis Harris and Associates, Inc.

third term: "Do you approve or disapprove of the way President X is handling his job?" This simple question is the means by which we gauge presidential popularity.

Every president takes office in an aura of public good will. Most presidents are never again as popular as in their first few months. Even Harry Truman, Jimmy Carter, and Richard Nixon, our most unpopular presidents since World War II, came into office with very high approval ratings. Indeed, Truman's 87 percent is the highest approval rating on record. Gerald Ford, who entered the White House with 71 percent approving, touched off a precipitous decline with his sudden pardon of Richard Nixon. Within three months Ford's popularity fell below 40 percent. His average popularity was only 46 percent. President Reagan's popularity, which had been high at first, was lower after six months in office than that of any of his recent predecessors at the same point in their tenure.

The trend in Carter's approval ratings is shown in Figure 6.1. His average rating was only 44 percent. The low rating before the Democratic convention in July 1980 is the lowest ever recorded for any president, even lower than the mere 25 percent who approved of Nixon's handling of the job in the darkest days of Watergate. Prior to Gerald Ford's administration, the average public approval rating was a relatively solid 61 percent.

Eisenhower's case is unique. Although there were peaks and valleys in his popularity (which never dropped below 49 percent), its trend line scarcely resembles the steady and significant declines experienced by all the other mod-

Figure 6.1 President Carter's Approval Rating in the Gallup Poll

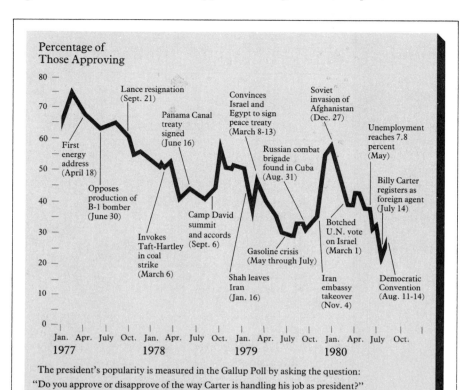

The president's popularity is measured in the Gallup Poll by asking the question: "Do you approve or disapprove of the way Carter is handling his job as president?" The graph shows the percentages of those who approve.

Source: *Congressional Quarterly*, September 13, 1980. Reprinted by permission.

ern presidents. One student of presidential opinion polls suggests that Eisenhower never experienced sharp declines in popularity because, especially on the domestic front, he did not do anything.[30] Lyndon Johnson and Harry Truman, both legislative activists, suffered greatly in the polls. This pattern is consistent with the American fear and distrust of presidential power: Those who do not act make few enemies; those who do act cannot fail to anger some and disappoint others.

This characteristic popularity decline also shows that Americans have at most times distinguished the institution of the presidency, which until Watergate had been held in high regard, from any given holder of the office, whose popularity generally declines steadily.

[30] John Mueller, "Presidential Popularity from Truman to Johnson," *American Political Science Review* 64 (March 1970): 31.

Rallying around the President Although presidential popularity rates tend to decline over the course of any given term, there are sudden temporary upturns, usually associated with dramatic international events in which the president is involved. Observe Jimmy Carter's high points in Figure 6.1. Many correspond to a diplomatic triumph (the Panama Canal Treaty, the Israeli-Egyptian peace accords) or to threats from abroad to perceived American interests (the discovery of Russian combat troops in Cuba, the Soviet invasion of Afghanistan). Such upturns in popularity have been called the "rally round the flag" phenomenon.[31] The American public generally closes ranks behind a president who takes bold and sometimes even risky actions in international affairs, *no matter what they are.* That is to say, any action by a president in foreign affairs increases his popular support.

Sometimes this support is won by the same president for diametrically opposed actions. For example, Lyndon Johnson's popularity reached high peaks shortly after his decisions to intensify the bombing of North Vietnam in 1966 and to halt that bombing in 1968.[32] Eisenhower's "rally points" included both the Korean armistice and the decision to send United States Marines into Lebanon. His popularity also spurted with a goodwill trip abroad and again a few months later with a decision not to go to Japan. Even failure in foreign adventures can increase a president's popularity: John F. Kennedy's ratings rose after the disastrous invasion of Cuba at the Bay of Pigs in 1961.

The most reasonable explanation of this rallying pattern is that the president serves for many people as the symbol and embodiment of the nation. In the international arena, it is he who commits the nation. When the country's prestige, international goals, or survival seem to be at stake, partisan differences and domestic complaints are forgotten as Americans close ranks. At such times people tend to be generous and uncritical in their support, providing, at least momentarily, vast leeway for a president to act.

Emotional Attachment to Presidents Americans have an emotional investment in their presidents that transcends partisan loyalties and the routine evaluations of politics that citizens make. This emotional attachment is apparently developed in childhood, before the individual has any sophisticated knowledge about the political system. The president is normally the first government figure of whom children become aware. Most American children have heard of "the President" by the time they are nine years old and can even name the incumbent.[33] Young children tend, in fact, to think that the president and the government are one and the same.

Children also tend to think of the president as benign, protective, helpful, and unusually powerful. More realistic perceptions of the president set in during the preadolescent years, but some scholars speculate that childhood idealization of the president has some carryover effects into adult political behavior.

---

[31] Mueller, "Presidential Popularity from Truman to Johnson," p. 21.

[32] Fred Greenstein, "What the President Means to Americans: Presidential 'Choice' Between Elections" in James D. Barber, ed., *Choosing the President* (Englewood Cliffs, N.J.: Prentice-Hall, 1974), p. 136.

[33] Ibid., p. 129.

However that may be, adult Americans do identify strongly with presidents and form strong psychological attachments to them. We see this most strikingly in the responses to deaths of presidents, events that assume personally traumatic dimensions for ordinary citizens. One survey conducted only days after Kennedy's assassination in 1963, for example, found that 25 percent of the sample reported having headaches in the four days after the shooting, 22 percent had upset stomachs, 48 percent had trouble sleeping, and 68 percent felt nervous and tense; others felt dizzy, had rapid heartbeats, experienced unusual sweating, and so on. Only 11 percent reported no unusual symptoms of distress.[34] These emotional and physical symptoms were shared by people who had been sympathetic to Kennedy and those who had not been, by northerners and southerners, by blacks and whites. It was as though all of America had lost a member of the family.

The depth of feeling displayed on the death of John Kennedy, a young, popular, and glamorous president (although his popularity was declining at the time of the assassination) seems natural. But there was a similar response to the death in 1901 — also by assassination — of William McKinley, a president of relatively insignificant accomplishment. According to one of McKinley's biographers, "Never was a man more deeply and widely mourned, not even the sainted Lincoln, nor the warmly esteemed Garfield. . . . The whole nation swung downward into the vale of grief."[35]

Even presidents who have died in office from causes other than assassination — FDR and Harding, for example — elicited extravagant displays of grief and mourning. Harding, indeed, was compared to Moses dying before he reached the promised land.

Although Americans may dislike, suspect, or criticize a particular president, although many of us scarcely pay attention to politics, we seem to have in some strange way a profound emotional tie to the president. It is this feeling, perhaps, as much as anything else, that makes a president so special, transforming an ordinary politician into a symbolic figure and universal family member of the American people.

THE CHARACTER OF PRESIDENTIAL POWER

The history of the American presidency can be read as the story of alternating periods of executive ascendancy, popular reaction, and executive decline. Clearly, a period of reaction set in at some point between the end of Lyndon Johnson's tenure and the midpoint of Richard Nixon's. Johnson, the visionary from the Pedernales country, who proclaimed the Great Society, promised blacks that "We Shall Overcome," and generated a legislative whirlwind in his first years in office, was all but hounded from the White House in 1968. Senator Eugene McCarthy, a political maverick and a harsh critic of our Vietnam venture, in effect vanquished Lyndon Johnson by promising that, if he were

[34] Paul B. Sheatsley and Jacob J. Feldman, "A National Survey of Public Reactions and Behavior," in Bradley S. Greenberg and Edwin B. Parker, eds., *The Kennedy Assassination and the American Public* (Stanford, Calif.: Stanford University Press, 1965), p. 158.
[35] Quoted in ibid., p. 169.

elected, he would avoid the power and majesty that had seemed to go with the job.

When Lyndon Johnson left office in January 1969, public reaction to presidential power had not yet permeated American society. But by the time Richard Nixon had established a record of warmaking, bombing, impoundment, executive privilege, deliberately mediocre Supreme Court appointments, and the crimes and deceits we know as Watergate, the reaction had become widespread and strong — and it forced him from office before the end of his term. The American people embraced Gerald Ford, who promised not programs, progress, or power, but openness and ordinariness. Ford's successor, Jimmy Carter, seemed to offer the American people much the same things.

The process of reaction to the "imperial presidency" of the 1960s was a piecemeal affair. It was in no way coordinated or directed, so we can see manifestations of this process in a variety of places, all aimed at cutting the president down to more human dimensions.

We can see reaction taking hold in the drive to unseat Nixon, which began as a very hushed discussion posed in hypothetical terms and culminated in a formal recommendation by the House Judiciary Committee on nationwide TV to impeach the president of the United States. We can see the attack on presidential power in congressional actions regarding the budget, warmaking powers, impoundment, and executive agreements. We can see it in the congressional investigations that laid bare presidential abuses of the intelligence services going back forty years. And we can see it in Jimmy Carter's continuation of the effort, begun by Gerald Ford, to dismantle the "imperial presidency." Within days after his inauguration, Carter had eliminated door-to-door limousine service for all White House staff members, forbidden the customary playing of "Hail to the Chief" in his honor, given a TV talk dressed in a sweater (and tie), and exhorted government officials to remember that they were public servants.

Carter soon discovered, however, that his efforts to "depomp the presidency," as his press secretary called it, did not sit well with the American people. Before long he had ordered the bands to resume playing "Hail to the Chief," and the informal "town meetings" with the public that marked his first years in office became less frequent. But to many Americans, Carter's brand of leadership was seen as ambivalent and ineffective, no matter what he tried. He appeared vacillating, buffeted by Iran, the Soviet Union, and OPEC. Some believed he had no stirring vision of America's future. For many voters the election of 1980 became a referendum on Carter's style of leadership and an opportunity to demand a more vigorous and self-confident presidency. "The 1980 results," one pollster commented, "were a call for order and stability. Things were out of control. The American people . . . were trying to say let's bring some control back to the system."[36]

Americans must still, however, face the question that has plagued them historically, namely, how to create a presidency that maximizes the possibility

[36] *The New York Times,* November 9, 1980.

for effective leadership in dealing with our problems while minimizing chances for abusing the trust of the people. No single election, no single candidate, is likely to provide a satisfactory answer to this old dilemma.

CONCLUSION We have explored two broad perspectives on the power of the presidency. Presidents themselves, burdened by the enormous expectations of the American people and indeed of the world, believe that their power is inadequate. Congress in particular has asserted itself in such areas as the control of American intelligence, warmaking, and budgeting, all at the expense of the president. To the American people, the president's power has often seemed both too great and too feeble. Abuse of presidential power in the late 1960s and early 1970s made it clear to the public that the man in the White House could act almost without meaningful constraints; but in the Carter years a diminished presidency came to seem acutely ineffective.

As the institution of the presidency exists today, many believe that occupants of the White House are destined to fail. Not only is the job too big and the expectations unrealistic, but the very problems that trouble people deeply these days — abortion, crime, drugs, gun control, busing — are not susceptible to resolution by presidential leadership. In the third century of the republic, the route to a restoration of public confidence in the presidency seems murky indeed.

SUGGESTIONS FOR FURTHER READING Barber, James D. *The Presidential Character,* 2nd ed. Englewood Cliffs, N.J.: Prentice-Hall, 1977. This is a highly readable and thorough exposition of the argument that personality shapes presidential performance.

Corwin, Edward. *The President: Office and Powers.* New York: New York University Press, 1980. An updating of a classic account of the institution of the presidency.

Cronin, Thomas. *The State of the Presidency,* 2nd ed. Boston: Little, Brown, 1980. Can we make the presidency safe for democracy?

Edwards, George. *Presidential Influence in Congress.* San Francisco: Freeman, 1980. One of the most comprehensive efforts to look at the relationship between the executive and the legislature.

Neustadt, Richard. *Presidential Power,* 2nd ed. New York: Wiley, 1980. An important treatment of how the use of power by individual incumbents fashions the institution.

Pious, Richard. *The American Presidency.* New York: Basic Books, 1979. One of the best of the recent comprehensive treatments of the presidency, focusing particularly on the weaknesses and contradictions in the institution.

Chapter 7 The Federal Bureaucracy

In the early 1970s, tensions between blacks and Chicanos in Bakersfield, California, increased; migrant workers in the Bakersfield area did not have dental care; and a bright, young idealist lost his job. This was the end product of well-intentioned efforts by federal bureaucrats working with a local community to implement legislation passed by Congress. The story is but one of many tragicomedies that can be told about the effect of bureaucratic rules and procedures on the best of motives. It is incidents like these that contribute to the public's image of the bureaucracy as a burden — if not a threat.

In March 1970 Congress passed the Migrant Health Act, which had been drafted by the Senate's Migratory Labor subcommittee.[1] The subcommittee's chairman, Walter Mondale, personally insisted that migrant workers, the population to be served, be involved in implementing the health-care programs. The federal agency responsible for administering the act was the Department of Health, Education, and Welfare (HEW), since 1980 known as the Department of Health and Human Services. This agency provided $2.6 million to its regional office in San Francisco and ordered it to establish a migrant workers' health program in accordance with the act.

---

[1] For further details, see Michael Aron, "Dumping $2.6 Million on Bakersfield (or How Not to Build a Migratory Farm Workers' Clinic)," *The Washington Monthly*, October 1972, pp. 23–32.

The HEW officials in San Francisco faced two serious problems. First, according to federal budget regulations, the money had to be spent by July 1 — now only six weeks away — or the funds would be forfeited back to the Treasury. Second, there were no known organizations in the migrant worker community through which the money could be channeled. The HEW bureaucrats responded to this situation by awarding the money to the Kern County Liberation Movement (KCLM), a black militant group in Bakersfield.

News of this action generated intense opposition from doctors, dentists, nurses, and public health officials in Bakersfield, who felt that they — not an inexperienced and militant group representing poor people — should administer such funds. Local opposition was also voiced by legislators, officials, and the press. This reaction prompted Dr. James Cavanaugh, HEW's deputy assistant secretary for health, to fly from Washington to San Francisco to question the behavior of that office. The result was a significant alteration of Senator Mondale's dictum regarding who should participate in the administration of the program. HEW established guidelines adding professional health-care providers to boards whose membership had been confined to health-care consumers.

The regional office of HEW resisted the direction of its headquarters in Washington, D.C. HEW officials in Washington suspended funds to the KCLM, but regional administrators kept providing it with "emergency" funds. The officials in San Francisco also selected as interim director of the project a young dental school graduate who was dynamic and competent, but unorthodox in his ideas and his dress. This appointment sparked a new round of controversy, which resulted in the dismissal of the interim director; the appointment of a more conventional public health official; and, for good measure, the cancellation of the dental health component of the program.

There still remained, of course, a major problem: The KCLM represented blacks, not migrant workers. After entrenching the Bakersfield medical establishment in the program's administration, HEW officials in Washington edged the KCLM out and brought Chicanos in. Naturally enough the black community resisted this shift, and HEW felt compelled to counter their resistance by mobilizing Chicano support. In February 1972 Chicanos demonstrated and blacks counterdemonstrated. Violence erupted, and the one clinic that had been built during the previous twenty-one months was seriously damaged. In April 1972 an uneasy and complicated agreement was reached between HEW, local health officials, the KCLM, and representatives of the Chicano community. Even after this agreement, however, there were controversial hirings and firings, rumors and resignations, and community tensions. What had begun as a new federal program to improve the health of migrant workers ended in administrative bungling that did more to aggravate problems than solve them.

WHAT IS BUREAUCRACY? To many people the words *bureaucracy* and *bureaucrat* are almost synonymous with "inefficiency," "red tape," "endless delay," "bungling," and so on. The Bakersfield fiasco described here helps explain how bureaucracy has gotten such a bad name among the citizenry. Bureaucrats also have another type of negative image. Some people complain that what happened in Bakersfield is another instance of administrative officials pushing and intervening beyond the intent of the law. In other words, sometimes the charge is that the bureaucracy is too sluggish to get anything done. At other times, it is felt that bureaucrats are too zealous and provoke too much change.

But the Bakersfield case should not be viewed as a condemnation of bureaucracy per se. Rather it should be seen as an example of the complex and at times almost insuperable problems government administrators face in implementing policy or, in more general terms, in "running things." Bureaucracies, like any human creation, are fallible; they often do not work the way they are supposed to.

Nevertheless — and this might surprise many people — bureaucracy is the most efficient system of administration known. Indeed, bureaucracies can be defined as "formally established organizations designed to maximize administrative efficiency." [2]

Advantages of Bureaucratic Organization   The foregoing definition states the goal of bureaucracy, but it does not tell us much about its nature. Bureaucracy, then, may be further defined as a type of administrative organization characterized by job specialization, hierarchy of authority, a system of rules, and impersonality of operation. [3] And a bureaucrat is simply someone who works in a bureaucracy. (In Europe, governmental administrative organizations are commonly called *bureaus;* in this country the words *department* and *agency* are more common. But the word *bureau* is often used here too — in the Federal Bureau of Investigation, for example, and in the New York State Bureau of Motor Vehicles.)

The administrative apparatus of every large organization, governmental or otherwise, is organized along bureaucratic lines. There is nothing new about this. Imperial Rome depended on its bureaucratically organized administrators two thousand years ago; so did ancient China; so does every modern state. So too does the General Motors Corporation, the International Ladies Garment Workers Union, the United States Army, the Boy Scouts of America, the company that publishes this book, and the college or university at which you are reading it. So, of course, does every department, agency, bureau, commission, and other administrative arm (by whatever name) of our federal government. As this list suggests, bureaucratic organization is essential to the *efficient* functioning of any large organization. Why? The answer is largely to be found in the four basic characteristics in the definition of bureaucracy just given.

Job Specialization.   Often called *division of labor*, job specialization means that each individual is responsible for specified tasks. Thus the contributions of many workers are needed to complete the organization's work. Job special-

---

[2] Peter M. Blau and Marshall W. Meyer, *Bureaucracy in Modern Society*, 2nd ed. (New York: Random House, 1971), p. 58. Our discussion of bureaucracy's general nature is based largely on Chapter 1 of Blau and Meyer's book.
[3] Ibid., p. 9.

ization has two great advantages: It permits an organization to do more things and more complex things than would otherwise be possible, and it enables the organization to do them better and faster. The automobile assembly line is a good illustration of job specialization in an organization.

Job specialization is important to government administration. The Department of Health and Human Services, for example, employs approximately 140,000 people, from file clerks and janitors to medical technicians, physicians, and chemists — and, of course, administrative specialists from typists and records clerks to examiners of project-funding applications. Examiners do not file, type, clean, conduct chemical analyses, or complete medical examinations. Moreover, those examiners who consider health-service-delivery grant applications do not evaluate applications for medical research grants; the expertise required is not the same.

Hierarchy of Authority. The hundreds of specialized skills that go into implementing a government policy must be coordinated, and coordination requires that each specialist be part of a chain of command. The secretary of Health and Human Services, Defense, or any other department cannot possibly consult with or check on every one of the workers in his or her department. All employees, from the agency head to the junior clerks, must rely on a hierarchy of authority by which instructions flow downward and information flows both upward and downward. Only by means of such a chain of command can a large organization develop and maintain the coordination — the teamwork — needed to execute its complex operations.

A System of Rules. Coordination depends not only on supervision but also on an understanding by all concerned of what should be done and how it should be done. In a large organization, hundreds or thousands of employees are performing dozens or hundreds of different specialized tasks, and no one person completely understands what everybody else is doing. Supervisors cannot be everywhere at once. Besides, their decisions and instructions must be consistent with those of other supervisors, with decisions made yesterday or last week, and with the organization's overall objectives. If the work of all employees is to be coordinated properly, there must be a formal, detailed system of rules — procedures and regulations — so that every employee knows what to do (and what *not* to do), and how to do it. Rules — whether formal or informal, general or specific, mutually agreed on or ordered from the top — are crucial to the smooth functioning of a large, complex organization.

Impersonality of Operation. If the administrative operations of any large organization are to proceed efficiently, employees must perform their tasks *impersonally.* That is, they must not let their personal feelings affect their administrative decisions. One main principle in bureaucracy, as in the legal system, is that power is vested in positions, not persons.

Bureaucracies strive to avoid situations in which feelings would be likely to interfere with the impersonality that is crucial to administrative efficiency. An agency head in a public bureaucracy, for example, is not permitted to hire a brother or daughter to work for the agency, because it would be difficult if not impossible to keep personal feelings from affecting such a hiring decision. Job applicants are evaluated according to their qualifications for the job in question; the ideal (not always realized, of course) is to hire the best-qualified applicant, not the one who is most in need of a job or who has the most winning smile or who is related to the boss.

Impersonality is also an essential characteristic of relations between bureaucrats and people outside the bureaucracy. Not only efficiency but also *fairness* depends on it, a fact that often goes unnoticed by the citizen who is frustrated or angered by a bureaucrat's "indifference" or "coldness." If a bureaucracy is to operate efficiently, similar cases must be treated similarly. For example, every application for a particular type of driver's license or tax refund should be processed the same way. This impartiality serves the public's interests: It means (at least in theory) that if you are eligible for a license or a refund, you will not be turned down because the bureaucrat who handles your case does not like your manner or accent or skin color. It also means that if you are ineligible you will be unlikely to get the license or the refund, no matter how pleasant you are to the person handling it.

Bureaucracy, then, is characterized by four features — job specialization, hierarchical authority, a system of rules, and impersonal operation — that make it the most efficient type of administrative organization. A large organization like the Department of Health and Human Services could not coordinate the work of its 140,000 employees or administer its huge annual budgets ($223 billion in 1981) if it were not bureaucratically organized.

Disadvantages of Bureaucratic Organization

And yet bureaucracy frequently is plagued by inefficiencies. These inefficiencies are extremely hard to root out:

> A fundamental dilemma of bureaucratic administration is that the very arrangements officially instituted to improve efficiency often have by-products that impede it. Centralized authority, even if it results in superior decisions, undermines the ability of middle managers to assume responsibilities. Detailed rules, even if they improve performance, prevent adaptation to changing situations. Strict discipline, even if it facilitates managerial direction, creates resentments that reduce effort. Generally, there are no formal arrangements that can assure efficiency because it depends on flexible adjustments to varying and changing conditions in the organization.[4]

Two other perennial problems of bureaucracy are *conflicting goals* and *divided allegiance*. These arise when different sections of a bureaucratic organization pursue different policies and have to satisfy different clienteles. The Department of Transportation, for example, includes units responsible for

[4] Ibid., p. 59.

The Bureaucratic Machine

"Golly, what a beautiful ship! What makes it go?"

The common image of the federal bureaucracy is that of a mysterious, cumbersome machine that produces little of value. Further, most Americans share the belief depicted in the cartoon: the bureaucracy is a parasitic organization that is powered by taxes paid by hardworking men and women in our society.

Ironically, the federal agency that most closely fits the image of a machine is the agency that collects taxes, the Internal Revenue Service (IRS). Applying tax formulas and checking income tax returns is fairly routine, mechanistic work. Much of what the IRS does is handled in an assembly-line fashion.

Not all administrative work is impersonal. In an attempt to counter the negative image of the IRS specifically and the federal bureaucracy in general, special efforts have been made to provide individual services to those filing income tax returns and to those who are having their returns audited. The IRS has insisted that those officials working in direct contact with the public act in a cordial, helpful manner. Given the reluctance and sometimes the hostility with which people pay taxes, this assignment is not always easy.

highways and units promoting the development of mass transit systems. These units not only compete with each other for funds but also quarrel about policies. Mass transit advocates, for example, argue that a national policy that focusses mainly on highways will ultimately discourage the development of efficient public transportation systems.

Another area of major concern relates to the central reason for establishing bureaucracies: to act efficiently. An emphasis on efficiency can frustrate the goals of justice and progress. The Bakersfield case illustrates how the traits of a bureaucracy can work against the purposes for which that bureaucracy was established. The rules governing budget years, for instance, were designed for efficient accounting. These rules do not accommodate particular program needs, such as the time required to work with migrant workers so that they might help set the direction for a health program. Impersonality, though necessary for efficiency, frequently closes the eyes of bureaucrats to what should be the basic concern of all government agencies: the needs of people. In short, a paradox of bureaucracies is that efficiency sometimes comes at the expense of effectiveness.

Some government employees respond to organizational rules and procedures with as much disdain and hostility as do people outside of government. Many individuals resent any infringement on their autonomy. They insist on exercising their own professional judgment. Rules can, in other words, generate defiance and conflict, even when they are designed to provide for coordination and cooperation. An example of this is when the officials in the San Francisco regional office continued to fund and encourage the black community in Bakersfield despite contrary orders from Washington.

STRUCTURE OF THE FEDERAL BUREAUCRACY

The term *federal bureaucracy* generally refers to the multitude of administrative organizations that enforce the laws and implement the programs legislated by Congress. These organizations — departments, agencies, commissions, bureaus, and so on — make up the executive branch of the federal government. In 1980 the executive branch had more than 2.7 million civilian employees and spent $332 billion.

The federal bureaucracy and the programs it administers extend far beyond the agencies and employees of the federal government itself. Increasingly, Washington works through state and local agencies and through contractors to get its jobs done. Largely because of the growth of federally funded programs administered by state and local governments, public employment at the state and local level increased more than 200 percent between 1950 and 1980, whereas the federal government grew only 35 percent during this period. In 1980, there were over 4 million state employees and over 10 million local government and school employees — in contrast to the 2.7 million in the federal government. Likewise, the federal government has preferred to contract out its tasks rather than to hire more employees to do the job itself. This is particularly appropriate when a task can be done within a definite time period and does not require an ongoing program. Contracting has grown to such proportions that no one is sure of its actual extent. Common estimates in 1980 were that over one-third of the federal government budget went to contractors and that there were more employees on the rolls of government contractors than in the federal civil service. Contractors do everything from producing nuclear weapons to providing care to the elderly.

The legislative and judicial branches also have bureaucratic components. The Congress is composed of 535 elected members, but it employs almost 40,000 people. Most of these people are bureaucrats — administrative personnel who assist Congress in its lawmaking and other functions, which we described in Chapter 5. The judicial branch has approximately 500 judges (including the nine on the Supreme Court), but it employs about 11,000 persons in all. This chapter, however, focuses on the bureaucratic apparatus of the executive branch.

The formal role assigned to bureaucracies in democratic societies is to ensure that legislated policy becomes reality. If Congress determines, for example, that certain efforts should be made to improve the health of migrant workers, then it is the responsibility of the bureaucracy to carry out that policy. The theoretical ideal is that those who hold office because they have been elected by the people will make policy, whereas those who hold office because they have been appointed for their expertise will implement policy.

The Constitution says nothing about the federal bureaucracy. Article II merely says that the president "shall take Care that the Laws be faithfully executed." Thus, the Constitution vests the president with the authority and responsibility for directing administration, but it provides no guidance as to the size, shape, or nature of the federal bureaucracy.

Laws passed by Congress establish the framework within which presidents must manage the government. Federal agencies must be authorized and funded by Congress, and Congress sets the salaries of administrative officials. When Congress creates a governmental agency, it will sometimes specify the terms of office and other conditions of employment for the agency's officials. Thus the commissioners of regulatory agencies like the Federal Trade Commission and the Interstate Commerce Commission are appointed, for staggered terms, by the president with the advice and consent of the Senate. When President-elect Jimmy Carter made his campaign pledge to reorganize the federal bureaucracy, he knew that he would need congressional approval to carry it out. Congress also specifies some of the ways in which legislation must be implemented, as in the provision for participation by migrant workers in the Migrant Health Act.

Cabinet Departments The most important and the largest federal administrative agencies are the thirteen cabinet-level departments: Health and Human Services, Agriculture, Defense, and so on. Each is headed by a secretary who is appointed by and serves at the pleasure of the president. By these crucial appointments the president seeks to coordinate governmental activity through officials who are directly accountable to him. Cabinet departments are established through legislation, and presidential appointments to the top departmental posts must have the formal approval of the Senate.

The cabinet came into being in George Washington's first administration. There were six departments in Washington's cabinet: War (which had responsibility for the Army), Navy, Treasury (charged with collecting revenue), State (concerned with foreign relations), Justice (law enforcement), and the Post Office. Each department had responsibility for a service or function that affected everyone throughout the country in approximately the same way. That is, there was a national constituency concerned about justice, defense, taxes, and postal service.

Since Washington's time, departments have been established in response to the expansion in the scope of issues with which government has become involved and to the needs of *particular* constituencies, or segments of society. (These constituencies are often called *interests* today, and the organizations that represent them are called *interest groups* — the subject of Chapter 12.) The Department of the Interior was created in 1849 to deal with the problems of land, natural resources, and Native Americans that developed as the United States expanded westward. The Department of Agriculture was established in 1862 to serve the small farmers of the northern states, a key constituency of the ruling Republican party. The industrial growth of the country made the departments of Commerce and Labor necessary. Initially, in 1903, there was an attempt to satisfy the needs of both business and labor in a single department. But this proved impractical, and in 1913 Congress and President Woodrow Wilson agreed to divide the Department of Commerce and Labor into two separate departments. The Department of Defense was created in 1947 during Harry S. Truman's presidency to include the new Air Force (formerly the Army Air Corps) with the old departments of War and Navy. The Department of Health, Education, and Welfare was established in 1953 at the initiative of President Dwight D. Eisenhower to cope with the often uncoordinated and overlapping agencies that had proliferated during the New Deal period. To implement his Great Society program, President Lyndon B. Johnson created two new cabinet departments: the Department of Housing and Urban Development, established in 1964, and the Department of Transportation, created in 1966. When Jimmy Carter took office in 1977, he set as a top priority the establishment of a Department of Energy. This department brought together the various agencies that had been dealing with energy-related issues so that the federal government might develop and implement a cohesive national energy policy. In 1980 President Carter fulfilled a campaign promise to teachers by separating education from Health, Education, and Welfare with the creation of the Department of Education, and renaming what remained the Department of Health and Human Services.

Figure 7.1 lists all the cabinet departments as of 1981. (The Post Office is not listed because in 1970 it was changed from a department to a government corporation.)

Figure 7.1 The Executive Branch of the Federal Government, 1981

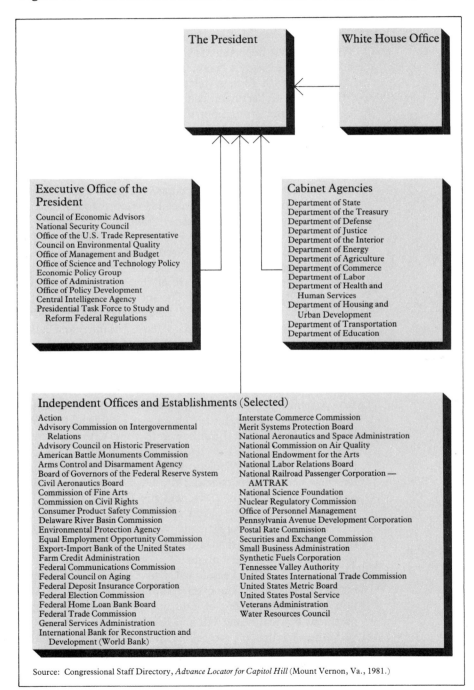

The President

White House Office

Executive Office of the President

Council of Economic Advisors
National Security Council
Office of the U.S. Trade Representative
Council on Environmental Quality
Office of Management and Budget
Office of Science and Technology Policy
Economic Policy Group
Office of Administration
Office of Policy Development
Central Intelligence Agency
Presidential Task Force to Study and
  Reform Federal Regulations

Cabinet Agencies

Department of State
Department of the Treasury
Department of Defense
Department of Justice
Department of the Interior
Department of Energy
Department of Agriculture
Department of Commerce
Department of Labor
Department of Health and
  Human Services
Department of Housing and
  Urban Development
Department of Transportation
Department of Education

Independent Offices and Establishments (Selected)

Action
Advisory Commission on Intergovernmental
  Relations
Advisory Council on Historic Preservation
American Battle Monuments Commission
Arms Control and Disarmament Agency
Board of Governors of the Federal Reserve System
Civil Aeronautics Board
Commission of Fine Arts
Commission on Civil Rights
Consumer Product Safety Commission
Delaware River Basin Commission
Environmental Protection Agency
Equal Employment Opportunity Commission
Export-Import Bank of the United States
Farm Credit Administration
Federal Communications Commission
Federal Council on Aging
Federal Deposit Insurance Corporation
Federal Election Commission
Federal Home Loan Bank Board
Federal Trade Commission
General Services Administration
International Bank for Reconstruction and
  Development (World Bank)

Interstate Commerce Commission
Merit Systems Protection Board
National Aeronautics and Space Administration
National Commission on Air Quality
National Endowment for the Arts
National Labor Relations Board
National Railroad Passenger Corporation —
  AMTRAK
National Science Foundation
Nuclear Regulatory Commission
Office of Personnel Management
Pennsylvania Avenue Development Corporation
Postal Rate Commission
Securities and Exchange Commission
Small Business Administration
Synthetic Fuels Corporation
Tennessee Valley Authority
United States International Trade Commission
United States Metric Board
United States Postal Service
Veterans Administration
Water Resources Council

Source: Congressional Staff Directory, *Advance Locator for Capitol Hill* (Mount Vernon, Va., 1981.)

The actual boundaries between departments are not as neat as their names imply. Agriculture, Commerce, Treasury, Energy, and, of course, Defense all share with the State Department the conduct of our foreign affairs. The wheat deals with the Soviet Union in the mid-1970s were a good example of bureaucratic overlap. As part of its so-called policy of détente (the easing of East-West tensions), the Nixon administration announced in 1972 that this country would sell $750 million worth of wheat over a three-year period to the Soviet Union. The State Department was, of course, deeply involved in all aspects of the détente efforts, which involved arms-control negotiations (a concern of the Defense Department as well), cultural exchanges, and other "initiatives" besides the wheat deals. The wheat sales were consistent with the Department of Agriculture's goals of increasing production on large farms. Because international trade, with all its necessary permits and regulations, was involved, the Department of Commerce had to participate. And because labor disputes arose over who would load the ships and what nations' ships would carry the wheat, the Department of Labor also had to participate.

To complicate further the general picture of bureaucratic organization and function, federal departments must work with and through various state agencies, local government offices, and private organizations. As we pointed out in Chapter 4 on federalism, the agencies in Washington accomplish their policy objectives by issuing rules that state and local governments must follow and by providing money for these jurisdictions to implement certain programs. An important part of this intergovernmental network is the monitoring by federal officers of what is actually happening with their rules and their money.

Other Federal Agencies   Although the cabinet departments are the best known, the federal bureaucracy includes more than a hundred other agencies. There are no systematic criteria that determine which agencies should have the prestige of cabinet status and which should not. Nor do any particular organizational features distinguish cabinet departments from others. The Veterans Administration, for example, is headed by a presidential appointee and in 1980 had a budget of $21 billion and a work force larger than those of cabinet departments like Housing and Urban Development, Transportation, Interior, Energy, and Education. Decisions about what agencies should be given cabinet status were frequently arbitrary.

The following list of types of agencies gives some idea of the scope of federal activity and the variety of federal bureaucracies.

Regulatory Agencies.   Regulatory agencies are established by Congress to regulate certain industries or activities. They do not provide services, but ensure that certain rules are being followed. The Environmental Protection Agency (EPA), for example, is supposed to see that the auto industry makes cars with exhaust emissions that meet federal air pollution standards and that other industries do not exceed certain limits set for air and water pollution. If the EPA is convinced that regulations in the laws are too harsh, Congress has given the agency some discretion in amending the regulations or in delaying their enforcement. Other examples of regulatory agencies are the Interstate Commerce Commission (which oversees the trucking and railroad industries) and the Securities and Exchange Commission (which establishes rules governing the operations of brokerage firms and stock exchanges).

Clientele Agencies. Many agencies are established to serve a particular group within society. The Veterans Administration, for example, administers insurance programs, loan services, hospitals, and other services to veterans and their families. The National Science Foundation funds scientific research and provides research-related services to the academic community. Agencies like these emerge in response to particular societal needs and to political pressure from important interest groups.

Corporations. Some government agencies have been created to perform tasks that are similar to those of private profit-making companies. The Tennessee Valley Authority is the most successful and the best known of these corporations. The TVA provides power to residents of the Tennessee Valley and also regulates use of the Tennessee River and adjacent land. The Postal Service is another major government corporation, which competes with United Parcel and other delivery services. The Federal Deposit Insurance Corporation insures money held by banks and is similar in many respects to other insurance firms.

Housekeeping Bodies. These agencies perform services to all government agencies except public enterprises and corporations. A notable example of a housekeeping agency is the General Services Administration, which constructs and operates most government buildings and helps other agencies contract for equipment or services. Another is the Office of Personnel Management, which helps administer the personnel system throughout the federal bureaucracy.

EMERGENCE OF THE CONTEMPORARY FEDERAL BUREAUCRACY

The problems of exerting presidential leadership over the variety of public agencies in the federal bureaucracy were not always as troublesome as they are now. As the federal bureaucracy grew in size, complexity, and power, the problems of controlling it have also changed and grown.

From the first administration of George Washington in 1789 to that of Andrew Jackson in 1828, the federal bureaucracy was very informal and personal. Washington hired "men of character" — nearly all of whom he knew personally — to do administrative work. Presidents from Washington through Jackson relied on people they trusted, gave their appointees a general idea of what should be done, and then let them use their good judgment in accomplishing the task.

Early Principles and Developments As the country grew, the personal, informal style characteristic of the initial small-scale operation of government increasingly became inappropriate. When Andrew Jackson became president, the federal government confronted problems in the nation's economy and banking system, the needs of the new territory added to the country with the Louisiana Purchase, and the demands of frontier voters. To meet these challenges, Jackson expanded the federal bureaucracy and initiated significant changes in existing agencies. It was in the Jacksonian period that the first steps were taken to make structures and procedures more regulated and systematic. The personal, informal traits of the earlier years were abandoned.

The Post Office. In the Post Office, for example, before Jackson's presidency virtually no records were kept, no accounting was done, and no regulations guided the administration and procedures of mail delivery. The common arrangement was for a postal official to define routes for service within an area that was generally regarded as his jurisdiction and then to contract with some firm to deliver the mail. No regulations stipulated how contracts were to be awarded. No procedures limited the arrangements for payment. Under such a casual system, patterns varied widely and corruption was common.

Jackson appointed his close friend Amos Kendall to head the Post Office Department and to improve its service. Kendall reorganized the department, primarily along geographical lines, and established a hierarchical supervisory system that specified the duties and responsibilities of each position within the department. Kendall also adopted an accounting system to record how money was spent and how much revenue was being earned. Contracts for mail delivery services were gradually replaced by the operations of the Post Office itself. The regulation, specialization, and routinization Kendall brought to the Post Office characterize much of federal bureaucracy today.[5]

The Spoils System. The Jacksonian period is also known for another change in the federal bureaucracy: the spoils system, the practice of rewarding one's supporters after an election with jobs in the bureaucracy. This practice did not originate with Jackson; at least since Jefferson's time political allies had been rewarded with public office. But Jackson engaged in it unashamedly and even enthusiastically.

Jackson's enthusiasm for the spoils system was not wholly cynical or opportunistic, however. He firmly believed that "rotation in office" (the change of administrators every few years) would make the federal bureaucracy more democratic — that is, more representative of the people. Jackson also believed that a specially trained bureaucratic elite, drawn from the educated upper classes, was quite unnecessary. He stated both beliefs this way in 1829 in his first message to Congress: "The duties of all public offices are . . . so plain

[5] Matthew Crenson, *The Federal Machine* (Baltimore, Md.: Johns Hopkins University Press, 1975).

and simple that men of intelligence may readily qualify themselves for their performance; and I can not but believe that more is lost by the long continuance of men in office than is generally gained by their experience."[6]

Jackson's successors also abided by the principle that "to the victor belong the spoils," and in time the abuses and excesses of this practice became so notorious that they aroused much concern in Congress. The spoils system was also the subject of derisive jokes. One story had it that the Union army retreated at the Battle of Bull Run because three vacancies had just been announced in the federal Customs Office.

After the Civil War the abuses and scandals in the federal patronage system grew worse. In 1881 President James A. Garfield was assassinated by Charles Guiteau, who thought that his support of Garfield in the presidential campaign should have been rewarded with a federal appointment after the election. Garfield's murder and the widespread unhappiness with the spoils system were major issues in the 1882 congressional elections, in which the Republicans lost badly. In the aftermath of these elections, Congress passed the Pendleton Act, named after Senator George Pendleton of Ohio, a Democrat who led congressional efforts for civil service reform. The Pendleton Act provided the foundation of the merit system currently used in appointing public administrators.

The Pendleton Act. The Pendleton Act (1883) provided that

1. Appointment to the civil service must be based on performance in competitive examinations open to all, regardless of political affiliation. The entrance tests (merit examinations) and other requirements must be designed to measure ability.
2. Once an individual has successfully completed a probationary period, he or she has *tenure* (job security) and can be dismissed only for "gross negligence," serious misconduct, or conviction on a criminal charge.
3. Civil servants cannot be required to make political contributions.
4. A Civil Service Commission of three members with staggered six-year terms is empowered to see that the merit principle is applied in personnel recruitment and administration. The commissioners are appointed by the president, with the advice and consent of the Senate, but they are not under presidential direction. No more than two commissioners can be from the same political party.

The Pendleton Act authorized the president to implement these reforms, but it did not require him to do so. President Chester A. Arthur (who had been vice-president when Garfield was assassinated) signed the bill, but applied the act to fewer than 14,000 government employees (about 10 percent of

---

[6] James D. Richardson, *Messages and Papers of the Presidents*, vol. 3 (New York: Bureau of National Literature, 1897), p. 1012; as quoted by Francis E. Rourke, *Bureaucracy, Politics, and Public Policy* (Boston: Little, Brown, 1976), p. 17.

the federal bureaucracy). Twenty-five years later, President Theodore Roosevelt, who had been a civil service commissioner, extended coverage to 60 percent of federal government employees. Succeeding presidents have extended the Pendleton Act's coverage, and today almost all federal bureaucrats are in the civil service. One reason that presidents have extended civil service protections to more positions is that this guarantees jobs for many of their own political appointees even after there is a new resident in the White House.

The extension of civil service coverage has been in the lower and middle ranks. Presidents have recognized the importance of having those in senior, policymaking positions serve at the pleasure of the president. In this way, a president can provide the day-to-day leadership over the federal bureaucracy that is consistent with both the president's wishes and his campaign promises. In addition to cabinet appointments, 5,000 positions outside the civil service system are filled by the president. Almost all of these require Senate confirmation.

The Hatch Act. To make certain that bureaucrats are politically neutral and available to serve elected officials regardless of which party is dominant, legislation prohibits civil servants from engaging in many political activities. The Hatch Act of 1939 provided that federal administrators may not

1. Campaign in partisan elections;
2. Be a political party's candidate in an election;
3. Collect funds for campaign treasuries (this provision is also designed to protect workers against having to make political contributions to keep their jobs or to get promotions);
4. Hold office in a political party;
5. Organize a partisan meeting or rally.

The Hatch Act does not deny civil servants all opportunities to participate in the electoral process. They can

1. Register to vote and vote;
2. Express opinions about candidates;
3. Campaign in nonpartisan contests (for example, a school board election);
4. Contribute money to political causes and campaign treasuries;
5. Express their political preferences by means of campaign buttons, bumper stickers, and the like.

The Classification System. Since the early 1900s, the merit principle in the civil service has been implemented by a classification system that evaluates all positions in the bureaucracy according to the skills they require, the responsibilities they entail, and the education and experience they demand. Positions with similar requirements are grouped together. Currently, federal civil service jobs are classified into eighteen basic grades. The lowest grade, Government

Service 1, or GS-1, includes those positions requiring the simplest skills and fewest responsibilities, such as janitors and low-level clerks. The highest, GS-18, includes the jobs with the most demanding qualifications and the most responsibilities. Most of the senior positions appointed by the president outside the civil service system are in an Executive Schedule, which is above the GS-18 grade. The classification of an individual's job determines his or her pay and position in the hierarchy of a government organization.

Recent Reforms The Pendleton Act, the Hatch Act, and the classification system addressed problems of corruption and patronage that are still potential threats. Today's reformers continue to be concerned about ensuring the selection of people who are competent, honest, and nonpartisan. Nonetheless, the National Civil Service League, which spearheaded the drive toward the end of the last century to establish a civil service system free from political patronage, is now arguing that too much has been done to keep politics out of the civil service. The League points out that earlier reform efforts were negative in focus; they were aimed at preventing patronage and spoils. The League observes that a more positive definition of what we want in our civil service system is needed today. The job security government employees enjoy needs to be balanced with incentives and sanctions that will ensure that they will work hard and effectively. Political neutrality must not be confused with isolation from the citizenry. Bureaucrats must be accountable to the elected representatives of the people. In short, contemporary reformers want to pursue the campaign against the abuse of privilege while at the same time emphasizing the need for government to work, and work well.

The 1978 Civil Service Reforms. Under the leadership of Alan K. Campbell, whom President Carter appointed as chairperson of the Civil Service Commission, the federal government adopted in 1978 the most comprehensive set of civil service reforms since the Pendleton Act of 1883. Campbell had the advantage of working in the post-Watergate atmosphere, in which Congress remembered vividly the massive and frequently blatant attempts of President Nixon to subvert the merit system and use political loyalty as a key criterion for appointment to a federal job. Congress also remembered the illegal and unethical harassment by the Nixon White House of those federal employees who helped bring public attention to waste and corruption in government.

Campbell, working with a special task force, compiled a package of proposals that included responses to these problems and also took aim at a number of longstanding public management issues. To address the needs raised by Watergate, the Civil Service Commission was dismantled. The commission had two contradictory roles: On the one hand, assisting the president in the management of federal personnel and, on the other hand, acting as a neutral arbitrator in complaints brought by federal civil servants about personnel management decisions. Clearly, it was hard to view the commission as really neutral when it was ruling on its own actions. The commission was replaced by the Office of Personnel Management, headed by a director who serves at the pleasure of the president and charged with helping the president run the federal bureaucracy; and the Merit Systems Protection Board, a bipartisan, independent body — as the Civil Service Commission was supposed to be — that hears employee appeals and protects the integrity of the merit system. Part of the Merit System Protection Board is the Office of the Special Counsel, which is charged with helping "whistleblowers" — federal employees who expose waste and corruption — from being mistreated by their superiors.

In addition to these changes, the 1978 Civil Service Reform Act attempted to improve management in federal agencies by linking the salaries and job security of top and middle managers to job performance. In order to utilize senior administrators in the most effective way, the act established the Senior Executive Service, a pool of top talent that can be shifted as agency needs vary. Those in the pool are officials in GS-16, GS-17, GS-18, and the Executive Schedule who have managerial responsibilities. Other features of the act include standards that make it easier to dismiss poor performers in the federal government, a new emphasis on performance appraisals, and a firm commitment to the establishment of a socially representative bureaucracy and to the collective bargaining process. These commitments had predecessors in Executive Orders of the president, but were given the firmer standing of law by being included in the act.

The impact of this law, like that of other laws, depends heavily on how seriously it is implemented. Many federal civil servants were opposed to the reforms and have resisted using the provisions of the new law. Initially, for example, few supervisors took advantage of the easier standards for firing their employees. In addition, problems with funding and the appointment of the special counsel of the Merit System Protection Board delayed protection for whistleblowers. Nonetheless, the law is in place, and the potential for significant change is there.

Representative Bureaucracy. A fundamental concern of reformers since the mid-1960s is that bureaucracies be demographically representative; that is, the bureaucracy's population makeup of civil servants should mirror that of society as a whole. Thus, if 10 percent of the population is black, then 10 percent of the federal bureaucrats should be black. If 50 percent of the society is female, then 50 percent of the administrators should be, also.

The progress in recent years toward a representative federal bureaucracy is the result of so-called affirmative action programs. As vacancies occur, attempts are made to fill them with members of minority groups. Although some progress has been made, demographic representation is far from equal at all levels; most women and minority group employees are in the lowest civil service grades (see Figure 7.2). In 1978, for example, nonwhites held 30.2 percent of the jobs in grades 1 to 4, but only 5.0 percent of the jobs in grades 16 to 18. The situation for women in 1978 was even worse. Although 78 percent of the civil servants in grades 1 to 4 and 62 percent of those in grades 5 to 8

Figure 7.2 Minorities and Women in the Federal Bureaucracy by Grades, 1966–78

	Number of Minorities	Percent of Employees	Number of Women	Percent of Employees
1966				
GS 1-4	83,000	23.4	280,000	75.1
GS 5-8	42,000	13.7	183,000	55.6
GS 9-11	17,000	6.6	39,000	14.1
GS 12-18	7,000	3.2	10,000	4.2
Total	149,000	13.1	512,000	42.4
1971				
GS 1-4	82,000	28.3	228,000	75.3
GS 5-8	74,000	18.9	234,000	57.4
GS 9-11	28,000	8.9	67,000	20.4
GS 12-18	15,000	4.9	18,000	5.5
Total	199,000	15.2	547,000	40.1
1978				
GS 1-4	85,000	30.2	213,000	77.7
GS 5-8	105,000	23.7	273,000	62.2
GS 9-11	49,000	14.3	103,000	29.7
GS 12-18	30,000	3.1	32,000	8.7
Total	268,000	18.8	626,000	43.6

The General Schedule classifies federal civil service jobs by grades ranging from GS-1 (routine, low-skill work) to GS-18 (includes bureau chiefs, national program directors).

Source: United States Office of Personnel Management.

were women, only 30 percent of the civil servants in grades 9 to 11 and 3.9 percent in grades 16 and 18 were women. In other words, the goals of affirmative action are a long way from full realization.

The merit system itself can be a major obstacle to the objective of equal access to careers in the bureaucracy for women, the handicapped, and minority group members, for traditional definitions of merit emphasize formal educational requirements and verbal skills that are most commonly found among middle-class white males. Concern arises when formal education requirements and verbal skills that are unrelated to jobs are used to screen people on the basis of culture rather than competence. The Civil Service Commission and a private firm, the Educational Testing Service, have attempted to weed out cultural biases in examinations used in the federal bureaucracy. Such efforts, which have changed the content and format of examinations, point to a need to reexamine the whole selection process used in the civil service.

There are two major arguments for having a representative bureaucracy. One is that minority groups are most effectively spoken for by their own members. The other is that a demographically representative bureaucracy is possible only when all groups in society have access to jobs in the federal bureaucracy, so that progress toward such a bureaucracy would be an indication of progress in overcoming discrimination.

The need for equal opportunity and open competition advocated by the second argument is compelling. Still, even if the federal bureaucracy's composition eventually mirrors that of society, such demographic representativeness cannot ensure that bureaucrats will reflect all the hopes and interests of the public. There is no guarantee that a black or a female administrator will advocate black or female interests as his or her agency debates and executes public policies. For one thing, minority groups are not monolithic; their members differ among themselves about what is the preferred course of action. Moreover, bureaucrats do not have the relationships with their constituencies that elected officials do with theirs. Minority groups cannot fire or "recall" minority bureaucrats who seem to have forgotten their roots.

Another major reason to doubt that demographic representation would affect public policy very much is that bureaucrats are constrained by the concerns of their agencies and by the authority attached to their positions. It matters little how officials in the Department of Defense feel about legalizing marijuana or how administrators in the departments of Justice or Health and Human Services felt about the war in Vietnam or our relations with communist countries. Likewise, a Chicano working for the State Department as a desk officer for Bolivia can do little to influence the federal government's response to the needs of migrant workers. What is crucial, of course, is how those who deal directly with the issues of migrant workers, foreign policy, or marijuana use feel about those subjects. Representativeness, then, may have symbolic importance, but cannot by itself make a bureaucracy responsive to the people it serves.

Although it is illegal for federal employees to strike, air traffic controllers in 1981 felt they had to take this step in order to make gains in collective bargaining over wages and working conditions.

Unionization. The growth of public-employee unions has brought about important changes in the contemporary federal bureaucracy. The unionization of federal employees began under President John F. Kennedy, who recognized the right of civil service workers to organize and ordered federal agencies to negotiate contracts with their employees. Collective bargaining in the federal government is over working conditions (hours, physical facilities, and the like) and grievance procedures. Public-employee unions have enhanced the protection of employee rights for federal civil servants. Civil servants who feel they are being mistreated by their supervisors or that they have been fired or demoted arbitrarily can seek redress through contractual grievance procedures and with union assistance.

Unlike many state and local governments, however, the federal government does not negotiate salaries with public-employee unions. There is one exception: The federal government does negotiate wages with employees of its largest corporation, the Post Office.

A potential problem of public-employee unionization involves the ultimate weapon of labor unions, the strike. Every person who enters the federal civil service must agree not to strike against the government. But if union members cannot strike — that is, if they cannot withhold their services from their employer (or threaten to do so) — then what bargaining chips do they really have in negotiations over salaries, working conditions, and so on? This question is more than academic; the no-strike pledge has been violated more than once by federal employees. In 1970, for example, Post Office workers struck. Not long after that, many air traffic controllers — employees of the Federal Aviation Agency — struck in fact if not in name by staying home on the pretense of being sick. Public-employee strikes are illegal in part because of a concern for public safety. Instead of enforcing this law, however, efforts typically focus on reaching an agreement with the employees and getting them back to work. In most jurisdictions, firing, fining, or jailing striking employees invites more political trouble — from private-sector unions as well as public employees — than it is worth.

To date, unions representing federal employees have done much to ensure employees' rights while doing little to threaten democracy. Whatever the problems and the potential dangers of public-employee unions may be, however, these unions seem to be here to stay, at the federal as well as at the state and local levels of government.

THE BUREAU-CRACY'S ROLE IN POLICYMAKING AND POLICY IMPLEMENTA-TION

A traditional concept of a public bureaucracy is that it implements the policies made by elected legislators and chief executives. From our description of the administration of the 1970 Migrant Health Act in Bakersfield, it should be clear that bureaucracies are not merely the passive instruments of legislators and other policymakers. Policy implementation by bureaucrats usually entails discretionary action; that is, bureaucrats must make choices among alternative courses of action that help determine the policy's effect. This is so because policy statements must be general statements, or guidelines: They cannot possibly specify how to handle every situation that will ever arise. Thus bureaucrats, like judges, often must decide how a given guideline will be interpreted in a given situation.

All societies hope that their bureaucracies are competent. Democratic societies seek, additionally, that bureaucracies be accountable to the people, through the people's representatives. Although bureaucrats are appointed, not elected, they must be responsive to the mood and desires of the voters.

The Legislative Connection

Administrators play an important role in *formulating* policy as well as in implementing it. In fact, many of the initiatives for changes in law come from administrative officials. Legislators must pass judgment on a wide variety of proposals, some of them very technical. In doing so they must rely on the advice and the evaluations of experts, many of whom are members of the bureaucracy. Formally, administrative officials are asked to provide information and evaluation at congressional hearings. Informally, civil servants work with members of Congress and their staffs on legislation throughout the initiation, drafting, and deliberation stages.

Interdependency and Tension. Despite the interdependency between politicians and bureaucrats, there is at times considerable tension between the two. As professionals, bureaucrats frequently consider themselves better equipped than legislators to handle a policy area. Indeed, some of them resent politicians for intervening in "their" work (the work of public agencies). They consider politicians, including the members of Congress with whom they must work, to be unqualified, intruding meddlers. Elected officials, on the other hand, sometimes sense a demand for change by the voters that they believe is being resisted, ignored, or misunderstood by bureaucrats who seem more concerned about preserving the status quo than about serving the public. At other times elected officials have the opposite problem; that is, the bureaucracy advocates a change that members of the public oppose.

Often the bureaucrats' problem is having somehow to accommodate conflicting demands — a problem that, as we saw in Chapter 5, legislators themselves continually face. Consider the conflicting demands of political and professional mandates faced by bureaucrats in the Agency for International Development (AID), which administers foreign assistance programs. An official charged with improving peasant agriculture in a Latin American country, for example, must simultaneously satisfy not only his or her own professional standards of how such a job should be done, but also (1) members of Congress, who want our aid to contribute to a stable, friendly, noncommunist world; (2) senior officials of AID, who want programs to be administered as efficiently as possible; (3) American private interests, who want the agency to use American goods and products and who hope that the agency's aid programs will provide more markets for American products; (4) officials in the Latin American country, who want changes that will contribute to their own support and stability; and (5) by the way, the peasant farmers. It is not easy to serve so many masters.

This problem of *divided allegiance,* as we called it earlier in the chapter, crops up often in relations between the bureaucracy and Congress. On the one hand bureaucrats report to, and are formally responsible to, their superiors in the executive department. On the other hand, they are expected to be responsive to congressional will, to agency clientele, and to the standards of their profession. When the president (or agency head) does not see eye to eye with Congress on how a given policy should be implemented, bureaucrats charged with implementing that policy can be in a very difficult position.

Sometimes, however, bureaucrats can turn the problem of divided allegiance to their own purposes — for example, when they disagree with a policy favored by their agency or department head or by the president himself. If the congressional committee or subcommittee that has jurisdiction in the matter sees the issue the way the bureaucrats do, they can often enlist the congressional group's support in opposing the departmental or presidential position. And this combined opposition can often prevail.

The interdependency and the tension between politicians and bureaucrats make any neat division of labor between politics and administration a practical impossibility.

Interagency Conflict.   Another factor that clouds any simple picture of bureaucrats as mere implementers of the legislative will is the potential for conflict between bureaucratic agencies. Different agencies often view the same or related problems from very different perspectives. Sometimes these different perspectives generate interagency conflict, or what we called *conflicting goals* in our earlier discussion of bureaucratic problems. For example, in 1975 and 1976, when Congress was considering legislation that would regulate the strip mining of coal, it received conflicting advice from different units of the federal bureaucracy. The Federal Energy Office was concerned about the need to increase coal production quickly, and it urged Congress to avoid regulations that would discourage stepped-up production. The Commerce Department, worried about the nation's depressed economy, gave Congress similar advice. But the Environmental Protection Agency (EPA) and the Council on Environmental Quality saw strip mining, which gets at coal by stripping away the overlying earth, as a serious threat to environmental quality (some 3 million acres of land had already been ruined). These agencies also viewed the burning of coal as an environmental threat because it causes serious air pollution. Therefore, they advised Congress to build tough regulations into any strip-mining legislation.

Agencies often find themselves working in pursuit of conflicting goals. Thus public health agencies administer programs and regulations designed to discourage people from smoking tobacco, even as agencies in the Department of Agriculture run programs to help growers improve and increase their tobacco crops. Similarly, the EPA had to fight in court with the Tennessee Valley Authority to get the TVA to reduce air pollution by its power-generating plants to legal levels.

Subgovernments for Policy Areas Probably the most important ties between the bureaucracy and the legislative branch are the informal relationships between congressional subcommittees and administrative agencies. Linkages frequently develop along the same interests, as for example between the Senate's Migratory Labor subcommittee and the agencies in the Department of Health and Human Services that administer programs for migrant workers. This subcommittee also has close ties with agencies in the departments of Justice and State that regulate the movement and the legal status of migrant workers, and the agencies in the departments of Agriculture and Labor that are concerned with migrant labor activities.

Relationships between agencies and subcommittees are so important that they can be referred to as *subgovernments*. Congress as a whole usually defers to the recommendations of its committees and subcommittees. Similarly, the federal bureaucracy is not a monolithic organization that speaks with one voice, but rather a loose collection of specialized agencies with enough autonomy to administer their own spheres of policy. Most of the time, if a congressional subcommittee and an agency agree on a policy, it will become the policy of the federal government.

These "subgovernments" are not entirely autonomous. When conflict develops, between subgovernments it must be resolved by Congress as a whole and at the cabinet or presidential level in the bureaucracy. For example, subcommittees and agencies that are concerned with the welfare of migrant workers may agree on policies that conflict with the policies of subcommittees and agencies concerned with other agricultural interests. Similarly, a disagreement within a subgovernment — between the subcommittee and the agency — may have to be resolved in the broader arenas of the federal government.

The Role of Interest Groups.   The web of relationships between bureaucratic and legislative units frequently also includes nongovernmental groups that are directly affected by the policies formulated by subgovernments. The legislation passed by Senator Mondale's subcommittee on migratory labor sought to make certain that migrant workers would be included in any subgovernment that might emerge from the new federal health program. But because of events in Bakersfield, health professionals and black leaders, rather than migrant workers, became involved.

Invariably, it is the best-organized groups in our society that are most closely involved in the formulation and administration of public policy. In the Bakersfield case, health professionals and blacks were both better organized than the migrant workers. Both groups had leaders to articulate their feelings and to represent them in negotiations and committee deliberations. The clout of an organized group is increased by the fact that for elected officials, organization implies the potential to mobilize support or opposition in election campaigns. The advantages of organization will be examined in more detail in Chapter 12, "Interest Groups."

Congressional Oversight.   Although Congress plays a crucial role in subgovernments through its subcommittees, the Senate and the House of Representatives are also supposed to act as watchdogs and overseers by providing legislative oversight, which was discussed in Chapter 5. Congress is supposed to make sure that the federal bureaucracy complies with the law and legislative intent, and that its activities are in the national interest. Yet Congress fulfills this role imperfectly. A major instrument of congressional oversight is casework for constituents. A citizen who is the victim of a bureaucratic delay or an interest group that feels wronged by a bureaucratic decision can contact a member of Congress. The legislator will in turn make inquiries of bureaucratic officials. Bureaucrats give legislators' inquiries prompt attention, and casework is often effective in prompting the bureaucracy to move.

Congress also oversees the federal bureaucracy through investigations. Senator William Proxmire of Wisconsin was noted for his investigations into Defense Department contracting for services and for military equipment. His success in showing that costs frequently exceeded those initially agreed to in contracts between the Defense Department and private industries prompted changes in the ways these contracts are written and resulted in significant savings to the taxpayers. Congressional investigations can uncover assaults on our liberties as well as our pocketbooks. It was through the investigations of the General Accounting Office, an agency of Congress, that legislators became aware of former President Nixon's efforts to use the Internal Revenue Service to harass his political opponents.

HOW CITIZENS VIEW THE FEDERAL BUREAUCRACY

The inefficiencies, complexity, and pervasiveness of the federal bureaucracy affect its image among citizens. The public image of government bureaucracies is not a favorable one. Few people distinguish among federal, state, and local bureaucracies; most lump them all together and discuss them in largely negative terms. In evaluating the bureaucracy, Congress as well as the public tends to focus its attention on inefficiency, waste, and corruption in the bureaucratic structure, and on procedures rather than the effects bureaucratic actions have on the implementation of policies. As pointed out earlier, the bureaucratic form of organization is designed for efficiency. The emphasis in the perspectives of Congress and the public, therefore, is generally understandable. However, because the focus on efficiency neglects fundamental questions about the purpose and the effect of public policies, the emphasis is unfortunate.

Bureaucratic Inefficiency

A large, complex organization like the federal bureaucracy is almost inevitably associated with waste and inefficiency. Some examples involve the purchase of millions of dollars worth of equipment that simply collects dust in warehouses. Frequently the smaller incidents, some amusing and some annoying, have the greatest impact on our image of the bureaucracy. In the spring of 1981, for example, a number listed in the Washington, D.C., phone book under "Federal Job Information" generated frustration instead of assistance. Almost any time someone dialed the number they got a tape recording saying that lines were busy, but that the tape would provide information while the caller waited for an official to answer specific questions. The only information provided was an observation that the lines were busiest between 11 a.m. and 3 p.m. After this message was repeated six times, the line was disconnected!

Bureaucrats subject themselves as well as the public to cumbersome procedures and jargon. The Justice Department has a gym for its employees. The gym is called an Occupational Health and Physical Fitness Program Facility. On the wall next to a telephone at this facility is a set of instructions for what to do if someone has a heart attack or suffers some injury. The list has nine steps, the first of which is to dial 911 and say: "There has been a life-endangering emergency at the Department of Justice exercise facility."

Similarly, there was groaning inside and outside of the Department of Defense when it was learned that a campaign to cut back on the number of forms used and paper consumed in the federal bureaucracy resulted in little more than a new agency with new forms. (The new agency was charged with studying what happens to used and unused paper within the Defense Department.)

The amount and complexity of the paperwork the bureaucracy imposes on itself — and on the citizenry — is notorious. In 1975, for example, the Office of Management and Budget calculated that more than 5,000 different forms were regularly sent by forty-four departments and agencies to people outside the government. This seemed a bit excessive to President Ford, who ordered a 10 percent cut in the number of forms. Ford got his wish; seven months later the number of forms sent to Americans had been reduced to 4,504. But this reduction hardly accomplished its intended purpose of reducing the government-generated paperwork burden on individuals, businesses, and other private organizations. In November 1976, the OMB calculated that whereas Americans had spent some 130 million hours filling out the 5,000 different forms (not including time spent on income taxes) in 1975 before the "reform," in 1976 they spent 143 million hours to complete the pared-down collection of forms. The reason, according to the OMB, was that more people than ever had to complete the forms. It attributed most of the increase to a new, complex, 247-page pension law designed to protect the retirement interests of the country's workers.[7]

The federal "paperwork problem" is compounded by another difficulty: a formidable language barrier. Many of the thousands of notices and regulations the federal bureaucracy issues each year are couched in impenetrable prose. Here, for instance, is an excerpt from a regulation issued in January 1977 by the Economic Development Administration:

> Projects assisted through the use of funds in supplementing EDA grants or loans under Titles I, II, other than planning grants authorized under sections 301(b) and 302, IV, and IX of the Act or in providing basic grants or loans shall be subject to the same procedures and requirements relating to post approval compliances, construction management, and disbursement as applicable to projects funded under Titles I, II, III, IV, and IX of the Act.[8]

Is such language necessary? In 1977 President Jimmy Carter announced that he did not think so, and he instructed his cabinet secretaries to make sure that regulations issued by their departments were written in "plain English." But the prospects for real improvement are dim. For years the bureaucrats who publish the *Federal Register,* the government's daily record of its new notices and regulations, have tried to get agency bureaucrats to write more clearly. "The problem," according to a lawyer who has tried to help the authors of regulations make their products more intelligible, "is that few government employees are ever trained to write regulations."[9]

Perhaps the most telling criticism of the bureaucratic language barrier is that even cabinet secretaries sometimes cannot decipher the forms and regulations issued by their departments. In 1977 Secretary of Agriculture Bob Bergland wrestled with the application for food stamps that his department inflicts on millions of needy Americans. Bergland found it so complicated that he complained, "Whoever wrote this ought to have to fill it out himself."[10]

The Bureaucrats   Surveys of public attitudes reveal that most people consider bureaucrats to be very cautious individuals who are tied to rule books and do little other than serve time in their jobs. Only 4 percent of those polled in a Harris survey described bureaucrats as creative and imaginative, and only 9 percent regarded

[7] *The New York Times,* February 19, 1977.
[8] Ibid.
[9] Ibid.
[10] Ibid.

them as idealistic.[11] A team of researchers at the University of Michigan found that only 30 percent of the people they questioned felt that government agencies do well at taking care of problems.[12]

Investigators have also surveyed the attitudes of elected leaders who work closely on a daily basis with career bureaucrats. Interestingly, the percentage of elected officials who have a negative image of administrators is higher than the percentage of the general public who feel the same way (see Table 7.1). Familiarity here seems to breed some contempt. Presidents have been particularly frustrated by the federal bureaucracy. Soon after the 1951 election, President Harry S. Truman sat in his office and mused on President-elect Dwight D. Eisenhower's initiation into the world of civilian (as opposed to military) bureaucracies when he took over as president. "Poor Ike," Truman said. "He'll sit here and say 'Do this' and 'Do that' — and nothing will happen."

The social status of bureaucrats is lower in the United States than almost anywhere else. In most European countries, jobs in the bureaucracy are coveted and are usually available only to members of the upper classes who have graduated from prestigious universities. In developing countries, those who succeed in landing administrative positions are envied. The generally negative image of bureaucracy and bureaucrats in this country makes it harder for government to recruit competent administrators. A major study conducted in the mid-1960s, for example, showed that working in a government bureaucracy

Table 7.1 How the Public and Elected Officials View Bureaucrats: Percentage Agreeing with Descriptions of Bureaucrats

Description	Public Percentage Agreeing	Elected Leaders Percentage Agreeing
Do things by the book	23	60
Play it safe	21	48
Bureaucratic	14	58
Make red tape	12	25
Dull	6	14
Honest	16	34
Corrupt	4	0

Source: *Confidence and Concern: Citizens View American Government,* A Survey of Public Attitudes by the Subcommittee on Intergovernmental Relations of the Committee on Government Operations (Washington, D.C.: December 1973), p. 310.

[11]*Confidence and Concern: Citizens View American Government,* a survey of Public Attitude by the Subcommittee on Intergovernmental Relations of the Committee on Government Operations (Washington, D.C.: U.S. Government Printing Office, December 1973), p. 306.

[12]Robert L. Kahn, "Americans Love Their Bureaucrats," *Psychology Today,* June 1975, p. 70.

ranked very low as a preferred career option among United States college students.[13]

Although the federal bureaucracy generally does not have an image of being corrupt, there are occasional scandals that cause public concern. During the Nixon administration, ITT (International Telephone and Telegraph) bribed Justice Department officials in order to keep them from prosecuting a case against the corporation. Officials in the General Services Administration, over a period spanning several administrations, profited from bribes and kickbacks that they acquired while securing supplies and property for government agencies.

The passage of the Ethics in Government Act in 1978 was a major step toward avoiding both the substance and the appearance of corruption and conflict of interest among federal officials. The approaches used include the disclosure by officials of their private holdings and associations, the divestiture of investments in businesses that might be advantaged by official decisions, and a ban on employment with firms affected by official decisions after leaving a federal government job.

Inevitably, this reform, although appropriate and effective, has proved counterproductive in one respect: It discourages government service by some very competent and doubtless ethically impeccable individuals who object to public scrutiny of their "personal" affairs. In 1980, for example, President Reagan's first choice for secretary of the Treasury appeared to be Walter Wriston, the chairperson of a large banking firm. But Wriston declined the post — apparently because he did not want to divulge details about his personal wealth.

Bribery, embezzlement, kickbacks and other forms of corruption have, of course, always been regarded as improper and illegal. The 1978 changes, in the aftermath of the Watergate scandals, were primarily an attempt to place the federal government, like Caesar's wife, beyond suspicion.

Bureaucrats have always borne a major share of the blame for government's failures, real and imagined, in meeting social and economic needs. A common caricature of the bureaucrat is that of an incompetent, petty tyrant who can do little but spout rules, lord it over those below him or her, and cower before those above. But how accurate is this popular image? When people are asked about their own encounters with bureaucrats, most of them report that they found these officials to be friendly, competent, efficient, helpful, and fair. A study conducted by Robert L. Kahn and his associates confirmed that although most Americans have stereotyped and derogatory mental pictures of public bureaucrats, they are generally quite satisfied with the behavior and attitudes of individual administrators with whom they have personally dealt (see Table 7.2).

A joke common in Washington, D.C., at one time was that civil servants and the early Vanguard missiles were similar: They don't work and you can't

[13] Franklin P. Kilpatrick, Milton C. Cummings, Jr., and M. Kent Jennings, *The Image of the Federal Service* (Washington, D.C.: Brookings, 1964).

Table 7.2 Public Satisfaction with Bureaucracy: Citizens' Opinions of Bureaucrats in General Versus Those They Have Dealt with Personally

	Percentage Satisfied or Highly Satisfied	
	General Evaluation	Own Experience
Overall satisfaction	65	74
Competence	31	72
Fairness	43	82
Consideration	38	77

Source: Robert I. Kahn, Barbara A. Gutek, Eugenia Barton, and Daniel Katz, "Americans Love Their Bureaucrats," *Psychology Today* Magazine. Copyright © 1975 by Ziff-Davis Publishing Company.

fire them. Yet, when a massive federal agency, the National Aeronautics and Space Administration (NASA), was faced with the challenge of landing an American on the moon within ten years, the agency generated an impressive number of technological advances, orchestrated a complicated network of interrelated efforts, and accomplished the task (in 1969) with almost two years to spare.

Citizen Access to the Bureaucracy Most citizens regard the federal bureaucracy, and bureaucracies generally, as immense, distant, and impersonal. Indeed, public bureaucracies *are* immense. Civil servants constitute one-sixth of the labor force and over one-third of all professional and technical workers in the United States. Contrary to a widespread popular belief the federal bureaucracy has not expanded as rapidly as state and local governments. Over the past three decades, the proliferation of federal agencies, which got under way in earnest during the New Deal, continued; but the size of the federal bureaucracy's work force has declined slightly in proportion to the population as a whole. In 1947 there were 14.4 federal workers for every 1,000 U.S. citizens. The ratio in 1981 was 12.7 per 1,000.

The gap between citizens and the federal bureaucracy is, of course, due to more than the size of government. The expertise that civil servants acquire in the details of regulations and the complexity of administrative agencies frequently remove the bureaucracy from meaningful control. The maze of procedures that provides the framework within which bureaucracies operate has made these agencies impersonal and their members insensitive to the differing needs of the individuals they serve.

For the most part, United States citizens seek to influence the federal bureaucracy through the Congress and the president. There are, however, some direct links between the citizenry and bureaucratic agencies. Thanks to the Freedom of Information Act — passed by Congress in 1966 and liberalized in 1974 and 1976 — citizens have at least theoretical access to the files and deliberations of their bureaucracy. Agencies are not supposed to refuse to show a citizen any records, or to exclude a citizen from a meeting, unless there is a good reason. Some things usually are kept confidential: personal information about individuals, strategies for combating crime, and national security matters.

Many agencies hold public hearings, either by tradition or by law, so that citizens can contribute — and react — to the proceedings. In addition, agencies sometimes ask citizens to sit on committees advising or directing administrative activity. The Migrant Health Act required such an arrangement. This device was also used extensively in the Community Action Programs, initiated by the Johnson administration in the mid-1960s to combat poverty. The experience of the Community Action Programs was sometimes frustrating for both bureaucrats and citizens. Members from the poor communities that sat on these committees frequently complained that they had little power and were often ignored, and administrators of the poverty programs felt that the citizens did not fully understand the intent and the methods of the government programs. These same frustrations are common among administrators and citizens who interact in hearings and other settings as well.

In short, although citizens have various opportunities to participate in governmental administration, their experiences have generally been unsatisfactory. The case of the migrant health program in Bakersfield is but one of many cases that illustrate this point.

CONCLUSION   Federal bureaucratic agencies are organizations designed to implement programs and policies authorized by Congress. The virtue of bureaucratic organization is supposed to be efficiency. In fact, however, public bureaucracies do more than merely implement legislation, and they frequently fall short of most measures of efficiency.

Elected officials who must rely on bureaucratic agencies for advice and for the implementation of legislation have learned to distrust bureaucrats generally and to regard administrative agencies as lethargic bodies that need to be pushed and prodded. Bureaucracies are, by their very nature, neither internally democratic nor easily controlled by more representative institutions. To assist them in their efforts to control and to guide the federal bureaucracy, both Congress and the president have hired ever growing staffs. Staff members are hired to provide alternative sources of advice and to provide closer oversight than legislators or the chief executive can do directly and personally. Of course, most of these staffs are also bureaucratically organized and, therefore, may be prone to some of the same problems they were created to overcome.

On the other hand, bureaucrats are equally disdainful of politics and politicians. Bureaucrats frequently regard demands made to satisfy political groups and to fulfill campaign promises as illegitimate intrusions. They fear that politically motivated demands will impinge on their ability to perform well as professionals. Increasingly, bureaucrats confront demands not only from politicians, but also from partially informed citizens seeking an input. If the bureaucracy has a negative image to the people and their elected representatives, then, from the bureaucrats' perspective, popular participation and legislative oversight are equally negative.

As governmental programs and policies increase in breadth and complexity, higher levels of competence and expertise will be needed from federal bureaucrats. At the same time, demands for accountability and political control over the bureaucracy are not likely to subside. Voters are going to take out their frustrations with governmental performance on elected officials; these officials, in turn, are going to want to ensure that they have a bureaucracy that responds to their leadership. The reaction to the evils of the spoils system resulted in a bureaucracy too far removed from the people and the ballot box. That reaction must be amended if democratic theory is to become more of a reality.

SUGGESTIONS FOR FURTHER READING

Downs, Anthony. *Inside Bureaucracy*. Boston: Little, Brown, 1967. This book outlines some of the pathologies of bureaucracies. Downs describes different types of bureaucrats and agencies and discusses how tendencies toward hierarchy and routine develop in organizations.

Heclo, Hugh. *A Government of Strangers*. Washington, D.C.: Brookings, 1977. This study of the relationships between senior civil servants and presidential appointees in the federal government is generally pessimistic about the ability of the latter to control the former. Heclo provides a vivid description of the tensions between the civil service and the White House.

Kramer, Fred A., ed. *Perspectives on Public Bureaucracy*. Cambridge, Mass.: Winthrop, 1973. Kramer has collected ten of the most famous essays on government administration and arranged them to show contrasting ways of viewing bureaucracy.

Nathan, Richard P. *The Administrative Plot That Failed*. New York: Wiley, 1975. As a member of the Nixon White House staff, Nathan viewed first hand the efforts of a president intent on securing control of the federal bureaucracy. Nathan describes three distinct strategies used by President Nixon and explains the limitations of each.

Rourke, Francis E. *Bureaucracy, Politics and Public Policy*. Boston: Little, Brown, 1969. One of the foremost authorities on the federal bureaucracy describes in this volume how administrative agencies participate in the policymaking process. The emphasis is on the political behavior of bureaucracies.

Seidman, Harold. *Politics, Position and Power. The Dynamics of Federal Organization*, 2nd ed. New York: Oxford University Press, 1975. Seidman draws on almost twenty-five years of experience in the Bureau of the Budget and presents a lucid and penetrating discussion of the federal bureaucracy. He provides a White House perspective on the reasons for organizational arrangements in government.

Thompson, Victor A. *Without Sympathy or Enthusiasm. The Problem of Administrative Compassion*. University, Alabama: University of Alabama Press, 1979. In this short book a scholar of public bureaucracies expresses his anger at bureaucrats who actively pursue social change.

Wildavsky, Aaron. *The Politics of the Budgetary Process*, 3rd ed. Boston: Little, Brown, 1979. The roles and strategies of Congress, the White House, and the bureaucracy in formulating a budget are discussed in this book. Wildavsky's analysis demonstrates the importance of political bargaining and of previous budgets in the budgetary process.

Chapter 8   The Legal System

American society is unusually law oriented. The "rule of law" — the idea that we are a nation ruled by laws and not by individuals — ranks high on our national scale of values. In the absence of a common religious or cultural heritage, Americans have often found in the secular law a means to define and regulate their common existence. Uncertainty about their democratic experiment pushed America's founders toward a strong faith in law as a reflection of transcendent and eternal values. Yet they also knew that law was to be made and enforced by ordinary people, and that in its emphasis on individual rights law might be a significant restraint on popular sovereignty. Their ambivalence about the law is understandable. In the words of historian Daniel J. Boorstin:

> We wish to believe both that our laws come from necessity beyond our reach, and that they are our own instruments, shaping our community to our chosen ends. We wish to believe that our laws are both changeless and changeable, divine and secular, permanent and temporary, transcendental and pragmatic.[1]

[1] Daniel J. Boorstin, "The Perils of Indwelling Law," in Robert P. Wolff, ed., *The Rule of Law* (New York: Simon and Schuster, 1971), p. 76.

THE FUNCTIONS OF A LEGAL SYSTEM Law has been defined as "the rules of conduct of any organized society . . . that are enforced by threat of punishment if they are violated."[2] Of course, merely passing a law does not guarantee that people's behavior will conform to it. Americans are strong believers in the concept of obedience to the law.[3] But there are exceptions, as the era of Prohibition and our more recent experience with marijuana laws clearly show. People may not obey a law that is contrary to strongly entrenched custom, that is morally offensive to them, or that disadvantages them in some important way.[4]

Any legal system, especially a democratic one, depends on people's willingness to comply with the law most of the time, whether or not they agree with it. A law that is intensely opposed by many citizens is likely to be unenforceable unless there are severe penalties for disobedience. A legal system that relies too heavily on such penalties is likely to invite opposition that can only undermine its legitimacy. For a democratic legal system to function effectively, it must have the trust and respect of its citizens.

Types of Law Law is more than rules and penalties. It is also the process and the institutions that create and enforce those rules. The basic theory of the American legal system is that it is the function of legislatures to create and abolish laws, and the function of the courts to interpret and apply them in resolving disputes. But that is much too simple a view. Legislatures are not the only "source" of law, and courts are not limited merely to enforcing statutes.

As we saw in Chapter 5 on Congress, many administrative bodies have been created in the federal bureaucracy to implement statutes passed by Congress. Thus, many — perhaps most — potential disputes over the law are resolved by administrative agencies. But not all problems involving legislation can be solved in this way, and so courts are constantly called on to interpret statutes. When a dispute arises, courts determine when, how, and to whom the statute in question applies. It is also necessary for the law to change to keep pace with new conditions of life and technological developments. Legislatures can and do modify statutes to meet these needs, but often the courts deal first with such problems. It is the interaction between courts and legislatures — between statutes and judge-made law — that produces "the law" in the United States.

What Does the Law Do? Legal systems differ, but in all societies the law is expected to serve certain functions. We have already noted that legal systems regulate behavior and resolve disputes. The legal system is also a means for establishing and protecting rights and for allocating resources. We shall look at each of these four important functions in turn.

---

[2] "Law," in *The New Columbia Encyclopedia* (New York: Columbia University Press, 1975), p. 1542.

[3] Harrell R. Rodgers, Jr. and Charles S. Bullock, III, *Coercion to Compliance* (Lexington, Mass.: Lexington Books, 1976), pp. 2–8.

[4] See Joseph Gusfield, *Symbolic Crusade* (Urbana: University of Illinois Press, 1963); and John Kaplan, *Marijuana: The New Prohibition* (New York: Pocket Books, 1971).

Regulating Behavior.   Law plays an important role in maintaining the social order by defining and regulating some relationships among members of a society. It specifies who can (or cannot) do what to whom. Sometimes the law reinforces relationships already established in custom, such as those between parents and children, or between parties to a business contract. At other times the law may be used to break down existing relationships or patterns of behavior, such as racial segregation, and replace them with others.

Regulative laws prohibit particular kinds of conduct regarded as harmful to other citizens, to the society as a whole, or to the violators themselves. For example, it is "against the law" to manufacture and sell an automobile that does not meet specified safety standards. It is against the law to cross the street against a red light. And it is against the law to practice the professions of law, medicine, and dentistry (to name just a few) without a license.

Resolving Disputes.   Law also helps to maintain social order by resolving disputes — disputes the anthropologist E. A. Hoebel once called "trouble cases." The vast majority of disputes in a society are never taken to court, but the law is (or should be) available to help resolve conflicts that cannot be settled elsewhere.

Some disputes may involve a criminal offense, the breaking of a law passed by government. Trespassing on your neighbor's property is a criminal offense, although most disputes about the ownership of property do not result in criminal charges. Most disputes that come to the courts, however, come in the form of "civil" rather than criminal cases. For example, persons sometimes cause injuries to others, either purposely or, more likely, by accident or negligence. This type of case is known as a *tort.* In such cases it is the victim's responsibility to seek a remedy, whereas when a crime has been committed, the wrongdoer is prosecuted by the state. A tort may or may not also involve a crime. The most common torts in today's society arise out of automobile accidents. But torts need not involve physical injury. A person's reputation may be injured by libel or slander, or his or her privacy may be invaded. Criminal and civil cases also differ with respect to the kinds of remedies that may be sought. In a criminal case, a fine or imprisonment is the most likely punishment for the convicted offender. In a civil case, the party responsible for the injury may be required to pay money damages or to provide other suitable compensation to the victim.

Establishing and Protecting Rights.   Laws also create or recognize rights and punish the violators or misusers of those rights. Some rights are open to all but require the permission of government before they can be exercised. This might be called the "licensing function" of law. The right to vote, to marry, to sell or purchase liquor, and to drive an automobile fall into this category.

The exercise of certain other rights — religious freedom, for example, or freedom of speech and of the press — does not require the permission of government, but often requires its protection. There are at least two reasons that government intervention is often needed to secure some rights. First, not all persons agree on their importance. Second, although most persons do believe in these rights in the abstract, they are less supportive when particular rights are exercised against what they see as their vital interests, or by persons of whom they disapprove. Freedom of speech is fine, but do we really want to allow a communist to speak at the neighborhood school? Racial equality is a constitutionally protected right, but does that require an affirmative action program that may prevent some whites from obtaining jobs or admission to professional school?

Allocating Resources. Law plays an important function in allocating a society's resources. It confers certain benefits on some persons or groups, but not on others. Not all citizens, for example, receive tax deductions for business expenses, or for interest payments on home mortgage loans. The grant of copyrights and patents to protect authors, artists, and inventors is an enormous benefit to some citizens. Government also provides huge subsidies to farmers, airlines, television networks, defense contractors, and other enterprises considered essential to the public interest.

Not all such resource allocations benefit the "haves" in our society, of course. The most controversial benefit laws today are those providing welfare payments, food stamps, and other subsidies to poor people. Income tax laws also redistribute resources from the rich to the poor, although the effectiveness of tax laws in redistributing wealth is a matter of dispute.

A special word needs to be said about the role of courts in allocating resources. Courts, unlike legislatures, do not possess the power of the purse. They cannot tax and, in theory, cannot spend. But in reality courts have come to play an important role in the law's allocation of resources. Court decisions may in fact require enormous public expenditures. For example, consider the cost of providing free legal services to indigent defendants, required as the result of several Supreme Court cases. Or consider the costs to Alabama when a federal district court found that the state's entire system of institutions for the mentally ill was below constitutional standards.[5] The state did not *have* to spend the money, but because the alternative of closing all such institutions and releasing the inmates was inconceivable, it complied. Court decisions may also lead to reallocation of resources in the private sector. Recent adoption by the courts of the doctrine of strict product liability has made it possible for consumers successfully to seek compensation from manufacturers for injuries caused by faulty merchandise.

LAW AND POLITICS Law is inextricably linked with government and the political process. There are, and must be, boundaries to define what is in the domain of the law, what

[5] *Wyatt* v. *Stickney*, 325 F. Supp. 781 (M.D. Ala. 1971).

belongs to the political system, and what is to be shared between them. But the boundary lines are not distinct.

Law and politics are competing but also interdependent forces that determine the allocation of values and resources. Yet they are judged by different standards. Law is often judged by its adherence to prescribed and fair procedures. In this sense, law is a particular way of doing things, and something is not truly "legal" unless it meets a high standard of internal consistency. If things are done the right way, it is often said, then, on the whole, the right things will be done.[6]

By contrast, politics is usually judged more by its results. To be sure, there are also unwritten "rules of the game" in politics that must be observed. But rules of this sort are means to various ends, not ends in themselves. Has the political process produced more justice and equality? Has it arrived at appropriate solutions to economic and social problems? It is largely by such results, or the lack of them, that we judge politics and politicians.

The distinctions between law and politics may be further clarified by reference to two important attributes of the legal system. One is the rule of *precedent,* or *stare decisis* (Latin for "let the decision stand"). *Stare decisis* is an important limitation on the freedom a judge has in deciding a particular case. It links past and present, and promotes continuity and stability. Politics, too, is concerned with continuity. But politics is, at least in theory, more open to change and less constrained formally by past practices and policies.

Another distinctive tradition of the law is *judicial independence,* symbolized by the principle that judges are accountable to the law, not to political authorities or to public opinion. Judicial decisions must accord with the law. They should neither be arbitrary nor reflect the personal bias of the judge. Judges should not be agents for any particular "cause" except the cause of justice itself. Political officials, by contrast, are expected to be guided largely by those they serve.

Politics sets many of the boundaries of judicial power. Judges, appointed or elected, are selected through the political process. There is a continual movement of personnel from the political world to the legal world and, to a lesser extent, back again. A large number of American judges have been involved in politics, and an equally large number of politicians have been trained in the law. This political connection brings strength to the law, but also makes it more vulnerable to political influence.

This intermixture of law and politics can also be seen in the overlap of their functions. The main function of courts is deciding disputes, but courts also play an important policymaking role. Partly by design and partly by tradition, American courts and judges make important policy decisions that would not be attempted by judges in other countries. In this respect they are centers of

---

[6] See Virginia Held, "Justification: Legal and Political," *Ethics* 86 (1975): 1–15; and Richard Richardson and Kenneth Vines, *The Politics of Federal Courts* (Boston: Little, Brown, 1970), pp. 7–11.

political power that compete with other — legislative and administrative — power centers. They are particularly receptive to groups that have been defeated or anticipate defeat in the political process. (This receptivity will be discussed further in Chapter 14.)

THE CULTURE OF AMERICAN LAW

The term *culture* refers to a set of enduring beliefs, symbols, and values that helps to define how a social system functions, and how its participants view and support that system. Thus we may speak of French culture, or American culture, or the culture of the French or American legal systems. We have already suggested that Americans are unusually dependent on the legal system for resolving disputes and in formulating public policy. What are some other distinctive attributes of the American legal culture, and what are their consequences?

Constitutionalism

Constitutionalism is the belief in the primacy of constitutional government. Every nation has a constitution in the sense of having a set of fundamental laws that provide for the basic organization of government, a basic statement of the society's foundation values, a specification of what powers government may and may not exercise, and an enumeration of those rights the people retain. But in many countries constitutions are not highly regarded; they are changed or discarded to suit the political needs of the moment. In some countries, such as Great Britain, constitutions are "unwritten" in the sense that they consist merely of selected documents or events in those nations' histories. In contrast, the American Constitution was one of the first written constitutions, and is the oldest of those still in effect. The framers deliberately made formal amendment of the Constitution difficult. But periodic interpretation by the Supreme Court and occasional amendments have kept the Constitution relatively up to date.

The American Constitution of 1787 was a pragmatic document, arising out of the experiences — and hopes — of the framers, many of whom were experienced politicians. This document established a model of compromise and accommodation that has structured American law and politics. It soon took on an aura of divine inspiration, becoming a symbol of political virtue whose appeal has improved with age. One result of this mystique is that judges are invested with a special responsibility to defend the constitutional system as they see it, and with a special legitimacy when they act in this role.

Legalism

Legalism refers to a strong tendency to use the law to resolve disputes and to regulate human conduct. Law is a set of procedures and a forum for resolving disputes, as well as a belief in a society that is governed by rules.[7] Many argue that the "rule of law" is an empty slogan that promises equality and fair treat-

---

[7] See Judith Shklar, *Legalism* (Cambridge, Mass.: Harvard University Press, 1964); and Philip Selznick, *Law, Society and Moral Evolution* (New York: Russell Sage, 1969), esp. chap. 1.

ment while concealing and perhaps even promoting injustice. As they see it, the equality the law professes to promote merely masks basic inequalities in our society. Worse still, it makes those inequities impervious to change. To such critics of the left, law can never be an instrument of justice or an effective agent of social change.[8] Despite such criticisms, however, faith in the law and legal procedures as a way of resolving disputes remains high.

Overcriminalization   The expression "there ought to be a law" aptly describes the American tendency to regulate by law behavior that, in some other societies, might be left to the control of custom or not regulated at all. If there is a problem, Americans often assume that a law will solve it. A good example is our use of the criminal law to impose moral standards, particularly those involving alcohol, drugs, or sexual behavior. Recent critics of this tendency have argued that "overcriminalization," or excessive reliance on criminal penalties to regulate moral behavior, is a major problem in our legal system. For one thing, laws that prohibit "crimes without victims," such as prostitution and the possession of marijuana, are often enforced unevenly. This violates basic principles of fairness and consistency. Such laws often foster social tension and hostility instead of stability and order.[9]

The passage of a law does not necessarily mean that it will be effectively enforced. It announces that a particular set of values is to be preferred and a particular standard of conduct followed, but actual enforcement is an entirely different matter. Laws are often passed without the provision of the resources necessary to implement them. For example, laws that regulate working conditions in dangerous occupations are often violated because there are not enough inspectors to enforce them. Often, only after a scandal or disaster does pressure mount to enforce some laws fully. The 1972 Buffalo Creek mine-disaster in West Virginia, a flood that killed 114 persons, is a case in point. Investigators found that the dangerous conditions leading to the flood had not been corrected, despite warnings and federal and state laws prohibiting them.[10]

Sometimes laws are underenforced by common consent. Today the police rarely make an effort to enforce marijuana laws against users. In a few states and communities marijuana possession has been decriminalized to a mere ordinance violation, and the attendant penalties have been reduced. But the mood of the public has been to ignore these statutes rather than repeal them, and this mood has been reflected in lax enforcement by the police.

Too Much Reliance on Courts.   The tendency to overuse the law is related to the widespread tendency to rely on the courts to establish public policy. *Litigation* is the process of invoking judicial intervention in a dispute, and

---

[8] See the various essays in Jonathan Black, ed., *Radical Lawyers* (New York: Avon, 1971).

[9] For an excellent discussion of this phenomenon, see Norval Morris and Gordon Hawkins, *The Honest Politician's Guide to Crime Control* (Chicago: University of Chicago Press, 1971), chap. 1; and Kaplan, *Marijuana.*

[10] Gerald M. Stern, *The Buffalo Creek Disaster* (New York: Random House, 1976).

Americans have become an uncommonly litigious people. In the last generation, individuals and groups have increasingly turned to the courts, particularly the federal courts, to challenge established values and practices and to bring about social change. In 1954 the Supreme Court ruled in the case of *Brown* v. *Board of Education* (of Topeka, Kansas) that racial segregation of the public schools is unconstitutional. This decision has become a model for the use of litigation to bring about social change.[11] Courts today are still involved in determining appropriate remedies for school segregation; one of these, school busing, has become a controversial national issue. The issues that come to the courts today mirror the problems of our society. They involve energy and the environment; the rights of consumers, students, prisoners, and welfare recipients; the financing of public education; decriminalization of certain sex offenses; sex and race discrimination and affirmative action programs.

Many people would agree with the charge that today "we have an imperial judiciary — intruding into people's lives in a manner unparalleled in our history."[12] The courts, these critics say, not only are intruding unnecessarily into the lives of people, but also are infringing outrageously on the traditional prerogatives of other governmental institutions in a way that weakens the authority of those institutions. "Government by lawsuit" contributes to a spiral of litigation that is rapidly becoming a burden on both state and federal courts.

Critics of "judicial imperialism" point out that a single judge can undo policy decisions by our elected leaders, as happened in 1976 when a judge overruled a cutback by the president and Congress in the federal food stamp program.[13] Some are dismayed that a federal court in 1976 told Mobile, Alabama, how its government must be organized.[14] Others are upset that federal courts have issued such detailed operating instructions for many state jails and hospitals that judges have become, in effect, the administrators of those facilities.

Defenders of "judicial activism," as this trend is often called, counter that Mobile's municipal government was structured in a way that denied its large black population political representation. They point out, too, that conditions in many jails and hospitals "taken over" by the courts were indisputably inhumane. The philosophy underlying such examples of modern judicial activism is summed up in a remark by United States District Judge Frank M. Johnson of Alabama:

> I didn't ask for any of these cases. In an ideal society, all of these judgments and decisions should be made by those to whom we have entrusted these responsibilities. But when governmental institutions fail to make these judgments and

[11] 347 U.U. 483 (1954). For the definitive treatment of this case and its aftermath, see Richard Kluger, *Simple Justice* (New York: Knopf, 1976).

[12] Nathan Glazer, "Toward an Imperial Judiciary?" *The Public Interest* 41 (1975): 104–23. See also Donald Horowitz, *The Courts and Social Policy* (Washington, D.C.: Brookings, 1977).

[13] *Dupler* v. *City of Portland*, 421 F. Supp. 1314 (1976).

[14] A federal court ordered Mobile to replace its commission form of government with a mayor-council type in order to increase the voting power of black citizens. The Supreme Court eventually reversed the lower court in *Mobile* v. *Bolden*, 64 L.Ed. 47 (1980).

decisions in a manner which comports with the Constitution, the Federal courts have a duty to remedy this violation.[15]

The Adversary System   The *adversary system* is the major structural feature of the American legal system. Once labeled by Jerome Frank the "fight theory of justice,"[16] the adversary system considers a court trial to be a contest between the disputants, with the judge (and the jury, if any) as the referee. Proponents of the adversary system assume that the best way to discover the truth is for each side to present the facts most favorable to its own position and make the strongest argument it can.

The adversary system leaves to the court the problem of determining who is telling the truth — or, more realistically speaking, who has the stronger case. Elaborate rules bar unreliable evidence (such as hearsay testimony) and test the truth of evidence that is presented. The parties do not merely present their case in narrative form. Instead, each witness may be subjected to intense cross-examination, that is, interrogation, by the opposing side. In most cases, the contest is carried out by highly skilled specialists (lawyers) and not by the disputants themselves.

The adversary system, then, emphasizes conflict over cooperation. The very words used to describe the process stress the element of conflict: Disputants "contest" a case and enjoy a "victory" or suffer a "defeat" in court. The system, which has strong roots in the American tradition of individualism and laissez faire, shows the great faith of Americans that "right" or justice will prevail when opposing parties clash under conditions of formal equality.[17]

Problems of the Adversary System.   Critics of the adversary system note, however, that in the courtroom the search for truth is often reduced to a battle to *exclude* relevant evidence. And they note the often false assumption that the contesting parties have substantially equal resources. Even with more free-legal-services programs, legal representation in the United States favors the wealthy. The underdog sometimes does triumph in court, but on the whole it is the "haves" who come out ahead. All too often, the winner in court is the party with the most skillful lawyer or the most resources, not necessarily the most just cause.[18]

Consensus and Plea Bargaining.   Although our courts are formally organized on the adversary system model, we have moved significantly away from it at the trial-court level. Most civil cases filed in the United States are now disposed of *consensually*, that is, by an agreement between the parties before

[15] Quoted in *The New York Times*, April 24, 1977.
[16] Jerome Frank, *Courts on Trial* (New York: Atheneum, 1963), chap. 6.
[17] For a brief treatment of these arguments, see Stuart Nagel and Marian Neef, "The Adversary Nature of the American Legal System from a Historical Perspective," *New York Law Forum* 20 (1974): 123–64.
[18] Marc Galanter, "Why the 'Haves' Come Out Ahead: Speculations on the Nature of Legal Change," *Law & Society Review* 9 (1974): 95–160.

the case goes to trial. The majority of criminal cases in the United States are concluded when the defendant enters a plea of guilty. In many of these cases the plea is the result of *plea bargaining* between the defendant's lawyer and the prosecutor.[19] Usually the defendant agrees to plead guilty to a less serious charge — one that carries a reduced maximum penalty. For example, he or she might plead guilty to manslaughter instead of second-degree murder, or to disorderly conduct instead of shoplifting. Sometimes the prosecutor also agrees to recommend that the judge impose a lenient sentence, or that the sentence be served in a local jail instead of the state penitentiary.

As in any bargain, both sides see an advantage. The prosecutor obtains a sure conviction without having to expend time, effort, and other resources preparing for a trial. The defendant, although conceding guilt and waiving the right to a trial, is able to get off with a significantly reduced penalty. Because the possibility of acquittal in a criminal trial is, at best, not very good, and because criminal defendants convicted at trial often receive more severe sentences than do those who plead guilty, it seems a good bargain. A defendant who is poor and unable to make bail may actually win release from jail by pleading guilty. If the defendant demands a trial, he or she will probably have to wait many months in jail because the court docket is already crowded with other cases. He will likely lose his job, making things even harder for his family. Thus he is under what many critics of plea bargaining regard as unfair pressure.[20]

In a plea bargain, although the prosecutor and the defendant are still adversaries, the most unpredictable elements of the conflict have been reduced. The formal adversary system, with its emphasis on the procedural rights of defendants, is replaced by a system that resembles an assembly line. Cases are processed rather than adjudicated, and the prosecutor and defense attorney, rather than a judge or jury, decide whether the accused is innocent or guilty. The degree of guilt and the penalty to be imposed are determined by negotiation subject to agreement by the judge; only the judge can impose sentence. Of course, discretion is a staple and unavoidable fact of modern government, and it is not surprising that it also permeates the legal system. The discretion of the prosecutor in processing guilty pleas is but one prominent example.[21]

AMERICA'S COURT SYSTEMS We have now described some of the main features of the American legal culture. Yet in doing so we have deliberately ignored a most important fact: There is no single court system in the United States. Rather, law in the United States is served by many court systems. There is a single, integrated system of

[19] Arthur Rosett and Donald R. Cressey, *Justice by Consent* (Philadelphia: Lippincott, 1976).

[20] Ibid., chap. 7. Also see James Eisenstein and Herbert Jacob, *Felony Justice* (Boston: Little, Brown, 1976); Malcolm Feeley, *The Process is the Punishment* (New York: Russell Sage, 1979); and Thomas M. Uhlman and N. Darlene Walker, " 'He Takes Some of My Time: I Take Some of His': An Analysis of Sentencing Patterns in Jury Cases," *Law & Society Review* 14 (1980), 323–42.

[21] Kenneth Culp Davis, *Discretionary Justice* (Urbana: University of Illinois Press, 1971), chaps. 6, 7.

federal courts, established by Congress under the Constitution. There is also a comparable system of courts in each of the fifty states. It would not be an exaggeration to speak of about a hundred court systems. At last count there were about 18,000 courts in the United States.

The American legal system is thus highly decentralized. State and federal courts overlap in function and *jurisdiction* (the types of cases courts may properly decide) and, to a lesser extent, in structure. The vast majority of both civil and criminal cases begin and end in the state courts. Yet the federal courts, our primary focus in this book, are very important. To understand the work of the federal courts, we must also look at the role and function of the state courts, and at the relationship between them.

Establishment of the Federal Courts The framers of the Constitution recognized the need for a central judicial authority and agreed on the need for a Supreme Court. But states' rights advocates opposed the creation of a separate system of lower federal courts that would parallel those already existing in each state. Such federal courts, they argued, would encroach on the jurisdiction of the states. The nationalists replied that a federal court system was needed to counter local and regional prejudices and to enforce federal laws uniformly. James Madison proposed that Congress be empowered to establish lower federal courts. That compromise was adopted by the Constitutional Convention, and Article III of the Constitution states: "The judicial Power of the United States shall be vested in one supreme Court, and in such inferior Courts as the Congress may from time to time ordain and establish."

Establishing a federal judiciary was a first order of business for the First Congress. The Judiciary Act of 1789 divided the country into thirteen districts, and established in each a federal district court, presided over by a federal district judge. These were trial courts of general jurisdiction, the initial point of access to the federal court system. In addition, an intermediate appellate or "circuit" court was established in each of three larger geographic regions. Each circuit court consisted of one local district judge and two Supreme Court justices who had to divide their time between the business of the Supreme Court in Washington and "riding circuit." It was not until 1891 that a permanent system of federal appellate courts was created and the onerous circuit-riding duties of Supreme Court justices were finally abolished.

The new federal district courts had a distinctly regional flavor. They were established within state lines and tended to be influenced by state concerns. Federal judges had to reside in the state where they held court, and, though appointed by the president, had to be confirmed by the Senate. It was expected that federal judges would thus be products of the local environment and sensitive to its needs.

The Federal Courts Today The federal district courts — the trial courts of general jurisdiction — are still at the base of the federal court system. At present there are ninety-five district courts: at least one in every state (as many as four in the larger states), as well as in the District of Columbia, Puerto Rico, Guam, the Virgin Islands, the Canal Zone, and the Northern Mariana Islands. Except in unusual circumstances, district judges sit alone in deciding cases. Currently about 550 federal district judgeships are authorized by Congress. Figure 8.1 shows the structure of the American court system.

Above the district courts there are twelve intermediate courts of appeal, one for the District of Columbia and eleven numbered circuits identified as the "Court of Appeals for the __th Circuit."[22] The courts of appeals have only appellate jurisdiction; that is, they hear only cases appealed from the district courts and from certain federal administrative agencies. The courts of appeals vary in size from 4 to 23 judges; in all there are about 132 appeals judges. Most cases brought to the courts of appeals are heard by panels of three judges, but a few extraordinary cases may be heard by an entire court.

At the top of the federal court system is the nine-member Supreme Court. The Supreme Court's legal and political roles are so important and complex that we shall devote the next chapter to them.

Besides these general courts, there are various federal courts of specialized jurisdiction: the Court of Claims, which hears claims against the United States government; the Customs Court; the Court of Customs and Patent Appeals; the Tax Court; and the Court of Military Appeals.

Cases Heard in the District Courts.   District courts hear both civil and criminal cases, including "diversity of citizenship" cases (in which a citizen of one state sues a citizen of another state). They review some actions by administrative agencies, enforce federal laws, and supervise bankruptcy proceedings and the naturalization of aliens.

In calendar 1979, 162,469 civil cases were commenced in the district courts, an increase of 12.5 percent over the previous year. Civil cases in the district courts have been increasing steadily for many decades. The 1979 figure is nearly 350 percent greater than the number of cases filed in 1940. Most civil cases are settled out of court; in 1979, only 6.6 percent were terminated by a trial.

Also in calendar 1979, 30,106 criminal cases were initiated, a *decrease* of 10 percent from the previous year. (Because the Constitution does not authorize Congress to enact a general criminal code, about 99 percent of all criminal cases in the United States arise in the state courts; those in the federal courts involve primarily the enforcement of federal statutes.) Of all the criminal cases finally decided in 1979, only about 17 percent were resolved by trial; the remainder were disposed by guilty pleas or dismissal of the charges by the prosecution.

---

[22] The twelfth circuit was created in 1981 by splitting the old 5th Circuit — the nation's busiest. The 5th Circuit will now comprise Louisiana, Mississippi, the Canal Zone, and Texas; Alabama, Florida, and Georgia will make up the new 11th Circuit.

Figure 8.1 Courts in the United States

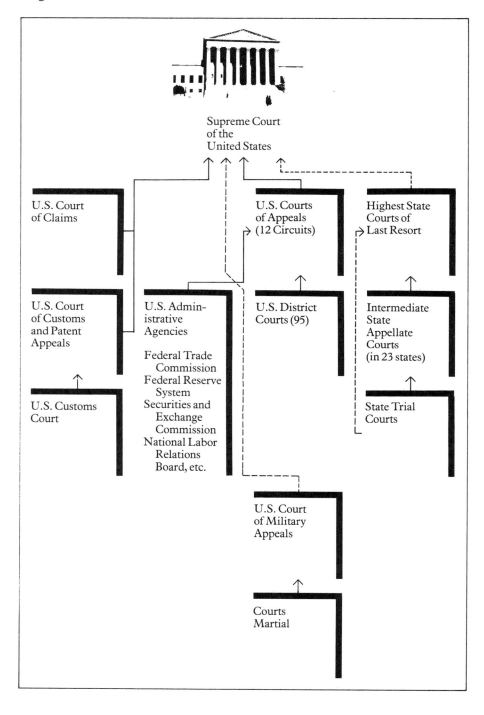

Cases in the Courts of Appeals. The courts of appeals hear cases from the district courts, the federal administrative agencies (such as the National Labor Relations Board or the Federal Trade Commission), and some of the specialized courts. In fiscal 1979, a total of 21,680 appeals were filed, an increase of more than 300 percent over 1961. The bulk of these were from the district courts. The vast majority of cases *filed* in the district courts never get to a court of appeals, but an increasing number of cases *decided by* the district courts — particularly criminal cases — are appealed. One of the distinguishing features of the American legal system is the relative ease with which cases can be appealed. It is not unusual for criminal cases to drag on for years, with successive appeals to different courts.

The State Courts In about half the states one finds the same three tiers of courts found in the federal court system: a set of trial courts of general jurisdiction, intermediate courts of appeals, and a state supreme court. In the other half there are no intermediate appellate courts, and appeals from the trial courts are taken directly to the state supreme court.

The modern trend is toward simplification and generalized courts, but there are still many specialized state courts. Most numerous are small claims courts, juvenile courts, traffic courts, probate courts, and domestic relations courts. Some cities have courts that handle only narcotics or gambling cases, and, perhaps, generalized misdemeanor courts known as magistrate's courts or police courts. Justice of the peace courts traditionally handled the first level of judicial business in rural America, but they have been abolished in many states. Generally, the more simplified and "modern" court systems are found in the newer, western states.

It is the state courts that most directly affect the lives of the ordinary citizens. Most civil suits are filed and adjudicated there, and most legal concerns of citizens are administered there: wills and estates, divorces, creditor-debtor actions, and so on. Most cases begun in a state court remain within the state judicial system, with final appeals being taken to the highest court of the state. State courts are independent of each other, although one state will normally enforce in its own courts decisions rendered in civil cases by judges in other states.

State Courts and The relationship between state and federal courts is complex and often quar-
Federal Courts relsome. The "supremacy clause" (Article VI, Section 2) of the Constitution requires state judges to obey and enforce the federal Constitution and the rights it protects, even if this means that a state law or even the state's own constitution must be disregarded. In practice, however, litigants must occasionally go to the federal courts to protect their federal constitutional rights. State judges, often elected for short terms, tend to be more responsive to state and local interests.

A good example occurred recently in a case from Utah. In 1975 the United States Supreme Court ruled that a Utah law establishing the age of majority as eighteen for women and twenty-one for men was discriminatory and prohibited by the equal protection clause of the Fourteenth Amendment. The case was returned to the Utah Supreme Court for appropriate action. But Utah's highest court was unwilling to accept the United States Supreme Court's decision. The Utah court held, 3–2, that the age of majority was a matter for the states to determine for themselves (as it is *unless* federal constitutional questions are raised) and rejected the interference of the Supreme Court. Somewhat testily, the Utah majority noted: "Regardless of what a judge may think about equality, his thinking cannot change the facts of life. . . . To judicially hold that males and females attain their maturity at the same age is to be blind to the biological facts of life."

When the case was appealed again to the United States Supreme Court, it held that the Utah court had obviously "misunderstood" the original ruling. Although the state could comply with the decision either by raising the age of majority for women or by lowering it for men, it could not maintain different ages for men and women.[23] This time the Utah court acquiesced.

State courts cannot interfere with cases in the federal courts, and a litigant or defendant cannot appeal a decision from a federal to a state court. But certain decisions of state courts may be brought to the federal courts for review. The state decision must be final, and all avenues of appeal *within* the state courts must have been exhausted. In theory, but not always in practice, this means that the case must have been reviewed by the state's highest court. The litigant must also be able to establish a *federal* question. This means that he or she must allege that the state law or decision is contrary to a federal treaty or statute, or to the United States Constitution itself. In criminal cases, a convicted defendant also has the right to petition a lower federal court for a writ of *habeas corpus*, by which he may seek federal review of his conviction by alleging that he has been deprived of federal constitutional rights.[24] But in the absence of a federal question, the federal courts have no jurisdiction to review state court decisions.

THE PARTICIPANTS IN OUR LEGAL SYSTEM Judges are the most visible symbols of the legal system and its goals of justice and equality before the law. Their black robes and solemn demeanor, their high seat at the front of the courtroom, and the deference shown to them by everyone else all emphasize the majesty and authority of the law. But very little of the business of the law is conducted in the courtroom, and judges are not the only important decision makers. Judges depend on the work of other officials in many important ways.

Prosecutors, defense attorneys, and juries play important roles in deciding cases. Their work and importance are generally understood, and will be dis-

---

[23]*Stanton* v. *Stanton,* U.S. 50 L Ed. 2nd 723 (1977).

[24]In 1976 the Supreme Court significantly limited the right of a state prisoner to challenge the constitutionality of his arrest and conviction in a habeas corpus proceeding. *Stone* v. *Powell,* 428 U.S. 465 (1976).

cussed later. But there are other, less visible courtroom personnel, such as the clerks of court, who have more influence than most people realize. Clerks do not decide cases, but, especially in large, urban courts, they play an important role in deciding when cases will be heard. Probation and parole officers provide important information about criminal defendants, such as their potential for rehabilitation. Such information often determines a judge's decision to impose or withhold a jail sentence. In the federal courts, the recently created position of United States Magistrate provides each federal court with an "assistant judge." Magistrates, appointed by the district judges, hold preliminary hearings, set bail, and perform other judicial and administrative tasks to free the time of busy judges. With the consent of the defendant, they may even conduct trials in misdemeanor cases. Misdemeanors are less serious crimes, usually punishable by small fines or by less than a year in jail, or both; felonies are more serious offenses, usually punishable by larger fines and/or more than a year in jail.

Judges Federal district judges do more than merely preside at trials. Indeed, as we have already noted, only a small percentage of cases brought to the courts actually go to trial. In criminal cases, the judge's pretrial role is minor. Guilty pleas must be stated in open court and accepted by the judge. The judge must determine that the defendant has been properly charged with a crime, that he is pleading guilty without coercion, that he has been advised by counsel, and that the prosecutor has evidence adequate to sustain a conviction if the case were to be tried. But the basic impetus for settlement is from the prosecutor rather than the judge, whose main function is to ratify an agreement already reached. In civil cases, the judge may play an active role as a mediator between the parties, by, for example, conducting pretrial conferences in order to facilitate a settlement that will satisfy both parties. But the judge's role in inducing settlements varies greatly in different courts and different states.

The Judge's Role at Trial. If there is a trial, the judge must conduct it and decide all questions of law that arise. If the trial is a *bench* trial — that is, if there is no jury — then the judge must determine the facts of the case as well. In a criminal bench trial, the judge also must decide whether the defendant is guilty or not guilty. If the former, sentence must also be pronounced. In a civil bench trial the judge must decide in favor of either the plaintiff (the person who initiates the lawsuit) or the defendant. If he finds for the plaintiff, he must decide what level of money damages to award, or what other remedy to apply.

If the case is tried to a jury, then the jury has the responsibility of determining the facts (Did Mrs. Smith willfully fail to file her income tax returns?) and the verdict. In a criminal case the jury must determine whether the defendant is guilty or not guilty; in a civil case it must find in favor of either the plaintiff or defendant and, if it finds for the former, decide on the amount of damages to award.

United States District Judge John Sirica's persistent questioning and threats of heavy sentences for the Watergate burglary defendants helped reveal their connections to the Nixon administration. Later Sirica ordered President Nixon to produce transcripts of the White House tapes, an important factor leading to Nixon's resignation. With these events, a relatively unknown judge became a household word.

Thus, the role of the judge depends on whether or not there is a jury. If there is a jury, the judge plays a more passive role, but he must also be more careful about such matters as the admissibility of evidence. The judge must protect the jury from influences that could unfairly affect its deliberations and contaminate its verdict. A judge may have considerable influence on the outcome of a jury trial. His rulings on evidence, his charge to the jury at the conclusion of the trial, his demeanor and conduct in the courtroom, and his attitude toward the defendant and key witnesses all can influence the jury's verdict.

The trial judge sits alone and is required to make on-the-spot decisions in public, often about highly technical points of law. Decisions will be scrutinized and often challenged during trial and, after trial, form the basis of an appeal to a higher court.

The Role of Appeals Judges.   The losing party in a federal district court has the right to appeal to a federal court of appeals. In American law, appeals are almost always limited to questions of law: Was the trial conducted fairly and in accordance with the rules? Was there a constitutional violation? Was there sufficient evidence to support the verdict? Appeals are decided on the basis of written briefs submitted by each side along with a transcript of the trial. In some cases oral argument is presented by the attorneys for each side. Appellate judges rarely come into direct contact with the litigants. And they do not normally review the correctness of the verdict unless it is without *any* basis in fact.

Unlike trial courts, appellate court panels always consist of more than one judge — usually three. Decisions are thus collegial rather than individual. Usually, they are made after deliberation and research rather than on the spot. Decisions of appeals courts are usually accompanied by written opinions stating the reasons for the decision. Dissenting judges may write separately to voice their own views. Thus, the setting in which appeals judges function, and the role they play, are quite different from those of the trial courts.

The Selection of Judges. From this brief description of the role and function of federal judges, it should be clear that who the judge is may make an important difference in the outcome of a case. Judges must enforce the law, but they have much discretion in interpreting what the law means, what the facts are, and how the law should apply to each case. Judgeships are also highly desirable patronage positions, one of the most lucrative and most prestigious rewards for political service.[25]

The Constitution, because it did not directly establish a federal judicial system, makes no provision for selecting federal judges. It does provide that judges of the Supreme Court, and of "such inferior courts as the Congress may from time to time establish," shall hold office during good behavior and shall not have their salaries reduced while in office. But there are no stated qualifications in the Constitution for any federal judgeship, not even requirements of age and citizenship, both of which are stated for the presidency and for Congress. Only custom dictates that all federal judges be lawyers.

The Judiciary Act of 1789 established that lower federal judges should be selected in the same way as Supreme Court justices — by the president with the consent of the Senate. In practice, this selection process is quite complex. The Senate plays a rather passive role; few federal judicial appointments are denied confirmation. However, individual senators have an important voice in the selection of district judges from their own states. This right — actually a custom that has grown into an unwritten rule — has behind it the force of *senatorial courtesy*. Senatorial courtesy is rarely formally invoked, but the Senate rarely confirms a judicial nomination opposed by a senator of the president's party from the nominee's state.

Beginning with the Eisenhower administration, the American Bar Association (ABA) has played a crucial role in the selection of federal judges. Its Committee on Federal Judiciary screens potential federal judicial nominees

[25] Federal district judges currently earn a salary of $61,000; courts of appeals judges, $65,000; and associate justices of the Supreme Court, $81,000. The Chief Justice of the United States receives $84,700. On the selection of federal judges generally, see Joel B. Grossman, *Lawyers and Judges* (New York: Wiley, 1965); and Harold Chase, *Appointing Federal Judges* (Minneapolis: University of Minnesota Press, 1972). For an interesting popular account, see Joseph Goulden, *The Benchwarmers* (New York: Weybright and Talley, 1974).

and advises the attorney general of their qualifications. Some presidents have accorded virtual veto power to the ABA, a private organization, by agreeing not to nominate persons the ABA committee disapproves. Presidents Kennedy and Johnson refused to make such a pledge, but often followed the committee's advice. The committee's role will always be controversial because there is disagreement on the qualities — apart from honesty, integrity, judicial temperament, and objectivity — and backgrounds one should seek in a prospective judge. It is accepted that a judge should be a lawyer. But must a judge have prior experience as a trial lawyer or prior judicial experience in a lower court, as the ABA recommends? Should there be an age limit? Should prospective judges have political experience?

President Jimmy Carter introduced a major change in the process of selecting judges for the courts of appeals. Instead of relying primarily on the suggestions of senators from the states involved (such as senators from the states in the circuit in which a vacancy was to be filled), Carter established ad hoc judicial nominating commissions to screen potential candidates and recommend up to five names for each vacancy. These commissions provided for increased citizen input into the selection process. They also contributed to the fulfillment of one of Carter's 1976 campaign promises — to appoint to the federal bench more members of minority groups and more women. All told, Carter made 265 federal judicial appointments; of these, 38 were members of minorities and 41 were women. He appointed more minority and more female judges than did all previous presidents combined. President Reagan abolished the judicial nominating commissions soon after taking office.

Who Are the Judges? Federal judges are almost always members of the political party of the president who appoints them. For example, President Carter, a Democrat, appointed 258 judges, 240 of whom were Democrats. Presidents Nixon and Ford, his Republican predecessors, appointed 288 judges, of whom 259 were Republicans.

Federal judges always come from the state, and usually from the district, in which they are appointed. Historically, they have also come from relatively privileged backgrounds, and a disproportionate number have gone to the most prestigious private law schools. As a group, federal judges have been disproportionately white, male, Protestant, and Jewish; blacks, women, and Catholics are underrepresented in proportion to their numbers in the population. But these proportions vary depending on which party controls the White House. We have already noted President Carter's attempt to redress the imbalance of race and gender.

Regardless of religion, race, gender, or social status, one attribute that most federal judges have shared is political experience. Many judges have had previous political careers; many have held either appointed or elected office. About 40 percent have had some prior judicial experience.

What attitudes, then, are federal judges likely to bring to the bench? The recruitment process for federal judges is political, and partisan. Judges chosen in this manner are likely to be sensitive to the realities of politics and, on some issues, are likely to reflect the values and attitudes of the presidents who appointed them. On others, the backgrounds of the judges themselves are likely to provide some cues to how they will act as judges.

Democratic judges tend to be more liberal on economic issues and on some civil liberties questions. Religion and age are also influential, but there is no automatic correlation between such background factors and judicial decisions. Age is a particularly tricky variable. Although they can retire at seventy, many judges remain in service much longer. Age is no sure barometer of conservatism, but some judges can always be expected to represent the political and legal views of a passing generation. For example, some judges who resisted enforcing the Supreme Court's school desegregation decision, *Brown* v. *Board of Education* (1954), were appointees of Presidents Coolidge and Hoover. They had received their legal training at the turn of the century, when the idea of racial equality was not widely held, and the rule of "separate but equal," repudiated in the *Brown* decision, was the law of the land. On the other hand, some of the most creative minds and the greatest responsiveness to new ideas in American politics today can be found among judges nearer the age of retirement than that of youthful rebellion. Thus it is wise to remember that the "lawyer is not always father to the judge,"[26] and that ascribing to any individual judge the characteristics of some larger category may be quite inaccurate.[27]

Lawyers Lawyers are the movers and shakers of our legal and political system. They occupy a majority of the important political positions and virtually all the judicial positions. About two-thirds of our presidents have been trained in the law (although only three of ten since 1929). Currently, more than half the members of Congress are lawyers, as are many top government officials and administrators.

America has been called a lawyers' paradise. There are about 500,000 lawyers in the United States today, more than all the lawyers in the rest of the world combined. We have one lawyer for every 530 citizens, the highest ratio in the world. The lawyer population is growing twice as rapidly as the population as a whole.[28]

These figures would not have surprised Alexis de Tocqueville, who in 1835 wrote — somewhat apprehensively — of the growing role of lawyers as the aristocracy of a society without a hereditary nobility or royalty. He saw lawyers as America's natural leadership class and as an effective counterpoint to the

[26] Paul Freund, *The Supreme Court of the United States: Its Business, Purposes and Performance* (New York: Meridian, 1961), p. 116.

[27] Sheldon Goldman, "Judicial Backgrounds, Recruitment, and the Party Variable: The Case of the Johnson and Nixon Appointees to the United States District and Appeals Courts," *Arizona State Law Journal*, 1974, pp. 211–22; and Sheldon Goldman and Thomas Jahnige, *The Federal Courts as a Political System*, 2nd ed. (New York: Harper and Row, 1975), pp. 46–73.

[28] Jerrold Auerbach, "A Plague of Lawyers," *Harper's*, October 1976; and Tom Goldstein, "Law, Fastest Growing Profession, May Find Prosperity Precarious," *The New York Times*, May 16, 1977.

Four Famous American Lawyers: Clarence Darrow, F. Lee Bailey, Melvin Belli, William Kunstler

Clarence Darrow (left), shown with William Jennings Bryan during the famous "Monkey Trial" in Tennessee in 1925, was the best-known criminal lawyer of his time. At this trial Darrow defended a young school teacher, John Scopes, not for a violent crime but for teaching the theory of evolution in violation of a state law. Assisting the prosecution was Bryan, thrice defeated Democratic candidate for president and an outspoken religious fundamentalist. Arguing before an unsympathetic jury in a hostile small-town environment, Darrow mercilessly cross-examined Bryan as an "expert" witness on the Bible. Bryan revealed his belief in a literal interpretation of the Bible and a woeful ignorance of modern science, exposing himself to much ridicule; the strain of the trial was too much, and he died shortly thereafter. Scopes was convicted, but received only a nominal fine;

history has regarded him as vindicated and Darrow as the victor. In Epperson v. Arkansas *(1968), an Arkansas statute modeled after the Tennessee evolution law was declared unconstitutional by the Supreme Court as contrary to the First and Fourteenth Amendments.*

Like Darrow, F. Lee Bailey established his reputation in criminal cases. Shown here with his most famous client, Patricia Hearst, Bailey gained attention in the 1960s by winning a reversal in the Sam Sheppard murder case. In probably the most notorious murder trial of the 1950s, Dr. Sheppard was convicted of murdering his wife, notwithstanding his insistence that the murderer had been a "bushy-haired intruder." The trial was a local and national sensation whose most salacious details were eagerly reported by the press, and the judge's unwillingness to impose any restraints further contributed to a circus atmosphere. Several years after Sheppard had begun serving a life sentence, Bailey was retained and won a reversal by convincing the Supreme Court that his client had not received a fair trial. Bailey's flamboyant and maverick life style have often obscured the fact that he is an excellent — if very expensive — lawyer. He was unable to win acquittal for Patricia Hearst in her bank robbery trial, but through a variety of legal maneuvers he secured her release on bail after serving only part of her sentence while the case remained pending on appeal.

Melvin Belli gained national recognition by his defense of Jack Ruby, the murderer of Lee Harvey Oswald, the accused assassin of John F. Kennedy. But this outspoken San Francisco lawyer has made his legal reputation and fortune as a personal injury lawyer, a specialist in representing injured persons who are suing for damages. Such suits run the gamut from automobile accident injuries to medical malpractice. In most such cases, the attorney representing the plaintiff does not receive a set fee for his services. Instead he is paid on a contingent basis — nothing if the case is lost and anywhere from one quarter to one half of the damages recovered if the case is won. The contingent fee system has many critics, partly because it tends to produce some very rich lawyers and partly because it may affect the lawyer's strategy. Instead of doing what is best for his client, a lawyer may either risk pushing for a big settlement or he may be overcautious and advise his client to settle for less money than the merits of the case would indicate. Defenders of the contingent fee system argue that it is probably the only way that some individuals could afford a lawyer at all.

William Kunstler, shown here about to address a 1970 Black Panther defense rally in Brooklyn, is widely regarded as America's leading radical lawyer because of his impas-

sioned defense of political radicals in the 1960s. He is best known as counsel for the "Chicago Seven," who were charged with various crimes arising from the demonstrations at the 1968 Democratic National Convention. Six of the "Seven" were convicted, but all appealed successfully to higher courts. Because of their unconventional and sometimes disruptive courtroom behavior, Kunstler and the defendants were cited for contempt of court and sentenced to prison. That sentence was also overturned on appeal. Kunstler and other radical lawyers have always regarded themselves as much attorneys for a cause as for specific clients. By using nonconformist and often outrageous courtroom tactics, they have sought to "demystify" the law, to expose its biases, and to win sympathy (if not always acquittal) for their clients. Often they have provoked prosecutors and judges into responding in kind. As in the Chicago Seven case, this judicial reaction has often provided the basis for reversing convictions on appeal.

turbulence of popular democracy, with its potential for a "tyranny of the majority."[29] The "rule of law," of which lawyers were seen as the chief curators, was an important adhesive in holding together a complex industrial society. But the growth of the legal profession, in both numbers and political dominance, would have upset the framers of the Constitution. They shared the then traditional distrust of lawyers as mere hired advocates — without scruples — for those who could afford them. Lawyers, considered to place a higher premium on winning a case than on doing justice, originally were barred in some states and discouraged elsewhere.[30]

The Legal Profession. Lawyers in the United States fall into three broad categories: those who are in private practice, those who work for corporations and other private institutions, and those who are employed by government. Lawyers in private practice are by far the largest group, constituting about 70 percent of the practicing bar.

Lawyers are unevenly distributed. The people with the most resources also command the lion's share of legal services. In the past generation there has been a proliferation of large law firms whose main clients are corporations. In 1980, the largest law firm, Baker and McKenzie in Chicago, employed 544 lawyers. There are still lawyers in smaller communities, and some in cities as well, who hang out the proverbial shingle and practice by themselves. But the "solo practitioner" is something of an anachronism in an increasingly urban society and corporation-dominated economy. The leaders of the bar have traditionally come from among those who represent wealthy, corporate clients. And the American bar is still predominantly white, male, and middle class.[31]

Lawyers for Indigents. The racial, social, and economic stratification of the bar contributes to the serious legal underrepresentation of minorities and the poor. Although there is a ratio of one lawyer for every 530 Americans, it has been estimated that there is only one lawyer for every 7,000 poor Americans.[32] Without adequate legal representation, it is nearly impossible to protect one's rights in a system so dependent on courts and the law.

Although the consequences of inadequate legal representation are severe in both civil and criminal cases, they are most visible in criminal cases. Not until 1938 did the Supreme Court hold that every person accused of a serious crime in the federal courts who could not afford to hire a lawyer was entitled to have

[29] Alexis de Tocqueville, *Democracy in America* (New York: Vintage Books, 1945, Phillips Bradley edition), pp. 282–90.

[30] Thomas Ehrlich, "Legal Pollution," *The New York Times Magazine*, February 8, 1976. Ehrlich adds (p. 17), 'In colonial Pennsylvania, it was said, "They have no lawyers . . . 'tis a happy country.' "

[31] For the best recent study of the American legal profession, see Jerrold Auerbach, *Unequal Justice* (New York: Oxford University Press, 1976). The number of female law graduates is increasing rapidly; however, the number of nonwhite law graduates, despite affirmative action programs, is still very small.

[32] Auerbach, "Plague of Lawyers," p. 44.

legal counsel appointed. In 1963 that principle was extended to all state and federal courts in a landmark decision, *Gideon* v. *Wainwright*.[33] In 1972 it was further extend to cover indigent defendants in *any* case in which a jail term might be imposed by the sentencing judge.[34]

Today only very minor infractions of the law are excepted from the general rule that a criminal defendant is entitled to court-appointed counsel if he or she cannot afford a lawyer. But there is still a wide gap between the equality of legal representation offered by private counsel and that offered by court-appointed counsel or public defenders. Appointed counsel or public defenders may be good lawyers, but they often do not have the investigative resources needed to mobilize the strongest possible case for their clients. And many citizens are neither poor enough to qualify as indigents nor affluent enough to hire a good lawyer. There is no right to counsel in civil cases. But at least a portion of the citizenry's legal needs in noncriminal cases is met by publicly financed legal services programs.

Traditional legal services programs, originally called "Legal Aid Societies," were aimed primarily at providing poor people with lawyers. As part of the "War on Poverty" of the 1960s, the federal government (and some private foundations) funded a large number of legal services programs throughout the country. The more traditional of these programs, modeled after the "Judicare" program in northern Wisconsin, concentrated merely on providing poor people with access to a lawyer.[35] Those eligible for the program could choose any participating lawyer, whose services, in turn, would be reimbursed by the program according to a set fee schedule. This kind of program was favored by the organized bar and by most lawyers because it came closest to duplicating the customary "fee for service" arrangements of most lawyers in private practice.

A number of legal services programs, however, were organized differently and had more ambitious goals. These programs relied on lawyers (often young lawyers) hired especially to represent poor people, much as in the traditional public defender or Legal Aid Society models. But many of these programs sought to do more than merely help poor people with personal problems, such as obtaining a divorce. They believed that poor people as a class would benefit more from broad "test" cases that challenged repressive government policies. Many successful cases were brought to challenge the benefits and procedures of welfare programs; others established more due process rights for debtors, students, agricultural workers, inmates in penitentiaries, and other groups largely unrepresented in the past. Many of these reform-oriented legal services programs were quite controversial. When the OEO Legal Services Program was disbanded and its functions transferred to the federal Legal Services Corporation, restrictions were placed on the types of cases that lawyers in these programs could bring to court. In 1981 the Reagan administration tried to

[33] 372 U.S. 335 (1963).
[34] *Argersinger* v. *Hamlin*, 407 U.S. 25 (1972).
[35] Samuel Brakel, *Judicare* (Chicago: American Bar Foundation, 1974).

eliminate the Legal Services Corporation entirely, but Congress voted to continue it at a lower level of funding.

The Public Interest Bar. A small corps of lawyers in the United States is concerned primarily with public interest law. Representing the indigent in civil and criminal cases is, of course, also in the public interest. But the term *public interest law* has been reserved for lawyers who have represented particular kinds of issues and interests, such as environmental protection and the rights of consumers. The NAACP Legal Defense Fund and the American Civil Liberties Union are the prototypes on which the public interest bar was modeled, although the LDF and the ACLU were and are devoted mainly to more traditional civil rights and civil liberties causes.[36] Public interest law was once the province of liberal groups such as Ralph Nader's Public Citizen Litigation Group, or the Environmental Defense Fund. But an increasing number of conservative public interest law firms have sprung up to defend interests attacked by the old public interest law firms — landowners and land developers; ranchers and others in the West who are opposed to restrictions on development of public lands and limits on the use of some pesticides; manufacturers who have been hit hard with antipollution and safety requirements for their plants and for the products they produce. President Reagan's secretary of the Interior, James Watt, was for many years director of a conservative public interest law firm known as the Mountain States Legal Foundation.

Lawyers for the Government. About 15 percent of American lawyers work for government at all levels. We shall focus on those employed by the federal government, particularly in the Department of Justice. The Justice Department is one of the major cabinet departments, headed by the attorney general and deputy attorney general. Although they are always lawyers, their primary concern is with administration and political matters, and they rarely appear in court. The government's chief lawyer is the Solicitor General, who is appointed by the president and serves at his pleasure. The Solicitor General and his small professional staff, which does not change with administrations, determine which of the government's cases lost in lower courts will be appealed to the Supreme Court. The Solicitor General can appear before the Supreme Court as an *amicus curiae* (friend of the court) in any case that interests the government, even if the government is not actually a party to the case. Because of the professional quality of his office and the high esteem in which it is held, the Solicitor General is an extraordinarily successful (and the most frequent) litigant in the Supreme Court.

Each federal judicial district has a United States Attorney, under the control of the Justice Department, who represents the government in all civil and criminal cases in that court. The position of United States Attorney is a pres-

---

[36] See Robert L. Rabin, "Lawyers for Social Change: Perspectives on Public Interest Law," *Stanford Law Review* 28 (1976): 207–61.

tigious one. Incumbents seek, and frequently get, federal judicial appointments themselves. Others seek higher political office. The United States Attorney in Chicago, James Thompson, who successfully prosecuted several henchmen of Mayor Richard Daley for fraud, was subsequently elected governor of Illinois in 1976.

The "People" in the Law
Law is an enterprise for trained professionals. The only role for the public is in those states (now about half) in which judges are elected. The only role for individual citizens is as litigants (plaintiffs or defendants) and witnesses in a case, or as members of a jury. It is only by serving on a jury that citizens participate directly in the legal decision-making process.[37]

Grand Juries. There are two types of juries, the *grand jury* and the *petit jury*. A grand jury is a body of citizens, usually numbering between twelve and twenty-three, that can be impaneled for as long as eighteen months. It considers evidence presented to it by a prosecutor about the commission of a crime, and determines whether there is sufficient evidence to return an *indictment* — that is, to require one or more individuals to stand trial for that crime. In about 95 percent of the cases presented to it, the grand jury returns an indictment. Grand juries deliberate in secret. There is no judge present, and no defense attorney. A majority vote is sufficient to indict. The accused has no opportunity to defend himself against this indictment; his chance will come at trial. Technically, an indictment means only that the grand jury believes that a crime has been committed and that there is sufficient evidence to charge someone with the offense. It remains for a judge or jury, absent a guilty plea, to determine guilt or innocence.

A grand jury may also investigate official corruption and wrongdoing on its own, without acting on a specific request from a prosecutor. Such findings are returned in the form of a *presentment,* which may become the basis for later official action. The grand jury investigating the involvement of President Nixon in the Watergate case performed both functions. It indicted several of Nixon's aides on charges of conspiracy to obstruct justice. When the special prosecutor, Leon Jaworski, advised the grand jury that in his judgment an incumbent president was not indictable for a criminal offense under the Constitution, the grand jury voted, 19 to 0, to name Mr. Nixon as an unindicted coconspirator. Its sealed presentment to that effect was given to Federal Judge John Sirica, who transmitted it to the Judiciary Committee of the House of Representatives for consideration in its impeachment investigation.

The Fifth Amendment to the Constitution requires indictment by a grand jury in all federal cases of capital or "infamous" crimes other than those arising in the military. Today, in the federal courts a grand jury indictment is required in all felony cases except that the defendant may waive indictment in noncapital cases. When such a waiver occurs, prosecution is by an *information,*

[37] See Harry Kalven and Hans Zeisel, *The American Jury* (Boston: Little, Brown, 1966).

which is simply the filing of charges by the prosecutor. The Supreme Court has held that the Fifth Amendment requirement of a grand jury indictment does not apply to prosecutions in the state courts.[38] As of 1977, only twenty-one states employed grand juries; in most states, criminal prosecution of a felony begins with an information.

In 1791, when the Bill of Rights was adopted, grand juries were regarded as a bulwark against government repression. But they are no longer so highly regarded. Because they operate in secret, because there is no opportunity to present a case for the defense, and because they rarely fail to return indictments requested by the government, grand juries today are often attacked as rubber stamps of the prosecutor and serious threats *to* civil liberties. The grand jury was abolished in England in 1933, and there are many who would consign it to a similar fate in this country — possibly excluding its very useful role in investigating official corruption.

Those favoring retention of the grand jury note that it is one of the rare opportunities left for citizen participation in the legal system on a long-term basis. Furthermore, they argue that requiring the grand jury to become an adversary proceeding would seriously constrain its latitude in searching for the truth.[39]

Petit Juries.   Petit juries have a different function. In criminal cases it is the *petit* jury that must determine whether the facts demonstrate, "beyond a reasonable doubt," that the defendant is guilty as charged. In a civil case it must determine whether "a preponderance of the evidence" sustains the plaintiff's case against the defendant.

The Constitution's Sixth Amendment guarantees trial by jury in all criminal cases in the federal courts. The Seventh Amendment extends that guarantee to all civil cases in which the amount in controversy exceeds $20. But jury trials have in fact never been available for petty offenses. About one-third of the criminal defendants in the federal courts who plead not guilty elect to be tried by a judge alone. Not until 1968 did the Supreme Court formally extend the constitutional right to trial by jury to defendants accused of serious crimes in the state courts.[40]

Historically, a jury consisted of twelve citizens and was required to reach a unanimous verdict. Although neither of these requirements is stated in the Constitution, both were regarded as part of the constitutional guarantee of trial by jury. However, many states now use six-person juries in both civil and criminal cases. Six-person juries are now also used in civil cases in some of the federal courts.[41] And in 1972, the Supreme Court held that the Constitution

---

[38] *Hurtado* v. *California,* 110 U.S. 516 (1884).

[39] See Marvin E. Frankel and Gary Naftalis, *The Grand Jury: An Institution on Trial* (New York: Hill and Wang, 1977).

[40] *Duncan* v. *Louisiana,* 391 U.S. 145 (1968).

[41] In *Ballew* v. *Georgia,* 435 U.S. 233 (1978), the Supreme Court ruled that a jury must consist of at least six persons.

does not require unanimous verdicts in noncapital criminal cases in the state courts. However, the Court specifically held that a unanimous verdict was still required in the federal courts, in both civil and criminal cases.[42] Nonunanimous verdicts in civil cases have long been the practice in some states.

Are Juries Representative?   Although juries are supposed to represent a cross-section of the community, they often do not meet this standard. Either law or custom often exempts from jury service those in certain occupations, such as lawyers, journalists, physicians, firefighters, law enforcement officers, teachers (in some jurisdictions but not others), and those in military service. Women have customarily been entitled to automatic exemptions if they did not wish to serve, although this practice is likely to end in light of a recent Supreme Court decision.[43] It is also easy in some jurisdictions to get excused from jury duty. Thus, citizens who serve on juries usually are those who are willing and able to do so.

Racial and other minority groups have traditionally been underrepresented on juries. Long after the Supreme Court outlawed explicit racial disrimination in jury selection,[44] black representation on juries has remained low, whereas middle-class, white-collar males continue to be overrepresented. There is no constitutional right to be tried by a jury with a particular racial or religious composition. But there *is* a constitutional right to be tried by a jury randomly drawn from a pool of citizens that is generally representative of the community.

The representativeness of juries is also skewed by the procedures used in selecting jurors. The final composition of a jury does not rest with the court clerks who compile the jury rolls, but with the judge and the attorneys for each side. Attorneys naturally seek to seat those jurors most likely to view their client's case favorably. At the jury selection proceeding before trial (known as the *voir dire*), each side questions prospective jurors. Any juror may be challenged for *cause* if there is evidence that he or she is biased or has prior knowledge of the case. Jurors may also be removed without cause by a *peremptory* challenge from either side. However, each side has only a limited number of such challenges. Peremptory challenges may in fact conceal racial prejudice, but in *Swain* v. *Alabama* the Supreme Court ruled that the reasons for a peremptory challenge are not subject to inquiry even if they affect the racial composition of the jury.[45]

In most cases, jury selection is completed with dispatch. But in some, hundreds of jurors may have to be questioned in a process that can take weeks,

[42] *Johnson* v. *Louisiana*, 406 U.S. 356 (1972); *Apodaca* v. *Oregon*, 406 U.S. 404 (1972).

[43] *Taylor* v. *Louisiana*, 419 U.S. 522 (1975). Indeed, women were not *permitted* to serve on juries until the late nineteenth century. In 1898, Utah became the first state to permit women jurors, and it was not until the Civil Rights Act of 1957 that women were allowed to sit on federal juries in all states.

[44] *Strauder* v. *West Virginia*, 100 U.S. 303 (1880).

[45] *Swain* v. *Alabama*, 380 U.S. 202 (1965).

Preventing Government Lawlessness

In its decision in the Nixon Tapes Case (United States *v.* Nixon, *1974), the Supreme Court stated emphatically that no man was above the law, not even the president of the United States. However, in his 1977 television interview with David Frost, former President Nixon continued to maintain the contrary:*

FROST: *"So what in a sense, you're saying is that there are certain situations, and the Huston Plan or that part of it was one of them, where the President can decide that it's in the best interests of the nation or something, and do something illegal."*

NIXON: *"Well, when the President does it, that means it is not illegal."*

Revelations about undercover activities by the FBI and the CIA, including breaking and entering of private property, illicit electronic surveillance, and the planting of agent provocateurs in dissident groups, demonstrate the pervasiveness of the Nixon attitude.

"Except for those of us who are above it."

How to prevent government lawlessness is a question of great current concern. Diligent investigative reporting of the kind made famous by Woodward and Bernstein of The Washington Post, *breaking open the Watergate burglary case, and of Seymour Hersch of* The New York Times, *exposing the My Lai massacre story, is one weapon. Another is the use of the grand jury, as in the Watergate case, to investigate corruption and official lawbreaking. (The Watergate grand jury's indictments are seen, right, handed over to Judge John Sirica's court.) But there are many critics who claim that the grand jury does not give sufficient protection to citizens called before it or under investigation by it. Current reform efforts focus on extending some due process procedural guarantees to witnesses before a grand jury, rather than abolishing it altogether.*

Grand juries: It's time to reform or abolish them

WILLIAM L. CLAY

If grand juries are not abolished, they ought to be altered to curtail the prosecutorial abuses inherent in the present system. The original intent of the grand jury was to protect the innocent who had been accused falsely. It supposedly was conceived as a group of peers deliberating in secrecy to determine if sufficient evidence existed to bring criminal charges against a neighbor.

However, in recent years grand juries have been composed almost exclusively of society's elite. The interest of the individual has been totally disregarded as prosecutors use the juries as a personal tool to harass, intimidate and frame those who espouse radical causes or differing political opinions.

Citizens who are targets of grand jury investigations, or more precisely the targets of prosecutors, are denied "due process" of law and most assuredly are not guaranteed the secrecy of the proceedings. In fact, most prosecutors have arrangements with the media to leak derogatory, unsubstantiated testimony to discredit and destroy the accused. In addition, the accused is not permitted legal counsel while appearing before the grand jury, not afforded the basic right to be confronted by his accusers nor is he allowed to cross-examine.

...In my opinion, the present system constitutes a blatant disregard of rights of the individual. Most grand jurors are pawns in the hands of many unscrupulous prosecutors who select what evidence will be considered, which witnesses will be called to testify, who will be granted immunity and which charges will be leveled.

Most indictments are written by the prosecutor independent of consultation with the jurors and then automatically signed by them. In effect, grand juries are no more than rubber stamps placing the onus of guilt on the accused.

There is a real need for the Congress to either reform the system drastically or abolish it. If evidence exists that indicates a person committed a crime, why not take that evidence before the court in a preliminary hearing and give the accused the right to cross-examine?...

William L. Clay is a Democratic member of Congress from Missouri. Reprinted by permission.

"A grand jury sitting in Terre Haute, Indiana, today handed up an indictment of society."

sometimes months. Over 1,100 prospective jurors were questioned before a jury could be empaneled in the 1970 Connecticut murder trial of Black Panther leader Bobby Seale. Indeed, defense attorneys sometimes petition the court for a *change of venue* — removal of the trial to another location — on the grounds that the nature of the alleged crime, or its notoriety, or both, make a fair trial impossible at the locality where the crime was committed. Until recently, for example, it probably *was* impossible in the Deep South to empanel an unbiased jury in cases where a black was accused of murder or rape and the victim was white. Prejudice was so widespread that even a change of venue would not have been of much help.

Many attorneys believe that a trial can be won or lost at the jury selection stage. They often spend much of their time and resources in efforts to empanel the "right" jury. In recent widely publicized trials there have been elaborate efforts to "shape" the jury according to some predetermined psychological profile of potentially sympathetic jurors. One example is the Watergate trial of John Mitchell and Maurice Stans, who were accused of concealing campaign contributions. The defendants' lawyers worked very hard to obtain jurors who were low-income, Catholic, blue-collar workers who, the lawyers believed, would be sympathetic to their clients. Ironically, the jury's verdict of acquittal was attributed to the influence of an alternate juror who did not fit this stereotype and was in fact reluctantly accepted by defense counsel.[46]

The United States is one of the few countries in which citizen juries are commonly used in criminal cases, and it is virtually the only country using juries in civil cases. Some legal scholars, judges, and lawyers argue that juries should be done away with. Juries are vulnerable to appeals to prejudice and sympathy, and jury trials are on the whole more time consuming and costly than bench trials. There seems to be little support for retention of the jury in civil cases; indeed, civil juries are used in a very small number of such cases. There is more widespread support for retaining the jury in criminal cases, and there is little chance that the criminal jury will be abolished. In both civil and criminal cases, juries are a potential bulwark against government repression. They do give some citizens a role and all citizens a stake in the legal system. The jury system is especially well suited to individualizing the law, to taking formal legal rules and applying them in individual cases with reason and compassion. In a way that no judge sitting alone can do, a jury can call on a variety of life experiences and perspectives in rendering justice in a case.

Who Uses the Legal System? Courts rely on others to initiate the cases that make up their agenda. Both custom and formal rules dictate that courts should not seek out cases or issues to decide. Because courts are thus primarily *reactive*, private decisions are immensely important in determining what cases and issues the courts will consider. Most disputes in our (or any other) society never come to the courts, or

[46] *The New York Times*, April 29, 1975.

even involve more than the disputants themselves. Formal recourse to the courts, by filing a lawsuit, is often a last attempt to resolve a dispute.

Access to the Courts.   In theory all citizens have equal access to the courts, but in practice some have more access than others. Moreover, even citizens with comparable resources have different propensities to use the courts. Apart from domestic-relations cases, such as divorce and child custody cases —which make up nearly half the civil dockets of many state trial courts — and automobile accident cases, the courts are not much used by "ordinary" people to resolve disputes. The federal government is the most frequent litigant in the federal courts, and large corporations and financial institutions are also frequent litigants. They often appear as creditors seeking the assistance of the courts in collecting debts.

Given the legalistic nature of our society, the real puzzle is why citizens are so reluctant to use the courts.[47] The reasons for this reluctance are not hard to identify. Litigation is expensive and time consuming; the costs may exceed the value of whatever is in dispute. Citizens do not, in practice, have equal access to lawyers. Only those who can afford to retain a lawyer, or who are poor enough to qualify for free legal assistance, may be able to bring a lawsuit. Any citizen may bring a case to court without an attorney, but this is very difficult and rarely attempted. Until recently, lawyers were prohibited by the Canons of Legal Ethics from advertising their services or otherwise "seeking out" legal business. Undoubtedly this contributed to the mystique that law and lawyers were for "other" people. But a recent decision by the Supreme Court, *Bates* v. *State Bar of Arizona,*[48] held that the right of lawyers to advertise their services was protected by the First Amendment. Advertisements for legal services can now be found in most major newspapers and telephone directories; it remains to be seen what effect such advertisements will have on opening up the legal process to the average citizen.

Citizens who are poor or are members of minority groups have also been reluctant to use the courts because the law often has been unfavorable to their interests. Recent reform efforts have altered this picture somewhat. Legal aid programs have provided some legal assistance, and under certain circumstances courts have been willing to waive filing fees necessary to commence a lawsuit. Both courts and legislatures have begun to recognize that tenants as well as landlords, debtors as well as creditors, and welfare recipients as well as businesses have rights that the law must protect. In general, the 1960s and 1970s witnessed a substantial rise in the "rights consciousness" of

---

[47] Donald Black, "The Mobilization of Law," *Journal of Legal Studies* 2 (1973): 125. See also Craig Wanner, "The Public Ordering of Private Relations," *Law & Society Review* 8 (1973): 421–40; and Wayne McIntosh, "150 Years of Dispute Settlement: A Court Tale," *Law & Society Review* 15 (1981): 823.

[48] *Bates* v. *State Bar of Arizona,* 433 U.S. 350 (1977).

Americans — an understanding that they had certain rights that might require judicial protection, and a willingness to fight for those rights in court.

HOW CITIZENS VIEW THE LEGAL SYSTEM

It is fashionable these days to criticize the legal system. We have already noted the views of some radical critics. They believe that the legal system will never sufficiently free itself from its social and cultural moorings to promote real social reform. Instead of leading the fight against inequality and injustice, these critics claim, the legal system reflects — and perpetuates — that inequality. Its halfhearted and formalistic efforts at reform not only are inadequate, but also undercut more radical efforts that might produce real reform.

Conservatives are equally unhappy with the legal system, but for different reasons. They oppose the courts' tendencies to expand and promote individual rights, particularly the rights of the disadvantaged and of minorities. Conservatives argue that the primary focus of the courts should be to strengthen and preserve the social order, not to undermine it. In particular, they single out the "misplaced" solicitude of the courts for the rights of criminal defendants and ask why the courts — and society — should not instead show more interest in the victims of crime.[49]

The dilemma has been to bridge this gap between conflicting sets of expectations about the role and function of courts. Historically, the legal system has managed, somewhat uneasily, to follow the liberal tradition of balancing individual rights with government's need for enough power to govern effectively. But for much of our history, this role has consisted of protecting property rights *from* governmental regulation.

Since the New Deal era, and particularly in the last two decades, the courts have been significantly more favorable to civil rights and civil liberties claims, while also supporting the broad governing powers of the welfare state. But no amount of support for individual rights and no amount of democratization can entirely eliminate the gap between the elitist tendencies of a legal system and America's commitment to liberal democracy. In a recent national survey, 57 percent of the respondents agreed with the statement, "The legal system favors the rich and powerful over everyone else."[50]

What are the causes of this gap, which seems easy enough to identify, but is apparently beyond our ability to control? *Delay* is a notorious problem. The old saying that "justice delayed is justice denied" is not always true, but it is true too often.[51] Lawsuits often take several years to reach trial. Even criminal cases, which under the Constitution's Sixth Amendment are entitled to a "speedy trial," are often postponed for unconscionable lengths of time. To

---

[49] Macklin Fleming, *The Price of Perfect Justice* (New York: Basic Books, 1974).

[50] Barbara Curran and Francis O. Spalding, *The Legal Needs of the Public* (Chicago: American Bar Foundation, 1974), p. 95.

[51] For an excellent review of the need for reforming the legal system, see Leonard Downie, *Justice Denied* (New York: Praeger, 1971). On why judicial reform is notoriously slow, see Herbert Jacob, *Justice in America* (Boston: Little, Brown, 1972), pp. 225–30.

alleviate this problem, Congress in 1974 passed the Speedy Trial Act, which requires that criminal cases be brought to trial within sixty days of arraignment. Many states have similar laws.

Inefficiency may be one cause of trial delay. Another is the limited — some say wholly inadequate — number of federal judges. Chief Justice Burger warned in 1976 that federal judges' case loads were "crushing" and "impossible." Yet Congress has moved very slowly to increase the number of judgeships. In 1978 Congress authorized the appointment of 152 new federal judgeships, an increase of more than 25 percent. The recent congressional authorization to federal magistrates to try some minor cases will also provide some relief. In 1979, for example, magistrates disposed of over 100,000 minor offenses that otherwise would have required judicial action.

Delay may impede reaching a just outcome in a particular case, but it has an even more serious effect. Delay fosters a lack of respect for the legal system, which in turn reduces the system's ability to deter crime and rehabilitate criminals. Spending months in jail before trial may embitter the accused against the system rather than help rehabilitate them. The common alternative to pretrial imprisonment — freedom on bail, often for several months, before trial — may not only postpone justice but actually thwart it. Witnesses may move away, or their memories of the crime may grow hazy. When the case finally does go to trial, an alert defense counsel often can get the case thrown out of court on grounds of insufficient evidence. This problem has reached crisis proportions in some urban areas, where it has greatly weakened the law's deterrent effect. Muggers and other criminals know that even if they are caught they have a good chance of avoiding conviction. A recent report showed that in New York City, in 1979, only one of every one hundred persons arrested on felony charges was sentenced to prison. The vast majority of persons arrested on felony charges had those charges dismissed or reduced to misdemeanors. A substantial portion of these dismissals or charge reductions is probably due to a backlog of criminal cases that has reached crisis proportions.

In the public outcry over the treatment of criminal defendants in our courts, the focus is on how efficiently criminal cases are processed and how severely criminals are punished. These are understandable concerns. But sometimes they make us forget that not all persons arrested and charged with a crime are guilty, and that the main function of criminal courts is to *determine* who is guilty under the law and who is not.

The *discretionary nature* of the legal system alarms many people. We have observed some of the ways in which discretion is built into the system — the decision to make an arrest, the decision to prosecute in criminal cases, plea bargaining, and sentencing. Discretion in sentencing is a particularly controversial issue. Its defenders point out that it permits the judge to fit the punishment to the criminal as well as to the crime. For example, an offender who shows signs of genuine repentance, of having "learned a lesson," can be given a more lenient sentence than one who shows no such signs.

Opponents of judicial sentencing discretion counter that many criminologists and judges admit they really know very little about how punishment affects offenders, or to what extent the threat of it deters potential offenders. They also point out that judges often dispense justice very unevenly, in a way that only aggravates the racial and social divisions of our society.[52] Criminal sentences, typically, have been "indeterminate." That is, the judge sentences the convicted criminal to a minimum and possibly also to a maximum term in prison, but the actual time served is determined by parole boards and by accumulated "time off" for good behavior. Today, with an increasing public concern for punishment rather than rehabilitation, the pendulum has swung back to favor "determinate" sentences. It is the judge and not the parole board who sets the actual sentence (minus a predictable discount for good behavior).

CONCLUSION The American legal system is a mix of tradition, rational goals, and adjustments to political reality. It has diverse and often conflicting functions, and it must be able to accommodate diverse constituencies. Ours is a government "of the people," yet the American legal culture is not uniquely a system "of the people." Constitutionalism, legalism, the adversary system, and professionalism are all constraints on the popular will and on the active involvement of the citizenry. They contribute to the gap between the people and the polity in a variety of ways — most importantly, perhaps, by walling off the legal system from true popular participation. Judges, many of whom are appointed rather than elected, play a substantial role in the making of government policy — from desegregating schools or protecting the environment to deciding how long the hair of schoolchildren and policemen may be.

Out of our description of the American legal system, several questions emerge: Is the legal system congruent with the basic values of our democratic system? Is it adequate to meet the needs of citizens in our highly mobile and technologically advanced society? What more can we expect from it, and what reforms are likely to achieve those expectations?

At various points in the chapter we have described two conflicting evaluations of our courts. One is that courts do too much, the other is that they do too little. The first argument is that we rely too heavily on our courts and expect too much of them. What we have as a result (with some exaggeration, no doubt) is "government by lawsuit," an imperial and elitist judiciary that dictates where society should be going and how it should get there. Neither the way judges are chosen nor the way courts operate (the adversary process) equips courts to play this role. In a futile pursuit of "progress" and "justice," the courts are in fact weakening the fiber of representative democracy. By promising more than they can deliver, they intensify demands that govern-

---

[52] Tom Goldstein, "Inequities Common in Jail Sentences," *The New York Times,* December 19, 1976, section 4. Also see Marvin E. Frankel, *Criminal Sentences: Law without Order* (New York: Hill and Wang, 1973).

ment is unable to meet and thereby increase popular frustration and disaffection toward government.

The counterargument emphasizes the role modern courts have played in expanding individual rights. It notes that, with all their shortcomings, courts are often the only political institution sufficiently unencumbered by political restraints to stake out bold and reformist positions on major social issues. It is argued that this activism is more important to the health of the system than preserving the traditionally limited but also conservative judicial role. If courts are to become again the forums of the people, then the courts must be willing to give serious consideration to what citizens want and need. If courts can in fact articulate the policies and secure the outcomes the people want, then there is no gap between "judicial" and "popular" sovereignty.

The next chapter, which focuses exclusively on the Supreme Court, expands our consideration of these issues by showing us the contending positions in their boldest relief in the highest court of the land.

SUGGESTIONS FOR FURTHER READING

Abraham, Henry. *The Judicial Process*, 3rd ed. New York: Oxford University Press, 1975. A richly detailed and insightful comparison of the American judicial system with courts and judges in France and England. A reliable source of important factual information.

Auerbach, Jerrold. *Unequal Justice*. New York: Oxford University Press, 1976. A fascinating historical study of the leadership of the legal profession and its lack of concern for securing equal justice.

Becker, Theodore. *Political Trials*. Indianapolis: Bobbs-Merrill, 1970. A collection of case studies about the breakdown of justice in the United States and other countries.

Downie, Leonard, Jr. *Justice Denied: The Case for Reform of the Courts*. New York: Praeger, 1971. A convincing case for judicial reform written by a reporter and editor of *The Washington Post*.

Frank, Jerome. *Courts on Trial*. New York: Atheneum, 1963. Originally published in 1949, this is still one of the most provocative critiques of the American legal system, by a renowned legal scholar and former federal judge.

Jacob, Herbert. *Justice in America: Courts, Lawyers and the Judicial Process*, 3rd ed. Boston: Little, Brown, 1978. A comprehensive survey of the judicial process, incorporating diverse research findings from scholars in many disciplines.

Chapter 9 The Supreme Court

In a political system that relies so heavily on law, it is paradoxical that so few Americans understand the Supreme Court. The Supreme Court is a unique hybrid institution whose role reflects a distant mixture of law and politics. It is essentially nondemocratic in its makeup and workings; yet it can and does overrule decisions made by the people's democratically elected representatives. Its job as a judicial body is to interpret the law; yet by its decisions it also makes law. Its commands are obeyed by the president, the Congress, and the citizenry; yet it has no visible means of commanding that obedience. It is at once vulnerable to public opinion and a powerful shaper of it. It is first and foremost a court; but, as journalist Anthony Lewis has written, "Its public image seems sometimes to be less that of a court than of an extraordinarily powerful demigod sitting on a remote throne and letting loose constitutional thunderbolts whenever it sees a wrong crying for correction." [1]

ORIGINS OF THE COURT The Supreme Court's powers were left largely undefined in the Constitution; its composition and most of its jurisdiction were left for Congress to decide.

[1] Anthony Lewis, *Gideon's Trumpet* (New York: Random House, 1964), p. 11.

Article III of the Constitution, which delegated the "judicial Power of the United States" to the Supreme Court and other federal courts that Congress might establish, did not make clear exactly what that power was to be. The great power of judicial review was not mentioned. However, as we saw in Chapter 2, some of the framers fully expected and wanted the Supreme Court to play a major role in the government.

Early Attitudes Toward Judicial Power The Constitution invited but did not ensure the strong exercise of judicial power. Several factors aided its development.[2] Most important was the colonists' own experience with arbitrary governmental power. Determined to prevent its recurrence, they set legally enforceable limits on government by means of a written constitution that delegated specific powers to separate branches of government and recognized the importance of the rule of law.

The framers were also sensitive to the potential for conflict between majority rule and the rights of minorities. The Constitution tried to resolve this inherent conflict, or at least postpone the day of reckoning, by making separate institutions the custodians for these competing principles of government. Congress, particularly the House of Representatives, embodied popular sovereignty, whereas an "independent" Supreme Court, as interpreter of the fundamental law, was to be specially concerned with minority rights — particularly the rights of the wealthy and propertied.

The Court's Political Role Law cannot exist entirely apart from politics. It is mainly through law that government expresses its policy choices, including (in the Constitution) the organization of government itself. The need to settle disputes about the meaning of statutes, treaties, and the Constitution inescapably draws the Supreme Court into questions of politics. The Supreme Court is involved in politics, as one observer has put it, "not as a matter of choice, but of function."[3] Were the Court to ignore or neglect its political role, it could not maintain its position as a genuinely coequal branch of government. Yet the Court's political role necessarily differs from those of Congress and the president. Certainly it is more indirect.

Alexander Hamilton spoke to the Court's distinctive political role in No. 78 of *The Federalist*. He defended the Supreme Court on the grounds that it would *not* exercise political power; it did not possess either the sword or the purse; it had no "will," only "judgment," and would never become a dominant sovereign. It was, in Hamilton's soothing words, "the least dangerous branch" of government. But he argued that the Court would review the constitutional validity of acts of the president and Congress — an inescapably political function.

Because the Supreme Court performs both legal and political functions, it

---

[2] One of the best interpretations of these events is Robert G. McCloskey, *The American Supreme Court* (Chicago: University of Chicago Press, 1960), chap. 1.

[3] Jack W. Peltason, *Federal Courts in the Political Process* (New York: Random House, 1955), p. 3.

has to satisfy diverse — and often opposing — constituencies. It must demonstrate its legitimacy in different ways: through the law, by appealing to reason, logic, and precedent; through politics, by responding to power and seeking an accommodation of interests. Throughout its history the Court has had to maintain its image as a legal institution in order to be politically effective; yet it has often found that "a good constitutional ruling is often a combination of sound policy and bad law."[4]

Judicial Review: The Supreme Court's Basis of Power
The power of the Supreme Court is a subtle blend of constitutional and statutory authority, a merging of what the framers intended and what history and tradition have produced. Scholars, judges, and practical politicians have long argued over its proper nature and limits. There are three main issues. What powers were actually given to the Supreme Court by the Constitution? What powers are justified, regardless of their origin, by the evolving needs of our political system? And — the most difficult question — is power exercised by nonelected judges compatible with the principle of majority rule?

Although the framers of the Constitution were committed to a strong legislative branch and very suspicious of executive power, they were not totally committed to majority rule or legislative supremacy. Agreeing with Madison's dictum that "ambition must be made to counteract ambition," they regarded a coequal Supreme Court as a necessary check on the excesses of majority rule. The framers were, in effect, "hedging their bet" on democracy.[5] But to do so they had to establish a nondemocratic institution — one with a role, not yet fully defined, that no court had ever played before. A necessary part of the constitutional formula was that the precise authority of the Supreme Court should remain ambiguous. Otherwise it might alarm the proponents of popular sovereignty, who would think it too strong, and anger critics, who would find it too weak.

Initially, two basic questions had to be decided. First, what authority would the Supreme Court have over the state courts? This question was not explicitly resolved in the Constitution, but an answer was strongly implied. The supremacy clause of Article VI made the Constitution, federal laws, and treaties superior to all state law and to the decisions of state courts. Article III gave the Supreme Court jurisdiction (authority) over types of cases and controversies that, at least initially, could occur only in the state courts. And the Constitutional Convention rejected a proposal to give Congress a veto power over state actions, assuming that the federal judiciary would exercise such a power. Accordingly, the Judiciary Act of 1789, which established the inferior federal courts, gave the Supreme Court limited jurisdiction to review the decisions of the highest state courts.

---

[4] Donald Kommers, *Judicial Politics in West Germany* (Beverly Hills, Calif.: Sage Publications, 1976), p. 303.
[5] McCloskey, *The American Supreme Court.*

Second, what authority would the Supreme Court have to pass on the validity of an act of Congress — the power of *judicial review*.[6] The convention considered several variations of judicial review. Much debate centered on Madison's proposal for a Council of Revision, to be composed of the president and several members of the Supreme Court, which would exercise a veto power. But this proposal was rejected three times, in part because the judicial members of the council would have had to review their own judgments if and when the validity of a law was later challenged in court. The convention then considered giving both the president and the Supreme Court independent power to revise legislation; if either objected to a bill, it would have to be repassed by a two-thirds vote in Congress; if both the president and the Court objected, it would have to be repassed by a three-fourths vote. This proposal was defeated by a vote of 8 states to 3. A presidential veto with a two-thirds override by Congress was accepted as an alternative, and nothing further was said about a reviewing role for the Supreme Court.

[6] The term *judicial review* has come to be applied to the review by a court of executive and administrative acts, as well as to the decisions of state courts.
[7] 1 Cranch 137 (1803).

Did silence at the convention imply acquiescence or rejection of the power of judicial review? Debate over ratification seemed to assume that some such review power would be exercised. To those who feared judicial tyranny, Alexander Hamilton responded that the power of judicial review was necessary to the operation of a written constitution, and that it did not imply judicial superiority.

Establishing Judicial Review: Marbury *v.* Madison.   In its early years, the Supreme Court reviewed and upheld several acts of Congress. In 1803, for the first time, it held that an act of Congress was repugnant to the Constitution and thereby null and void. This was the famous case of *Marbury* v. *Madison*,[7] which arose out of the bitter rivalry between the Jeffersonian and Federalist political factions. After the Jeffersonians swept the 1800 election, the Federalists sought to consolidate their remaining power in the federal courts before their terms of office expired. Outgoing president John Adams appointed his secretary of state, John Marshall, as chief justice. The outgoing Congress, controlled by the Federalists, did its part by passing several bills providing for new judgeships. Naturally, deserving Federalists were appointed to these positions. One of these "midnight appointments" was that of William Marbury as a justice of the peace.

Marbury's commission was not delivered before Jefferson's inauguration. The Supreme Court was asked to issue a *writ of mandamus* ordering the new secretary of state, James Madison, to deliver Marbury's commission. (Such a writ, as Marbury's purpose suggests, is a court order to compel a public official to perform a legal duty.) Chief Justice Marshall realized that the Court could never force Madison to deliver Marbury's commission. But he also saw an opportunity to claim the power of judicial review over acts of Congress while at least rebuking his political adversaries, the Jeffersonians, for their failure to obey the law.

Marshall first held that Marbury was entitled to his commission, and that the laws of the country afforded him a remedy. He next ruled that the writ Marbury sought could not, under the Constitution, properly issue from the Supreme Court. Thus, the portion of the Judiciary Act of 1789 that gave that power to the Supreme Court was unconstitutional. The result of Marshall's strategy was one of the best bargains since the purchase of Manhattan Island. In return for "giving away" the minor power to issue writs of mandamus (and with it Marbury's commission), Marshall firmly grasped the great power of judicial review.

Marshall argued that "it is peculiarly the province of the judiciary to say what the law is." Judges would be violating their oaths of office if they enforced unconstitutional acts. Of course, *all* officers of the government, including members of Congress, take the same oath to preserve and defend the Constitution; but Marshall conveniently ignored this fact. Nor did he consider the possibility that the framers had intended each branch of government to be responsible for the constitutionality of its own actions. For Marshall, the logic of a written constitution (and the political necessities of the case) compelled the conclusion he reached. It was substantially the same argument made earlier in *The Federalist* by his ally, Alexander Hamilton. No other act of Congress was invalidated until 1857, when, in the case of *Dred Scott* v. *Sandford,* the Supreme Court declared portions of the Missouri Compromise unconstitutional.[8]

Judicial Review in Practice. Although it remains controversial, judicial review has survived for several reasons. First, it has made a practical contribution to the operation of government. Judicial review may not be necessary in order to preserve a written constitution, as Marshall claimed, but it has given the American political system both a means of preserving traditional values and a degree of flexibility when the need for change arises. Some agency must perform the role of interpreting the meaning of the Constitution, and over time the Supreme Court has done an acceptable job.

Second, judicial review has been responsive to Americans' unwillingness to make the final commitment to unlimited majority rule. Judicial review has enabled the Supreme Court to intervene in behalf of individual rights and liberties, although the Court has not always played this role.

Third, judicial review prevails because it appeals to the traditional American suspicion of government power. The case of *United States* v. *Nixon* (1974), in which the Court ruled that President Nixon had to surrender tape recordings of his conversations to the special prosecutor, enhanced that appeal. It demonstrated that judicial review can be used to check arbitrary and corrupt presidential power, as well as legislative power.

From 1789 to 1979 the Supreme Court declared a federal law invalid approximately 120 times. Since the Civil War, the average has been just under once per year. But more than half the cases invalidating federal statutes have come since 1943; the vast majority of these cases protected civil liberties and civil rights. The Burger Court, contrary to its "nonactivist" image, has invalidated 33 parts of federal laws in 21 cases.[9] The increased incidence of judicial review of acts of Congress increases the chances of another constitutional crisis comparable to the great confrontation between President Franklin Roosevelt and the Supreme Court in 1937. (If such a crisis materializes, however, it most likely would stem from issues arising more frequently in review of state court decisions — on abortion, school prayer, or criminal justice.) In 1937 Roosevelt threatened the independence of the Court — unsuccessfully — by trying to "pack" it with additional justices who would be more sympathetic to his New Deal programs. In 1935 and 1936, the Court had invalidated several key New Deal measures; Roosevelt retaliated by asking Congress to authorize the appointment of as many as six new justices, one for each sitting justice on the

---

[8] *Dred Scott* v. *Sandford,* 19 How. 393 (1857).

[9] Henry Abraham, *The Judicial Process,* 3rd ed. (New York: Oxford University Press, 1975), pp. 279–93; and P. Allan Dionisopoulos, "Judicial Review in the Textbooks, 1979," *DEA News,* Spring 1980, pp. 1, 3.

Court who had already reached the age of seventy-five. Roosevelt's proposal was widely denounced, and ultimately was soundly defeated in the Senate. But it might have succeeded if the Court itself had not, in the interim, made some conciliatory decisions, yielding to political pressure in what one wit called "a switch in time that saved nine."

As judicial review of acts of Congress has become more frequent, it has shifted in scope and direction. Until 1943, its main use was to protect property rights against government regulation. Since then, however, the Court has used it most frequently to invalidate federal statutes limiting individual constitutional rights.

The Supreme Court has been much less deferential toward state legislation than toward federal. It has struck down more than 900 state laws and judicial decisions as repugnant to the Constitution. Justice Oliver Wendell Holmes once said, "I do not think the United States would come to an end if we lost our power to declare an Act of Congress void," adding, however, "I do think the Union would be imperiled if we could not make that declaration as to the laws of the several states."[10]

Yet the actual effect of judicial review is difficult to assess. Justice Benjamin Cardozo once observed that the real effect of judicial review lies not in the Court's relatively rare invalidation of an act, but in the implicit threat of invalidation.[11] The ever present possibility of judicial review encourages legislators and other public officials to respect constitutional limits and conditions citizens to regard judicial intervention as a normal fact of political life. Its continued vitality is a recognition that political legitimacy need not reside in majority rule alone.

In order to protect individual rights — one of the main goals of constitutional government — it may be necessary on occasion to limit majority rule. Judicial review, therefore, contributes to the tension between citizens and government but also reduces that tension by protecting individual rights and providing a means for citizen oversight of elected officials. It is an essential part of the system of checks and balances.

THE SUPREME COURT AND ABORTION: A CASE STUDY Our understanding of how judicial review functions and what issues it raises may be aided by reference to an actual case. The case discussed here is one of the most controversial decided by the Supreme Court in recent years. Indeed, few public issues have been more hotly debated than the right of a woman to end an unwanted pregnancy. Abortion arouses strong moral fervor, cutting across political party and social class lines. It mobilizes citizens who ordinarily have little interest in the Supreme Court or in politics. It raises questions of women's rights and of the right of privacy. To what extent is a woman free to

[10] Oliver Wendell Holmes, "Law and the Court," in *Collected Legal Papers* (New York: Harcourt, Brace and World, 1920), p. 295.

[11] Benjamin Cardozo, *The Nature of the Judicial Process* (New Haven: Yale University Press, 1921), pp. 93–94.

make decisions about her own body? How much should that freedom be restrained by the rights of the unborn fetus? Is the fetus a "person" within the meaning of the Constitution? Finally, what about the responsibilities of the states to regulate the public health and welfare? Do the states have unlimited power to regulate abortions? If not, what are the limits?

The Origins of *Roe* v. *Wade* On January 22, 1973, the Supreme Court of the United States decided by a 7–2 vote, in the case of *Roe* v. *Wade*,[12] that the abortion laws in virtually every state were unconstitutional. The case began on March 3, 1970, when Jane Roe (a fictitious name but a real person) filed a suit in the federal district court in Dallas, Texas, against Henry Wade, the district attorney of Dallas County. Roe was a divorced bar waitress who had become pregnant. She asked the court to hold unconstitutional the Texas law that made it a crime to perform an abortion except to save the life of the mother. She also asked for an *injunction*, or legal order, barring Wade from enforcing the law. Roe stated that having an illegitimate child would cause her substantial economic hardship and stigmatize her socially, and that her inability to secure an abortion had caused her to suffer severe emotional trauma. She could not afford to travel to another state where a legal abortion could be secured, and she did not want to risk an illegal abortion. Denial of an abortion, Roe claimed, violated her rights under the Ninth and Fourteenth amendments to the United States Constitution. (The Ninth Amendment states that "The Enumeration in the Constitution, of certain rights, shall not be construed to deny or disparage others retained by the people." The provisions of the Fourteenth Amendment invoked here prohibit a state from depriving "any person of life, liberty or property, without due process of law.")

On June 17, 1970, the federal court decided, in Roe's favor, that the Texas abortion law was in violation of the Ninth and Fourteenth amendments. However, not wanting to intrude more than necessary on the state's powers, the federal court refused to issue an injunction formally barring Texas from enforcing its statute. Both Roe and Wade appealed to the federal Court of Appeals for the Fifth Circuit, in New Orleans. Because the case was so important, they also asked the Supreme Court to review it directly, and the Court agreed to do so. By now the case was receiving national attention, and attorneys for many organizations — some supporting abortion, some opposing it — joined the litigation as *amicus curiae* (friend of the court).[13] The case was set for oral argument before the Court in December 1971. By this time, Jane Roe had already borne a son and put him up for adoption. The Supreme Court could not make up its mind initially, and the case was reargued in October 1972.

[12] 410 U.S. 113 (1973).

[13] For example, organizations such as Women for the Unborn, Americans United for Life, and the National Right to Life Committee filed as amicus curiae in favor of the Texas law. Organizations such as the Planned Parenthood Federation, the National Welfare Rights Organization, the American Association of University Women, the American College of Gynecologists and Obstetricians, and Zero Population Growth filed as amicus curiae opposed to the Texas law.

The Continuing Abortion Controversy

The issue of abortion was far from resolved by the Supreme Court's 1973 decision in Roe v. Wade. That decision brought forth both ardent supporters and bitter opponents who resorted to mass demonstrations and political lobbying in support of their respective views. Those favoring a woman's right to have an abortion, such as the demonstrators at a rally in Washington, D.C., argued that the issue was a woman's right to choose. Those in opposition said that the real issue was the "right to life" of the unborn fetus.

Efforts to reverse the Supreme Court's decision continue undiminished. Spearheading the attack on abortion is a group which calls itself "The Moral Majority," led by the Rev. Jerry Falwell, a Baptist minister from Lynchburg, Virginia. Falwell's supporters worked hard in the 1980 elections to support Ronald Reagan (who opposes abortion) and to defeat congressional and senatorial candidates who did not favor reversal of the Supreme Court decision. Falwell initially opposed Reagan's nomination of Sandra Day O'Connor to the Supreme Court because her record on the abortion issue as a state legislator was ambiguous. Later, O'Connor testified before the Senate Judiciary Committee that she was personally opposed to abortion and the Senate confirmed her nomination by a vote of 99–0.

Deciding
Roe* v. *Wade   The Court's majority opinion was written by Justice Harry Blackmun. Before considering the substantive issues in dispute, Justice Blackmun had to dispose of a thorny preliminary question: Did Jane Roe have *standing* to challenge the Texas statute? That is, did she have a legally protected personal interest that was threatened by the statute? The Constitution limits the exercise of federal judicial power to "cases or controversies." The Supreme Court does not have the authority to decide *abstract* constitutional issues, no matter how important. Attorneys for Wade argued that the case was *moot*. Because Roe was no longer pregnant, there was no longer a real controversy; a nonpregnant woman cannot be legally injured by a statute prohibiting abortions.

Technically, Wade's attorneys were correct. But Justice Blackmun rejected such a narrow view. He noted that the normal gestation period of 266 days made it unlikely that litigation dependent on the plaintiff's being pregnant would ever survive beyond the trial court stage. Thus, appellate review would be effectively foreclosed. He observed that "Pregnancy often comes more than once to the same woman, and in the general population, if man is to survive, it will always be with us. Pregnancy provides a classic justification for a conclusion of nonmootness."

Blackmun then held that the constitutional right to privacy protected a woman's determination to terminate her pregnancy. But that right was not absolute. Rather, Blackmun said, it was a matter of balancing the interests of the mother against those interests asserted by the state in protecting the mother *and* in protecting the potential right to life of the unborn fetus. Blackmun held that since the fetus was not a "person" in the constitutional sense, the state had no compelling reason to intervene in a purely medical decision until the fetus was capable of life outside the womb. As for the state's interest in protecting the mother, Blackmun noted that under modern conditions abortions in early pregnancy are relatively safe and easy medical procedures. Indeed, he pointed out, the mortality rates for early abortion were lower than those for normal childbirth.

Balancing the mother's rights against the state's interest in protecting the health of the mother and the unborn fetus, Justice Blackmun developed an unusual sliding-scale policy. For the first trimester of pregnancy, the right of the mother to have an abortion was absolute. It could not be regulated or prohibited by the state. In the second trimester of pregnancy, the risks of abortion increase, and so does the state's permissible interest. At this point the state, although still foreclosed from prohibiting an abortion, is entitled to regulate where, how, and by whom the procedure is performed. The regulation must be "reasonably related to the preservation and protection of maternal health." The legitimate interest of the state in protecting the fetus increases markedly at viability. Thus, in the third trimester, the state may forbid abortion except when it is necessary to preserve the life or health of the mother. As the state's legitimate interests increase, the mother's right of privacy necessarily decreases.

Should the Court Have Intervened?   Several justices who joined in the majority opinion wrote concurring opinions to express their personal views. Two justices, Byron White and William Rehnquist, dissented. Their dissenting opinions raised crucial issues. For Justice White, the Court was not following any existing rule of law, or even interpreting the intended meaning of a provision of the Constitution. It was, instead, simply fashioning an arbitrary rule to serve the convenience of pregnant women. Whether abortions should be permitted or not, White argued, was not legitimately a decision for the Supreme Court to make. It was a decision to be made by the people through their state legislatures, allowing for differences of opinion on a controversial subject. Although he did not use these words, Justice White obviously believed this to be an improper use of judicial power.

Justice Rehnquist, the Court's most conservative member, agreed with Justice White, and added some additional objections. One was that this was not even an issue of "privacy" as he understood the term. Roe was not seeking to protect her privacy but seeking medical intervention in a hospital to end her pregnancy. Another of Rehnquist's objections was that his colleagues were misinterpreting the meaning of the Fourteenth Amendment. When that amendment was adopted in 1868, at least thirty-six state or territorial legislatures had already enacted laws limiting abortion; indeed, the Texas law was first enacted in 1857. Because none of these laws was regarded then as contrary to the Fourteenth Amendment, Rehnquist argued that the amendment could not now be interpreted to nullify such statutes.

Roe v. *Wade* raises many fundamental questions about the Supreme Court's role in the political system. As a court of law, for example, the Supreme Court cannot openly decide cases merely according to its own view of right and wrong. It is bound by the commands of the Constitution and of federal statutes and treaties. But the meaning of the Constitution is often vague, and the justices have ample opportunity to incorporate their own values into their decisions. In fact, the Constitution does not specifically mention any "right to privacy," although the concept of privacy is implicit in the First, Third, Fourth, and Fifth amendments. But the constitutional "right" of privacy was not spelled out by the Supreme Court until 1965, in a Connecticut birth control case.[14] In that case, as in *Roe* v. *Wade*, the Supreme Court was substituting a set of values, at best implicit in the Constitution's general language, for a policy established by an elected state legislature.

A Blow to Federalism?   The issue of federalism posed still another problem for the Court. Under what circumstances, and with what justifications, should the national government, through its highest court, intervene in an area of policy generally reserved to the states by the Constitution or its amendments? Primary responsibility for protecting the health, safety, welfare, and morals of

---

[14]*Griswold* v. *Connecticut*, 381 U.S. 479 (1965).

the people — known as the "police power" — rests in the states. Justice Blackmun's opinion tried to draw a balance between this traditional power of the states, on the one hand, and Roe's claimed right to control over her own body on the other.

It is always difficult to justify a ruling that withdraws power from elected legislatures. It is particularly troublesome when public opinion is badly split (at the time of *Roe,* a slight majority favored abortion), and when the state of knowledge and understanding of the subject ruled on is imperfect. There is far more disagreement among medical experts about when a fetus becomes "viable" outside the womb than Justice Blackmun's opinion suggests. And these experts still debate the relative safety of abortion after the first trimester of pregnancy. On the other hand, if the Supreme Court always stayed its hand until scientific knowledge was complete or until there was a national consensus on moral and ethical questions involved in a particular controversy, it would decide few important cases.

"Activism" versus "Restraint." The terms *judicial activism* and *judicial restraint* are labels often used to define competing conceptions of the Court's proper role. But these terms can be simplistic and misleading. Generally, *activism* refers to the tendency of a court to intervene in the policymaking process. Defenders of judicial activism hold that the Supreme Court must be bold in its defense of constitutional principles, and sensitive and responsive to the changing needs of society. If necessary, it must take the lead in meeting those needs. *Judicial restraint* is a philosophy of nonintervention, a more orthodox conception of the judicial role. Judges should invalidate a challenged law only when it is clearly repugnant to specific constitutional principles. The rule of precedent — *stare decisis* — should be more than a convenient rule of thumb, to be discarded at will. *How* things are done may be more important in the long run than the results of a case, because the legitimacy of the Supreme Court, like that of the law itself, depends on its internal consistency and rationality. The law is not hostile to all change, but neither is there "under our Constitution a judicial remedy for every political mischief, for every undesirable exercise of legislative power." In the words of the late Justice John Marshall Harlan, the Constitution cannot be a panacea for all public ills or "a haven for reform movements." [15]

Today, judicial activism is associated with a liberal political philosophy. It may have reached its epitome in the work of the Warren Court (1953–1969). But much of the debate over judicial activism versus restraint is partisan and shifting. The conservative justices on the Court who attempted to block New Deal legislation in the 1930s were also accused of being activists; it was the liberals on the Court at that time who counseled restraint.

To those in favor of judicial restraint, *Roe* v. *Wade* was the essence of what the Supreme Court should *not* be doing. It was not necessary to decide the

---

[15] Dissenting in *Reynolds* v. *Sims,* 377 U.S. 533 (1964).

case. The constitutional rules applied were largely judicially created and tailored to this particular case, rather than neutral principles transcending the issues in the case. The Court was substituting its own judgment about abortion for that of elected legislatures.

To judicial activists, *Roe* was a forceful statement of human liberty, whatever its technical imperfections. It showed that the law could change to meet changing social conditions and values, and that the Constitution was a dynamic instrument of government. They realized, however, that *Roe* did not contain a full and affirmative proabortion policy. By invalidating existing state laws, it merely removed one major obstacle to the actual availability of abortions.

The Aftermath of *Roe* v. *Wade* Like most Supreme Court decisions, *Roe* v. *Wade* was neither the beginning nor the end of a political controversy, but merely a phase in a continuing political and legal battle. The Court's decision stimulated further controversy, which has been escalating ever since. Proabortion forces have been fighting to preserve the "right to choice"; antiabortion groups have mobilized under the banner of "right to life." The battle continues in the courts, but it has also spilled over into the legislative arena and electoral politics. The 1980 Republican platform supported the antiabortion position, and candidate Ronald Reagan said he would consider a candidate's position on abortion when making appointments to the federal judiciary. A number of proposals for constitutional amendments have been introduced in the Congress, and a number of states have called for a constitutional convention to draft such a measure.[16]

Notwithstanding the political strength and intensity of the antiabortion forces, a significant majority of Americans favor legalized abortion in some circumstances. A 1979 Gallup poll reported that 22 percent of those surveyed favored legalized abortion in all circumstances, 54 percent favored it in certain circumstances, and 19 percent opposed it under all circumstances.[17]

Antiabortion forces in Congress have been successful in legislating against Medicaid-funded abortions each year since 1976. In the most recent (1980) form of what are known as the "Hyde amendments" (after their principal sponsor, Illinois Congressman Henry Hyde), the use of federal funds for abortions was prohibited except where the life of the mother would be endangered if the fetus were carried to term, or if the pregnancy was the result of incest or rape reported promptly to law enforcement or public health authorities. As a result of these congressional prohibitions, Medicaid abortions for poor women have dropped to just a few thousand per year, from a high in 1976 of about 250,000. Surprisingly, however, the national abortion rate apparently

[16] Article V of the Constitution provides two methods for amending the Constitution: (1) passage of an amendment by two-thirds of each house of Congress and ratification by three-fourths of the states (either by the state legislatures or by special ratifying conventions); (2) a call by two-thirds of the states for Congress to set up a constitutional convention, followed by ratification by three-fourths of the states of any amendments flowing from that convention. The second method of amendment has never been used. And only one amendment, the twenty-first, has been ratified by conventions.

[17] *Facts on File*, 1979.

has not decreased. The United States Disease Control Center in Atlanta reports that, despite the Hyde amendment, many poor women are neither bearing unwanted children nor having back-alley abortions. Many women seeking abortions live in the states that still fund abortions despite the loss of federal funds. Private funds are available to help many others.[18]

The Supreme Court's response to these antiabortion efforts has been mixed. In July 1976, in *Planned Parenthood of Central Missouri* v. *Danforth*,[19] the Court held that a state could require a pregnant woman to consent in writing to an abortion. But it also ruled that a state could *not* require prior consent of a woman's spouse, nor could it, in the first trimester, require parental consent for an unmarried minor seeking an abortion. Missouri had also prohibited the use of saline amniocentesis, the most common method of abortion, after the first twelve weeks of pregnancy. The Court held this to be unconstitutional, and it also invalidated a portion of the statute that required the physician to preserve the life and health of the fetus. The Court said that this requirement was intended to obstruct the patient's right to an abortion by dissuading physicians from performing one.

A number of states have prohibited the use of state Medicaid funds for nontherapeutic abortions, a practice that was upheld in *Maher* v. *Roe*.[20] A state was entitled to make "a value judgment favoring childbirth over abortion," the Court said. In *Harris* v. *McRae*, the Court upheld the Hyde amendment by a 5–4 vote. A woman may indeed have the freedom to choose whether or not to terminate her pregnancy, Justice Potter Stewart wrote, but

> it simply does not follow that a woman's freedom of choice carries with it a constitutional entitlement to the financial resources to avail herself of the full range of protected choices . . . although government may not place obstacles in the path of a woman's exercise of her freedom of choice, it need not remove those not of its own creation. Indigency falls in the latter category.[21]

THE SUPREME COURT AS POLICYMAKER The justices of the Supreme Court must often choose between competing social policies. Should the states be permitted to regulate and prohibit abortions, or does a woman have a constitutional right to terminate her pregnancy? Under what circumstances is the death penalty consistent with the Eighth Amendment's prohibition of cruel and unusual punishments? Can Congress impose the same minimum-wage and maximum-hour standards on the employees of state and city governments as on employees in the private sector? These are just three of the many policy questions that have come before the Court in the last few years.

There is nothing mechanical or automatic about the process by which such choices are made, in spite of Justice Owen Roberts's famous dictum:

[18]*New York Times*, Sec. IV, September 6, 1981.
[19]428 U.S. 52 (1976).
[20]432 U.S. 464 (1977).
[21]65 L Ed. 2d 784 (1980).

> When an act of Congress is appropriately challenged in the courts as not conforming to the constitutional mandate, the judicial branch of the government has only one duty: to lay the article of the Constitution which is invoked beside the statute which is challenged and to decide whether the latter squares with the former.[22]

Yet it would be wrong also to assume that judicial decisions are merely the personal preferences of the justices. Justices take seriously their obligation to interpret and apply the law. But judging is a dynamic process, and judges inevitably "make law" as they interpret statutes and the meaning of the Constitution.

There are many perspectives from which to interpret the Constitution, as well as ample precedents for justices to cite in support of almost any conclusion they wish to reach. Justice William O. Douglas once remarked, perhaps a bit too cavalierly, that there were "plenty of precedents to go around," and that a capable judge could always find legal authority to support the decision he wanted to make.[23] Yet the rule of precedent is not merely a cynical ploy to deceive the public. Justices understand well that the rule of law requires a high degree of predictability and continuity.

What Cases Does the Court Decide? The myth that any citizen can take a case "to the top" is particularly resistant to fact. Because under the law every person is equal, each has (or should have) an equal chance to petition the Supreme Court for a redress of grievances. It is also believed that the Supreme Court is not too distant and elevated to respond to the pleas of the ordinary citizen. But in fact very few citizens have a chance of getting a case decided by the Supreme Court.

Numbers tell much of the story. At present, 4,000 new cases come to the Supreme Court each year. Thirty percent come from the state courts; most of the remainder come from the federal courts of appeals. These 4,000 cases represent an unknown but minute fraction of all the cases processed in American courts in a single year.

Each year the Supreme Court decides about 150 cases in which it issues full opinions after hearing oral argument in open court. It rules on another 150 or so by short, unsigned *per curiam* (by the court) opinions, on the basis of briefs submitted by the parties, but usually without oral argument. The other cases that reach the high court are not accepted for review; these remain as decided by the lower courts.

The Court's Jurisdiction.   What cases get to the Supreme Court? *Jurisdiction* is the legal power to hear a case. If the Supreme Court has no jurisdiction over a matter, then it cannot act on it. Under Article III of the Constitution, the Supreme Court has *original jurisdiction* in only a few types of cases. That is, only a few types may begin in (rather than be appealed to) it. The Court has

[22] *United States* v. *Butler*, 297 U.S. 1 (1936).
[23] William O. Douglas, "Stare Decisis," *Columbia Law Review* 32 (1949): 735–55.

Figure 9.1 Jurisdiction of the Supreme Court

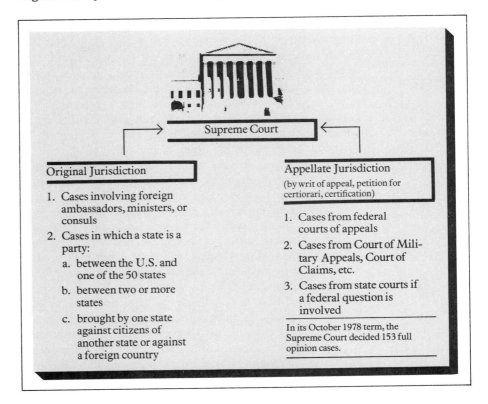

Supreme Court

Original Jurisdiction

1. Cases involving foreign ambassadors, ministers, or consuls
2. Cases in which a state is a party:
   a. between the U.S. and one of the 50 states
   b. between two or more states
   c. brought by one state against citizens of another state or against a foreign country

Appellate Jurisdiction
(by writ of appeal, petition for certiorari, certification)

1. Cases from federal courts of appeals
2. Cases from Court of Military Appeals, Court of Claims, etc.
3. Cases from state courts if a federal question is involved

In its October 1978 term, the Supreme Court decided 153 full opinion cases.

decided only about 150 original jurisdiction cases in its entire history. Virtually all the Supreme Court's cases come under its *appellate* jurisdiction. These are cases already decided by one or more lower courts, which the Supreme Court is asked to review. Congress regulates the appellate jurisdiction of the Supreme Court. It decides which kinds of cases may be heard by the Court (see Figure 9.1).

Before cases from the state courts can be reviewed by the Supreme Court, they must meet two conditions. First, and most important, the Supreme Court can review only cases that raise "federal questions," that is, issues involving the Constitution or federal law or treaties. Second, the case must have been decided by the highest state court in which a decision was possible. The remedies within the state's own legal system must have been exhausted.

The Decision to Review. A case is accepted for review only if four or more of the nine justices vote to hear it. There are two basic forms of review: writs of *appeal* and writs of *certiorari*. A writ of certiorari is an order directing a lower court to produce all the records of a case for review by a higher court.

The Supreme Court has complete discretion to grant or deny a petition for certiorari. Technically, it must review every case properly brought to it by a writ of appeal. But in practice the Court treats all petitions substantially alike — that is, as discretionary. At present only about 5–7 percent of all petitions for review are accepted by the Supreme Court. A substantial number of petitions for certiorari are filed by prison inmates seeking to overturn their convictions. Because almost all of these inmates are indigent, these are known as *in forma pauperis* petitions. Less than 1 percent of all such petitions are granted. The Court normally does not give reasons for denying review, nor does it offer much explanation when review is granted. In the final analysis, what four or more justices think is important is the standard.

The issues of a case are not the only factor determining whether or not it is reviewed. Cases brought by the solicitor general on behalf of the United States government are accepted at a much higher rate than petitions brought by private litigants. Also, several cases often raise the same or similar issues, and the Court may choose among them. The Court may reject a petition because the record in the trial court is deficient, or because the issues have not been skillfully presented. The Court may reject a petition because there are doubts whether the plaintiff has standing to sue, or because the issue is moot or not yet ripe for decision by the Supreme Court. For example, in 1961 the Supreme Court refused to hear a challenge to the Connecticut birth control law because, despite the plaintiffs' allegations that they feared prosecution under the statute, the record showed that no person had been prosecuted in twenty years.[24]

Sometimes the Court will refuse to hear a case simply because it is "too hot to handle" (although it would never formally state this as a reason for denying review). The Court declined to hear a case challenging state laws prohibiting miscegenation (racial intermarriage) in 1955, but declared all such laws unconstitutional in 1967.[25] Public attitudes had changed in the intervening years, and the justices might well have thought that such a decision would no longer risk defiance by the civil authorities.

For similar reasons, the Court consistently refused to consider the constitutionality of the war in Vietnam, despite countless opportunities to do so. Even after the war had become unpopular, it is likely that the justices feared the patriotic backlash judicial intervention might have precipitated. More important, perhaps, they may have hesitated to issue a decision that could not necessarily be implemented. Would President Nixon have withdrawn American troops from Vietnam merely because the Supreme Court declared the war unconstitutional in the absence of a formal declaration of war by Congress? Would the Congress have obligingly declared war?[26]

---

[24] *Poe* v. *Ullman*, 367 U.S. 497 (1961).

[25] *Loving* v. *Virginia*, 388 U.S. 1 (1967).

[26] Because the Supreme Court never issued an opinion expressing reasons for not deciding the Vietnam War issue, this analysis is necessarily speculative. But it is informed by the repeated dissents written by Justice Douglas to protest the denial of review in Vietnam War cases. See *Massachusetts* v. *Laird*, 400 U.S. 886 (1970).

Over time, the Court has created a category of cases known as *political questions*. These are cases that fall within the jurisdiction of the Court, but seem inappropriate for decision. There is no distinct category of such cases, but there are some loose standards to be followed in determining whether or not a case constitutes a political question. Is the issue one that has been specifically entrusted by the Constitution to another branch of government? For example, the Court has long regarded most foreign affairs questions as belonging in this category. Is the issue judicially manageable, and one for which appropriate constitutional standards for a decision exist? Until 1962 questions of legislative apportionment were nonjusticiable political questions. But in that year, in the decision Chief Justice Warren regarded as the most important of his career, the Supreme Court held that federal courts could decide questions of reapportionment. The doctrine of "one man–one vote" soon followed in another case.[27] Today, federal (and state) courts are regularly involved in monitoring the decennial reapportionment process in every state.

The Court's Docket. Is the Supreme Court's workload too great? In fact, the flood of certiorari petitions and the time needed to process them has become a problem. A commission appointed by Chief Justice Burger recommended in 1973 that a new national court of appeals be established to review certiorari petitions and choose about 400 each year to be considered by the Supreme Court.[28] That proposal had little chance of acceptance. But debate over the commission's report called attention to the importance of case selection. Choosing what cases to decide is crucial to the Court's policymaking autonomy.

The Supreme Court at Work In an age of big government, the Supreme Court is a relatively small institution. Its staff and budget are smaller than those of many administrative agencies. But its stature as the third branch of government is symbolized by the enormous marble palace, across from the Capitol, in which the justices work. The building is magnificent but austere. Visitors can enter the courtroom when the Court is in public session, but the seats are few, the rules of silence strictly enforced, the acoustics terrible, and the overall effect one of solemn dignity.

The Supreme Court is part of the political system, but visitors are reminded at once of its independence and special role. The black robes worn by the justices, the barely audible and unfailingly polite exchanges between the justices and the attorneys arguing cases, the formal morning coat still worn by the solicitor general (and once donned by all counsel), the often inscrutable language of the law used by the participants — all create an atmosphere reminiscent of a conservative religious institution. The image, no doubt, is intended. In recent years the Supreme Court has made a few concessions to

[27]*Baker* v. *Carr*, 396 U.S. 186 (1962); *Reynolds* v. *Sims*, 377 U.S. 533 (1964).
[28]*Report of the Study Group on the Caseload of the Supreme Court* (Washington, D.C.: Federal Judicial Center, 1972).

modernity in the ways it announces its decisions and helps the media communicate those decisions to the public. But its venerable routines are not designed in any way to bring the Court "closer to the people." Indeed, in an age when secrecy in government is on the defensive, and increased popular participation in government is a common slogan if not a reality, the Supreme Court has made no concessions whatever. In its public face, at least, the Court remains professionalized, somber, deliberate, and elitist.[29]

The Supreme Court meets once each year. Its term begins on the first Monday in October and ends late the following June. When in session, the Court alternates between two-week periods devoted to oral argument and equal periods spent in conferences and opinion writing. Petitions for review arrive throughout the year; each is considered by every justice and his clerks. Any justice can request that a petition for review be considered at conference. If no justice requests discussion of a case, it is automatically rejected. About 70 percent of all petitions for review are thus rejected without discussion. Cases that make the "discuss list" circulated by the Chief Justice are considered at the next available conference.

Deliberation at these conferences is secret; no formal written records are kept. Only the justices are permitted to attend; if books or papers are needed, the "junior" justice (often a man over sixty years old) passes a message to the bailiff waiting outside the door. The Chief Justice begins the discussion of each case, and then each justice speaks in descending order of seniority. Until recently, voting in each case followed the reverse order; the junior justice voted first and the Chief Justice last. Under Chief Justice Burger some modifications in this procedure have taken place. Each justice indicates a tentative vote when he takes his turn discussing a case; thus the initial voting follows the same descending order of seniority as the discussion. In some cases this is sufficient. However, when a formal vote is taken, the votes are cast in the traditional manner — in reverse order of seniority. By whichever method, any case that receives four or more votes, as we have seen, is docketed for oral argument and full consideration. Cases that fail to receive four votes for review are rejected.

Cases are normally scheduled for oral argument several months after they are accepted for review. In the interval, the parties submit new briefs detailing the major arguments to be considered by the Court. Except for a few cases of special importance, each case is allotted one hour of oral argument, equally divided between the petitioner and the respondent (the party against whom the case is brought). Unlike a trial, in which the adversaries are usually present and witnesses testify, oral argument in the Supreme Court is carried on only by attorneys. The justices frequently ask questions from the bench; often attorneys spend most of their time answering these questions and have little time for their prepared remarks.

[29] Recent publication of *The Brethren* has contributed to piercing the veiled curtain of conference secrecy and giving the Court a somewhat more "human" image. Bob Woodward and Scott Armstrong, *The Brethren* (New York: Simon and Schuster, 1979).

Shortly after oral argument, each case is again considered at conference. The justices follow the same procedure as in the prehearing conference, with the Chief Justice speaking first, except that now a majority vote is needed to decide the case. After this conference, the Chief Justice circulates a list of opinion-writing assignments for all cases in which he voted with the majority. Opinions for all other cases are assigned by the senior associate justice voting with the majority. Each justice who voted with the majority is free to write his own concurring opinion, and each dissenting justice may write to express his views. Dissent has become common. Only about 25 percent of full opinion Supreme Court cases are decided unanimously.

Opinion drafts are prepared by the Court's private printer and circulated to each member of the Court. Some win easy acceptance; others undergo considerable revision before they satisfy all members of the majority. Occasionally, an opinion written initially to express the views of a conference majority ends up as a dissent, and vice versa. Those initially in dissent may persuade other justices to join their opinion and so end up as supporters of the majority opinion. A justice's vote can be changed until the decision is announced in open court.

When decisions are announced in open court, copies of each opinion are distributed to the news media and sent to the litigants and lower courts. Until recently it was customary for each opinion to be delivered orally by its author. This practice was very time consuming, and today most justices merely summarize and quote from their opinions. For a few momentous cases, decision day is one of high drama; for most cases, the public reading of opinions could easily be eliminated. Yet there is a strong feeling that this one direct communications link between the Court and the public, however slight, ought to be maintained.

THE JUSTICES OF THE SUPREME COURT The Constitution established "one Supreme Court," but left its size for Congress to determine. Since 1869, there have been nine justices on the high bench. Until then the number fluctuated between five and ten, with periodic alterations made, usually for political purposes.

Justices are appointed by the President, with the advice and consent of the Senate. They serve in office during "good behavior," which in practice means for life or until voluntary retirement. The average length of service has been just under fifteen years. A Supreme Court justice can be removed from office only by conviction following impeachment; this has never happened. A few justices have served into their eighties, and Oliver Wendell Holmes retired at 90. Justice William O. Douglas, at age 39 the youngest man ever appointed to the Court, retired in 1975 for reasons of health after a record thirty-six years of service.

The Constitution does not prescribe any qualifications for appointment to the Supreme Court, as it does for election to Congress or the presidency. Custom alone dictates that all justices are lawyers. This custom is unlikely to

Three Pathbreaking Appointments to the Supreme Court

When the Supreme Court began its October, 1981 term, Sandra Day O'Connor of Arizona became the first woman to sit on the high bench. Justice O'Connor served as a state Appeals Court judge and legislator before President Reagan chose her to replace Justice Potter Stewart. Stewart, appointed by President Dwight Eisenhower in 1958, had been one of the youngest justices appointed to the Court (he was forty-three at the time) in the twentieth century. Justice O'Connor is expected to follow Stewart's moderate-conservative voting record; if so, her appointment will probably not have much initial impact on the Court's decisions. Its symbolic significance, and its impact on the women's rights movement, cannot be underestimated.

O'Connor's appointment recalls two others of comparable importance. In 1916, President Woodrow Wilson nominated a Jewish Boston lawyer named Louis D. Brandeis. An outstand-ing lawyer and an aggressive advocate of progressive economic policies and social justice, Brandeis was opposed by the pillars of America's legal establishment. Former President William Howard Taft and six other former presidents of the American Bar Association claimed that Brandeis' "reputation, character, and professional career" made him "not a fit person to be a member of the Supreme Court." The spectre of anti-semitism lay just below the surface of this opposition, but Brandeis was confirmed by the Senate and became one of the Court's greatest justices. The subsequent appointment of four other Jewish justices — Benjamin Cardozo in 1932, Felix Frankfurter in 1939, Arthur Goldberg in 1962, and Abe Fortas in 1968 — reinforced the philosophy that religion should not be a barrier to judicial appointment.

In 1967, President Lyndon Johnson's nomination of Thurgood Marshall broke the Court's color barrier. Marshall was serving as Solicitor General of the United States, the government's chief advocate in the Supreme Court. Before that he had been appointed by President John F. Kennedy to the Court of Appeals for the Second Circuit. But Marshall was most famous for his years as chief counsel of the NAACP's Legal Defense Fund. Marshall argued, and won, some of the most important cases on racial discrimination to come before the Supreme Court. The most famous of these, of course, was Brown v. Board of Education of Topeka (1954), in which the Court unanimously ruled that racial segregation had no place in the public schools of our nation. As a member of the Court Marshall continued his forceful advocacy of racial, personal, and social equality. But as the Court has become more conservative, his voice is heard most often in dissent.

change, but another — that only men are appointed — was broken by Ronald Reagan's appointment of Sandra Day O'Connor.[30]

The President has the dominant role in choosing Supreme Court justices; the Senate "consents," but does not "advise." In the 20th century, the Senate has more or less routinely approved most Supreme Court nominations. Some nominees may be roundly denounced by one political faction or another; but until 1968 only one nominee, Judge John Parker in 1930, was formally denied confirmation. In 1968 the Senate did block Lyndon Johnson's nomination of Abe Fortas, then an associate justice on the Court, to become Chief Justice. Fortas asked that his controversial nomination be withdrawn when it became apparent that confirmation was unlikely. Johnson's nomination of federal Judge Homer Thornberry to replace Fortas as an associate justice was thus also blocked.[31]

In 1970 the Senate rejected two nominees of President Nixon: Clement Haynsworth and G. Harrold Carswell, both court of appeals judges from the South. Haynsworth was rejected because of allegations of conflict of interest, but he was also opposed by liberal and labor groups, which disliked his conservative views on school desegregation and labor unions. Carswell, who was nominated after Haynsworth's rejection, was successfully opposed by the same labor-liberal coalition. His record on civil rights, both before and after he became a judge, was even more conservative than Haynsworth's. His critics contended that, in addition, his "mediocre" record did not qualify him to serve on the Supreme Court.

The American Bar Association Committee on Federal Judiciary, which screens prospective nominees to lower federal courts, plays a lesser role in Supreme Court appointments. Some recent presidents have asked the ABA to evaluate a prospective nominee, but most often only after the president has settled on one candidate. The ABA, like any private group, is free to oppose judicial nominees in hearings before the Senate Judiciary Committee. It has never formally opposed a nominee to the Supreme Court.

A Supreme Court vacancy often triggers an intense political struggle. It is expected that the president will choose a candidate who shares his general political outlook or who represents values or interests he wishes to recognize. Presidents usually nominate members of their own political party, although a nominee's record may be more important than any formal political label. For President Nixon, Lewis Powell's conservatism was more important than the

---

[30] Possibly in anticipation of the appointment of a woman justice, the Court recently "neutralized" its form of reporting decisions. Instead of reporting an opinion written by "Mr. Justice _____," for example, an opinion is now reported as written by "Justice _____."

[31] See Robert Shogan, *A Question of Judgment: The Fortas Case and the Struggle for the Supreme Court* (Indianapolis: Bobbs-Merrill, 1972). On the role of the Senate, see Joel B. Grossman and Stephen L. Wasby, "The Senate and Supreme Court Nominations," *Duke Law Journal*, 1972, 557–591.

fact that he was a nominal Democrat. For similar reasons, Wilson nominated Louis Brandeis and Roosevelt selected Felix Frankfurter: Both were progressives, though not Democrats. Pressure to appoint a justice from the opposite political party usually builds up when one party holds all the other seats on the Court.

There are also pressures on a president to secure a balance of religious, racial, and geographic representation, and to have several members of the Court with experience as trial judges. In 1956, President Eisenhower selected William Brennan, a state court judge in New Jersey, because he was a Democrat, a Catholic, and had prior judicial experience. Eisenhower had been under attack for his earlier appointment of Earl Warren as Chief Justice in 1953. Warren, then the governor of California and the Republican party's vice-presidential candidate in 1948, had no prior judicial experience. He proved to be a more liberal justice than anyone expected, including the president who appointed him. Brennan likewise turned out to be a strong liberal on the Court, not unexpectedly to those who knew his record.

President Nixon was more candid about his Supreme Court appointments than most presidents. In his 1968 campaign and thereafter, he made it clear that he would appoint "strict constructionists" to the Supreme Court. What he meant by this term was justices who shared his opposition to many of the liberal decisions of the Warren Court, particularly those concerning the rights of criminal defendants. Nixon was also determined to appoint one or more justices from the South, in recognition of the increased support that region had been giving Republican presidential candidates. Nixon's "southern strategy" was stalled by the defeat of Haynsworth and Carswell, but redeemed — at least in part — with his later appointment of Powell, a Virginian. Many would argue with Nixon's interpretation of a "strict constructionist," but the record amply attests to his success in choosing more conservative justices.

A profile of the 101 men appointed to the Supreme Court prior to 1981 shows that, at least until recent years, most have been well-born, upper-middle-class, white Protestants. All have been lawyers, but few had primarily legal careers. Almost all were involved in politics. Most of the justices have been of English or Irish origin, though very few have been foreign born. Thurgood Marshall was the first — and so far the only — black appointed to the Court. Justice O'Connor, the first woman on the Court, is also a well-born, upper middle-class white Protestant. Yet, proportionally, more of the recent appointees have been from humble origins, and in time the Supreme Court probably will become more respresentative of our society's diversity. Yet the Court's small size and the infrequency of its vacancies ensure that change in its social profile will not be rapid. Only four presidents other than George Washington — Franklin Roosevelt, Jackson, Lincoln, and Eisenhower — have ever appointed a majority of the Court. In his twelve years in office, Roosevelt made nine Supreme Court appointments.

EXPLAINING THE COURT'S DECISIONS

"All attempts to explain Supreme Court decision-making stumble on the same barrier: the lack of data." Thus observes one leading commentator on the American legal system.[32] As we have already noted, the Court itself is largely responsible for this barrier. The Court's secrecy about its decision-making process means that one can never be absolutely sure how it has arrived at a given decision. The justices' recorded votes and written opinions seldom illuminate the bargaining and the give and take of views that occur as opinions are drafted and circulated to all justices. No single formula can "explain" the outcome of the Court's decisions. But there are several ways to look at the decision-making process; each contributes something to our understanding.

The Role of the Law

We have already noted the inadequacy of the theory of mechanical jurisprudence in explaining Supreme Court decisions. The rule of precedent, *stare decisis*, is not a rigid constraint. The Supreme Court has never hesitated to overrule a past decision that it believes to have been wrongly decided or that, over time, has simply not worked very well. Yet it would be a mistake to assume that precedent means nothing at all. The law does play an important role in structuring judicial choice. Supreme Court decision making, like most public policy formation, is incremental: it builds on existing case law (unless that law is regarded as wrong or no longer controlling). In most cases the Supreme Court will not decide more than is necessary to dispose of a particular case. "The law" is thus the initial basis for the justices' consideration and probably controls the outcome of most cases. Even if the Court decides to modify or overrule an existing precedent, it must explain in its opinion why that precedent was wrong, unfair, not working, obsolete, or simply not applicable to the case at hand. Courts have an obligation to provide *reasoned* judgments, a major distinction between them and the other branches of government.

The Role of Interest Groups

Interest groups play an important role in mobilizing and sponsoring litigation. Their activities often symbolize to the Court and to the country what the great issues of the time are. Cases brought by organized groups usually concern broad policy goals. Indeed, litigants are often recruited by organizations, instead of the reverse.[33]

The cumulative effect of such group activities has been a "politicization of litigation." It is not a new development, but all indicators suggest that it is a growing one. The number of litigation-oriented interest groups, and the resources they command, are now vastly greater than in the 1950s, when *Brown v. Board of Education* seemed to open the floodgates of interest-group litigation. Social reform groups, which have moved beyond more traditional civil

---

[32] Herbert Jacob, *Justice in America: Courts, Lawyers, and the Judicial Process*, 2nd ed. (Boston: Little, Brown, 1972), p. 204.

[33] See Peltason, *Federal Courts;* and David B. Truman, *The Governmental Process* (New York: Knopf, 1951), pp. 479–98.

liberties issues to such concerns as environmental reform and energy conservation, are opening up the judicial process to groups and interests formerly not well represented there. The Supreme Court itself noted, in 1963, that "Under the conditions of modern government, litigation may be the sole practicable avenue open to a minority to petition for redress of grievances."[34]

Once it was thought that litigation was a second-strike strategy pursued by a few minority groups or other interests that had "lost" in the political process or were excluded from effective participation in it. Certainly this was an adequate description of the early activities of the NAACP, in its efforts to eradicate racial discrimination, or of the Jehovah's Witnesses in seeking relief from ordinances against religious proselytizing.[35] But interest-group activity in litigation dates back at least to the end of the nineteenth century, and spans the political and socioeconomic spectrums. Furthermore, litigation today is often a primary strategic activity of groups, as we will see in Chapter 12.

Test Cases. Test cases are a leading tactic of judicial lobbyists. A test case is one in which an organization seeking to establish a new rule of law develops a case, provides attorneys, and pays all legal expenses. Sometimes it recruits the litigants; sometimes the litigant approaches the organization seeking help, and the organization decides to build a case on that request. A classic test case was the NAACP Legal Defense Fund's fight, over twenty years, to eliminate racially restrictive deeds in the sale of private housing. As part of its campaign, the Fund had to coordinate the activities of many civil rights groups. It stimulated favorable articles in law reviews, to which it could later refer in its arguments to the Supreme Court. And in 1948 it won its case, *Shelley* v. *Kraemer*.[36]

On a much larger scale, the Legal Defense Fund has recently coordinated and argued virtually all the capital punishment cases heard by the Supreme Court.[37] The Fund intervened in hundreds of cases across the country, securing stays of execution where necessary, so that no one would be executed before the Supreme Court could rule on the constitutionality of the death penalty. By the time the Court acted, in June 1972, the fate of more than six hundred persons lay in the balance.

The Court decided, in *Furman* v. *Georgia* (1972), that capital punishment, as then administered in the United States, was unconstitutional — a violation of the cruel and unusual punishment provision of the Eighth and Fourteenth amendments. The Court's ruling was based on its finding that the death penalty was applied in an arbitrary manner. Thirty-five states responded to the *Furman* decision by passing new death-penalty statutes designed to meet the Court's objections. Courts again began sentencing criminal defendants to death, and again the Fund intervened. By 1976, another four hundred persons

---

[34] *National Association for the Advancement of Colored People* v. *Button*, 371 U.S. 415 (1963).

[35] See Clement Vose, *Caucasians Only* (Berkeley: University of California Press, 1959); and David Manwaring, *Render Unto Caesar* (Chicago: University of Chicago Press, 1962).

[36] 334 U.S. 1 (1948); for the classic account of this case, see Vose, *Caucasians Only.*

[37] Michael Meltsner, *Cruel and Unusual* (New York: Random House, 1973).

were awaiting execution. In *Gregg* v. *Georgia* (1976), the Supreme Court found that some of the new death-penalty statutes were constitutionally valid, whereas others had to be revised yet again. In some states, therefore, the last constitutional barriers to executions had been removed. In January 1977, a convicted murderer named Gary Gilmore was executed by firing squad in Utah, the first legal execution in the United States since 1967. Several additional executions have taken place since then, but the number of persons awaiting execution continues to grow, and the Legal Defense Fund continues to represent many condemned persons in an effort to thwart the further resumption of the death penalty.

Amicus Curiae Briefs. Amicus curiae briefs, like test cases, have become a major tactic of interest groups. *Amicus curiae* means "friend of the court" in Latin. However, *amici* (the plural form) rarely appear as neutral advisors solicited by the court itself, but more often act as advocates of one side or the other. Interest groups have made increasing use of this tactic over the last two decades. Groups advocating social reform have filed a large number of such briefs. Only the solicitor general, the government's chief lawyer, has filed more. An amicus brief may be filed with the consent of both parties to a case or by permission of the Court. The solicitor general can appear as amicus, on behalf of the United States, in any case in which the government asserts an interest.

The success of an amicus depends not only on the quality and persuasiveness of the argument, but also, inevitably, on how receptive the Court is to a particular line of reasoning or a particular set of values. Between 1920 and 1936, corporations filed 24 percent of all amicus briefs before a Supreme Court whose policies were sympathetic to business interests. The NAACP and the ACLU, during the same period, filed only 2 percent of the amicus briefs. During the Warren Court period, from 1953 to 1969, the percentages were reversed. Corporations filed only 8 percent of these briefs, and the NAACP and ACLU filed 22 percent.[38] Clearly, amicus briefs tend both to reflect judicial preferences and to encourage the expression of those preferences. In the affirmative-action case, *California Board of Regents* v. *Bakke*, decided in 1978, 51 amicus briefs were filed by over 100 organizations.[39]

The Justices' Attitudes and Backgrounds One response to the question "Why do the justices vote as they do?" is simply that they vote in favor of outcomes they prefer. After all, Supreme Court justices have value preferences, like everyone else, and their preferences are not totally repressed when they don the black robe of the judge.

We might expect the justices' personal biases to show up more strongly in the opinions they write. Only rarely, however, does the language of a Supreme Court opinion reveal the personal feelings of its author. Opinions are much

---

[38] Robert Scigliano, *The Supreme Court and the Presidency* (New York: Free Press, 1971), chap. 6.
[39] 438 U.S. 265 (1978).

more likely to speak of "the requirements of the Constitution," even when it is the justices who have decided what the Constitution means and how it should be applied in a particular case. Justices rarely speak as candidly as Potter Stewart did in one obscenity case, when he said that he could not define hard-core pornography, "but I know it when I see it." [40]

The personal preferences of the justices are more likely to be revealed in their votes, particularly when these votes follow a consistent pattern over time. There are many techniques for measuring the consistency of judges' votes, but even a simple counting of votes for and against claims of individual rights shows a marked difference among the justices that is consistent over time. As Table 9.1 shows, there is a wide gulf between justices Brennan and Rehnquist; the former almost always supports civil liberties claims, the latter almost never. It is unlikely that this pattern of responses could have occurred by chance; the likelihood is that it reflects fundamentally different sets of attitudes.

We have noted that about three-fourths of the Supreme Court's full-opinion cases are not unanimous, and it is the votes in these nonunanimous cases that are recorded in Table 9.1. But the justices also dispose of nearly 4,000 other

Table 9.1 Percentage of Civil Liberties Votes of Supreme Court Justices (Nonunanimous and Unanimous Decisions) in Favor of Civil Liberties Claims, 1970–75 Terms

	Term					
Justice	1970	1971	1972	1973	1974	1975
Douglas	90	96	91	92	92	—
Brennan	77	84	86	87	76	85
Marshall	80	88	89	85	75	83
Black	51	—	—	—	—	—
Stewart	47	72	58	50	54	41
Stevens	—	—	—	—	—	44
White	46	58	33	42	42	31
Burger	35	36	28	28	32	18
Blackmun	35	42	36	34	39	27
Harlan	43	—	—	—	—	—
Powell	—	36	37	42	40	28
Rehnquist	—	27	16	21	26	13
Total Court	50	56	41	44	44	31

Source: Sheldon Goldman and Austin Sarat, *American Court Systems* (San Francisco: Freeman, 1978).

[40]*Jacobellis* v. *Ohio*, 378 U.S. 184 (1964).

cases each term by denial of review without significant disagreement in the vast majority of them. This suggests that the outcome of many cases is fairly clearly dictated by the legal factors involved or that the cases do not provoke disagreements over policy positions. Still, it is clear that all justices — and some more than others — have attitudes about the political world that shape their decisions. No explanation of Supreme Court behavior can fail to acknowledge this fact.

What are the sources of the personal attitudes that, it seems, have such an effect on judicial choices? Some researchers concentrate on the justices' backgrounds: Whether one is a Catholic or a Protestant, a Democrat or a Republican, a labor lawyer or a corporation lawyer, black or white, male or female is bound to influence one's values. There are two problems with this approach, however. The first is that such simple categorizations cannot pinpoint one's truly formative life experiences; they are at best clues to what those experiences are likely to have been. Each of these categories covers a range of values, any one of which may be crucial in a particular case. The second problem is that whatever attitudes a judge brings to the bench are likely to be modified by the experience of being a judge, including the influence of other justices.

Political scientists have sought to relate judges' backgrounds to their voting behavior. One important study of court of appeals judges' backgrounds has shown that their political party affiliation had a moderate effect on their votes in cases involving economic issues, and a smaller effect on their votes in civil liberties cases. Age and religion produced occasional positive correlations. To the extent that this study yields a composite picture, it suggests that judges who were young, Catholic, and Democrat were likely to be more liberal than those who were older, Republican, and Protestant.[41] But such a profile must be treated with extreme caution. Its application to a body as small as the Supreme Court is problematic at best. The effect of Supreme Court justices' social backgrounds on their decisions, then, must be regarded as indirect and uncertain.

Group Influences on Judicial Decisions So far we have emphasized the individual nature of judicial decisions. A justice's votes are also influenced by the social and pyschological pressures involved in collegial decision making. Certain of these influences — especially the size of the Court and its internal decision-making norms — may affect the outcome of its deliberations. Social psychologists have found that individuals behave differently in groups than they do, or would, if acting alone. For example, research indicates that individuals acting in groups sometimes are more willing to take risks than those acting alone, and that group decisions are, on the whole, more accurate than individual decisions.[42]

[41] For the best recent study of the social backgrounds of federal judges, see Sheldon Goldman, "Voting Behavior on the U.S. Courts of Appeals Revisited," *American Political Science Review* 69 (1975): 491–506.

[42] S. Sidney Ulmer, *Courts as Small and Not So Small Groups*, (New York: General Learning Press, 1971).

Two Chief Justices and the Presidents Who Appointed Them

In the summer of 1953, President Eisenhower nominated Governor Earl Warren of California as chief justice of the United States. Warren had been the Republican vice-presidential candidate in 1948 and a contender for the 1952 presidential nomination. At the 1952 Convention Warren threw his support to Eisenhower. Warren's subsequent selection as chief justice was widely regarded as an acknowledgement by Eisenhower of a political debt to Warren. If matters of judicial philosophy concerned Eisenhower, they were not apparent at the time. Warren had a distinguished record as a district attorney, attorney general, and governor, but had no prior judicial experience.

In the spring of 1954, Chief Justice Warren announced the Court's unanimous decision in Brown v. *Board of Education, holding that racial segregation in public schools was unconstitutional. The decision was the most controversial, and probably the most important, so far in this century. President Eisenhower made it clear publicly that he opposed the decision. Relations between president and chief justice cooled to an icy formality, the minimum required by the dignity of their respective offices. Eisenhower once referred to his appointment of Warren as a "damn fool mistake." In the 1960s, with a solid majority, Warren led the Supreme Court in an even more liberal direction, especially in the area of the rights of criminal defendants. Even if Eisenhower had paid closer attention to Warren's political philosophy before appointing him, it is* doubtful he could have predicted the course of the "Warren Court," the most liberal in the nation's history.

Upon Warren's retirement in 1969, President Nixon nominated Judge Warren Burger to replace him. A Minnesota lawyer, Burger had managed Eisenhower's successful convention fight in 1952. He later served as an assistant United States attorney general and from 1953 to 1969 on the Court of Appeals for the District of Columbia. Unlike Eisenhower and Warren, Nixon and Burger knew each other personally and politically. Burger had established himself as the most conservative member of that Court of Appeals, especially on criminal justice issues. And Nixon had made "law 'n' order" and the appointment of more conservative Supreme Court justices a major campaign issue in 1968. Unlike Warren, Burger had the prior judicial experience that many observers believed a Supreme Court nominee should have. Burger's conservative leadership of the Supreme Court in most instances cannot have been a disappointment to the president who appointed him. But, in one of the ironies of history, it was Chief Justice Burger who wrote the Supreme Court's unanimous opinion in the Nixon Tapes Case (1974), holding that the president must surrender certain tapes of White House conversations to the Watergate prosecutor. Revelation of the contents of these tapes was so damaging that Nixon resigned shortly thereafter.

Collegial decision making also creates interdependencies. No justice of the Supreme Court can decide a case alone. To secure a majority, a justice must obtain at least four additional votes. Of course there are many cases in which all justices, or a majority of them, agree on a decision without significant debate. But bargaining, accommodation, and persuasion are often a necessary part of forming a majority.

The Chief Justice's Leadership. Opportunities for leadership are open to all justices. But the Chief Justice is in the best position to exercise both task and social leadership. *Task leadership,* as defined by David Danelski, is concerned with getting the job done, seeing to it that the Court does not get bogged down in trivial or unresolvable conflicts, and that it stays abreast of its docket. A good *social leader* tries to maintain good personal relationships among the justices and to foster an *esprit de corps* that facilitates the Court's work. Combining the two types of leadership requires considerable skill. It means knowing when to push for accommodation, and when to hold out for a particular position.[43]

The Chief Justice has the tools with which to lead. He is the conference leader: Discussion begins when he states the facts of each case and his own opinion of how it should be decided. If he votes in the majority, he decides who will write the majority opinion. The chief can assign the opinion to a justice with views similar to his own, or can write the opinion himself, as Chief Justices have often done in important cases. He must keep in mind the need to maintain a majority; in closely divided cases, the opinion may be assigned to a justice in the "middle" of the court, rather than to one with more extreme views. Earl Warren's marshaling of a divided Court to present a unanimous front in *Brown* v. *Board of Education* (1954), the school desegregation case, is widely regarded as the supreme modern example of effective judicial leadership.[44] On the other hand, at least according to Bob Woodward and Scott Armstrong, authors of *The Brethren,* Warren Burger has been inept at both the task and social leadership functions. Although he was the nominal author of the Court's unanimous opinion in the Nixon Tapes Case, most of the opinion was written by other members of the Court.[45]

Voting Blocs. It is often useful to characterize the Supreme Court in terms of voting blocs, that is, justices with similar attitudes who often vote together. Justices do not formally identify with a "bloc" as members of Congress might. The Court's tradition of individuality is too strong. But justices who share the

[43] David J. Danelski, "The Influence of the Chief Justice in the Decisional Process," in Walter F. Murphy and C. Herman Pritchett, eds., *Courts, Judges and Politics* (New York: Random House, 1961), pp. 497–508. See also Walter F. Murphy, *Elements of Judicial Strategy* (Chicago: University of Chicago Press, 1964).

[44] See, for example, Richard Kluger, *Simple Justice* (New York: Vintage Books, 1976), pp. 678–99.

[45] Woodward and Armstrong, *The Brethren.*

same general outlook may find it useful to work together to achieve common goals.

In the early 1970s it was common to depict the Burger Court as loosely divided into three blocs: a liberal bloc of Justices Douglas, Brennan, and Marshall; a center or "swing" bloc of Justices White and Stewart; and a conservative bloc consisting of the "Minnesota Twins" — Chief Justice Burger and Justice Blackmun, and Justices Rehnquist and Powell. In 1976 President Ford appointed federal appeals judge John Paul Stevens to replace Douglas. Stevens quickly established himself in the center of the Court. In the meantime, the conservative bloc became somewhat unglued, with Blackmun moving to the left on issues such as abortion, and the Chief Justice moving somewhat to the right. Predictions are that Justice O'Connor will follow the moderate conservative philosophy of the man she replaced, Potter Stewart. A new "picture" of the Court in 1982 thus might find Brennan and Marshall well to the left, Burger and Rehnquist far out on the right, and the remaining five justices clustered loosely in the center, but too fragmented to be called a "bloc."

THE IMPACT OF THE COURT'S DECISIONS   Although the Supreme Court may have the final word on the meaning of the law, it does not always determine the final outcome of a case. There is no certainty that a Supreme Court decision will be carried out. Furthermore, a decision may not have its intended effect because it is not carried out fully; or it may have a different effect than the Court anticipated, even though it is fully complied with.

In theory, the American legal system is hierarchical: The Supreme Court, at the apex, interprets the law and decides important policy issues, and its decisions are enforced by lower federal court judges and state court judges. In fact, although the Supreme Court is the nominal head of the judicial system, its authority is diffuse and its enforcement powers uncertain. Lower federal courts come directly under the administrative control of the Supreme Court, but they nonetheless have considerable independence. State courts are subject to Supreme Court control only when "federal questions" or constitutional issues are involved, and they are thus even more independent of Supreme Court control.

Limits on the Court's Reach   Lower federal court judges escape direct supervision by the Supreme Court for several reasons. First, the high court can review only a handful of cases each year; case-by-case supervision of lower court judges is impossible. Further, the Court seldom bothers with cases in areas of the law not of great current public interest, or that concern mostly private disputes. Most supervision of these cases is done by the courts of appeals. Second, the majority of lower court cases are not appealed. Third, even in cases that raise major public issues, trial judges control scheduling, motions, penalties, and remedies, and thus substantially and irrevocably affect the rights of the litigants. Fourth, on many issues federal judges are more responsive to local and regional values and pressures than to Supreme Court policies.

Outright defiance of Supreme Court decisions is rare. Judges usually do what the Supreme Court tells them to do. On the other hand, clear, direct orders by the high court are also rare. Supreme Court decisions may be clear with respect to the immediate parties to the case but ambiguous in their broader meaning.

A good example is the aftermath of *Tinker* v. *Des Moines School District* (1969). In that case, the Supreme Court held that students protesting the Vietnam War by wearing black armbands could not be suspended unless there was evidence that wearing the armbands actually disrupted school life and activities. The Court also held, however, that students do not have an absolute right to wear black armbands, and that its decision did not automatically extend to other forms of nonverbal political speech. Still, the decision was a strong affirmative statement upholding the First Amendment rights of students. By implication it could easily apply to other forms of political expression, such as long hair or particular forms of dress. Were students now free to make these choices themselves, or were school authorities still entitled to enforce hair and dress codes? Lower courts are substantially divided on this, and the Supreme Court has never seen fit to resolve the issue. Whether a school administrator can enforce such a code depends, at present, on which federal judicial circuit the school is in. The fact that the law is not, and need not be, uniform throughout the United States is often difficult to accept, but it is nonetheless true.

The Problem of Enforcement.   Even when the Supreme Court has made an authoritative decision, it has limited means to ensure full compliance. It (or the courts of appeals) can reverse a lower court judge. But that action alone is a mild sanction, especially for a judge whose opposition to a Supreme Court decision is rooted in conscience or in local popular sentiment. The Court can directly order a judge to decide in favor of one or another party to the case, but it rarely does so. Removal of a case from a judge's docket is also rare. A recalcitrant judge can be cited for contempt, and judges are subject to removal by impeachment under Article II, Section 4 of the Constitution. But no federal judge has ever been removed for failure to carry out the orders of the Supreme Court.

The problems of enforcement are magnified when it is the state courts that refuse to carry out a Supreme Court order. The Supreme Court can review only the federal and constitutional issues that such a case may present. It cannot review questions of state law. Thus, state courts can evade Supreme Court review by deciding strictly on the basis of state law — that is, by avoiding any "federal questions." Elected state judges are especially careful to protect local interests and reflect local values. Supreme Court review of the decisions of state courts has been a point of contention since the beginning of the Republic.

The problem of enforcing Supreme Court decisions is not just a matter of noncompliance by lower court judges. Bureaucrats and the general public also sometimes resist complying. One study of local responses in several midwestern states to the Court's controversial 1962 and 1963 school prayer decisions found that state and local leaders had little incentive to comply. In the absence of a direct order from a court or a higher state official, none wished to take the responsibility of carrying out unpopular Supreme Court decisions they also personally opposed.[46] As far as many hard-pressed local school officials were concerned, the benefits of retaining prayers in the schools were far greater than the political costs of trying to abolish them. To do the latter would provoke conflict and instability — conditions local officials wanted to avoid. Those officials who wanted to enforce the Supreme Court's decision, either because they agreed with it or because they felt an obligation to obey the law, were isolated and unable to mobilize support.

Efforts to overturn an unpopular decision may continue indefinitely, with varying degrees of intensity, and such activity may encourage noncompliance. The prayer decisions, for example, are still highly controversial. The U.S. Catholic Conference has long favored a constitutional amendment to permit prayers in the schools. Recently, right-wing Protestant groups have joined the cause, supported by many people who perceive a religious and moral degeneration in the country and see the restoration of school prayer as a means of correcting it.

Early efforts to reverse the Supreme Court's prayer decisions by a constitutional amendment failed, but a resurgence of effort to overrule the Court is now occurring. In 1979 the Senate passed a rider sponsored by Senator Jesse Helms (R-North Carolina) which would have prevented the Supreme Court from reviewing any state law related to voluntary prayers in the public schools. Whether or not the Congress may limit the Court's jurisdiction in that way is unclear; if the law is ultimately passed by Congress, a judicial test of its constitutionality is certain. But whether or not the Helms rider is constitutional, there is no mistaking the strong sentiment behind a revival of prayers in the schools.

Along with efforts to overturn the prayer decisions are a spate of efforts to evade their spirit by substituting other religious symbols or exercises. Currently, ten states have laws either requiring or permitting a "moment of silence" for student meditation. Tennessee and Mississippi have laws requiring "voluntary" prayer, and legislation supporting voluntary prayer is pending in six other states. The Massachusetts law, which required teachers to invite students to say prayers if they wanted to, was declared unconstitutional by that state's highest court. In 1980, in *Stone* v. *Graham*,[47] the Supreme Court struck down a Kentucky law that required the posting of a copy of the Ten Com-

[46] See, for example, Kenneth M. Dolbeare and Phillip Hammond, *The School Prayer Decisions* (Chicago: University of Chicago Press, 1971). On the need for coercion to enforce some unpopular decisions, see Harrell Rodgers, Jr. and Charles Bullock, III, *Coercion to Compliance* (Lexington, Mass.: Lexington Books, 1976).
[47] 449 U.S. 39 (1980).

mandments in every classroom in the state. Posting the Ten Commandments, the Court said, is "plainly religious in nature" and thus violates the First Amendment requirement of separation of church and state.

Inducing Compliance. If the Supreme Court is unable to count automatically on full compliance with its decisions, it may nevertheless increase the likelihood of compliance in a number of ways. A decision should state clearly what the Court expects will be done. Too often, Supreme Court decisions are couched in general policy terms and their application to persons other than the litigants is unclear. But clear and direct orders may not be enough. The *Miranda* decision made it very clear that law enforcement officers, on taking a criminal suspect into custody, were required to inform the suspect of the constitutional right to remain silent and the right to have an attorney appointed. The problem was not that police officers did not understand, but that they understood all too well and did not like what they were being told to do.

A second way the Court can induce compliance is to identify who is responsible for carrying out its decisions. Few public officials are likely to volunteer to implement an unpopular Court decision without some incentive to do so. In many cases, including but not limited to the prayer decisions, the interest groups who brought the cases did not have either enough incentive or sufficient resources to monitor compliance throughout the country.[48]

Effects of Court Decisions We have said that the Supreme Court is part of the political process and an important contributor to the making of public policy. Its decisions enter a larger arena of conflict, where their effect is often reduced by forces outside the Court's control. Yet these facts should not be allowed to detract from the real influence the Court has in our society.

Even if compliance is not always immediately forthcoming, the effect of the Court's major decisions can be seen over time. When a decision is aimed at changing an entrenched custom, or when it requires officials to act contrary to their own values, some initial resistance should be expected. Yet, despite the pockets of disobedience and recent resurgence of effort to restore prayers to the public schools, most communities in the United States still do not allow prayers in the public schools; most police officers do give the *Miranda* warnings most of the time (even on television); and racial segregation by law has ended in the public schools (although, as we shall see in Chapter 14, segregated schools still exist for other reasons).

What the Court decides also may have an important effect on the opinions, habits, and attitudes of the citizenry. Who can doubt the effect of *Brown* (and many other decisions on the same subject that followed) on American racial

---

[48] For a fascinating study of the development of litigation in the prayer cases and in other freedom of religion cases, see Frank Sorauf, *The Wall of Separation: The Constitutional Politics of Church and State* (Princeton, N.J.: Princeton University Press, 1976).

attitudes? Even if no clear link is established, who can doubt that the Court's many decisions on civil liberties influenced recent legislation by Congress prohibiting electronic surveillance without a court order? And who can doubt the effect of the Court's permissive decisions on pornography and obscenity on the ongoing revolution in sexual mores in the United States?[49]

HOW CITIZENS VIEW THE SUPREME COURT

Public opinion is an important part of the Supreme Court's decision-making environment. But it is not well understood. The very notion of public opinion affecting how judges decide cases contradicts the accepted view of courts as insulated from outside pressure. Courts are not supposed to be representative institutions. Their decisions should rest not on the ebb and flow of popular opinion but on sound reasoning, the logic of the law, and an objective reading of the needs of the society.

But judges cannot be oblivious to the times in which they live or to the changing norms of a society. It is simplistic to say that the Supreme Court "follows the election returns," but it would be foolhardy to claim that the Court pays no heed whatsoever to popular opinion. A Court so out of step would risk its legitimacy. It would come into increasingly hostile conflict with the Congress, arouse the ire of the citizenry, and risk massive noncompliance by public officials and the public itself.

What Does the Public Know about the Court?

For most citizens the Supreme Court is just a blur on the political landscape.[50] They do not perceive it as having much direct effect on their daily lives. Of course this perception varies somewhat with particular decisions by the Court. A few decisions — often in clusters on a particular subject — are known to the public in a general way. Surveys have shown that there is widespread awareness of decisions on racial segregation in the public schools, school prayers, abortion, and some aspects of the criminal justice system such as the right of an arrested person to obtain a lawyer and to remain silent. By contrast, there was little public awareness of the Court's important decisions on legislative reapportionment.[51] Opinion surveys support the conclusions that the public has little knowledge or understanding of the Supreme Court. Not only are citizens poorly informed about Supreme Court decisions, but they are also poorly informed about how the Court functions. Typical survey questions reveal that many citizens do not know such basic facts about the Supreme Court as the number of justices. One recent survey showed that only 7 percent of the

[49] See *Report of the President's Commission on Obscenity and Pornography* (New York: Bantam Books, 1970), pp. 42–51, 346–442.

[50] Among the many treatments of the subject, one of the best is Walter F. Murphy, Joseph Tanenhaus, and Daniel L. Kastner, *Public Evaluations of Constitutional Courts: Alternative Explanations* (Beverly Hills, Calif.: Sage Publications, 1973).

[51] See Walter F. Murphy and Joseph Tanenhaus, "Public Opinion and the United States Supreme Court: A Preliminary Mapping of Some Prerequisites for Court Legitimation of Regime Changes," in Joel Grossman and Joseph Tanenhaus, eds., *Frontiers of Judicial Research* (New York: Wiley, 1969), pp. 273–303.

respondents followed the Supreme Court closely, compared with 20 percent for the Congress and 60 percent for the president.[52] Lack of press and TV coverage is undoubtedly responsible for much of this gap.[53] But the Supreme Court also contributes to its own low visibility, as we have already suggested.

Citizens who know some details about the Supreme Court and follow its work are said to constitute its "attentive public." How large is this public, and who are its members? A good estimate, based on many surveys over time, is that this group does not exceed 40 percent of Americans. It consists mostly of affluent, well-educated citizens who are interested in and knowledgeable about politics generally. Perhaps another 30 to 40 percent, called the "marginal" public, know a few facts about the Court, such as the number of justices. The remaining 20 to 40 percent (estimates vary) have neither interest in nor knowledge about the Court. These people tend to be apathetic about politics generally.[54]

Who Supports the Court? It is useful to distinguish between public attitudes toward the Supreme Court as an institution, and attitudes toward specific decisions. Prevailing attitudes toward the Court consist of a general reservoir of good will, which is affected very little by particular decisions. In a sense this good will helps to set a protective boundary within which the Supreme Court can operate relatively free of political interference. Attitudes toward the Court's specific decisions, although they do contribute to general support, are analytically separate.

Public confidence in the Supreme Court as an institution has varied over the years. During the late 1960s, its support appeared to decrease markedly — both absolutely and in comparison with support for Congress and the president. This was a time generally of diminished respect for and confidence in our governmental institutions. The greater decline in support for the Court may have reflected public dissatisfaction with the liberal trend of the Warren Court's decisions on school desegregation and the rights of those charged with crimes, and its "permissiveness" in obscenity cases. Since 1972, perhaps fueled by Watergate and the conservative leaning of the Burger Court, popular confidence has risen markedly, approaching its mid-1960 levels.[55]

Regarding the Court's actual performance, surveys reveal some concern among citizens that the Court is too "political," and perhaps not always as objective and impartial as befits the highest court in the land.[56] However, few citizens have definite and informed opinions about specific Supreme Court decisions. Of those who do, more express discontent with certain decisions than

[52] Jack Dennis, "Mass Public Support for the U.S. Supreme Court," unpublished paper, 1976, p. 8.

[53] Publication of the best seller, *The Brethren*, may contribute to improved public understanding of the Court.

[54] Sheldon Goldman and Thomas Jahnige, *The Federal Courts as a Political System*, 2nd ed. (New York: Harper and Row, 1975), pp. 143–46.

[55] Dennis, "Mass Public Support."

[56] Summarized in ibid., pp. 18–19.

approval of others. But this disparity may just be due to the disproportionate publicity the media give to the Court's most controversial decisions. Even the better-informed citizens base their judgment of the Court's work on an unrepresentative sample of its decisions. Public attitudes toward specific decisions also vary over time by group, region, and subject. For example, some of the northern white liberal support for school desegregation evaporated as de facto segregation and busing became an issue in northern cities in the late 1960s. A 1975 resurvey of citizens who had been questioned in 1966 showed that they had become much more negative in their views of Supreme Court policies on civil rights.[57]

The Influence of Public Opinion   Public opinion rarely has a *direct* effect on Supreme Court decisions. As our brief survey suggests, the Court can count on little *active* public support. The public knows little about the Court, and, except for a few publicized decisions, cares even less. Some of the Court's most consistent support comes from citizens who are not politically powerful and who tend to be politically apathetic. But their support, though widespread, may only be skin deep. They are as unlikely to rise to the Court's defense in time of crisis as they are to support political attacks on the Court. Still, in this way they may provide an important buffer between the Court and its active critics.[58]

Public opinion may have an *indirect* and *long-term* effect on Supreme Court decisions, but evidence is difficult to obtain. The long-term influence of public opinion is most likely to be expressed through the appointment of new justices by a president who shares public dissatisfaction with some of the Court's work and who exploits that dissatisfaction to his own political advantage. President Nixon's appointments to the Court, which we have already described, are a good example. Long-term, if more specific, effects are also likely to be felt in the occasional reversal of unpopular Supreme Court decisions by constitutional amendment. The *Dred Scott* decision of 1857, which supported slavery and racial inequality, was effectively overruled by the results of the Civil War, and by the Thirteenth, Fourteenth, and Fifteenth amendments, which were passed after the war. More recently, a Supreme Court ruling that Congress did not have the power to impose an eighteen-year-old voting age on state elections was superseded by the Twenty-sixth Amendment, which established a national minimum voting age of eighteen for all elections.[59] Finally, Congress, through its control of the appellate jurisdiction of the Court, can withdraw jurisdiction over subjects or areas in which the Court has made particularly unpopular decisions.

Public opinion may have an effect on the Supreme Court in another way. In several recent decisions the Court openly considered the weight of public

[57] Walter F. Murphy and Joseph Tanenhaus, "Patterns of Public Support: A Study of the Warren and Burger Courts," paper presented to the X World Congress, International Political Science Association, Edinburgh, Scotland, August 1976, p. 17.

[58] Goldman and Jahnige, *Federal Courts as a Political System*, pp. 148–49.

[59] *Oregon* v. *Mitchell*, 400 U.S. 112 (1970).

opinion. Justice Blackmun's opinion in *Roe* v. *Wade* noted the growing public support for legalized abortion, although he was careful to base his opinion squarely on the Constitution. Public opinion was also an issue in the death penalty cases. Those cases turned, as we saw earlier, on the "cruel and unusual punishment" clause of the Eighth Amendment, a clause that has been interpreted as reflecting the "evolving standards of decency" of the American people. In 1972, when *Furman* v. *Georgia* was decided, several justices noted the fact that public opinion supporting capital punishment was at its lowest level in years. In *Gregg* v. *Georgia* (1976), the majority opinion of Justice Stewart noted that thirty-five states had reinstituted the death penalty after 1972, and that public opinion had swung strongly back in favor of capital punishment.

Levels of public support for the Supreme Court may be more important in determining the *effect* of the Court's policies than in influencing the making of those policies. There is some evidence that citizens who support the Court as an institution may be predisposed to support its decisions. But as we noted earlier, citizens who agree with a particular decision — and those whose actions on the matter are directly supervised by public officials — are most likely to comply.

CONCLUSION Most citizens have little knowledge about the Court and few feel able to affect its decisions. With some exceptions, people are only vaguely aware of a few especially well-publicized and controversial decisions. The Supreme Court, in turn, has not shown much interest in what citizens think about the cases it has decided, or about how it conducts its business. Is this a major weakness in our political system? We have seen that, at least on the surface, the Court is not a democratic institution. But is it so remote and elitist as to be incompatible with a democratic system?

The Supreme Court is certainly less subject to direct popular control than either Congress or the presidency. Otherwise it would hardly be a court. Perhaps a more relevant question is: How responsive has the Court been to the major social and political currents of society? Have the Supreme Court's decisions contributed to the enhancement of our processes of self-government?[60] These questions raise others. What interests has the Court represented, and how important to our system is it that those interests be represented in the courts? Could they be represented more effectively by another institution? Would the gap be lessened significantly if Supreme Court justices were popularly elected?

Only the brief outline of an answer to these questions is possible here, and that answer is mixed. For most of its existence the Supreme Court was predominantly sympathetic to the claims of wealth and privilege. Yet such a

---

[60] See David Adamany, "Review of Alexander Bickel's *The Morality of Consent*," *Wisconsin Law Review*, 1977, pp. 271–92.

stance was also consistent with nationalist policies important to the development of a new nation. As the nation's values have changed, so too the Court's role has changed. Since the New Deal the Court has been much more responsive to a liberal conception of human rights, and it has been a leader in articulating and protecting these rights. Many of its decisions have contributed to greater popular participation in, and control of, all political institutions, although, as we have noted, in the Burger Court, the pendulum is slowly swinging back again on some issues.

It is difficult to square this recent performance by the Supreme Court with the picture painted by many of its critics on the left. An elitist restraint on popular government is precisely what many of the framers of the Constitution expected the Supreme Court to be. If we use these early expectations as our baseline for comparisons, then in both function and performance the Supreme Court has come a long way toward easing the tension between itself and the people. Tension still remains, but it is extremely unlikely that, as the political system as a whole moves toward greater popular participation and accountability of institutions (though also toward the political right), the Supreme Court will regress completely to its elitist origins.

SUGGESTIONS FOR FURTHER READING

Baum, Lawrence. *The Supreme Court.* Washington, D.C.: Congressional Quarterly Press, 1980. An excellent description of the Supreme Court and its procedures.

Bickel, Alexander. *The Supreme Court and the Idea of Progress.* New York: Harper Torch Books, 1970. The late Yale Law School professor and scholar argues against the activist trends of the Warren Court. The Supreme Court, in his view, cannot operate effectively or legitimately as the vanguard of social movements.

Lewis, Anthony. *Gideon's Trumpet: The Poor Man and the Law.* New York: Random House, 1964. Still the best single case study of a Supreme Court decision. Lewis describes Gideon's successful effort to reverse his conviction for burglary in a Florida court. The Supreme Court accepted Gideon's claim that he had a constitutional right to have a lawyer appointed to defend him.

McCloskey, Robert. *The American Supreme Court.* Chicago: University of Chicago Press, 1960. Although the book's coverage ends with the early years of the Warren Court, it is still the best short historical interpretation of the Court.

Murphy, Walter F. *Elements of Judicial Strategy.* Chicago: University of Chicago Press, 1964. A fascinating "inside" look at the internal politics and decision-making strategies of Supreme Court justices, based on revelations of the private papers of former justices.

Sorauf, Frank. *The Wall of Separation.* Princeton, N.J.: Princeton University Press, 1976. A study of the mobilization of litigants and the development of litigation in cases raising constitutional issues of church and state.

Woodward, Bob, and Armstrong, Scott. *The Brethren: Inside the Supreme Court.* New York: Simon and Schuster, 1979. Two investigative reporters provide an inside view of how the Court functions and how a number of its most important cases in the 1970s were decided.

Chapter 10 Elections

American political ideals emphasize the citizen's power in a democracy. Although the country's founders knew that tensions between leaders and led are inherent in any political system, they hoped to minimize them in America. But the *means* of bridging the gap between citizens and their government took time to develop. Today, three primary links connect the people with political institutions and officials: elections, political parties, and interest groups. The performance of each of these links determines just how large the gap between citizens and government becomes in America. This chapter examines the electoral connection.

Regular and meaningful elections are a major fact of political life in America. We take elections for granted, but many countries have no regular electoral process at all, and even the most democratic countries have been known to suspend elections for longer or shorter periods. In communist societies elections are held regularly; usually, however, only candidates who belong to the Communist party are actually elected. In many Asian, African, and Latin American countries, elections are a kind of cruel, on-again, off-again charade; powerful leaders call elections only when it pleases them to do so. Military governments, of course, suspend free elections when they believe that such elections threaten the country with "disorder." Meanwhile, in countries emerging from long periods of authoritarian control, such as Spain and Portugal, the cry goes up for "free elections," and the establishment of an electoral process whereby parties compete peacefully with each other becomes a proud hallmark of a newly established democracy.

Why are free elections widely desired, yet vulnerable to disruption? The answer is that free elections are an essential part of democratic politics and, therefore, constitute a potential *threat* to political leaders. Free elections can be a powerful instrument in the hands of the people. Realizing this, leaders try to protect themselves from elections when they can.

Elections can perform several important democratic functions. First and foremost, they enable citizens to choose their leaders. Elections thus afford the opportunity for a circulation of political leadership. Elections also provide the opportunity for a general debate over public policy. The alternative policy approaches the candidates offer usually generate public discussion and may determine many voters' decisions. As a result, elections may allow the general public to influence the course of public policy. Finally, elections sometimes allow winning candidates to claim a "mandate from the people." This mandate, or vote of confidence, provides a justification for leaders to undertake major policy initiatives and thus to govern from a position of great strength.

It is little wonder, therefore, that political leaders bent on monopolizing political power should fear a system of free elections. More puzzling, however, is the fact that ordinary voters often become cynical about electoral politics — even though they apparently have the most to gain. Why? The answer is that the electoral process is a delicate mechanism that only *promises* to circulate leaders, to provide public debate and popular influence on policy, and to revitalize commitments to democracy. Nowhere is there an electoral system that succeeds entirely in performing these functions. It is not surprising, then, that people occasionally become impatient with the electoral process.

THE ELECTORAL PROCESS The United States is one of the most "electoral" political systems in the world. Americans always seem to be going to or coming from the polls. A great many state and local offices are filled by the ballot. Each state chooses its governor and state legislators at the polls; some choose their judges in this manner. Some states even choose important cabinet officers, such as superintendent of public instruction (California) or secretary of state (Wisconsin), by the ballot. Localities fill every office from mayor to dogcatcher by voting. Officers of "special districts" (governmental units responsible for crucial local services such as education and the water supply) may also be chosen at elections.

The Constitution provides for the election of presidents and vice-presidents every four years, members of the House of Representatives every two years, and senators every six years. Technically, the president and vice-president are chosen by the electoral college, not directly by the electorate as a whole. The electoral college consists of a slate of representatives from each state, called *electors;* it is for these electors that we actually vote when we cast a presidential ballot for one candidate or another on election day. The winning slate of electors in each state then almost invariably casts its votes for the candidate to whom it has pledged itself. After the election, the electoral college dissolves until a new one is elected by the people four years later.

There also exists a growing system of primary elections in which the people choose the candidates who will run in the general election. In 1980, thirty-seven states chose their delegates to the presidential nominating conventions in primaries, and most states choose candidates for state offices this way.

How and why did this proliferation of electoral mechanisms develop? Does it fulfill the electoral functions outlined earlier? We turn to the first question next and will consider the second later in the chapter.

Why So Many Elections? Why do we have so many elections, and what are the consequences of this situation? Four factors bear mention.

The Separation of Powers. One of the factors most responsible for the proliferation of elections in the United States is the doctrine of the separation of powers. As seen in Chapter 2, the Founding Fathers were anxious to prevent any single group of political leaders from dominating government. Hence, they designed a political system in which the main branches of government would depend on different sources of power. To help ensure that this separation would work, they deliberately split off the election of the president from the election of members of Congress. The president must muster a national coalition of voters; members of Congress depend only on local coalitions. Moreover, by staggering the elections of senators (one-third are chosen every two years) and by limiting members of the House of Representatives to a two-year term, the founders tried to prevent a tyrannical combination of executive and legislative power from emerging in any single election.

The separation-of-powers principle was designed by the Founding Fathers for application only to the federal government. However, the states adopted it for their own internal organization, thus producing a proliferation of state and local elections paralleling the federal electoral system.

Federalism. The practice of federalism is a second factor responsible for the proliferation of American elections. The founders divided power not only functionally (through the separation of powers) but also geographically. The Tenth Amendment to the Constitution gives the states sovereignty over many of their own internal affairs. The Constitution says little about the organization of state elections; therefore, the states varied considerably in their electoral development. The result is an amazing number and variety of state, county, city, and special district elections.

The Progressive Movement. A third factor that helps explain the proliferation of American elections is the Progressive Movement of the early twentieth century. Indeed, as early as the 1880s many white middle-class Americans had come to believe that, without reform, our country's electoral politics would become increasingly corrupt. Already the "spoils system" of political patronage had produced a number of boss-dominated political machines, which flourished both in cities and in rural areas. The machines commonly practiced vote fraud and bribery.

The Progressives argued that these practices were systematically destroying public faith in the electoral process. Accordingly, they proposed electoral reforms. They spearheaded the movement to introduce the primary election as an antidote to bossism, to introduce the secret ballot, and to enable voters to vote for each office individually rather than for a party bloc. Primaries loosen the hold of party leaders by permitting the people to choose their own party candidates for the general election. The Progressives also helped introduce the "nonpartisan" election, in which no party label appears on the ballot, as an antidote to machine control.[1] As a result of these efforts, American elections became even more common than before.

The urge for electoral and party reform has continued into our own time. Since the late 1960s both parties have introduced a number of reforms that have increased opportunities for Americans to use the ballot. In particular, both parties have attempted to ensure that more delegates to the national party conventions come from local districts, rather than from the state as a whole. As a result, in a number of places delegates to the national convention are chosen by voting in party "caucuses," which are limited to declared party members and do not involve a statewide electorate.

The Electoral College. We have already examined the contribution of federalism to the proliferation of American elections. Federalism is also an important force in determining the composition of the electoral college, which actually elects the president. Each state is allotted one elector for each of its senators and representatives. In addition, the District of Columbia casts three electoral votes. The distribution of electoral votes is recalculated every ten years according to changes in state populations as reported in the census, which the Constitution stipulates be taken every ten years. The result is an electoral college composed roughly according to state populations.

A candidate need win only a small number of highly populated states in order to win the required majority of 270 electoral votes (of the total 538) and thus to become president. Consequently, campaigners generally focus their attention on the large industrial states, where substantial concentrations of electoral votes are to be had. This "large-state" strategy is also encouraged by the "winner-take-all" rule, whereby the winning candidate in each state wins *all* the state's electoral votes. Typically, therefore, the division of the electoral vote is somewhat less even than the overall popular vote totals for president.

---

[1] For a description of the Progressives' reforms, see Samuel P. Hays, "The Politics of Reform in Municipal Government in the Progressive Period," *Pacific Northwest Quarterly*, October 1964, pp. 157–69. The best study of nonpartisan elections is Willis Hawley, *Nonpartisan Elections and the Case for Party Politics* (New York: Wiley, 1973).

For example, in 1960, although John Kennedy won only 49.9 percent of the popular vote to Richard Nixon's 47.7 percent, he captured 56.4 percent of the electoral college vote (303 votes). The disparity was even more glaring in 1980, when Ronald Reagan won 51 percent of the popular vote but 90 percent of the votes in the electoral college. Thus it is evident that the electoral college usually strengthens the power of small voting majorities.

The Constitution provides that if no candidate secures a majority of the electoral college vote, the president shall be chosen by members of the House of Representatives, with each state casting only one vote, and with a majority of states necessary to win. In this extraordinary procedure the importance of a state's population is totally nullified. The House has chosen the president by this method twice, once in 1800 (Thomas Jefferson) and again in 1824 (John Quincy Adams). For a while it seemed possible that this method might be employed in 1968, when a strong third-party candidate, George Wallace, ate into the electoral vote totals of candidates Nixon and Humphrey. Some felt that John Anderson's independent candidacy in 1980 might have the same result, but Anderson won only 7 percent of the popular vote and no electoral votes.

Features of American Elections
Although there is a great variety of American elections, most have certain things in common. The features most important to understand are the fixed timing of elections, the reliance on the single-member district, the winner-take-all rule in the electoral college, and the institutional barriers to parties and candidates wishing to appear on the ballot.

Fixed-Interval Elections. American elections occur at fixed intervals determined by either state or federal law. In some cases the interval is short — two years, for example, for the House of Representatives. Presidential elections occur every four years, senatorial elections every six.

An important consequence of this system is that election day itself may not coincide with decisive points in the policymaking process. Therefore, it may be difficult for voters to relate important issues to the positions of candidates and hence to use their vote either to support or to oppose the candidates' issue positions. They therefore lose important leverage in the electoral process.

Obviously, fixed elections have their drawbacks. At the same time, fixed elections give leaders "breathing room" to make temporarily unpopular decisions. Such decisions may win public approval in the long run. In any event, fixed elections obviously do not encourage immediate public control over policy.

Single-Member Districts. A second common feature of American general elections is the single-member district, in which voters choose only one candidate to represent a district. For example, a state's members of the House of Representatives are not selected as a group by all the state's voters; rather, each one is elected as the representative of a certain area within the state. This system narrows responsibility for representing a group of voters down to a single person and permits the voters in an area to focus all demands on a single representative. At the same time it alerts the representative to the need to represent *all* the people in his district, not just those who voted for him or her.[2] The single-member district system thus encourages leaders to pursue moderate policies that are compromises between the demands of major constituent groups. To continue to win elections as the district's representative, a leader obviously needs as broad a base of support as possible.

Plurality Winners. A third common feature of American elections is the *plurality,* or winner-take-all, provision. In the plurality situation — the usual one in American general elections — a candidate need not get any stated number of votes or percentage of the vote to win. In other words, no matter how few votes a candidate gets, he or she wins as long as each of the other candidates gets fewer.

There are exceptions to this rule. In some primary elections, chiefly in the South, the top *two* candidates face each other in a runoff election in order to ensure that the winner is chosen by a majority of voters. In presidential elections, the winning candidate must gain a majority of electoral votes — not popular votes. Typically, the popular and electoral votes coincide, but in three cases — the elections of Benjamin Harrison, John Quincy Adams, and Rutherford Hayes — the leader in the race for electoral votes won fewer popular votes than his major opponent.

The plurality procedure has profound consequences. Consider, for example, an election in which Candidate X is opposed in the election by two other candidates, Y and Z. On election day Candidate X receives 40 percent of the vote; Candidate Y, 38 percent; and Candidate Z, 22 percent. But only 75 percent of the eligible voters actually went to the polls. A little arithmetic shows that Candidate X attracted only 30 percent of the total electorate. Nevertheless, this is sufficient to give Candidate X a vote *plurality,* enough to elect Candidate X under the winner-take-all system (see Figure 10.1).

This system works a special hardship on small parties and insurgent candidates at the national level. If the foregoing example represents a presidential race, Candidate Z, through winning 22 percent of the vote, is unlikely to win any electoral votes unless his support is highly concentrated in a particular region or a few states. If his support is widely distributed — as it must be if he is to be taken seriously as a possible winner nationally — he will probably lose everywhere. The result is that, in practice, his 22 percent of the voting public will enjoy no representation of their views. It is evident from this example that the plurality system discourages challenges to two large, dominant parties; prospective third-party voters have good reason to fear that their votes will go for naught. As a result, initial enthusiasm for third-party candidacies

---

[2] This does not eliminate the problem of representation, however. For a discussion, see Hannah Pitkin, *The Concept of Representation* (Berkeley: University of California Press, 1971).

Figure 10.1 Plurality Winners in American Elections

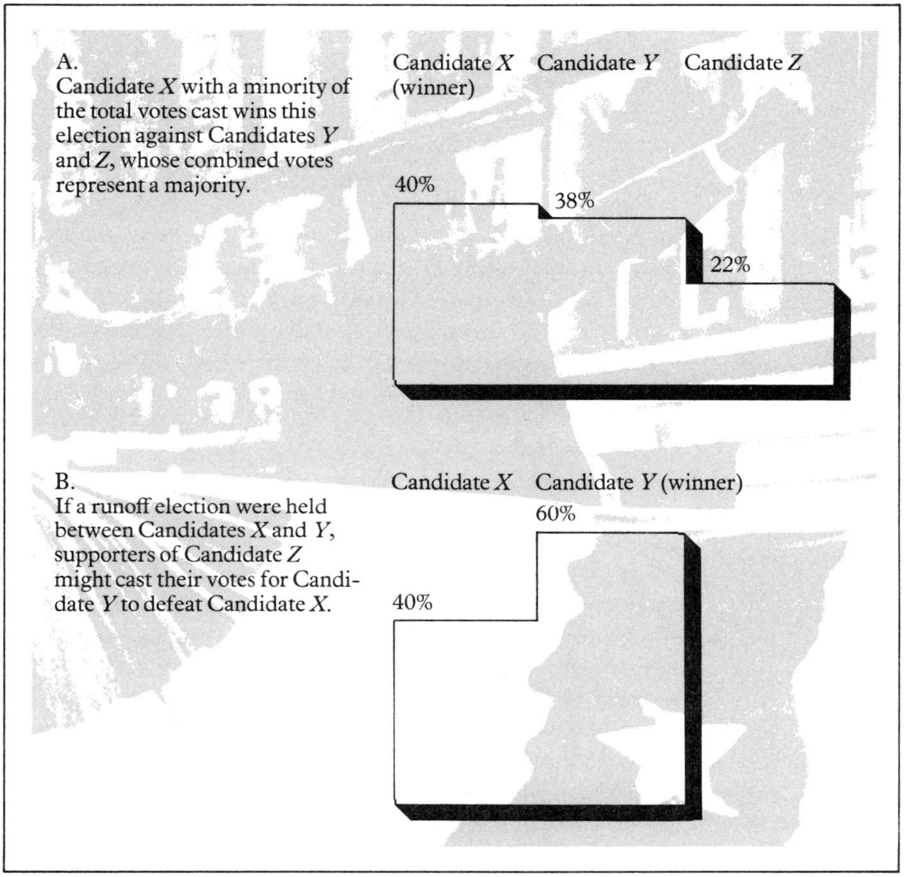

A.
Candidate *X* with a minority of the total votes cast wins this election against Candidates *Y* and *Z*, whose combined votes represent a majority.

Candidate *X* (winner)   Candidate *Y*   Candidate *Z*

40%

38%

22%

B.
If a runoff election were held between Candidates *X* and *Y*, supporters of Candidate *Z* might cast their votes for Candidate *Y* to defeat Candidate *X*.

Candidate *X*   Candidate *Y* (winner)

60%

40%

often deteriorates as election day nears. In 1980, support for candidate John Anderson declined rapidly as election day neared; he wound up winning only 7 percent of the vote.

It is easy to criticize this system. After all, the majority of voters *rejected* Candidate X, the winning candidate in our hypothetical election. And many voters, fearful of voting for a "sure loser," may have voted for their second choice or for no one at all. But this criticism overlooks two major aspects of the plurality system. First, the system forces all serious candidates to search for a winning coalition of voters. Naturally, each will seek out policies and programs designed to appeal to a broad segment of the electorate. In the process, each candidate will act as a mediator between groups in conflict.

Second, the winner-take-all system reduces the amount of bargaining between elected officials after the election. It almost always produces a majority *party* both in Congress and in state legislatures. An alternative system, such as proportional representation, might represent minority views more fairly in the distribution of offices, but in so doing it would make governing more difficult because government itself could be divided. This is often the situation in some European countries with *multiparty* systems. To govern the country, several parties must form a working group or *coalition*, agree on a legislative program, and decide how to divide up the government positions among themselves. Sometimes the necessary coalition cannot be formed or, once formed, rapidly disintegrates. Either situation can, and often does, result in stalemate or chaos. For example, between 1946 and 1958 France was ruled by a bewildering succession of coalition governments, most of which lasted only a few months. Under such conditions the formulation and execution of governmental policy can be seriously obstructed or halted altogether. The winner-take-all system, then, favors political continuity and stability over precise representation of the electorate's policy preferences.

Thus an important consequence of the plurality system is that it pushes the country toward a two-party system. Suppose a party wins 51 percent of the vote in every congressional district across the nation. That party would win *every* congressional seat; the opposing party, which garnered only 2 percent fewer votes, would win *no* seats. In practice, of course, this outcome never occurs. Each of the two major parties always has some regional pockets of strength to sustain it. Nevertheless, the smaller the party, the smaller the chance that it will win a seat anywhere and, therefore, the greater the chance that its supporters' votes will be wasted. The winner-take-all system thus encourages the formation of two large competitive parties with national followings.

Getting on the Ballot. A candidate or party cannot count on automatic access to the ballot. Each state differs in the requirements it places on candidates and parties wishing to run, but most state practices harm insurgent candidates and third parties. Many states require that a designated proportion of the voting-age electorate in the state sign petitions requesting that a candidate's name appear if the candidate wishes to run as an independent or if the party has never appeared on the ballot before. Often these signatures must be gathered long before election day and, therefore, long before many voters have become interested in the candidate or the new party. These requirements can be met only with the aid of substantial financial outlays and the work of dedicated volunteers in each state, two resources that new parties and independent candidates are likely to have trouble locating on a national level. The established parties — Republican and Democratic — are, however, assured ballot places by their previously strong showings in state elections.

The Federal Election Campaign Act of 1974 has further handicapped the independent candidate and the third party. This act provides federal money on a matching basis to presidential candidates who are able to raise a minimum of $5,000 in amounts of $250 or less in each of 20 states. This is an easy task for the Republicans and Democrats but is much harder for the independent and the third party. The federal government roughly matches the amounts raised by parties and candidates in this way, up to approximately $5 million in all. Consequently, the federal government's allocation puts at a further disadvantage insurgent and third-party candidates as opposed to the candidates of the two major parties. Indeed, a candidate receiving less than 5 percent of the vote loses his federal subsidy. For the third party, the risk of financial ruin is high.

The broad outlines of the American electoral system now come into view. The system is characterized by a proliferation of electoral procedures that encourage moderate policies, two large heterogeneous parties, and an emphasis on negotiation and bargaining. The system underrepresents minority viewpoints and disperses governmental responsibility among a large number of officials; but it does provide for a continuous process of public consultation and discussion, and for more or less stable governance.

WHO VOTES? The composition of the American electorate has altered considerably through history. Over time, American elections have been opened to an increasing number and variety of people.

The first major expansion of the American electorate occurred in the early nineteenth century. Although the Constitution made no provisions for disqualifying potential voters who did not own property, some state constitutions did disqualify such persons. By placing property restrictions on the vote, members of the propertied classes hoped to prevent the propertyless from changing the balance of power in their states. Not until the 1830s did property restrictions on voting disappear in the wake of Andrew Jackson's rise to national power as the first real president of the "common man."

The second major change in the composition of the electorate occurred immediately after the Civil War. At that time blacks became legally enfranchised in states of the old Confederacy and for some time thereafter voted in great numbers. As a result, black representatives soon became common in southern state legislatures.

But these gains proved short lived. The federal government was reluctant to coerce southern states into permitting blacks to vote. A combination of state legal regulations, such as the *grandfather clause* and the *white primary*, helped reduce black voting to a trickle after 1876. The grandfather clause provided that no citizen whose grandfather had not been a voter in 1867 could himself become a voter. The white primary closed primary elections to nonwhites. These legal maneuvers, coupled with *poll taxes* (taxes a citizen must pay at the polls in order to vote) and *literacy tests* (administered by white voting officials), effectively barred blacks from the polls. Not until the Voting Rights Act of 1965 did black registration really spur in the South. The 1965 act stationed federal registrars throughout the South to enforce the rights of prospective black voters. Soon blacks were registering — and voting — in strength, not just in the South but throughout the entire country. By 1968, 62 percent of voting-age blacks were registered, compared with only 5 percent in 1940.

The third major change in the composition of the American electorate came about after sex restrictions on voting were abolished. The Nineteenth Amendment, adopted in 1920, gave women the right to vote. Women were slow to develop the habit of voting, but in recent years their participation has accelerated dramatically. Today, women turn out to vote as often as men.[3]

The most recent major change in the composition of the electorate occurred with the lowering of the voting age from twenty-one to eighteen. Until 1971 only Kentucky and Georgia permitted eighteen-year-olds to vote, but the Twenty-sixth Amendment lowered the voting age to eighteen in all fifty states. However, young voters have low turnout rates. For example, in the 1972 general election, in which George McGovern articulated issues supposedly attractive to many young voters — such as disengagement from Vietnam — voters between the ages of eighteen and twenty-four, who constituted 17.9 percent of the voting-age population, made up only 14.2 percent of the turnout. The young voter is underrepresented at the polls.

Influences on Voter Turnout It is evident that not everyone who is entitled to vote actually does vote. How many Americans actually go to the polls, and how often, depends on many factors. Three factors in particular are worth consideration: how voters are registered and mobilized at election time, the relationship between party competition and voting turnout, and variation among social groups in their propensity to vote.

In many western democracies levels of voter turnout are consistently higher than they are in the United States. Why is this so? The answer has partly to do with how one becomes eligible to vote in the first place. In the United States, new residents of a locality may have to wait between thirty days and six months before they can vote in local elections. In presidential elections, states require residency for anywhere between one and sixty days. In a mobile society such as ours, these residence requirements disenfranchise many potential voters.

Another problem is that Americans must register themselves if they want to vote. In contrast, in many other countries local government authorities keep and update voter registration lists; when a voter moves, his registration follows him to his new address. Voter turnout in United States presidential elections could be increased by as much as 10 percent (about 15 million voters) if registration laws in all the states were made to correspond with those in states that make registration easiest. If this country employed an automatic, government-initiated registration system, the turnout would be raised by "substantially" more than 10 percent.[4]

[3] Sidney Verba and Norman Nie, *Participation in America* (New York: Harper and Row, 1972), p. 98.

[4] Based on an article by Robert Reinhold in *The New York Times*, September 7, 1976, p. 27.

Other technical requirements also play a role. In most places people must register no later than two or three weeks before the election. Some states provide ample places and times to register, but others do not. Finally, nonvoting among registered voters usually results in their being "purged from the rolls" in an effort to prevent vote fraud. Habitual nonvoters must therefore reregister if they wish to exercise the franchise. If some of these technical impediments were eliminated — that is, if there were no "closing date" on registration, so that people could register right at the polls; if there were more access to registrars; and if registration among absentee voters were made easier — there would be, one study estimates, a 9.1 percent total national increase of voters and an even greater increase among less affluent voters.[5]

Perhaps as important as any of these technical factors, however, is the fact that organizations that could help stimulate voter registration are often weak. This is particularly true of political parties, which vary in strength from place to place and may almost disappear between election periods. *During* election periods, parties are often too involved in their candidates' campaigns to undertake large voter registration drives.

Still, the 1980 presidential election provides an example of how effectively organizations can stimulate voting. The Republican National Committee, under its chairman, Bill Brock, spent money extensively prior to election day — reaching voters via mail and telephone solicitation, raising money for campaigning, and registering potential Republicans. The use of computer-generated voter lists and sophisticated direct mail techniques, combined with much personal grass-roots contact, paid off not only in the presidential election but also in the House and Senate races. The greatest testament to Brock's success was the grudging admission by Democrats that they had simply been "outmuscled" organizationally, and needed to adopt some of the same techniques themselves.

A second factor that affects voter turnout is competition between candidates. When parties and candidates are evenly matched, voters realize that every vote may be important. However, when one party regularly dominates electoral office in an area, the voter may conclude that his or her vote is unimportant. Historically, this problem has particularly affected the southern states, where turnout rates have been quite low. It is no accident that until recently these were one-party states, dominated by the Democratic party.[6] Traditionally, southern voters concentrated on the Democratic primary election, in which the choice of the eventual officeholder was for all practical purposes decided. The general election between the major parties thus became almost an afterthought.

Many elections are afflicted by the problem of low participation because of an absence of perceived competition. As many as fifty to seventy congressional

---

[5] Raymond Wolfinger and Steven Rosenstone, *Who Votes?* (New Haven, Conn.: Yale University Press, 1980).

[6] Donald R. Matthews and James Prothro, *Negroes and the New Southern Politics* (New York: Harcourt, Brace and World, 1966), chap. 3.

seats are uncontested in each general election because of one-party dominance. Obviously people are not attracted to vote in such elections. By contrast, primary elections, though often quite competitive, are also characterized by low turnout, chiefly because primary competition is intraparty. Therefore, many voters who need the party label to bring them to the polls are untouched by primaries. Competition must be *perceived* in order to be effective in attracting voters.

Finally, social groups differ in their propensity to vote. Higher-income people are more likely to vote than lower-income people. Until recently, men were more likely to vote than women. Blacks have usually voted in smaller proportions than whites; Jews have turned out more regularly than white Protestants; white Protestants have voted slightly more regularly than Catholics. These generalizations do not always hold. For example, in cities where there have been black mayoral candidates, the black voting rate has jumped to over 70 percent from averages of 50 percent or less.[7] In 1960, when John Kennedy became the first Catholic presidential candidate since Al Smith, who ran in 1928, he mobilized not only many Catholics who had voted for the Republican candidate, Dwight Eisenhower, in 1956, but also many other Catholics who had not voted at all in 1956. The result was a net gain of 2.5 million votes for Kennedy — votes that could be traced mainly to his Catholicism.[8]

The single most important group factor influencing voting turnout is education. For example, among voters in the $10,000–15,000 income range in 1972, only 4 percent more of those who possessed a grade school education voted than would have had they no education at all; by contrast, in the same income range people with five or more years of college were 41 percent more likely to vote than they would have been had they no education at all. A college education often produces information, interest, and a secure issue orientation, all of which facilitate voting. Thus a more equal educational level among rich and poor, black and white, rural and urban people would significantly alter the composition of the voting public.

The Current Drop in Turnout One might have expected that with the gradual trends toward quicker, more efficient registration, on the one hand, and toward a more highly educated population on the other, voter turnout would increase. But this has not been the case. Instead, presidential voting hovered around 60 percent of those eligible to vote from 1952 until 1972, when it dipped sharply, first to 55.6 percent and then, in 1976, to 54 percent. In 1980 turnout fell again, to slightly over 52 percent. Voter turnout reached an all-time high in the period 1860–96, when it averaged 78 percent, and has fallen off slowly ever since.

It is difficult to account for this puzzling pattern, but some writers maintain

---

[7] Thomas F. Pettigrew, "When a Black Candidate Runs for Mayor: Race and Voting Behavior," in Harlan Hahn, ed., *People and Politics in Urban Society* (Beverly Hills, Calif.: Sage Publications, 1972), pp. 95–118.

[8] Philip E. Converse, "Religion and Politics: The 1960 Election," in Angus Campbell, et al., eds., *Elections and the Political Order* (New York: Wiley, 1955), pp. 96–125.

For all its shortcomings, judged only from the shallow views of today, the voluntary system of government worked better, involved more people and did more good than any other system invented by man up to that point. And it was not necessary to plead and beg to carry it out.

Somewhere in the middle of the twentieth century, perhaps because of a rampant guilt complex about the bad old days when not all persons could vote, Americans acquired an obsession that if only we could get all eligible people to register and vote, we could attain some sort of political Nirvana. If all voted, then all would be free. This became a dogma atop a dogma within the dogma of democracy.

Not so. Why, for God's sake, should we all suffer from the negative legacy of shared ignorance? Why should we encourage those who do not care and do not know, those whose vote can be bought for a catchy jingle, to dominate elections? Heaven knows that among the caring and informed there are strong differences of opinion. Must we deliberately count the lowest common denominator among us by drafting the uncaring and trying to compel them to vote?

The Voter as Citizen

Who votes matters. Southern politicians knew this basic fact better than anyone else in the century after the Civil War. They knew they might well be out of jobs if the large black population of the South were enfranchised and politically active. And they were right, as demonstrated by the dramatic increase in the number of black officeholders after the Civil Rights Act of 1965. Here we see lines of black voters waiting to use the franchise to obtain some of the political "sugar" previously denied to them.

Of course, voting is not the only measure of "good citizenship," nor is it a guarantee of good leadership. But the commentator quoted here might want to consider whether people fail to vote because they genuinely "don't care" (as he seems to think), or because they believe they gain no benefits from politics. If those pressured into voting still come away empty-handed, then perhaps the whole exercise is futile. But that is more a judgment on the electoral system than a condemnation of the voters.

that the Progressive reforms introduced in the late nineteenth and early twentieth centuries cut down voter participation. Nonpartisan local elections, the primary system for choosing candidates, the reduction in party-controlled patronage appointments, more stringent systems of voter registration designed to reduce bogus ballots, the introduction of poll watchers (party-designated observers at the polls to prevent vote fraud) — all these reforms undoubtedly weakened the capacity of parties to obligate voters to themselves and to control voters on election day. Once the party was weakened, these observers believe, the major American institution for the mobilization of voters ceased to function.

Progressive reform extended even to the act of voting itself. In 1876 the Australian, or secret, ballot system was introduced into the United States. Until then each party had printed and distributed its own ballots, and party officials had "helped" voters make the right choice. The secret ballot virtually eliminated these practices, but in the process it reduced the ability of parties to mobilize their supporters. Moreover, as part of the reformers' efforts to break the political machines, the ballot was lengthened. Previously, voters had cast their ballots for only one or two offices, or perhaps just for the party whose name was printed on their ballot. The new *long ballot*, as it was called, listed every candidate running for every office. Now voters could choose among offices and candidates and could even abstain from voting for some offices. Naturally, voting began to drop off for lower offices, and voters began splitting their tickets among candidates of more than one party.

Another influence on voter turnout has been recent changes in the composition of the electorate. Groups that were formerly disenfranchised compose a greater part of the potential voting public than ever before. Thus, younger voters have been recently enfranchised, and blacks in large numbers have entered the electorate as a result of civil rights policies initiated in the 1960s. Members of both groups are less likely to vote, on average, then are other potential voters; therefore, their presence in the electorate holds voting levels down.

A more speculative possibility — but one with the most far-reaching implications — is that declining turnout amounts to a vote of "no confidence" in the American political system, or at least in recent candidates. The problem of a long-term decline in voter confidence in candidates or in the system itself is only part of a larger issue — a possible increase in political alienation affecting all aspects of American politics — that runs through all chapters of this book. Does the decline in voting signify increased tension between leaders and followers in the United States, or is it a transient phenomenon?

WHO RUNS FOR OFFICE AND WHY? The electoral mechanisms described in this chapter provide only the setting in which candidates and voters operate. This section examines the role played by those at the center of the electoral process: the candidates.

Certain social characteristics of American candidates lead us to expect a large gap between candidates and voters. Candidates' backgrounds differ from those of most of their constituents, as do their policy preferences. In addition, most candidates have little reason to fear that if they do not do what the voters want, they will suffer at the polls. Some candidates are not ambitious enough for reelection to worry much about their constituents, and all candidates have trouble discovering what their constituents want. These factors reduce the effectiveness of the electoral process by loosening the tie between candidates for office and the electorate.

A Look at the Candidates   Consider first the social backgrounds of candidates. Compared with their constituents, disproportionate numbers of the candidates are male, white, Protestant, middle-aged, propertied, and well-educated. As for occupations, law and other middle-class professions are heavily overrepresented, manual work drastically underrepresented. Candidates of the Democratic party — which relies on a base of voter support that is heavily black, lower and working class, Catholic and Jewish — do not generally differ markedly from Republican candidates. As a result, Democratic candidates for office resemble their prospective constituents even less well than do Republican candidates.[9]

On some issues, candidates will be directly influenced by their backgrounds (Jewish candidates are likely to be concerned with the fate of Israel, for example). In most cases, however, the influences of social background seem to be indirect or even entirely absent. Even when social background has no direct effect, however, there is always the possibility of an indirect effect — that candidates very different in background, education, and experience from their constituents will have difficulty appreciating the voters' concerns. A candidate from a particular social background, then, may subtly screen out certain issues and overemphasize others.

The question of social background would be unimportant if candidates always shared the policy perspectives of their constituents, but often they do not. For one thing, candidates possess more definite and well-grounded political views than do most of their constituents. Their policy ideas are generally coherent and integrated, often falling into ideologically consistent programs of liberalism or conservatism. Candidates also believe strongly in the "rules of the political game" in the United States. They celebrate the *procedural* underpinnings of American politics — free speech, a free press, and so on. Despite the damage done by some political leaders to these freedoms through Vietnam and Watergate, political leaders in general are still more consistent democrats than are their constituents.[10] Thus, at crucial points we can expect politicians and their constituents to part company.

---

[9] This is equally true for leftist parties in other western democracies. In Britain, for example, the disparity between Labour party members of Parliament and Labour voters is profound. See W. L. Guttman, *The British Political Elite* (London: Macgibbon and Kee, 1965), chap. 9.

[10] Herbert McClosky, "Consensus and Ideology in American Politics," *American Political Science Review* 58 (1964): 361–82. For a critique, see Robert Jackman, "Political Elites, Mass Publics, and Support for Democratic Principles," *Journal of Politics* 34 (August 1972): 753–73.

Some people have argued that the possibility of a closer fit between the policy perspectives of candidates and those of their constituents is increasing. During the 1970's the parties were opened to more diverse channels of recruitment for both candidates and other party members. The McGovern-Fraser commission advocated changes in the recruitment of 1972 convention delegates in the Democratic party, most of which were implemented. These changes moved delegate recruitment away from professional politicians toward greater representation of the mass base of the party, opening the possibility of choosing a new kind of candidate. The Republicans adopted similar, though less extensive, reforms. By 1980 the largest single contingent of delegates to the Democratic nominating convention were not from the traditional groups — lawyers, politicians, union officials, businessmen — but were *teachers*. As Jeanne Kirkpatrick has put it, more diverse sources of recruitment are producing a "new breed" of politician, more issue oriented, less loyal to party organization, better educated, and more amateur than professional.[11] After their 1980 defeat, however, the Democrats began to rethink these reforms in an effort to re-establish tighter party control over the nominating process.

Evidence does not support the argument that a more representative recruitment process makes for better representation of mass opinion among candidates or their organizations. Richard Hofstetter found, for example, that in 1972 the socially more representative body of Democratic campaign activists was only 22 percent more likely than chance to represent the view of Democratic constituents, and Republican activists only 12 percent more likely to reflect the views of Republican constituents.[12] Thus candidates and the activists who work for them in campaigns remain quite different in their policy views from the main body of voters.

Advantages of Incumbency Of course, the voters' ultimate source of control is their opportunity to turn officeholders out of office. But do most officeholders really have to fear being turned out by their constituents? Perhaps not. As Table 10.1 shows, far more incumbents are returned to office than are defeated.

Incumbents standing for reelection enjoy several advantages over their challengers. First, the chances are good that they will not face primary election challenges from within their party. In 1978, for example, 70 percent of congressional incumbents faced no primary challenge. Incumbents who do not face a primary have the advantage of not having to mend the wounds created by intraparty dissension. Their challengers are usually less fortunate. Most have had to fight off a number of other hopefuls to win the nomination. Second, incumbents have already *been* in office for some time) they know the informal rules by which the political game is played, which their challengers have yet to learn. Incumbents further enjoy "name recognition" among voters;

---

[11] Jeanne Kirkpatrick, *The New Presidential Elite* (New York: Russell Sage, 1976).
[12] Richard Hofstetter, *Bias in the News: Network Coverage of the 1972 Election Campaign* (Columbus: Ohio State University Press, 1976).

Table 10.1 The Incumbency Factor in House and Senate Elections, 1954–80

Year	Number of House Incumbents Running	Number Reelected	Percentage Reelected	Number of Senatorial Incumbents Running	Number Reelected	Percentage Reelected
1954	401	379	94.5	26	22	84.6
1956	405	389	96.0	29	25	86.2
1958	391	354	90.5	26	17	65.4
1960	398	372	93.5	28	27	96.4
1962	382	368	96.3	30	27	90.0
1964	389	345	88.7	30	28	93.3
1966	402	362	90.0	26	25	96.2
1968	405	396	97.7	24	20	83.3
1970	397	384	96.7	30	24	80.0
1972	382	369	96.6	25	20	80.0
1974	383	343	89.6	25	23	92.0
1976	382	369	96.6	25	16	64.0
1978	382	368	96.3	25	15	60.0
1980	392	361	92.1	24	15	62.5
Totals	5,491	5,159	94.0	373	304	81.5

Source: Warren Lee Kostroski, "Party and Incumbency in Postwar Senate Elections: Trends, Patterns, and Models," *American Political Science Review* 67, no. 4 (December 1973): 1217; and *Congressional Quarterly*. Reprinted by permission.

challengers must struggle to become well known and to dispel the uncertainties often generated by new figures on the political scene. Finally, incumbents have been doing favors for their constituents; this gives them a set of obligations they can call in at election time. Challengers have no such credit with voters.

In recent years, however, as Table 10.1 suggests, the advantages of incumbency appear to have diminished slightly, at least among senators. This is also true at the presidential level, where since 1968 one sitting president withdrew because of opposition to his policies in Vietnam; another resigned in disgrace following revelations of White House wrongdoing; his successor was unseated by a rank newcomer in national politics; and, in turn, the newcomer was himself ousted after his first term by an ex-governor of California who had received his political tutelage as president of the Screen Actors Guild, not as a professional politician.

It is hard to know exactly why incumbency does not carry the weight it once did in the Senate and the presidency. A possible explanation is a downturn in the country's economic fortunes. In addition, partisan identification does not hold voters to candidates as closely as it used to; since incumbents usually do represent the dominant party in a district, the shakiness of partisanship may work to their disadvantage. Finally, in times of economic decline the media may focus negative attention on the most visible officeholders, such as senators and presidents, who become in effect lightning rods of discontent.

Obstacles to Representativeness

In this chapter we have assumed that elected officials are ambitious people who want either to keep their jobs or to move on to higher office. But many elected officeholders apparently do not harbor such ambitions. In a study of cities and towns around San Francisco, one investigator discovered that 25 percent of the local officials did not plan to run again and that only 29 percent wished to pursue higher office. Similar findings come from a study of Connecticut state legislators, many of whom apparently found their jobs so unpleasant that they did not plan to repeat the experience. Others admitted to using their political positions as a way of making contacts that would help them in their private capacities as businessmen or lawyers.[13] Surely politically unambitious officials have little motive to conform to the wishes of their constituents. Instead, their perspective on their jobs leads them to care little about electoral controls and drives a wedge between them and the public.

Of course, even conscientious elected officials sometimes have a hard time finding out what their constituents want. Many politicians now employ polling techniques, but good polling is expensive and time consuming; and not all candidates can afford it. Nor are polls foolproof methods for ascertaining citizen views. Finally, most candidates are interested mainly in issues that promise to win them votes; these may not be the issues that most concern the electorate. If his or her own views on an issue do not conform to those of a large portion of the electorate, the candidate usually prefers to avoid the whole question if at all possible.[14] In a politically heterogeneous election district or in a statewide or national campaign, this can mean having to avoid a large number of issues voters may feel strongly about.

Thus there are many reasons that elections do not necessarily recruit candidates who will assure the public of much control over the political process. Elections simply do not always reduce tension between the governors and the governed.

Campaigning: What Does It Really Accomplish?

Candidates do not simply announce their availability for office and then sit back to await the voters' decision. Each candidate strives to get his or her name before the voters; to keep it there; and to persuade the voters that he or she, not somebody else, deserves to be elected. In short, candidates *campaign,* usually with a great deal of help. They head massive organizational efforts that generally include large staffs of volunteer workers and professional politicians. How does this process work?

[13] James David Barber, *The Lawmakers: Recruitment and Adaptation to Legislative Life* (New Haven, Conn.: Yale University Press, 1965), chaps. 2–4.

[14] Benjamin Page, "The Theory of Political Ambiguity," *American Political Science Review* 70, no. 3 (September 1976): 742–53.

Figure 10.2 Political Expenditures in the United States, 1952–80*

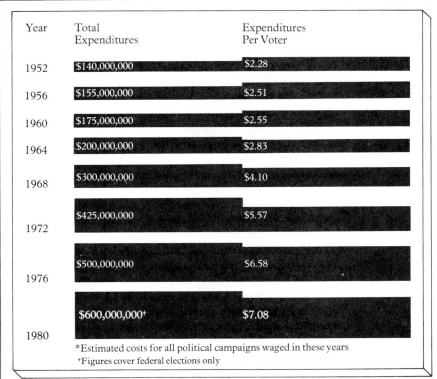

Year	Total Expenditures	Expenditures Per Voter
1952	$140,000,000	$2.28
1956	$155,000,000	$2.51
1960	$175,000,000	$2.55
1964	$200,000,000	$2.83
1968	$300,000,000	$4.10
1972	$425,000,000	$5.57
1976	$500,000,000	$6.58
1980	$600,000,000†	$7.08

*Estimated costs for all political campaigns waged in these years
†Figures cover federal elections only

Source: David W. Adamany, *Campaign Finance in America* (North Scituate, Mass.: Duxbury Press, 1972), p. 31; Herbert E. Alexander, *Money in Politics* (Washington, D.C.: Public Affairs Press, 1972); 1976 figures courtesy of Herbert E. Alexander; 1980 figures from David Adamany, "Political Finance in Transition," *Polity* (forthcoming), p. 7.

Consider first the problem of money. Until the Federal Election Campaign Act of 1974 limited campaign expenditures, the costs of recent elections were skyrocketing. Three major factors help account for the increased cost of campaigning. First, there is the growth of the electorate itself. The larger the number of people a campaign attempts to reach, the more expensive the campaign becomes. (In Figure 10.2, the slower rate of increase in total spending in 1976 may be attributed to the 1974 campaign law.)

The problem would be eased if candidates did not feel that they had to reach the greatest possible number of people. But the psychology of campaigning is largely one of fear. Every candidate worries that if he does not make a maximum effort, his opponent will. Such thinking naturally produces a vicious upward spiral of expenditures.

The ratio of money spent to number of votes cast has also risen in recent years because of the high cost of television campaigning. Television gives campaigners the opportunity to reach great numbers of constituents in their own homes, but TV time is expensive, as are the consultants who help candidates plan and execute a television campaign.

Other technological advances also have increased campaign costs. For example, many candidates now engage in massive direct mail operations. Although highly efficient in their coverage, such efforts are extremely costly. So is air travel by jetliner. In addition, there are the costs of polling, of renting headquarters space around the country, of putting together telephone banks, of leafletting. Finally, there is the longer period of campaigning that has been dictated by the growth of the primary and caucus systems, which require candidates to deploy their forces much earlier than they used to and to reach many more voters than they ever had to in the past. It is hardly surprising that so many candidates end their campaigns with debts to pay.

How are these costs met? The traditional method was to rely on rich private contributors. The big financial winners under this system are those who have access to corporate sources of money, and the losers are those with little access. This typically means that Republican candidates outspend their Democratic opponents. For example, Gerald Ford reported that his 1976 reelection effort cost about $30 million, whereas Jimmy Carter reported that his victorious campaign that year cost $20 million.

In 1974 campaign finance legislation (the Federal Election Campaign Act) was enacted in the aftermath of the Watergate scandal. The law attempts to reduce the dependence of campaigners on a few large contributors. The law limited primary expenditures to $10 million per presidential campaigner and to $20 million for the general election. The law also limited individual contributions to $1,000 and organizational contributions to $5,000, and provided that as much as $5 million of each presidential candidate's primary campaign may be financed from public funds. Finally, it permitted taxpayers to deduct small political contributions from their taxes. With more recent amendments, it made the two major parties eligible for $29 million each to finance their 1980 presidential campaigns.

Yet the 1974 reforms have not met with uniform success or approval. The fact that small campaign contributions are deductible from one's taxes has not really stimulated many private contributors to support their parties or candidates. Limitation on the amount of money that can be given by any particular individual or corporation has somewhat reduced dependence on a few big contributors, but "big money" remains a financial backbone of most campaigns, particularly state and congressional campaigns. Also, candidates need not accept federal money if their private fortunes are large enough to finance their campaigns. Thus, John Heinz III of Pennsylvania spent $1.5 million of his own money on his successful 1976 Senate race. On balance, the reforms have helped the Democratic party overcome the previous financial superiority of the

Republicans. But most candidates still devote a lot of their time to raising money.

Of course, money cannot win elections — for that, candidates need votes. Thus, although Republicans have usually outspent Democrats, Democrats have held their own by using their large population base and mobilizing large amounts of volunteer help provided by organized labor.

It is obvious that the American electoral process is far from perfect. Large numbers of voters do not turn out, and many others waste their votes. Incumbents have little to fear from their challengers, and parties are only weak links between candidates and the electorate. As a result, the electoral process often does little to reduce the tension between leaders and followers.

HOW CITIZENS VIEW THE ELECTORAL PROCESS

To the political candidate, the electoral process has a certain logic. His own policy preferences, the nature of his constituency, the structure of his campaign organization and campaign strategy, his debts and obligations to supporters and contributors — all these give his effort a pattern. His knowledge-ability about politics, his comparatively well-defined political views, and his relation with advisors and supporters provide him with a coherent view of the electoral process.

The voter, however, has no such vantage point. All too often voters see only confusion in the electoral process. Indeed, so gross is the disparity between the electoral process voters see and the one in which candidates participate that one wonders whether they are the same process at all. What are the consequences of this problem for the cleavage between the electorate and its leaders?

Public Support for Elections

Whether citizens can use the electoral process successfully depends at the very least on their belief in that process. *Do* Americans believe in the electoral system? The answer seems to be an unequivocal yes, at least in one respect: Americans almost unanimously equate the electoral process with the very meaning of democracy. Indeed, their support for the electoral process contrasts vividly with their distrust of the political party system. Many Americans apparently feel they could get along quite well without parties. But no such reservations apply to the electorate's view of elections. People seem almost to be saying that elections are fine but that the institutional paraphernalia surrounding elections is anything but fine.[15]

A particularly graphic example of the American faith in elections can be found in recent research on the presidential elections of 1968 and 1972. The

[15] For a comparison, see Jack Dennis, "Support for the Institution of Elections by the Mass Public," *American Political Science Review* 64 (September 1970): 19–35; Jack Dennis, "Trends in Public Support for the American Party System," Paper presented at the annual meeting of the American Political Science Association, Chicago, August 29–September 2, 1974.

mere act of voting, regardless of whether a person voted for the winning or losing presidential candidate in each of those elections, was associated with increased public trust in government. In 1972, for example, of those voters who had negative conceptions of their "say" in government before the election, 26.5 percent became positive after the election, even though they had voted for the loser, McGovern. The effect was even more pronounced among those who voted for the winner, Nixon. Here, 48.3 percent of those negative before the election became positive after the election. In both instances the "positivity" effect of having voted exceeded any such effect among nonvoters. In short, the mere availability of elections is a potent source of faith among Americans in the responsiveness of their system.[16]

How, then, can we explain the fact that although most Americans equate being a "good citizen" with voting, large numbers of them do not vote regularly? In this instance, as in others, merely holding a belief does not guarantee that a person will act accordingly. In addition to the factors already discussed that affect people's propensity to vote, there are certain psychological factors that help determine whether general approval of voting will be transformed into the act of voting.

Most important, although people may believe in the abstract goodness of the vote, they do not always feel confident that politicians will respond to those who elected them by doing what the electorate wants. Many people are not even confident of their own ability to understand politics. As a result, they may feel that voting is a fruitless endeavor.

Thus, the citizen's attitude toward voting is shaped by a complex combination of forces. Given what we know about many citizens' feelings on these subjects, it is not surprising that large numbers of people vote intermittently and others not at all, even though voting itself produces a surge of confidence in the political system.

The Influence of Partisanship

If a person chooses to vote at all, how does he or she decide which way to vote? Despite the current weakness of American parties, one of the most important factors affecting a person's voting decision is *partisan identification* — the long-lasting psychological ties many people have to a particular political party, reflecting their belief that that party usually represents their interests (Figure 10.3). A voter's partisan identification does not always prevent him or her from switching a vote when a unique candidate or issue appears, but strong partisan identification normally reduces the likelihood of such deviations.

For most of recent American electoral history, partisan identification has been the best single predictor of the individual's vote. However, the importance of partisanship in controlling electoral behavior has declined in recent years.

---

[16] Benjamin Ginsberg and Robert Weissberg, "Elections as Legitimizing Institutions," in Jeff Fishel, ed., *Parties and Elections in an Anti-Party Age* (Bloomington: Indiana University Press, 1976), pp. 170–89.

Figure 10.3   Relationship between Party Affiliation and Voting for President, 1952–80

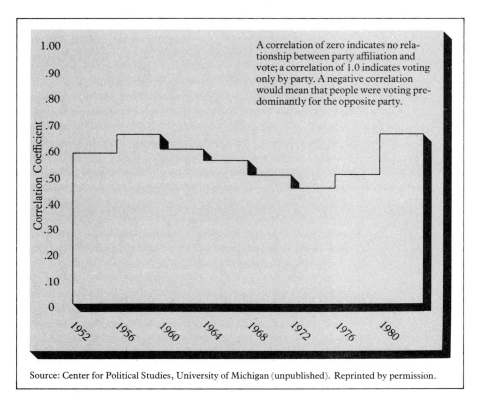

Source: Center for Political Studies, University of Michigan (unpublished). Reprinted by permission.

For one thing, a growing number of Americans do not consider themselves members of any party, as we shall see in Chapter 11. Furthermore, growing numbers of Americans now "split their tickets" by voting for candidates of different parties for different offices.[17]

The large number of independents should not be misinterpreted, however: many self-proclaimed "independents" actually vote consistently for one party. Indeed, weak partisans seem actually to be slightly more inconsistent in their party voting choices over time than are independents. Furthermore, most new independents are not converts from strong partisanship. The electorate *is* volatile, but less so than a superficial glance at partisan identification suggests.

A major contribution to the weakening capacity of the parties to control voting through identification is the unpopularity of parties among young voters.

---

[17] Everett Carll Ladd, Jr. with Charles D. Hadley, *Transformations of the American Party System* (New York: Norton, 1975), p. 296.

Gerald Pomper shows that in 1972 new voters were overwhelmingly either weak partisans or independents, as opposed to strong partisans (89 percent versus 13 percent). By contrast, in the 1960 election 18 percent of new voters were strong partisans and the remaining 82 percent weak partisans or independents.[18] In short, the party system seems to have a harder time attracting young voters now than in the past.

It also appears that partisan identification is more subject to change over the life cycle than was once true. For a long time it was assumed that partisan identification, once acquired in childhood, was quite stable. But between 1972 and 1976 fully 50 percent of adult Americans altered their positions on a seven-point scale measuring partisan identification.[19] In most cases the change was not dramatic, but it cannot be assumed that partisanship, once acquired and even once exercised in the voting booth, remains stable enough to predict the vote over time.

Of course, partisanship is important only if it is a guide to the voter. For example, if partisan identification helps organize a person's political attitudes, then it will almost certainly influence the vote. The key question, therefore, is how partisan identification is connected to the individual's other political attitudes. The answer seemed to be, at least in 1972, that although the majority of people had political attitudes that favored the party they eventually voted for, almost everyone shared some views with the opposing party. Thus, partisan identification did not by any means produce total consistency between party choice and issue position.[20] The relationship varies from issue to issue. For example, evidence suggests that racial attitudes are unusually closely related to partisan choice in the United States. Before 1964 supporters and opponents of racial desegregation could not easily choose between the parties in this respect. However, following the clear choice between Goldwater and Johnson in that year, the Republican party became the home of those opposed to racial changes mandated by the federal government, whereas the Democratic party became the home for those believing that the federal government should play the leading role in racial integration.[21]

Despite these uncertainties, *strong* party identification at election time still manages to predict voting very well, with 92 percent of strong Democrats voting for Carter in 1976 and 97 percent of strong Republicans for Ford in that same year. However, the electorate as a whole seems to move rather more readily between partisan and independent roles than was once thought to be the case.

---

[18] Gerald Pomper, "The Decline of Partisan Politics," in Louis Maisel and Joseph Cooper, eds., *The Impact of the Electoral Process* (Beverly Hills, Calif.: Sage Publications, 1977), pp. 13–39, 30.

[19] Kessell, *Presidential Campaign Politics*, p. 238.

[20] Ibid., p. 233.

[21] Edward G. Carmines and James Stimson, "The Racial Reorientation of American Politics," in John C. Pierce and John L. Sullivan, eds., *The Electorate Reconsidered* (Beverly Hills, Calif.: Sage Publications, 1980), pp. 199–219.

The reason for these changes in partisanship is a topic of much debate. One possibility is that the weakening of party control over candidate nominations serves to make the partisan label less useful to voters as a means of deciding how to vote. Voters then turn to the candidates' "images" or issue positions in order to make a choice. Changes in the electorate may also be important, however. One political scientist argues that an increasingly well-educated electorate, which is able to use complicated information about candidates and issues, does not need partisan identification to help it make its political choices. If this is true, then partisan identification will become useful primarily to the relatively small number of poorly educated Americans, and may thus permanently lose some of its traditional power.[22]

Still, the distribution of partisanship continues to have an important bearing on contemporary American politics. Those who call themselves Democrats continue to outnumber self-styled Republicans. Democratic dominance, which began during the 1930s, has persisted down to this day and in itself usually gives Democratic candidates an initial advantage over their Republican opponents. On the other hand, Democrats are somewhat more prone to deviate from their partisanship than are Republicans, for several reasons. A large proportion of Democrats occupy the lower socioeconomic rungs of society. They usually have had less education than Republicans and, consequently, assimilate less political information. This means that many Democrats are weakly attached to their party and are therefore likely either to stay home on election day or to vote Republican in response to particular candidates or issues. Republicans, by contrast, find it psychologically easier to stay loyal. It is partly for this reason that Republicans manage to hold their own in the electoral process despite the fact that they are outnumbered by Democrats in the electorate.

The big event in recent American electoral history, of course, has been the growth in the percentage of Americans who claim allegience to no party at all, yet who vote in elections regularly. Independents are comparatively open to the pressures of particular issues and candidates. A case in point is the election of Dwight Eisenhower, whose appeal to independents overcame the disadvantages of being the candidate of the minority party, the Republicans. Eisenhower won over 80 percent of the independent vote in both 1952 and 1956. Not surprisingly, independents tend to be more sensitive to the short-range power of issues and candidates' personalities than are party loyalists. This gives them a pivotal role in deciding the outcome of elections. Of course, no single segment of the electorate can itself determine an electoral outcome. The forces that swing elections affect *all* segments of the electorate. But independents are more responsive to these forces than are other voters.[23]

[22] W. Phillips Shively, "The Development of Party Identification in Adults," *American Political Science Review* 73 (December 1979): 1039–54.

[23] For an indication of how short-term issue and candidate factors usually affect all segments of the electorate in roughly similar ways, see Warren Miller and Teresa Levitin, *Leadership and Change: The New Politics and the American Electorate* (Cambridge, Mass.: Winthrop, 1976).

Thus for many Americans partisan cues provide a general guideline in choosing between candidates. However, they do not provide a very comprehensive or clear picture of the political process. Partisan identification provides the voter with a political cross-country map that shows only freeways, not interesting side roads.

Candidate Orientation

Most people are not so wholly controlled by partisan cues that they ignore the characteristics of the candidates. Of all the modern presidents, Franklin Roosevelt and Dwight Eisenhower had the strongest personal holds on the electorate. Roosevelt's personal attractiveness was strong enough to win him four consecutive terms in the White House, more than any other president. And Eisenhower's popularity level, unlike that of any other modern president, remained high throughout his eight years in office. Yet even these highly popular figures had their detractors. As noted earlier, many conservative Republicans suspected that Roosevelt was a closet socialist, whereas many liberal Democrats disliked Eisenhower's apparent passivity and withdrawal on important moral issues, such as civil rights.

By contrast, of modern presidential candidates, George McGovern suffered from a uniquely unfavorable candidate image, not only among Republicans and independents but also among many members of his own Democratic party. McGovern appeared rash to many voters; in particular, his advocacy of sharp reforms in tax policy and welfare programs seemed to them irresponsible and poorly conceived. Worse, when McGovern attempted to modify these proposals, he was perceived as hesitant and confused. Similarly, when he first reacted to charges about the history of mental stress of his running mate, Thomas Eagleton, by claiming he was "1,000 percent behind" his choice, then — under pressure from his own campaign staff — immediately accepted Eagleton's withdrawal, McGovern again appeared uncertain, indecisive, and insincere. Candidate image perhaps did as much to injure the McGovern candidacy as did his views on controversial issues, such as the war in Vietnam, affirmative-action programs, and legalization of abortion and marijuana.

Qualities of a Good Candidate

In recent years, many people have written about "charismatic candidates" and "image politics." Some observers argue that television has turned the contemporary presidential campaign into a contest dominated by the superficial appeals of personality. In this view, each candidate strives to project an image of responsibility and honesty while ignoring thorny political and ideological questions.[24] To this end, all presidential candidates employ "media consultants" to whom they defer in the "image-building" process. But the importance of images should not be exaggerated. For one thing, if images were all important, by now it should be clear just what voters look for in a candidate. However,

[24] Indeed, this is a view widely propagated by mass media commentators themselves. It is reflected in Dan D. Nimmo, *Popular Images of Politics* (Englewood Cliffs, N.J.: Prentice-Hall, 1974).

we still know very little about the components of a good personality "image." Indeed, certain aspects of a candidate's personality seem to be simultaneously engaging and upsetting. Many of the same people who found Gerald Ford reassuringly "safe" were unhappy about his "unimaginativeness."

Ingredients of Appeal. Some things about candidate image do seem to hold true over time, however. First, Americans like presidential candidates with previous executive experience either inside or outside government. A hero's reputation certainly does not hurt, either. Dwight Eisenhower was an ideal presidential candidate in these respects; as supreme commander of the victorious Allied forces in Europe during World War II, he had developed a reputation for both leadership and competence. John Kennedy's exploits as a PT-boat skipper during World War II were, likewise, an asset in his candidacy.

Americans also like candidates who are (or appear to be) open to public questioning. The career of Richard Nixon is instructive in this respect. Nixon's apparent aloofness from the public hurt him in his first (1960) presidential campaign. Careful structuring of his 1968 campaign aimed at creating spontaneity and give and take between the candidate and the public. These included television presentations in which representative Americans questioned Nixon spontaneously. The fact that the entire process had been carefully designed and rehearsed by Nixon's staff did not detract from its appearance of spontaneity.[25] Later, however, after the Watergate affair broke, Nixon again retreated into his defensive unresponsiveness to questions.

Finally, Americans prefer their candidates to appear active, dynamic, and competent. Indecision— even reflectiveness — can hurt. Since it is hard to know what competence in politics *really* is, we often use activity and dynamism as an index of ability. Thus John Kennedy profited in his initial television debate with Richard Nixon in 1960 by his apparent command of relevant facts, the energy and precision of his presentation, and the apparent quickness of his thought processes.[26] In 1976 Jimmy Carter made a somewhat similar impression. By contrast, Adlai Stevenson suffered in his 1952 and 1956 presidential campaigns against Eisenhower by what seemed an unwarranted psychological distance from the political fray and a somewhat inappropriate sense of humor.

At least until recently, Americans also seemed to prefer candidates who had been around the political scene for some time and who, therefore, were known political quantities. Candidates who are best known at the outset of a campaign enjoy a natural advantage. In seven of the eight contested nominations for president prior to 1976, the candidate who stood first in the polls at the beginning of the campaign won both the nomination *and* the election. In 1980, the

---

[25] The standard, if somewhat distorted, interpretation of this strategy is found in Joe McGinnis, *The Selling of the President, 1968* (New York: Trident, 1968).

[26] See the articles in Sidney Kraus, ed., *The Great Debates* (Bloomington, Ind.: Indiana University Press, 1962).

same was true among Republicans. In 1976 Jimmy Carter *became* the best-known Democratic candidate early in the primary season.

   The Influence of Image.   The relative importance of partisan attachment and candidate image in presidential contests varies from election to election. In recent American history the candidates' images have been central to the outcome. In 1952 and 1956 Dwight Eisenhower's nonpartisan, personal appeal in a time of comparative political tranquility convinced many Democratic and independent voters to support him. The purely personal nature of Eisenhower's appeal is indicated by the fact that in 1960 voting behavior returned to its normal partisan lines. In 1964 Barry Goldwater's attempt to provide a conservative Republican alternative to the drift of American public policy suffered because of his extremely negative image as a candidate. The fact that large numbers of Americans believed Goldwater to be both an extremist of the right and an impulsive person did him no good in his campaign. George McGovern's attempt to provide a liberal Democratic alternative to American public policy in 1972 produced much the same response. Even among those voters who agreed with McGovern's policy views, almost half believed that Nixon was the better *candidate.* Among those voters who accepted Nixon's policy positions, almost none found McGovern the personally more acceptable candidate.[27] Thus, under suitable conditions, the image of one or both candidates can become the central issue in a campaign.

The Influence of Issues   Perhaps the key question in the study of voting is the extent to which issues decide votes. Voting on the basis of the candidates' issue positions is one way a voter can perhaps influence public policy. But what role does the voter's perception of issues really play in his or her decision making?

   In order to use an issue to decide whom to vote for, a citizen must first feel he or she understands the issue well enough to form an opinion on it. Some issues can be fairly easily understood by the voter, but others cannot. Consider, for example, the Vietnam War. By 1968 most Americans were concerned with this painful issue, but few of them hinged their presidential votes on that concern. Why? The war was a complex and uncertain undertaking in a far-off land. What was at stake in the war was a matter of hot dispute. Small wonder, then, that voters had difficulty with the war as an issue and that policy options in the Vietnam War were not easily translated into votes for or against a presidential candidate.

   Domestic issues usually generate widespread interest, and voters often feel comfortable with such issues. Occasionally, controversial issues such as race can fuel an entire political career — for example, that of George Wallace. As governor of Alabama, Wallace cried, "Segregation forever!" and fought federally mandated integration, a major issue in his presidential campaigns of 1964, 1968, 1972, and 1976. Largely because of his stance on school integra-

[27] Miller and Levitin, *Leadership and Change,* chap. 6.

tion, he gained widespread support among conservative, low-income whites in northern industrial states as well as in the South. In 1976 he got off to a strong start, placing third in the Massachusetts Democratic primary. But by then his health had failed, and his fellow southerner Jimmy Carter had eroded his strength in the South. Wallace's national career did not survive the 1976 campaign.

Issue voting also depends on the positions taken by candidates and parties. By 1968, despite the complexities of the issue, some Americans did have well-formed views on Vietnam; but the two major party candidates offered little choice on the issue. Both Humphrey and Nixon made vague promises about a policy change, the former edging away from Lyndon Johnson, the latter asking the people to trust in a "secret plan" he would unfold to them after the election. Thus the Vietnam issue was effectively neutralized as a major determinant of voting.[28] By contrast, when busing to achieve racial balance in the schools became an issue in 1972, the major party candidates took quite different positions. President Nixon early signaled his dislike of busing. His Democratic opponent, George McGovern, reluctantly associated himself with the proponents of busing. Their differences on this issue were sharply enough drawn that voters could, and did, use their racial attitudes in making a choice between the two candidates.

Further complications arise in the public's attempt to vote for candidates on the basis of issues. For one thing, candidates do not regularly address policy issues in their campaign rhetoric. In 1968, a time when issues of busing, civil rights, and racial confrontation were central to American life, only 3 percent of candidate Nixon's speeches dealt with these issues. Candidates tend instead to focus their remarks on questions of personal style, broad and vague policy directions, and records of accomplishment.

Moreover, even when candidates do address issues, they often fail to make their positions clear. Indeed, the larger the audience the candidate addresses, the greater the incentive to be ambiguous, out of fear of alienating any special constituency. Further, more often than one might think, the candidates actually agree in substance about issues. As already mentioned, in 1968 candidates Nixon and Humphrey seemed too close in their statements on Vietnam for many voters' comfort. Verba and his colleagues observe that "In 1976, fewer respondents used issue and ideological terms to describe candidates than in any election year since 1960" (only 7 percent).[29] Carter in particular defied ideological or issue analysis.

There is also the problem of news media coverage of the candidates' policy positions. Most candidates "bury" their most specific policy pronouncements in long press releases or position papers, making it difficult for journalists to

---

[28] For a full discussion, see Richard Brody and Benjamin Page, "Policy Voting and the Vietnam War Issue," *American Political Science Review* 66 (September 1972): 979–95.

[29] Sidney Verba, Norman Nie, and John Petrocik, *The Changing American Voter* (Cambridge, Mass.: Belknap Press, 1979), p. 366.

locate, digest, and present them. Moreover, most journalists believe that specific policy views are difficult to explain to readers or television viewers, and most also believe that audiences are uninterested in specific policy positions. Campaign coverage therefore concentrates on other aspects of the contest.

In short, the cost to the voter of acquiring issue-based information about the candidates tends to be high and, in particular, to work against less well educated elements of the electorate. The candidate, the news media, and even voters themselves often conspire to reduce the frequency of issue-based choices that might reduce the tension between the public and its leaders.[30]

Campaigning for President   Issues, parties, and candidates combine in complicated ways in election campaigns. Technically, presidential campaigns begin immediately after the nominating conventions of the two major parties, usually in June or July, and continue until election day. However, the expansion of the primary season and the openness of the national parties to capture or challenge by insurgent candidates mean that the presidential campaigns now actually begin long before the nominations themselves, as evidenced by Jimmy Carter's two-year search for the Democratic nomination he secured in 1976.

Types of Campaigns.   Generally speaking, we can divide campaigns into three different kinds which have three different types of effects. The first sort is the partisan, issue-oriented campaign, typified by the presidential campaign of 1948. Harry Truman, the incumbent Democratic president, began at a great disadvantage in the polls. Most knowledgeable political observers had all but conceded the election beforehand to Truman's Republican opponent, Thomas Dewey. On election day, however, Truman staged a dramatic upset and retained the presidency. His success was due in part to his stress on "bread and butter" domestic issues. Recognizing his vulnerability on foreign policy issues, Truman emphasized the domestic welfare programs he had inherited as successor to the New Deal coalition forged by Franklin Roosevelt. In the last weeks of the campaign he hammered hard at New Deal themes, playing on the class antagonisms that divided the two parties. Truman's strategy worked. He succeeded in snatching victory from defeat by winning back many of the Democrats who had been planning to vote Republican or not vote at all.

A second type of campaign, especially appealing to candidates of the minority party, is the "nonpartisan" campaign, typified by the elections of 1952, 1956, and 1972. Here, Republican candidates Eisenhower and Nixon were men known for their previous experience and proven executive ability. Both candidates emphasized these personal qualifications and avoided divisive, partisan issues that could have cost them the Democratic votes they needed in addition to those of the outnumbered Republicans. Eisenhower and Nixon both emphasized their trustworthiness, their experience, and their personal

---

[30] Most of this material is drawn from Benjamin I. Page, *Choices and Echoes in Presidential Elections* (Chicago: University of Chicago Press, 1978).

moral convictions. For both, the strategy worked, because both enjoyed enormous advantages in personal image over their opponents.[31]

A third type of campaign exploits dramatic, fortuitous events to win votes. A candidate who is not well known at the outset of the campaign often can gain ground by exploiting every chance to make news and impress potential voters. John Kennedy was especially skillful at capitalizing on fortuitous events during his 1960 campaign. When Martin Luther King, the black civil rights leader, was jailed in Atlanta, Kennedy telephoned King's wife to reassure her, thus appealing to many previously undecided black voters. When it became clear that Kennedy's Catholicism would be an important issue in the campaign, Kennedy decided to address the matter dramatically and directly at a conference of Baptist ministers in Houston, Texas. He could not have chosen a more spectacular forum in which to focus public attention on himself. Finally, Kennedy got his opponent, Richard Nixon, to agree to a series of television debates. Millions who watched the first debate were struck by Kennedy's apparent intelligence and alertness. He answered questions quietly and articulately, conveying a desirable image of competence.

The 1980 presidential campaign resembled this third type of campaign in some respects. The incarceration of American hostages in Iran was a dramatic issue that strongly aroused Americans. President Jimmy Carter planned the early stages of his reelection campaign around his dedication to the release of the hostages. Thus he employed the "Rose Garden strategy," staying off the campaign trail and pursuing efforts toward the release of the hostages. However, after the failure of the dramatic attempt to rescue the hostages by force, his strategy could no longer work. Carter, finding himself increasingly vulnerable on domestic issues that attention to Iran could no longer defer, plunged into partisan campaigning. Nevertheless, rumors persisted that Carter had arranged for the hostages to be released close to election day, further evidence of the sensitivity of campaigners to last-minute turns of fortune that can make winners out of losers.

The News Media and Presidential Campaigns. The effect of news media, particularly of television, is a major concern of many observers of presidential politics. In the view of some, television presents a major opportunity for candidates to reach voters in unprecedented numbers, thereby increasing the interest, awareness, and rationality of the voting public. Others — perhaps a majority — believe that television has significantly distorted both the actions of candidates and the reactions of voters and that this phenomenon has debased campaigns and lowered the quality of voter choice.

Three aspects of television coverage are important in structuring campaigning. First, there is the visual appearance of the candidate him- or herself. The

[31] On Eisenhower, see Angus Campbell, Phillip Converse, Warren Miller, and Donald Stokes, *Elections and the Political Order* (New York: Wiley, 1965), chap. 15. On Nixon in 1972, see Gerald Pomper, *Voter's Choice* (New York: Dodd, Mead, 1975), p. 48.

The Medium and the Message

The 1960 Kennedy-Nixon television debates led many to conclude that presidential politics had become a forum where "the medium is the message," in sociologist Marshall McLuhan's phrase. Here we see an apparently calm, self-assured John Kennedy and an apparently tense, self-conscious Richard Nixon waiting to go at one another before the cameras. To many observers, Kennedy epitomized the "cool" politician able to exploit the medium of television to his advantage.

But what happens when television as a channel of political communication is no longer fresh and new? What happens when the issues at stake take on more significance than the personalities involved? Jimmy Carter found in 1977 that despite the careful attention of his make-up man and an effective television speech on energy problems, the hoped-for groundswell of support for his energy program failed to materialize. No one yet knows what the laws of media and politics are — or even if there are any. Until more is known, media-conscious candidates like Representative Toby Moffatt of Connecticut will continue to hire media consultants in the quest for electoral victories. (Photo credits: top and center, Wide World; bottom, Michael D. Sullivan) television camera can be merciless, exposing every line of fatigue, every gesture and facial expression. Some candidates are simply more visually appealing than others. Thus, Lyndon Johnson's slow drawl may have been less appealing on radio and television than John Kennedy's brisk, clipped phrasing. How could a crippled candidate, such as Franklin Roosevelt or George Wallace, conceal his disability in the television age, thereby preventing inevitable questions about suitability?

Second, today's candidates must rely heavily on both television and newspapers to become known to the electorate. Early in the primary season name recognition is vital for all candidates. In 1976, for example, this was a particular concern of candidate Jimmy Carter who was little known nationally. Carter therefore entered the presidential race early, and favorable media evaluation of his early primary and caucus victories soon made him the best known of all the Democratic contenders. This stood him in good stead later on when he faced strong challenges from Henry Jackson and Jerry Brown.

Finally, a candidate seeks not only media attention, but also publicity as a *winner*. But what is a winner? In primaries and early caucuses it is often hard to tell. There may be several candidates; rules for the appointment of delegates are often complex and hard for the voter to understand; and public interest may be low. Thus it is up to television reporters and media journalists to decide for themselves what an "acceptable" candidate performance is, and often they decide in what appears to be an illogical way. In 1972, heavily favored front-runner Edmund Muskie lost his leading position after the New Hampshire primary, when the media decided his victory margin over George McGovern (46 percent to 37 percent) was "too small." In 1976, Jimmy Carter became the front-runner for the Democratic nomination by winning only 28 percent of the caucus nominating vote in Iowa. The media's early perception of winners or losers, therefore, may bear little relation to the actual distribution of votes, although it may influence who ultimately wins nomination and election.

Clearly, then, any presidential candidate will attempt to be visually "right," well known quickly, and a perceived primary winner early. A fourth rule that a candidate will follow is to avoid, if at all possible, embarrassing public mistakes, even if they are trivial in policy terms. The media — television in particular — play up such mistakes. Thus Carter's "ethnic purity" remark in 1976, Ford's debate mistake about Poland being outside the Russian orbit of influence, or even Carter's label as a "mean" campaigner in 1980 may seriously alter media treatment of the candidate and, hence, the public's perception of the candidate. These slips of the tongue have one thing in common; though distracting, they are quite peripheral to major policy issues.

Why does television emphasize such trivial items in its coverage? Television news in its coverage of campaigns is primarily interested in the conflict-ridden, "horse-race" element of the campaign. Fully 58 percent of network newscasts were directed to this aspect of the 1976 presidential campaign. Most news stories focus on who seems to be doing well, who is falling behind, and why this seems to be so. Dramatic and colorful occurrences in the course of the campaign fit into this framework because they provide quick explanations of why a candidate is doing well, and can be discussed in terms of their impact on winning and losing.

By contrast, television in particular seldom succeeds in discussing candidate issue positions effectively. Television discussion of the Ford-Carter debates in 1976 — in which the candidates elaborated on many issues — was primarily devoted to which candidate had "won" and to how they had performed. Half of the network news time relating to the debates discussed this issue; during only one-third of the time were issue differences between the candidates discussed. Television has a hard time focusing on issues partly because issues themselves are too complicated to fit comfortably in the short time span television can devote to them. In addition, it is hard to dramatize issues effectively. Finally, candidates usually develop their basic issue positions early in the campaign and keep them comparatively unchanged. Over a long campaign, it would become tedious for television simply to repeat unchanging issue positions.

Under these conditions, it is perhaps not surprising to discover that people who spend most of their time following the campaigns on television show no appreciable gain in their issue awareness with respect to the election. Television simply does not meet the issue "needs" of such people. Thus, so far at least, those who charge television with having degraded the electoral process would seem to be right.

Yet it would be wrong to come to an entirely pessimistic conclusion about media coverage of campaigns. For one thing, from one-quarter to one-third of the general public continues to rely mainly on newspapers rather than on television for campaign coverage. Many television viewers also use newspapers to some degree. Therefore, television's impact on creating a less issue-oriented campaign is not pervasive.[32]

The Effects of Campaigns on Election Outcomes What effects does campaigning itself have on the outcome of an election campaign? This is a vital question. Campaigners spend millions of dollars to influence voters. Further, campaigns are supposed to help the public consider issues and vote intelligently, thereby injecting their own preferences into public policy. Is this hope well founded?

Campaigns *can* make a difference, particularly at the presidential level. Here the public's high interest and the campaign's high visibility help create an involved but swayable electorate. Nevertheless, even the most carefully constructed presidential campaigns must contend with several hard facts of

---

[32] Material in this section is drawn primarily from the following sources: Thomas E. Patterson, *The Mass Media Election: How Americans Choose Their President* (New York: Praeger, 1980); Doris Graber, *Mass Media and American Politics* (Washington, D.C.: Congressional Quarterly Press, 1980); David Paletz, "Candidates and the Media in the 1976 Presidential Election," in Fishel, *Parties and Elections*, pp. 256–63; Thomas Patterson and Robert D. McClure, *The Unseeing Eye: The Myth of Television Power in National Politics* (New York: Putnam, 1976).

political life. First, many of the likely voters in any presidential election will have made up their minds about how they intend to vote by the time the campaign proper begins. Early deciders have high levels of involvement that lead them to strong political convictions. In turn, these commitments permit them to resist the blandishments of the campaigners. Thus, ironically, those who might make real voting use of the information a campaign provides are often deaf to it. For example, in the 1980 presidential campaign 54 percent of the voting public claimed to have decided whom to vote for by the end of the primaries.

Many other potential voters do not make up their minds early but nevertheless pay little attention to the campaign. They are easily swayed if they are exposed to campaign rhetoric, but the chances are good that their exposure will be limited and superficial.

Between the uninvolved and the highly involved lies a segment of the electorate that the campaign may reach. But *how* to reach this group is by no means clear. An important problem is the voter's perception of campaigning itself. Despite all the efforts of ingenious advertising agencies and campaign consultants, most voters are well aware that campaign rhetoric is designed with the interests of candidates, not those of voters, in mind. They therefore discount much of the campaign imagery they receive. In fact, an influential recent study suggests that as few as 3 percent of the electorate are swayed by televised campaign advertising.[33] A more generous estimate — which considers all components of a campaign, not just television — concludes that effective presidential campaigners can increase their vote by as much as 20 percent.[34] The effects of most campaigns undoubtedly fall below this figure, but campaigns clearly make enough of a difference to determine the outcome of many elections.

The 1980 Election The 1980 presidential election once more raises the question of realignment in American politics. Despite the numerical domination of the Democratic party and the candidacy of an incumbent Democratic president, the Republican challenger — an unabashed conservative, Ronald Reagan — succeeded in winning a smashing electoral vote victory. The Senate also became Republican for the first time in over a generation. Did this election signal a long-term movement to the political right as a culmination of electoral instability in the United States and the unseating of the Democratic party as the majority party in American politics?

Fundamental electoral realignments can never be accurately charted immediately after their occurrence. Thus the key test of the realignment thesis of the 1980 election will come in 1982 and 1984, when the electorate decides whether the Republicans deserve to be returned to power. Nevertheless, there are some reasons to doubt the realignment argument.

[33] Patterson and McClure, *The Unseeing Eye*, p. 135.
[34] William Crotty, "Party Effort and Its Impact on the Vote," *American Political Science Review*, 65, no. 2 (June 1971): 439–51.

The seeds of President Carter's defeat were planted from the very outset of his term in office. In 1976 Carter won few states outside his native South; he began his term, therefore, with a narrower electoral and popular vote base than most Democratic presidents. The key problem he faced, therefore, was expanding and consolidating this base during his four years in office. He did not succeed. Instead, major voting groups outside the South — especially Jews and union members — actually rejected his 1980 candidacy in substantial numbers. Within the South, the most conservative region of the United States, the appearance of a genuinely conservative Republican candidate drew many voters away from Carter and back to the Republican party, which they had begun in some numbers to support with Dwight Eisenhower. Thus part of the 1980 outcome can be attributed as much to Carter's particular weakness as to any strength his opponent mustered.

Another element of Carter's failure was his inability to dominate the party he represented. In particular, Carter could not surmount the challenge of a more liberal Democratic candidate, Teddy Kennedy. Kennedy, though not able to wrest the nomination from Carter, did divide the Democratic party bitterly in some places. Although efforts were made to patch over these differences, the Democrats found themselves a less efficient campaigning force in 1980 than they needed to be.

Of course, it can be argued that these Democratic weaknesses are themselves reflections of a move to the right and to the Republican party in the United States. At present, however, the Democratic failure of 1980 does not appear to be the result of an ideological rejection of the Democratic party in American politics. For one thing, self-proclaimed Democrats continue to outnumber self-proclaimed Republicans. More important, most Americans do not consider themselves ideological conservatives. Immediately after the election, *The New York Times* discovered that conservatives accounted for only 28 percent of the voters, moderates for 46 percent, and liberals for 17 percent. Thus a self-conscious realignment clearly has not occurred.

Why, then, did Carter lose? Three factors seem to have played a major role. Of these, the most important was the impact of inflation and economic hard times on the electorate. Whereas in 1976 Carter had gained a 3-to-1 margin among those voters who felt that their family finances were in worse shape than they had been the previous year, in 1980 Carter lost the same group by 2 to 1. Because of the economy's general distress, this group constituted a substantial 34 percent of the voting public.

A second important factor was Carter's inability to articulate an image of decisiveness and strength in the conduct of the presidency. A substantial 38 percent of Reagan voters claimed as the major reason for their vote that "it was time for a change." It is hard to interpret so general a sentiment, but it may reflect a compound of frustrations associated with the inability of the Carter administration to prevent the capture of hostages in Iran or to effect their release; a sense of drift in military policy; and a feeling of uncertainty about domestic policy, especially about problems associated with energy.

Finally, Carter failed to capture the liberal strength of the Democratic coalition. For example, Jews, who had voted for him by a 2-to-1 margin in 1976, could muster only 45 percent of their votes for him in 1980. Union members were also 12 percent less likely to support him in 1980 than in 1976. Only among black voters did he hold his strength. It seems clear that Carter's policies never fully placed him within the liberal mainstream of his own party and thus left him vulnerable to major defections from the heretofore normal Democratic coalition.

Contrary to the belief that the 1980 election depended heavily on a *moral*, fundamentalist reaction to liberal policies of permissive abortion, equal rights for women, and the abolition of prayers in the public schools, evidence does not suggest that Carter lost because of the efforts of right-wing Christian groups. Among fundamentalist white Protestants, Reagan received only 5 percent more votes than he did among nonfundamentalist Protestants. Of course, many such voters were southerners who may have voted for Carter in 1976. Still, for most voters the 1980 election was not a referendum on public morality.[35]

What, then, is the likelihood of a Republican realignment? As in 1932 and 1936, all depends on whether the party in power can convince voters that it is dealing effectively with economic problems. Just as in the 1930s, the substantial numbers of nonideological Americans who are suffering from economic distress hold the key to realignment. If Republican economic policies succeed, the prospects for realignment may be strong. If these policies fail, the chances are good that Republicans will suffer in 1984 from their perceived failures, just as the Democrats did in 1980.

The Changing Electorate Well into the 1960s, the traditional electoral connection between candidates and voters was fairly straightforward. Candidates organized their lives around electoral competition, spent as much money and energy as possible pursuing and holding onto public office, and in the process generated much information and some issues for voters to consider. The electorate, by contrast, considered elections a brief, one-day respite from their normal routines, an obligation cheerfully enough undertaken. Normally, voters brought little information to their voting decisions, saw only marginal differences between the parties, and relied mainly on their partisan identifications and their perceptions of the candidates in deciding how to vote.

Recent American electoral history suggests that this picture is no longer accurate. Both the electorate and the candidates have apparently entered a period of flux; out of which may come a wholly new connection between candidates and voters.

Perhaps the most important change in the contemporary American electorate, as already mentioned, is its retreat from partisan identification. Estimates of the percentage of independents varies, but most observers agree that Americans are less and less attracted to the present system of political parties.

The reasons for this decline of partisanship are hotly debated. Some observ-

[35] Material in this section comes from *The New York Times*, November 9, 1980.

ers trace the decline to the expansion of the primary system. Others attribute it variously to the breakdown of strong political party organizations, the rising educational level of the electorate, the incorporation of more young people into the electorate, or the intrusion of the media into campaigning. More fundamentally, some debate the *extent* of the change, whereas others argue the question of whether declining partisanship will produce lasting changes in American politics.[36]

Although Americans are less attracted to the political parties than they once were, they have not lost touch with the things parties stand for. Indeed, they appear increasingly able to distinguish between the issue positions of the parties. During the 1950s "party images," as they were perceived by the voters, were comparatively vague. These images have become increasingly clear in recent years.[37] Might there be a link between the growing clarity of "party images" and the decline of partisanship itself? Could it be that as people find it easier to distinguish between the parties, they also discover that their own views and those of the parties do not match? Such a discovery might be unsettling enough to generate considerable political change.

Of course, the decline of partisan identification means little in itself, as long as people continue to *vote* according to their traditional party preferences. But voters seem increasingly unwilling to do this. The proportion of voters who regularly split their ticket is a convenient measure of deviation from partisanship. The ranks of split-ticket voters, like those of independents, have increased in recent years. Thus, in 1952, 58 percent of Democrats, 38 percent of Republicans, and 50 percent of independents split their tickets. In 1972 the comparable figures had grown to 69 percent, 49 percent, and 73 percent. In 1952 only 12 percent of voters split their tickets between presidential and House candidates. The comparable figure in 1976 was 25 percent.

Voter dispositions are but one contributor to electoral flux. Perhaps equally significant is the kind of political stimulation voters receive. In a time of economic instability and widespread feelings of economic hardship, voters look for help. When they do not think they are being helped, they are in the mood to consider change — in the form of third-party candidates; challenges to incumbents; and, finally, throwing the "in"s out. Chronic instability created by a party system and an economy in seemingly permanent disarray contributes considerably to voter fluidity. Thus, for both institutional and psychological reasons, we may have entered a period of electoral uncertainty, the dimensions of which we have yet to perceive clearly.

CONCLUSION This chapter began with the argument that elections constitute an opportunity for citizens to reduce the tension between themselves and their leaders. This

---

[36] For the strongest statement of this position, see Walter Dean Burnham, "American Politics in the 1970's: Beyond Party?" in Louis Maisel and Paul M. Sacks, eds., *The Future of Political Parties*, Sage Electoral Studies Yearbook, vol. 1, (Beverly Hills, Calif.: Sage Publications, 1975), pp. 238–78.

[37] Pomper, *Voters' Choice*, chap. 8.

section addresses, in conclusion, the question of whether elections perform this bridging function successfully. The answer is that elections are effective connectors for only a relatively few Americans — those lucky enough to be well informed politically; to have political preferences that accord with those of winning candidates; and, finally, to be able to distinguish between the issue positions of the candidates.

For most of us, these conditions do not exist. The distribution of political information in the United States is imperfect, and the growing domination of television in this respect produces great superficiality in our political knowledge. Most Americans still lack the sharp sense of issues and ideologies that could force a specific political course on political leaders. Finally, the fixed, single-member district election format, with its reliance on pluralities, makes it difficult for issue preferences to control election outcomes. Instead, compromise and blurring of issues become the usual course for politicians.

Nevertheless, the situation has been changing in recent years. More people are now projecting their ideological and issue concerns onto elections than at any time in the recent past. As the next chapter shows, elections have to reach out more to minorities and small groups of intense campaigners. The fragmentation of the traditional party system has opened the way for candidates such as Jimmy Carter in 1976 and John Anderson in 1980, who represent, at least to some extent, "antiestablishment" views. And in 1980 the presidential election did allow Americans to select a candidate with a quite distinctive program. Thus some elections do provide an important choice.

SUGGESTIONS FOR FURTHER READING

Asher, Herbert. *Presidential Elections and American Politics: Voters, Candidates, and Campaigns since 1952.* Homewood, Ill.: Dorsey, 1976. A good general overview of recent controversies in electoral behavior.

Burnham, Walter Dean. *Critical Elections and the Mainsprings of American Politics.* New York: Norton, 1970. A provocative argument about the decay of electoral politics in the United States. Confusing, flawed, but extremely interesting.

Campbell, Angus; Converse, Philip; Miller, Warren; and Stokes, Donald. *The American Voter.* New York: Wiley, 1960. The modern classic of voting research, a taking-off point for all subsequent work.

Miller, Warren, and Levitin, Teresa. *Leadership and Change: The New Politics and the American Electorate.* Cambridge, Mass.: Winthrop, 1976. Particularly useful for the study of the 1972 presidential election.

Niemi, Richard G., and Weisberg, Herbert F., eds. *Controversies in American Voting Behavior.* San Francisco: Freeman, 1976. An excellent anthology of influential recent journal articles, with some original material.

Pomper, Gerald. *Voter's Choice.* New York: Dodd, Mead, 1975. The most optimistic assessment currently available of the voters' rationality.

Verba, Sidney; Nie, Norman; and Petrocik, John. *The Changing American Voter.* Cambridge, Mass.: Belknap Press, 1976, 1979. The richest, most careful reconsideration of American electoral politics since *The American Voter.*

Chapter 11 Political Parties

Political parties . . . are the only devices thus far invented . . . that can, with some effectiveness, generate countervailing collective power on behalf of the powerless against the relatively few who are individually or organizationally powerful.[1]

Walter Dean Burnham

Through the mechanism of elections, political parties can provide an important link between those citizens who are ruled and those few who do the ruling. Such a bond is hardly automatic, however; effective linkage through political parties must also include a continuing exchange of ideas between elected officials and their constituents. For instance, the parties distribute information about candidates and policies; citizens respond with approval or disapproval, often expressed in their votes — or their failure to vote. In addition, as the official force behind a wide range of candidates and policies seeking public support, parties can be held accountable for the performance of their elected officials and the success of their programs.

The Republicans, Democrats, and myriad minor parties in the United States are much more loosely organized than their counterparts in many other countries. American parties do not solicit large numbers of formal members who pay dues, attend meetings, and regularly perform party-related work. If

[1] Walter Dean Burnham, "The End of American Party Politics," *Trans-Action* 7, 1969, p. 20.

they cannot depend on "card-carrying" members, then, what holds them together? In the United States, the parties' glue is simply people's identification. By *party identification*, or *partisanship*, we mean a longstanding psychological attachment to a particular party. Many citizens have such attachments, and this gives each major party a firm base in the electorate. These attachments occur even where formal mechanisms for declaring one's partisanship, such as registration, do not exist. In other words, if you choose to call yourself a Democrat or a Republican or a Libertarian, then you *are* one.

Increasingly, however, individuals (especially the young) are spurning party affiliation (see Table 11.1). Partisan ties have traditionally been passed from one generation to the next within a family, as part of the political socialization process (see Chapter 3). In recent years, however, the partisan element of this learning experience has weakened considerably. About 60 percent of all adults consider themselves to be Republicans or Democrats, but only half of those in the 18 to 25 age group express partisan allegiance. Americans are no longer depending on parties as heavily as they did twenty years ago, when three of four adults were self-proclaimed partisans.

This weakened linkage has not gone unnoticed. Indeed, many political analysts have seriously questioned the parties' capacity to establish any meaningful bonds between citizens and elected officials. Such observers have pictured the parties as "decomposing" or "disintegrating," descriptions that are often buttressed with citations of shrinking voter turnouts and ever smaller numbers of party loyalists in the electorate.

For most of the post–World War II era, parties have performed poorly in bridging the constitutional gap between Congress and the president. Jimmy Carter, for instance, enjoyed substantial Democratic majorities in both houses of Congress throughout his four-year term of office, but could not rally his legislative troops with any consistency. In fact, Carter virtually stopped trying to "twist congressional arms" in the latter stages of his presidency.[2] Just as

Table 11.1 Party Identification in the United States, 1952–80 (Percentage of Sample Polled)

	1952	1956	1960	1964	1968	1972	1976	1980
Democrat	47	44	46	51	45	40	40	37
Independent	22	24	23	23	30	34	36	40
Republican	27	29	27	24	24	23	23	24
Apolitical/Don't know	4	3	4	2	1	3	1	*

*not measured

Source: Center for Political Studies, University of Michigan. Used by permission. 1980 figures from Market Opinion Research.

[2]*Congressional Quarterly Weekly Report*, September 13, 1980, p. 2700.

Richard Nixon did not much care about his GOP brethren in the Congress, Carter seemed indifferent to his would-be legislative allies on Capitol Hill. This split between the executive and the legislative branches stems largely from forces beyond the control of individual politicians. The president and the individual members of Congress have distinct electoral bases. Despite the oft-discussed notion of "coattails," the president and the legislators are not dependent on each other for their election victories. Partisans are often encouraged to go their separate electoral ways — little wonder, then, that parties, both inside government and out, are viewed as declining in importance.

Although the contemporary role of American political parties is ill defined, they continue to serve as our major avenues to elective office. The 1976 Republican and Democratic presidential candidates, Gerald Ford and Jimmy Carter, won 99 percent of the total vote; Carter and Reagan drew 92 percent of the 1980 vote, despite a strong challenge from independent John Anderson. The demise of the major parties, then, does not appear imminent. Yet the mere survival of these parties does not signal any continuing success in their ability to link the public with its elected officials. To assess the quality of party linkage we must first examine what parties actually do. Only in that context can we evaluate the strength of party-based bonds between the rulers and the ruled.

WHAT PARTIES DO

Time was when a precinct captain was king. When someone needed something done, he'd call the precinct captain. . . . That's the way it was. You did favors and got favors in return. Times were bad, but no one in our ward who needed clothes went without. Nobody who needed food went without. The organization provided.[3]

Aaron Burr and Boss Tweed of the nineteenth-century Tammany Hall Democratic machine in New York; Huey Long of Louisiana; Chicago's Mayor Richard Daley — all these men gained notoriety as "bosses" of strong political organizations. But aside from a few well-preserved holdouts, the boss and his machine are things of the past in American politics. Although machine politics was frequently tinged with corruption, it had many important virtues. The political party of the bosses' heyday could recruit electable candidates, conduct rousing and effective campaigns, "get out the vote" on election day, provide jobs for loyal workers, and dominate the policymaking process of most cities and many states.

American political parties may now be in partial eclipse, but they still make important contributions by playing roles in the selection of candidates, the conduct of campaigns, and the development of policies.

Selecting Candidates

Obtaining the Republican or Democratic nomination for office is a crucial step toward winning elective office in the United States.

[3] Sam Goodman, Chicago Democratic precinct captain, quoted in *The Galesburg Register-Mail*, October 29, 1975.

Once the major parties have made their nominations only two out of millions of persons meeting the constitutional requirements of the office have a realistic chance of entering the White House. . . . Viewed qualitatively, nominations are equally important. If the two major parties select well-qualified candidates, the voters cannot make a really bad choice; if the two parties both nominate fools, the electorate cannot win.[4]

For congressional, state, and local offices, control over candidate selection is equally important. Nominees win the right to attach a well-known "label" to their name — a label that will attract considerable support from the electorate (at least when it reads "Republican" or "Democrat").[5] Until the late nineteenth century, party leaders dominated the nomination process.

Beginning around the turn of the century, reformers sought to wrest the power to select candidates away from the party bosses. Their chief weapon was the direct primary election. If a party's nomination is contested, for any office except president, primary elections decide who will run in the general election as the party's designated nominee. In short, it is the voters, not the party leaders, who have the final say in selecting candidates for most American elective offices. This loss of control has posed serious problems for the major parties.

First, primaries raise the cost of politics.[6] This gives well-heeled candidates a great advantage, as has been amply demonstrated by such millionaires as ex-Pennsylvania governor Milton Shapp and Ohio senator Howard Metzenbaum, who spent their way to name recognition and ultimate victory in statewide races despite being virtually unknown at the start of their initial campaigns.

Second, primaries diminish the power of party organizations to reward the faithful (through nomination for office) or to obtain loyalty among the party's office holders (who must seek renomination). For instance, Georgia Representative Larry McDonald, a Democrat, voted with his party colleagues only 5 percent of the time in 1979–80. Yet despite some stiff challenges in the Georgia Democratic primaries, he has won renomination, and reelection to the House, since 1974. Neither the Democratic party in the House nor the party in Georgia can exercise any real control over his actions, which are vigorously conservative to the point of being reactionary. As Sorauf points out,

> The primary permits the nomination of a candidate (1) hostile to the party organization and leadership, (2) opposed to their platforms and programs, or (3) out of key with the public image the party wants to project — or all of the above! At the worst it may permit the nomination of an individual under the party label who will be, intentionally or not, a severe embarrassment to it.[7]

[4] Donald R. Matthews, "Presidential Nominations: Processes and Outcomes," in James David Barber, ed., *Choosing the President* (Englewood Cliffs, N.J.: Prentice-Hall, 1974), p. 36.

[5] See Leon Epstein, *Political Parties in Western Democracies* (New York: Praeger, 1967) for a fuller explanation of parties as "labels."

[6] The following section draws heavily on the discussion by Frank Sorauf in *Party Politics in America*, 4th ed. (Boston: Little, Brown, 1980), pp. 212–13.

[7] Ibid., p. 212.

Finally, the primary may encourage or produce a weak ticket for the general election. Primary voting turnout is usually much lower than in subsequent general-election campaigns. Relatively small groups of voters can thus have a magnified effect on the outcome. Given their constituency, candidates with identifiable ethnic names may have an advantage, regardless of their records, in heavily ethnic districts. In the past party leaders may have selected some poor candidates, but minimal competence was usually assured. The primaries guarantee neither political nor governmental strength in their results.

Primary elections increase citizen participation in politics and open up the party to its voters. But the reliance on primaries for selecting candidates allows the parties little control over their nominees. Therefore, even if a candidate wins election as a Democrat and then supports policies most Democrats oppose, it is difficult for the party to deny him or her renomination for reelection. Incumbents generally are renominated, even when challenged in a primary contest. The party's label thus may convey little meaning, and those who vote for a candidate on the basis of party affiliation may seriously misjudge his or her philosophy.[8]

Conducting Campaigns

Political campaigning takes extensive resources, the most important being money, campaign workers, and technical expertise in matters like public relations, organizing, scheduling, and advertising. It is often said that "the Democrats" or "the Republicans" ran an effective (or ineffective) campaign in one race or another. Such generalizations mask the fact that few party organizations — whether local, state, or national — have enough resources to play a major role in a large-scale campaign.

Who does provide the finances, personnel, and organization needed to run an effective campaign? In presidential campaigns, public financing is significant. In 1976 and 1980 all major presidential candidates relied completely on public funds for the general election. They (like the numerous other contenders for the Democratic and Republican nominations) received more limited financial assistance in the presidential primaries, when individual contributions, up to $250, were matched by government funds.

Although congressional candidates do not receive federal campaign funds, they rely no more heavily on party organizations than do presidential aspirants. House and Senate campaigns have grown increasingly expensive, and candidates must obtain money from: (1) political action committees (PACs), which represent special interests ranging from labor to business to advocates

[8] Sullivan and O'Connor report that in any given congressional race the party label does convey some useful information. Working with a unique poll of House candidates, they find that in almost every instance the Democratic candidate was more liberal than the Republican. Thus, even though some Democrats may be very conservative and some Republicans reasonably liberal, their opponents are likely to be even more conservative or more liberal, respectively. See John H. Sullivan and Robert E. O'Connor, "Electoral Choice and Popular Control of Public Policy," *American Political Science Review* (1972): 1256–68.

of handgun reform; (2) individual donors (up to $1,000 per campaign); and (3) their own personal wealth. Political parties do contribute, but the sums are paltry compared with the total cost of mounting a competitive campaign (see Table 11.2).

Campaign organizations follow a similar pattern. Parties remain important where some patronage (jobs, contracts, etc.) still exists and for some minor offices; but in most instances candidates build their own organizations and recruit their own volunteers. As Fenno reports in one intensive study of House members' district activities:

> [In] only two or three [of 18] cases is there an integrated working relationship between the congressman's personal organization and the local party organization. That is exactly the way most of our House members want it — separate organizations pursuing separate tasks. The task of the congressman's personal organization is to keep him in Congress. The task of the local party organization is to keep the party in control of local affairs.[9]

And never the twain shall meet.

Reinforcing this trend toward candidate-centered campaigns have been the growing numbers of free-lance political consultants. Such individuals as David Garth, John Deardourff, Doug Bailey, and Richard Wirthlin, among others, provide sophisticated campaign advice, organization, survey research, advertising, voter targeting, and any number of other services that a candidate might want to purchase.

Although most forces — whether organizational, financial, or technological — have served to remove campaigning from party control, the major parties have fought to retain an important role in the campaign process. As we shall see, Republican organizers have achieved much greater success in this endeavor than have their Democratic counterparts.

Posing Policy Alternatives American political parties — unlike those in many other countries — have rarely formulated coherent policy programs for their candidates to run on. In recent years, however, the parties' presidential platforms have presented some well-defined ideological positions. The 1980 Republican platform, for example, took a strongly conservative approach to government: less domestic spending, a strong military, and fewer restraints on private industry. If conservatives continue to dominate the Republican party, we can expect more such pronouncements in the future.

---

[9] Richard J. Fenno, Jr., *Home Style* (Boston: Little, Brown, 1978), p. 113.

Table 11.2 Political Action Committees and the Party Leader: Contributions to Senator Howard Baker's 1978 Campaign Made During the 1979–80 period.

Type of Interest	Number of Groups	Largest Single Contribution Amount	Largest Single Contribution Source	Total Contributions
Agriculture	14	$ 8,000	Associated Milk Producers	$ 17,950
Business				
Aerospace and Defense	10	5,000	Grumman	12,450
Automotive	5	10,000	National Auto Dealers Association	13,000
Chemical	10	1,500	Monsanto	6,350
Communication	13	2,800	ATT	8,350
Energy and Utilities	44	3,000	National Rural Electric Cooperative	35,255
Finance	30	5,000	American Bankers Association	21,554
Food and Restaurant	26	5,000	Malone and Hyde	19,200
Forest and Paper Products	13	9,400	International Paper	20,035
Insurance	13	5,000	NLT Corporation	21,700
Manufacturing	38	3,000	Westinghouse	32,350
Metals	9	5,000	Alcoa	9,450
Pharmaceutical	8	2,500	Pfizer	5,300
Real Estate/Construction	9	9,600	National Association of Realtors	16,900
Transportation	20	3,100	American Trucking Association	16,200
Other	42	3,000	Republic Steel	26,950
Health	10	15,000	American Medical Association	31,400
"No-Connected" Organizations	3	2,200	National Rifle Association	3,800
Labor	9	5,000	International Airline Pilots Association	11,550
Professional	9	5,000	Association of Trial Lawyers	7,850
	336*			$341,743*

*Includes one group labeled "miscellaneous" with a $200 contribution.

Source: *A Common Cause Guide to Money, Power, and Politics in the 97th Congress.* Copyright © 1981, Common Cause. Reprinted by permission.

Democrats, on the other hand, have not generally expressed a consistent set of positions; but a comparison of 1980 platform statements does reveal an array of real differences between the announced positions of the two parties (see Table 11.3).

**Some New
(and Renewed)
Party Roles**

So far, our picture of the current status of political parties has not been optimistic, nor does it bode well for the parties' future prospects. But although primary elections and independent campaigns have contributed to political parties' loss of power, a few opposing trends have developed in recent years. For example, the parties' national committees have begun to provide more extensive services to Senate and especially to House candidates. The national committees operate independently of Congress; Republicans and Democrats in both the House and the Senate mount their own campaigns. But by offering pre-election polling, fund-raising assistance, and issue-related information, the national parties can absorb some of a candidate's overhead costs and thereby enable him or her to concentrate more on specific local problems.

Although the Democratic party has strengthened itself along these lines, it is the Republicans who have led the way. This makes sense, because since the 1930s the Republicans have been a minority party — in the Congress and among all citizens who identify with one party or the other. The Republican party has not had the luxury of relying on large numbers of incumbents to win reelection with ease. The GOP's organizational renaissance began after Lyndon Johnson's 1964 landslide victory over Republican Barry Goldwater. A nonideological party veteran, Ohio's Ray Bliss, took over the Republican reins and proceeded to strengthen both the party's base of financial support and its organization. Building on growing numbers of small contributors initially attracted to the party by Goldwater, Bliss was able to construct a firm financial foundation built on a large number of modest (under $100) annual contributions. At present this figure has risen to about 500,000 donors — each giving an average of $20 per year.[10] In addition, national-level Republicans began to provide campaign assistance to many candidates through party-sponsored campaign schools. In these settings electioneering professionals could instruct novice candidates and campaign managers on an array of techniques and strategies ranging from television use to the care and feeding of volunteer workers. Both parties conduct these schools at present, but the Republican efforts have usually been more regular and more thorough.

Although Richard Nixon did little to strengthen the Republican party, the base provided by Bliss's operations in the 1960s allowed the party to weather the Watergate affair reasonably well. A second generation of party rebuilding began in 1977, under the direction of Republican National Chairman Bill Brock, a former senator. Brock strengthened the party's financial underpinnings and increased GOP campaign contributions to congressional and state-legislative candidates.

Beyond this, Brock and his national GOP colleagues worked diligently at recruiting attractive candidates, especially for state-legislative seats. This combination of strong candidates and sophisticated campaign assistance helped the party gain about 500 state legislature seats in the 1978 and 1980 elections. In concert with the Reagan and GOP Senate victories in 1980, this trend bodes

---

[10]*Congressional Quarterly Weekly Report*, April 28, 1979, p. 775.

Table 11.3 The Parties on the Issues: Platform Statements, 1980

Republicans	Democrats
Defense	
Republicans commit themselves to an immediate increase in defense spending to be applied judiciously to critically needed programs. *We will build toward a sustained defense expenditure sufficient to close the gap with the Soviets, and ultimately reach the position of military superiority* that the American people demand.	Our fourth major objective is to strengthen the military security of the United States and our Allies at a time when trends in the military balance have become increasingly adverse. *America is now, and will continue to be, the strongest power on earth.* It was the Democratic Party's greatest hope that we could, in fact, reduce our military effort. But realities of the world situation, including the unremitting buildup of Soviet military forces, required that we begin early to reverse the decade-long decline in American defense efforts.
Health	
Republicans recognize that many health care problems can be solved if government will work closely with the private sector to find remedies that will enhance our current system of excellent care. We applaud, as an example, the voluntary effort which has been undertaken by our nation's hospitals to control costs. The results have been encouraging. More remains to be done. *Republicans unequivocally oppose socialized medicine,* in whatever guise it is presented by the Democratic Party. We reject the creation of a national health service and all proposals for compulsory national health insurance.	The answer to runaway medical costs is not, as Republicans propose, to pour money into a wasteful and inefficient system. The answer is not to cut back on benefits for the elderly and eligibility for the poor. *The answer is to enact a comprehensive, universal national health insurance plan.*
Energy	
Republicans believe this disappointing cycle of shrinking energy prospects and expanding government regulation and meddling is wholly unnecessary. We believe that *the proven American values of individual enterprise can solve our energy problems.* This optimism stands in stark contrast to the grim predictions of the Democrats who have controlled Congress.	We must continue on the path to a sustainable energy future — a future based increasingly on renewable resources and energy conservation. Our national goal of having 20 percent of our energy from renewable resources in the year 2000 must become a working target, not a forgotten slogan. *Conservation must remain the cornerstone of our national energy supply.*

Republicans	Democrats

Judicial Appointments

Under Mr. Carter, many appointments to federal judgeships have been particularly disappointing. By his partisan nominations, he has violated his explicit campaign promise of 1976 and has blatantly disregarded the public interest. We pledge to reverse that deplorable trend, through the appointment of women and men who respect and reflect the values of the American people, and whose judicial philosophy is characterized by the highest regard for protecting the rights of lawabiding citizens, and is consistent with the belief in the decentralization of the federal government and efforts to return decisionmaking power to state and local elected officials.

We will work for the appointment of judges at all levels of the judiciary who respect traditional family values and the sanctity of innocent human life.

Note: Emphases added.

One of President Carter's highest priorities has been to increase significantly the number of women, Blacks, Hispanics, and other minorities in the federal government. That has been done.

This record must be continued. The Democratic Party is committed to continue and strengthen the policy of *appointing more women and minorities to federal positions at all levels including the Supreme Court.*

well for the Republicans, even though only about one citizen in four currently identifies with them.

The national parties played much greater and more visible roles in 1976 and 1980 presidential campaigning than in some earlier elections. This turn of events was brought about by the Federal Election Campaign Act of 1974, which limited campaign spending by presidential candidates. The law was designed to end the financial excesses and abuses that had characterized earlier campaigns. Prior to 1974, presidential candidates acting independently of their parties had raised and spent huge amounts of money. This practice culminated in Richard Nixon's 1972 fund-raising drive, conducted by the independent Committee to Reelect the President, which raised $60 million — much of it illegally.

The 1974 campaign law also gave candidates a choice: They could either raise their own general-election (postprimary) campaign funds, subject to no limitations; or they could accept public financing. If they opted for public financing, they could not accept private contributions. Since the law went into effect, before the 1976 election, all the major party candidates (Ford, Reagan,

Carter) have chosen to receive the public funds, which came to about $21 million in 1976 and about $29 million in 1980. Independent candidate John Anderson was alloted $4.2 million in public money after his 6.5 percent showing in the 1980 election. No other candidate or party has come close to obtaining the 5 percent of the total vote essential to qualify for public funding.

These limits on spending, along with public financing, meant that in 1976 and 1980 the major-party candidates became at least partially dependent on their parties for both money and services in the campaign. Each national party can supplement the public funds with a limited amount of its own money (approximately $4 million in 1980), and state and local party organizations can provide unlimited voter registration and get-out-the-vote services to further their presidential candidate's cause. The public-financing reforms, ironically, have served to strengthen party efforts in presidential electioneering, although the candidates and their personal organizations remain at political stage center.

What, then, can we safely say political parties do? Without question, they act as "labels," to be attached to whoever wins their nomination, whether for president, state legislator, or county coroner. Because most adults still do identify with either the Democratic or the Republican party, the party label is no small asset, despite the declining significance of party identification in determining voting decisions.

What else, then, do parties do? In some circumstances they can recruit candidates and assist their campaigning. But as we have seen, candidates more often run their own campaigns, and primary elections select the candidates. Further, neither Republicans or Democrats look to their party as a major source of policy proposals.

In short, although political parties are widely seen as playing an important role in the American political process, we should be skeptical of their current performance while being aware of their potential strengths.

WHAT IS A POLITICAL PARTY?

What is a political party? Is it all the people who call themselves Republicans or Democrats (or Socialist Workers or whatever)? Is it precinct organizations such as those controlled by Chicago's Democratic machine? Or does the political party consist of public officials who have won election under a given party's banner? All these descriptions are appropriate, but none is complete.

Over time, the two major parties have developed general images that attract distinct types of voters. Since the 1930s Democrats have been considered the party of the "poor" or the "little man," and 80 percent of voters in one study were able to identify the Democrats as the more "liberal" of the two parties.[11] In recent years the Democratic party's image has broadened to include advocacy of blacks and Chicanos, and, more generally, civil rights legislation and programs. Many voters also associate the Democrats with economic "good times," free government spending, inflation, and high employment.

[11] Gerald M. Pomper, *Voter's Choice* (New York: Dodd, Mead, 1975).

The Republican party, in contrast, is seen as having a wealthier and more conservative bent. Republicans are viewed as more predictable than Democrats, more efficient as managers of government, better at managing foreign policy, and tougher on crime. More specifically, in 1980 the Republican nominee, Ronald Reagan, won support disproportionately from those who (1) saw inflation as a more significant problem than unemployment; (2) thought that federal spending on domestic programs should be decreased; (3) felt the United States should be "more forceful" with the Soviet Union; (4) thought that too much attention was being paid to needs of minorities; and (5) did not support the Equal Rights Amendment.[12] At the same time, many voters continued to see few real differences between the major parties. One recent study reported that six citizens in ten thought there were "no real differences" between the Democrats and Republicans.[13]

Whatever party images do exist give us little help in understanding the real nature and roles of American political parties. We find the most useful description of the political party to include three distinct, but related, major components: the *party in government*, the *party organization*, and the *party in the electorate*. Each maintains its own identity and can be treated separately; yet the continuing interaction among the three components creates a political party we can view as a single phenomenon.

We will focus on each of these components in turn. It is important to remember, however, that a party's ability to link citizens with their rulers depends in turn on how strongly its three components are tied together.

THE PARTY IN GOVERNMENT Gaining control of the government, and with it the right to govern, is the immediate goal of most major party activity, at least in the United States. In common parlance, parties "organize" the Congress or "capture" the presidency. However, given the relative weakness of party organizations and the decreasing partisan attachments of many citizens, does it really make a difference which party wins? Can we expect the victor (or its members who hold office) to provide alternative policy directions, along the lines suggested in the campaign?

There are no clear-cut answers to these questions. On the one hand, party workers and candidates are likely to exaggerate the differences between the competing parties' policy positions, especially during election campaigns. In spite of campaign rhetoric, some critics of American parties see the Democrats and Republicans as representing a nonchoice between interchangeable sets of office seekers. For example, many observers noted little difference between presidential candidates Richard Nixon and Hubert Humphrey in 1968, despite their long-standing disagreements over a wide range of policies.

[12]*Public Opinion*, December 1980–January 1981, pp. 34–35. Source: CBS News/*New York Times* survey, November 4, 1980.
[13]Carll Everett Ladd, *Public Opinion*, October–November 1980, pp. 54–55.

On the other hand, looking back, we can see that in terms of both economic policies and general confidence in government, a Humphrey presidency probably would have been very different from the Nixon-Ford administration that came to pass. And Ronald Reagan's election as president has produced trends in policy emphasis (the elimination of public service jobs) and policy development (proposed tax cuts) that are quite different from what a second-term Carter administration probably would have produced. In short, the choice between candidates that the parties offer us can be important, although much of the difference lies in how the successful candidate acts once in office.

Partisanship is widespread in government, yet party-based considerations rarely dominate the making of public policy. The potential for party-based linkage between citizens and elected officials is nevertheless real. For even if the electorate can only throw the current bunch of rascals out, replacing them with another gang of rascals, operating under a different label, the threat to a party's office holders remains. Thus in 1980 the defeat of nine Democratic senators, along with the election of Ronald Reagan as president, illustrates a partisan housecleaning; as the 97th Congress (1981–82) progressed, and the Senate approved a host of spending cuts, the policy implications of such a housecleaning began to take shape.

Chief Executives: Restrained Partisans Most candidates for executive office — whether president, governor, or mayor — are partisans, running under a Democratic or Republican label. When they are elected, the question becomes: To what extent can they, or will they, choose to govern as partisans?

The answers are complex; but in general, an executive who tries to govern according to his or her party's policies runs into serious obstacles. Many governmental bodies, such as regulatory agencies, are independent of direct control by elected officials. Even the national bureaucracy, although nominally under the president's control, must maintain a close working relationship with the Congress, a necessity most bureaucrats take seriously.

The President versus Congress. Often in the past the conflicting demands of a Republican president and a Democratic Congress have effectively prevented the bureaucracy from following the policy leadership of either. For fourteen of the years between 1955 and 1977, a Republican president sat in the White House; at no time during this period did the GOP control either the Senate or the House of Representatives. Thus neither party could dominate national policymaking, even though the Democrats had substantial congressional majorities in some of these years. As we saw in Chapter 6, Republican presidents Eisenhower, Nixon, and Ford used their veto powers with great effect, only occasionally being overridden by the necessary two-thirds majorities in both House and Senate. Thus, neither Republicans nor Democrats have been able to implement their policies in any comprehensive way.

Even when a single party controls both the Congress and the presidency, strictly partisan decision making remains the exception. Between 1955 and

1980, despite continuing Democratic majorities in the House and Senate, enough conservative (and often southern) Democrats ordinarily defected from their party's ranks to place in doubt major changes proposed by Democratic administrations.

Even a strong electoral showing does not translate easily into legislative success. The 1980 Reagan victory, coupled with the Republicans' Senate majority, remained offset by continuing Democratic control of the House.

This post-1955 period of government without strong partisan direction has generally served the purposes of Republican presidents better than those of Democratic ones. This is partly because of the Republican tendency to support the status quo; for instance, despite overall increases in federal spending, Republican presidents have been able to frustrate some Democratic calls for more spending and larger programs. But the presidential veto is a negative power. The more important question is how much the president can initiate and infuence governmental changes advocated by his party at the federal level. To a genuinely conservative Republican, the goal of reducing governmental intervention may be as difficult to achieve as was the initial Democratic goal of expanding the role of the federal government in the 1950s and 1960s.

A President's Partisan Powers.   The president draws little power from his role as leader of his party; but opportunities to push partisan programs do arise through his control of White House resources. The president can fill over 2,000 high-level jobs, and the vast majority of these go to fellow partisans. In addition, there are large numbers of honorary, advisory, and ceremonial positions to be filled; again the president has the opportunity to reward deserving partisans. Finally, the president appoints Supreme Court justices to lifetime positions. The potential for a long-lasting impact is clear. Justice William Rehnquist, a 1972 Richard Nixon appointee, at age 47, may well still be serving on the court in the twenty-first century.

Beyond these appointment powers, the president generates tremendous amounts of news coverage, and the attention given the chief executive is necessarily partisan. Covering the presidency means covering the partisan politician who occupies the Oval Office. This political fact of life has continually bedeviled opposition-party spokespersons, who often receive time from the television networks to rebut presidential messages. Almost without exception, these presentations have little effect.

One observer has called American parties "national executive-centered coalitions" — coalitions that are held together by partisan identification and some shared policy goals but that require the president's skillful leadership to provide direction and reinvigoration.[14] The president must provide energy for much of the policymaking process, and thus usually he must attempt to build temporary alliances of support that extend beyond his own party. This lead-

[14] Judson L. James, *American Political Parties in Transition* (New York: Harper and Row, 1974), pp. 240 ff.

ership function may have reduced the significance of the chief executive as a party leader, simply because so many of his responsibilities and goals transcend partisanship, and because even his partisan efforts so often require broad public support that far transcends his partisan political base.

Parties in the Legislature Most legislators, like most executives, are elected under a party label. As we saw in Chapter 5, the party affiliation of a member of Congress is one of his or her most important characteristics in the legislature. But even the most partisan representative, senator, or state legislator is influenced by other political forces as well — constituents' pressures, committees' dictates, lobbyists' pleas, or a president's desires. The party is only one source of influence among many that a lawmaker ordinarily takes into account. Knowing the party affiliation of a member of Congress will allow us correctly to guess his or her vote on most issues, but we cannot know exactly what influence partisan affiliation actually had on that vote.[15]

The initial, procedural phase of organizing the Congress (and most state legislatures) after each election is almost completely a partisan affair. Democrats held a majority of both House and Senate seats from 1954 through 1980. This allowed them to name the Speaker of the House and the majority leader of the Senate in each Congress during those years, as well as to control all the committee and subcommittee chairmanships and the resources that go with these positions. More generally, such power to organize any legislative body permits party leaders to control much of the pace and content of the legislative process, even though much of the program itself has been developed at the executive's behest.

Every two years, however, when a new Congress gets underway, the effect of parties declines precipitously. John Kennedy, for instance, entered the presidency in 1961 with a comfortable 262-to-173 Democratic House majority. He immediately sought to change the composition of the important Rules Committee in order to eliminate some procedural logjams that its conservative majority was using to block his legislative program. Kennedy discovered, however, that his majority had shrunk from 89 to 5 (217 to 212) with the defection of many conservative southern Democrats, based on their opposition to his liberal program. Kennedy's subsequent wariness in approaching the Congress with controversial legislation undoubtedly reflected the lesson he had learned about the limits of his party tie to Congress.

Although the short-term effect of party on policy is inconsistent, and often minimal, a national legislative party may exert a substantial effect on policymaking over a longer time span. As James Sundquist noted, the "out-party" (the one not controlling the presidency) can create a series of policy proposals, which it then acts on if there is a reversal in the next presidential election.[16]

[15] See Julius Turner, *Party and Constituency: Pressures on Congress*, rev. ed., ed. Edward Schneier (Baltimore, Md.: Johns Hopkins University Press, 1970); also see John Kingdon, *Congressmen's Voting Decisions* (New York: Harper and Row, 1973), chap. 4 and p. 236.

[16] James Sundquist, *Politics and Policy* (Washington, D.C.: Brookings, 1968), chap. 9.

This appears to have happened in the mid-1960s, as Democrats enacted policies that had been stewing in their congressional pots through the 1950s and early 1960s. The outpouring of legislation such as Medicare and massive federal aid to education following the 1964 presidential and congressional landslides were the results of seemingly endless debates and maneuvering in the House and Senate — the apparently fruitless work of Democrats in the 1950s, which bore substantial returns once they won the White House and dominated the Congress in 1965–66.

The Party in Government: Accountability
During the 1980 presidential campaign, Republican Ronald Reagan often argued that he should be elected in order to check the free-spending Democrats. His Democratic opponent, incumbent Jimmy Carter, emphasized the themes of leadership and stability, while playing down the nation's economic woes. The crushing Reagan victory was open to numerous interpretations, ranging from the personal rejection of Jimmy Carter to a sign that a rising conservative tide was sweeping away a great number of nonresponsive Democrats. In general, Democrats were held accountable for national conditions, even if those conditions were beyond their control. Many Reagan voters (38 percent) observed that it was "time for a change."[17]

What do we mean by accountability? First, that the electorate must be able to assign credit or blame for governmental policymaking. And second, that the citizens must be able to act on their assessment. A single party's control of both the presidency and the Congress thus is an important step in making office holders accountable because it enables voters to hold their representatives responsible for achieving promised goals, and to remove them in the next election if they fail. Of course, such control must be exercised in retrospect, after a party has had an opportunity to govern. Accountability is also limited by the degree of choice offered the electorate by the major political parties. Thus, to remove a current set of Democratic "ins," voters must usually be willing to elect the Republican alternative.

The quality of party-based accountability is suspect, but it offers a better chance to assign responsibility for policies than does a divided government. President Carter could not criticize congressional decisions without attacking fellow Democrats, and vice versa. A Reagan presidency gives Democrats much more freedom to attempt to hold the administration accountable, whereas Republicans face the prospect of moving beyond their electoral successes to confront the problems of governing. As one prominent GOP congressman observed, "We're very aware of the fact that we won, we won big, and now we've got to produce."[18]

The party in government extends into every branch of the federal government (including, on occasion, the judiciary), which means that its members often find themselves cooperating and competing at the same time. Party ties

[17] *Public Opinion*, December 1980–January 1981, p. 43.
[18] *The New York Times*, November 6, 1980, p. 18.

among governmental officials can be extremely important in at least two respects. First, a party can control the levers of the governmental machinery, such as the president's power to appoint Supreme Court justices or to make up the budget. Second, a political party can encourage and regularize cooperation among the separate branches of government, along with the top levels of the bureaucracy. Such coordination does not imply a lock-step response to the dictates of party leaders, but it does mean that the electorate can hope for enough coherence in policymaking that it can hold the decision makers accountable for their behavior.

Nevertheless, the political parties' effect on governmental policymaking has declined in recent years. Divided partisan control of government has been commonplace since the 1950s, and the independent power of the presidency has grown tremendously in this same period. The party in government does have its roots in the electorate, but the voters' controls over government are imperfect and occasional. One potential source of linkage may come through the party organization, and we now turn to an examination of that possibility.

PARTY ORGANIZATION As we saw earlier, party organizations — the second aspect of the three-part political party — were often depicted in terms of an autocratic boss and his well-oiled machine. Unquestionably the political machine has played an important role in American politics and continues to do so in a few locations. But the machine is scarcely an accurate representation of most contemporary party organizations.

Is the political party generally so well organized that it can crush its opposition, reward only its own loyalists, and exercise power far out of proportion to its limited number of active workers? On every organizational level — local, state, and national — the answer is a clear-cut "no." Political parties are ordinarily so fragmented, in fact, that they fall well outside any conventional description of "organization." If we speak of Republicans, for instance, we may mean the national party. But what of the fifty state parties, not to mention the thousands of county units, which often have no real structure at all?

Nor do the Democrats have any firmer an organizational base. Even the legendary Chicago mayor, Richard J. Daley, had begun to lose his hold on some party activities before his death in 1976. Since then the Cook County (Illinois) Democratic "machine" has become increasingly divisive and ineffective — to the point that in 1980 Richard J. (Richie) Daley, Jr., ran for state's attorney against the regular Democratic organization, which was under the control of insurgent-turned-regular Jane Byrne.

Although, as we saw earlier, Republicans are better organized at the national level, neither party can consistently put together strong organizational efforts at all levels and in all areas (urban and rural, Northeast and Southwest, etc.). Because their organizations are fragmented, American parties find it very difficult to connect citizens to their leaders in any systematic fashion. Despite their fragmentation, however, party organizations do have the potential for funneling public sentiments to elected officials, who are — almost without exception — partisans. To understand both the reasons for party fragmentation and the potential for party-based linkage, let us examine the basic work force of party organizations at the local level.

The Activists: Who Participates and Why? Like almost all other regular avenues for political activity, partisan politics draws most of its participants from the more affluent and well-educated segments of society. American political parties do not seek vast numbers of dues-paying members; rather, they usually rely on occasional volunteer help from interested individuals. These citizens make up the activist core of parties at the local, state, and even national levels. Delegates to national party conventions are good examples of party activists, and Table 11.4 illustrates the substantial differences between them and the population at large.

In general, individuals with certain talents or resources, such as writing or speaking abilities, wealth, or high position, participate most easily and effectively in party affairs. For instance, because of their specialized skills and flexible working hours, lawyers are disproportionately involved in party matters.

Table 11.4 Delegates to the 1980 National Conventions, Compared with the American Population (Percent)

Demographic Characteristics			
	GOP	Democratic	General Population (1980 Census)
Youth (20–34)	5	11	25.8
Black	3	15	11.6
Women	29	49	51.4
College education	65	65	17.0

General Ideology Self-Ranking			
GOP Delegate	GOP in Population	Democratic Delegates	Democrats in Population
Liberal	2	13	46	21
Moderate	36	40	42	44
Conservative	58	41	6	26

Source: All figures except census data are drawn from Warren J. Mitofsky and Martin Plissner, "The Making of the Delegates, 1968–80," *Public Opinion*, October–November 1980, pp. 41–43.

Are Activists Representative? A different and perhaps more important question is the extent to which activists' issue positions reflect those of party supporters as a whole. Republican activists have consistently held somewhat more conservative positions than have other Republicans in the electorate. In general, however, Republican activists and voters both see themselves as rather conservative. Among Democrats, over the past two decades there have been considerable changes in the relative issue positions of the activists and the other partisans. In the 1950s the ideological character of both groups was similar — moderately liberal.[19] Since then Democratic activists have moved sharply to the left; by the 1970s the Democrats had come to resemble the Republicans in that their activists were more ideologically extreme than their ordinary supporters. Indeed, the Democrats' problem is more serious than the Republicans', because GOP activists and supporters are all generally conservative, whereas the liberal Democratic activists are faced with many moderate and sometimes conservative Democrats in the electorate (see Table 11.4).

Professionals and Purists. The differences between each party's issue-oriented activists and less ideological followers is compounded by substantial internal divisions among the activists of both the major parties. Traditionally, activists have embarked on party work not out of concern with issues or ideological positions, but for "professional" reasons; that is, they have sought jobs, career advancement, or government contracts. In short, they have participated largely in hopes of sharing the spoils of victory. Members of political machines, from the boss on down, are examples of activists in the traditional mold. But in an era when most government workers are made secure in their jobs by civil service protection, when candidates are selected in wide-open primary elections, and when party service counts for little, the "professional" incentives for party activism have greatly diminished.

In recent years, more and more party activists have become involved for "purist" reasons of issue positions and ideology. Purists often believe in a cause, expect no reward from a candidate in return for their support, and are reluctant to compromise any of their ideals.[20] Their incentives flow from convictions that certain policies (and candidates who support them) are greatly preferable to the alternatives. Such activists derive their satisfaction from seeing that policy is altered in certain directions, not from obtaining such rewards as a sewage construction contract or a political job. The success of two bands of purists, Goldwater's supporters in 1964 and McGovern's in 1972, in dominating the two major parties shows how influential such issue-oriented amateurs can be.

---

[19] See Herbert McClosky, Paul J. Hoffman, and Rosemary O'Hara, "Issue Conflict and Consensus among Party Leaders and Followers," *American Political Science Review* 54 (1960): 406–27; also, Everett C. Ladd and Charles D. Hadley, *Political Parties and Political Issues: Patterns of Differentiation since the New Deal* (Beverly Hills, Calif.: Sage, 1973).

[20] See Nelson W. Polsby and Aaron Wildavsky, *Presidential Elections: Strategies of American Electoral Politics*, 5th ed. (New York: Scribners, 1980).

What are the implications for the parties in the trend toward political activity based on purist issue goals instead of the traditional desires for gain? First, selecting candidates comes to focus on who is "right" on the issues rather than who is most "electable." Especially in the primary-election stage, candidates are linked, often superficially, to particular issue positions. In 1976 Ronald Reagan, with strong conservative credentials, was perceived as less electable than was President Gerald Ford, who ultimately won the GOP nomination. Four years later Republican purists and professionals alike came to support Reagan, who consistently (if incrementally) modified his conservative image throughout the campaign.

In recent years, much purist activity has taken place on the fringes of party politics. Some liberal groups, such as the National Committee for an Effective Congress, have been active since the 1960s. Several Republican Senate candidates were assisted in the 1980 election by well-organized conservative groups (Committee for the Survival of a Free Congress, National Conservative PAC) and evangelical groups such as the Moral Majority. As time passes, there will be considerable tension between such groups' purist goals (banning abortions, permitting prayer in schools) and the professional realities of making and implementing policy.

On the whole, the infusion of issue-oriented activists may lessen the parties' ability to mediate and compromise — an ability essential to forge the conditions on which election victories depend. Traumatic intraparty showdowns over economic, foreign, or other policies divide the party into warring factions instead of bringing together broad and diverse segments of the party's electorate. Conservative Republicans, for instance, will have to decide whether they want to help govern or remain opposed to any compromise. In 1981 most Republican members of Congress went along with President Reagan's request to raise the national debt ceiling — a policy that many of them had fought bitterly during the Carter administration. At the same time, some conservative senators found ways to escape the Reagan administration's budget cuts. The usually tight-fisted Senator Orrin Hatch (R-Utah), chairman of the Labor and Human Resources Committee, protected the federally funded Job Corps, which operates a large training facility in his home state.[21] Even for a "purist" conservative like Hatch, the lure of pork-barrel politicking (one base of the political professional) was too much.

The "purist-professional" division is not as absolute as it appears. Party activists are human; other incentives besides pet policies or patronage can induce them to work. For many activists, party work provides large doses of social and psychological satisfaction. Working closely with others who share the same goal, be it electoral or ideological, can be immensely rewarding. Nowhere are these potential rewards greater than in that political hothouse, the political party's convention.

---

[21] Timothy Noah, "Republican Pork Barrel," *The New Republic,* April 4, 1981, p. 10.

National Conventions Every four years Republicans and Democrats alike stage national conventions, where they nominate their presidential candidates. These extravaganzas present a rich and tumultuous flow of activity characterized by widespread participation, intricate organization, and broadly based (and sometimes unlikely) coalition building. The national nature of a major-party convention is very significant: Only at these gatherings are party politicians from all over the country able to congregate as a body, renewing personal friendships as well as forging political alliances. With thousands of delegates and alternates circulating on the floor and meeting in hundreds of smaller gatherings inside and outside the convention hall, much of the politicking is informal. As one convention watcher notes,

> Normally a national convention gathers in a huddle of close-clustered downtown hotels at the center of some clotted city, so that simple nearness throws delegates together at cafe, bar, sidewalk, lobby. Then in the daily bustle and jostle they rub on one another and rub and rub and whisper and gossip and mill and churn, until summer heat, strained emotions and growing tension bring them to a common boil out of which decision erupts.[22]

On the other hand, former president Richard Nixon, one of the most experienced of all current students of political conventions, senses that conventions are outdated in an era of television and primary elections.[23] What is it, then, that these gatherings accomplish?

Choosing a Candidate. First, the convention is where the party's presidential candidate is selected. Even though both parties have chosen their nominees on the first ballot in every convention since 1956, rarely has the nomination been completely certain until shortly before that point. Edward Kennedy's 1980 challenge to Jimmy Carter showed that even a party with an incumbent president may find itself awaiting a convention decision that goes down to the wire. Nevertheless, it is fair to say that conventions no longer actually *choose* the parties' candidates, even though they have the formal power to do so.

Generating Publicity. A second function of national nominating conventions is to generate publicity for the party and its candidates. Convention goings-on have long been front-page news, and television coverage has greatly increased this free publicity. But TV coverage has forced changes in the scheduling and pacing of convention business: Convention officials now must watch the clock. In the past, balloting for the standard bearer often dragged on and on (through 103 ballots at the Democrats' convention in 1924, for example). In the age of television, however, party leaders and candidates are under enormous pressure to reach their decisions while the televised proceedings have the

---

[22] Theodore H. White, *The Making of the President 1960* (New York: New American Library, 1967), p. 174.
[23] Televised interview with Theodore H. White, September 9, 1980.

nation's fleeting attention. Democratic party leaders still shudder when they think of the drawn-out squabblings over the 1972 vice-presidential nomination, a delay that left George McGovern making his acceptance speech at 3 a.m. — long after most TV viewers had gone to bed. Still, what this leaves us — stage-managed shows of party unity that encourage commentators to attempt to drum up a little excitement — is not a great bargain. Advances in communications and travel technology may have left the conventions with diminished roles in choosing and publicizing the party candidates.

Writing the Platform. A third convention (and preconvention) activity is writing the party's *platform,* a set of positions and goals that the party endorses. The conventional wisdom of politics plays down the importance of party platforms. The sentiments of David Truman are typical:

> The platform is generally regarded as a document that says little, binds no one, and is forgotten by politicians as quickly as possible after it is adopted. . . . Considered as a pledge of future action, the party platform is almost meaningless and is properly so regarded by the voters.[24]

Indeed, few voters ever read the platform statements. Nevertheless, each of the major parties has suffered divisive battles over platform proposals, such as the 1976 struggle between the Ford and Reagan forces over whether to endorse a strong stand against surrendering control of the Panama Canal. If the platforms go unread, then why do fierce disputes develop over them?

First, party positions as presented in the platform may have a greater effect on policy decisions than is commonly believed. For instance, Gerald Pomper has found that policy statements included in the party platform of the minority party have more often than not been enacted, even if the electorate as a whole pays little attention to specific provisions.[25]

Second, platforms indicate those broad bases of electoral support most important to a party at a given time. They allow the activists, the candidates, and interested spectators a chance to see what policies are currently acceptable to the party as a whole. Today's struggles over platform "planks" are often tomorrow's legislative battles. Consider civil rights, for example. The 1948 Democratic convention produced a bitter fight over an antidiscrimination plank, ending with a walkout by the southern "Dixiecrat" faction and the emergence of Hubert Humphrey, then a Senate candidate, as a national leader in the civil rights movement. This platform controversy was the opening skirmish of a battle that was to rage, with increasing intensity, for the next twenty years.

Although platform fights can be divisive, the platform-writing process can

[24] David B. Truman, *The Governmental Process* (New York: Knopf, 1951), pp. 282–83.
[25] Gerald M. Pomper, with Susan S. Lederman, *Elections in America,* 2nd ed. (New York: Longmans, 1980), chap. 8.

Political Conventions

Every four years Americans are treated to the spectacle of a pair of party conventions. In one way, these quadrennial gatherings have lost some of their importance; not since 1952 has the voting for a party's presidential nominee gone beyond a single ballot. In fact, the candidates usually have won the party nomination before the convention convenes. These often-tumultuous events remain important for various other reasons, however. Each party, for instance, hammers out a platform on which its presidential candidate will run. Both parties have experienced heated debates over numerous platform planks, ranging from abortion to welfare reform to ratification of the Panama Canal Treaty.

Conventions also provide party activists an unparalleled opportunity to get to know each other, to exchange views, and to renew old acquaintances. The parties are, in a sense, restored every four years. In addition, conventions allow the parties a chance to present themselves to the American people, who, by watching the proceedings on television, may glean some notion of how the parties might deal with the important issues of the next four years.

also help to hold together various groups of party loyalists. The unifying potential of the platform is great; as Herbert Agar observes,

> A Senator, or a state legislator, or a city boss, can go proudly home to his people as a power in the party, as a man who must still be reckoned with, if he can show that although he did not get the presidential or the vice-presidential candidate of his choice, his favorite "plank" was included in the platform.[26]

In 1980 the Republicans, conservative to the core (see Table 11.3), could easily write a platform that virtually all the delegates could endorse. The Democrats, however, produced a platform considerably more liberal than were the policies generally espoused by President Carter. The platform planks served both to soothe the bruised feelings of Senator Kennedy's supporters and to bring the senator back into the party fold. Indeed, Kennedy campaigned vigorously for a Carter reelection, in part because the party platform allowed him to move beyond merely supporting many of the president's more moderate positions.

There are no guarantees that a convention will successfully rebuild the party coalition, as has been amply demonstrated by the nominations of Goldwater, Humphrey, and McGovern. In 1964 supporters of Senator Goldwater shut out Republican moderates from both the nomination and the platform-building process; the moderates responded by giving the conservative ticket only half-hearted support. Similarly, the Vietnam War, with its domestic repercussions of protest and student unrest, created divisions among Democrats that went unbridged in both 1968 and 1972. Dissident Democrats (Kennedy supporters) in 1980 and disenchanted Republicans (Reagan supporters) in 1976 generally backed their party's nominee, but convention rhetoric and camaraderie could scarcely heal the wounds of months of rough campaigning.

Conventions do not necessarily excite, energize, or bind together the party base within the electorate. The voters must evaluate their party's choices in a broader social context. It is this "party-in-the-electorate" that must provide the base of popular support for both the party organization and the party in government. In an era of declining trust for all political institutions, this is a tall order.

THE PARTY IN THE ELECTORATE   Above all else, the partisan attachment or identification among the electorate generally is what gives political parties their coherence, continuity, and influence. In Chapter 10 we discussed the role of citizen partisan preferences in deciding their votes; but partisanship is more than just a voting cue.

Some of the electorate's partisan predispositions are weakening — leading more and more people to split their tickets and fewer and fewer to vote at all. In addition, even though a majority of Americans call themselves Democrats or Republicans, most citizens have little direct contact with political parties.

---

[26] Herbert Agar, *The Price of Union* (Boston: Houghton Mifflin, 1950), p. 348.

As we noted in Chapter 10 on elections, television advertising has become the most popular way of reaching large numbers of voters; in 1980, less than 30 percent of "likely voters" were contacted either in person, by telephone, or through the mail by *any* presidential campaign worker.[27] In the past, political machines maintained continuing contact with citizens, at least in cities where precinct captains and ward heelers often made the local party as important an institution as the parish Catholic church. With a few notable exceptions, such as the Chicago Democratic organization, such regularized direct contact between citizen and party is a relic of the past.

Television coverage of partisan activities (conventions, campaigns, some congressional hearings, etc.) seem to offer us direct contact between ourselves and the parties; but we are increasingly cast as spectators, not participants. Even when activists canvass door to door, they are more and more likely to seek our support for a single candidate in a single race, rather than for a party slate.

Citizens do have *indirect* contact with parties through the news media — TV, radio, newspapers, magazines — which present much information about partisan office holders and candidates and, to a lesser extent, about party matters themselves. Party officials do not get information in return from the citizenry (except for the occasional poll result, letter, or phone call). In the longer run, however, party officials hear from citizens in the form of votes, for a citizen's voting behavior is shaped by the information he or she receives.

The information that citizens receive indirectly affects their attitudes toward partisanship. In the post-Vietnam, post-Watergate political world, much of this information is negative. As a result, younger voters increasingly opt for "independent" status and skepticism toward the major parties rather than adopting the partisan loyalties of their parents. As Crotty and Jacobson conclude,

> Any change toward increased partisanship by the new voters of the last decade is unlikely. The point cannot be proven, obviously, but it is likely that strong partisanship for older voters is a product of the time and political conditions in which they entered the electorate. Different generations of voters are socialized in different states of political party significance. As they mature their political ties become stronger. New voters have weaker ties. The political situation at present encourages independence; the political parties do not attract the new voters. Unless there is some unforeseen unheaval, these conditions are not likely to change. Partisanship is dying. The strongest party identifiers are consistently being phased out of the electorate. Time is on the side of the independents.[28]

Some recent campaign-law modifications may improve the parties' abilities to attract the uncommitted. In 1980 Congress removed all limitations on state and local party funds raised and spent for registration, get-out-the-vote activi-

---

[27] Report of NBC News/Associated Press survey, *Public Opinion*, December–January 1981, p. 44.

[28] William J. Crotty and Gary C. Jacobson, *American Parties in Decline* (Boston: Little, Brown, 1980), pp. 40–41.

ties, and some campaign material. The Republicans in particular have taken great advantage of this freedom. Many state parties hosted fund-raising events by the presidential and vice-presidential candidates, who benefited in turn from the parties' organizational efforts. As we have noted, the Republicans have led the way in providing their candidates with costly and sophisticated services in large numbers. Although Democrats outnumber Republicans within the electorate by about a 3-to-2 margin, Republicans have historically been much more active participants in the political process, both as financial supporters and as workers.

These prospects for either stronger identification or greater participation are bucking the overall trend toward ever weaker ties between the party and the electorate. The party in the electorate is not something tangible but, rather, a state of mind shared by an indeterminate number of voters — and we cannot read the voters' minds. The available evidence shows, however, that the citizens' strong attachments to parties are weakening. Party identification has declined markedly over the last twenty years, and today's party organizations lack the personnel and other resources to make frequent contact with the citizenry. Strong groups of partisan identifiers in the electorate have been the base of the American political parties since the 1830s; this base may no longer be secure.

HOW CITIZENS VIEW POLITICAL PARTIES

As we have seen, Americans are often indifferent to, and sometimes suspicious of, their political parties, even though the parties attempt to provide regular connections between the electorate and the government. Not only are citizens currently suspicious of parties, but such hostility has roots in our founding, and offshoots throughout our political history. This widespread public skepticism seriously threatens the parties' ability to link citizens and leaders at all effectively.

Citizens express their attitudes about political parties both in what they *say* (to pollsters and others) and in what they *do* (in the voting booth). When asked directly how they feel about parties, citizens have voiced little confidence in their performance. Simultaneously, there has been a rise in the number of self-proclaimed independents (now almost 40 percent of the electorate), who profess no party ties. These trends indicate widespread public skepticism toward the value of parties as useful political "signposts." Other data confirm the low levels of citizen confidence. Between 1964 and 1974, for example, support for keeping party labels on the general-election ballot fell from two-thirds of the public to less than 40 percent. Likewise, most voters reject the notion that parties "help a good deal . . . in making the government pay attention to what the people want."[29]

The electorate's declining reliance on party cues in voting also illustrates

[29] See Jack Dennis, "Trends in Public Support for the American Party System," *British Journal of Political Science* 5 (1974): 204.

the general skepticism toward political parties. In 1980 Jimmy Carter won only 66 percent of the total Democratic vote. One of every three self-proclaimed Democrats turned his or her back on the party candidate — hardly an auspicious performance.

Other actions of the electorate reinforce this conclusion. First, voting turnouts are low and have dropped steadily over the past twenty years. Only a little more than half the electorate (53 percent) voted in the 1980 presidential election, compared with 61 percent in 1960. In off-year (nonpresidential) elections, the turnout is even lower. Less than two voters of every five cast ballots in the 1978 congressional elections. The parties' nominees, both presidential and congressional, are failing to attract large segments of the population to the polls.

Second, as we noted in Chapter 10, voters are "splitting their tickets" in record numbers. Utah voters, for instance, gave Ronald Reagan a massive margin (73 percent to 21 percent) over Jimmy Carter in 1980; they returned Republican Senator Jake Garn to office with 74 percent of the vote; yet they elected Democrat Scott Matheson to the governorship in a 55 percent to 45 percent count over his GOP opponent. These citizens voted for the candidates they saw as most qualified, regardless of party label.

Neither public attitudes nor voting trends demonstrate much contemporary support for political parties. This lack of support can only make the parties' task of linking citizens to the government more difficult — a problem that may further increase the public's skepticism toward the parties in the future.

AMERICAN PARTY SYSTEMS: PAST, PRESENT, AND FUTURE

Unlike many other Western democracies, such as Italy, France, and Germany, the United States traditionally has nurtured only two major political parties. Most other democracies have multiparty systems, each party representing a single political faction. Thus, in the wake of elections, coalition governments are often formed by two or more parties that share power.

Why have we not experienced similar party fragmentation? Although there is no simple or complete answer, several reasons exist. First, we choose our most important office holders by *plurality elections* in *single-member districts*, as was noted in Chapter 10. The winner of the general election is that candidate who receives the most votes (a plurality); there are no second or third prizes. Thus, to ensure a win in such an election, a candidate often needs a majority of the vote. This feature of our electoral system has favored the development of two parties.

Second, many observers have noted a *natural dualism* in the United States. It began with a split between eastern merchants/financiers and western frontiersmen/farmers in the early 1800s and changed to a North-South tension from the Civil War on. Yet underlying such sectional differences has been a broad *social consensus* that accepts the basic American rules of the game — ranging from the rule of law under the Constitution to the free-enterprise economic system. The issues separating Americans, with rare exceptions, have not been so divisive as to rule out compromise.

Within this setting of social consensus, natural dualisms, and institutional mechanisms such as single-member districts and plurality elections, Americans formed two conglomerate, majority-seeking parties. Once launched, the parties perpetuated themselves by creating strong identifications within the electorate and by acting as forces of moderation and compromise in a society that highly values those qualities.

The Two-Party System and Political Change

Since the creation of a two-party system of Federalists and Republican-Democrats in the 1790s, American political parties have time and again exhibited tremendous capabilities for survival. The price of this survival has been change, and those parties that could not adapt to new issues or attract new followers, such as the Federalists in the early 1800s and the Whigs in the 1850s, have been replaced by more vigorous and electorally successful alternatives (see Table 11.5)

What, exactly, do we mean by a two-party system? The important characteristics are that (1) two major parties share most of the votes and elective offices and (2) each of the two dominant parties periodically wins elections. Some states, notably in the South, have traditionally been dominated by a single party (the Democrats). At the national level, however, we have had continuous and strong two-party competition since the early 1800s. This competition has forced the parties to attune themselves to the citizenry, at least when major, society-wide issues are at stake. The resulting balance of power in American politics has produced a series of partisan regroupings at remarkably regular intervals.

Typical of such a change was the Republican party's pre–Civil War replacement of the Whigs. The Whigs, a loosely knit coalition of northern merchants, farmers, and southern gentry, could not come to terms with the slavery issue. The Republicans coalesced into a major party around their opposition to slavery, and their meteoric rise to national office (founded in 1854, they captured the presidency in 1860) was the last instance of a major party being replaced by a new, third party.

American political parties represent coalitions of interests. Indeed, one of their chief functions is bringing together diverse groups and philosophies under a single banner. Such coalition building is vital for electoral success, and a party's support for a set of fundamental issue positions also provides a rallying point for diverse interests. But party coalitions that exist merely to win elections, such as the Whigs, find it difficult to remain unified in the face of an extremely divisive issue (e.g., slavery) that cuts across the party's base of support.

Although most Americans do not expect their politics to be heavily laden with issues, parties must take a stand on important new problems or risk losing a crucial part of their electoral support. As James Sundquist and Walter

Table 11.5 The Five American Party Systems and Their Major
Characteristics

1. The Experimental System, 1789–1820. Major Parties: Federalists, Republican-Democrats	Relatively few activists, better organized at national level than in states or towns. Party divisions based largely on foreign policy grounds. Rival parties identify "the national good with their own partisan views."
2. The Democratizing System, 1828–54/60. Major Parties: Democrats, Whigs	Emphasis on mobilizing large numbers of grassroots supporters. Presidential nomination by conventions. Higher rates of participation. Parties more election oriented in their goals.
3. The Civil War System, 1860–93. Major Parties: Democrats, Republicans	Explicitly sectional party lines (post-1876 solid Democratic South); extremely close elections nationally. Great political strength held by industrializing elites.
4. The Industrialist System, 1894–1932. Major Parties: Democrats, Republicans	Extreme sectionalism (South still solidly Democratic); Republicans dominate national elections. Industrial elites, mostly Republican, insulated from political attacks of working classes.
5. The New Deal System, 1932–present? Major Parties: Democrats, Republicans	Nationalization of party voting and alignment, with Democrats dominant, especially at subpresidential levels. Much partisan deadlock after 1952 between Republican presidents and Democratic Congresses.

Source: Data based on *The American Party Systems: Stages of Political Development*, 2nd ed., by William Nisbet Chambers and Walter Dean Burnham. Copyright © 1975 by Oxford University Press, Inc. Reprinted by permission.

Burnham have carefully documented, party systems are not static.[30] As issues emerge, parties and candidates must cope with them or face the possibility of being abandoned by the electorate.

[30] Walter Dean Burnham, *Critical Elections and the Mainsprings of American Politics* (New York: Norton, 1970); and James L. Sundquist, *Dynamics of the Party System* (Washington, D.C.: Brookings, 1973), esp. chaps. 13, 14.

Party Realignments *Party realignment* is the term frequently used to describe this process of widespread political change. Most simply, such realignment is a lasting alteration in patterns of political behavior. Realignment also can be seen as a visible manifestation of political disarray: The parties respond publicly to social unrest by making changes in their nomination of candidates, writing of platforms, and attempts to govern. Not only the party's organization but also its office holders and its electorate all must react to changing political conditions. The stakes during a period of realignment are high, and great uncertainty arises over which party will emerge as the dominant force in organizing the government and setting the nation's political agenda.

One of the most interesting facets of American party systems has been the almost clocklike regularity with which the partisan balance of power has shifted over the past 180 years. As Burnham has pointed out, "Crucial realignments have historically been periodically recurring phenomena, with peaks spaced approximately 36 to 38 years apart."[31] Has this regular recurrence been just coincidence? Or is there something in the way parties operate, perhaps in the way they try to build coalitions, that dictates such a cyclical pattern? This is not simply idle speculation: The last major realignment was completed in 1936, and we appear overdue for a substantial alteration.

No current evidence points to a pervasive change like the GOP ascension to a period of dominance in 1896 or the Democratic turnabout in 1932. But neither have we enjoyed "politics as usual." For example, between 1954 and 1976, Democrats captured both houses of Congress at every election, but controlled the presidency for only eight years — scarcely the mark of a successful majority party. In addition, George Wallace's American party won almost 15 percent of the 1968 presidential vote, indicating substantial dissatisfaction with the two major parties. As previously mentioned, both presidential and congressional election turnouts have decreased steadily over the past twenty years, to the point that only 53 percent of the electorate voted in 1980.

Add to these trends an increasing reluctance of most voters to call themselves "liberal" and the growing skepticism of citizens toward party politics, and one might conclude that the era of Democratic dominance, ushered in by Franklin D. Roosevelt's administration, is over. Yet no obvious replacement has emerged. Indeed, scholars and practicing politicians alike disagree heatedly over the shape of any developing party system. Some fascinating possibilities do arise, however. Let us look at five of them.

An Emerging Republican Majority? Some conservatives have argued that a coming realignment will favor a Republican party centered on an explicitly conservative philosophy. The strength of American conservatism extends beyond the bounds of the Republican party. One 1980 survey found that only 17

---

[31] Walter Dean Burnham, "American Politics in the 1970s: Beyond Party?" in William Nisbet Chambers and Walter Dean Burnham, eds. *The American Party Systems*, 2nd ed. (New York: Oxford University Press, 1975), pp. 309–310; see also Ladd and Hadley, *Transformations of The American Party System*, 2nd ed., (New York: Norton, 1978).

percent of the population was willing to be called "liberal," whereas 28 percent felt comfortable with the "conservative" label. Ronald Reagan fashioned a conservative-moderate coalition in winning the 1980 presidential election, and many of his appeals went directly to the heart of the Democrats' blue-collar constituency.

In the wake of its 1980 presidential and congressional election victories, the Republican party must be concerned with grasping possibilities for becoming a majority party. No independent group seems capable of organizing a strong, conservative third-party challenge. Rather, most observers would probably agree with Richard Scammon and Ben Wattenberg, who see the continuing need to "capture the center" of American politics as crucial to any GOP-dominated realignment. They write:

> a Republican realignment would do those things Americans have already decided they want done. That is reinforced by the likelihood that any realignment, although viewed historically as a sudden break at a particular election, is more likely to be a process than an event. [Reagan's election], for example, . . . could be a first step, but sustainable only if Republican policies were deemed worthy by specific groups. Remember, blacks voted for Hoover in 1932 — not for FDR until 1936. Republican prime targets in the eighties would be Southerners, union members, ethnics, Jews — yet they can add numbers if and only if they stay near the potent center.[32]

A New Party? Since the 1850s, when the Republican party replaced the Whigs, the two major American parties have remained dominant, though not unchallenged. Scarcely a decade has gone by without a serious attempt to supplant one of the major parties, but the record shows that such efforts have little chance of success.[33] Most third-party efforts have arisen at the presidential level; George Wallace's American Independent party won 13.5 percent of the 1968 popular vote for president but had virtually no impact on state or local election outcomes. In almost all instances, third parties play one or both of two roles: (1) to articulate issues or to protest conditions that the major parties have ignored and (2) to serve as vehicles for individual candidates who have lost (or failed to contest) a major-party nomination. The Populist party of the 1890s illustrates the former role, whereas Theodore Roosevelt's Progressive (Bull Moose) party falls into the latter category. The American-Independent party combines the roles, in that Wallace, seeing that he could not hope to win the Democratic nomination, formed a third party to "send a message to Washington" in opposition to much of the liberal social policy of the 1960s.

[32] "Is It an End of an Era?" *Public Opinion*, October–November 1980, p. 12.

[33] Third parties clearly have roles other than that of displacing a major party. As Daniel Mazmanian notes: "Third parties dramatize and help to crystallize minority positions on issues. Unimpaired by continuing commitments or the need to seek the middle of the road, they have repeatedly forced controversies into the open, compelling the major parties to respond." See Mazmanian, *Third Parties in Presidential Elections* (Washington, D.C.: Brookings, 1974), p. 4.

Prior to the 1980 election, many conservative strategists aggressively advocated the formation of a new party that would hew faithfully to conservative principles. Such a movement might attract a great many Republicans, a host of Democratic conservatives, various independents, and some apolitical individuals who felt unrepresented by the ongoing parties. The election of Ronald Reagan, a genuine conservative, has effectively halted many of these plans. Even without Reagan's election, however, in practical terms the creation of a new party truly capable of displacing a major party is an extraordinarily difficult task. This is especially true because contemporary parties are more easily taken over from the inside than overwhelmed from the outside (see the later discussion of political parties as "empty vessels").

A Reinvigorated Democratic Coalition?   In the 1930s Franklin D. Roosevelt constructed a strong, broad electoral coalition composed of the South, various ethnic groups, labor unions, blacks, Catholics, intellectuals, and the poor. This alliance, commonly called the New Deal coalition, provided Roosevelt's base of support in his four presidential victories. But in presidential elections since the late 1940s, voters from many of the coalition's groups have defected in large numbers. Although many more citizens identify themselves as Democrats than as Republicans, neither Hubert Humphrey in 1968 nor George McGovern in 1972 got over 44 percent of the total popular vote for president. Many southerners deserted the Democratic party in the 1940s and 1950s. Still other crucial elements of Roosevelt's New Deal coalition, such as ethnics, Catholics, and labor union members, left the party's presidential ranks in 1972, when McGovern won only Massachusetts and the District of Columbia. The election of Jimmy Carter to the presidency temporarily reversed the disintegration of the traditional Democratic coalition, but his 1980 election defeat, in which he received only 42 percent of the popular votes, bodes ill for any major reconstruction.

As we have seen, in 1980 Democrats failed to rally many elements of their basic coalition, such as labor, Catholics, Jews, and the poor (see Table 11.6). These defections, however, may simply be symptoms of the current weakness of key New Deal notions of governmental intervention and increased federal spending. If, as an out-party, the Democrats can develop new ideas and instill a renewed sense of purpose into their efforts, they might well engender a new coalition strong in both philosophy and electoral possibilities.

Parties as "Empty Vessels?"   In 1972 and 1976, the Democratic party selected George McGovern and Jimmy Carter, respectively, as its presidential candidates. Was the Democratic party of 1976 the same as that of 1972? For the most part, it was. But, as we noted earlier, different segments of the party's activists and voters dominated the nomination process in the different years. Such adaptability has always been a part of American party politics, but never, perhaps, a more important part than at present.

As one unabashed defender of American parties notes:

Table 11.6   The Disintegrating Democratic Coalition, 1976–80

Coalition Groups	Percentage of Group Voting for Carter	
	1976	1980
Liberals (self-identified)	70	57
Southerners	54	44
Blacks	82	82
Hispanics	75	54
Catholics	54	40
Jews	64	45
Less than $10,000 annual income	58	50
$10,000–15,000 annual income	55	47
Blue-collar workers	57	46
Labor union households	59	47

Source: CBS/*New York Times* exit poll, November 4, 1980. © 1980 by The New York Times Company. Reprinted by permission.

It seems to me the beauty of our two party system is that the two parties are not rigid or doctrinaire or terribly ideological. They are pretty much empty vessels, and because of the unique nature of our primary system, these . . . empty vessels can accept any color liquid you choose to put in them.[34]

Our understanding of political parties is enhanced by following up on this imagery. The Republicans, for instance, took on a particularly conservative shading with Goldwater's 1964 nomination; likewise, with their selection of George McGovern, the Democrats took on an especially liberal coloration in 1972. The strength of both the Carter and Reagan candidacies illustrates the very real opportunities for party outsiders to capture a major party's presidential nomination.

In other electoral arenas, many outsiders have penetrated the ranks of the party regulars. An obscure but colorful university president, Lee Dreyfus, won the Wisconsin governorship; Senator Lawton Chiles, as a political unknown, first won election to the Senate by walking across Florida; and airline pilot Gordon Humphrey gained a New Hampshire Senate seat in his initial campaign for public office. Dreyfus and Humphrey ran as Republicans, Chiles as a Democrat; but their respective state parties were little more than shells, waiting to be filled in, during a statewide campaign.

For the foreseeable future, parties are likely to continue to attract relatively small groups of activists — narrow bases of support. In the midst of cam-

[34] Ben Wattenberg, quoted in *National Journal Reports*, May 31, 1975, p. 811.

paigns, the backers of major candidates may well "take over" the party, perhaps changing its character, as the Goldwaterites changed the Republican party in 1964 and the McGovernites altered the Democratic party in 1972. In the aftermath of a campaign, however, the base of working partisans tends to shrink back to a core of activists. This shrinkage is inevitable, given the lack of incentives the party can offer to the only occasionally active citizenry.

This decline in the number of dedicated party activists has paralleled the decline of committed partisan voters. At the same time, activists and citizens have increasingly come to think of politics in terms of issues. Thus both parties are open to capture by issue-oriented factions. For the Republicans, well-organized conservatives have been in control of the national party since Barry Goldwater won the presidential nomination in 1964. The flexible nature of the Democratic "vessel" has led to fierce primary-election competition between liberal and moderate activists at both state and national levels. The 1980 Carter-Kennedy confrontation for the presidential nomination was only one in a series of battles that periodically divide the Democrats.

If Republicans and Democrats continue on this "narrow-base" footing, there will be a substantial alteration in the meaning of party. With fewer reliable party voters and with an organization susceptible to capture by a narrowly based faction, the parties will continually react to ongoing political change. The politics of the 1960s and 1970s may well have produced a realignment, but without any obvious alteration in the balance of party power. Rather, the role of American parties as linkages between the citizenry and its elected officials may have been inalterably weakened. This version of a realignment, therefore, would be unique in affecting the balance of power *against* parties, not *between* them.

Politics without Parties? The notion of American politics without parties sounds outlandish. Parties have been an integral part of our history, and they continue to be regarded as important political forces. Yet, given the current distrust of parties, the increasing independence of voters, and the ability of candidates to conduct campaigns without much party assistance, such a possibility may not be so far fetched. According to Walter Dean Burnham, it may already be happening: "We start with the premise that the United States is now living through a critical realignment to end all critical realignments in the traditional meaning of the term. *This is a realignment whose essence is the end of two-party politics* in the traditional understanding."[35] Burnham envisions American party politics as "decomposing," with the increasingly independent electorate encouraging candidates and elected officials to reduce their reliance on party backing. Party organization would eventually wither away, playing no important role in linking citizens to their government.

The implications of a politics without meaningful parties are striking, es-

[35] Burnham, "American Politics," p. 308; see also Carll Everett Ladd's discussion of "dealignment" in *Public Opinion*, October–November 1980, pp. 13–15.

pecially in terms of the public's ties to its rulers. One possibility is the development of a new political phenomenon, made up of a temporary coalition of voters, united around a single major issue, but dissolving and reforming as the major issues changed. This would be very similar to some tactics used by interest groups in mobilizing "grass-roots" support on a specific issue (see Chapter 12).

Less optimistic about any kind of effective citizen linkage is Burnham, who sees the end of effective political parties as a signal to societal elites (whoever controls money, skills, and opportunities) that they can dominate policymaking without much intervention from partisan forces. As Burnham pessimistically observes, "The old-style American major party-in-the-electorate may very well be on its way out as a channel through which the collective power of the many can at least occasionally control the behavior of the elites who run the political system."[36]

CONCLUSION   We have considered political parties as one of the main potential links between citizens, their leaders, and political institutions. Do parties actually fulfill this function today? In an era when political party organizations possess a fraction of their former power, when mass identification with parties has sharply declined, when divided party control of government is commonplace, what can we conclude about the role of parties in American politics?

First, parties are often ignored. Voters use party cues less regularly than in the past; candidates often campaign apart from the party organization; elected officials make little policy that is clearly partisan. Second, parties are distrusted. The public is skeptical both of the value of parties and of the quality of party-based bonds between citizens and rulers. In addition, the ties that have bound the party in government to the party organization and the organization to the party in the electorate are weakening steadily. All the elements of the "three-part" political party are in disrepair, and many observers feel that parties will continue to diminish in importance.

We should be skeptical, however, of those who foresee a quick demise for American parties. Even though some scholars see the parties as decomposing, we agree with Sundquist's statement that "You can't win an election or run the government as a group of unorganized individuals; the individuals are going to organize and at that point where they organize, they are a party."[37]

The question is not so much *whether* parties will survive, but *how* they will survive — in what form. Of the alternative futures for parties noted previously, the image of political parties as empty vessels seems most accurately to capture their nature in our changing society. The quality of the linkage be-

---

[36] Burnham, "American Politics," p. 349.

[37] James L. Sundquist, in Jonathan Moore and Albert Pierce, eds., *Voters, Primaries, and Parties* (Cambridge, Mass.: Institute of Politics, Harvard University, 1976), p. 39.

tween citizens and their officials will depend in part on which party activists gain the right to pour their political wine into the empty party vessels. American parties thus remain open to change, as they must if they are to be capable of offering alternative sets of rulers and ideas to a skeptical, yet still partisan, electorate.

SUGGESTIONS FOR FURTHER READING

Burnham, Walter Dean. *Critical Elections and the Mainsprings of American Politics.* New York: Norton, 1970. Burnham's thesis of a decomposing American party system has set the stage for many of the controversies over the roles of parties in the 1970s.

Chambers, William Nisbet, and Burnham, Walter Dean, eds. *The American Party Systems: Stages of Political Development,* 2nd ed. New York: Oxford University Press, 1975. An excellent set of essays on the development of and prospects for the American party system.

Crotty, William, and Jacobson, Gary. *American Parties in Decline.* Boston: Little, Brown, 1980. A first-rate, brief survey of the continuing weakness of American parties.

Ladd, Everett Carll, with Charles Hadley. *Transformations of the American Party System.* 2nd ed. New York: Norton, 1978. Examination of changing coalition bases of the parties.

Ranney, Austin. *Curing the Mischiefs of Faction: Party Reform in America.* Berkeley: University of California Press, 1975. Ranney perceptively traces the attempts of political parties to reform themselves. This is particularly apt in light of Democratic party reforms of the past decade.

Sorauf, Frank J. *Party Politics in America,* 4th ed. Boston: Little, Brown, 1980. The best current text on political parties. Sorauf is both comprehensive and insightful.

Sundquist, James L. *Dynamics of the Party System.* Washington, D.C.: Brookings, 1973. This is the most complete theoretical treatment of the realignment process, brought to life with three extended historical examples.

Tolchin, Martin, and Tolchin, Susan. *To the Victor: Political Patronage from the Clubhouse to the White House.* New York: Vintage, 1972. The best recent treatment of patronage politics.

Chapter 12   Interest Groups

Like political parties and elections, interest groups help link citizens to those who rule them — but with some marked differences. Parties, especially during election campaigns, seek to build broad coalitions within the electorate and to play down differences among their various subgroups. Interest groups, by contrast, usually represent narrow concerns that parties may gloss over. In this chapter we will look closely at interest groups and examine their accomplishments and shortcomings in linking parts of our society to the decision-making process.

WHAT IS AN INTEREST GROUP? What do we mean by an interest group? One leading scholar, David Truman, sees it as "any group that, on the basis of one or more shared attitudes, makes certain claims upon other groups in the society."[1]

This definition has two key components. First comes the essence of an interest — *shared attitudes*. Executives in the American auto industry, for example, work for different companies, but share certain attitudes about the role of the automobile in the nation's economy and in American life. The country's

---

[1] David B. Truman, *The Governmental Process* (New York: Knopf, 1951), p. 33.

gun enthusiasts belong to different political parties, profess different religions, have different jobs, enjoy different pastimes, and hold different views on everything from capital punishment to rock music. But most of them share at least one attitude or concern — that there should be a minimum of government restrictions on the citizen's right to bear arms.

The second key component of our definition is *making claims on other groups*. The auto companies seek, and often get, certain things they want from other groups: certain provisions in their contracts with labor unions, compromises on air pollution standards from the federal government, and so on. Making claims requires some degree of *organization* by which to coordinate and press those claims on other groups. Thus, the country's several million gun owners are not an interest group, but the million or so who belong to the National Rifle Association are.

An interest group becomes political when it makes claims on the government or on other groups through the government. The auto industry, for example, has recently sought both to limit the number of cars imported each year (a claim on other interests through the government) and to eliminate many allegedly unnecessary and expensive regulations (a claim on the government itself).

Interest groups are generally organized formally. Although some interests, like auto manufacturers, do not require much organization outside their own large corporate structures, most interests find it essential to organize. The shared attitudes of gun enthusiasts, environmentalists, doctors, or lawyers are expressed through formal interest groups, whose representatives, called lobbyists, can communicate their members' needs to governmental policymakers. As Ziegler and Baer note, "Interest groups are 'transmission belts' between individual needs and governmental institutions."[2] In short, groups provide links between interests and decision makers.

Traditionally, interest groups have been viewed as selfish, as seeking narrow and sometimes unfair advantages. As was noted in Chapter 2, America's Founding Fathers warned of the dangers of factions. James Madison wrote in *The Federalist* No. 10:

> By a faction, I understand a number of citizens, whether amounting to a majority or a minority of the whole, who are united and actuated by some common impulse of passion, or of interest, adverse to the rights of other citizens, or to the permanent and aggregate interests of the community.

In discussing "factions," Madison meant what we mean by "interest group" today, although he also viewed the political parties of his era as a species of faction. Madison saw the existence of factions as perfectly natural and predictable. At the same time, factions, though free from direct controls, needed to be checked — largely by (1) encouraging competition among them and (2)

---

[2] Harmon Ziegler and Michael A. Baer, *Lobbying: Interaction and Influence in American State Legislatures* (Belmont, Calif.: Wadsworth, 1969), pp. 2–3.

using the separation of powers, dual legislative chambers, and federalism to reduce the potential of one group to embrace a majority of citizens, who then might run roughshod over minority factions.

Such negative views of interest groups were also common throughout the nineteenth century. They are reflected, for example, in the words of a New York State judge who in 1855 complained about a system in which legislators and executive officials were "surrounded by swarms of hired retainers of the claimants upon public bounty or justice."[3] Such views persist today. Many journalists, reformers, and ordinary citizens still look at interest groups with alarm, suspicion, or cynicism. Typical of such sentiments is a recent Common Cause report:

> The Special Interest State is a system in which interest groups dominate the making of government policy. These interests legitimately concentrate on pursuing their own immediate — usually economic — agendas, but in so doing they pay little attention to the impact of their agendas on the nation as a whole.[4]

In recent years, however, many other people, including numerous political scientists and politicians, have come to the defense of groups' legitimate activities. They reason that if all interest groups can enter the political fray with roughly balanced resources, then equitable policy decisions will be made. Yet this ideal of a pluralist society remains largely just that — an ideal. Some interests' resources and ties to the government are much stronger than others', and policy decisions often reflect these inequalities. Interest-group politics is, above all, the politics of obtaining and maintaining access to important governmental policymakers. Some groups are more successful at it than others. And those with the best access usually have the best chance of pressing their claims successfully — that is, the best chance of influencing policy in the directions that will most benefit their members.

Both the public at large and political analysts, then, express mixed feelings about the role of interest groups in American politics; these are summarized as follows:

Generally Positive	*Generally Negative*
1. Interest groups are important and useful political organizations in a complex society.	1. Interest groups most often represent "special interests" and should be viewed with suspicion.
2. America is a nation of "joiners," and groups play a great role in holding together our diverse society.	2. There is a distinct social bias to group membership, which tends to favor the upper and middle classes.

[3] From Robert Luce, *Legislative Assemblies* (Boston: Houghton Mifflin, 1924), p. 385. Quoted in Truman, *The Governmental Process*, p. 4.
[4] *The Government Subsidy Squeeze* (Washington: Common Cause, 1980), p. 11.

Generally Positive	*Generally Negative*
3. Although all interests do not possess equal political resources, all are likely to have adequate resources to make their policy desires known to decision makers.	3. Crucial political resources are unequally distributed, and many groups generally lacking in funds, education, or communications skills may be heard weakly, if at all.
4. Tangible benefits of group activity are distributed throughout the society, albeit without perfect equality.	4. Tangible benefits are distributed with great inequality; many groups are systematically shortchanged.
5. Lobbyists pursue group goals by facilitating communications between group members and policymakers.	5. Lobbyists often provide not only information to decision makers, but also enticements in the form of personal favors, campaign contributions, or outright payoffs.
6. Groups play an important role in accurately representing citizens before political decision makers.	6. The top officials, lobbyists, and staff of interest groups often pursue substantially different goals from those of their constituencies.
7. All important political issues are likely to be aired through interest-group activity.	7. Issues related to the interests of *producers* (business, labor) generally receive greater attention than *consumer* interests.
8. One important side benefit of interest-group politics is a general adherence to the "rules of the game," under which political competition is carried out openly and fairly.	8. Interest-group politics often encourages secrecy and bends the "rules of the game."
9. The interplay among interests that are continually forming and reforming coalitions will, in the long run, best serve the "public interest."	9. Narrow interests are usually accorded more attention than groups that claim to represent broader interests. The broadest interest, that of the "public," is impossible to determine, let alone serve.

Regardless of how we will view them — and we will examine many of these views in this chapter — interest groups do link us, in specific ways, to our rulers. Big government and complex problems have bred a profusion of sophisticated interest groups at all levels of government.

The number and diversity of well-established interests is astonishing. As federal programs have grown in scope and number, more and more interests have set up shop in Washington. The Great Society programs initiated by President Johnson brought dozens of education-related organizations to Washington; tough safety, health, and pollution regulations encouraged many industry and trade groups to increase their representation; and an array of cities, counties, and states have opened Washington offices to fight for more federal aid and generally favorable policies. As Stuart Eizenstadt, the Carter administration's top domestic policy advisor, noted:

> We have a fragmented, Balkanized society, with a proliferation of special economic interest groups, each interested only in one domestic program — protecting it, . . . unwilling to have it modified.[5]

Groups with similar interests often band together — sometimes formally under a single umbrella organization (the Clean Air Coalition), but more frequently in informal ways. A single large Washington office building, One DuPont Circle, houses many education organizations. Similarly, the "Hall of the States" building is home to over sixty state offices. "There's symbolic strength in this building," observes one National Governors' association official.[6]

Many interests are well entrenched *within* government circles — at federal, state, and local levels. The National Education Association enjoys strong ties with the Department of Education, as well as with many state education agencies. Likewise, environmentalists have generally built working relationships with the Environmental Protection Agency, as have farm groups — especially the American Farm Bureau Federation — with the Department of Agriculture. The list of such pairings is endless. As Theodore Lowi and others have noted, such a thorough pattern of interest representation may render powerless most would-be advocates of major changes.[7]

President Reagan has challenged this situation with his budget cuts proposals and his desire to reduce many interests' apparent dependence on federal support — ranging from legal services for the poor to automatic increases in subsidies for dairy farmers. Reagan, a conservative, won backing from many quarters for his efforts to loosen the ties between the government and a host of interest groups. Even the liberal *New Republic* editorialized:

> The [Reagan] administration deserves support on most of these cuts from anyone, liberal or conservative, who wants to break up the conspiracy of special interests against the general interest that is strangling our economy.[8]

---

[5] "Special Interests Gaining Power as Voter Disillusionment Grows," *The New York Times*, November 14, 1978.

[6] *National Journal*, September 6, 1980, p. 1437.

[7] See Theodore J. Lowi, *The End of Liberalism*, 2nd ed. (New York: Norton, 1979), for the most complete statement of an immobilized society.

[8] *The New Republic*, February 28, 1981, p. 5.

"Conspiracy" may overstate the case, but interest groups do play major roles in shaping almost all public policies. In fact, groups have become central parts of the policymaking process — frequently providing crucial information and acting as part of the bargaining arrangements that lead to policy decisions. Most groups seek to become part of the policymaking process in order to exert influence on decisions from within. But one relatively new set of groups appears most comfortable and most effective working from the outside; these are *single-issue* groups, which have added new dimensions to interest-group politics.

SINGLE-INTEREST GROUPS: A CHALLENGE TO "POLITICS AS USUAL" Many groups organize around and lobby on single issues, such as the Equal Rights Amendment (ERA) or busing policies; others make campaign contributions to a favored candidate on the basis of the candidate's stand on a single issue. Although some consumer and environmental groups engage in such actions, the vast preponderance of such funds comes from conservative groups. In 1979–80, for example, the National Conservative Political Action Commit-

"*Senator, according to this report, you've been marked for defeat by the A.D.A., the National Rifle Association, the A.F.L.-C.I.O., the N.A.M., the Sierra Club, Planned Parenthood, the World Student Christian Federation, the Clamshell Alliance . . .*"

tee (NCPAC) spent $1.2 million in its attempts to unseat six liberal Democratic senators. These funds went directly into anti-incumbent advertising, and NCPAC's only real function was to defeat selected senators (its candidate won in four of the six races, but it is unclear exactly to what extent NCPAC was responsible).

The Reverend Jerry Falwell, founder of the Moral Majority, and ERA opponent Phyllis Schlafly have become important political figures in recent years, as they have developed vast followings based on wide media exposure on a narrow range of issues. They, and many others like them, differ from traditional "special-interest" representatives, who usually seek some concrete economic advantage. Single-interest groups, be they antiabortionists, nuclear power opponents, clergy who mix fundamentalist religion with political preachments, or opponents of the Panama Canal treaty or the Strategic Arms Limitation Treaty (SALT II), are rarely interested in winning "half a loaf" through compromise. Rather, these groups emphasize absolute answers and a certainty of their convictions that do not allow for compromise on substance.

Such predispositions have direct political consequences. First, there is little room for maneuvering. In discussing one of his 1980 senatorial targets, NCPAC head Terry Dolan stated, "I personally believe [that Senator] Frank Church is a baby killer."[9] Who, Dolan implicitly asks, would deal with such a person?

A related characteristic is the group's focus on emotional issues, such as abortion or busing, which encourages intense involvement by group identifiers. Such intensity, coupled with emotional issues and no sense of compromise, leads single-interest groups to practice a kind of blackmail in dealing with legislators. Antiabortionists, for example, want to know where a legislator stands on "right-to-life" issues — and only those issues. Opponents of busing or the ERA often voice similar sentiments, refusing to acknowledge that politicians must, first of all, confront a wide range of issues and, second, use compromise as an important and essential tool.

To the extent that single-interest groups succeed in electing candidates sympathetic to their concerns, their ability to judge these legislators' performances will be tested severely. As officeholders, they will have to concern themselves with many policies and may discover complexities even on single-issue matters. (Would a Reagan SALT treaty look better than a Carter treaty? How much better?)

President Reagan won strong support from the so-called evangelical Right, but he will have to be very wary of pushing for a constitutional amendment allowing prayers in the public schools. Such a measure would please his evangelical clients but might cost him precious political support in other quarters. Single-issue politics seems more easily practiced outside the government than within it.

[9] L. J. Davis, "Conservatism in America," *Harper's*, October 1980, p. 26.

GROUP GOALS, RESOURCES, AND TECHNIQUES

More than any other political institutions — legislatures, executives, courts, or even political parties — interest groups differ widely in their composition and actions. "Interests" are conventionally defined as shared attitudes, and — as we have seen — an interest group represents the people who share one or more attitudes, or interests. Thus we can expect that doctors or auto workers or firearms enthusiasts will develop organizations to represent their interests. And indeed, the American Medical Association (AMA), the United Auto Workers (UAW), and the National Rifle Association (NRA) are three of the strongest interest groups in our political system.

This does not mean, however, that the primary purpose of such groups need be political. The AMA, the UAW, and the NRA were not originally organized to pursue political goals, nor does political action absorb most of their efforts today. Rather, these groups were first developed to protect and advance the common interests of many individuals, whether the concerns were professional (AMA), economic (UAW), or recreational (NRA). Of course, the goals of the organizations have changed over time, as the government has increasingly entered into health, labor-management, and firearms policymaking; but political activity remains a secondary concern for these three groups, as it does for most interests.

Goals

"No nukes!" "Freedom now!" A shorter workweek. Extra fringe benefits. Fewer imported cars. A stronger national defense. The goals pursued by interest groups are endless in number and diversity. Goals may change, as when long-time adversaries, such as General Motors and the United Auto Workers, unite to fight tough pollution standards or the influx of foreign cars. Goals often help to determine how interest groups will act, and certain regularities do emerge. Two key goal-related aspects of interest-group activity are: (1) breadth and (2) orientation toward positive governmental involvement. A group may emphasize a single goal or a wide array of issues, and its goals may lead the group to encourage or resist governmental intervention (usually at the federal level).

Some groups focus on limited sets of issues. The current goals of the NRA, for example, often relate to its central aim of preventing the government from further regulating the ownership and use of firearms. The Southern Christian Leadership Conference (SCLC) was at its strongest in lobbying singlemindedly against segregation laws. Other groups, such as the AFL-CIO, Common Cause, and the National Association of Manufacturers, take positions on a wide range of issues because their policy goals are more diverse than those of the NRA or ERA opponents (see Figure 12.1).

In addition, most groups are organized around goals that are quite specific and include little active desire for major change away from the status quo. Many such groups represent economic interests, and their desire for change, if any, is for less governmental interference in the private sector. Also, many groups we ordinarily think of as favoring change may find themselves fighting

New Wrinkles in
Interest-Group Politics

Given an array of new tactics, new issues, and
new leaders, American interest-group politics has
changed greatly in recent years. Such leaders as
Phyllis Schlafly, the Rev. Jerry Falwell of the
Moral Majority, and the National Conservative
Political Action Committee's Terry Dolan (all
pictured here) have focused attention on a host
of conservative issues, ranging from abortion to
defeat of the Equal Rights Amendment to defense
policy. Although some liberal groups have also
formed in recent years, it is the new conservatives, like Schlafly, Falwell, and Dolan, who
have taken advantage of television, direct mail,
and mass solicitations to create a variety of
pressure-group organizations.

Although some of these organizations may emphasize a single issue, such as the ERA or opposition to abortion, most groups attend to larger
numbers of issues — often seen through an
ideological lens, whether liberal or conservative.
Many of the new groups emphasize membership
participation and financial support. Thus, some
citizens may be mobilized for the first time — not
by a political party or a candidate for office —
but by a group that seeks particular policies from
the political system.

Figure 12.1 Interest-Group Focus and Orientation to Positive Governmental Intervention

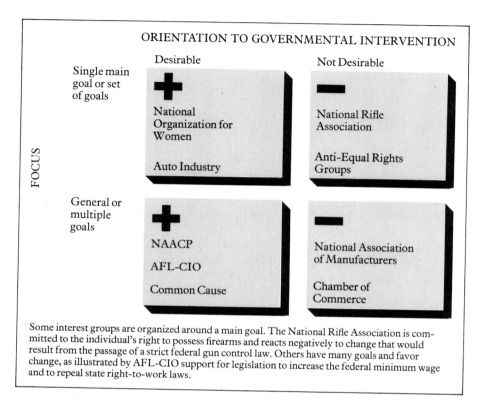

Some interest groups are organized around a main goal. The National Rifle Association is committed to the individual's right to possess firearms and reacts negatively to change that would result from the passage of a strict federal gun control law. Others have many goals and favor change, as illustrated by AFL-CIO support for legislation to increase the federal minimum wage and to repeal state right-to-work laws.

for the status quo once they achieve their basic goals. For instance, in the wake of the passage of civil rights legislation in the 1960s, many black groups are currently working for the enforcement of existing laws rather than pressing for additional legislation.

At one extreme, some groups may be able to exercise an effective "veto" over some key policies. The National Rifle Association and its ability to side-track gun control legislation is the clearest contemporary example, although other groups, ranging from antiabortionists to oil producers, have exercised such power over specific policy proposals and personnel decisions.

The goals we have considered so far are interest groups' "ultimate" objectives — their long-term policy preferences. Nearly all groups have several other goals as well, some of which are common to all of them. These include organizational necessities, such as maximizing membership support while minimizing internal conflicts. Beyond such internal requirements, the most widely shared intermediate goal is continuing *access* to decision makers. Access consists of any channel, formal or informal, by which a group can bring its views to the attention of those with the power to help it achieve its goals. Access may take the form of a campaign contribution, a lobbyist's friendship with a key member of Congress, or a group's testimony before a congressional committee on behalf of a pending bill or on behalf of an executive-sponsored policy proposal. However created, a group's access is crucial to the communications process. The ability to convey information to an important decision maker does not guarantee influence with the decision maker. But without access the chances for receiving a favorable decision are much reduced.

Consider this summary of how groups obtain access to, and influence with, legislators:

> Today's lobbyists . . . are not *buying* congressmen with their money — they are only buying *access*, which can turn out to be just as important. With their access, they are able to tell their side of the story, and, all too often, that is the only version that the congressman will hear in any detail. . . . So, if a group is willing to spend the time and money, it can get just what it wants.[10]

Can we reach any conclusions about a group's goals and how these relate to the group's effectiveness in achieving its desired policies? Recalling the resistance to change that is part of the Congress (Chapter 5) and the bureaucracy (Chapter 7), we might expect groups guarding the status quo to fare better than those advocating political change. Generally this is the case. Change is difficult to accomplish, although groups like the NAACP or Common Cause have had their share of successes.

Second, groups are more likely to achieve narrow, rather than broad or multiple, goals. The National Association of Manufacturers, for instance, wields less power than it might, largely because its member firms find it hard to agree on a single policy agenda. In contrast, the specific goals of sugar producers (high prices, protection from foreign competition) helped them to dominate United States sugar policy for many years.

Finally, regardless of a group's ultimate goals, obtaining regular and easy access to decision makers remains a basic intermediate goal for all groups whose interests are affected by governmental policies.

Resources Access is not achieved in a political vacuum; usually a group's resources determine the amount of attention it gets from policymakers. Whether or not a group's goals are realistic — that is, capable of being achieved — depends less on their merits than on the resources the group can muster in their support. And resources vary almost as much as the specific goals of interest groups.

Money, organization, information, expertise, position, size: These are among the most important conventional resources that groups employ. Obviously they are not evenly distributed among groups hoping to shape policies. The Ford Motor Corporation, for instance, has at its command virtually lim-

[10] Arthur Levine, "Getting to Know Your Congressman: The $500 Understanding," *Washington Monthly,* February 1975, p. 48.

itless financial resources for lobbying. In addition, its combination of information, expertise, and corporate reputation afford it easy access to the councils of government. Conversely, although an active group of poor people may be (but usually is not) large, this potential resource of size requires the discipline of organization before it can have much effect. And organizational strength is difficult to build without substantial communications skills and adequate funding.

Money and Organization. The cost of running for office has risen sharply in recent years. Although presidential campaigns are largely supported by public financing, congressional candidates (and those for state offices) remain dependent on private sources. As expenses have escalated, interest-group involvement in campaigns has grown increasingly important.

The chief vehicle for groups is the political action committee, or PAC. Some PACs, like the AFL-CIO's Committee on Political Education (COPE) have long histories of campaign activity, but most PACs have grown up and flourished in the wake of the 1974 amendments to the Federal Election Campaign Act. Between 1975 and 1979, the number of PACs grew from 608 to 1840. Total PAC spending increased sharply in this same period — from $36.9 million in 1975–76 to $130.3 million in 1979–80 (see Table 12.1).[11] Although

Table 12.1 Total Political Action Committee Spending, in Millions: 1976, 1980 Elections*

Type of Sponsor	1976	1980	Percentage Increase, 1976–80
Labor	17.5	25.0	43
Corporate	5.8	31.8	440
"No-Connected" (often ideological, such as NCPAC or NCEC)	†	37.8	
Trade, Member, Health	†	32.1	
Other	†	3.6	
	36.9	130.3	253

*Figures for 1976 include all spending in the 1975–76 period, 1980 figures are for the 1979–80 period. These expenditures include campaign contributions and independent spending.

†Not computed separately.

Source: Federal Election Commission.

[11] Edwin M. Epstein, "Business and Labor under the Federal Election Campaign Act of 1971," in Michael Malbin, ed., *Parties, Interest Groups and Campaign Finance Laws* (Washington: American Enterprise Institute, 1980).

labor PACs and ideological PACs (such as the conservative Committee for Survival of a Free Congress or the liberal National Committee for an Effective Congress) spend a good deal of this money, it is corporate-sponsored PACs that have grown the most in recent years. In 1974, for example, none of the corporations ranked in the *Fortune* top 500 had established a political action committee. By 1980, 212 of these corporations had done so. Total corporate contributions still lagged behind those of labor, but business interests are becoming more sophisticated in their approach to electoral politics. In both 1978 and 1980, for example, corporate PACs gave, early in the campaign, to incumbents of both parties. This conventional strategy was supplemented by later contributions to (mostly) Republican challengers, who appeared to have a good chance to unseat an incumbent or to win an open seat (where no incumbent was running).

Few analysts claim that interest-group contributions, through PACs, directly buy congressional votes, but as Common Causes's Fred Wertheimer notes,

> It's a question of relationships that get built, obligations and dependencies that get established. It puts PACs at the head of the line, as opposed to the great bulk of a congressman's constituents.[12]

Wertheimer's fears seem justified in light of the growth and patterns of PAC financing, which tend to link major interests with congressional incumbents (see Table 12.1). Such patterns also exist at the state level. As the *Kansas City Times* reported:

> Everybody loves a winner — especially special interest groups. Within a few weeks *after* [emphasis added] state Rep. Bob Griffin was named Speaker of the Missouri House last November (1980), his campaign committee received $12,000 in donations from more than 50 political action committees, lobbying organizations and individual lobbyists tied to various business and labor concerns.[13]

To the extent that corporations, labor unions, or other special interests seek to "buy an interest in a candidate," PAC's have become a potentially decisive force in American politics.

Information and Expertise. Both Capitol Hill and the Pentagon depend on "defense lobbyists" — the representatives of such companies as Northrop (fighter planes); Pratt & Whitney (aircraft engines); and General Dynamics (submarines, aircraft, missiles). These lobbyists are steeped in technical and financial data about their complex products, and they provide legislators as well as Defense Department bureaucrats with information these decision mak-

---

[12]*Congressional Quarterly Weekly Report*, May 17, 1980, p. 1333.

[13]*Kansas City Times*, February 2, 1980. See also Russell Getter, *Campaign Finance in Kansas Elections* (Lawrence: Division of Continuing Education, University of Kansas, 1980).

ers need when they shape weapons programs and buy weapons systems. In 1979, for instance, Congress approved a $15 billion program for 850 F-18 fighters, produced by Northrop, for the Navy. It did so over the objections of the Navy, which wanted F-14s built by Grumman (and, of course, over the objections of Grumann's lobbyists). Northrop won largely because of the efforts of its own lobbyists and those of the lobbyists for its subcontractors. George C. Troutman, a lobbyist for General Electric, was in the forefront of Northrop's effort because GE makes engines for the F-18. "Troutman made me look smart in front of my colleagues," said Representative James F. Lloyd, a member of the House Armed Services Committee. "He kept feeding me information on the performance and cost advantages of the F-18 — sometimes practically on the House floor." [14]

A different but equally important type of information comes from various "institutes" or "think tanks," where elected officials seek to find support for their broad, strategic policies. The Georgetown University–affiliated Center for Strategic and International Studies, for example, provided President Reagan with personnel for many of his appointments to national security and foreign policy positions.

Position. One of the crucial elements in the influence of both the defense contractors and the Georgetown institute is their position within the policy-making process. The companies become partners of the United States government in arms sales abroad, and the defense intellectuals set out rationales for future actions they may implement as government officials. In this vein, Reagan's United Nations Ambassador Jeanne Kirkpatrick is now in a position to act on her previous assertion that "U.S. interests and human rights are often best advanced by supporting 'traditional autocracies' " (military dictatorships for the most part). [15]

Position can be extremely important in more mundane circumstances as well. City sanitation workers enjoy a similarly advantageous strategic position, which allows them to bargain effectively with municipal governments. A garbage strike has much more drastic and dramatic effects than a strike by most other municipal employees, such as teachers or bus drivers (without the obvious threat to public safety posed by police or fire department strikes). Thus sanitation workers have fared well in labor negotiations with urban governments, because city officials are highly motivated to end garbage strikes quickly.

Size. The most ambiguous resource, perhaps, is group size. The AFL-CIO and the Chamber of Commerce, for instance, represent large constituencies, and when the member unions or chambers are united on an issue, their impact is great. Frequently, however, they are not united. As one top union

---

[14] "How the Weapons Lobby Works in Washington," *Business Week*, February 12, 1979.
[15] *National Journal*, January 24, 1981.

lobbyist said of labor's tendency toward fragmentation: "If members of Congress sense that the labor movement is split, they figure they've got a free ride. They say, 'Maybe the AFL-CIO is for it, but X, Y, and Z unions are against it.' "[16] Take, for example, the important labor-related issue of expanding day-care facilities. In 1975 the American Federation of State, County and Municipal Employees (AFSCME), representing day-care workers, was opposed by the American Federation of Teachers, which called for schools to control all day-care programs. The result? The AFL-CIO failed to adopt a strong position, and the labor movement's vast size was rendered impotent as a political resource — despite the fact that the overall membership solidly supported the expansion of day care.

Less Obvious Resources. Beyond such straightforward resources as money, expertise, and numbers lies an array of less tangible assets that groups can often employ effectively. The Southern Christian Leadership Council, during the early and mid-1960s under the leadership of Martin Luther King, possessed a "moral strength" in its civil rights arguments that was a potent, though intangible, resource. Moral strength is more limited in its uses than tangible assets such as money. But in certain situations, especially when abetted by effective publicity (such as TV news footage of passive demonstrators facing snarling, lunging police dogs or club-wielding policemen), it can be a powerful resource indeed.

Two other intangible resources are the *intensity of group opinion* and the *trust* that can develop between group representatives and decision makers. A group strongly committed to its goals can often prevail over a much larger, but less concerned, opposition. For example, although various surveys have reported that a majority of Americans are in favor of stricter gun control laws, the National Rifle Association can, and frequently does, muster extremely intense opposition to any such proposal: Letters, telegrams, and phone calls flow into congressional offices in overwhelming numbers. State or local efforts to restrict gun use run into similar NRA efforts, as became evident in the 1976 Massachusetts referendum in which a gun control measure was soundly defeated after a vigorous and expensive anticontrol campaign. Even the shock of John Lennon's murder and the attempted assassinations of President Reagan and Pope John Paul II, did little to move politicians toward regulating handguns. Although some gun control groups do exist, they have made little impact. On the whole, support for gun control is lukewarm and fragmented; decision makers feel, apparently correctly, that they can easily ignore it.

Trust is a resource that usually develops in long-term relationships between decision makers and groups (and often with particular spokespersons for groups). When a lobbyist maintains contact with a congressional subcommittee chairman or an agency head over the years, there is little occasion for threats or exorbitant promises by either side. As one congressman put it, "What [we]

---

[16] Quoted in *Congressional Quarterly Weekly Report,* July 19, 1975, p. 1536.

appreciate in a lobbyist is knowing he's a professional and will be back. . . . If he gives you bum information, he won't be welcome back."[17] Strong bonds often form between interest-group spokespersons, congressional subcommittee members and staff, and bureaucrats who share an interest in the same issues and policies over an extended time. As we saw in Chapter 7, these informal alliances among groups, members of Congress and their staffs, and bureaucrats, are sometimes labeled "subgovernments"— a term suggestive of the potential for influence available to lobbyists if they can establish systematic communications with governmental policymakers.

Not only are resources unevenly divided among groups, but the inequities tend to be cumulative. That is, a trade association, a national union, or a large corporation has the financial resources and expertise to present its position clearly (and often persuasively) to decision makers. This situation in turn may help an interest group develop a strong continuing relationship with important congresspersons, staffers, and executive bureaucrats. Such a link may even become formalized in a governmental advisory panel or temporary study commission. For instance, presidential commissions have been formed to study such specialized subjects as American shipbuilding and international radio broadcasting. The members of these and other commissions are leaders in their fields, rather than members of the public at large. Interest-group representatives, as commission members, provide only an indirect and ill-defined link between governmental policymakers and the citizenry.

Techniques of Influence Virtually all the techniques interest groups use in attempting to influence decision making can be labeled either "inside" or "outside" strategies. We will outline a few of the general aspects of these techniques and will proceed to consider in detail one organization, the AFL-CIO, that relies heavily on a combination of these two styles.

Inside Strategies. These usually involve establishing close ties between group and government at the highest levels of decision making. When a large defense contractor such as General Dynamics or Litton Industries chooses someone to lobby for a new weapons system, that person is likely to be a former military officer who knows exactly which people to see at the Pentagon. The chief advantage of the inside strategy is that it can have a sustained effect on policymaking without drawing much attention to a group's efforts. Interest groups with strong governmental ties shun publicity because it may call into question their special relationships to decision makers. In many instances, groups may use well-paid (and confidential) consultants or lawyers to make their case. A phone call from consultant Charls Walker or attorney Clark Clifford may unlock a key piece of information or cement a difficult bargaining arrangement.[18] In addition, Walker, an ex-Treasury official, and Clifford, a

---

[17] Quoted in Elizabeth Drew, "Charlie," *The New Yorker*, January 9, 1978, p. 40.

[18] The best presentation of an insider at work is Elizabeth Drew's portrait of Charls Walker, ibid.

Democratic insider since the New Deal, can give invaluable advice — on whom to approach and how — without doing any of the work themselves.

Outside Strategies.   These efforts emphasize issue-oriented campaigns and publicity to "educate" both the public and the appropriate decision makers. There are two basic types of outside strategies. A group can present its positions to the press, hoping that news coverage will magnify their importance in the eyes of those they desire to influence. Or a group's leaders can attempt to mobilize its members in a *grass-roots* campaign to express themselves (through letters, telegrams, phone calls, petitions, etc.) directly to decision makers.

With the growing sophistication of computer-based direct-mail technology, Washington-based lobbyists can alert group members (be they individuals or

In 1978 Californians voted to reduce their property taxes (and eventually, their governmental services) in a hotly contested referendum, placed on the ballot by a strong ad hoc grassroots lobbying effort.

trade groups or corporations) to impending actions and solicit communications to the appropriate policymakers. The U.S. Chamber of Commerce, for example, has become very adept at using grass-roots methods to mobilize its vast and diverse membership. When President Reagan announced his extensive 1981 budget cuts, the Chamber machinery swung into action — sending Mailgrams urging strong backing of the president to 2,200 state and local chamber heads, 1,000 corporate chief executives, and 1,300 national and regional trade associations.[19]

Combining Inside and Outside Strategies.   Most groups do not rely solely on either inside or outside techniques, but use combinations of both, including different approaches for different decision makers. Consider, for example, the breadth of tactics employed by the AFL-CIO as it lobbies in behalf of its diverse interests. Because the federation's goals range from basic economic objectives (such as raising the minimum wage), to reducing restrictions on union organizing, to broad defense and foreign policy concerns, its targets and strategies also must vary.

As we have noted, the most obvious potential resource of the AFL-CIO, its size — millions of members and 110 affiliated unions — may not represent its greatest strength, given the breadth of interests found within the union movement. Individual unions often find it more productive to lobby on their own for specific objectives than to depend on the clout of the AFL-CIO as a whole. For example, the American Federation of Teachers, whose members are preoccupied with educational policy and have little or no interest in raising the minimum wage or unionizing farm workers, institutes its own inside and outside strategies to pursue its own goals. As one Senate staff aide notes, "I hear as much from individual unions as from the AFL-CIO itself. . . . They leave a lot of decisions to the individual unions."[20] Nevertheless, as Representative Richard Bolling states, "They [the AFL-CIO] still have an enormous constituency they can mobilize on the outside. . . . They don't use it very often. But they can argue beautifully on the outside."[21]

The AFL-CIO's most effective technique, however, is undoubtedly its day-to-day inside lobbying, which has produced extremely strong ties between its staff and numerous powerful legislators and bureaucrats. The AFL-CIO staff does its homework; its members can talk to legislators and congressional staffers with the authority of experts on labor matters. These lobbyists have rightly been called the "professional Washington representatives" of the labor movement.[22] Their job, which they perform assiduously, is communication —both to the decision makers and back to the top union officials. In addition, the relationships created by these professionals become more than a lobbyist-leg-

[19] From *Congressional Quarterly Weekly Report,* March 7, 1981, p. 406.
[20] *Congressional Quarterly Weekly Report,* July 19, 1975, p. 1535.
[21] Ibid., p. 1536.
[22] Lewis Anthony Dexter, *How Organizations Are Represented in Washington* (Indianapolis: Bobbs-Merrill, 1969), chap. 1.

islator exchange of information; personal *alliances* are forged between the lobbyist and the legislator that stand the test of time and are mutually beneficial.

Access does not guarantee influence, as the AFL-CIO learned the hard way in the early months of the Carter administration and the 95th Congress. In the spring of 1977 it backed a bill that would have permitted a single picketing union to shut down all building activity on a construction site. AFL-CIO lobbyists and legislative strategists thought they had the votes in Congress to pass the bill, but the House unexpectedly rejected it by a vote of 217 to 205. The next day, according to one congressional staffer, "Everybody [on Capitol Hill] was talking about how labor wasn't as powerful as people thought."[23]

One top AFL-CIO official who backed the abortive picketing bill was Sol Chaikin, the president of the International Ladies Garment Workers Union. Chaikin delivered this post mortem:

> The building trades didn't do their homework. They didn't touch base with the people whose votes they were counting on. The Right to Work Committee and the Associated General Contractors did the job of arousing public sentiment that we of labor should have been doing, and we have no right to cry that they beat us.[24]

The day after it lost on the picketing bill, the AFL-CIO received another setback. The secretary of labor, Ray Marshall, recommended that Congress increase the minimum wage to $2.50 an hour instead of $3.00, as the unions had lobbied for. Speaking of the AFL-CIO's picketing and minimum-wage defeats, a labor spokesman said: "We learned some lessons last week. We learned we can't take the House of Representatives for granted. We learned we have to lobby back home to get legislation in Washington. And we learned we need friends. We can't win battles alone."[25]

Another major avenue of AFL-CIO influence lies in the campaign contributions and other electioneering assistance provided by the AFL-CIO's "political arm," the Committee on Political Education (COPE). COPE representatives and the AFL-CIO lobby team usually work separately; the lobbyists see their roles as influencing policy decisions, not playing electoral politics. Kenneth Young, an AFL-CIO lobbyist, put it this way:

> COPE people don't lobby on the Hill and we don't get involved in political contributions. . . . When I go to see a member, I think he may be worried about the impact of a bill on local labor in his district. But I don't think his mind is on the contributions. I don't get asked for contributions. . . . If we got

---

[23] Philip Shabecoff, "Organized Labor's Power in Washington: Setbacks Indicate Its Influence Is Less Strong Than Was Expected," *The New York Times*, April 5, 1977, p. 18. See also, Norman Ornstein and Shirley Elder, *Interest Groups, Lobbying and Policymaking* (Washington, D.C.: Congressional Quarterly Press, 1978).

[24] *The New York Times*, March 26, 1977.

[25] Shabecoff, "Organized Labor's Power."

involved in [electoral] politics, every time I went to see a member he'd be talking about funds. And I'd never get anything done.[26]

This is not to say that individual unions or other interests (such as dairy co-operatives) have not used campaign contributions as political bait. And COPE certainly takes stock of members' records when it distributes its funds (about a million to House and Senate candidates in 1980) with almost all funds going, as usual, to Democrats.

In sum, the AFL-CIO pursues a wide range of interests with a variety of techniques designed to communicate information to and influence potential allies within the Congress and the bureaucracy. The key to its daily political operations is not its numbers or its campaign clout, but the strong, professionally based relationships that its lobbyists have developed. For any interest group — whether the labor movement with its broad and complex concerns or the National Barrel and Drum Association, with its very specialized and occasional interests — some variety of an inside strategy is probably the most effective technique for influencing policy decisions.

Litigation. The legal system offers an additional channel for those who would influence policy. As we saw in Chapter 8 on America's legal system, in certain circumstances groups with few resources can compete effectively with other interests or with various governmental agencies by taking them to court. This process, known as *litigation*, simply means that a group works through the judicial process, in a formal court setting, rather than carrying its pleas to legislators, executives, or bureaucrats. The courts may be willing to tackle difficult problems that elected officials would rather not face directly.

The civil rights movement has long relied heavily on litigation to achieve its overall goal of obtaining equality before the law. Various rights groups have time and again sought, often successfully, to have discriminatory statutes declared unconstitutional. Similarly, "public interest" lawyers representing environmental and consumer groups have increasingly used litigation to contest both governmental policies and projects of corporations and other private interests. Many large construction projects have been stopped or modified by environmentalists' court suits; one recent court decision prevented a Florida land developer from further draining the wetland refuge of many endangered bird and animal species. Consumer groups, too, have won notable victories in removing unsafe toys, drugs, and other products from the market through the threat of litigation. Finally, although the Reagan administration has reduced the scope of this program, government-financed lawyers, paid in part through federal Legal Services Corporation funding, have often effectively represented the interests of many relatively powerless groups of people — ranging from tenants to migrant workers to homosexuals.

There is, however, another side to the use of legal action to pursue a

[26]*Congressional Quarterly Weekly Report,* July 19, 1975, p. 1538.

group's interests. Civil rights groups, environmentalists, and consumer advocates have won some important court victories, but in our political system the wealthy usually have the advantage in litigation. The costs of court action are extremely high, especially in suits requiring years of effort by many lawyers. Generally, wealthy interests want to maintain the status quo. Thus, even when a large and powerful interest has little chance of ultimate victory, its ability to force long delays may ensure short-term profits that far outweigh the costs of a court fight.

A notorious example of such a delaying action was the Reserve Mining Company's long-term success in dumping 67,000 tons of potentially hazardous taconite tailings each day into Lake Superior despite intense opposition from the federal and state governments and from environmental groups. The tailings, a form of iron or waste, contained asbestos fibers, a known cancer-causing agent. Several lakeshore municipalities, including the city of Duluth, Minnesota, get their drinking water from the lake. But Reserve Mining and its parent companies, Armco Steel and Republic Steel, found it cheaper to invest in protracted legal stalling tactics than to develop an on-land dumping site. So this corporate interest group held off its critics in the courts for eight years — from 1969 to 1977 — during which it dumped more than 170 million tons of its health-endangering wastes into Lake Superior.

Reserve Mining finally lost its legal battle, as it doubtless knew it would. But even after the courts ruled that it must switch to an on-land dumping site, the company gained the right to continue dumping in the lake during the two years it would take to construct the new facility.

Still, on some occasions the legal advantages of the status quo position belong not to the wealthy, established interests, but to their opponents. The air and water pollution laws passed during the 1970s have generally favored environmentalists. It has become easier to use the courts to block actions potentially dangerous to the environment. Antinuclear organizations have proved especially effective in thwarting the construction of new nuclear power facilities. In fact, such litigation has contributed significantly to the virtual abandonment of plans for any new nuclear plants, aside from those already under construction.

Litigation, then, does offer some substantial opportunities to groups with relatively few resources, because they may receive a more complete hearing in the courts than in other political arenas (especially at the federal level). On the other hand, a group's ability to use the legal system usually depends on its financial resources, and here the inequities of group politics are just as severe as they are in gaining access to top-level legislative or executive decision makers.

Unconventional Tactics: Protest and Civil Disobedience. After the Vietnam War and the civil rights movement of the 1960s, it may seem strange to label protests or civil disobedience "unconventional tactics." Such efforts can be very effective as a means of dramatizing group demands. Often it is a lack of other resources that encourages a group to use legal protests or actions in which the letter of the law is broken. Southern blacks in the early 1960s possessed few conventional group resources, but they could mount protests and refuse to obey laws mandating segregation, by demanding service at "white-only" lunch counters or refusing to sit only in the rear seats of public buses. The protests and the civil disobedience in themselves did not produce sweeping changes, but they did generate publicity and elicit great sympathy at home and abroad. In turn, public sentiments and media exposure pressured the president and Congress to rectify the most blatant racial inequities, such as the segregation of public places and the denial of blacks' voting rights.

The success achieved by civil rights and antiwar groups has not gone unnoticed by other interests. Independent truckers, faced with higher fuel costs and lower speed limits after the 1973 Arab oil boycott, soon formed their own group, the Independent Truckers Association, and staged numerous protests to dramatize their plight. Likewise, the late 1970s found many farmers engaged in demonstrations, traffic-snarling "tractorcades," and protests in state capitals and in Washington, D.C., under the umbrella organization of the American Agriculture Movement.

Policemen and other public employees who are often legally prohibited from striking have staged "job actions," such as massive sick calls (the "blue flu") or enforcement crackdowns (for example, traffic tickets for every minor violation). Opponents of court-mandated busing or the integration of white neighborhoods have also adopted protest tactics to dramatize their cause, as have opponents of nuclear power plants.

Protests like farmer tractorcades, sanitation workers' strikes, and police "sick-outs" run the risk of generating a backlash of antagonism and opposition from the people they inconvenience. After all, few citizens relish crawling along for hours in traffic jams or seeing their garbage pile up on the sidewalks. Interest groups that resort to such protests must try to determine whether their actions will ultimately help their cause more than hurt it — and this is not always an easy calculation. Sometimes a group knows that resentment over its disruptions will outweigh sympathy for the cause, but members go ahead in the hope that policymakers will acquiesce to their demands nevertheless. This strategy underlies many strikes and slowdowns by government employees, although the strategists will rarely admit it publicly.

In sum, many different tactics are available to interest groups, and the tactics a group chooses depend on the resources at its disposal. But great resources or dramatic tactics cannot ensure success.

Unconventional Tactics: Illegal and Unethical Behavior. Political scientists have not been overly concerned with the seamy side of American politics, but a continuing series of examples show illegal and/or unethical tactics as the tools of some lobbyists. One state-house lobbyist in Olympia, Washington, boasted that he could deliver a prospective governor–attorney general team to a gambling syndicate for the "bargain" price of $84,000. And seven members of

Congress were convicted of influence-peddling in the FBI's ABSCAM investigation (see Chapter 5).

Illegal payments and contributions can also enter into international lobbying activities. In 1977 a South Korean agent admitted to channeling hundreds of thousands of dollars to dozens of congressmen, through illegal campaign contributions, bribes, gifts, and favors. Other nations, such as Taiwan, have remained within the bounds of legality, but have provided many free "fact-finding" trips to United States legislators.

At the presidential level, public financing of campaigns currently blocks some of the avenues for unethical lobbying; but in 1972 individuals, corporations, and other organizations made massive illegal contributions to Richard Nixon's reelection campaign. Democratic hopefuls also received substantial sums from similiar sources.

The politics of bribery, kickbacks, and payoffs may not be practiced as widely now as they were during the nineteenth and early twentieth centuries. But some elected (and appointed) officials can be "reached" by such tactics, and it is naive to think otherwise. Obtaining billion-dollar weapons contracts or arranging multi-million-dollar milk-price deals virtually invites illegal tactics in an age when even payoffs reaching into the millions (such as those that Gulf and Lockheed have admitted to) are considered by some businessmen just one more form of corporate investment.

How Effective Are Interest Groups? It is virtually impossible to say precisely how effective interest groups have been in their attempts to influence policy. Group goals are often imprecise; resources are difficult to compare. Then, too, successes may go unnoticed by the public or press, and even well-publicized successes may come about independently of an interest group's efforts. But we can make some general observations.

Gaining access is the first step toward effectiveness. Without access to decision makers, a group cannot get its position across, and if it cannot communicate its position it cannot hope to be effective. As we noted earlier, however, access does not guarantee influence. A lobbyist's campaign contributions may assure him or her of contact with a legislator; but even a legislator who votes with the group's interests might have cast the same vote without the lobbyist's intervention.

Persistence, unity of effort, and clarity of goals are also extremely valuable in achieving success. The actions of another truckers' group, the American Trucker's Association (ATA), illustrate the virtues of being persistent and having clear goals, even in the face of strong opposition.[27] For over six years the ATA sought to increase the weight trucks could carry on federal highways; larger loads would mean higher profits, although at the costs of reduced safety and greater road damage. The group concentrated its efforts on members of the congressional committees handling interstate commerce. The onset of the

---

[27] Levine, "Getting to Know Your Congressman," p. 50 ff.

energy crisis in 1973 brought the ATA its golden opportunity: Lower speed limits provided a perfect rationale for less stringent weight restrictions and hence "greater productivity." The proposed weight increase was made part of a broad package of transportation legislation in 1974. The result was a policy decision that gave the truckers the weight increase they wanted, even though the decision was opposed by many private and public groups, ranging from the Teamsters Union to the National Association of Counties.

The unity of the trucking industry contributed mightily to its effectiveness against a broad but disjointed opposition. In their detailed 1963 study of the role of interest groups in the policymaking process, Bauer, Pool, and Dexter noted the general ineffectiveness of a fragmented business community in its attempts to influence trade and tariff policies.[28] Later studies, however, showed that businessmen often succeeded in such attempts when industrial and commercial interests joined forces to promote specific policy initiatives. Likewise, a single industry whose members are all affected in the same way by governmental policies can lobby very effectively, because they can speak with one voice to policymakers through their trade association (such as the ATA).

Although single-interest groups ordinarily find it easier to present a united front than do groups with more diverse interests, many of these latter groups have found ways to develop greater unity. The Chamber of Commerce, for example, operates a strong communications network from its Washington office, coordinating the flow of information to the local level. As with many organizations, the Chamber's Washington representatives increasingly set the group's agenda. Environmental groups faced a different type of internal divisiveness. In the early days of the movement, through the mid-1970s, most environmentalists distrusted any deviation from absolute purism — no cost was too great to preserve a completely clean environment. More recently, however, as environmental groups have seen many of their policies implemented, at least in part, there is a greater tendency for most groups to adopt more conventional, compromise-oriented tactics. As Conservation Foundation president William Reilly notes: "I don't think environmentalists would have wanted to sit down with industry in 1968, when there were very few [protective] charters for the environment, and [there was] a diffuse and largely unprofessional environmental community. Now there's a much more equal balance of power."[29]

In short, interest-group effectiveness, like beauty, may lie in the eye of the beholder. That is, lobbyists may portray themselves as influential in order to cement relationships with their clients. Or campaign contributors may claim great victories based on flimsy evidence. Or corporations may disclaim any influence, when in fact they operated very successfully behind the scenes. For the most part, however, interest groups and lobbyists know that today's vic-

---

[28] Raymond A. Bauer, Ithiel de Sola Pool, and Lewis Anthony Dexter, *American Business and Public Policy* (New York: Atherton, 1963), chap. 22.
[29] *Congressional Quarterly Weekly Report*, January 31, 1981, p. 216.

tory may turn into tomorrow's setback — such is the continuing and fluid nature of bargaining-oriented group politics. As Charls Walker concludes in describing the nature of his job:

> I keep trying to see if there's anything behind the smoke that I ought to know about. I'm trying to find out, by talking to people, by my clients' talking to people. I don't know — you just keep going around and talking.[30]

CITIZENS AND INTEREST GROUPS

Interest groups are firmly established as major forces in American politics. Groups provide organized means for many interests, especially the most powerful, to have their voices heard regularly by key decision makers. But what can groups do for individual citizens?

As a link between decision makers and the public, interest groups render three major potential benefits to both citizen and society. First, groups are one of the most important avenues (along with political parties and elections) by which citizens can influence policy decisions without going through the prescribed (but often unproductive) government channels. For example, a group of apartment dwellers in New York City may protest welfare or housing policies directly to their representatives in Congress, avoiding the administrative maze of the welfare or housing bureaucracies. Second, groups often encourage citizens to participate in political activity, thus making them feel more a part of the political system. And third, groups are open to everyone; any set of like-minded individuals can create an organized group to press for their goals. Environmental and consumer lobbies are two examples of groups that have been created for and by ordinary citizens in the past two decades.

Before looking more closely at the potential benefits of joining and participating in groups, let us first note how Americans view interest groups and how much they actually participate in group politics.

Why Belong?

For many years Americans have been pictured as a nation of "joiners." We are said to belong to more organizations than do people from almost any other country. (Recent estimates, however, depict us as roughly equivalent to citizens of other industrialized nations in our tendencies to join organizations.) Moreover, Americans tend to be active within their organizations and to join groups that engage in discussion about politics and community affairs (see Table 12.2). Even in ostensibly "nonpolitical" organizations — veterans' groups, farmers' organizations, and service clubs (such as the Lions or Rotarians) — three out of every five individuals report frequent political discussions. Joining groups, becoming active, and talking politics are commonplace in American society.

We have already noted that many citizens belong to more than one group. This tendency can reduce conflicts within the society by forcing an individual

---

[30] Elizabeth Drew, "Charlie," *The New Yorker*, January 9, 1978, p. 89.

Table 12.2 Organizational Involvement of American Population

Percentage of Sample Reporting	
That they belong to an organization	62
That they belong to more than one organization	39
That they are active in an organization	40
That they belong to an organization in which political discussion takes place	31
That they belong to an organization active in community affairs	44

Source: Sidney Verba and Norman N. Nie, *Participation in America*, p. 176. Copyright © 1972 by Sidney Verba and Norman H. Nie. Reprinted by permission of Harper & Row, Publishers, Inc.

to divide his or her loyalties among groups viewing various political situations from more than one perspective. Probably of greater importance is the fact that most Americans identify with more than one reference group (that is, a population grouping set apart by a distinguishing characteristic, such as race or ethnicity). Blacks or persons of Irish descent can perceive themselves as black Americans or Irish-Americans, thus identifying both with the nation and a specific population segment of the nation. Reference groups rarely harbor only a single interest group. For example, the Urban League, the Congress of Racial Equality, the NAACP, and many other groups each seek the support of different (but overlapping) segments of the black community.

Of special importance are the psychological benefits of maintaining a dual identity (as a Mexican-American or Italian-American, for instance). Identifying with both a reference group and the nation offers a firm sense of belonging that is often absent in contemporary American society. Such feelings are amplified when a person's interest-group memberships reinforce his or her reference-group identification, while creating an organized political resource.

A Nation of Joiners? People join groups for many different reasons. Some professions put direct or indirect pressure on their members to join one or more of the occupation's interest groups. Doctors, for example, are expected by their peers to join their state and local medical associations; most do. Or stronger coercion may occur, as in "closed shop" situations, where labor unions can require new workers to join within a certain number of working days. As we have seen, an individual may join an organization to "get things done" (work for certain policy changes), or merely to enjoy the fellowship of the group's members. Although motives vary widely, people join interest groups in response to three basic types of incentives: material or economic, social, and issue-related.[31]

On the basis of our discussion so far, we might expect that political issues

[31] See James Q. Wilson, *Political Organizations* (New York: Basic Books, 1973). Also, Mancur Olson, an economist, presents a cogent discussion in *The Logic of Collective Action* (Cambridge: Harvard University Press, 1971).

and policy questions would be the greatest spurs to interest-group membership. But we must remember that few organizations are primarily motivated by political goals. A retail merchant who joins the Chamber of Commerce may become politically active at times, but the major initial reason for his or her membership is likely to be material gain (better business) or peer pressure. Sometimes, too, individuals join organizations for material or issue-related reasons, but their incentives for remaining in the group are social.

Organizations usually provide a mixture of benefits to their members. A state medical association, for instance, is organized around a profession, so its members share similar occupational interests; however, their main reasons for joining may be specific material benefits, such as a journal subscription or a group insurance plan. The American Civil Liberties Union (ACLU) is an almost purely issue-related organization; its meager newsletter offers no great inducement to join. But the ACLU, and its state and local affiliates, may also provide its members with personal satisfactions: One derives a sense of fellowship from knowing that many other individuals are also fighting for a certain cause, such as freedom of speech.

Groups that rely on such issue-related benefits may lose members if they take unpopular stands. The ACLU, as we saw, supported the rights of American Nazis to stage a march through Skokie, Illinois, in 1980. This issue position, consistent with the ACLU's traditional support for freedom of speech, caused many members both in Illinois and across the country to resign from the organization. ACLU membership subsequently rebounded, as new "freedom of speech" and other Bill of Rights issues arose. The ACLU in a sense, relies on various groups' continuing challenges to basic civil liberties. From censorship controversies to the rights of prisoners to opposition to the military draft, the organization never lacks for causes that will bring in new members and revitalize the interest of the faithful.

Who Participates?   As important as the reasons that people join interest groups are the kinds of people who join and participate. Who uses the potentially great power of this link between citizens and polity?

As we have seen, almost any group of individuals, rich or poor, can benefit from being well organized. In 1955, with almost no conventional political resources, blacks in Montgomery, Alabama, organized a bus boycott under the leadership of Martin Luther King, Jr., to desegregate the city's public transportation facilities. They succeeded. Black Americans have increased their political strength tremendously by organizing into groups like the NAACP, the Reverend Jesse Jackson's People United to Save Humanity (PUSH), and many others. Such organizations have mobilized large numbers of black members; obtained substantial publicity; and won sympathy, support, and concessions from the dominant (mostly white) power structure.

Organizations like the NAACP and PUSH are notable exceptions to the more general pattern in group participation. For the most part, people who are well off and well educated participate more actively in interest groups than do their less affluent, less well educated fellow citizens. One result is that organized activity may magnify the differences between those citizens who control many and those who control few political resources.[32] A lawyer, with communications skills, wealth, and free time, is probably more active in his interest groups than is an unskilled laborer in his. The lawyer, with his skills and resources, can forge even closer ties to decision makers by his interest-group participation. Thus the difference in their potential for political influence, already great, is magnified by their group activities.

In addition, most interest groups are oligarchies; that is, relatively small groups of activists make most policy decisions without consulting the rest of the membership. Limited active participation stems either from most members' apathy or from the difficulties involved in dislodging any given set of leaders. In well-established groups (for example, the American Medical Association, the National Rifle Association, most labor unions), the leadership elites retain the apparent support of the entire organization without continually having to demonstrate their members' backing. Thus, spokesmen for automobile or labor interests, such as Henry Ford or AFL-CIO President Lane Kirkland, often express their own policy preferences; their positions as representatives of broad constituencies give considerable weight to their statements, and they need not continually seek backing from their constituents (in this case, either the Ford Motor Company or the AFL-CIO member unions).

Spokespersons for most newer, less well established groups do not enjoy such leeway. In such organizations, especially those representing interests that have not yet won wide political recognition (for example, tenants, the poor), leaders must continually demonstrate that they have the support of their constituents. For instance, welfare recipients make up a potentially powerful interest group. On occasion some local "welfare-rights organizations" have been politically effective.[33] Their successes, however, have usually been short lived, mainly because most of their members respond well to their leaders only as long as tangible benefits are forthcoming. Once these benefits level off or decrease, the group's leaders lose much of their following, and government officials can safely ignore the organization's demands.

Who Is Represented? Interest groups are generally more successful in linking special interests to the government than in linking broad "citizen" interests to it. The manufacturer of a prescription drug may have no larger stake in the government's regulation of its product than do the citizens whose health or even lives depend on that product. But the manufacturer's stake lends itself better to interest-group action. The drug company's continued success — indeed, its very survival — depends on its ability to manufacture and sell its products. Therefore it can (and must) afford to promote and defend its interests to the policymakers who reg-

---

[32] For a fuller discussion, see Sidney Verba, Norman H. Nie, and Jae-on Kim, *Participation and Political Equality* (New York: Cambridge University Press, 1978).

[33] Frances Fox Piven and Richard A. Cloward, *Regulating the Poor: The Functions of Public Welfare* (New York: Vintage, 1971), chap. 10.

ulate those products. This it does by forming or joining a well-financed, well-organized interest group, as well as in lobbying on its own.

The users of the company's drug are in a less favorable position to defend *their* interests regarding the drug's safety, purity, effectiveness, price, and so on. Yet the entire consuming public has a tremendous stake in the safety, cost, and effectiveness of any widely prescribed drug. Can a group represent the "public interest" by acting on behalf of the entire citizenry?

Strictly speaking, it is probably impossible to determine *the* public interest. People usually have a variety of interests, based on their attitudes and roles as workers, bosses, consumers, producers, environmentalists, strip miners, or whatever. Thus, what is good for Smith in any particular case is not necessarily good for Jones. Is it, for example, in the public interest to ban DDT and other chemicals that pollute the environment if doing so cuts farmers' incomes, reduces food production in a hungry world, endangers vast tracts of insect-threatened timberland, and leads to a risk of new outbreaks of human disease? Is it in the public interest to legislate tougher strip-mining regulations if they will throw thousands of coal miners out of work and more quickly deplete our oil and gas reserves? Is it in the public interest to stimulate the economy in order to create more jobs if doing so will trigger more inflation? Such questions point up the difficulty of determining what "the" public interest is.

Nevertheless, the answer to our earlier question — Can a group represent the public interest? — must be a strong, if qualified, yes. Groups can represent "the public interest" in much the same sense that the president of the United States can represent "the people." They, like he, can strive to determine what is in the best interests of most of the people, and then work to further those interests.

Perhaps it would be more accurate to speak of "citizens' interests" and "citizens' interest groups" instead of "the public interest" and "public interest groups." But the latter terms are in common use, so we shall employ them here — bearing in mind that what the president of Common Cause has emphasized about his own group applies equally well to all such groups: "We are *a* citizens' lobby, *a* public interest group. The difference between 'a' and 'the' is very important. We don't define 'the public interest' in the sense that one group represents it while others don't."[34]

Over the last decade public interest groups have grown in numbers and strength; today government officials take very seriously such groups as Common Cause, Ralph Nader's Public Citizen, and the Sierra Club. Let us look more closely at organizations that seek to define and represent the public interest.

Public Interest Groups Two very different types of organizations seek to represent the public interest in contemporary American politics. One type has a broadly based membership and equally broad objectives; the other has a narrower membership and inter-

[34] Quoted in *Congressional Quarterly Weekly Report*, May 15, 1976, p. 1197.

ests. Most prominent among the broad-based groups are Common Cause and Public Citizen (the umbrella organization for Ralph Nader's various groups). Both Common Cause and Nader's groups have undertaken a wide variety of projects, ranging from campaign reform (Common Cause) to analyses of corporate accountability (Nader).

Although both groups deal with some matters of substance, many of their concerns are procedural. John Gardner, Common Cause's first chairman and a former secretary of the Department of Health, Education, and Welfare, says that his previous experiences as a policymaker taught him that "process determines substance."[35] Accordingly, Common Cause has lobbied for such "process" reforms as the eighteen-year-old vote, the Equal Rights Amendment, and campaign reform. Public financing of presidential campaigns resulted largely from persistent lobbying by this group. Procedural matters such as campaign reform are also less divisive than specific substantive concerns, like health care; and divisions among Common Cause members could be especially damaging to its credibility and clout as a representative of the public interest.

Both Common Cause and Nader's groups have worked to make people more aware of governmental processes and decisions that benefit special interests at the expense, in their opinion, of the general public. Nader, in particular, is a master publicist who usually backs up his claims with documentation. His Tax Reform Research Group helped to prompt a congressional revision of a tax bill by showing that the original bill would have benefited many special interests, and his Health Research Group successfully petitioned the FDA to ban certain dangerous food additives and packaging materials. During the Carter administration, several Nader associates served in important posts, most notably Joan Claybrook as head of the National Highway Safety Administration. And although the organizations' memberships are not immense (224,000 for Common Cause, 195,000 for Public Citizen), their members are active and have begun to exert pressures at the state and local levels.[36]

The strengths of the citizen-government linkages provided by public interest groups are still spotty; Common Cause and Nader's groups exist on shoestring budgets compared with the corporate or labor lobbies. Common Cause membership costs $15 a year (although many members give more). But the consuming public does have two substantial voices that speak often and articulately; the interests of citizens, however defined, are better represented now than they were before these groups became part of the Washington scene.

The other type of citizens' group specializes, concentrating its efforts on a narrow range of interests. Many environmental groups — the Sierra Club, for example — fit this mold. So do various farm, welfare, and consumer groups. Although the general public may benefit from their actions, these groups usually attend to the narrow interests of specialists, such as ecologists, consumer advocates, or health-care experts.

[35] Ibid., p. 1200.
[36] See Neal R. Pierce and Jerry Hagstrom, "The 'Open Government' Lobby Is Closing in on New Frontiers," *National Journal*, December 12, 1977, pp. 2012 ff.

As with Common Cause, the backbone of these groups is their membership. Public interest groups have been extensive users of direct mail technology. "Donors do not just contribute, they 'belong' — which for dues of $15 to $25, guarantees them regular magazines and newsletters, an occasional exhortation to write their congressmen, and pleas for more contributions."[37] Jeffery Berry observes that a variety of other conditions encouraged the growth of citizen groups at the very time that political parties were weakening.[38] Aside from broad initial causes such as antiwar and civil rights activism, and books like Rachel Carson's attack on pesticides, *Silent Spring*, Berry sees several more immediate bases for the growth of public interest groups. Philanthropic organizations provided some initial backing; the Ford Foundation, for instance, gave almost $10 million to public interest law groups in the years 1970–74. An alienated and disheartened public saw public interest groups as "honest brokers" who were not out for personal gain. And many government programs required citizen participation, which in turn created opportunities for the formation of organizations to represent various citizen groups, ranging from neighborhoods to environmentalists to consumer advocates.

The specialization of many public interest groups often pays off in influence beyond what mere numbers and other resources might suggest. One 1980 study listed sixty environmental groups in Washington, D.C., ranging from the Alaska Coalition to Zero Population Growth.[39] Such diversity allows for specific groups to perform particular tasks. Thus the Solar Lobby can argue its specific issues, whereas Environmental Action, with a more urban focus, can take on issues of air pollution and toxic substances. At the same time, as we noted earlier, many environmental groups have become more attuned to bargaining and have turned away from confrontation as a way of life. The Wilderness Society, for example, has named former senator Gaylord Nelson as its chairman; likewise, Rupert Cutler, a former assistant secretary of the Agriculture Department, has assumed control of the National Audubon Society's Washington office. Not only do environmental public interest groups employ technical experts, but they also have reached out to hire political experts who know how to bargain and negotiate in an era in which environmental interests must coexist with harsh energy and economic realities.

Self-styled public interest groups, whether broad or specialized, do attempt to link citizens with their government. Although the Nader organizations and Common Cause are dominated, like other interest groups, by small managing elites, they do carry on numerous activities aimed at educating citizens; they also try, on occasion, to sample their members' opinions. In this sense they facilitate greater communication between citizens and policymakers. Even if the ties between the average citizen and these organizations are tenuous, governmental decision makers are increasingly apt to call on umbrella public in-

---

[37] *Congressional Quarterly Weekly Report*, January 31, 1981.

[38] This section was adapted from Jeffery Berry, "Public Interest vs. Party System," *Society*, May–June 1980, pp. 42–48.

[39] "See *Congressional Quarterly Weekly Report*, January 31, 1981, p. 213.

terest lobbies, environmental groups, and consumer groups for their opinions and advice before policies are made. And with this access comes greater power and, perhaps, more responsive policies.

OIL AND INTERESTS: A CASE STUDY Since the early years of this century, when a successful antitrust action was brought against John D. Rockefeller's mammoth Standard Oil Corporation, the "politics of oil" have been marked by sporadic interest-group conflicts. Reformers have contended that the oil industry's profits have gone under-taxed, but the oil interests have maintained that high profits are essential to the financially risky business of oil and gas exploration. Until recently these conflicts were muted, because energy costs in the United States have been among the lowest in the world and our economy has thrived under these "cheap energy" conditions. But times have changed; the age of cheap, seemingly inexhaustible energy is over. As our dependence on ever more costly foreign oil has grown, so have the controversies over such oil-related issues as gasoline prices, utility rates, pollution control, and nuclear energy. The politics of oil illustrates some of our more general observations about interest-group politics.

Resources and Tactics of "Big Oil" The best-organized energy interests are, without a doubt, the individual oil companies. Although these firms have created their own interest group, the American Petroleum Institute, industry giants such as Exxon, Texaco, and Mobil do massive lobbying in their own right. Through campaign contributions, professional public relations, and careful monitoring of governmental actions, each of the oil industry giants is a strong lobbying force by itself. The API is a significant interest group, but the corporations also act as independent "interests" in the policy process.

The financial resources of the oil industry are vast. In addition, it controls energy-related information, such as the costs of production and the amounts of remaining domestic oil and gas supplies. This means that most of the government's information about energy in the United States comes from the oil companies — hardly an objective source. Oil interests also have been able to rely on a strong base of support in the Congress, and especially in the Senate. Oil companies have made heavy, sometimes illegal, campaign contributions in the past. Perhaps more importantly, many states are energy producers, and their congressional representatives are naturally sympathetic to the oil interests. One study of oil politics between 1950 and 1970 estimated that a minimum of thirty senators could be found in the pro-oil camp regardless of the question at hand.[40] And in the 1950s and early 1960s, pro-oil representatives and senators dominated the taxing committees in the Congress.

In short, the oil industry, as well as its largest individual companies, pos-

[40] Bruce Oppenheimer, *Oil and the Congressional Process* (Lexington, Mass.: Lexington, 1974), p. 25.

sesses substantial resources that are easily converted into influence. Money, access, and information are a powerful combination, to which the oil industry can add a further advantage: Its basic goal — to maximize profits — is strikingly unambiguous.

To achieve its objectives, the oil industry has employed a variety of tactics. It has obtained easy and frequent access to decision makers and has told the public that it is not to blame for the energy crisis (or for pollution or inflation). As we have said, interest-group politics is basically a communications process, and the oil industry works diligently at explaining its positions both to policymakers (congressional subcommittees, the Federal Energy Administration, the White House) and to the American people through sophisticated media presentations. For instance, in the late 1970s, Mobil Oil regularly purchased the only quarter page of advertising on the prestigious "opinion-editorial" pages of *The New York Times;* Mobil thus assured itself of an influential set of readers. Exxon reached a wider audience by sponsoring the weekend NBC evening news.

The oil industry has also sought to influence the communications process by making massive campaign contributions. In 1972 oil companies and their officers contributed about $5 million, much of it illegally, to the Nixon campaign. Big oil's "investments" in American party politics have been paralleled by its even more substantial political contributions abroad. Standard Oil, for example, through its Italian subsidiary, gave $46 million to Italian political parties between 1970 and 1975.[41] Adding insult to injury, these contributions have often been treated as business expenses and as such have served to reduce corporate taxes.

Oil interests have not ignored the Congress, where crucial policy decisions (on taxes, for example) are made. The number of "oil and gas PACs" grew from 12 in 1974 to 133 in 1979.[42] These groups contributed over $2.5 million to congressional candidates in the 1977–79 period. Given the rapid expansion of these PACs, contributions should rise sharply in the future. But studies illustrate that oil and gas PAC funding may be just the "tip of the iceberg." In 1978 Oklahoma's David Boren announced that his Senate campaign would not accept any PAC money, but the *Tulsa Tribune* reported that he did accept $320,000 from individuals with oil connections. And a 1979 *Washington Post* analysis shows that twelve of twenty members of the Senate Finance Committee, which is responsible for writing tax laws, received over $370,000 in oil industry money since 1977. Our earlier cautions still apply. Those who make large contributions do not automatically gain great influence. There is little question, however, that the specific oil and gas interests that came up with $67,000 for William Armstrong's (R-Colorado) successful Senate campaign

---

[41] *The New York Times,* June 13, 1975.

[42] The following section is based largely on Alan Berlow and Laura B. Weiss, "Energy PACs: Potential Power in Election," *Congressional Quarterly Weekly Report,* November 3, 1979, pp. 2455–2459.

will enjoy excellent access to Senator Armstrong. To repeat, obtaining access is a central, if intermediate, goal for almost all groups.

As Figure 12.2 indicates, major oil companies have been able to take advantage of favorable political circumstances in recent years. Their profitability (reported in net, after-tax earnings) increased sharply (1) after the 1973–74 Arab oil embargo and (2) in 1979, as more oil could be sold at "deregulated" prices. Deregulation — allowing domestic oil prices to rise to the inflated levels set by the Organization of Petroleum Exporting Countries (OPEC) — was the most important aim of the oil industry in the 1970s. By 1981 it had achieved this goal, and oil profits were limited only by the public's decreased consumption.

In short, the oil interests have a clear-cut goal of corporate profitability. To this end they employ various resources we discussed earlier — including money, expertise, information, and position — to maintain a strategic interdependence with government. The ties they have fashioned with state and federal bureaucrats and elected officials are strong. Given their resources, the

Figure 12.2 Selected Oil Company Profits, 1973–80, in Millions of Dollars

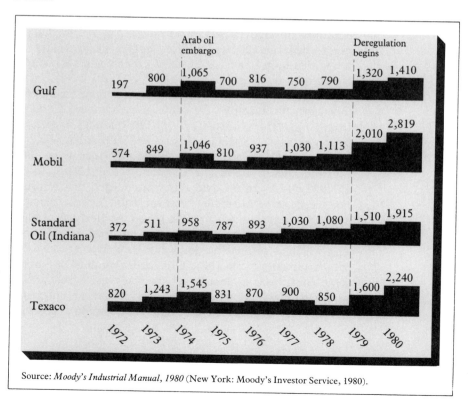

Source: *Moody's Industrial Manual, 1980* (New York: Moody's Investor Service, 1980).

success of their communications efforts, and our national reliance on oil, it is no wonder that oil interests have been generally successful in obtaining favorable policies over the years.

Opponents of "Big Oil"   In spite of the advantages just mentioned, all is not well in the oil industry. Its rising prices, high profits, and pollution problems have led many other interest groups to challenge the oil companies' behavior and the governmental policies that favor the oil industry. The oil industry's main opponents are consumer-oriented interests, such as Ralph Nader's Public Citizen organization and various environmental groups. But growing numbers of other economic interests, such as the tourist and electric power industries, may come to oppose the oil companies as rising energy costs hurt their own profitability.

In contrast to big oil's clear goals and abundant resources, the opposing groups have multiple, and often contradictory, goals and few resources. The goals of the public interest lobbies are fragmented in two ways: First, the oil industry represents only one target among many for such groups; second, the "solutions" endorsed by various groups are frequently in conflict. Environmentalists are especially concerned with "wasteful" consumption and pollution, whereas the broader public interest groups stress the effect of rising energy prices on low-income consumers. And some potential anti-oil allies, such as the politically strong electric utility industry, have generally succeeded in passing along their higher fuel costs to their customers and therefore have not felt constrained to oppose the oil interests.

The resources of big oil's opponents are equally problematic. First of all, most public interest lobbies lack money. Although some groups — notably Common Cause, the Nader organization, and various environmental interests — do provide data and analyses for policymakers, they have not generally enjoyed the access to decision makers that the oil interests have nurtured for decades. In addition, such resources as publicity or moral outrage (over oil profits, prices, or pollution) are not easily convertible to resources that can effectively combat the oil industry's advantages of funding, expertise, and position.

Publicity is an essential resource of the oil industry's opponents. The most valuable exposure is that which costs nothing, because it is legitimized in the public eye as "news" (rather than discounted as "paid propaganda" or "PR"). Many public interest groups have employed their publicity skills, often to good advantage. Their lobbying accomplishments, such as those of Common Cause and the Nader group cited earlier, have frequently been due at least in part to their skill in marshaling public opinion behind their positions, as well as in establishing some strong ties to congressional supporters.

Confronted with serious and organized opposition for the first time, the oil industry has been dealt some setbacks in the past decade. The oil depletion allowance, which granted large tax deductions on oil exploration costs, was first cut and then eliminated; and increasingly strong water and air pollution standards have been legislated. However, it is questionable whether the oil industry has been seriously hurt by these regulations, given their 1979–80 profit levels. Even the widely heralded "windfall profits tax" on oil companies' postderegulation revenues may prove little more than a symbolic gesture. It touches only the highest levels of additional profits that come about from the rise in domestic oil prices to the much higher world levels.

In the 1970s the politics of oil have become increasingly open and well publicized, as the oil industry has emphasized the "energy crisis" and the dream of American independence from foreign suppliers as reasons that decision makers should support policies that would allow them even greater freedom to pursue corporate profits. On the whole, the oil industry has come through the turbulent 1970s in excellent shape. Although there have been challenges from interests within the government (such as the Environmental Protection Agency) and outside it (such as consumer groups) the oil industry remains, as an interest, well connected and well protected. As energy policy becomes more and more important to the economy, oil companies are entering related fields (coal, nuclear power) that will require even more political involvement. In their new role as "energy" companies, they will be at least as formidable as they have been as (largely) oil companies.

CONCLUSION

We have viewed interest groups as significant links between citizens and the government. Unlike political parties, these groups usually represent narrow interests and often make narrow policy demands — that is, demands intended first and foremost to meet their specific needs. Narrow, of course, need not mean small or unimportant: A fifty-cent change in the government's support price for a bushel of wheat can mean a difference of many millions of dollars to American farmers. Groups with clear, nonconflicting goals and ample resources are likely to be effective in influencing policies, especially if their lobbyists can create and maintain trusting relationships with key bureaucrats and congressmen.

Many individuals participate actively in interest groups, and with some exceptions the patterns of citizen participation reinforce disparities within the population. That is, the influence possessed by affluent, well-educated, articulate individuals is greatly magnified when they join together in groups. Citizens may, however, be increasingly well served by public interest groups. Often ill-funded, sometimes obscure, these groups nevertheless develop information and expertise that provide decision makers with alternative views to those offered by corporate, labor, professional, and other special-interest groups. This is extremely important if, in our plural society, the whole range of interests are to be capable of presenting their cases effectively. Ironically, to the extent that such presentations are effective, political change and the capacity to establish clear policies will be hindered, in that all groups seek to protect their own narrow interests.

There are reasons to be suspicious of special-interest pressures on government. Unethical and sometimes illegal behavior does occur. The legal goals and tactics of special-interest groups also deserve scrutiny. There is no assurance that "What's good for General Motors is good for the country," as one former chairman of GM put it while he was the country's secretary of defense. But we should not overlook the fact that all of us — whether as students, professors, labor union members, corporate executives, environmentalists, or whatever — pursue our own special interests. Many, perhaps most, of us tend to think that we ourselves are in the best position to determine what is best for us as students, professors, union members, and so on. And in order to get what we think is best, those of us with like interests often join together in groups. Our political system of federalism and separation of powers encourages attempts to gain access to and influence governmental officials at many levels. Although decision makers must reconcile the many demands of our society's diverse interests, it remains the citizens' obligation, through their groups, to be both heard and listened to. Effectively presenting one's case is not sufficient to create influence, but in our system it is a necessary first step.

SUGGESTIONS FOR FURTHER READING

Bauer, Raymond A.; Dexter, Lewis A.; and de Sola Pool, Ithiel. *American Business and Public Policy*. New York: Atherton, 1963. An exhaustive and illuminating study of business interests' interactions with government on United States trade policy, and of their frequent lack of impact.

Berry, Jeffery. *Lobbying for the People*. Princeton, N.J.: Princeton University Press, 1977. The best book-length treatment of the public interest phenomenon.

Dexter, Lewis A. *How Organizations Are Represented in Washington*. Indianapolis: Bobbs-Merrill, 1969. In a brief and enlightening treatment of "lobbying," Dexter pins down the group representative as just one more professional within the policy process. Along with *American Business and Public Policy* (above), this book usefully destroys some myths surrounding interest-group activities.

Lowi, Theodore J. *The End of Liberalism*, 2nd ed. New York: Norton, 1979. A critique of American group politics, attacking the deadlock created by the continuing need for the accommodation of interests.

Ornstein, Norman, and Elder, Shirley. *Interest Groups, Lobbying and Policymaking*. Washington, D.C.: Congressional Quarterly Press, 1978. A contemporary, but sketchy, view of the interplay between lobbying and policies, this book includes three extended case studies.

Schattschneider, E. E. *The Semisovereign People*, 2nd ed. Hinsdale, Ill.: Holt, Rinehart and Winston, 1960. A classic book on the whole of American politics. *The Semisovereign People* is excellent in relating group politics to the actions of other political institutions and to the role of the citizen in public decision making. Like fine wine, this book improves with time.

Truman, David. *The Governmental Process*. New York: Knopf, 1951. This book is *the* primer for those seeking to understand American politics from a group perspective.

Chapter 13

The Making of Public Policy

Hospitals in Maryland are required by state law to keep their hot water temperature at *no less* than 110 degrees. By federal law, hospitals must keep their hot water temperature at *no more* than 110 degrees. The public policy objective of the state is to make sure that the water is hot enough to wash effectively. Federal public policy is concerned with the possibility that patients or staff may scald themselves. With some pretty precise controls, hospitals in Maryland can satisfy the mandates of both policies.

Public policies relating to a similar area do not always come so close in finding common ground. Indeed, there often simply is no common ground. In Chapter 7, for example, we noted the conflict between the policies followed by two federal agencies, one providing assistance and subsidies to tobacco growers and the other encouraging people to quit smoking.

Ideally, the process by which our government formulates public policies would include all relevant agencies and all available expertise. Presumably, it is desirable to avoid contradictory programs and mandates and to ensure that government actions resolve the problems to which they are addressed. Ideally, too, the democratic institutions involved in policymaking should make sure that there is no gap between the needs and wishes of the people and the decisions of their government.

But just as there are contradictory public policies, so also are there many examples of a gap between the sentiment of the people and the policies of government. Since 1977, for example, public opinion polls have consistently indicated that a majority of the American electorate favors the ratification of the Equal Rights Amendment (ERA) prohibiting discrimination on the basis of sex. Nonetheless, at the beginning of the 1980s, the prospects for ratification seemed almost hopeless. When the United States was mired in a bloody, frustrating war in Indochina in the 1960s and 1970s, the federal government seemed to be the last to learn that most people wanted to admit error and defeat and get out of that war.

Policymakers sometimes have trouble understanding and responding to public sentiment. Taxpayers demand reduced government expenditures and balanced public budgets, while at the same time exhibiting an insatiable appetite for government services and programs — increased defense budgets, subsidies for mass transit systems, improved recreational facilities, cancer research, the development of alternative energy sources, and so on. On other occasions — as with the issues of equal rights for women and the war in Indochina — public officials are simply unwilling to be consistent with public opinion.

In this chapter we will examine the public policymaking process. We will discuss the role of the various political institutions and individuals that have been described in previous chapters as they interact to formulate public policy. First, however, we should be clear about what our terms mean.

WHAT IS PUBLIC POLICY?	Generally speaking, *policy* is government's general direction or course of action. *Decisions,* on the other hand, can be either general or specific. Some decisions are choices to pursue certain policies (general courses of action) and not to pursue others. Other decisions follow from general goals and represent choices about how best to achieve those goals. For instance, when Congress enacted Medicare legislation in 1965, it decided that the federal government would pursue a policy of ensuring medical care to the elderly, regardless of their ability to pay. This then required other decisions: Should health-care providers be paid directly? Should limits be set on how much is paid for specific services?

Public policies are made by government officials. Someone with recognized, formal authority must be committed to a certain course of action before we can regard that course as public policy. Informal and group pressures may prompt an official to make a certain decision, but it is the school board, not parent-teacher organizations, that makes educational policy; the mayor, not neighborhood groups, who sets city policies; the Congress, not lobbyists, that legislates federal policies; the president, not presidential advisors, who provides executive direction to the federal government. Advisors, lobbyists, and citizen groups often give conflicting cues to government officials. These officials must weigh these messages, consult their personal value systems, and make a decision. When they do this, they participate in public policymaking.

In our system of checks and balances, frequently more than one government official or group of officials must agree on a common policy before it can be regarded as public policy. President Carter announced in 1977 that the United States had a new energy policy, but he had to get congressional approval of fundamental components of his proposals before the country actually had a new set of public policies on energy. Likewise, President Ronald Reagan needed congressional approval in order to get the cuts in taxes and government spending that are key to his economic policy. Many federal programs dealing with social welfare and transportation require not only the approval of both houses of Congress and the president, but also the approval and cooperation of state and local government officials. Local units of government must agree to participate in many federal programs and often must be willing to meet requirements such as providing matching funds, expanding or creating local agencies, and complying with certain personnel regulations.

HOW POLICIES ARE MADE

There is no one way in which public policies are made. Setting the course of government in any issue area is as varied and complex a process as are the individuals and organizations that are involved in government. Nor is there a single logical method that determines the content of public policies. Identifying which issues should be on the agenda of government policymakers often is a process of struggle and debate, and resolving a problem, is not simply a matter of finding the most effective solution. Frequently, experts do not agree on what the best solution is or even on what the problems are. Even if they do, in a democratic society elected public officials are naturally concerned with the preferences and prejudices of constituents. Individual government leaders have *their* own personal attitudes and value systems. Finally, we must remember that government does not operate in a vacuum; sometimes public policies are determined by specific crises, by economic developments, or by international events.

But complexity should not be confused with chaos. We can identify some major forces and patterns of the policymaking process. One important consideration is that both individuals and institutions are actors in the policymaking process. Let us begin with some reflections about ourselves as individual decision makers.

Individuals as Decision Makers

Our first inclination is to regard ourselves as rational beings who make decisions based on calculations about what course of action is most likely to help us attain our goals. The basic steps in the rational decision-making process are:

1. Identify the problem or opportunity.
2. Rank personal goals, values, or objectives in order of importance.
3. Identify the various alternatives for responding to the problem or opportunity.

4. Analyze and weigh the costs and benefits of each alternative as it relates to one's goals and values.
5. Compare the alternatives, and their costs and benefits.
6. Select the alternative that maximizes the attainment of goals and values at the lowest possible cost.

Although we frequently distinguish ourselves from other species of animals by referring to this capacity for rational choice, there is considerable evidence that this is an ideal process, not an actual one. Charles Lindblom has written a critique of the rational model of decision making.[1] He argues that the time, information, and energy needed to follow the six steps listed here are so demanding that in fact we muddle through our decisions instead of adhering to a rational decision-making process. Lindblom describes the process we actually follow as "incrementalism" — that is, we respond to problems and opportunities by searching in a limited way for alternatives and information, and we select an alternative that promises satisfactory results and differs only marginally from what we have been doing. In other words, we do not make the considerable effort to maximize goal attainment; instead, we limit our examinations and analyses to a search for satisfactory solutions. If, in this limited search, we hit on an optimal solution, it is more through luck than anything else. In other words, in real life we often must — and are often willing to — settle for *the acceptable*, rather than strive for the optimal.

Recent social-psychological research supports this description of individual decision making.[2] This research points out that, when we confront a situation, our first preference is to avoid having to make a decision at all. Our basic inclination is not to maximize goals or values but, rather, to reduce uncertainty. Thus, we tend to associate a problem or opportunity with one we have confronted before, and to respond in a manner similar to whatever produced a satisfactory result previously. In other words, we rely more on learned, reflex responses than on comprehensive or even limited calculations. Social psychologists go on to tell us, however, that we do have the capacity to make decisions in a careful, rational way. The key to doing so is to recognize a situation as serious and as significantly different from anything we have dealt with satisfactorily before. Without this recognition, we will not make the effort necessary to identify and weigh a broad range of alternatives.

For example, consider the decisions we make about our living arrangements. A thoroughly rational process would require us first to identify and rank all of our relevant goals, values, and objectives. These would probably include completing a degree program, affording the accommodations, being safe and comfortable, being located conveniently for classes and/or work, having rewarding social relationships, and providing for eating and entertainment.

[1] Charles E. Lindblom, "The Science of Muddling Through," *Public Administration Review* 19 (1959): 79–99.
[2] Irving L. Janis and Leon Mann, *Decision Making* (New York: Free Press, 1977).

Just the task of ranking these objectives in some order of importance is likely to be a major effort. The next step would be to identify the alternatives: rent or buy; apartment, room, dormitory, house, condominium, or mobile home; live alone or with someone — with whom? how many?; live near or far from campus; for transportation, rely on bus, bike, walking, motorcycle, or car; buy or rent furniture; and so on. These alternatives can be combined in an almost infinite number of arrangements, which complicates the next step: examining the costs and benefits of each. Likewise, the tasks of weighing and comparing the alternatives are complicated by the divergent nature of the consequences with respect to finances, study time, personal comfort, and individual preferences. How many of us actually went through a rational decision-making process in selecting our living arrangements? No doubt, the answer is few, if any.

It is much more likely that the range of choices we considered was far more limited. Someone going away to college may simply have applied for a room in a dormitory because he or she did not want to make the effort to investigate thoroughly all the other alternatives. Issues of roommate, food, and study facilities, as important as they are, were not addressed. Instead, if one drew an unsatisfactory roommate, one would switch or make some other adjustment. If dormitory food became tiresome, one would begin a search either for some other eating arrangement or for an apartment. Decisions would be prompted by problems that needed to be resolved or by opportunities that emerged, and choices would be based on a minimal effort to be reasonably certain that a change would be acceptable (not necessarily optimal).

On the other hand, a decision about living arrangements may involve a relationship with another person. A change in housing may involve a change in that relationship. Although obviously one might not think of all the alternatives and consequences for both housing and the personal relationship, the decision-making process here is more likely to follow the steps of the rational model.

Government officials face decisions about whether to recommend a policy change to a superior, how to vote on an issue, and how to interpret a legislative mandate. They must make these decisions in ways that are not dissimilar from the ways we decide the structure of our living arrangements. There are the same inclinations to avoid the rational decision-making process, and the same capacity to use that process if the situation seems to require it.

Groups as Decision Makers   Many policy decisions by government officials are made in small groups of three to fifteen people — task forces, committees, and so on. As we pointed out in our discussion of Congress, many of the major decisions seemingly made by the Senate or the House voting as wholes are really just the ratification of decisions made by small groups — committees and subcommittees. There are also groups of legislators, administrators, and advisors that continually discuss and decide on agendas and strategies that they will pursue. Small groups are more than an aggregation of individuals. There is an interpersonal dynamic within these groups that we must understand if we are to have a clear comprehension of public policymaking.

We frequently consider small-group decision making as having the advantage of pooling ideas and perspectives. In contrast to an individual who is limited to his or her own experiences and knowledge, a small group can draw on the collective expertise of its members and, ideally, can overcome the limited search for solutions that is so characteristic of decision making by individuals.

In fact, this ideal is elusive. The tendency of small groups is to seek a consensus, not to engage in the kind of open debate and interchange that might generate a wide range of alternatives and objective, detailed analyses.[3] Sometimes this consensus seeking represents an effort to anticipate and to bolster the preferences of the leader. Advisors to a governor or an agency head at times seek to curry favor by telling the governor or the agency head what he or she wants to hear, or to vie with one another by strategically providing or withholding information. Sometimes this same dynamic is evident in classroom discussions. A student's question or comment may be designed more to impress the instructor than to probe for a greater understanding of the material.

One of the most dramatic and disastrous instances of faulty small-group decision making in United States history occurred prior to the attack by the Japanese on Pearl Harbor in 1941.[4] In staff meetings that Admiral Kimmel held to set policies determining the state of readiness of the forces stationed at Pearl Harbor, participants considered intelligence reports that the Japanese were planning a surprise attack against the United States somewhere in the Pacific. When Admiral Kimmel hinted that he thought any such attack would be somewhere other than Pearl Harbor, his staff made more of an effort to give reasons why he should feel confident in this assessment than they did to probe assumptions, test alternative interpretations, or develop contingency plans. When they received further information indicating that an attack, possibly on Pearl Harbor, seemed imminent, everyone continued to bolster the existing consensus view that Pearl Harbor was not the target. They left unchanged the policy of maintaining normal routines, rather than placing forces on alert and dispersing the ships anchored in the harbor. When, in the minutes before the attack, trainees questioned activity on the radar screen caused by the approaching Japanese planes, they were brushed aside, the warnings were ignored, and U.S. planes remained neatly parked, close together, on the ground.

The consensus-seeking tendencies of small groups do not always revolve around the preferences of a leader. Sometimes the goal of maintaining at least a minimum level of cordiality among the members of a group will prompt

[3] Ibid., pp. 107–34.
[4] R. Wohlstetter, *Pearl Harbor: Warning and Decision* (Stanford, Calif.: Stanford University Press, 1962).

individuals to go along with what appears to be the feeling of the group. To challenge and dissent is to risk exclusion and resentment. Instances of this range from decisions we make with friends about where to go to eat to decisions made in an office about what objectives need to be emphasized. An effective legislator knows not only when to fight for his or her constituents, but also when to compromise so that the committee or the whole body can continue to function and complete its business. Adhering to group norms for arriving at a consensus is important. However, the price for consensus is frequently a less than complete consideration of the issues and a second-best solution.

The faults that we have identified with small-group and individual decision making plague the efforts of government to design programs and policies that respond to public needs and concerns. Most would agree that we need careful, rational decisions to cope effectively with problems of inflation, poverty, crime, energy, hazardous waste, and unemployment. Yet, although rational choice is possible, it is unusual. The impediments to rational decisionmaking are not confined to government. What we have discussed so far are general features that apply to decision making regardless of where it occurs.

Institutions, Processes, and Policymaking The making of public policies involves more than the problems and possibilities of decision making generally. The procedural and institutional characteristics of government affect the content of public policy in important ways. In addition to the limitations of individuals and small groups, there are the hurdles and delays posed by formal rules, limited authority, and political pressures.

In order for the Environmental Protection Agency, for example, to establish a public policy for managing hazardous waste, individuals within the agency must consider what the most effective approach would be, and there must be staff meetings to discuss the issues so that the agency can take a position. But the process does not end there. Government procedures require that there be public hearings and that drafts of new EPA policies be circulated and publicized before they can become effective. The agency may have to seek new funds or law changes from Congress. The president will have to be persuaded not to veto what Congress does. State and local government officials will have to understand and support the new policies if they are to be implemented effectively. All of this will have to be accomplished in a setting in which those who produce waste can be expected to argue that they should be exempt from government regulations or that EPA policies should be structured so that the cost of safe disposal of waste should be paid by someone other than those who produce the waste. Communities will be concerned that disposal sites be located in someone else's back yard. Environmentalists will protest efforts to use wilderness areas as dumping grounds.

The system of checks and balances in American government has the effect of assigning primary responsibility for each major phase of the public policymaking process to a separate institution. These assignments are presented in

Table 13.1   Formal Policymaking Roles

Process	Institution
Agenda setting	Interest groups
Policy formulation	Congress
Implementation	President and bureaucracy
Evaluation	Courts and interest groups

Table 13.1. Although these formal roles provide some limits on what each institution can do, the boundaries defining these roles are not clear and firm. Courts cannot, for example, pass laws or budgets. But they can and do make policies when they interpret a statute, and they affect the agenda when they declare a law unconstitutional. Likewise, although the primary task of the bureaucracy is the implementation of congressional decisions, administrators make policy when they exercise discretion in applying the law, and they make evaluations and promote agenda items when they sense that the government is pursuing the wrong objectives or that government could be more effective in what it wants to do.

Policymaking is a complex and often inadvertent process. The variety of actors and the dynamics of conflict involved in many policy areas defy any orderly description. Nonetheless, it is possible to identify four major phases through which policies usually evolve.

Agenda Setting.   For a policy to be made, the need for one must first be established. Thus, the first phase involves convincing the appropriate people that a problem exists that they ought to consider. In the federal government, where many problems are competing for the attention of officials, the problems must be seen as both real and important if it is to become part of an agenda.

Frequently a specific conflict or crisis makes a more general issue visible. The shootings of prominent people like John and Robert Kennedy, Martin Luther King, Jr., George Wallace, and Ronald Reagan have renewed debate over whether or not the government should place more controls on handguns. The financial problems of major American automobile makers in the early 1980s, and the effects of these problems on jobs and on the economy of the midwestern states specifically and the country generally, prompted consideration of new trade and economic policies.

Crises are not the only way for an issue to reach the agenda of government officials and institutions. The campaigns of elected officials involve promises and pledges that result in the consideration of certain policies. An interest-group representative seeks to persuade some members of Congress of the need for specific kinds of legislation. Administrators in the federal bureaucracy

Setting the Policymaking Agenda

Public participation in public policymaking is most critical in identifying what issues need to be addressed. The process of deciding how government will resolve social problems requires the application of expertise and the careful and sometimes delicate negotiation of compromises and agreements. This process does not lend itself to meaningful, active public participation.

Public concern arises in response to a variety of events and manifests itself in a variety of ways. The need for government to control oil companies, for example, was initially part of a general reaction against the emergence of monopolies (as seen in this 1884 cartoon attacking John D. Rockefeller's Standard Oil Company). This concern was high on the government's agenda from the 1880s to the 1930s. The energy crisis that become highly visible in the 1970s and 1980s again raised the question about what public policy should be towards oil companies. Debates emerged. Senator Henry Jackson (facing page, top left), other officials, and consumer groups complained that oil companies were not taking adequate steps to prevent shortages of energy supplies, but were instead exploiting the energy crisis to reap high profits. Oil companies responded that they were trying to increase energy resources and that profits were necessary for exploration and for greater production. Likewise, disagreements between those concerned with protecting the environment and those anxious to do whatever is necessary to exploit energy resources became part of public policymaking discussions.

Government officials hear demands through public demonstrations, like those protesting rising food prices, and through organized interest groups, such as labor unions concerned with the effect of imports on American jobs. In addition, public decision makers face conflicting demands. It is not easy to satisfy consumer pleas for low oil prices and to answer oil company arguments for adequate profits. The policy response to the unemployed, such as these people in a Detroit unemployment office, tends to add to inflationary pressures and conflict with strategies for keeping the price of food and other goods and services low. In other words, concerns reach the public policymaking agenda in large part because of the political activity of affected groups. The fact that government officials discuss and consider an issue does not necessarily mean, however, that the problem will be resolved.

identify problems that must be addressed as they apply regulations or implement programs. An individual politician may sense an opportunity to get favorable publicity by advocating the need for a new policy in a particular area. In short, although we frequently think of interest groups and crises as responsible for what gets the attention of government, the sources of agenda items are many and varied.

Policy Formulation. Once a problem has become part of government's agenda, the branch or agency involved next seeks remedies for it. This means that the policy must be made in accordance with the rules and procedures of that branch or agency. If the policy is being formulated in Congress, it must be acceptable to a majority of the 100 senators and 435 representatives, and it must be approved by the president. If the Supreme Court is faced with resolving a problem presented to it in a case, the decision must be suited to the particulars of that case and limited to the specific controversy involved. A regulatory or administrative agency is guided by the discretion and procedures provided for it in the laws establishing the agency. Within the various institutional guidelines, of course, there are the deliberations of individuals and small groups that we have described earlier.

Implementation. As was pointed out in Chapter 7 on the federal bureaucracy, what finally determines the effect of a governmental policy is its implementation. Those who carry out policies hold a staggering amount of important discretion. Not surprisingly, Congress, the courts, and interest groups all have tried to monitor the behavior of administrative agencies entrusted with this phase of the policy process. This monitoring is not always confined to watching bureaucrats. Sometimes an interest group or a president who loses at the policy-formulation stage may try to pursue the same cause at the implementation phase, persuading administrators to interpret or enforce legislation in a favorable way. A notable example of this is the Medicare program, which was opposed vigorously by the American Medical Association when legislation was first introduced in Congress but which eventually provided a major source of income for members of the medical profession.[5] Lobbyists for doctors are now among the loudest protestors of attempts to control and reduce the costs of this program.

Evaluation. Groups and individuals that oversee the implementation phase are in effect evaluating both the agency and the policy. One fundamental question that is posed is: "Did the policy have its intended effect?" For example, does punishing convicted criminals deter crime very severely? Do farmers innovate and work hard when the government provides them with income stability through guaranteeing minimum prices for their crops and livestock? Another concern in policy evaluation is whether the agency or agencies

[5] Theodore R. Marmor, *The Politics of Medicare* (Chicago: Aldine, 1973).

responsible for implementing a policy did what was intended and made the best use of available resources. Are courts and penal institutions in fact treating criminals in a punitive manner? Are agricultural agencies setting minimum prices at a level that guarantees an adequate income, and are they processing payments in a timely fashion? Evaluation — the answers to these and other questions — leads to agenda setting and starts the policy process over again. If a policy is not resolving a problem effectively or if there is a sense that improvements are needed, government needs to act again.

Subgovernments   The complexity of American politics may require us to draw from a variety of sources to explain public policymaking. One concept that is especially useful in describing how most policymaking that is no more than moderately controversial occurs is that of *subgovernments*, outlined in Chapter 7. Subgovernments, as we noted, are informal networks that link administrative agencies, interest groups, and congressional subcommittees involved in the same public-policy area. As long as these three groups agree among themselves and as long as the issues they deal with do not become a matter of visible national controversy, public policymaking is largely accomplished at this level. If they disagree, or if an issue is on a national agenda, then the arena of participants widens to include Congress as a whole, the president, and competing interest groups.

Some of the most stable subgovernments have been in economic areas, where our society tends to be best organized. Table 13.2 summarizes the major participants in policymaking affecting agricultural commodities. Those primarily responsible for federal activity in setting cotton prices and defining cotton production goals, for example, are: (1) the Agricultural Stabilization and Conservation Service (ASCS) — the cotton agency in the Department of Agriculture; (2) the House Cotton Subcommittee (which is traditionally dominated by representatives from the cotton-growing states); and (3) the National Cotton Council, an organization speaking for cotton growers.

Subgovernments provide an imperfect solution to the problem of obtaining the expertise of those who have special interest and knowledge in a policy area while keeping government from being responsive only to parochial, well-organized interests. Government must itself specialize — and rely on outside "special interests" — in order to serve a diversified, complex society. However, serving an aggregate of special interests is not the same as serving the needs of the country as a whole. Because the weak and unorganized elements of society usually go unrepresented in subgovernments, and because there is no central review of subgovernment activity, subgovernments have closer ties with particular interest groups than with the general public. The president, who has a national constituency and who therefore must attempt to serve the broad "national interest," can intervene in agency–congressional–interest group relationships. But because his time is limited, he can do so only if an issue of visible national importance is at stake.

John W. Gardner, a former cabinet officer and national chairperson of Com-

Table 13.2 Agency, Congressional, and Interest-Group
Relationships: Commodity Subgovernments

Commodity	Subgovernment Members		
	Congress	Bureaucracy	Interest Group
Cotton	House Cotton Subcommittee	Agricultural Stabilization and Conservation Service (ASCS) cotton program	National Cotton Council
Oilseeds and Rice	House Oilseeds and Rice Subcommittee	ASCS programs for peanuts, rice, tungnuts, flaxseed, soybeans, dry edible beans, and crude pinegum	Soybean Council of America
Tobacco	House Tobacco Subcommittee	ASCS tobacco program	Tobacco Institute
Dairy and Poultry Products	House Dairy and Poultry Subcommittee	ASCS milk program	National Milk Producers Federation; National Broiler Council
Livestock and Grains	House Livestock and Grains Subcommittee	ASCS programs for wheat, corn, barley, oats, grain, sorghum, rye, wool, and mohair	National Association of Wheat Growers; National Wool Growers Association

Source: Randall B. Ripley and Grace A. Franklin, *Congress, the Bureaucracy, and Public Policy* (Homewood, Ill.: Dorsey Press, 1976), p. 78. Reprinted by permission.

mon Cause, a large "citizens' lobby," once made this sour observation about the congressional, administrative, and special-interest representatives who interact in what we have called subgovernments:

> In a given field, these people may have collaborated for years. They may have formed deep personal and family friendships. They have traded innumerable favors. They have seen Secretaries of departments come and go. Often they couldn't care less about White House messages or pronouncements from the top of the Department. They have a durable alliance that cranks out legislation and appropriations in behalf of their special interest.[6]

[6] Quoted in *The New York Times*, November 28, 1976.

THE BUDGET AND POLICYMAKING An important process in which subgovernments are integrally involved is the establishment of the federal government's annual budget. Budgets can be viewed as government approval of the agenda and activities of subgovernments. Because there is never enough money to give all agencies everything they ask for, subgovernments must compete for funds. That is, each must argue that its programs deserve higher priority and more money than other programs. These arguments must be accompanied by the mobilization of political support within Congress and among the public, and subgovernments play an obvious and crucial role here.

As Figure 13.1 illustrates, several activities in the federal budgetary process are often going on simultaneously; from January until about July every year, the final steps in establishing a budget for one year overlap with the first steps

Figure 13.1 The Budgetmaking Process

Approximate Time Period	Executive Branch			Legislative Branch		
	Agencies	Office of Management and Budget	President	Budget Committees	Appropriation Committees	Full House and Senate
January ↓ May	Defend requests before Congress for Budget Year I	Conduct economic forecasts and set general budget ceilings for Budget Year II	Submit budget to Congress for Budget Year I and Set policy guidelines for agencies for Budget Year II	Conduct economic forecasts and set general budget ceilings for Budget Year II	Consider presidential budget request for Budget Year I	Pass resolutions on budget ceilings for Budget Year II
June ↓ July	Submit requests and justifications for Budget Year II					Pass budget for Budget Year I and send to president for signature
August ↓ October		Consider requests from agencies for Budget Year II and prepare to submit to President		Make any necessary revisions in economic forecasts and budget ceilings for Budget Year II		Pass resolution on revised budget ceilings for Budget Year II
October 1	Federal fiscal year begins for Budget Year I					
November ↓ December	Revise justifications for requests in accordance with OMB decisions for Budget Year II		Consider budget developed by OMB for Budget Year II			
January ↓	Defend requests before Congress for Budget Year II	Conduct economic forecasts and set general budget ceilings for Budget Year III	Submit budget to Congress for Budget Year II and Set policy guidelines for agencies for Budget Year III	Conduct economic forecasts and set general budget ceilings for Budget Year III	Consider presidential budget request for Budget Year II	Pass resolutions on budget ceilings for Budget Year III

in formulating a budget for the next year. Furthermore, the process of making a budget is approached from two levels. At a general level, both the Congress, through the House and Senate Budget committees, and the Office of Management and Budget simultaneously but separately make economic forecasts and set spending limits for the various policy areas, such as defense, agriculture, transportation, and welfare. The Budget committees aim to introduce a resolution for passage by both houses of Congress by May 15 each year setting forth guidelines for the committees and members of Congress when they make decisions on the budget. The Office of Management and Budget, which is an arm of the presidency, issues its conclusions and guidelines to administrative agencies.

Whereas the OMB and the congressional budget committees approach the budget from the top down, agencies and their partners in the various subgovernments use a bottom-up approach. Agencies, with one eye toward the OMB instructions and congressional resolutions and another toward their own needs and wishes, construct a budget request for submission to OMB and the president. Smaller agencies submit their requests directly to OMB. Agencies that are parts of larger departments must go through department heads, who usually modify agency requests so that they fit within the agenda of the depart-

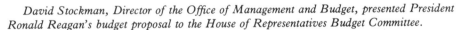

David Stockman, Director of the Office of Management and Budget, presented President Ronald Reagan's budget proposal to the House of Representatives Budget Committee.

ment as a whole. Anticipating these alterations, agencies ι
requests larger than what they expect they will get.

Likewise, there is an expectation that OMB will trim bacl
they get. Department and agency heads typically leave eι
requests so that when the inevitable scalpel of the OMB cut
the department budget will not be fatally wounded. OMB cuts, in turn, represent the president's policy preferences and priorities, as well as an expectation that Congress will make further cuts when it receives the president's budget proposal.

When the president submits the budget to Congress, it is first considered by the House Appropriations Committee. At this point, the subgovernments, which until now have been operating behind the scenes, become visibly active. The various subcommittees of the Appropriations Committee, organized according to policy areas, hold hearings and receive testimony from interested agencies, legislators, and lobbyists. The House Appropriations Committee adheres as closely as possible to the ceilings set by the Budget committees. Invariably, this means cutting the president's budget proposal in some policy areas.

After the House Appropriations Committee completes its deliberations, it sends the budget to the Senate Appropriations Committee. The Senate committee frequently acts as a "court of appeals," restoring some of the cuts if an agency and its supporters can convince the senators that the cutting process has been too severe or unwise in some way. Differences between the House and the Senate may have to be reconciled in a Conference Committee. When both chambers have agreed on a budget bill, they send it to the White House for the president's signature, or veto. Given the complexity of the budgetary process, vetoes are very unlikely. Once presidential approval is given, the federal government has both a budget and a policy agenda.

The budgetary process is like a game in some ways. Agencies and departments, anticipating cuts at various points in the process, are careful to leave in some fat to be cut while arguing that they have proposed a "bare bones budget." OMB and the House Appropriations Committee, on the other hand, assume that agencies have "padded" their requests on the assumption that the requests will be cut. Thus, regardless of the protestations, the cuts are made. Table 13.3 shows the typical fate of an agency's budget request at various points in the process.

There have been attempts to make the process less like a game. President Johnson tried to introduce a system called the Planning-Programming-Budgeting System, which required the definition of policy and program development for a five-year period, as well as cost-benefit analyses to justify expenditures. President Jimmy Carter introduced zero-base budgeting to the federal government; agencies were told to identify what could be cut as well as what they would like to be expanded in their programs, and to document their requests with relatively detailed cost-benefit analyses. Although both of these approaches had considerable intellectual and intuitive appeal, they required so

Table 13.3 Human Resource Training Activity Budget Request, 1980

Estimate to Office of Management and Budget	$1,912,775,000
Budget Estimate to Congress	1,636,615,000
House Allowance	790,775,000
Senate Allowance	1,546,775,000
Final Appropriation	1,389,215,000

much work that they could not be fully implemented. Moreover, both approaches assumed a lack of competition and a presence of rationality that were unrealistic. Both these approaches were abandoned as soon as their proponents left the White House.

TYPES OF PUBLIC POLICIES

One can at least partly understand the different processes through which public policies are made if one recognizes the type of policy issue that is being considered. Theodore Lowi has proposed a useful typology of public policies.[7] *Distributive* public policies provide support to a particular group in society in a noncompetitive manner. *Regulatory* policies represent general agreements to limit or restrict the behavior of certain individuals or groups. *Redistributive* policies are designed to take some resources or opportunities from some groups and give them to others. Let us look at these types of policy.

Distributive Policies

Subgovernments play a particularly important role in distributive public policymaking. The fragmented character of policymaking at this level provides a noncompetitive arena in which it appears that, for example, government assistance for cotton growers, for rice farmers, and for tobacco growers can be arranged without these groups having to compete with one another. The cotton subgovernment is mainly concerned about what policy would be most responsive to the needs of cotton growers. It does not consider what rice and tobacco farmers need, nor does it openly devise strategies to compete with rice or tobacco farmers for something that all of them want but only one can have. Price supports for one commodity are not viewed as potentially eliminating the possibility of price supports for the others.

Regulatory Policies

Regulatory policies, on the other hand, invariably involve conflict, typically, between those whose activities are being restricted and those who argue for the restrictions. The establishment of the Environmental Protection Agency represented a victory for environmentalists over developers and polluting in-

[7] Theodore J. Lowi, "American Business, Public Policy, Case Studies, and Practical Theory," *World Politics* 16 (July 1964): 667–715.

dustries. But this victory did not mean the end of conflict. New issues arise and old ones continue. The energy crisis of the 1970s prompted efforts to reduce reliance on foreign oil and to revive the use of domestic coal. Although that strategy helped meet energy needs, it also required the suspension of some air pollution controls and regulations on strip coal mining. At the same time, newer issues were being hotly debated: how to dispose of hazardous waste without poisoning groundwater or making farmland unsafe for growing food. What environmentalists gained in the creation of the Environmental Protection Agency was a critical group of experts and government officials as allies in the policymaking process. Although sometimes agencies established to limit the activities of a particular group end up as protectors of that group against those who wish to impose new regulations, the element of conflict and debate is a constant feature of regulatory policymaking.

Redistributive Policies The conflict that accompanies redistributive policymaking is over fundamental issues, and the debate is ideological in nature. Rarely is there a consensus to provide resources and opportunities for one group in society at the expense of others. Even when it would seem callous to fail to express a concern for the less fortunate, opponents of redistribution question the effectiveness of assistance programs or attribute the causes of poverty and misfortune to traits of the victims themselves. In 1964, when the mood of the country favored the so-called War on Poverty, opponents of this policy were accused not of heartlessness, but of naivete: of believing that the way out of poverty was to "inherit a department store," as the political cartoonist Herblock put it. In contrast, when a more conservative country began dismantling the War on Poverty programs in the mid-1970s, the supporters of those programs were portrayed as naive in their faith about what government spending — "throwing money at problems" — might accomplish, and as ignorant about the benefits derived by the poor from the profits and investments of private businesses. Closure on these issues reaches far beyond the boundaries of subgovernments. Major political and governmental leaders play decisive roles, and the news media typically provide extensive coverage of the dispute, which informs and involves the general public. Pollsters report public opinion on the issue, and thousands of constituents write letters to their representatives and senators.

POLICY EVALUATION The rise and fall of the War on Poverty is not atypical of public policies. Public policies are not inalterable decisions carved in stone. Our society changes, as do our preferences, and some policies simply do not work. Government officials continually reevaluate existing policies, reacting in turn as groups and individuals respond to how government affects them. Every year, public policies are evaluated as part of the budget process. When problems reach a crisis stage or receive much public attention, a special task force may be established to evaluate current public policies and suggest improvements.

Policy evaluation, in short, is an integral and ongoing part of public policy-making — and one that can prompt new policies.

Most public-policy evaluation is done "by the seat of the pants." Ideally, there would be periodic reviews to match the goals of public policy with what has been accomplished. Is the social security program keeping the elderly from being destitute? Are regulations on pollution improving the quality of our environment? Does our arsenal of weapons deter aggression and provocation? Although these questions seem straightforward and should provide a base for conducting sound, objective inquiries, the realities of public-policy evaluation present a different picture.

Policy evaluations are frequently based on anecdotal evidence rather than on sound empirical data, and all too often conclusions do little more than generalize the complaints or praise the few individuals and groups that take the time to make them. It is not unusual for legislators or presidents to hear, either directly or through a staff member, about someone who has been cheating in collecting welfare, or about an owner of a business who quit because he or she could not comply with minimum-wage regulations and still make a profit — and conclude from these examples that current welfare policies or labor policies are faulty.

To say that public policymaking is frequently based on impressions and partial evidence is not to imply that few evaluative efforts are made. There are no precise figures on how much time and energy are spent on evaluating public policy, but the amounts are considerable. Researchers at universities and private consultants to government are engaged in studies that both assess the consequences of current public policies and anticipate the effects of proposed alternatives. Interest groups, citizen organizations like Common Cause, congressional committees, and administrative agencies conduct evaluations of existing and proposed policies. Media investigations not only generate news, but also influence public decisions. Congress created the General Accounting Office to evaluate policy implementation and thereby assist the legislature both in making policy and in overseeing administrative agencies.

This list of some of the major actors involved in public-policy evaluation provides some hints as to why that process does not always operate in an ideal manner. Each actor approaches the analysis with a different set of concerns. These differences influence the questions that are and are not asked. Consider, for example, the policy that motor vehicles should not travel more than 55 miles per hour. Those concerned with energy will focus on how much gas this policy has saved per mile driven. The trucking industry, however, is also concerned with the increased time it takes to move goods from one place to another. The longer delivery time resulting from this policy means that the industry can serve fewer customers. The National Safety Council may share an interest in energy conservation, but its main concern is how the 55-mile-per-hour speed limit affects the rate of accidents and the number of traffic fatalities. Legislators must be responsive to the feelings of their constituents. The public may support the policy, it may tolerate the policy, or it may oppose the policy as a nuisance and an inconvenience.

If each of these actors comes to a different conclusion about the value of the policy from his or her perspective, conflict will occur, and compromise may be necessary to continue the policy in modified terms. On the other hand, everyone may agree that the policy seems desirable. Or there may be a general feeling, perhaps supported by evidence, that the policy would be more effective if the law were enforced more stringently. (This conclusion might, in fact, be urged by police officers seeking to expand their forces.) Some might focus renewed attention on the condition of roads, the energy efficiency of cars and trucks, the availability of mass transit, the use of seat belts and safety devices, and so forth.

Public-policy evaluation, then, always involves many actors and employs many criteria. There are, of course, the explicitly stated goals of the speed-limit policy — to save energy and save lives. In addition, there are the political goals of maintaining constituent support, and the administrative criteria concerned with efficient and effective enforcement or implementation. The ratio of costs to benefits is a common yardstick in evaluating public policies. The clearest example of this ratio in our discussion of the 55-mile-per-hour speed limit is the calculation that the trucking industry might make in comparing the savings in fuel and accidents with the costs incurred by not being able to serve as many customers within the same period of time.

Outputs and Impacts Public-policy evaluation is never easy. Government decisions are rarely the only influence to be considered. A distinction must be made between the outputs of the policymaking process and the impact of those policies. Outputs are the direct actions taken by government itself: New signs with the lower speed limit are posted, highways are built, food stamps and checks are distributed, teachers are certified. These outputs are designed to produce certain results, but we cannot assume that they actually will. The posting of a speed limit does not ensure that every driver will stay within that limit, or that accidents will be reduced or energy saved. Nor does the certification of teachers guarantee that students will be taught more competently.

To understand the impact of a public policy, we must identify and examine factors other than the government's action. To determine the extent to which the 55-mile-per-hour speed limit has reduced the consumption of motor fuel, one needs to know — for the periods both before and after the imposition of the lower speed limit — the speed at which drivers actually traveled, the number of miles driven on the highway as opposed to city streets, the effects of current pollution-control devices and tires on gas mileage, the kinds of vehicles driven, and the amounts of gas consumed by those vehicles at various speeds. As is usually the case, all the necessary data are not available for earlier years, and are difficult to gather for the current period. Although one might be able to make some fairly good estimates, they are only estimates and are therefore vulnerable to challenge by someone opposed to whatever conclusions might be drawn.

In some policy areas, research on the impact of public policies is further complicated because we cannot agree on what we should try to measure. There are major differences of opinion, for example, about what constitutes high-quality education. These differences in part reflect disagreement about the relative importance of personal happiness, practical skills, cultural heritage, and analytical thinking. Such differences are probably irreconcilable, and their existence limits severely the kinds of assessments of educational policies that can be done.

Likewise, how do we determine whether our policies toward the elderly are enabling them to live with financial security and personal dignity? The vagueness of these objectives defies efforts to measure goal achievement. Vague goals are sometimes intentional — the result of political compromise. In such cases, any attempt to clarify legislative intent may only revive old battles and foreclose any hope of agreement on goals.

In many instances, policymakers can do little more than infer causal relationships between government outputs and the desired policy impact. They set qualifications for teachers and doctors, and machinery to ensure that the qualifications are met, on the assumption that the individuals who meet the qualifications will provide us with satisfactory service. They increase police patrols and add street lights in a high crime area and then conclude that the subsequent crime rate is not as high as it otherwise would be. Unfortunately, the intuition and impressions so frequently relied on for public-policy evaluation are the only tools that are available.

The Use of Public-Policy Evaluation Ideally, the evaluation of public policies would be conducted so that we might improve successful policies and discard those that are not accomplishing what was intended. Here, too, we have frequently seen a deviation from the ideal. Uses for parochial interests were hinted at in the discussion of the various actors involved in evaluation. The lesson here is that analyses can be designed and used to justify a particular position.

Several important considerations affect the use of public-policy evaluations. Frequently, if one wants to halt or delay an impending change, a useful ploy is to urge that a study of the implications of the proposed change be conducted first. One can use the study itself to drag out the delay further in arguments about how the study should be conducted, who should do it, whether it was done properly, and what the most appropriate conclusions are from the research. One of the most common ways of thwarting construction of nuclear power plants, dams, waste disposal sites, and urban-renewal projects is to challenge the methodology of the required study of the environmental impact of the construction and call for a new study. In some instances the arguments over environmental-impact statements have been prolonged so that the price of construction rises so high or the need for the project becomes so remote that nothing ever happens.

If, on the other hand, one favors change in a policy and encounters opposition, a useful strategy may be to propose a sunset for the policy, with a provision for renewal dependent on a study of the effects of the policy. The purpose of sunset legislation — that is, a law that expires after a certain specified time — is to avoid the establishment of policies and agencies that outlive their usefulness. However, this approach is often used when there are doubts about whether the proposed policy will be useful at all. The 55-mile-per-hour speed limit and federal revenue sharing with local and state governments are two of many examples of policies adopted for a period of several years, with the provision that their continuation would be based on an evaluation of their effects. This use of policy evaluation does not, of course, mean that the studies that are conducted are any more or less parochial or objective than studies conducted for other purposes.

Finally, public-policy evaluations are used for symbolic purposes. To assure the public that he was concerned about rioting in urban areas, President Johnson appointed the Kerner commission. Everyone knew that the problem of urban rioting was complex and that there was no single, easy solution. But the evaluation of urban and policing policies was important to convey the impression that the government was doing something.

Public-policy evaluation, in short, is an integral part of politics and policy-making. Persuasive arguments require supporting data and evidence. Public-policy evaluations are incorporated into the rhetoric and the reasoning of the political process.

It is rare for all the participants in the process to have their positions fixed at the outset and the policy evaluations to be merely façades. In virtually all cases, some policymakers are undecided and do in fact pay attention to the studies that are done. They must realize, however, that the evaluations they examine are likely to present a particular perspective.

CONCLUSION The process of making public policy involves all the institutions and actors in the American political system. This is the arena of interaction. Formal, legal powers are separated and shared by governmental institutions, whereas informal, political power is divided among both governmental and private groups. To arrive at an authoritative agreement on the direction of our society and the role of government in heading in that direction requires the participation of diverse elements of American politics. Because of this, we should expect public policies to reflect conflict and power and to be vague and contradictory at times. That, after all, is the nature of our politics.

Different policies involve different actors. The cozy relationship between some administrative agencies, congressional subcommittees, and interest groups, allows these groups to develop policies in their particular areas of concern, out of sight of the rest of us. Policies that structure the redistribution of resources and opportunities, on the other hand, tend to be very visible and to involve virtually everyone. We draw on the most fundamental values of our society when we make policies about how to distribute wealth and opportunities.

Public policies and popular preferences are not always identical. The existence of subgovernments maintains privileges and services for specific groups and interests, sometimes beyond the time when there is general agreement that this is important. Procedures for making significant changes are cumbersome and designed to give undue weight to minority views and interests. The requirements that vetoes be overridden by two-thirds in both houses of Congress and that three-fourths of the state legislatures must approve constitutional amendments have blocked the adoption of changes that a majority of the electorate favor. Public-policy evaluations are difficult to conduct because of the vague or contradictory nature of some policies, or because social goals frequently defy attempts at measurement. Moreover, evaluators and those who use evaluations tend to have a perspective that looks only at parts of a policy, to the neglect of other concerns.

ECONOMIC POLICYMAKING: A CASE STUDY

Since 1965, inflation has replaced unemployment as the major economic fear of the American people. This is not because we have few people out of work or because people no longer care if they are working. Inflation is frightening because it erodes the buying power of those who *are* working and destroys the plans of those who have been saving for retirement, a trip, or a major purchase. Inflation is also frightening because it is not understood very well.

Most people identify inflation with increases in prices. Groceries, heating fuel, books, services all keep costing more. These price increases are particularly devastating if a person's income is not going up, as is the case with many of those living on retirement pensions or other fixed incomes. People start realizing that they are only hurting themselves when they save money because their money will buy less tomorrow than it will today. Common responses to inflation are to demand higher wages — a demand that contributes to higher prices (since the company will have to get more money to pay those wages) and to more spending, which also contributes to higher prices (since the demand for goods may be greater than the supply). Another problem with a pattern of high spending and low saving is that little money is then available for investing in remodeling old plants, developing new technologies, building new plants, and taking other steps to improve productivity — that is, producing more goods and delivering more services at the same cost that was incurred for fewer goods and services. One view of inflation, in other words, is a spiral of higher prices and higher wages, but without higher productivity.

Another way of viewing inflation is as a situation in which there is too much money in the economy. The monetarist school of economics defines inflation as "too much money chasing too few goods." [1] The generation of money through government budget deficits, banking policies, and low interest rates can produce more money than is justified by the production of goods and services in the total economy. When there is too much money, the value of the money is less, and prices rise — that is, we have inflation.

AGENDA SETTING As we have learned, the first step in government policymaking is recognizing that an issue is important enough to be moved to the top of the long list of items on the agenda of government officials. Invariably, economic issues are among those that receive the most attention. The *kind* of economic issues change, however. As we mentioned, unemployment has frequently been regarded as more important than inflation. During the first part of the Carter administration, unemployment and inflation were both regarded as serious issues, but unemployment won the place of primary concern. When the inflation rate had exceeded 10 percent for several years in a row, frustrations and discontent mounted. As theories emerged about the causes of inflation, the American public developed a list of enemies: the deficit spending of the federal government; the rise in oil prices engineered by the Arab governments; the cost and wastefulness of government regulations; the craftiness of the Japanese auto industry; the consumptionist character of the American public; the greed of American businesses and labor unions. The concern expressed itself in opinion polls and at the ballot box. In his bid for reelection, President Carter was defeated by Ronald Reagan. Furthermore, the Democratic party lost control of the United States Senate as Republicans running on an anti-inflation platform took the lion's share of the seats being contested. Inflation clearly had reached a visible position on the agenda. Upon taking office, President Reagan promised major proposals for new policies to reduce the rate of inflation. Both Republican and Democratic legislators promised to cooperate. The press and the public applauded.

POLICY FORMATION Consensus that something must be done about inflation is not the same as agreement about *what* must be done. The process of determining what to do is not simple. In many ways, it represents in microcosm the more general pattern of politics in America. The participants in the process include a variety of actors — individuals, small groups, and institutions — all with their own interests and their own perspectives on the problems of inflation and on possible solutions. In 1981, as the new Reagan administration initiated anti-inflation policies, the actors included:

1. *Individuals:* Although small groups and institutions are, of course, composed of individuals, several prominent persons with important formal au-

---

[1] Edgar R. Fiedler, "Inflation and Economic Policy," in Clarence C. Walton, ed., *Inflation and National Survival* (New York: Academy of Political Science, 1979), p. 114.

thority and informal influence played distinctive roles. Because of their importance in the policymaking process, how they make decisions, what values they pursue, and what kinds of evidence they find persuasive were crucial both to the conflict that accompanied policy formulation and to the content of the final decision. Prominent individuals in the 1981 economic policymaking process included President Reagan, David Stockman (director of the Office of Management and Budget), Dan Rostenkowski (chair of the House Ways and Means Committee), James R. Jones (chair of the House Budget Committee), Carl Perkins (chair of the House Education and Labor Committee), and Peter Domenici (chair of the Senate Budget Committee).

2. *Small groups:* Although the individuals just listed must at some point make their own decisions, virtually all of them relied on the advice and expertise of small groups. Some participants in the policy-formulation process, such as interest-group spokespersons, agency heads, and committee chairs, see their role as representing and pressing for the decisions reached by the small groups to which they belong. Some of the small groups involved in 1981 economic policymaking were President Reagan's White House staff, Office of Management and Budget staff, the House and Senate Budget Committees, the House Ways and Means Committee, cabinet secretaries and their staff, and informal coalitions of interest-group representatives.

3. *Institutions:* Institutions that have formal authority, such as Congress, the Federal Reserve Board, and the presidency, must participate in economic policymaking and must interact with each other. Decisions about tax cuts, spending limits, and budget allocations must be made jointly by Congress and the president. To get a majority vote in both houses of Congress and to get the president's signature — especially with a Democratically controlled House and a Republican Senate and president — is likely to require bargaining and compromise.

Even an independent body like the Federal Reserve Board must interact with other institutions. The Federal Reserve Board regulates how much money banks must have on hand, how much they can invest, and how much interest they can charge on loans. Thus, it has an important impact on the amount of money available in the economy. The members of the Federal Reserve Board are nominated by the president and confirmed by the Senate. The board is a creature of Congress. It exists because of congressional action, and if Congress is sufficiently upset with what the board does, it can pass a law curtailing the board's authority.

Institutions are important not only for how they interact with other institutions, but also because they, unlike individuals and small groups, have procedural rules that they must follow. Rules can affect the content of a policy or even whether a policy gets changed at all. Chapter 5 cited examples of how filibusters in the Senate and actions by committees in Congress affect policymaking in the legislature.

With the election of Ronald Reagan to the presidency, the aforementioned cast of characters moved toward the formulation of new economic policies for the federal government. President Reagan presented a general blueprint for these new directions in his campaign speeches. In the days after his election in November 1980, he organized task forces to translate these into more specific proposals. When he was inaugurated in January 1981, he was ready to forward his proposals to Congress.

The major provisions of President Reagan's initial proposals were:

1. Cut personal income taxes by 30 percent over a three-year period, with 10 percent to come in the first year.
2. Cut $48.6 billion from the budget proposed by the Carter administration for the fiscal year beginning October 1, 1981, and promise to balance the federal government's budget by 1984. The cuts were concentrated in the social service area. Defense spending was to increase by $4.3 billion.
3. Allow businesses to take larger deductions for new capital equipment when calculating their income taxes.
4. Cut government jobs by 43,000 the first year and 83,000 the next.

The intent behind these proposals was to attack inflation by decreasing the supply of money through decreasing the federal budget deficit, and by increasing productivity through encouraging more investment in new plants and technologies by businesses and higher-income groups. Ideally, in other words, money would be channeled into new investments rather than into higher prices; the new investments in turn would generate new jobs and more revenue for government and the economy generally. As in most other instances of policymaking, data indicating whether or not the proposals would achieve their goals were not available. Decision makers were forced to make important guesses and assumptions — such as what the inflation rate was likely to be, and what people were likely to do with any extra income, and whether interest rates would go down for those borrowing money to invest in new plants and technologies.

The Reagan proposals were generally well received, but they also generated doubts and criticism. Some economists disagreed with the assumptions and theory behind the proposals. Some worried about the data and the projections on which the formulation of the anti-inflation strategy was based. A major fear was that, even with budget cuts, the loss of revenue from lower taxes would mean more borrowing by the government to meet expenses and that this borrowing would drive interest rates up. High interest rates would, of course, make it costly to invest and increase productivity, thus defeating a major goal of the Reagan administration.

Criticisms also came from those whose own interests or causes were being hurt. Federal employees nervously calculated the effects of cuts on their agencies and themselves. Representatives from the so-called Frostbelt (the Northeast and Midwest) objected to the incentives for *new* capital investment. They perceived President Reagan to have accepted a recommendation from President Carter's

Commission for a National Agenda for the 1980s that the federal government accept the decline of Frostbelt industries and concentrate resources on growth and development in the "Sunbelt" (the South and Southwest). The Frostbelt needed incentives to rehabilitate and modernize existing plants and capital more than it needed incentives for new capital. Midwestern dairy farmers questioned whether the rationale behind the president's proposals was economic or political. They noted that whereas dairy price supports were being cut substantially, tobacco subsidies (important to Senator Jesse Helms, chair of the Senate Agriculture Committee and a strong supporter of President Reagan during his campaign) were left untouched.

In late February 1981, a coalition of 150 liberal organizations formed to fight the proposals to cut social service spending. The lobbyists for this coalition had a friend in Carl Perkins, a Democrat from Kentucky who has chaired the House Education and Labor Committee since 1967. Representative Perkins illustrated the importance of an individual in the policymaking process. Representative Perkins is a big man in a rumpled suit who speaks with the twang that is common among the people in Appalachia that he represents. His colleagues in the House agree that his style combines a quiet, disarming smile with a hard determination to get what he believes is right. Representative Perkins personally authored most of the $34 billion in federal programs that his committee oversees.

In response to the budget cuts proposed by President Reagan, Representative Perkins orchestrated twenty-four days of hearings in which his committee met with coal miners wheezing from black lung disease, family court judges worried about rehabilitation programs, unemployed factory workers, disabled children, malnourished pregnant women, and the like. Administrators in affected agencies openly and covertly provided Representative Perkins with data supporting his efforts. At the end, in a move that seemed totally out of touch with the general mood of government and the country, his committee voted for a budget increase of $3.9 billion over what had been recommended by the Carter administration and $18 billion over the Reagan proposal. Meanwhile, other Democratic committee chairs were seeking compromises with the Reagan administration budget cutters.

In a separate strategy move to wrest some of the visibility and policy initiative from the Republicans, Democratic leaders in the House worked through James R. Jones and the Democratic majority on the House Budget Committee to offer a substitute to the Reagan anti-inflation plan. The major features of the Democratic plan were:

1. Deeper cuts in the federal budget than those proposed by Reagan.
2. Only half the cuts in social program spending proposed by Reagan.
3. Less money for defense than proposed by Reagan ($189.7 billion instead of $194 billion). The reduction in defense expenditures was based on eliminating a pay raise, blocking the addition of 30,000 civilian employees, and delaying or changing a number of weapon programs.

Simultaneously, Representative Dan Rostenkowski, a Democrat from Illinois and chair of the House Ways and Means Committee, offered an alternative to President Reagan's tax cut proposal. The Democratic alternative included a one-year cut, aimed mainly at families with incomes below $50,000 a year, that would cost $40 billion, in contrast to President Reagan's 30 percent across-the-board cut over three years that would cost $53.9 billion the first year. To encourage investments, the Democratic plan included a reduction of the maximum tax on investment earnings from 70 to 50 percent immediately, rather than the gradual reduction as proposed by the president. To help the Frostbelt, the Democratic plan included tax write-offs for rehabilitating old industries, as well as for building new ones.

One effect of the Democratic proposals, for both spending and taxation, was that there would be a smaller deficit in the federal budget ($25.9 billion instead of President Reagan's $50.5 billion). Also, the Democrats promised a balanced budget one year earlier and did their calculations on the assumption that inflation would be 10 percent annually, rather than 8.3 percent, the rate used by the Reagan administration.

Clearly, the Democratic party was acting in a partisan fashion and trying to embarass the Republicans by going farther than they seemed prepared to go in responding to the public's concern about inflation. On the other hand, that partisan effort did provide an alternative proposal. Initially, the Democratic strategy seemed to have some effect. The Republican-controlled Senate Budget Committee had considered the spending and taxation proposals of the president separately and voted in favor of them. Committee procedures, however, required a vote on the package as a whole. That vote, taken on April 9, 1981, the same day that the House Budget Committee and the House Ways and Means Committees approved the Democratic alternatives, went against the president. The three Republicans who voted with the nine Democrats to form the 12–8 majority explained their votes as concerns about the budget deficit and its possible impact on continued inflation if the president's proposals were adopted. The vote was a signal that compromise was necessary.

Indeed, two weeks later President Reagan agreed to accept and support a compromise budget drafted by a coalition of conservative Democrats and Republicans in the House. This version passed both houses of Congress by substantial margins. The compromise split many of the differences between the initial Reagan proposal and the Democratic alternative, but it was clearly closest to President Reagan's version. Ironically, just as this agreement was reached, the inflation rate dropped from a projected 12 percent to 7.5 percent, endangering support for the drastic measures proposed by the conservatives. Rather than taking credit for the drop, White House aides cautioned against optimism and warned of bad economic news on the horizon.

Policy formation, in short, involves more than the collection of information and the testing of theories about cause and effect. The process includes the wisdom and the limitations of individuals, small groups, and institutions, and takes place at the confluence of a variety of interests. In government, the adage "knowledge is power" only partially applies. Power also comes from representation and from the ballot box. It comes from the influence of friends and aides on individuals. It comes from wealth and social status. And power, as well as knowledge and reason, is important in policy formation.

IMPLEMEN- Some of the implementation of the economic policymaking initiated with Pres-
TATION ident Reagan's inauguration began before the policies were actually formulated and adopted. The handwriting on the wall was clear: There would be extensive cuts in federal expenditures in almost every area other than defense. Although Republicans and Democrats, conservatives and liberals, Frostbelt and Sunbelt differed on some of the details and priorities, there was little disagreement that there would be cuts — serious cuts. With this in mind, federal agencies, state and local governments, and private organizations with government contracts began thinking about how they were going to cope with less money from Washington. The mood of the public was such that state and local governments gave little serious consideration to the option of increasing taxes in order to make up the losses in federal dollars. Like others, they discussed how to cut.

In many ways, this anticipatory implementation both reflected and contributed to the apparent consensus that government spending and taxation must be cut in order to combat inflation. Within the federal government, President Reagan pursued a shrewd strategy that had the effect of discouraging most federal agencies from mobilizing the clientele and legislative committees in what we have called subgovernments to resist the formulation and implementation of budget cuts. President Reagan delayed filling thousands of positions at the level just below cabinet agency heads until well into his first year in office. Although he was criticized for interrupting the flow of government operations and for postponing decisions by not appointing people to these senior management posts, President Reagan made the process of cutting back on government easier. Typically, a career civil servant was appointed to fill one of these positions on an acting basis. That appointment usually represented an important promotion, albeit temporary and tentative, for the individual employee. There was personal satisfaction with this. Recognizing that they were only "Acting" and frequently not wanting to jeopardize the possibility that the president might make their appointment a regular one, these individuals were generally much more compliant than might otherwise have been the case.

Economic policies, particularly those that rely on patterns of consumption and investment for their success, depend on implementation in the private sector as well as by government agencies. The mandate to government agencies was to cut. The wish was expressed to individuals and institutions outside government that they invest in ways that would increase America's productivity. The Regan administration was encouraged by public opinion polls, taken in February and March 1981, that indicated that people would invest extra money if they had it, rather than use it to purchase something. If money from a tax cut were to contribute to the fight against inflation, then it could not be used to purchase luxury items, or to invest in diamonds or gold to hedge against further inflation, and it must not be swallowed by tax increases at the state or local level. Ideally, neither would it be absorbed by price increases due to an event like crop failures or an oil embargo. Full implementation required the right private, as well as public, response. As 1981 came to a close, the major obstacle to implementation was an interest rate that refused to go below 20 percent. Questions emerged about whether more time was needed for implementation or whether something was wrong with the policies and strategies themselves.

EVALUATION Just as there was some anticipatory implementation, so also was there some anticipatory evaluation. Not surprisingly, many opponents were quite ready to pronounce as failures policies they regarded as misguided even before those policies were adopted. Those concerned about cuts in social services were pleased with the action of Carl Perkins's committee. Other legislative committees quarreled about how much to cut, rather than whether to cut. From the perspective of those who appeared before Perkins's committee, the casualties in the battle against inflation were going to be the poor. They had already evaluated the policy.

There are, of course, other standards for measuring the success or failure of the policies adopted to lower the rate of inflation. One can use the aggregate rate of inflation for the country as a whole. One can use the impact on various regions of the country. One can use public satisfaction, perhaps as expressed in the ballot box, as a measure.

At this point, it is too early to make a judgment. Time must pass, and information must become available. Even then, there will be questions that are difficult to answer. In part, this is because we still do not fully understand the causes and the nature of inflation. In part, this is because we are dealing with so many factors. For example, a balanced federal budget, in itself, will not remove enough money from the economy to have an effect on the inflation rate of much more than 0.5 percent. What is more important is the effect of a balanced budget on the perceptions of the public — and the guess was that the effect will be to restore confidence and investment in the economy. Evaluation of the economic policies adopted in the first years of the Reagan administration might also be complicated by external events like those cited before, such as crop failures and oil embargoes.

Our evaluations of public policy tend to be incomplete and confined to short time spans. President Carter's policies were judged to be inadequate — in part because of their limitations but in part, too, because of factors beyond his control. In any case, we act on those evaluations. The assessment of the effects of a policy becomes an agenda item.

Carter's failure became Reagan's mandate. What happens if the policies of the early 1980s fail? Will we blame Reagan? the approach? Congress? labor unions? businesses? the weather? an event or organization outside our boundaries? Wassily Leontif, the Nobel Prize winner in economic science in 1973, has nominated yet another possible culprit — the policymaking process itself. Although he hopes that inflation will no longer be a problem, Leontif suggests that, if there is failure, it may be the result of the lack of rationality in our manner of making decisions.[2] The lack of systematic information, the political compromises, and the cumbersome procedures may be imperfections we cannot afford. Yet resolving these problems may necessitate the sacrifice of cherished parts of our democratic system. This is most obvious when we think about what would be lost if we did not allow political compromises. The result is that we accept some of the inefficiencies and tensions in our policymaking process.

SUGGESTIONS FOR FURTHER READING

Allison, Graham. *Essence of Decision: Explaining the Cuban Missile Crisis.* Boston: Little, Brown, 1971. Allison applies three major approaches to the study of policymaking in an attempt to understand the behavior of Soviet and American agencies during the Cuban missile crisis of 1962. He concludes that although each approach effectively helps explain some decisions, no single approach explains all the actions taken.

Braybrooke, David, and Lindblom, Charles E. *A Strategy of Decision.* New York: Free Press, 1963. This book elaborates the argument that most policies are the result of decisions to pursue small, incremental changes in the status quo. Braybrooke and Lindblom discuss the reasons for this pattern and some of its implications.

Etzioni, Amitai. "Mixed-Scanning: A Third Approach to Decision-Making." *Public Administration Review,* December 1967. The approach outlined in this article acknowledges that most decisions are incremental, but also recognizes that at times policymakers make special efforts to consider new directions and to weigh a wide variety of alternatives.

Lowi, Theodore J. *The End of Liberalism.* New York: Norton, 1969. After reviewing the structures and institutions involved in policymaking, Lowi concludes that governmental direction is bound to be set by powerful special-interest groups unless there are significant changes in the organization and processes of the federal government. Lowi challenges traditional definitions of democracy and public interest in the United States.

Ripley, Randall B., and Franklin, Grace A. *Congress, the Bureaucracy and Public Policy.* Homewood, Ill.: Dorsey Press, 1976. Ripley and Franklin specify the changes in the roles and relationships between institutions of government with different kinds of policy issues and different levels of political conflict. Case studies are used to illustrate general patterns.

Wildavsky, Aaron. *Speaking Truth to Power. The Art and Craft of Policy Analysis.* Boston: Little, Brown, 1979. The basic argument presented by Wildavsky is that our

[2] Wassily Leontif, "If Mr. Reagan's Policies Flop, Then What?" *The New York Times,* February 22, 1981, p. EY21.

governmental system is incapable of either conducting or using comprehensive, systematic policy analyses. Values, more than objective analyses of facts, are of primary importance in policymaking. Wildavsky illustrates by examining several attempts at policy evaluation.

Chapter 14 Individual Rights

Freedom is not free . . . the cultivation of civil liberty can be no more passive than the cultivation of a farm. . . . It requires resolution, faith, and courage to maintain what Madison called "the great rights of mankind."

— Edmond Cahn, *The Great Rights* (1963)

RIGHTS AND THE CONSTITUTION The framers of the Constitution believed that individual rights were embodied in the people, individually and collectively, were inalienable and were not given *to* the people by kings or governments. John Locke, the English philosopher whose views played such a large role in the making of our Constitution, had argued that the sole purpose of government was to prevent individuals from infringing on the rights of others. These rights inhered in persons in nature; government could neither expand nor contract them. But the framers of the Constitution did not hold so negative a view of government. They recognized the need for governmental power that *also* protected, or at least did not threaten, the rights of the people. But they were also fearful of governmental tyranny, and wrote a constitution of "enumerated powers." They believed that the best way to protect the people's rights was to give government no power to violate those rights. If government could exercise only those powers delegated to it, then it could not use its power to deprive citizens of their rights.

Because the framers were men of practical experience, they recognized that merely enumerating the powers government might exercise did not ensure that fundamental rights would be respected. They wrote into the Constitution a number of specific prohibitions, which apply either to the federal government or the states alone, or to both state and federal governments. Both the state and federal governments were forbidden to pass bills of attainder (legislative punishments) or ex post facto laws. Congress was prohibited from suspending the "great writ" of habeas corpus except in situations of emergency.[1] Trial by jury was required in criminal cases in the federal courts; religious tests or qualifications for office were banned; and limitations were placed on the definition of treason and on the punishment for conviction of that offense.

Even these measures were not sufficient for those whose distrust of the federal government threatened to block ratification of the new Constitution. James Madison, among others, initially opposed inclusion of a bill of rights in the Constitution. Since any list of the rights of citizens would necessarily be incomplete, he reasoned that other rights might later be rejected simply because they were not on the original list. He believed that a constitution of limited powers simply did not give the federal government the lawful authority to infringe these rights. Nevertheless, the need to secure ratification of the Constitution led to the introduction of a bill of rights in the First Congress. Twelve amendments were proposed, ten of which were ratified and became known as the Bill of Rights. One of these amendments, the Ninth, attempted to meet the "inadvertent exclusion" problem by stating that "the enumeration in the Constitution, of certain rights, shall not be construed to deny or disparage others retained by the people."

The Bill of Rights and the prohibitory clauses of the original Constitution reflect what Americans then believed to be the most important rights — or at least the governmental excesses they most feared. We have already noted, in Chapter 2, the inconsistencies in those beliefs and the limitations on realization of protected rights brought about by social and economic inequalities. The Constitution and the Revolution may have done away with the last vestiges of hereditary aristocracy, a pervasive state bureaucracy, the medieval guilds, and other "paraphernalia of the old world," but the equality of opportunity created in its wake was nonetheless limited primarily to property-holding white males. Property qualifications for voting still existed; women could not vote; and slavery and the slave trade still flourished.

Even with these inconsistencies, the Constitution and the Bill of Rights provided a new concept of the relationship between government and the governed. The Constitution did not specify a particular "method" or institution

---

[1] An *ex post facto* law retroactively defines a certain act as a crime. The writ of *habeas corpus* is a court order that challenges the illegal detention or incarceration of an individual. Federal courts today are empowered by Congress to issue a writ of habeas corpus to any prisoner held "in violation of the Constitution or of any treaty or law of the United States."

with primary responsibility to protect individual rights, but the document as a whole (including the Bill of Rights) created a system of protection. First, as already noted, a government of limited and enumerated powers, reinforced by a complex system of checks and balances, was created. Second, protections of individual rights were stated clearly as legally enforceable restrictions on government, not mere admonitions as were characteristic of the English Bill of Rights and the Virginia Declaration of Rights. Finally, the opportunity for judicial enforcement of constitutional rights was implied.[2]

THE BILL OF RIGHTS AND THE STATES The words of the Bill of Rights seem to apply as much to the states as to the federal government. Only the First Amendment ("Congress shall make no law . . .") and the Seventh Amendment refer specifically to the federal government. The others state general principles that appear to apply to both the states and the federal government. Historians have disputed the meaning of these differences in language, but the controversy was settled for political and legal purposes by the opinion of Chief Justice John Marshall in the case of *Barron* v. *Baltimore* (1833).[3] Barron owned a wharf that became obsolete when municipal construction of a road diverted the streams that led to it. Speaking for a unanimous court, Marshall denied Barron's claim that this constituted a taking of private property, without due process of law or just compensation, in violation of the Fifth Amendment. Marshall observed that the Bill of Rights was drafted in response to fear of abuse by the *federal* government. The Constitution did contain some express limitations on the states; but these, Marshall noted, were always stated quite specifically. General constitutional limits, he said, should be construed to apply only to the federal government.

Ratification of the Fourteenth Amendment in 1868 provided an opportunity to reexamine the relationship of the Bill of Rights to the states. This amendment imposed certain prohibitions on the states. They were required to observe the norms of "due process of law" before depriving any person of life, liberty, or property; they were prohibited from making laws abridging the privileges and immunities of citizens of the United States; and they were prohibited from denying to any person the "equal protection of the laws." But just what did these majestic phrases mean?

Did these prohibitions of the Fourteenth Amendment, taken together, "incorporate" the first eight amendments of the Bill of Rights and apply them to the states? Initially, the Supreme Court rejected this contention. To accept it, the Court said, would contradict the intention of those who wrote and voted for the amendment and would radically alter the relationship between the federal government and the states. The federal government, not the states, would

[2] Edmond Cahn, "A New Kind of Society" in Edmond Cahn, ed., *The Great Rights* (New York: Macmillan, 1963), p. 4.
[3] 7 Pet. 243 (1833).

be the government to which the people looked first for protection of their rights. Furthermore, the Court said, since the due process clause of the Fourteenth Amendment was identical to the due process clause of the Fifth Amendment, the two were obviously meant to have the same meaning.[4]

Periodic efforts to incorporate the Bill of Rights into the Fourteenth Amendment continued. In 1925 the Supreme Court announced that the free speech provisions of the First Amendment applied to the states.[5] However, the push to incorporation was slowed in 1937 by the Court's decision in *Palko* v. *Connecticut*,[6] when the Supreme Court ruled that the Fifth Amendment prohibition against double jeopardy did not necessarily apply to the states. For an 8-to-1 majority, Justice Benajmin Cardozo rejected the contention that *all* provisions of the Bill of Rights became applicable to the states via the Fourteenth Amendment. Some provisions were "absorbed" by the Fourteenth Amendment, such as the First or Sixth Amendments' guarantee of right to counsel. The dividing line, Cardozo wrote, was whether or not the particular provision was "of the very essence of ordered liberty, . . . [or constituted] a principle of justice so rooted in the traditions and conscience of our people as to be ranked as fundamental." The principle of double jeopardy, he said, as applied in this case to permit the state to retry Palko for first-degree murder after his earlier conviction of second degree murder had been reversed, was not so fundamental.

Cardozo's opinion rejected the doctrine of "total incorporation," but acknowledged that individual provisions of the Bill of Rights deemed to be fundamental could be absorbed into the Fourteenth Amendment, a process that became known as "selective incorporation." One of the justices who agreed with Cardozo's opinion in *Palko* was Hugo Black, a former senator from Alabama then just appointed to the Court by Franklin Roosevelt. Eleven years later, however, Black emerged as the leader of a group of justices seeking to discard Cardozo's opinion and adopt the total incorporation doctrine.[7] Black argued that the framers of the Fourteenth Amendment *intended* to incorporate the Bill of Rights, an interpretation that historians generally have not accepted. He also contended that Cardozo's selective incorporation thesis gave judges excessive power to "pick and choose" among the provisions of the Bill of Rights in determining which were, and which were not, "essential to a scheme of ordered liberty." For Black, this gave Supreme Court justices the authority to declare unconstitutional laws they did not like.

Black and other adherents of the total incorporation doctrine were never able to persuade a majority of the Court to accept it. One by one, however, most of the key provisions of the Bill of Rights have been applied to the states in a process of expanding selective incorporation. By the end of the 1960s only

---

[4]*Hurtado* v. *California*, 110 U.S. 516 (1884); *Twining* v. *New Jersey*, 211 U.S. 78 (1908).
[5]*Gitlow* v. *New York*, 268 U.S. 652 (1925).
[6]302 U.S. 319 (1937).
[7]*Adamson* v. *California*, 332 U.S. 46 (1947).

a few provisions remained unincorporated.[8] And the Court's focus has shifted from incorporation to defining other rights in *addition* to those enumerated in the Bill of Rights. For Black, who claimed to hold a literal view of the meaning of the Constitution, this was as indefensible as permitting judges to decide which rights were "fundamental" enough to apply to the states, and which were not.[9]

Dispute about incorporation of the Bill of Rights was a debate over the fundamental question of national versus state protection of individual rights, and in particular over whether rights should be the same throughout the United States. What would be the consequences if the right to trial by jury or the protections against self-incrimination existed in some states but not in others? How important is it to have a *uniform* policy defining the constitutional protections for speech and religion? Does the existence of a federal system require local or regional autonomy in matters of individual rights?

IS THE BILL OF RIGHTS ENOUGH? Supreme Court Justice William O. Douglas once suggested that the Bill of Rights "may not be enough."[10] The rights protected by the Bill of Rights are dependent for enforcement on legislative or judicial action. Rights are often meaningful only to those who already possess certain minimum resources and skills. The effective existence of rights depends on social, economic, and political factors over which the law, or government, may have little control. Most important, Douglas wrote, the rights stated in the Bill of Rights are not adequate for the times in which we live. Most of the provisions of the Bill of Rights, he observed, prohibit government from engaging in certain activities, or establish procedures that government must follow when acting against citizens (as in the criminal process).

Douglas was arguing that the Bill of Rights, essentially a negative document, was better suited for a time when government played only a small role in the lives of the people. In a welfare state, threats to liberty may come as much from what government fails to do as from the abuses of government officials. For example, some would argue that the failure of government to protect individuals effectively against economic deprivation is the greatest of all threats to individual liberty.

RIGHTS IN REALITY The framers of the Constitution believed that rights are "natural" and not something the government gives to its citizens. In practice, the rights a citizen can exercise often depend on government action or protection. For example,

[8] After *Benton* v. *Maryland*, 395 U.S. 784 (1969), which reversed *Palko* and incorporated double jeopardy, only the Second, Third, and Seventh Amendments, the grand jury provisions of the Fifth Amendment, and the right against excessive bail of the Eighth Amendment, remained applicable only to the federal government.

[9] See, for example, Justice Black's strong objections, in *Griswold* v. *Connecticut*, 381 U.S. 479 (1965), to a judicially created constitutional right to privacy.

[10] "The Bill of Rights Is Not Enough," in Edmond Cahn, *The Great Rights*, pp. 117–58.

the courts (and other law enforcement officials) may be called on to protect the free speech rights of an unpopular minority group. If the courts are unwilling to enforce such a claim, then free speech exists in only a theoretical sense for members of that group. Furthermore, freedom of speech — like most constitutional rights — is not absolute. Exercise of that right is dependent on the context in which it is claimed. Supreme Court Justice Oliver Wendell Holmes once wrote that there is no right to falsely shout "fire" in a crowded theater. Likewise, there is no constitutional right to utter slanderous words, or to advocate directly the overthrow of the government by force and violence.

The contingent nature of rights was recognized in the Supreme Court's treatment of the abortion controversy. Its decision in *Roe* v. *Wade*,[11] establishing the right to an abortion free of governmental interference in the first two trimesters of pregnancy, was qualified in practice by the Court's later decision in *Harris* v. *McRae* (1980),[12] which upheld the power of Congress to prohibit the funding of abortions under the Medicaid program. In his opinion for a 5-to-4 majority in that case, Justice Stewart put it succinctly:

> Although the liberty protected by the Due Process Clause affords protection against unwarranted government interference with freedom of choice in the context of certain personal decisions, it does not confer an entitlement to such funds as may be necessary to realize all the advantages of that freedom. To hold otherwise would mark a drastic change in our understanding of the Constitution.

The right to counsel in criminal cases, which applies to all but the most minor offenses, may be a hollow right without adequate provisions for public defenders or assigned counsel. And it may be detrimental if it does not mean the right to effective counsel. The right to equal employment without discrimination on account of race or sex may be little more than symbolic if administrative enforcement apparatus is not adequately funded or if not enough jobs are available.

The ability of the law and the courts to articulate and protect our most cherished rights is a necessary but not sufficient condition for the enjoyment of those rights.[13]

The late Judge Learned Hand once wrote:

> I often wonder whether we do not rest our hopes too much upon constitutions, upon laws, and upon courts. These are false hopes. . . . Liberty lies in the hearts of men and women; when it dies there, no constitution, no laws, no court can save it; no constitution, no law, no court can even do much to help it. While it lies there it needs no constitution, no law, no court to save it.[14]

---

[11] 410 U.S. 113 (1973).

[12] 65 L. Ed. 2d. 684 (1980).

[13] Stuart Scheingold refers to this belief as the "myth of rights" in *The Politics of Rights* (New Haven: Yale University Press, 1974).

[14] *The Spirit of Liberty* (New York: Vintage, 1959), p. 144.

But Judge Hand overstated his case. Law can educate and help create the conditions of liberty. In a divided community, it may provide crucial support to the defenders of liberty. Judge Hand was right, however, in stating that liberty cannot survive if it is supported by the law alone and is not embodied in the popular culture.

Recent studies show that "support for civil liberties among the American public is as shallow as it is broad."[15] Americans value their own freedom. They strongly support the slogans of freedom — free speech, freedom of the press, due process, equality, and so on. But citizens seem curiously reluctant to apply these slogans to persons different from themselves or in situations in which they expect to suffer some personal disadvantage as a result of extending rights to others. As one scholar has observed,

> Most Americans want to be treated as well as anyone else, but do not mind if others are treated less well than they are. This kind of commitment reflects a long-standing American ambivalence about privilege and disadvantage. . . .
>
> Americans seem too willing to tolerate restrictions on the rights of those who are strange, different or threatening even as they profess devotion to the principles from which those rights derive.[16]

Ambivalence about the meaning and extent of individual rights, which seems to develop early in life,[17] is inherent in a free society that places a high value on *both* liberty and order. Freedom is not absolute. There is a constant need to balance the rights of individuals with the rights of society, although these are certainly not mutually exclusive. Society as a whole is well served, for example, by maximizing freedom of speech and press. But there may be circumstances in which this is not always true. Where is the line to be drawn, for example, when the magazine *The Progressive* planned to publish an article purporting to show how a hydrogen bomb is built?[18] Where is the line to be drawn when an individual or group advocates the overthrow of government itself?[19] Similarly, society as a whole is well served by the various protections in the Bill of Rights for persons accused of crime. But when do the protections accorded criminal defendants, which are in reality protections for us all, threaten the safety and security of other citizens?

Conflict between asserted rights of private property and public regulation of the use of that property is also common. Some types of regulation, designed to protect the public's health and safety, are long established and generally

[15] *Austin Sarat*, "Studying American Legal Culture: An Assessment of Survey Evidence," *Law & Society Review* (1977): 444.

[16] Ibid., pp. 444, 448.

[17] Ibid., p. 445.

[18] A federal judge issued an injunction against publication. When the essential facts of the article were published by a newspaper in Madison, Wisconsin, the government withdrew its lawsuit and the article was published. See Howard Morland, "The H-Bomb Secret: How We Got It — Why We're Telling it," *The Progressive*, November 1979, pp. 14–23.

[19] Generally speaking, the line, the Supreme Court has said, is between the advocacy of abstract ideas and the advocacy of direct action. See *Yates* v. *United States*, 354 U.S. 298 (1957).

accepted. The Supreme Court decided long ago that property "affected with a public interest" was subject to regulation by the government.[20] Thus, the law may not compel you to clean the bathrooms in your home, but restaurants and other similar establishments are required to keep public restrooms clean. But even government regulation designed to protect the public may not be acceptable if it is believed to be unreasonable. In 1980 the Supreme Court invalidated an Occupational Safety and Health Administration (OSHA) regulation reducing the permissible amount of a toxic substance — benzene — in industrial plants.[21] The Court upheld a challenge by the American Petroleum Institute that the secretary of labor did not have sufficient evidence of an asserted relationship between benzene and leukemia to justify the standard he had set. In effect, the Court was balancing the rights of industrial workers to an environment free of toxic substances with the cost to private industry (and, ultimately, to consumers) of maintaining that environment.

Ambivalence about individual rights is particularly acute when rights conflict with one another. The classic example is the conflict between the right to a fair trial protected by the Sixth Amendment and the rights of a free press protected by the First Amendment. A defendant's rights can be undermined by prejudicial publicity before and during a trial.[22] The Supreme Court has held that a trial judge must protect the defendant's rights; yet he cannot do so by imposing a gag order on the press or excluding it from coverage of the trial, except under the most extreme circumstances.[23]

ENFORCEMENT OF RIGHTS   The Constitution does not specify which branch of government is responsible for enforcement of the rights it defines, but there is evidence that many of the framers believed that judges would come to assume the role of guardians. Federal judges, and the Supreme Court in particular, play a critical role in enforcing constitutional protections. But the judicial record in effectively enforcing rights is uneven. Furthermore, protection of rights almost always involves more than a favorable Supreme Court decision. Popular acceptance, presidential and congressional support, and sympathetic bureaucrats and lower court judges all have a critical role to play.

The three Civil War amendments, as well as the Nineteenth, Twenty-fourth, Twenty-fifth, and Twenty-sixth, give special enforcement powers to Congress. But in all cases the development of rights policies and levels of rights enforcement are the product of interaction among Supreme Court decisions, legislation, and bureaucratic rules. The student must be careful to observe where government's commitment to enforcement of a particular right is

---

[20] *Munn* v. *Illinois*, 94 U.S. 113 (1877).

[21] *Industrial Union Department, AFL-CIO* v. *American Petroleum Institute*, 65 L. Ed. 2d. 1010 (1980).

[22] As, for example, when jurors — or potential jurors — read in the newspapers about an alleged confession by the person accused of the crime.

[23] See *Sheppard* v. *Maxwell*, 384 U.S. 333 (1966).

purely symbolic, and where it goes beyond mere symbols to the allocation of resources necessary to protect that right fully. In the most common situation, however, different agencies of government, representing different constituencies and perhaps different values, are contending *against each other*. Thus, lack of enforcement of a right articulated by the Supreme Court may reflect opposition to that right that has coalesced in other branches of government. The continuing battles over abortion, school prayer, and busing are examples of this phenomenon.

THE RIGHTS OF CITIZENSHIP   The Constitution does not define citizenship. It delegates to Congress the power to establish a uniform rule of naturalization, and Congress has made several efforts to define citizenship and the rights of citizens. However, the Supreme Court's decision in the infamous *Dred Scott* case in 1857 underscored the need to have a uniform definition of citizenship.[24] Dred Scott was a black slave from Missouri whose master had taken him to the free state of Illinois and to the Wisconsin territory, also free soil under the Missouri Compromise of 1820. Scott's master eventually returned to Missouri, and upon his death, title to Scott passed to a citizen of New York named John Sandford. Scott sued for his freedom, first in the state courts of Missouri and then in the federal courts. Scott's immediate claim was that a slave taken into free territory automatically became a free man. But the case became embroiled in pre–Civil War politics, and Chief Justice Taney's opinion addressed the question of whether Scott could *ever* become a citizen of the United States. Taney wrote that he could not, for two reasons: because Scott was black and because he was a slave. The Fourteenth Amendment directly overruled the *Dred Scott* decision. In its first sentence it formally defined national citizenship and made state citizenship dependent on it: "All persons born or naturalized in the United States, and subject to the jurisdiction therefore, are citizens of the United States and of the State wherein they reside."

Citizenship may well be the most fundamental of rights — "the right to have rights," as Chief Justice Earl Warren once wrote.[25] In a series of cases beginning in 1958, the Supreme Court concluded that citizenship is so fundamental that it may not be taken away by Congress for desertion from the armed forces in wartime, for leaving the country in wartime to avoid conscription, or for voting in a foreign election. In the military desertion case, Warren wrote that to deprive a soldier of his citizenship was cruel and unusual punishment prohibited by the Eighth Amendment — "a form of punishment more primitive than torture," which involved "the total destruction of the individual's status in organized society.[26]

Generally speaking, naturalized citizens have the same rights as native-born citizens. In *Schneider* v. *Rusk* (1964) the Court invalidated an act of Congress

[24] *Dred Scott* v. *Sandford*, 60 U.S. 393 (1857).
[25] *Trop* v. *Dulles*, 356 U.S. 86 (1958).
[26] Ibid.

that deprived naturalized citizenship of their citizens if they returned to their native land[27] and lived there for three years or more. And in *Afroyim* v. *Rusk* (1967), the Court held that Congress could not take away citizenship — natural born or naturalized — unless it was freely renounced.[28] Renunciation of citizenship must be a "knowing" act, not merely an inference drawn from some other act. Afroyim, who was also a citizen of Israel, had voted in an Israeli election. However, the Court has upheld various congressional requirements for *obtaining* citizenship (becoming "naturalized") and for maintaining that status.[29]

The Constitution did not enumerate the "rights" of citizens, merely stating in Article IV that the privileges and immunities of citizens of one state may not be withheld from the citizens of other states. The framers of the Constitution probably intended only to protect citizens of one state from being discriminated against when they traveled to, or lived in, another state. In fact, neither of the Privileges and Immunities clauses (of Article IV and of the Fourteenth Amendment) has proved to be a significant factor in establishing and protecting individual rights.[30] The *rights* of citizenship have been derived largely from other constitutional provisions. Most constitutional protections extend to all persons, not just citizens. Of the rights that are said to be the rights of citizenship, the most important, the right to travel, is not mentioned in the Constitution. In 1941 the Supreme Court invalidated California's "anti-Okie" law, which made it a misdemeanor to bring indigent persons into the state.[31] In 1966 the Court held that the constitutional right to travel was protected by federal civil rights laws.[32] And in 1969 it held that a state could not deny welfare assistance to persons who had not been residents of the state for at least a year. This "durational residency requirement," the Court said, inhibited the constitutional right to travel.[33] The right to travel abroad, though more limited, has generally been protected by the Court. In *Haig* v. *Agee* (1981), however, it upheld the State Department's revocation of a former CIA officer's passport. The officer, Philip Agee, had exposed foreign intelligence operations and the identities of a number of CIA agents. Chief Justice Burger's opinion was that Congress has allowed the president broad discretion in regulating the foreign travel of American citizens. Many critics charged that the Supreme Court was granting the government a veritable license to restrict the travel, and thereby limit the speech, of political dissidents.[34]

[27] 377 U.S. 163 (1964).

[28] 387 U.S. 253 (1967).

[29] Most recently the Court upheld a lower court decision to strip a former Nazi concentration camp guard of his naturalized U.S. citizenship. The guard had lied about his wartime activities in order to enter the United States and eventually to obtain that citizenship. See *Fedorenko* v. *United States*, 66 L. Ed. 2d 686 (1981).

[30] The Privileges and Immunities Clause of the Fourteenth Amendment was severely limited by the Supreme Court's decision in the *Slaughterhouse Cases*, 83 U.S. 36 (1873).

[31] *Edwards* v. *California*, 314 U.S. 160 (1941).

[32] *United States* v. *Price*, 383 U.S. 787 (1966).

[33] *Shapiro* v. *Thompson*, 394 U.S. 618 (1969).

[34] *Aptheker* v. *Secretary of State*, 378 U.S. 500 (1964).

EQUALITY   Equality, like liberty and justice, is a fundamental ideal of our political system. Unlike the Declaration of Independence, the original Constitution made no mention of equality. The need to compromise on the issue of slavery was one reason. Another was that equality was an unsettling and perhaps radical notion. Nevertheless, the idea of equality pervades the Constitution. The Privileges and Immunities Clause of Article IV requires equal treatment of citizens. The due process clause of the Fifth Amendment implies equal treatment before the law. Equality of representation was the guiding principle for the House of Representatives, even though it was left to the states to set qualifications for voting, thus ensuring the continuance of property qualifications. The prohibition against "religious tests" for holding office, and the religion clauses of the First Amendment, were designed to ensure that no religion would be given preference over others — that there would be no "state religion." The various provisions of the Constitution and the Bill of Rights dealing with guarantees to defendants in criminal cases presuppose at least a formal equality of treatment.

Passage of the Fourteenth Amendment (along with the Thirteenth and Fifteenth), however, constituted the nation's first formal commitment to protecting equality. The prime concern of the framers of the amendment was to protect the rights of newly freed black slaves in the southern states. But the words of the amendment are general: "Nor shall any *state* . . . deny to any person within its jurisdiction the equal protection of the laws." Congress was given full authority to enforce the amendment.

The amendment applies only to the actions of *states* (which includes local governments as well). It does not directly prohibit discrimination by private individuals, and it does not apply to the federal government. The Supreme Court has held, however, that the equal protection guarantees of the Fourteenth Amendment are applicable to the federal government through the Due Process Clause of the Fifth Amendment.[35]

The Equal Protection Clause of the Fourteenth Amendment prohibits classifications that are "invidious" or discriminatory. Government may validly establish classes of individuals and treat the members of those classes differently from others if there are good reasons for doing so. But members of the same class must be treated similarly. For example, government may set different tax rates for persons with different income levels. It may establish a particular age — currently 65 — as the dividing line for Medicare eligibility. Welfare benefits may be limited to persons who are bona fide residents of a state. The Equal Protection Clause, however, does not require government to establish *any* of these programs. There is no constitutional obligation to provide for public education for an old-age pension system (Social Security), or a health care system for the elderly (Medicare) or the indigent (Medicaid). But *if* Congress or a state chooses to establish such programs, then the standards of the Equal Protection Clause apply.

---

[35] *Bolling* v. *Sharpe*, 347 U.S. 497 (1954).

Generally speaking, the Equal Protection Clause permits "reasonable" classifications. But certain types of classifications are so likely to be discriminatory that they are regarded as *suspect classifications*. The Supreme Court has held that race is a suspect classification; so too are classifications based on alienage or national origin. Gender and wealth, on the other hand, are not suspect classification.[36] Whereas ordinary classifications are valid if they are merely reasonable, suspect classifications are regarded by the courts as presumptively *invalid*. A suspect classification can be justified only by demonstrating that the government has a compelling interest in maintaining it. With the exception of certain affirmative-action programs, it is difficult to conceive of a valid racial classification today.

Racial Equality Black people have been victimized by discrimination more visibly — and certainly longer — than any other racial or ethnic group in the United States. However, Native Americans, Hispanics, Orientals, and many white ethnic immigrant groups (Jewish, Irish, and Italian, among others) have also endured significant deprivations. The seeds of "legal racism" were in the Declaration of Independence, which did not condemn slavery, and in the Constitution, which tolerated it.[37] They were underscored by Chief Justice Taney's opinion in the *Dred Scott* case, in which he recalled the general belief at the time of the Constitution that blacks were "so far inferior that they had no rights which the white man was bound to respect," and could be reduced to slavery for their own benefit.

The post–Civil War amendments put a formal end to slavery and overruled the *Dred Scott* decision. But the objectives of those amendments, and of civil rights laws passed during the Reconstruction period, were undermined by several Supreme Court decisions and by development of the "Jim Crow" system of racial segregation. In the *Civil Rights Cases* (1883),[38] the Court overturned the Civil Rights Act of 1875 — the nation's first public accommodations statute — and in so doing interpreted narrowly the power of Congress to implement the Fourteenth Amendment. And in *Plessy* v. *Ferguson* (1896),[39] the Court upheld a Louisiana law requiring separation of the races on passenger trains. The Court said that racial segregation was not inconsistent with the Fourteenth Amendment as long as equal facilities for both races were provided; forced separation of the races did not stamp "the colored race with a badge of inferiority." The lone dissenter, Justice John Marshall Harlan, argued that "Our Constitution is color-blind, and neither knows nor tolerates classes among citizens. In respect of civil rights, all citizens are equal before the law."

[36] *San Antonio Independent School District* v. *Rodriguez*, 411 U.S. 1 (1973); *Frontiero* v. *Richardson*, 411 U.S. 677 (1973).

[37] This is often referred to as "overt" discrimination — laws that *required* discriminatory treatment on the basis of race.

[38] 109 U.S. 3 (1883).

[39] 163 U.S. 537 (1896).

The Court's ruling in the *Civil Rights Cases* impeded congressional efforts to protect civil rights, and the *Plessy* doctrine of "separate but equal" turned the words of the Fourteenth Amendment into an empty guarantee. Segregation in the public schools and in most other walks of life became a permanent fixture in the southern and border states, and in the District of Columbia. The requirement that separate facilities also be "equal" was generally ignored. Not until the mid-1930s did the Supreme Court begin seriously to examine whether segregation was in fact "equal." Until then, only the more obvious forms of racial discrimination had failed to gain the Court's tacit approval. The Court outlawed overt racial discrimination in the selection of juries, for example, but more subtle tactics of intimidation kept black citizens from serving as jurors.[40] It outlawed simple-minded attempts to exclude blacks from voting, such as the notorious "grandfather clause,"[41] but accepted more subtle and effective barriers, such as the white primary, which prevented blacks from voting in Democratic Party primaries. It invalidated a discriminatory municipal housing ordinance, but was reluctant to prohibit other tactics that effectively restricted blacks in our large cities to living in ghetto areas.[42]

Three Supreme Court decisions marked a turning of the judicial tide against racial discrimination. In *Smith* v. *Allwright* (1944) the Court outlawed the white primary.[43] Although this decision did not immediately result in substantial increases in black voting in the South, it did clear away a major legal obstacle and open the door for the political action that would ultimately bring about that result. In *Shelley* v. *Kraemer* (1948), the Court held that judicial enforcement of racially restrictive housing covenants was discriminatory "state action" within the meaning of the Fourteenth Amendment.[44] This decision had no immediate impact on the housing market, but it swept away a major obstacle to achievement of a fair housing policy. By these two decisions the Court signaled a turn away from a policy of tolerating racial discrimination. The edifice of "separate but equal" was in the process of being torn down.

In the landmark case of *Brown* v. *Board of Education of Topeka*, (1954) the Supreme Court held that racial segregation in the public schools violated the Equal Protection Clause even if the physical facilities of black and white schools had been equalized.[45] The separate-but-equal test was rejected:

> Does segregation of children in public schools solely on the basis of race, even though the physical facilities and other "tangible" factors may be equal, deprive

[40]*Strauder* v. *West Virginia*, 100 U.S. 303 (1880).

[41]*Guinn* v. *United States*, 238 U.S. 347 (1915).

[42]*Buchanan* v. *Warley*, 245 U.S. 60 (1917). But in *Memphis* v. *Greene*, 67 L. Ed. 2d 769 (1981) the Court approved the closing of a street linking white and black communities in Memphis, Tennessee. The Court determined that no racially discriminatory intent or purpose had been proved, and that there was adequate evidence the street had been closed to promote traffic safety and to reduce pollution in the white neighborhood.

[43]321 U.S. 649 (1944).

[44]334 U.S. 1 (1948). Also see Clement Vose, *Caucasians Only* (Berkeley: University of California Press, 1959).

[45]347 U.S. 483 (1954).

the children of the minority group of equal educational opportunities? We believe that it does. . . .

To separate children in grade and high schools from others of similar age and qualifications solely because of their race generates a feeling of inferiority as to their status in the community that may affect their hearts and minds in a way unlikely ever to be undone . . . separate educational facilities are inherently unequal.

The same principle was applied to the schools of the District of Columbia under the Due Process Clause of the Fifth Amendment.[46]

Although the *Brown* decision technically applied only to the public schools, its pervasive principles were quickly applied in other cases to ban governmentally established or sanctioned racial segregation of all kinds. *Plessy* v. *Ferguson* was explicitly overruled, and the legal foundations of *Jim Crow* toppled. Even more important, perhaps, was the immense psychological impact of the decision. The nation's highest court had spoken directly and unanimously about the injustice of racial discrimination, and the reverberations of that decision were heard throughout the nation and the world.

Southern white resistance to the *Brown* decision was intense. Federal troops were required to quell disturbances brought about by attempts to integrate the high schools of Little Rock, Arkansas.[47] Angry white mothers picketed the integration of grade schools in New Orleans. Some southern counties closed their schools rather than integrate, and private academies sprang up to educate the white children who would not attend the gradually integrated public schools.[48] The Supreme Court, condemning the defiance that led to Little Rock, invalidated the closing of schools to avoid integration.[49] But little progress toward desegregation was made. The turning point came only with the intervention of Congress. The Civil Rights Act of 1964 formally endorsed the *Brown* decision. In Title VI of that act, Congress prohibited racial discrimination in all institutions receiving federal funds. In 1965, when Congress for the first time provided large scale financial assistance to public schools, the Department of Health, Education and Welfare (now the Department of Education) established a set of guidelines for integration that school districts had to meet as a condition of receiving federal funds. The Supreme Court approved these guidelines, and southern school districts slowly began to fall in line.[50]

The *Brown* decision had focused on "legal" segregation. Every southern and border state at the time had on its books, or had enacted in the past,

---

[46] *Bolling* v. *Sharpe*, 347 U.S. 497 (1954).

[47] These events are well described in Richard Neustadt, *Presidential Power* (New York: Wiley, 1960), pp. 16–17, *passim.*; See also J. Harvie Wilkinson, *From Brown to Bakke: The Supreme Court and School Integration, 1954–1978* (New York: Oxford University Press, 1979), Part II.

[48] Ibid.

[49] *Cooper* v. *Aaron*, 358 U.S. 29 (1958); *Griffin* v. *County School Board of Prince Edward County*, 377 U.S. 218 (1964).

[50] See *Green* v. *County School Board of New Kent County*, 391 U.S. 430 (1968).

legislation that required or permitted segregation in the public schools. Segregation in the schools of these states was thus presumed to flow from state laws, and was known as *de jure* segregation. It was quickly recognized, however, that, many schools in the north, particularly those in large urban areas, in fact were also segregated, usually because of segregated housing patterns combined with a "neighborhood school" policy. This situation is known as *de facto segregation* — segregation that ostensibly is not "intended" but that simply results from social and economic conditions over which school officials have no control. De jure segregation is an obvious violation of the Constitution, but the Supreme Court has held that defacto segregation is not.[51] But the de facto segregation becomes the equivalent of de jure segregation and violates the Constitution where it can be shown that the policies of local officials — policies concerning assignment of pupils, teacher assignments, school building patterns, and the like — have had a segregative intent and effect.[52]

Where the courts have found evidence of de jure or intentional de facto segregation, they can authorize remedial integration of the schools to "right the constitutional wrong" that has been committed. But what if, as is often true, there are too few white students left in the inner-city schools for integration actually to be achieved? In 1972 a federal judge in Detroit ordered what became known as a "metropolitan" or "interdistrict" remedy. He ordered that city schools be combined with adjacent suburban schools so that integration, involving some busing of students, could take place across district lines. Without such an extraordinary remedy, he concluded, no effective integration was possible.

By a 5-to-4 vote, the Supreme Court in *Milliken* v. *Bradley* (1974) reversed the lower court.[53] There was no evidence, Chief Justice Burger wrote, that the suburban districts were in any way implicated in the constitutional violations that had resulted in school segregation in Detroit. The Chief Justice did say that an interdistrict remedy would be acceptable if there was evidence of complicity by the suburban districts. Since such evidence is often impossible to obtain, the Court's decision placed important — perhaps fatal — restraints on urban school integration efforts. Chief Justice Burger's opinion reiterated that the Constitution does not require integration; it merely forbids governmentally fostered or sanctioned segregation. Integration — the remedial shift from a "dual" to a "unitary" school system — may be ordered by the courts only in school districts that experienced de jure segregation or where the complicity of governmental or school officials in de facto segregation could be shown.

Unquestionably the most explosive racial issue today is "school busing." Of course a large number of America's school children have always been bused to school. Busing was never a political issue until federal judges began to order it as a means to achieve integration. The issue became prominent in the 1968 and 1972 elections, and many assumed that a Supreme Court dominated by

[51]*Keyes*, v. *School District #1*, 413 U.S. 189 (1973).
[52]Ibid. See also *Washington* v. *Davis*, 426 U.S. 229 (1976).
[53]418 U.S. 717 (1974).

appointees of President Nixon would rule against busing. But the Court surprised everyone by declaring unanimously, in *Swann* v. *Charlotte-Mecklenburg Board of Education* (1971), that busing was appropriate to remedy a long history of racial segregation, especially where, as in this district, busing of school children had been in effect for years, and where the travel time of most children was actually reduced under the busing-for-integration plan.[54]

Congress was unable to pass a constitutional amendment prohibiting school busing for integration. But in 1977 it passed a rider to an appropriations bill that prevented the Department of Health, Education and Welfare (HEW) from threatening to cut off funds for school districts not complying with school busing orders. Two federal courts upheld the validity of the rider, but only because it appeared that there was another way in which the federal government could comply with constitutional requirements that busing be utilized, if necessary, to desegregate formerly segregated school districts: HEW could refer such cases to the Justice Department for court action.

After the 1980 election, however, Congress passed a bill barring the Justice Department from taking court action to enforce the use of busing to achieve desegregation. The new bill, however, did not challenge the power of the courts to order busing as a means of desegregation. In one of his last official acts President Carter vetoed the bill, but the issue is far from settled.

The twenty-eight years since *Brown* was decided have witnessed eradication of the structure of legal racism in the United States. Laws requiring segregation in public accommodations and recreation facilities, as well as laws forbidding racial intermarriage (miscegenation), have been struck down by the Supreme Court.[55] Passage by Congress of the Voting Rights Act of 1965 broke the back of white resistance to black voting in the south; blacks now vote there in increasing numbers, and black legislators and mayors are no longer a rarity.[56] Both the Supreme Court and Congress moved to abolish discrimination in housing.[57]

Eradicating the last vestiges of *overt* legal racism in the United States is only a step in the direction of undoing the effects of slavery and segregation on blacks as well as whites. There is substantial evidence that *covert* racism still exists in many of our public institutions, and that it is pervasive in the private sector as well. By covert racism we mean the effective continuation of disadvantages to a racial or other minority group within a system of formal equality. It need not be intentional. Job test requirements that bear no real relationship to job performance are one example. Another is apprenticeship programs in craft unions which serve more to exclude "outsiders" than to prepare skilled craftspersons. Still another would be ostensibly "equal" academic requirements for entrance to professional schools which do not take account of a minority group's past experience with discrimination and assume

[54] 403 U.S. 912 (1971).
[55] *Loving* v. *Virginia*, 388 U.S. 1 (1967).
[56] The act was upheld in *South Carolina* v. *Katzenbach*, 383 U.S. 301 (1966).
[57] *Jones* v. *Mayer*, 392 U.S. 409 (1968).

that merely because formal barriers to equal opportunity have been torn down, opportunities are in fact equalized.

Affirmative action programs have been the primary means of redressing-racial (and gender) inequality. Through the establishment of "targets" or "quotas," women and members of disadvantaged minority groups have been accorded preference in employment hiring and promotion and in admissions to educational institutions. Opponents contend that this is really "reverse discrimination" and that there is no such thing as a "benign" quota. They argue, quoting Justice Harlan's opinion in the *Plessy* case, that our Constitution must be "color blind" and that no racial distinctions are permitted. Proponents of affirmative action argue, on the other hand, that in order to make our society truly color blind, the Constitution and the laws must be "color conscious" in devising remedies for the lingering effects of past racial inequality.[58]

The Supreme Court, like the nation, has been divided on the issue. In its first major affirmative action opinion, *Board of Regents of California* v. *Bakke* (1978), the Court considered the validity of a program at the University of California–Davis Medical School that voluntarily set aside 16 out of 100 places in the entering class for qualified minority students.[59] Such students would be admitted for these 16 places in preference to nonminority students who had ranked higher in admissions evaluation. Bakke was a white student who would almost certainly have been admitted were it not for the minority quota. Instead, he was rejected twice. By a 5-to-4 vote, the Supreme Court ruled that Bakke should be admitted because inflexible racial quotas, even those established to achieve benign goals, were in conflict with the Fourteenth Amendment. But the Court also ruled that properly devised "race conscious" university admissions programs were acceptable in order to secure student diversity, provided that race was only one of many factors considered.

One year later, in *United Steelworkers of America* v. *Weber*,[60] the Court upheld the validity of a collective bargaining agreement between the United Steelworkers and the Kaiser Aluminum Corporation that established minority hiring goals and established training programs to enable minority workers in unskilled positions to compete for promotions to skilled positions. Fifty percent of the positions in these training programs were reserved for black workers, even though they may have had less seniority than some white workers who also wanted to enter the programs. Weber, a white worker who had been excluded from the training program, filed a lawsuit charging that this plan violated Title VII of the Civil Rights Act of 1964.[61] Despite what seemed to be words to the contrary in the statute, the Court approved the agreement,

---

[58] Thus Archibald Cox, arguing before the Supreme Court in behalf of the University of California in the *Bakke* case, told the justices: "There is no racially blind method of selection which will enroll today more than a trickle of minority students in the nation's colleges and professions."

[59] 438 U.S. 265 (1978). For a good description of the case, see Allan Sindler, *Bakke, De Funis, and Minority Admissions* (New York: Longman, 1978).

[60] 443 U.S. 193 (1979).

[61] Title VII prohibits discrimination in employment on the basis of race, color, religion, sex, or national origin.

stating that "Congress did not intend wholly to prohibit private and voluntary affirmation action efforts."

In *Fullilove* v. *Klutznick*, decided in 1980, the Court upheld a provision of the Public Works Employment Act of 1977 that, following the determination of Congress that minorities were underrepresented in the construction industry, required that 10 percent of the federal funds allocated for local public-works projects be used by states and local governments to procure services or supplies from minority owned businesses.[62] The act defined minority group members as United States citizens who are "Negroes, Spanish-speaking, Orientals, Indians, Eskimos and Aleuts." A majority of six justices held that this statute did not violate either equal protection under the Fifth Amendment or Title VI of the Civil Rights Act of 1964.

Of course, "affirmative action" is more than quotas or goals. Those are just its most visible aspect. Affirmative action is a personal and institutional commitment to racial minorities and women to compensate for past discrimination. Achieving an acceptable balance between advocates and opponents of affirmative action is no easy task especially during a recession when the economy is contracting and the paucity of new jobs defeats even the strongest commitments to affirmative action. When layoffs are required, is seniority to be the only criterion? If it is, then even the modest successes of affirmative-action hiring will be undone.

The hope of equality kindled by the *Brown* case has been only partially fulfilled. The Jim Crow system of segregation in the South and other overt forms of legal discrimination have been abolished. Blacks have made great advances in voting, and increasing numbers of blacks and other minorities have been elected or appointed to public office. President Carter, as we have seen, appointed more women and members of minority groups to federal judgeships than did all previous presidents combined. Yet the 1980 Annual Report of the National Urban League argues, along with others, that racism is "alive and well in the American body politic." There is, for example, still a sizable economic gap between black and white America, revealed in indicators of income and unemployment.

In 1963 the median income of black families was about 53 percent of the income of white families. The gap appeared to be closing gradually; by 1970 black income was more than 60 percent that of whites. But during the 1970s the gap widened again; in 1979 the black income ratio had dropped to 57 percent. Unemployment figures tell a similar story. In 1970 black unemployment was 8.2 percent; in 1979 it had risen to 11.9 percent. For the same years, white unemployment increased from 4.5 to 5.2 percent. In every major city, black unemployment in 1979 exceeded white unemployment; for the United States as a whole, the ratio was 1.8:1. Not all the economic disparity between blacks and whites can be attributed to racism. But the bleak picture of chronic black unemployment and continuing income disparities is dispiriting, particu-

---

[62] 65 L. Ed. 2d 902 (1980).

larly in light of the enormous number of laws and government programs passed since the early 1960s to promote racial equality.

Gender Equality Whereas the structure of legal discrimination against blacks had to be dismantled piece by piece, the legal props of gender discrimination have come tumbling down in very rapid order. Discrimination against women in our society is in some respects even more ingrained in the social fabric than discrimination against blacks. But gender discrimination never reflected the ravages of slavery, and women are not a minority group. As the principle of equality established in the *Brown* case became widely accepted, its extension to women's rights was inevitable.

The Fourteenth Amendment always applied to women as persons or citizens. But until recently it was never successfully invoked against discriminatory classifications by gender. A Supreme Court decision in 1873, upholding the right of a state to exclude women from the practice of law, cited

> The natural and proper timidity and delicacy which belongs to the female sex [which] evidently unfits it for many of the occupations of civil life. The constitution of the family organization, which is founded in the divine ordinance, as well as in the nature of things, indicates the domestic sphere as that which properly belongs to the domain and functions of womanhood. . . . The paramount destiny and mission of women are to fulfill the noble and benign offices of wife and mother. This is the law of the creator.[63]

The following year, the Court ruled that women had no constitutional right to vote,[64] a decision eventually overruled by the Nineteenth Amendment. Women did not generally serve on juries; Utah, in 1898, became the first state to allow women jurors. During the Progressive era, women became the special object of reform efforts. Protective legislation was passed limiting their hours of employment, prescribing the conditions under which they could work, and excluding them from "morally polluting" occupations such as bartending.[65] Many laws, particularly those dealing with the control and disposition of property, still discriminate against women.[66]

In the post–World War II period, a time of much ferment in thinking about racial inequality, little attention was paid to gender equality, at least not by the Supreme Court. In 1948 the Court upheld a Michigan statute that prohibited women from serving as bartenders except where the woman was the wife or daughter of the male owner of the bar. Writing for the Court, Justice Frankfurter observed: "The fact that women may now have achieved the virtues that men have long claimed as their prerogatives and now indulge in vices

---

[63]*Bradwell* v. *Illinois*, 83 U.S. 130 (1872).

[64]*Minor* v. *Happersett*, 88 U.S. 162 (1874).

[65] The Supreme Court, which at the time was quite hostile to laws regulating wages and working conditions, nonetheless upheld many laws regulating the working conditions of women. See *Muller* v. *Oregon*, 209 U.S. 412 (1908).

[66] For a good summary of these laws, see Leo Kanowitz, *Women and the Law* (Albuquerque: University of New Mexico Press, 1970).

that men have long practiced, does not preclude the States from drawing a sharp line between the sexes, certainly in such matters as the regulation of the liquor traffic."[67] As late as 1961 the Supreme Court upheld a state law providing that women should be included on jury lists only if they *volunteered*, whereas men were included unless they requested an exemption. The Court said that notwithstanding the recent "enlightened emancipation of women . . . woman is still regarded as the center of home and family life."[68]

Significant changes in the legal status and rights of women began in the 1960s. Congress prohibited gender discrimination in the Equal Pay Act of 1963, and discrimination against women in employment in Title VII of the Civil Rights Act of 1964. Title IX of a law known as the Education Amendments of 1972 prohibited gender discrimination in school activities. In 1972, Congress finally passed the Equal Rights Amendment (ERA), which had been introduced unsuccessfully in every Congress since 1923. The amendment, which provides that "Equality of Rights under the law shall not be denied or abridged by the United States or by any state on account of sex," was ratified by thirty-four states in the first year, but the drive for ratification stalled as opposition grew. As of the spring of 1981, the amendment had been ratified by thirty-five states, three short of the required thirty-eight. But four states that ratified the Amendment — Idaho, North Dakota, Nebraska, and Tennessee — later voted to rescind their ratification, a move of uncertain constitutionality.[69] When it became clear in 1979 that the ERA would not be ratified within the statutory limit of seven years from the date of its passage, pro-ERA forces in Congress extended the time limit for ratification to June 30th, 1982.

What would the ERA accomplish? Its proponents claim that, at the very least, it would make gender a constitutionally "suspect" classification, like race. This means that the only gender based classifications that would be acceptable would be those that could be justified by a state or federal government in the strongest terms. The Supreme Court might go further and hold that the ERA prohibited *all* gender classifications, without exception.

Many of the objectives of the ERA have already been accomplished by court decisions and legislative actions during the 1970s. The Supreme Court has invalidated most laws that prefer one sex over the other or that establish sex-based age distinctions, such as the age of majority, drinking age, and the age of marriage without parental consent.[70] Many distinctons between men and women in the social security system and in the allocation of benefits to military

---

[67] *Goesaert* v. *Cleary*, 335 U.S. 464 (1948).

[68] *Hoyt* v. *Florida*, 368 U.S. 57 (1961).

[69] The Supreme Court has never directly considered whether a state may rescind an earlier ratification. There is, however, little question that a state may vote to ratify an amendment after an earlier failure to do so.

[70] *Craig* v. *Boren*, 429 U.S. 190 (1976). In *Michael M.* v. *Sonoma County*, 67 L. Ed. 2d 437 (1981), the Supreme Court backtracked from that policy. It held valid a California statute that punished boys but not girls for the crime of statutory rape. This gender distinction was acceptable, the Court said, because the state had a legitimate interest in discouraging premarital pregnancy, and also because punishing the male "equalized" the risks since only the female could become pregnant.

dependents — some favoring men and some favoring women — have been eliminated. Gender-based differences in the operation of the criminal law would also become constitutionally suspect if the ERA was ratified. Prostitution laws and enforcement practices would have to be amended to punish the prostitute and the customer equally. Juvenile courts would have to equalize sanctions imposed on boys and girls who have engaged in sexual misconduct; it would no longer be acceptable to impose restrictions only on girls for conduct in which boys have also engaged. And any military draft might have to include women as well as men, something that is *not required,* the Supreme Court has said, by the Constitution as it now stands.[71] On the other hand, despite the allegations of ERA opponents, no expert seriously believes that an ERA would require unisex bathrooms or locker rooms.

Defeat of the ERA would not signal either the end of the women's movement or an abridgement of the many gains in real equality that women have achieved over the last decade. But there is no denying that the protests and fears of the anti-ERA forces have struck a responsive chord. Fears about the disintegration of the family and the erosion of traditional women's "privileges" (special labor laws, jury exemptions, and so forth) have become linked with other issues such as the growth of the gay rights movement and sexual permissiveness generally. The link between the anti-ERA and antiabortion forces has forged a powerful coalition, at least symbolically.

More and more women are gaining access to the professions and to better jobs. More women are now employed outside the home — about 50 percent — but women are still disproportionately confined to the least desirable and lowest-paying positions. The median income for all women in 1977 was $8,600, less than 60 percent of the $14,500 median income for males. Disparities between the earnings of men and women are not uniform. In some occupations, such as engineering and the sciences, and in some professional business positions, women are catching up. But in others — sales, services, and so forth — women's earnings still lag far behind.

Unequal pay for women is rapidly becoming a major issue in the courts. The Equal Pay Act, ironically, is the main obstacle to overcome. The act requires "equal pay for equal work" but implicitly rejects the broader standard of "equal pay for jobs of comparable worth." Since so many women hold traditionally low-paying jobs, wage differentials are difficult to challenge as intentionally discriminatory. The Supreme Court has just decided a case, however, that may help to bridge the "equal work" barrier. In *County of Washington* v. *Gunther* (1981), the Court said that women may challenge wage differentials under Title VII of the Civil Rights Act of 1964, even when they hold different jobs than men do. Evaluating the monetary worth of different jobs is extremely difficult. There is no expectation that the courts will become involved in a wholesale reevaluation of the wage levels of traditional "women's jobs," or that Congress will broaden the coverage of the Equal Pay Act to cover jobs of comparable worth.

---

[71] *Rostker* v. *Goldberg,* 69 L. Ed. 2d. 478 (1981).

'Of course my hair transplants will be covered by sick pay. Baldness is a disease.
Pregnancy, on the other hand, is the natural state of women.'

Continued social and economic disparities between blacks and whites and between men and women suggest the limitations of the law, and of the Supreme Court and the Constitution in particular, in bringing about this kind of social change. In each instance the traditional inequality persists long after the discriminatory laws and overt practices have been cast aside. Although the Constitution and the Court are important factors in formally defining the rights of Americans, they are most adept at clearing away legal barriers to equality. Creation of the social and economic conditions for achieving real equality is a far more difficult task.

FREEDOM OF EXPRESSION The Constitution assigns no priorities to the rights it protects. But the guarantees of the First Amendment to freedom of speech and of the press, and the freedom to assemble and petition the government for redress of grievances, are often regarded as first among equals. Writing about the First Amendment in *Palko* v. *Connecticut* (1937), Justice Cardozo spoke of freedom of thought and speech as "the matrix, the indispensable condition, of nearly every other form of freedom. . . ."

Freedom of Speech Who can doubt the central importance of freedom of expression for a democratic society? One of the best arguments against suppression of speech came from Justice Oliver Wendell Holmes in the case of *Abrams* v. *United States* (1919).[72] Abrams and others had been convicted of violating the Espionage

[72] 250 U.S. 616 (1919).

Act by circulating pamphlets attacking President Wilson's decision to send troops to Russia during World War I, and calling for a strike by munitions workers. The Supreme Court affirmed their convictions. Said Holmes in dissent:

> Persecution for the expression of opinions seems to me perfectly logical. If you have no doubt of your premises or your power and want a certain result with all your heart you naturally express your wishes in law and sweep away all opposition. To allow opposition by speech seems to indicate that you think the speech impotent, as when a man says that he has squared the circle, or that you do not care whole-heartedly for the result, or that you doubt either your power or your premises. But when men have realized that time has upset many fighting faiths, they may come to believe even more than they believe the very foundations of their own conduct that the ultimate good desired is better reached by free trade in ideas — that the best test of truth is the power of the thought to get itself accepted in the competition of the market, and that truth is the only ground upon which their wishes safely can be carried out. That at any rate is the theory of our Constitution.

Holmes's argument is essentially utilitarian. The metaphor of the marketplace symbolizes the competitiveness of ideas in a forum in which all can participate on an equal basis. It suggests, as Professor Thomas Emerson has written, that "freedom of expression is an essential process for advancing knowledge and discovering truth."[73] But there is also an argument of principle to be made.[74] As Emerson says, "freedom of expression is essential as a means of assuring individual self-fulfillment. The proper end of man is the realization of his character and potentialities as a human being. For the achievement of this self-realization, the mind must be free."[75]

The First Amendment is written in terms that seem to be absolute: "Congress shall make *no* law . . . [emphasis added]." Some scholars and Supreme Court justices have maintained that it should be interpreted that way. But the dominant view is that although expression is entitled to the strongest constitutional protection, that protection is not absolute. Certain kinds of speech, for example, are not protected. In upholding the conviction of a man who called a police officer a "God damned racketeer" and a "damned Fascist," the Supreme Court said in 1942:

> There are certain well-defined and narrowly limited classes of speech, the prevention and punishment of which have never been thought to raise any Constitutional problem. These include the lewd and obscene, the profane, the libelous, and the insulting or "fighting" words, those which by their very utterance inflict injury or tend to incite an immediate breach of the peace. It has well been

---

[73] Thomas I. Emerson, *The System of Freedom of Expression* (New York: Random House, 1970).
[74] Ibid., p. 7.
[75] Ibid., p. 6.

observed that such utterances are no essential part of any exposition of ideas and are of such slight social value as a step to truth that any benefit that may be derived from them is clearly outweighed by the social interest in order and morality. . . .[76]

More recently, however, the Court has substantially narrowed the "fighting words" exception. In *Gooding* v. *Wilson* (1972), the Court reversed the conviction of a black man in Georgia who called a white police officer a "son of a bitch" and threatened him with mayhem. The Georgia statute under which Gooding was convicted prohibited "opprobrious words or abusive language"; the Court ruled that this language was unconstitutionally broad because it was not limited just to fighting words.[77]

There is a federal law that punishes any person who threatens the life of the president. But in *Watts* v. *United States* (1969), the Court reversed the conviction of a man who said at a public rally that if drafted into the military and given a weapon, "the first man I want to get in my sight is LBJ." The Court said this speech was mere "'political hyperbole" and, no matter how crude and offensive, could not be punished.[78]

These are examples of what is often referred to as "pure speech" — speech without any associated conduct. It includes the printed as well as the spoken word. It includes the outrageous, the shocking, and the blasphemous as well as the benign. The Supreme Court has assigned the highest constitutional protections to this kind of speech. On the other hand, the Court has recognized that much communication occurs not by speech alone, but by speech plus various forms of conduct. These were described by the Supreme Court in 1965 as communication of "ideas by conduct such as patrolling, marching, and picketing on streets and highways." This is commonly known as "speech plus." Finally, ideas may be communicated by conduct alone. This is known generally as "symbolic speech."

Restrictions on pure speech have rarely been upheld. Neither symbolic speech nor speech plus, because they involve conduct as well as speech have been accorded the same degree of protection. Parades, demonstrations, and picketing, for example, may be restricted to certain "times, places and manners" provided that all groups who seek these privileges (such as a parade permit) are treated equally. There is no constitutionally protected "right" to hold a mass meeting at a busy traffic intersection, or to parade down a main street during the rush hour, or to hold a noisy demonstration with a bullhorn at night in a residential neighborhood. But there is a right to communicate ideas on public issues in what the Supreme Court has called the "public forum." "Wherever the title of streets and parks may rest," Justice Roberts once wrote, "they have immemorially been held in trust for the use of the public and time out of mind have been used for the purpose of assembly,

---

[76]*Chaplinsky* v. *New Hampshire,* 315 U.S. 568 (1942).
[77]405 U.S. 518 (1972).
[78]394 U.S. 705 (1969).

communicating thoughts between citizens and discussing public questions."[79] The use of the public forum may be regulated *because* it is a public resource available to all citizens. Its use cannot be abridged merely because the authorities do not favor the ideas being discussed.

These rules seem simple enough, but they are often the object of intense controversy. A particularly good example is the planned march of uniformed members of the American Nazi Party through the village of Skokie, Illinois, a suburb of Chicago with a heavily Jewish population. A significant number of the Jewish residents of the village are themselves survivors of Hitler's death camps or are relatives of those who perished there. Skokie was selected by the Nazis for precisely that reason.

The village won a court order prohibiting the march. The Illinois Supreme Court refused to lift that injunction while it was considering the case, but the United States Supreme Court intervened and ordered the injunction removed. A state appellate court then decided that the Nazis were entitled under the First Amendment to proceed with their march in uniform and to distribute pamphlets and display other materials along the route of the march. However, that court held that display of the swastika, the hated symbol of Nazism, amounted to "fighting words" and thus was not protected by the Constitution.

The Illinois Supreme Court held that the march could go on, and that the swastika could be displayed. "The display of the swastika," the Court said, "as offensive to the principles of a free nation as the memories it recalls may be, is symbolic political speech. . . . It does not . . . fall within the definition of 'fighting words.' " Display of the swastika by those engaged in peaceful demonstrations, the Illinois Court said, cannot be prohibited merely because it might provoke a violent reaction, especially where there has been advance notice of the march so that those who find it offensive are "forewarned" and need not attend.[80]

The Skokie case pushes the First Amendment to its limits. Many argued that the repulsiveness of Nazism is irrelevant in determining whether to issue a permit. The First Amendment, they say, does not — indeed cannot — distinguish between "good" speech and "bad" speech. Once government sets itself in the role of censor, free speech is a myth. The very strength of the First Amendment and of our commitment to its principles is vindicated by extending its protection to the most hateful groups and ideas. This was the position of the American Civil Liberties Union, which undertook to represent the American Nazi Party. A Jewish lawyer named David Goldberger handled the case. As a result, many ACLU supporters around the country canceled their memberships.

Others, equally committed to the defense of free expression, argued that permitting uniformed Nazis to march in Skokie, and allowing them to display the swastika, would undermine the real meaning of the First Amendment. By

[79]*Hague* v. *C.I.O.*, 307 U.S. 496 (1939).
[80]*Village of Skokie* v. *National Socialist Party*, 69 Ill. 2d 605, 373 N.E. 2d 21 (1978).

protecting speech so hateful and incompatible with democratic ideals, they argued, the meaning of free expression would be distorted. Such a parade fell within the "fighting words" exception to the First Amendment. Under the circumstances, they said, it was an incitement to violence of the kind that the law has traditionally condemned.[81]

The Skokie case is a recent reminder that the communication of ideas, particularly in the electronic media age, is often carried on by conduct without a significant verbal (spoken or written) component. Is the First Amendment broad enough to protect nonverbal communication on an equal basis with verbal communication? What of the Vietnam War dissenter who burned his draft card? Or the student who peaceably wore a black armband in school to protest the Vietnam War? Or the black citizen convicted for burning an American flag in protest against an attack on civil rights leader James Meredith? Or the citizen of New Hampshire charged with obliterating the state motto, "Live Free or Die," from his automobile license plate?

The Supreme Court has been sympathetic to protecting symbolic speech that is peaceable and not disruptive of the legitimate activities of others, but it has stopped short of saying that symbolic speech is always entitled to the same constitutional protections as "pure" speech. In the draft card burning case, *United States* v. *O'Brien* (1968), the Court upheld O'Brien's conviction under a 1965 law that prohibited the knowing destruction or mutilation of draft cards. Chief Justice Warren denied that an "apparently limitless variety of conduct can be labelled 'speech' whenever the person engaging in the conduct intends thereby to express an idea." When speech and conduct are combined, Warren added, then a sufficiently important government interest in regulating the nonspeech element can justify "incidental" limitations on speech otherwise protected by the First Amendment. In this case, such an interest was clearly present in the aim of Congress to protect the military draft.[82]

On the other hand, in *Tinker* v. *Des Moines School District* (1969) the Court upheld the right of public school students peaceably to wear black armbands in school. There was no evidence of disorder or disruption in school caused by the protesting students. "Undifferentiated fear or apprehension of expression," Justice Fortas wrote, "is not enough to overcome the right to freedom of expression." The First Amendment clearly applied to students, who "may not be regarded as closed-circuit recipients of only that which the state chooses to communicate." But Fortas drew the line at the peaceful and nondisruptive wearing of symbols; the same constitutional protections surely would not apply to noisy demonstration on school property during regular school hours.[83]

In the flag burning case, the Court was badly divided. Justice Harlan's majority opinion reversed the flag burner's conviction under a state law that made

[81] See, for example, Irving Louis Horowitz and Victoria Curtis Bramson, "Skokie, the ACLU, and the Endurance of Democratic Theory" *Law and Contemporary Problems* 43 (1979): 328–49.

[82] 391 U.S. 367 (1968).

[83] 393 U.S. 503 (1969).

it a crime to "publicly mutilate, deface, defile or defy, trample upon or cast contempt upon, either by word or act, the state or national flag." "Disrespect for the flag is to be deplored," Harlan wrote, but "the right to differ as to things that touch the heart of the existing order, encompass[es] the freedom to express publicly one's opinions about our flag, including those opinions which are defiant or contemptuous."[84] In the New Hampshire license plate case, the Court held, similarly, that the state's interest in enforcement of its statute prohibiting defacement of license plates was insufficient to justify restriction of a person's constitutionally protected expression. New Hampshire was prohibited from requiring display of the state motto on license plates.[85]

Freedom of the Press   The First Amendment protects "freedom of the press." But what is this freedom, and to whom does it extend? The second question can be answered quickly. For constitutional purposes, "the press" refers to all the various media of communication: television, radio, handbills, books, magazines, films, newsletters, and of course newspapers. However, there may be certain permissible restrictions of the visual media that are not allowed for the print media. The reason for this is the need to protect special groups from unwanted exposure to harmful ideas; for example, the Supreme Court recently upheld a decision by the Federal Communications Commission censuring a radio station that ran in prime time the famous "dirty words monologue" of comedian George Carlin. No book or magazine would ever be legally restrained or its publisher punished for printing that monologue.[86]

In what ways does the First Amendment protect the press? An early interpretation by the Supreme Court contended that the First Amendment prohibited only "prior restraint" of the press.[87] But it is now accepted that the protections of the First Amendment extend considerably beyond that. The First Amendment also guarantees to the press the right of access to criminal trials, and no less access than the public at large to other arenas of government and public activity. The First Amendment prohibits punishment for seditious libel. It now extends substantial protection to the dissemination of materials depicting explicit sexual activity, which formerly were regarded as obscene. Let us look briefly at each of these areas.

Prior Restraint.   Prior restraint is censorship. It is universally accepted that the First Amendment prohibits prior restraint of the press by government. And it is remarkable how few exceptions to that prohibition have been tolerated. The reasons, perhaps, are obvious. Prior restraint is a drastic action which cuts off communication in advance and makes free trade in ideas impossible. The whim of the censor replaces the judgment of the press or of the people.

[84] *Street* v. *New York*, 394 U.S. 576 (1969).
[85] *Wooley* v. *Maynard*, 430 U.S. 705 (1977).
[86] *Federal Communications Commission* v. *Pacifica Foundation*, 438 U.S. 726 (1978).
[87] *Robertson* v. *Baldwin*, 165 U.S. 275 (1897).

Two recent cases illustrate the principle in operation. One was known as the *Pentagon Papers* case.[88] In June 1971 *The New York Times* (and later *The Washington Post* and other newspapers) began serial publication of a secret government study of United States policies and conduct of the war in Vietnam. The study had been leaked by a former government employee who had participated in writing it. The Nixon administration, claiming that publication of "sensitive national security" materials was harmful to American interests, asked the *Times* to cease publication. When the newspaper refused, the government sought a federal court injunction to prohibit further publication. A similar order was sought against the *Post*. The trial courts in New York and the District of Columbia both denied the government's request for a gag order; and the Supreme Court also ruled against the government, holding that it failed to meet the very heavy burden of justifying prior restraint. The vote was 6 to 3, and several of the dissenting justices observed that by publishing purloined classified documents the newspaper was risking subsequent criminal action — something not forbidden by the rule against prior restraints. In fact, no such prosecutions took place.

The circumstances of the *Pentagon Papers* case were unusual. The issue of *prior restraint* arises more often in the context of press reporting of criminal trials where the right of the press to report events may be challenged as detrimental to the defendant's right to a fair trial, protected by the Sixth Amendment. A trial judge may take a number of steps to ensure a fair trial for the defendant. The trial may be moved to another location; witnesses and attorneys may be ordered not to discuss the case with anyone outside the courtroom; and, most drastically, the jury may be sequestered for the entire trial so that it is not exposed to information not admitted as evidence. The question is: May a judge also issue a gag order directly to the press to prevent it from disseminating certain kinds of information about the case that it already has in its possession and that may be prejudicial to the defendant?

In a recent case involving the trial of an alleged mass murderer in a small Nebraska town,[89] the Supreme Court held that the trial judge could not bar reporting of the gruesome facts of the case unless it could be shown, with very strong evidence, that press coverage would irreparably damage the right of the accused to a fair trial. Chief Justice Warren Burger wrote for the Court: "We reaffirm that the guarantees of freedom of expression are not an absolute prohibition under all circumstances, but the barriers to prior restraint remain high and the presumption against its use continues intact."

Right of Access. The rule against prior restraint does not foreclose other means of averting adverse publicity, both before and during a criminal trial. Pretrial publicity is often especially harmful to the defendant since it may disseminate false and misleading information in the community *before* a jury

---

[88] *The New York Times* v. *United States*, 403 U.S. 713 (1971).
[89] *Nebraska Press Association* v. *Stuart*, 427 U.S. 539 (1976).

Prior Restraint

The Supreme Court has consistently held that prior restraint of the press — censorship — is forbidden by the First Amendment except in extraordinary circumstances. But what are these circumstances?

The issue of prior restraint occurs most often today in two situations: in the context of a criminal case, when the trial judge seeks to prevent publication of material prejudicial to the defendant; and when the government seeks to ban publication of material it deems to be obscene, libelous, or contrary to the interests of national security.

An individual charged with a crime is entitled to a fair trial. This right is protected by the Sixth and Fourteenth Amendments to the Constitution. The public also has a "right to know" protected by the First Amendment. The framers of the Constitution did not assign a priority either to the right to a fair trial or to the rights of a free press, yet there is an essential incompatibility between them. Charles Simants was accused of the brutal slaying of six members of a family in a small Nebraska town. To protect his right to a fair trial, the judge ordered the press not to divulge certain information about the defendant (who was a neighbor of the victims), his arrest, and the nature of the crime. These restraints were to apply until a jury had been selected and sequestered. The Supreme Court unanimously reversed the gag order and held that the judge had not met the very heavy burden of showing that such restraints were necessary to protect the defendant. Until that burden of proof could be met, the Supreme Court said, prior restraints on the press are presumed to be unconstitutional. Simants was eventually convicted of murder and sentenced to death.

In June, 1971, The New York Times *began to publish exerpts from a classified government study of American policy in Vietnam, later known as "The Pentagon Papers,"* The Washington Post *and other newspapers followed suit, and the government asked the newspapers, in the interests of national security, to*

cease publication of the materials. When the Times *and the* Post *refused, the government sought an injunction in the Federal District Courts in both cities. These courts denied the government's request, and the Supreme Court, acting with unusual haste, also held in favor of the newspapers by a vote of 6 to 3. Justices Black and Douglas held that prior restraint should never be permitted: ". . . every moment's continuance of the injunctions against these newspapers amounts to a flagrant, indefensible and continuing violation of the First Amendment." Other justices in the majority agreed that the government had not made a substantial case for an injunction, but they refused to interpret the First Amendment absolutely to bar all prior restraint. For them it was enough to conclude that the government had not demonstrated that publication would result in "direct, immediate and irreparable damage to our nation or its people." Following this decision, newspaper serialization of the Pentagon Papers continued; eventually they were published in book form.*

A similar situation occurred in the spring of 1979. A federal judge in Milwaukee enjoined publication of an issue of The Progressive *magazine which contained an article explaining how to construct an H-Bomb: "The H-Bomb Secret: How We Get It, and Why We're Telling It." Unlike the Pentagon Papers case, these were not purloined documents; rather the author had pieced together the information from sources already available to the public. But, the government contended, publication would violate a provision of the Atomic Energy Act which stated that information about nuclear weapons was "restricted data" deemed to be "classified at birth." In other words, the government asserted it was a crime to publish information about nuclear weapons even if that data were the product of divine revelation or the reporter's own logical thinking.*

So fearful was the government that this information would be released that it imposed a lid of secrecy on briefs and exhibits submitted to the court. One of Judge Robert Warren's opinions, in which he declined to lift the injunction, was not even shown to The Progressive's *lawyers. Before the case*

could be considered by the Court of Appeals, however, a newspaper in Madison, Wisconsin (where The Progressive *is also published), independently published nearly all the same details about the H-Bomb. The government then asked that the case be dismissed and the article appeared in the November, 1979 issue of the magazine.*

has been selected, thereby contaminating the adversary process irreparably. On the other hand, there are two constitutional provisions that seem to set a standard of open and public trials. One is the First Amendment's free press provisions; the other is the Sixth Amendment's guarantee of a speedy and "public" trial. The Court has held that a defendant's rights are violated by a secret trial, but that they are not violated by the televising and broadcasting of a trial without the defendant's consent. In 1979 the Court held in *Gannett* v. *De Pasquale* that there was no Sixth Amendment barrier to closing a pretrial hearing in a sensational murder case when both the defense attorneys and the prosecution agreed to do so.[90] Much confusion surrounded the decision in this case, in part because the Court refused to consider whether the First Amendment, independently of the Sixth, gave the press a right to attend all criminal trials.

Some of this confusion was resolved in 1980 in *Richmond Newspapers, Inc.* v. *Virginia.*[91] By a 7-to-1 vote, the Supreme Court held that the First and Fourteenth Amendments contained a guaranteed right of access of the public (including the press) to attend criminal trials *unless* there was overwhelming evidence that an open trial would be prejudicial to the accused.

Political Expression. Protection of political expression was a primary concern of those who wrote the First Amendment. Under English law at the time, a citizen could be prosecuted for mere criticism of the government or of public officials (this was known as *seditious libel*). Such prosecutions are notoriously subject to abuse. (Even today, British libel laws restrict criticism of the government far more than American laws do.) The First Amendment notwithstanding, the Federalist-controlled Congress could not resist prohibiting just that kind of "seditious libel" in the Sedition Act of 1798. The act was allowed to expire in 1801 after the Jeffersonians took power, and the fines levied against those convicted under it were eventually paid back.[92] In 1964 the Supreme Court declared that the act had been unconstitutional, and stated that the First Amendment abolished the crime of seditious libel.[93]

Government cannot prohibit mere criticism of its policies, but it can penalize expression combined with action, or expression likely to lead to action, that threatens the nation's security. Apart from clearly illegal actions, such as espionage, sabotage, incitement to riot, or obstruction of government activities, the question remains: How threatening must mere words become before they lose their constitutional protection? A good example is the famous case of *Schenck* v. *United States* (1919).[94] Schenck was convicted of conspiracy to violate the Espionage Act of 1917. His crime was to print and distribute

[90] 443 U.S. 368 (1979).
[91] 65 L. Ed., 2d 963 (1980).
[92] See Leonard Levy, *Legacy of Suppression* (Cambridge, Mass.: Harvard University Press, 1960).
[93] *New York Times* v. *Sullivan*, 376 U.S. 254 (1964).
[94] 249 U.S. 47 (1919).

through the mails circulars calling on citizens who had been drafted into the military to assert their constitutional rights and refuse induction.

A unanimous Supreme Court affirmed Schenck's conviction. Justice Holmes attempted to draw the line between utterances that were protected and those that were not:

> The character of every act depends upon the circumstances in which it is done. . . . The most stringent protection of free speech would not protect a man in falsely shouting fire in a threatre and causing a panic. . . . The question in every case is whether the words used are used in circumstances and are of such a nature as to create a clear and present danger that they will bring about the substantive evil that Congress has a right to prevent. It is a question of proximity and degree. . . . When a nation is at war many things that might be said in time of peace are such a hindrance to its effort that their utterance will not be endured so long as men fight and that no Court could regard them as protected by any constitutional right.

Notwithstanding the distinction that Holmes was trying to draw between protected and unprotected speech in formulating the "clear and present danger" test, the Supreme Court was not favorably disposed to those punished under these laws. Tolerance for different political views declined further with the approach of World War II. In 1940 Congress passed the Alien Registration Act. The Smith Act, as it was known, was the first peacetime sedition act since 1798. It prohibited the advocacy of overthrowing the government by force and violence, the printing and distribution of materials advocating such ideas, and the organization of, or membership in, any group that advocated such ideas. The law made it a crime merely to belong to such a group. The Communist party was never mentioned, but its suppression was obviously intended.

In 1948 the government charged eleven leaders of the American Communist Party with conspiring to organize that party and to advocate the duty and necessity of overthrowing the government. No overt illegal acts of sabotage or violence were alleged. Their conviction after a lengthy and tumultuous trial gave the Supreme Court its first opportunity to consider the validity of the Smith Act, in a case entitled *Dennis* v. *United States* (1951).[95] If the Court was to apply the clear and present danger test literally, the convictions should have been reversed, since there was no danger that was either clear or present. But a 6-to-2 majority of the Court, affirming the convictions, adopted a different test; instead of clear and present danger, it said that the "gravity of the evil, discounted by its improbability" justified the convictions. Under this test, if the evil was great enough, the threat need not be very imminent.

Additional prosecutions of Communist Party leaders brought the Smith Act to the Supreme Court again in 1957, with quite different results. The defendants in *Yates* v. *United States* had been charged with conspiring to organize

[95] 341 U.S. 494 (1951).

the Communist Party and advocating the overthrow of the government. But the Court held that the statute prohibited only the initial organization of the party (it was "reorganized" after World War II) and not the continued recruitment of members. Thus, further prosecutions for "organizing" were prohibited. More important, the Court held that there was a difference between advocating an abstract doctrine of overthrow, and the direct advocacy of unlawful acts. The convictions of five of the fourteen defendants were reversed; new trials were ordered for the remainder. The government then decided that prosecutions under the Smith Act, as now interpreted by the Supreme Court, were impossible. All the indictments were dismissed; the Smith Act today, though unrepealed, is unused and probably unusable.[96]

By the end of the 1960s, most of the laws designed to outlaw the Communist Party had been invalidated by the Supreme Court or, like the Smith Act, rendered unusable by very strict evidentiary requirements. Communists could not be denied passports and could no longer be required to register as members of subversive organizations. Mere membership in the Party could no longer be the basis for denial of jobs and professional certification. Loyalty and security oaths, and the controversies that always surrounded the administration of these devices, receded in use and importance.[97] Symbolizing the reduced national concern with internal subversion, the House Internal Security Committee, formerly the House Committee on Un-American Activities, was disbanded in 1975; the Internal Security Subcommittee of the Senate Judiciary Committee, once the main forum for Senator Joseph McCarthy's assaults on communism, was abolished in 1978, then re-established in 1981 as the subcommittee on Security and Terrorism when the Republicans gained control of the Senate.

Obscenity.   The constitutional status of obscenity has never been in doubt; it has long been regarded as one of the exceptions to the speech protected by the First Amendment. But the definition of what constitutes obscenity has never been satisfactorily resolved. In part this has been a failure of words, the inability of language to define adequately what kinds of sexual expression are permitted or prohibited. This is a problem, of course, only as long as *some* sexual expression is permitted. If *all* such expression or all references to sex are prohibited, then the problem of definition is minimized.

Prior to the 1930s there was little difficulty in "drawing the line." American courts followed the rule of the English courts that a book could be declared obscene if it tended to "deprave and corrupt those whose minds are open to such immoral influences, and into whose hands a publication of this sort might fall." Even a great work of literature might be suppressed if it contained one salacious passage, and if its *tendency* to corrupt was measured by its effect on the most vulnerable groups, such as children. A federal court of appeals re-

---

[96] *Yates* v. *United States,* 354 U.S. 298 (1957).
[97] See, for example, *United States* v. *Robel,* 389 U.S. 258 (1967).

pudiated this rule in 1934 and held that James Joyce's book, *Ulysses*, was not obscene. It was the "dominant effect" of a book, the Court said, and not a few isolated passages, that determined whether the book could be brought into the United States.[98]

The constitutional definition of obscenity was not addressed by the Supreme Court until 1957. In *Roth* v. *United States* the Court upheld Roth's conviction for sending obscene circulars through the mails. Obscenity was not protected by the Constitution, the Court said, because it was "utterly without redeeming social importance." But all treatments of sex were not obscene, Justice Brennan wrote. The test was "whether to the average person, applying contemporary community standards, the dominant theme of the material taken as a whole appeals to prurient interests."[99] Subsequent cases interpreted this test strictly, and few books or movies were found to be obscene. "Contemporary community standards" was held to be a national and not a local standard. By 1966 the *Roth* test had been applied to permit the suppression only of the worst hard-core pornography. In fact, the test was so difficult to explain that most obscenity cases coming to the Supreme Court were decided without opinion on a case-to-case basis, after the justices had looked at the book or magazine, or viewed the film.

In *Miller* v. *California* (1973),[100] and in six other cases, a reconstituted Supreme Court reexamined obscenity standards and made three important changes. First, it held that "community standards" meant state or local standards; the mores of New York or Las Vegas, the Court said, should not control the definition of obscenity everywhere. Second, it held that state law might specifically define the particular types of sexual activity whose portrayal was prohibited. Third, instead of determining whether the work was "utterly without redeeming social importance," it was only necessary now to show that "the work, taken as a whole, lacks serious literary, artistic, political or scientific value."

The Court's new test for community standards ran into trouble almost immediately. A small-town jury in Georgia found the nationally distributed film *Carnal Knowledge* to be obscene. Clearly, this was not what the Supreme Court had in mind; in a unanimous opinion written by Justice Rehnquist, it held that the film was simply not "the public portrayal of hard core sexual conduct for its own sake" that could be deemed obscene.[101]

Prior to *Miller* it might have been said that the only legitimate objects of antiobscenity laws were restrictions for minors and protection for adults against having unwanted obscene materials "thrust upon them." The *Miller* case did nothing to change that. Children may still be denied access to materials not regarded as constitutionally obscene for adults, such as *Playboy* magazine; and restrictions on advertising pornographic materials to avoid offend-

---

[98] *United States* v. *One Book Entitled "Ulysses,"* 72 F2d 705 (1934).
[99] 354 U.S. 476 (1957).
[100] 413 U.S. 15 (1973).
[101] *Jenkins* v. *Georgia,* 418 U.S. 153 (1974).

ing sensitive persons are generally still valid. But the *Miller* doctrine has not produced the rash of prosecutions and convictions its sponsors had sought.

In 1970 the President's Commission on Obscenity and Pornography recommended that government "not seek to interfere with the rights of adults . . . to read, obtain, or view explicit sexual materials." It did endorse regulation of the sale of sexual materials to children without parental consent, and laws to protect persons from being exposed unwillingly to such materials. The Commission majority found no empirical evidence to link exposure to explicit sexual materials with various forms of deviant or antisocial behavior. It noted the lack of success of attempts to regulate obscenity. Such efforts often resulted in inconsistent and often discriminatory law enforcement, a problem common to attempted enforcement of other "crimes without victims." The commission also noted the absence of consensus among citizens about the availability of explicit sexual materials.[102] In fact, Americans seem to treasure both their vices and their morals. They support the passage and retention of "antivice" ordinances, but are also content with the underenforcement of these ordinances. One obvious reason is that many citizens patronize such businesses.

Barring a major reversal by the Supreme Court in its application of the First Amendment to obscenity and pornography, or a constitutional amendment overruling Court decisions that some regard as excessively permissive, explicit sexual materials will continue to be available to those who want and can afford them. In this context, the rise of radical feminist objections to pornography is a fascinating contemporary development. Increasingly, radical feminists assert that pornography not only degrades women but also stimulates men to commit sexual assaults and engage in sexual harassment of women. Thus, conservatives who have criticized the availability of pornography are gaining a new and unexpected ally.[103]

FREEDOM OF RELIGION The First Amendment provides that "Congress shall make no law respecting an establishment of religion, or prohibiting the free exercise thereof." But these simple and direct commands do not mean exactly what they seem to say. First, we know that the First Amendment was incorporated into the Fourteenth, so that both the federal government *and* the states are limited by it. Second, "no law" does not mean "no law," but something less than that, since the Supreme Court has rejected an "absolutist" interpretation of the First Amendment. In fact, as we shall see, what these constitutional commands mean is that government and religion must not be *unduly* intertwined or *excessively entangled.*

In his famous letter to the Danbury Baptist Association in 1802, Thomas

---

[102] *Report of the Commission on Obscenity and Pornography* (New York: Bantam Books, 1970), pp. 43–48 and passim.

[103] See, for example, Irene Diamond, "Pornography and Repression: A Reconsideration," *Signs: Journal of Women in Culture and Society* 3 (Summer 1980): 686–701.

Jefferson argued that the First Amendment built a "wall of separation between Church and State." Yet the simplicity of this metaphor, which has come to dominate constitutional and political rhetoric about religion and the state, obscures the competing interests that the First Amendment was designed to protect. Jefferson, for example, was most concerned with protecting the state from the encroachments of the church. On the other hand, Roger Williams, who established the colony of Rhode Island in the seventeenth century, was most concerned with protecting the church from the state. Both were concerned with avoiding the destructive quarrels between state and church, between politics and conscience, that had characterized the English experience.

The Establishment Clause At the very least, the Establishment Clause of the First Amendment meant that government may not prefer one religion to another, or set up an established church. But as Jefferson's metaphor suggests, it means more than that; the predominant view has been that the Establishment Clause implies not merely an evenhanded treatment of different religions, but a complete *separation* between the state and all religions. The Supreme Court has generally accepted the second and broader view of the Establishment Clause.

Unquestionably the most volatile church-state issue of our time concerns the validity of school prayers. In *Engel* v. *Vitale* (1962) the Supreme Court outlawed a local school board requirement in Nassau County, a suburb of New York City, that all school children recite daily a "nondenominational" prayer composed by the Board of Regents: "Almighty God, we acknowledge our dependence upon Thee, and we beg Thy blessing upon our parents, our teachers, and our country." For a 6-to-1 majority, Justice Black wrote that "in this country it is no part of the business of government to compose official prayers for any group of the American people to recite as part of a religious program carried on by government."[104] Just one year later, in *Abington School District* v. *Schempp* and in *Murray* v. *Curlett* (1963), the Court incited a storm of protest by holding that the First Amendment also prohibited recitation of the Lord's Prayer and the daily reading of Bible verses in the public schools.[105]

Efforts to reverse the Court's decisions by constitutional amendment failed. Many schools stopped requiring prayers, but in a substantial number prayers continue to be said. According to one study, nearly one-third of the schools in the South continued to require prayers long after the Court's decision.[106] Some states have provided for voluntary prayers, others for a period of silent meditation before each school day. Kentucky required the posting of a copy of the Ten Commandments in every classroom in the state, but this was struck down by the Supreme Court in *Stone* v. *Graham* (1980).[107] As noted in Chap-

[104] *Engel* v. *Vitale*, 370 U.S. 421 (1962).
[105] 374 U.S. 203 (1963).
[106] Reported in "Spring Survey of Education," *The New York Times*, April 20, 1980, p. 3. See also Kenneth M. Dolbeare and Phillip Hammond, *The School Prayer Decisions* (Chicago: University of Chicago Press, 1971).
[107] 449 U.S. 39 (1980).

ter 9, current efforts to undermine the school prayer decisions continue in the Congress. Most prominent among these efforts was Senate passage in 1979 of the so-called Helms amendment, an appropriations bill rider that would have deprived the Supreme Court of jurisdiction to hear school prayer cases, and thus insulated from constitutional attack those states wishing to reinstitute school prayers. A 1981 *New York Times*–CBS survey reported that approximately three-fourths of its sample supported the resumption of school prayers.

A major constitutional issue today is whether government can provide financial assistance to religious schools. Both the states and, since 1965, Congress have provided subsidies to religious schools. Some have been upheld, others have not. The Supreme Court held that a state could lend secular textbooks to parochial school students, but invalidated a program of salary supplements to parochial school teachers who taught secular subjects.[108] It upheld construction grants for parochial school facilities designed for secular purposes, but in 1973 it invalidated a program providing for tuition reimbursements and tax credits for parents whose children attended parochial schools.[109] In 1975 the Court invalidated the direct loan to parochial schools of various educational equipment, but in 1977 it upheld an Ohio law providing counseling and diagnostic services for parochial school children held *off* school premises.[110]

All these decisions, however confusing, ostensibly were decided by applying a three-part test that the Court has developed: a statute must have a secular purpose; its primary effect must be neither to advance or inhibit religion; and it must avoid excessive entanglement of church and state. In effect, the Court has recognized that although separation of church and state can never be absolute, relations between church and state can develop only so far. The Court has recognized that religion plays an important role in American life. Our coins bear the motto "In God We Trust." Many important affairs of state including each session of the Senate, begin with a prayer. Church property, the Supreme Court has said, may be exempted from state taxes lest disputes over tax assessments produce that feared "excessive entanglement."[111]

The Free Exercise Clause The Establishment and Free Exercise clauses of the First Amendment are closely related in purpose, but their origins were different. The Free Exercise Clause protects religious toleration. As Pritchett has noted, the principle was already firmly grounded in 1791 in both England and the United States.[112]

---

[108]*Board of Education v. Allen*, 3924 U.S. 236 (1968); *Lemon v. Kurtzman* 403 U.S. 602 (1971).
[109]*Committee for Public Education and Religious Liberty v. Nyquist*, 413 U.S. 756 (1973).
[110]*Wolman v. Walter*, 433 U.S. 229 (1977). In *Committee For Public Education and Religious Liberty v. Regan*, 63 L. Ed. 2d, 94 (1980), the Supreme Court upheld a New York statute authorizing public funds to reimburse church related and secular private schools for the direct costs of carrying out state-mandated testing programs. Said Justice White for a 5-to-4 majority, ". . . Establishment Clause cases are not easy; they stir deep feelings; and we are divided among ourselves, perhaps reflecting the different views on this subject of the people of this country."
[111]*Walz v. Tax Commission of the City of New York*, 397 U.S. 664 (1970).
[112]C. Herman Pritchett, *The American Constitution* (New York: McGraw-Hill, 1977), p. 390.

The Establishment Clause, on the other hand, was a clear break with the English tradition of an established church and, indeed, with similar practices found in many of the American states.

There are few if any instances in American history in which specific religious *beliefs* have been subject to official coercion. But such beliefs often involve actions that come into conflict with secular regulations. In such instances the court must balance the competing claims. The general rule is that there is no constitutionally sanctioned religious exemption from laws with a legitimate secular purpose — the assumption being that religious *belief* is absolutely protected, but that actions (or inactions), even those that flow from religious conviction, are subject to regulation.

Unquestionably the most famous case of this kind involved the Mormon practice of polygamy. In *Reynolds* v. *United States* (1878), the Supreme Court upheld the validity of an act of Congress prohibiting polygamy in the territories. The act was said to violate the Free Exercise clause. The Court reasoned, however, that Congress had a clear power to prohibit polygamy in the territories, and that to grant an exemption to Mormons would be tantamount to favoring one religion over others — a violation of the Establishment Clause. Freedoms otherwise protected by the First Amendment, the Court said, may be subject to *incidental* regulation as part of an otherwise proper secular legislative scheme. Thus this statute could be upheld even though inevitably it did impinge on the religious beliefs of Mormons.[113] A similar result was reached in 1961, when the Court upheld the validity of Sunday closing laws (known as "blue laws") against challenges by orthodox Jewish businessmen. The merchants contended that since they had to observe their own sabbath on Saturday, forced closing on Sunday limited them to a five-day business week and thus aided competitors who could stay open six days.[114]

Can school children be required to salute the American flag even when doing so violates their religious convictions? When first confronted with a challenge to such a law by Jehovah's Witnesses, the Supreme Court held in 1940 that requiring *all* children to salute the flag did not violate the constitutional rights of any of them.[115] But the decision was controversial, several justices changed their minds, and new appointments to the Court further undermined the original majority. Three years later, in *West Virginia State Board of Education* v. *Barnette* (1943), the Court reversed its earlier ruling and held that the First Amendment prohibits requiring *any* school children from saluting the flag, not just members of the Jehovah's Witnesses faith.[116]

Exemptions for certain sects or certain types of beliefs have been approved, however. In *Wisconsin* v. *Yoder* (1972), the Court held that application of an eighth grade compulsory school attendance requirement violated the constitutionally protected beliefs of the Old Order Amish. But the Court went to some

[113]*Reynolds* v. *United States*, 98 U.S. 145 (1878).
[114]*Braunfield* v. *Brown*, 366 U.S. 599 (1961).
[115]*Minersville School District* v. *Gobitis*, 310 U.S. 586 (1940).
[116]319 U.S. 624 (1943).

lengths to emphasize that it was not approving a general religious exemption from such laws, but only balancing the state's interests in fostering education against the interests of the Amish children (at least those asserted by their parents, as Justice Douglas observed).[117]

Religious exemptions are also at issue in the practice of granting conscientious objector (CO) status and exemption to those who oppose military conscription on the basis of religious beliefs. The Court has never required that Congress permit such objections. Rather, a series of cases have tested whether Congress, having elected to establish a conscientious objector category, can limit its benefits to objectors holding certain kinds of religious beliefs. The Draft Act of 1917 exempted only those affiliated with a "well-recognized" pacifist religion — a distinction that would almost certainly be constitutionally invalid today. The 1940 draft law extended CO status to those whose opposition to war was based on "religious training and belief." After World War II, this was defined by statute to mean "an individual's belief in relation to a Supreme Being involving duties superior to those arising from any human relation, but not including essentially political, sociological, or philosophical views or a merely personal moral code."

When the statute was challenged in *United States* v. *Seeger* (1965), the Supreme Court interpreted the words "Supreme Being" to encompass not only an orthodox religious belief, but a belief that "occupies a place in the life of its possessor parallel to that filled by the orthodox belief in God of one who clearly qualified for the exemption." Thus, according to the Court, one could qualify as a conscientious objector without belonging to a pacifist religion or without even a belief in God, as long as one's objections to war were more than merely a personal moral code.[118] On the other hand, in *Gillette* v. *United States* (1971), the Court held that there were valid neutral reasons for Congress's policy that limited CO status to those who objected to *all* wars, thus excluding selective objectors.[119]

PRIVACY The Ninth Amendment to the Constitution was proposed to allay fears that enumeration of certain rights in the bill of Rights would be interpreted as excluding other rights. Over the years the Supreme Court has acknowledged that there are significant rights not enumerated in the Constitution that nonetheless are entitled to the fullest constitutional protection. For example, the presumption of innocence of the defendant and the standard of "beyond a reasonable doubt" in criminal trials are found nowhere in the Constitution. Neither is the right to travel, as already noted, nor the right of association and the right to attend criminal trials, the latter two read into the First Amendment.[120] Unquestionably the most controversial of the "unenumerated" con-

---

[117] 406 U.S. 205 (1972).

[118] *United States* v. *Seeger*, 380 U.S. 163 (1965).

[119] 401 U.S. 437 (1971).

[120] The right of association, for example, is derived from the freedoms of speech, press, and religion, and from the right of assembly, which *are* directly protected by the First Amendment. See *NAACP* v. *Alabama*, 357 U.S. 449 (1958).

stitutional rights is the right to privacy, announced for the first time in *Griswold* v. *Connecticut* (1965).[121]

The concept of privacy has antecedents in both English and American law before the Constitution. Moreover, the framers of the Bill of Rights were certainly sensitive to privacy rights. The First Amendment implicitly addresses the question of religious privacy and the privacy of thought. The Third Amendment's prohibition of the quartering of soldiers in private homes speaks to a major privacy concern. The Fourth Amendment is directly concerned with the right of the people "to be secure in their persons, houses, papers and effects." And the Fifth Amendment prohibits forced self-incrimination.

In 1928 Justice Louis Brandeis, dissenting in a wiretapping case, *Olmstead* v. *United States,* gave classic expression to the importance of privacy:

> The makers of our constitution undertook to secure conditions favorable to the pursuit of happiness. They recognized the significance of man's spiritual nature, of his feelings and of his intellect. They knew that only a part of the pain, pleasure, and satisfaction of life are to be found in material things. They sought to protect Americans in their beliefs, their thoughts, their emotions, and their sensations. They conferred as against the government the right to be let alone —the most comprehensive of rights and the right most valued by civilized men.[122]

But not until the *Griswold* case was the right of privacy given formal constitutional recognition. The case involved a challenge to Connecticut's restrictive (but generally unenforced) birth control laws. Mrs. Griswold, an officer of a birth control clinic established in New Haven, was convicted of violating the statute. In overturning her conviction, the Supreme Court, in an opinion by Justice Douglas, found a right to privacy contained in the "penumbras" (or shadows) of the First, Third, Fourth, Fifth, and Ninth Amendments; and it held that the intimacy of the marital relationship is protected by that privacy right. Later cases extended the right of privacy to unmarried persons: "If the right of privacy means anything, it is the right of the individual, married or single, to be free from unwarranted governmental intrusion into matters so fundamentally affecting a person as the decision to bear or beget a child."[123] Unquestionably the most controversial extension of this right was in the abortion case, *Roe* v. *Wade* (see Chapter 9).

Claims that one's privacy has been infringed occur with increasing regularity in the courts, in a bewildering array of circumstances. Thus, in 1967 the Supreme Court declared that law enforcement officers could not "bug" a public telephone booth without a judicial warrant, even though they had information that the booth was used for bookmaking purposes. The Constitution "protects people, not places," the Supreme Court said; besides, even though a person is visible when using a public telephone, "what he sought to exclude when he entered the booth was not the intruding eye — it was the uninvited

---

[121] 381 U.S. 479 (1965).
[122] *Olmstead* v. *United States,* 277 U.S. 438 (1928).
[123] *Eisenstadt* v. *Baird,* 405 U.S. 438 (1972).

ear."[124] In 1969 the Court held that the constitutional right to privacy protects an individual watching pornographic films in his own home.[125] But in 1973 it held that the right of privacy *did not* protect one's right to view comparable films in a public theater.[126]

These decisions may have encouraged the development of personal autonomy in sexual activity. But the Supreme Court, like many Americans, has not yet come to terms with homosexuality. According to public opinion polls, most Americans believe that sexual relations between consenting adults of the same sex is wrong. But nearly half believe that such relations should not be illegal; better educated, younger respondents living in the east or west are the most favorably inclined; grade school educated, older persons living in the south or midwest much less sympathetic.[127] The Supreme Court's contribution to the gay rights movement has been to do nothing. In 1976 it affirmed, without opinion, the validity of Virginia's law against sodomy between consenting male adults.[128] And it has denied certiorari in several cases involving the rights of gay teachers.[129] It would appear, from this limited evidence, that the Court is not (yet) willing to extend the constitutional right of privacy to sexual practices it regards as deviant, notwithstanding the mobilization of gay rights organizations or the increase in public tolerance for (though not approval of) gay life-styles.

Most Americans take an expectation of privacy for granted. The problems we have just described happen not to them but only to "other" people. Birth control information and devices are freely available, as are abortions, at least for those who can afford them. Most Americans make telephone calls without fear of electronic surveillance, do not watch pornographic films in their homes, and are not homosexually inclined. But with the development of high technology information retrieval and transfer systems, the increasesd use of credit in purchases, and the need in dealing with various public and private agencies to provide personal information, more is known about our private lives than ever before. These concerns normally fall under the rubric of "informational privacy." Prevention of abuse of informational privacy has become a major public-policy — largely legislative — concern.

Congress has passed a number of statutes seeking to regulate the flow and potential misuse of personal information. The Fair Credit Reporting Act of 1970 imposed regulations on consumer reports. The Crime Control Act of 1973 limits access to individuals' criminal records. The Family Education Rights and Privacy Act of 1974 limits access to student educational records.

---

[124]*Katz* v. *United States*, 389 U.S. 347 (1967).

[125]*Stanley* v. *Georgia*, 394 U.S. 557 (1969).

[126]*Paris Adult Theatre I* v. *Slaton*, 413 U.S. 49 (1973).

[127] As reported in *Public Opinion* (July/August, 1978), p. 38.

[128]*Doe* v. *Commonwealth's Attorney*, 403 F. Supp. 1199 (E.D. Va., 1975), aff'd mem, 425 U.S. 901 (1976).

[129]*Gaylord* v. *Tacoma School District*, 434 U.S. 897 (1977). Also see David Adamany, "The Supreme Court at the Frontier of Politics: The Issue of Gay Rights," *Hamline Law Review* 4 (1981): 185–285.

The Freedom of Information Act of 1966 gives individuals access to federal records, but exempts disclosures constituting a "clearly unwarranted invasion of personal privacy."

The major federal legislation is the Privacy Act of 1974. The act affirms that "the right of privacy is a personal and fundamental right protected by the Constitution of the United States." It limits the kinds of information federal agencies may collect; for example, it forbids collection of information on political and other activities protected by the First Amendment. It places restraints on how information that can be collected is to be maintained, and the conditions under which it is to be disclosed. There is a built-in conflict between the Freedom of Information Act, which "encourages agencies to err on the side of disclosure," and the Privacy Act, "which permits disclosures only when required." [130] There are also many technical inconsistencies between the two laws that have hampered their effectiveness and perhaps diluted the protections they afford. But the overall congressional approach is to secure to individuals a legal right to some measure of control over information collected by government about them, *not* primarily to regulate what government "ought to know" about each of us.

THE RIGHTS OF CRIMINAL DEFENDANTS

Criminal justice and law enforcement in the United States are primarily the responsibility of the states. Since the Bill of Rights did not apply to the states, virtually no criminal cases reached the Supreme Court prior to passage of the Fourteenth Amendment. A new concern with the rights of criminal defendants developed slowly on the Court in the 1930s and reached a peak in the 1960s, when most of the rights of defendants protected by the Bill of Rights were applied to the states.

Incorporating the Bill of Rights

We have already described the constitutional arguments for and against incorporation. The Sixth Amendment right to counsel was applied to the states as early as 1932, and the protections of the Fourth Amendment in 1949. [131] But not until the 1960s did incorporation become virtually complete. In 1961, in *Mapp* v. *Ohio*, [132] the Court applied the exclusionary rule to the states. In 1962 the Cruel and unusual punishment clause of the Eighth Amendment was incorporated. [133] The next year, in *Gideon* v. *Wainwright*, the Court held that all indigent persons accused of a serious crime were entitled to counsel provided by the state. [134] The rights against self-incrimination and double jeopardy, and the right to trial by jury were subsequently added. [135] By "nationalizing" the

---

[130] David M. O'Brien, *Privacy, Law and Public Policy* (New York: Praeger, 1979), chap. 6.
[131] *Wolf* v. *Colorado*, 338 U.S. 25 (1949).
[132] 367 U.S. 643 (1961).
[133] *Robinson* v. *California*, 370 U.S. 660 (1962).
[134] 372 U.S. 335 (1963).
[135] *Malloy* v. *Hogan*, 378 U.S. 1 (1964); *Duncan* v. *Louisiana*, 391 U.S. 145 (1968). See footnote 8.

Bill of Rights, the Court effectively "constitutionalized" the criminal justice process, making it directly subject to policies established by the Supreme Court.

Defining new rights to apply uniformly in both state and federal courts is easy compared with the task of implementing those rights. In such matters, the willingness of law enforcement officials to respect constitutional rights cannot be assumed, especially where protection of those rights makes the law enforcement task more difficult. Therefore, the Court devised three types of strategies for implementation. First, it decreed that evidence obtained by the police in violation of constitutional rights could not be used against the defendant. This is known as the *exclusionary rule*. Second, the Court established a number of "prophylactic" (preventive) rules to ensure that the police did protect constitutional rights. The most famous of these are the *Miranda* rules, which police must read to suspects before questioning them. Third, the Court substantially enlarged the scope of the constitutional right to counsel on the assumption that the presence of a lawyer would ensure that basic rights were protected.

The Exclusionary Rule The exclusionary rule provides that evidence obtained by the police in violation of constitutional rights, such as evidence obtained by an illegal search, cannot be used against the defendant at trial. The Supreme Court adopted this rule for use in the federal courts as early as 1914, but did not apply it to the states until 1961, in *Mapp* v. *Ohio*.[136] The exclusionary rule is unique to American courts. It is contrary to past and current practice in Great Britain. In British courts, the only standard for admitting evidence into a criminal trial is whether the evidence is reliable. The arguments for the exclusionary rule are that it is the only effective judicial sanction against illegal police behavior and, further, that it preserves the integrity of the courts by not making them a party to illegal conduct.

One argument against the rule is that it often results in freeing defendants who might be guilty: "Is the criminal to go free because the constable has blundered?" Justice Cardozo once asked. A second argument against the exclusionary rule is that it does not work very well. Studies also show that the exclusionary rule encourages police perjury on the witness stand.[137] It is also extremely costly and time consuming, since it is necessary to have a pretrial "suppression" hearing before a magistrate to determine whether evidence against the defendant can be used against him.

Although the principle of the exclusionary rule applies to all protected rights, it is most centrally concerned with the Fourth Amendment. The Fourth Amendment protects individuals from *unreasonable* searches and seizures of their "houses, papers, and effects." A search is unreasonable if it is obtained without first securing a warrant from a judge. A judge may only issue

[136] 367 U.S. 643 (1961).
[137] Dallin Oaks, "Studying the Exclusionary Rule in Search and Seizure," *University of Chicago Law Review* 37 (1970): 665–757.

a search warrant if the police can show "probable cause" that a particular piece of evidence is to be found in a particular location. "General warrants" to search for evidence are prohibited.

As a matter of fact, the majority of police searches in the United States are carried out *without* a search warrant. This is legal because the Supreme Court has recognized certain exceptions to the warrant rule, and most searches can be carried out within those exceptions. The police may search without a warrant where consent has been given, where the search is made pursuant to a lawful arrest, or where evidence of a crime or contraband is observed by a police officer in "plain sight." Evidence may also be seized without a warrant when it might otherwise be destroyed. Thus, for example, the police are empowered to search in the course of "hot pursuit" or when evidence is believed to be located in a burning building. There is also a special exception for automobiles (and similar vehicles) that may be driven out of the jurisdiction. Searches without a warrant, however, must still satisfy the constitutional requirement of probable cause. Whether or not evidence has been properly obtained in a particular case is often a judgment call. Generally speaking, the Supreme Court has held that, except for special circumstances, a warrant is required where an individual's expectations of privacy are greatest — in his or her own home.[138]

The "Miranda Rule" In many criminal cases the primary — often the only — evidence against the accused is a confession. Yet it is said that our system is "accusatorial" rather than "inquisitorial," meaning that it is society — the "people" — that bears the burden of proving (beyond a reasonable doubt) that the defendant committed the crime charged against him. Traditionally, a confession was admitted as evidence in a criminal case if it was judged to be voluntary. Such a determination could be made only on a case-by-case basis, and thus was not an effective check on police misbehavior. Furthermore, the "voluntariness" test worked best to exclude confessions that resulted from brutal force; it was ineffective in preventing nonphysical and often subtle forms of coercion.

To protect defendants against this kind of coercion, the Supreme Court decided in *Miranda* v. *Arizona* (1966) that no admission of guilt (either a formal confession or any other "inculpatory" statement by the accused) would be admissible in a trial unless the defendant had first been read his constitutional rights.[139] The defendant must be told that he need not say anything, that everything he did say might be used against him, and that he was entitled to consult with a lawyer — prior to or during police questioning — at the government's expense if he was indigent. An individual who wished to make a statement to the police could do so, but a court would admit that statement into evidence against him if there was evidence that the right to remain silent

[138]*Katz* v. *United States*, 389 U.S. 34 (1967); see also *Payton* v. *New York*, 63 L. Ed. 2d. 639 (1980).
[139]*Miranda* v. *Arizona*, 384 U.S. 436 (1966).

had been "knowingly" waived. Likewise, an accused person could waive his right to a lawyer, but the police had to be sure that it was a voluntary decision. Otherwise, any statement that the defendant made would be inadmissible at trial even if it might otherwise be deemed voluntary and reliable. For the police, the risk of not following these prophylactic rules was great, since in many cases statements by a defendant were the best, or the only, admissible evidence.

The political reaction against *Miranda* was especially severe. Prophecies of how it would "handcuff" the police abounded, and the backlash included several proposed constitutional amendments and related efforts in Congress to retaliate against the Supreme Court. Yet such prophecies were premature. The police still obtained confessions. Many accused persons elected to "come clean," and some preferred not to have a lawyer — at least not (if they were indigent) a government-appointed one.[140]

Miranda became the focal point of criticism of the Supreme Court in the 1968 and 1972 presidential elections. The Burger Court has not reversed *Miranda,* as liberals feared and many conservatives wished. But it has sought to limit the impact and scope of the decision. Yet the fact is that all over the United States, police carry wallet-sized "*Miranda* cards" and automatically read arrested persons their constitutional rights. It was reported that Miranda himself, killed in a barroom brawl after his release from prison, was carrying a *Miranda* card; the first thing the police did when they apprehended his suggested killer was to read *him* his *Miranda* rights!

The Right to Counsel It was not until 1963, when the Court decided *Gideon* v. *Wainwright,* that the appointment of counsel was required in all serious criminal cases in both states and federal courts. In succeeding cases, the "right to counsel" was extended to pretrial lineups and similar identification procedures; as we have just seen, in *Miranda* it was extended from the courtroom to the station house. It has also been extended to some misdemeanor cases.[141] Counsel must also be provided for at least the first appeal of a criminal conviction. The right to counsel also applies in juvenile proceedings, but not, the Court has said, in prison disciplinary hearings. Parenthetically, there is no right to appointed counsel in civil cases.

The Supreme Court has stated that counsel must be provided to indigent defendants, but it is the states that determine both standards of indigency and the form in which counsel is provided for most defendants. Most large cities today have public defender systems that provide state-hired lawyers to most criminal defendants. In smaller communities, where a public defender system is not feasible economically, members of the local bar may be appointed by the judge to represent indigents accused of crime. In an interesting twist, the

---

[140] See, for example, Michael Wald, et al., "Interrogations in New Haven," *Yale Law Journal* 76 (1967): 1521–1648.

[141] *Argersinger* v. *Hamlin,* 407 U.S. 25 (1972), and *Baldasar* v. *Illinois,* 64 L. Ed. 2d 169 (1980).

Supreme Court ruled in *Faretta* v. *California* (1975) that an indigent defendant need not be required to accept counsel provided to him. The Sixth Amendment guarantees the right to conduct one's own defense as well as the right to counsel.[142]

The Right to a Fair Trial What is a fair trial? The Sixth Amendment provides a good short definition, yet not a complete one. It requires a *speedy* and *public* trial, by an *impartial* jury locally drawn. It requires that the accused be informed of the nature of the charges, that he be confronted with witnesses against him, that he have compulsory process for witnesses in his favor, and that he have the assistance of counsel. So far, so good! But what of the coerced confession, improper search and seizure, biased lineup, hurried and perfunctory reading of the *Miranda* rule, and prejudicial pretrial publicity, all of which may undermine the defendant's position irreparably? What about the diligence of the defense lawyer and the resources available to him? What about the conduct of the trial judge and the fairness and correctness of his handling of the trial?

Is it less fair to the defendant to confront a jury of only six citizens instead of the traditional twelve (as the Supreme Court has said is possible in the state courts)?[143] Is a jury that returns a less than unanimous verdict for conviction (as the Supreme Court has recently said is possible in the state courts) upholding the defendant's constitutional right to conviction only on evidence "beyond a reasonable doubt"?[144] What about the effectiveness of counsel? Can we expect a public defender to expend the same effort and resources investigating a defendant's claims that F. Lee Bailey spent in behalf of Patricia Hearst? If the verdict is guilty, what about the fairness of the sentence? Other than sentences grossly disproportionate to the crime, such as capital punishment for rape or loss of citizenship for military desertion, few punishments have been struck down by the Supreme Court.[145] As long as a judge sentences within the legal limits set by law, the sentence will stand, even though defendants committing similar crimes may fare quite differently before the same judge, or before different judges. Is it fair, for example, for a defendant who declines to plead guilty and elects a trial — as few do — to receive a more severe sentence if found guilty. There is evidence that such is the case,[146] yet no constitutional violation is involved. In United States law there is generally no appeal of sentences imposed by the trial judge.

The preceding paragraphs are an implicit answer to the question with which

[142] 422 U.S. 806 (1975).

[143] See *Ballew* v. *Georgia*, 435 U.S. 223 (1978), where the Court held that six was the *minimum* permissible size of a state criminal court jury.

[144] *Johnson* v. *Louisiana*, 406 U.S. 356 (1972).

[145] In *Rummel* v. *Estelle*, 63 L. Ed. 2d 382 (1980), for example, the Court rejected a claim that a life sentence under a recidivist (repeat offender) statute was grossly disproportionate to the crime and hence unconstitutional. Rummel had committed three minor felony thefts, the last for $120.

[146] Thomas M. Uhlman and N. Darlene Walker," 'He Takes Some of My Time; I Take Some of His'! An Analysis of Sentencing Patterns in Jury Cases," *Law & Society Review* 14 (1980): 323–42.

this section began: What is a fair trial? The Constitution requires a fair trial, but an appellate court's judgment of whether or not a trial is fair in most cases touches only the tip of the iceberg. There are so many discretionary elements in the criminal justice system, and such interdependence between the many components of the system, that it is very easy not to have a fair trial and quite difficult to have one, even assuming the best of intentions on the part of officials. Opportunities for unfairness abound. The Supreme Court can establish broad constitutional rules, but some trials will always be less fair than others.

CONCLUSION   Everyone believes in individual rights, but how are these rights to be translated from abstract principles to real situations? Everyone believes in the principle of free speech, no doubt, but does that principle encompass the right to wear an American flag sewn to the seat of one's pants? No one denies the value of personal privacy, but should that principle extend to a woman's right to an abortion? When government acts against a citizen, it must act according to due process of law. Should that principle be interpreted to require a hearing for a high school student faced with a short suspension for misconduct? a college student charged by an instructor with plagiarism? an inmate accused of a breach of prison disciplinary rules?

Equally difficult questions arise about who, or which instituion, is to make these decisions. When should the Supreme Court defer to the other branches of the national government? When should it defer to the laws and courts of the several states? When is it necessary — or at least appropriate — for individual rights to be uniform throughout the country? And when is diversity to be encouraged or tolerated?

In a healthy, democratic society, these kinds of questions can never be entirely laid to rest. Interpreting, claiming, and enforcing rights is an inevitable part of the dynamics of political democracy. Our society's concern with individual rights is one of its most distinctive and healthy features. Yet there is also a tendency to be excessively self-congratulatory, and to succumb to what Scheingold has called "the myth of rights." [147] This myth is the assumption that rights asserted by our courts automatically become "accomplished social facts." In truth, as Scheingold argues, such rights are not nearly so secure or widely recognized. They may be inalienable, but they are not cost free, and guaranteeing them requires a considerable and continuous investment of our collective and individual resources.

SUGGESTIONS   Berns, Walter. *The First Amendment and the Future of American Democracy.* New York:
FOR FURTHER   Basic Books, 1976. Following up on his earlier work, *Freedom, Virtue and the First*
READING   *Amendment*, Berns argues against the trend of recent Supreme Court decisions that have taken a permissive view of First Amendment rights.

---

[147] Scheingold, *The Politics of Rights.*

Emerson, Thomas I. *The System of Freedom of Expression*. New York: Vintage Books, 1970. A modern classic, this book explores the meaning and importance of free expression, and analyzes the major constitutional doctrines that set the boundaries of government intervention and protection.

Harris, Richard. *Freedom Spent: Tales of Tyranny in America*. Boston: Little, Brown, 1976. A prize-winning journalist's account of three cases in which American citizens had to fight for their rights *against* government.

Kluger, Richard. *Simple Justice*. New York: Vintage Books, 1977. A rich and detailed account of the Supreme Court's historic school-desegregation decision, *Brown* v. *Board of Education of Topeka* (1954).

Meltsner, Michael. *Cruel and Unusual*. New York: Random House, 1973. An insider's view of the campaign by the Legal Defense Fund to end capital punishment in the United States, a campaign that ended successfully — but only temporarily, as it has turned out — with the Supreme Court's decision in *Furman* v. *Georgia* (1972).

Sorauf, Frank J. *The Wall of Separation: The Constitutional Politics of Church and State*. Princeton, N.J.: Princeton University Press, 1976. A study of all major church-state litigation from 1951 to 1971, including interviews with the parties and their attorneys. A fascinating view of how interests are aggregated and channeled into the judicial arena.

Wilkinson, J. Harvie, III. *From Brown to Bakke: The Supreme Court and School Integration, 1954–1978*. New York: Oxford University Press, 1980. An accurate portrayal of the aftermath of the *Brown* decision, the law and politics of school-integration efforts, and the continuing controversy over school busing.

Chapter 15 The American System and Its Critics

As we have seen throughout this book, governing the United States is a huge, demanding, and complex undertaking. The diversity of American life necessitates some agency to guide our mutual affairs as a people, if only to resolve our many conflicts. America's great population and the intricate economic, transportation, and communication networks on which we depend impose the same requirement. These needs ensure that the United States will always have a government. Yet they do not necessarily mean we will or must have the kind of government we now have. Nor do they guarantee that the complaints that are now heaped on our political system are inevitable. This chapter has two aims. First, it attempts to explain exactly what kind of political democracy we have. Second, it considers the types of complaints our system of government now confronts. Chapter 16, the concluding chapter, will explore some alternative ideas of democracy and contrast them to our own.

It may seem odd to ask what kind of government we have after so many chapters describing the institutions, policies, and processes of the American system. It is far from an idle question, however. It is not enough to look at policies or institutions. At some point we must stop and ask what they constitute: What is the American political system? We soon discover that there is no one idea about its nature.

Most American versions of what democracy should be stress that a democratic government should make collective decisions by applying two principles. The first is the principle of *popular consent*. As the Declaration of Independence reminds us, a democratic order obtains its right to rule only from the consent of the governed. A government that does not have the ultimate support of its people lacks moral authority to rule. After all, what right would any government have to rule if its people rejected it? Second, a democratic government must be subject to popular participation and control. It must have regular channels through which people may express their choices about rulers and public policies. At the very least, the citizenry must have the right and opportunity to choose among alternative candidates who seek to rule, the right to express political opinions freely, and the right to organize into political parties and interest groups to press for particular government policies. This is the principle of *popular influence*.

Besides these two principles, however, most supporters of democracy believe democratic politics must meet another, more pragmatic standard. They contend that legitimate government not only must be open to citizen influence and constraint, but also must accomplish a good deal of what people want from government. A political system that does not fulfill citizens' needs, whether for clean, well-lighted streets or for a fair tax policy, will not long be considered representative, under citizen control, or just. Nor will it command much popular esteem. Supporters of democratic politics realize that government's record of providing benefits is often the norm people use to judge how democratic it is. This is the standard of *popular benefit*.

THE PLURALIST INTERPRETATION

The most common view of our system of politics is that it is *pluralistic*. The term *pluralism* refers to the crucial role American government assigns to interest groups. Most pluralists describe American politics as interest-group politics; they see intense group activity everywhere they look in our political life. They contend that this is a happy fact about our nation, since a system in which most people can organize to represent their ideals and interests is impressively democratic. Pluralism allows many people access to political decision making — what could be more democratic? Moreover, pluralists believe that the record of pluralism in the United States, though not unblemished, is basically a success story. Pluralism has provided enough popular influence and control and has produced enough popular benefit.

Pluralism and Popular Representation

As seen in Chapter 12, interest groups strive to advance their objectives in the Congress, with public opinion, within the bureaucracy, and within our political parties. Organizations as different as Gulf Oil, the International Ladies Garment Workers Union, and the Sierra Club are able to obtain a hearing and perhaps affect policy judgments at all levels. At its best this arrangement greatly expands the opportunities for representation and democracy. Interest groups also can give citizens many opportunities to restrain or even block the acts of politicians or bureaucrats. Strong pressure groups can halt actions of public officials or administrators long before the next election comes around.

With a wide variety of groups busy in their political role as lobbyists for their point of view, American politics emerges in theory and often in fact as an endless process of competition and bargaining among interests. This bargaining reflects the vast range of perspectives and groups in the United States. Tax bills are compromises. Labor bills represent some reconciliation between various business and labor forces. Medicare was a closely bargained compromise between the American Medical Association and advocates of national health insurance. Although this process does not ensure that all groups will win their objectives, its enthusiasts claim that one of its great advantages is the political stability for which the United States is known. Bargaining requires that people be prepared to accept half a loaf — to compromise.

Pluralists do not assert that everyone in the United States has equal political power. They realize that within all groups there are bound to be elite members who have greater influence than does the ordinary member. They see this as inevitable but also consider it useful, since not every member can be or wants to be as active as every other. Moreover, they note that the possession of more power than other group members have does not necessarily keep a leader from accurately representing the general membership's wishes in the process of group bargaining — not at all.

Finally, pluralists do not claim either that each interest group has equal power within the American political order, or that all people or all interests are organized. For pluralists the openness of American democracy is more important than absolute political equality, although they sometimes worry about the political advantages available to unusually monied and established interests. They argue that any pressure group can increase its influence if it appeals to more of the public and if it can draw more financial support and gifted leadership. They also assume that any group of citizens can get organized if they really want to. They cite the growth of the American labor movement in the 1930s as an example of what a determined group can accomplish. As another illustration, they point to the rise during the 1960s of black organizations such as Martin Luther King's Southern Christian Leadership Conference (SCLC) and the Congress of Racial Equality (CORE). They also note the growth of public-interest organizations like Common Cause in the 1960s and 1970s and conservative Christian and other right-wing groups in the 1980s as proof of the enduring openness of American political processes.

Pluralism and Popular Control Although lobbying is probably the most important instrument interest groups have in the short run, it is not their only one. Interest groups also often play a role in choosing and backing candidates in our electoral system.

Pluralists recognize that elections are a crucial arena for their efforts. They know that elections play an important role in our form of democracy, providing for an orderly selection of leaders, popular representation through voting on competing candidates, and public debate over major issues to inform the public. Elections can also have a significant part in policymaking, especially when opposing candidates take sharply different positions on central issues — as happened in the presidential elections of 1964 (liberal Lyndon Johnson versus conservative Barry Goldwater), 1972 (liberal George McGovern versus conservative Richard Nixon), and 1980 (moderate Jimmy Carter versus very conservative Ronald Reagan). Moreover, elections are a powerful device for controlling and changing leaders by removing from office those the public does not like or trust. Finally, many pluralists like electoral democracy (one in which citizens elect representatives to govern) because, they say, it suits the realities of the modern world. It permits a realistic division of labor, allowing a few to govern and most to choose.

Pluralists warn, however, that elections are not sufficient to provide significant popular representation and checks. They insist that pressure groups that operate continuously — not just at election time — can and do keep the most effective watch on our elected officials. Such groups often have the time and the trained staff to present views to political elites and to investigate whether or not campaign promises become postelection realities. They also may have the money to pay lobbyists to talk to representatives and to compile careful voting records of what decisions legislators make.

Interest groups sometimes are willing to expose corruption, incompetence, or abuse of power, at least when it does not hurt them to do so. Civil rights organizations in the 1960s reported numerous abuses of authority by local sheriffs and others in public positions in the South — sometimes aided by the malfeasance of the FBI — in treatment of blacks. Common Cause has drawn attention to cases of abuse of power by members of Congress and has been influential in pushing our government closer to public financing of elections in an attempt to reduce corruption. Finally, the efforts of a few newspapers (a very potent interest group in our age) were essential in uncovering Richard Nixon's dangerous misuse of his office and in ending his presidency. More and more interest groups flex their muscles when they confront assorted examples of illegality and immorality in government. They are heard and feared by many elected and nonelected figures in public office.

COMPLAINTS ABOUT OUR PLURALIST SYSTEM This book has returned repeatedly to the theme that there is a gap between the government and the citizen that poses potentially serious problems for democracy in the United States. The fact is that a good many Americans both in and out of government are not sure pluralism is working in a way that produces democratic and effective government. The gap is based in doubt. Objections come from three not always separate corners: (1) that our government is too elitist — that only a few rule; (2) that our institutions simply do not work well anymore because of fragmented power, structural limitations, and value conflicts; (3) that our citizens are incompetent and that they, not our governors or our institutions, are at fault.

The Complaint about Elite Rule Many people in the United States today argue that isolated, insulated ruling elites now dominate American politics and government. They say that the average person has no significant input and that it is clear that our leaders like it that way. They contend that the gap is caused by the desire of rulers to rule alone and by the popular discovery of this travesty of democracy. It forces us to ask whether our pluralism is really open to popular representation and control. Pluralists insist it is, but are they right?

For many years people have charged that our political system at both the national and the local levels is in fact undemocratically closed to input from ordinary citizens. Twenty years ago, sociologist C. Wright Mills, in his landmark book, *The Power Elite,* made perhaps the most famous argument to the effect that a small coterie of men rules the United States. All those who claim to see such a power elite declare that the evidence is strong that this power elite, rather than our elected representatives, makes the crucial decisions for our society, and that such a state of affairs naturally alienates citizens. They point to crucial foreign policy decisions as cases in point. They cite the manner in which the United States edged into World War II or decided to drop the atomic bomb on Japan, noting correctly that these momentous moves were made by tiny elites. The record of policymaking during the Vietnam War under both the Johnson and Nixon administrations in particular convinced many observers that only a few carefully chosen voices were ever heard in the deliberations leading to such key decisions as the secret bombing of Cambodia, which affected the lives of millions and the fate of nations. Critics contend that the same situation prevailed after Iran captured American hostages in 1979 and 1980. Here again, all the thinking and deciding about how to bring them home was done by a small elite.

The usual explanation for the gap between citizen and state leans on elitism as the principal cause, identifying a collection of political, corporate, and (sometimes) military leaders as the powerful persons who work together to rule the United States. No one suggests that they share identical concerns or goals. Critics argue, however, that they do share an interest in stability, economic gain, and maintenance of their own power. Similarly, few doubt that there are policy differences within the power elite, but critics assert that these disagreements fade away whenever opponents threaten the power, prestige, and established distribution of goods and services that are the elites' chief concerns.

There is considerable agreement among sophisticated proponents of this critique that issues that do *not* touch the basic prerogatives of the elite often are subject to public debate and public resolution. These critics acknowledge that Congress is the institution in which matters such as the size of social security payments and the placement of dams, roads, and new government facilities are considered. On the other hand, they say, it is the power elite that discusses and decides fundamental questions concerning the economy, the military, and international affairs. Thus compared with the ruling elite Congress is unimportant, just one of the many American institutions, groups, and forces that supposedly have major power but actually do not. No wonder that critics find little truth in the idea that the problem in the United States is that power is too dispersed among different parts of government and a multitude of competing pressure groups. For them, power is all too concentrated. The strength of the power elite renders mythical the notion that there is too much pluralism in American politics. Indeed, these critics charge that even to talk about American politics and pluralism in one breath is farcical.

Some critics of the power elite devote most of their attention to the role of the very rich, who, they charge, rule the United States, usually through the power of the major corporations operating both in and out of our government. Many of these critics are Marxists or are influenced by the theories of Karl Marx. They often describe American elitism as a natural expression of what they see as our capitalist society, and they maintain that the United States will never become a democracy until we destroy capitalism and with it our corporate rulers.

Other critics are uncomfortable with this version of the power elite complaint. They acknowledge that large corporate elements are tremendously influential in our country, but they believe that other parts of the elite (for instance, the military) cannot be neatly explained in this manner. Moreover, they usually resist sweeping analyses that consider people only in class terms, single-mindedly focusing on how the rich exploit the poor. They know this analysis is not always useful in a country in which most citizens are members of the middle class. Yet both Marxists and non-Marxists who make the power elite analysis remain convinced that fundamentally rule by a few exists only for the benefit of the few. These critics unite in denunciation of such a perversion of democracy.

Other citizens who are skeptical of most social science or ideological disputes nonetheless suspect that our political system does normally help some citizens far more than it does others, despite the supposedly equal resources we all have as citizens. There is no doubt that the systematic favoritism shown to well-established wealthy groups and individuals in our political arrangements is a tremendous built-in advantage. It allows beneficiaries to maintain their position of authority and privilege by mobilizing the bias already existing in the system for their future goals and interests. Some critics suggest that this explains why many aspects of our society rarely come up for discussion or reconsideration. Our capitalist economic order, for instance, goes essentially unchallenged; even when inflation and unemployment are rampant, no one in the political arena seriously considers replacing capitalism with some other form of economic organization. Currently the argument is that the ills of capitalism come from government and, hence, that the cure for capitalism is more capitalism.

It is true that when we study American politics and closely examine the policymaking process, we see that some people do have more say than others; but there is much more evidence of popular input and conflict among elites than power elite theorists suggest. Their reply is that to study only the decision-making process and conclude that there is no power elite may be to ignore basic, unchanging aspects of society that elitist forces continue to sustain. Advocates of this view insist that there are "two faces of power" and that the hidden face, undetected in ordinary studies of government action, is the more important one.[1]

The Group Elite Thesis. Proponents of a closely related view usually deny that any single power group controls national or local politics. They maintain, nonetheless, that our democracy gives citizens little representation or control. They agree that the existence of so many and such varied interest groups prevents any single group from running the political order, but they argue that the result is less democratic than many people may think. The reason, they say, is that pressure groups themselves are largely run by elites — and therefore are not really vehicles for broad public participation or representation. Group leaders, in this view, often care more about keeping their own personal power than about articulating members' needs or encouraging active involvement. This ensures feelings of powerlessness among the citizenry. These theorists also note that even the most enthusiastic pluralists admit the reality of our elite-dominated group life. Pluralists may use other terms, the best known being *active minority,* but the meaning is largely the same.[2]

The crucial question is: What does the existence of such ruling elites within groups tell us about democracy in the United States? Those who are unworried about the existence of elites declare that elite groups are inevitable unless we demand that all members participate equally — something few members of organizations either want or are able to do. They suggest that this arrangement has a great practical advantage for the membership. It is efficient because it lets most members go about their business while a few concern themselves with conducting the group's business. Furthermore, these theorists remind us again that an elite can accurately reflect membership wishes. The problem, then, is not whether there are elites, but whether they are representative of their constituencies and checked by them.[3]

Do Groups Compete? Another question often posed is: Does competition among interest groups really exist? Many citizens complain that particular groups such as veterans, the oil companies, or the television networks have little competition and therefore control the areas of public policy that most concern them. Such pressure groups seem to be the power elites in their own policy areas. If they do not compete, then the vaunted open and representative aspects of our democracy are a myth.

---

[1] The classic statement is found in Peter Bachrach and Morton Baratz, "Two Faces of Power," *American Political Science Review* 56 (December 1962): 947–52.

[2] David Truman, *The Governmental Process* (New York: Knopf, 1960), pp. 139–55.

[3] A point drawn from William Kelso, "In Defense of Pluralism," Ph.D. diss., University of Wisconsin, 1974, chap. 7.

Critics of American pluralism insist that citizens can easily see how often policy arenas are closed to them. Many government agencies that are supposedly set up to regulate interests actually work hand in hand with those interests to ward off any public interference. Federal regulatory agencies such as the Federal Trade Commission (FTC) and the Federal Communications Commission (FCC) have been attacked for having too cozy relationships with the industries they are supposed to regulate. Other interests obtain grants of government authority to regulate themselves, an arrangement that normally leaves citizens out in the cold and frustrated. Doctors, lawyers, professional educators, and even barbers resist nearly every regulation that is not self-imposed, even as many citizens fume at incompetent doctors or dishonest lawyers who go on practicing. Still other organizations arrange to avoid bargaining with competitors for government aid. For example, highway interests in many states have been able to establish separate government accounts that may not be used for purposes other than road building, not even for the financing of mass transit. Or consider the Department of Agriculture, which has within its jurisdiction many separate and virtually self-governing units, from soil conservation districts to price support districts, each run largely by farmers and bureaucrats closely associated with farmers, and each with power to block government policies it does not like. Nor is such a situation unique to the Department of Agriculture. The Department of Interior, for instance, has been characterized as a collection of "little fiefdoms" by former President Jimmy Carter's secretary of the interior, Cecil D. Andrus.

These examples could be multiplied endlessly. Instead of competing groups, all too often we have groups that have succeeded in insulating themselves from competition. This situation casts doubt on the vitality of American pluralist democracy. Our political system, in other words, has less openness and more self-interest and self-protectiveness than its ideals proclaim.

Do Citizens Have Equal Access?   Still another hotly disputed question about elitism and democracy in our system is: Do citizens really have access to government decision makers to an approximately equal degree? Some observers contend that woefully unequal resources among individuals and groups make open access a fiction. The mere fact that many organizations are active in the policy processes of the United States is not the only important point. At least as important is the fact that some groups, such as the powerful General Moters Corporation or the United Auto Workers, have vastly greater resources than do other interst groups, such as those who lobby for overburdened taxpayers or for safety improvements in American cars.[4]

The perception of unequal access is now widely shared, as is the belief that inequalities in the United States are cumulative. Those who lack resources of

[4]Charles Lindblom discusses this problem extensively in his impressive *Politics and Markets* (New York: Basic Books, 1977).

Access to Power

No question is more important in a democracy than that of how citizens gain access to power in order to present their views and control their leaders. A government that is not open to its citizens, that does not listen to them, and that does not ultimately respond to their wishes is hardly democratic.

But how do citizens make their voices heard? We know that in America, as elsewhere, some citizens have more access to power than others. The influential corporate executive (Henry Ford, testifying before Congress) or important labor leaders are examples of those who often have ready access to the seats of power. What about most citizens? They can vote, write letters, and give money. They can also form or join lobbying organizations which sometimes can gain access even to the President. Here, representatives of Right-to-Life groups, a remarkable illustration of the results of citizen organization in politics, confer with President Reagan.

one sort are likely to lack others and to be unable to acquire them, with the result that they have no real chance to influence policies.[5] The chief resource at issue, of course, is money. Despite campaign-financing laws, skeptics say, there is little real opportunity in the United States for the average citizen or group to compete equally with the wealthy. After all, one-fifth of the population controls more than three-quarters of the national wealth and about half the national income; the richest 5 percent of the citizenry controls over half the national wealth and 20 percent of the national income.[6]

The Complaint A second complaint focuses on the alleged inability of our government to pro-
That Government duce policies that the citizens want. According to this view, the problem is not
Does Not Deliver the lack of openness of the political order but, rather, its failure to organize itself to function well. If it did, critics suggest, citizen dissatisfaction would decline. Who, they ask, can expect people to be happy with a government that fails to deliver what they want and yet calls itself democratic?

The principal objection today is that our national political institutions do not act decisively to address domestic problems and concerns. This is partly a matter of divided opinions and limited wills. Another and larger part, according to critics, derives from the fact that power is so divided among different agencies of government, parts of Congress, meddlesome courts, and influential interest groups that it is hard to get anything done, especially anything that involves changes. This thesis holds that where government power is too fragmented for action, as in the United States, there will be many angry and frustrated citizens who know this makes a mockery of democracy.

A good example of the problem has been the nation's energy policy — or lack of one. Since 1974, confusion has reigned. Presidents simply have not been able to overcome all the power bases that fought (and still fight) for their self-interest, precluding any action. Oil companies, congressional committees, environmental groups — all struggle with each other and with the White House. The result is anything but a strong, coherent, effective energy policy. Meanwhile, the cost of energy — at the gas pump and in the furnace — continues to rise, affecting all of us. The process has been repeated all too often in recent years with such issues as inflation and unemployment, taxes and housing, and many others. No wonder government seems ineffective, somehow trapped by its internal divisions and the swirl of interest groups surrounding it. No wonder citizens become frustrated with political institutions. No wonder public dissatisfaction mounts. Whether Ronald Reagan's decisive early start as president will continue and will allay some of this dissatisfaction in the long run remains to be seen. Only an optimist would bet on it.

[5] Compare Robert Dahl's two discussions in *Who Governs?* (New Haven: Yale University Press, 1961); and *After the Revolution?* (New Haven: Yale University Press, 1970).
[6] The national income situation is well discussed in Herbert Gans, *More Equality* (New York: Pantheon Books, 1973).

Structural Limitations   Although the main problem today is power diffusion and consequent government ineptitude, according to this view it is fair to observe that sometimes citizens expect too much from government and suffer the pangs of disillusionment when it cannot deliver. There are inherent limitations to government structures, some theorists say. Government may be equipped to accomplish much less than some of us insist it should. One reason many people today are deeply disillusioned with the American system as an agency of their wishes is that they asked more of it in the past than it could deliver. The ambitious anti-poverty programs of the 1960s produced few positive results, despite their enormous cost; the urban renewal programs of the 1950s and 1960s tore up cities but advanced no one's conception of justice; and that the present welfare system has delivered large tax bills but little human dignity. Indeed, even when people agree on what policies would be just, human problems prove immensely hard to solve; the machinery of a large and not always responsive or capable bureaucracy guarantees few quick, complete successes.

The resistance of the real world around us is strong. We should be skeptical of how much any government, including our democracy, can achieve in a world filled with intractable human problems and affected by unforeseen consequences of our actions. This view suggests we must recognize the continuing relevance of Samuel Johnson's observation: "How small of all that human hearts endure, that part which law or kings can cause or cure." The same moral is conveyed in a story about Charles Parnell, the nineteenth-century Irish nationalist. Once he encountered an old laborer working on a road. Recognizing Parnell, the old man was overjoyed. "Calm down," said Parnell. "Whether I win or lose, you will still be breaking rocks." [7]

Conflict with Other Values   Even when government is organized for action and can make a difference, yet another obstacle may stand in its way. Because values conflict, it is not enough to know whether people favor a policy. The question is: Do they favor it understanding that it will cost them something in terms of other goals they seek? If they do not, their initial support for an objective may vanish. Politicians tend to be wiser in this matter than citizens. They are less likely to take polls showing support for a policy at face value.

An example or two is in order. The tremendous interest today in the media and among some politicians in "liberty" (at least for business) and in a smaller government reflects an old American concern. There is no doubt that many corporate and media leaders — and intellectuals responsive to them — support "liberty" as a value more important than anything else government could encourage. In part this is because they believe they will benefit economically from strengthening this norm. In part it is because they genuinely believe our society is overregulated at the expense of the flowering of the entrepreneurial individual who, they think, made the United States what it is today. These

---

[7] Samuel Johnson, *Lines Added to Goldsmith's Traveller*, in David N. Smith and Edward McAdam, eds., *The Poems of Samuel Johnson* (Oxford: Clarendon Press, 1941), p. 380; quoted in George F. Will, "The Disease of Politics," *Newsweek*, November 1, 1976.

ideas have strong support from President Reagan, as well as from most Republican and many Democratic voters. The strength of such views among the public can be measured by both poll and election results. They appear to be very popular, but actually feelings are mixed, even in this age of support for budget cuts and tax cuts. People do want the number of government programs and bureaucrats reduced and taxes cut. However, they are not as interested in slashing most specific programs about which they are well informed, and they support increased defense expenditures.

There is also conflict over which meaning of *liberty* should be promoted. Most of those who cry loudest for liberty are imprecise about exactly what kind of freedom they favor. In its most general sense liberty is the absence of restraint so that someone may do what he or she wishes. Some people emphasize economic liberty, others social liberty (such things as the right to have an abortion if one chooses) Often those most in favor of economic liberty are among those most vehemently against social freedoms, and vice versa.

The clash over racial integration in many big northern cities in the mid-1970s provides another painful illustration of the need to balance values. Even though there is little disagreement that justice requires guaranteeing every American child an equal education, many whites (and some blacks) do not favor busing for school integration. For the whites the crucial values in question are not those of racial justice but, rather, the importance of neighborhood schools and of democracy. Residents of South Boston do not want children from other parts of the city bused to their neighborhood schools, and they do not want their own children bused far from home to achieve some federal judge's plan for integration. Moreover, to them court-ordered busing is the height of elitism, denying their right to govern themselves.

Likewise, those who argue for ensuring due process for every person accused of a crime — an often elaborate due process that may set many criminals free — are often in conflict with the increasing portion of our population concerned about the sharp deterioration of public safety. Many Americans are worried about crime and markedly uneasy over their personal safety, especially in large cities. What is at issue is a question of priorities: Is government's obligation to ensure legal justice more important than its obligation to provide safety from violence and crime? Civil libertarians insist that people accused and even convicted of crimes must have every right strictly enforced for their protection, including a list of their rights read to them upon arrest, the right to a lawyer, the right to be spared too rough questioning by police, and the right to have no conviction based on illegally obtained evidence.

They maintain that if government does not protect those suspected of crimes, why should we expect it to safeguard the rest of us? Their critics reply that they too want a fair trial and fair treatment for everyone, but that things have gone so far toward protecting the rights of the accused and the criminal that the rights of the vast majority to have public order are regularly sacrificed. More and more the papers are filled with stories of criminals who were obviously guilty but who got off on some legal technicality.

Do Citizens Deserve Much of the Blame? A final view sees the gap between citizen and state originating in the failure of citizens to live up to the ideal on which our system depends.[8] Our vision of the best citizen has always been one who was rational, informed, and participatory; yet there are disappointingly few such persons today.

The great bulk of social science data of the last thirty years throws doubt on the idea that most of us are very rational, well informed, or even interested in politics. Recent findings improve the picture somewhat, but most research continues to show that the average voter is surprisingly ignorant about candidates, issues, and the political system, with the partial exception of voters in presidential elections. These findings contrast sharply with the notion of the mythical citizen of a democracy. When Americans do talk politics, too often the discussion focuses on personalities and gossip rather than on substantive information or issues. Voters also know little about public officials other than the president. Moreover, studies demonstrate that only half of the American public knows that there are two senators from each state; less than half knows that members of the House of Representatives serve for two years; most do not know the number of Supreme Court justices; less than one-quarter can state even one article of the Bill of Rights.

Most citizens are equally poorly informed on the issues. Those about which they are at all well informed are limited to major economic and foreign affairs matters, and even here much of what passes for information is little more than casual opinion. To be sure, public information about issues in presidential elections increased in the 1960s and early 1970s, although it has not risen since. Even now, no more than two-thirds to three-quarters of the voters (only about half the electorate) make any reference whatsoever to issues or begin to use them in deciding how to vote for president. Beyond the presidential race the percentage falls drastically, and many voters have no opinions whatsoever about issues.

Even if more people were aware of issues, had opinions on them, and understood how American government works, they would still have to know how their representatives in Congress vote in order to exercise any check on them. But most constituents have only the slightest awareness of their representatives' voting records. How could they — a majority of citizens do not even know who their representatives in Congress — or at the statehouse — are? At congressional election time only about half the voters know the name of one candidate; far fewer know the name of that person's opponent; and fewer than 10 percent are aware of the issues under discussion in the campaign.[9]

Finally, even in this age of declining allegiance to political parties and rising respect for the independent label, party loyalty continues to be an important determinant of many attitudes and votes. We may like to think that citizens

---

[8] See, for example, Giovanni Sartori, *Democratic Theory* (New York: Praeger, 1965), p. 91.

[9] Warren Miller and Donald Stokes, "Constituency Information in Congress," *American Political Science Review* 57 (1963); B. Hinckley, *Stability and Change in Congress* (New York: Harper and Row, 1971), pp. 14–15.

Balancing Private and Public Roles

Citizens are partly responsible for weaknesses of our democracy in operation. They are
often uninformed and uninterested in political
matters. Some do not even vote. We have to keep
in mind that people are not only citizens. They
have many interests and obligations other than
political activity. Most of us like to relax in
various ways and most of us have family
responsibilities. The demands and pleasures of
private life take time or energy that are not
devoted to politics. Both the pursuit of private
happiness and the fulfillment of the public
responsibilities of citizenship are important in a
complete life. Achieving a healthy balance
between the private and public spheres is an
ongoing problem in a democracy.

earnestly study issues and candidate records, but the reality is otherwise. Even many so-called independents who claim to vote on the basis of issues or "the man" are not independent at all; they actually vote consistently by party label.[10]

POPULAR MISCONCEP-TIONS Critics charge that another, closely related problem is the ignorance revealed in some popular misunderstandings about government and politics. Two of these often receive attention. First, there is the idea that representative government can somehow speak for the public will and that something is wrong with American democracy if it does not. Critics say that such a belief is hopelessly naïve. There are simply too many citizens in our country for their diverse opinions to be reflected accurately. Moreover, it is false to assume that there is a majority out there, at least a durable one. Public opinion on rulers and on issues, insofar as it may be determined at all, is always shifting and thus is difficult to translate into law.[11]

Others suggest that many citizens become dissatisfied and withdraw because they have the "illusion" that our government will be much more open to citizen participation and much less the province of elites than it turns out to be. Pluralists maintain that this is a serious error. They say that such people simply do not understand that considerable leadership is essential if government is to accomplish anything, and thus the price we pay for effectiveness is a certain amount of elitism. We want a government that responds to the people's wishes, and we demand an effective government — but can we really expect both at the same time?

Moreover, many policy decisions involve complex and often quite technical issues. It makes sense to turn over such decision making to a small number of specialists. Sound judgments about banking policy, weapons systems, forest management, and so on require technical expertise. The broadest outlines of policy may be properly determined by the popular will, but beyond that there is no substitute for the knowledge of a few. Again, according to this view, citizens must make a choice: They cannot complain endlessly about the inefficiencies of government and then charge that it is undemocratic. If they want government that deals expertly with their needs, then they must be prepared to give up some participation in order to get it. This is a considerable gamble, but so is the chance of inaction resulting from a more democratic but woefully ineffective state.

A similar argument defends leadership by a political elite on the ground that both stability and effectiveness grow in this way. Mass participation, it is sometimes proposed, could be dangerous to the stability of the American po-

[10] Robert Lane, *Political Life* (New York: Free Press, 1959), p. 300; Norman Nie, Sidney Verba, and John Petrocik, *The Changing American Voter* (Cambridge, Mass.: Harvard University Press, 1976), chap. 4; and a tide of other literature.

[11] The classic statement: Robert Dahl, *A Preface to Democratic Theory* (Chicago: University of Chicago Press, 1956).

litical order because citizens are often mercurial, passionate, and uninformed. It is sometimes even suggested that apathy on the part of much of the general population is not a danger signal for any democracy. Indeed, one commentator argues:

> It is not an established truth that democracy suffers from voting apathy, or that any democracy has fallen because of it . . . the evidence points overwhelmingly the other way, that there has always been wide, almost feverish public interest in politics and voting in countries where democracy has collapsed, e.g., in the Weimar Republic.[12]

It is not really clear that more leadership and less mass participation are incompatible with democracy, as long as the opportunity to participate is available to every citizen. Indeed, there is evidence that political elites tend to know more about current issues and the principles of democratic government than does the average citizen. Some evidence shows that elites in the United States are also likely to be more committed to the rights of unpopular political minorities than is the average person.

The Irrational Citizen? A darker view argues that voters are not just uninformed or misinformed but that voter interest in candidate personality and psychology reveals the irrational nature of much of the electorate. There is no doubt that voters take seriously their judgments about the personal strengths and weaknesses of the individual candidates before them when they vote. Studies have repeatedly shown that contemporary voters evaluate known candidates more by their perceived personalities than by their stands on issues.[13]

There are those, however, who believe psychology plays a much greater role than this. They suggest that political behavior in most contexts may be less a matter of a more or less rational citizen seeking to satisfy his or her self-interest (or the public interest) than a search for the fulfillment of psychological needs. A pioneer political psychologist, Harold Lasswell, argues that:

> The findings of personality research show that the individual is a poor judge of his own interest. The individual who chooses a political policy . . . is usually trying to relieve his own disorders by irrelevant palliatives. An examination of the total state of the person will frequently show that his theory of his own interests is far removed from the course of procedure which will give him a happy and well-adjusted life.[14]

This patronizing observation is an exaggeration, but there is no doubt that some citizens are so involved in acting out their personal needs in politics that

---

[12] Henry Mayo, *An Introduction to Democratic Theory* (New York: Oxford University Press, 1960), p. 123.

[13] Nie, Verba, and Petrocik, *The Changing American Voter*, p. 167.

[14] Harold Lasswell, *The Political Writings of Harold Lasswell* (New York: Free Press, 1951), p. 891.

they cannot begin to approach any kind of rational perspective. Some students of political psychology note that politics seems to attract a surprisingly large number of people driven by hostile and aggressive sentiments toward the world because it provides them with many opportunities to vent their antagonisms. In politics there are always endless enemies to denounce. There has also been interest in the role politics may play for some citizens as an outlet for frustrated sexual drives.[15]

Probably the greatest effort has gone into examining the function of politics in meeting people's need to be reassured. People seem to need reassurance from their political order that all is well — reassurance that is often provided by symbols rather than by a rational examination of the current condition of state and society. Large numbers of us respond to flag waving, presidential reassurances, and patriotic songs in a manner that critics think is quite contrary to the image of a rational citizen. Rather than striving in some superhuman way for understanding of an issue or policy, we settle for some pretty — or not so pretty — symbol. Many people may hope a leader's smile or patriotic tiepin, or his utterance of political code words about law and order, or his receipt of a blessing from a prominent religious leader, will substitute for their own efforts to be rational, probing citizens.

This fact points to a picture of citizen behavior that is far from flattering. One student, for example, claims: "It is characteristic of large numbers of people in our society that they see and think in terms of stereotypes, personalization, and oversimplifications, that they cannot recognize or tolerate ambiguous and complex situations, and that they accordingly respond to symbols that oversimplify and distort."[16] At its most pessimistic, this analysis sees the typical citizen as thirsting for "symbolic reassurance" and easily fooled into believing that this is the same thing as achieving concrete goals. In this view, although most of politics may seem to be about great issues and momentous decisions, it is really about comforting psychologically vulnerable people with a good show. Years ago the economist Joseph Schumpeter summed up this pessimistic perspective when he dismissed the will of citizens as "an indeterminant bundle of vague impulses loosely playing about given slogans and mistaken impressions."[17]

Are Most Citizens Apathetic? Those who criticize the model of the rational, informed, issue-oriented American have an even more telling argument. They note that many people are plainly apathetic and display none of the idealized interest and involvement that classical democratic theory assumes is characteristic of the average citizen. Indeed, the interested are hard to find. Seldom does more than 10 percent of

[15] Lane, in *Political Life* has a particularly intriguing, if speculative, discussion of this subject.
[16] Murray Edelman, *Symbolic Uses of Politics* (Urbana: University of Illinois Press, 1964), pp. 31 and 164–65.
[17] Joseph Schumpeter, *Capitalism, Socialism and Democracy* (New York: Harper and Row, 1950), p. 254.

"FRANKLY, I DON'T CARE ONE WAY OR THE OTHER ABOUT VOTER APATHY"

the American population get involved in politics beyond voting, and except in presidential elections less than half bother to vote.

Taken together, the available data on Americans' political behavior support those who assert that if our system has failings, it is partly because we fail as citizens. If we are disillusioned, perhaps we should be disillusioned with ourselves and be thankful that democracy has endured in spite of us.

CONCLUSION   We have seen that a number of commentators blame the citizenry for the gap between citizen and state. Voters and citizens, they declare, all too often lack information and let illusions guide them. We have noted that others blame power elites in government, in key interest groups, and elsewhere. Still others fault the nature of our political institutions, their failure to produce what citizens want because of fragmentation, value conflicts, and inherent limitations. And this does not exhaust the list.

We need to realize that some gap between citizens and their leaders is inevitable. Its existence in so large and diverse a nation as our own should not come as a surprise. Yet we know that the gap at present is larger than we can be comfortable with and still be confident that the United States achieves our democratic aspirations. Achieving and maintaining popular consent, popular influence, and popular benefits requires effort to reduce the gap between rulers and citizens in every polity. This is doubly true in our own, where the storm signals of popular dissatisfaction and apathy are clear.

This book has looked at the dimensions of the gap from several perspectives: historical, institutional, policy, and theoretical. We have probed the subject in detail. We hope the reader has learned a great deal in the process about how our government operates, as well as about its history and ideals. In the first chapter we raised two questions: Is our government democratic enough, or is the gap between citizens and rulers too great? And is it possible today for any democratic polity to survive the challenges and complexities of the modern era? In the ensuing chapters we have seen that many citizens' fears are well grounded, that popular influence and popular benefits do not seem to include enough citizens — at least, many citizens believe they do not. Thus American government falls short, not just of the democratic ideal, as is inevitable, but also of what many Americans consider a reasonable approximation of the ideal. The gap appears unreasonably large to many citizens. It is painfully obvious that this poses a great potential problem for maintaining the degree of pluralist democracy we now have.

We observed in the first chapter that any democracy is fragile. The proof is that few countries have had, or maintained, anything ordinarily called a democracy. Thus we should appreciate how remarkable it is in our pluralist democracy that we have the degree of citizen consent, influence, and benefit that we do have. At the same time, the gap remains as both a danger to our democracy and a challenge to us as citizens. The danger is that dissatisfied citizens may sometime sweep democracy away. The challenge — one we must worry about — is to reduce the inevitable gap, to make the democratic promise in the United States more a reality and less a remote ideal.

SUGGESTIONS FOR FURTHER READING

Dahl, Robert. *Who Governs?* New Haven: Yale University Press, 1961. An impressive explication and defense of pluralism.

Dolbeare, Kenneth, and Edelman, Murray. *American Politics: Policies, Power, and Change,* 3rd ed. Lexington, Mass.: D. C. Hearth, 1977. A skeptical, radical analysis of American government and politics.

Domhoff, G. William. *Who Really Rules?* New Brunswick, N.J.: Transaction Books, 1978. An attack on Dahl, Polsby, et al.

Mayo, Henry. *An Introduction to Democratic Theory.* New York: Oxford University Press, 1960. A standard pluralist view.

Mills, C. Wright. *The Power Elite.* New York: Oxford University Press, 1960. The classic presentation of the power elite theory.

Polsby, Nelson. *Community Power and Political Theory.* New Haven: Yale University Press, 1963. A hard-hitting attack on power elite theory.

Chapter 16 Alternative Forms of Democracy

Does American democracy work well? The answer depends on whom you ask and on what criteria you think are important. We know that citizens differ on the answer to this question, but more and more people in recent years have said no. The next question arises immediately: Are there alternatives to our pluralist democracy, and would they successfully address some or all of the complaints our system faces? It is clear that there are alternatives. Whether they would solve current problems is another matter.

The American system is hardly the only version of democracy either in theory or in practice, and there is no shortage of alternative ideas about the proper nature of democracy. We will explore four major ones: reform pluralism, participatory democracy, populism, and democratic socialism. Although these four are not the only alternatives worth considering, they are the most important ones today in the ongoing debate over the best form of democracy. In each case we will frame the debate as much as possible in terms of the three issues about a democratic system that, as we saw in Chapter 15, form the principal complaints about our democracy. We will ask how elitist (as opposed to participatory) they are; how capable of decisiveness they are (as opposed to fragmented or limited by structural and value constraints); and how attuned to real citizens and real people they are (as opposed to either too idealistic or too pessimistic about citizen capabilities). This is the only way to probe whether any of these competitors really could close the gap between citizen and state.

513

REFORM PLURALISM

Reform pluralism holds a critical view of American democracy, although it proposes less sweeping changes than participatory democrats or social democrats would require.[1] Reform pluralists see our system as a flawed pluralist one — that is, as composed of a limited number of organized interests, brought together by bargaining and compromise. Reform pluralists' major complaints are that our political system is too elitist. They want to transform it from what they see as a private preserve for just a few groups to one in which (1) elite interests have fewer advantages because (2) all elements of the public are organized and participate in making decisions that influence the entire political community. Common Cause and Ralph Nader are two well-known examples of those who often speak in reform pluralist language.

The Case for Reform Pluralism

Reform pluralists complain that the reality of American government does not fit its supporters' image of it as a remarkably open political order. They agree with the classic remark that although our government may be some people's idea of heaven, "the heavenly chorus sings with a strong upper-class accent."[2] To be sure, a majority — though less than two-thirds — of the adult American public does claim membership in at least one interest group.[3] Yet what about the massive numbers who do not belong to one? Reform pluralists find it shocking that so many are missing in a political system that congratulates itself on its democratic nature. The poor, in particular, are frequently left out of the group interactions that determine so much of American politics. Reform pluralists also worry that some broad public concerns of vital importance to every citizen are represented by few significant organized groups. They insist that too few groups exist that are concerned with what they consider to be issues of public interest — the environment, campaign reform, and so on.

Government Help for Interest Groups. Reform pluralists agree that aggressive government intervention is necessary to make our system less elitist. They believe that government can help people become organized. It can do so by law, as with Provision 7a of the Wagner Labor Relations Act, which legitimized collective bargaining in the 1930s. Or it can sponsor agencies like ACTION, VISTA, Community Action Commissions, and publicly funded legal aid organizations, which in the mid- and late 1960s funded community organizers who helped many people come together and pressure government to be more responsive to their interests. Such proposals are not revolutionary. In earlier years the government performed similar functions for many groups that are now well established. It helped business by creating the Department of

---

[1] The best theoretical formulation of this type of pluralism is in William Kelso, *American Democratic Theory* (Westport, Conn.: Greenwood, 1978). I found Kelso's arguments and footnotes useful in this entire chapter.

[2] E. E. Schattschneider, *The Semi-Sovereign People* (New York: Holt, Rinehart and Winston, 1960), p. 35.

[3] S. Verba, *The Civic Culture* (Boston: Little, Brown, 1963), p. 247; S. Verba and Norman Nie, *Participation in America* (New York: Harper and Row, 1972), pp. 41–42.

Commerce and by aiding the Chamber of Commerce, and it helped farmers by facilitating the creation of the powerful farm lobby, the Farm Bureau. Government employees and politics directed at organizing, recognizing, and supporting groups have long been common. Why should this old practice not continue in our own day?

Reform pluralists do not expect government and money to do all the work and, in fact, do not want government to do any of it except where necessary. John Gardner's building of Common Cause into an influential public-interest group is a recent example of what private means and private citizens can do. But reform pluralists know that middle-class people have far more of the money, skills, and information needed to fashion organizations like Common Cause that lead to political clout than poor people do. Government help will be needed for the poor.

Besides favoring government aid through money and organizers, reform pluralists also urge government to take other steps to break through the cozy arrangements that keep unrepresented interests outside the government process. For instance, Common Cause's struggle to get adequate regulation and public financing of political campaigns is an effort to open the political process to citizens who are less well organized and have fewer resources than established groups. In this case and in others, the argument of reform pluralists is the same: American democracy is good in principle, but its actual structure needs to be — and with the help of the state can be — more genuinely democratic; elitism must be curbed.

Keeping Power Divided. Reform pluralists favor change for another reason. They think a reformed pluralism will keep power genuinely divided in our system. They are usually indifferent to the current charge that government power is already too fragmented. They believe that power in reform pluralism will be so widely distributed among different people and groups that no person or group will lose and no group will be in a position to dominate. They claim they want to stay in the tradition of the Founding Fathers and respect the truth that individual liberty can exist only where power is divided. To be sure, they appreciate that they are in fact calling for government intervention to encourage the creation of a more democratic pluralism, but they insist that the long-term results will produce a government not only more democratic but also less active, at least in serving the interests of the established few.

The Case against Reform Pluralism   Critics sometimes accuse reform pluralists of suffering from the weakness of political naïvete. They criticize them for being naïve about why people join or do not join interest groups and why certain interests are underrepresented in American politics. One fashionable thesis is that people will join nothing if they think they can get as much without doing so — that people will, in other words, seek a free ride in every way they can. This view supposedly explains, for example, why unions have had to impose union or closed shops. Workers will not join a union otherwise, these theorists contend, because if the union is able to achieve a pay raise, nonunion workers can get it also without paying dues, and if it does not, then nonunion employees have not lost anything in a futile struggle. According to this analysis, the only way to promote membership in groups is to coerce people into joining or to offer them some selfish inducement. This assumption casts doubt on reform pluralists' hopes for greater organization and thus for wider representation.

Reform pluralists reply that this argument underestimates the complexities of human motivation. They believe the success of an established group, or the likely success of a new group, often determines whether people will join it. Claiming that the history of pressure groups supports this view, they cite the experience of the union movement in the 1930s, which, they say, succeeded when people saw that it could wrench contracts out of obdurate employers. Pluralists are convinced that duty and even altruism can be powerful motivations too. People often join groups or causes without being forced or offered special inducements — even when they do not think they will win.[4]

Despite this observation, however, it is no surprise that there is considerable unease over reform pluralists' refusal to explore seriously the theories that maintain that part of the problem really has to do with the citizen. It is only reasonable that Common Cause, a self-styled citizens' organization, is reluctant to bite — or even think about biting — the hand that feeds it. What is true of Common Cause, however, is true of reform pluralism in general. It looks everywhere for fault but to the human being as citizen. And, its detractors complain, it rarely even tries to explore what people are like. It just goes on affirming that changing institutions and organizing the unorganizing will cure our ills.

More radical democrats accuse reform pluralists of simply accepting the present less-than-democratic order with a few minor, cosmetic changes here and there. They contend that if reform pluralists were really serious about opening up the political system, they would mount a massive campaign aimed at forcing the government to help the poor get their heads sufficiently above water. Only then can the poor concern themselves with organizing for their own interests. These theorists say that the tremendous expansion of the welfare rolls in the 1960s was a prerequisite for the creation of welfare-rights organizations. These organizations turned out to be a weak reed for the very poor, but they were at least a start. Now, critics say, much more needs to be done, to make equal representation among groups a reality; but they think reform pluralism is for the middle classes and that its supporters do not propose to challenge the basic economic and social inequalities of capitalism that render political equality a fiction in the United States.

Those who want more leadership in American politics are also critical of reform pluralists. Reform pluralists favor more representation for additional

---

[4] Brian Barry, *Sociologists, Economists and Democracy* (London: Macmillan, 1970), p. 29; R. E. Wolfinger, K. Prewitt, and S. Rosenhach, "America's Radical Right: Politics and Ideology," in David Apter, ed., *Ideology and Discontent* (London: Free Press, 1964), pp. 262–93.

Reform Pluralism

Reform pluralist groups are composed of all sorts of people involved in various projects and campaigns. Three approaches are seen here. Common Cause is well known for its efforts to make American pluralist democracy work better. Its members have been active in movements to establish public financing of political campaigns and to require government to conduct its operations more openly. The Sierra Club crusades "in the public interest" to preserve the environment for present and future generations. Finally, this local Community Action Agency is an example of organizations that have been funded by the federal government in order to get dormant groups and interests organized to represent previously missing points of view. These organizations usually aim at bringing poorer members of our population into the representative process thereby making the process more democratic. Each group seeks different objectives, but this does not bother the reform pluralist, who wants all portions of our diverse population involved in the process of government.

groups but do not see that the result would almost certainly increase the likelihood of a system so blocked on all sides that it could not act. Fragmentation is ignored in reform pluralism, skeptics insist. They contend that until group vetoes are overcome and government can form and carry out politics, our democracy is in trouble. Although reform pluralism guarantees that everyone will belong to a group, popular dissatisfaction will continue to soar as groups endlessly check each other and governmental inaction is the rule.

Still others doubt that reform pluralism allows for the present evidence of citizen apathy and ignorance. Reform pluralists propose more involvement when most citizens evidently want little. But the reformers insist that a good deal of citizen disinterest derives from lack of hope and lack of resources to be heard. If these were present, they predict, we would see a different, more impressive citizen. Moreover, reform pluralists believe they can provide realistically for people's complex and not very political lives, and they are not against leadership.

To the second objection, reform pluralists reply that one has to deal with political realities. Whether or not drastic schemes to transform the lives of the poor, steps toward a socialist and egalitarian economy, are attractive does not matter because they are unrealistic. For the moment, the much more conservative reform pluralist strategy promises more change.

Meanwhile, reform pluralists admit they have reservations about too much leadership. They rarely fail to cite the case of Richard M. Nixon as an example of the dangers of unchecked leadership. Checks slow down change, they realize. But checks also prevent the abuse of power, and it has mostly been the unorganized who have suffered from such abuses in the past. Democracy may be slow, they say, but it is better than government by a few leaders — or a few groups.

PARTICIPATORY DEMOCRACY   In the mid- and late 1960s, perhaps the most talked about alternative to the American form of government was participatory democracy. It continues to be discussed today, much to the annoyance of many self-styled social science "realists." Its proponents insist that democracy really is alive only when people govern themselves directly in decentralized communities, assemblies, or town meetings.

Any major move toward the participatory ideal in the United States today would require an enormous upheaval in our political order, which allows relatively little *significant, direct* decision making by citizens on the local level. Drastic decentralization of federal, state, and even municipal decision making would be necessary before citizens could come together to make the policy choices that would govern their existence.

A host of political experiments in the last twenty years have drawn on the participatory model, from school decentralization in New York City to rural communes dotting the American countryside. These experiments join a long history of such endeavors. New England town meetings operated as a type of participatory government for hundreds of years, as they still do in a few towns.

The earliest and best-known example of participatory democracy was Athens of the fifth century B.C., the Athens of Pericles and Socrates. Vote of the Athenian Assembly resolved major policy questions. All citizens could participate, and there was no separate representative body comparable to our Congress. The role of leadership and bureaucracy was small. Although it is true that women and the large slave population were excluded from citizenship, in the context of the time Athens had a remarkably participatory government.

Over the centuries, however, few governments — none with extensive territory or population — have been participatory democracies.[5] Participatory politics has existed largely as an ideal, one to which many thinkers have turned as they observed what they considered to be the miserable, despotic results of governments that ruled *over* citizens. Some political theorists have called for participatory democracy even at the cost of abandoning the large modern state. Others have recognized the futility of trying to realize the ideal but have nonetheless urged that there be as much citizen participation as possible: "Political machinery does not act of itself . . . it has to be worked by men, and even ordinary men. It needs, not their simple acquiescence, but their active participation."[6]

The Case for Participatory Democracy Enthusiasts advance four justifications for a more participatory government. The most common is also the oldest: that participatory democracy, with its emphasis on local control and widespread participation, is the only true democracy, the kind we must adopt if we really believe in democratic principles. Advocates of participatory politics contend that democracy means active citizen involvement above all else, and that no government is democratic that does not seek to encourage involvement to the maximum extent possible. Although supporters of participatory politics realize that the sheer size of the modern state precludes giving local, participatory assemblies complete power, they continue to insist that every citizen could play a larger role in making the decisions that affect his or her life. These supporters see too much power in the hands of giant corporations, unions, and the federal and state governments, and too little in the hands of people in their local neighborhoods, places of work, and churches.

A second argument for participatory democracy — and the most controversial one — is the claim that participatory politics encourages the growth of a distinctly better human being. This ambitious claim has been made by those attracted to the participatory ideal in all ages. From Pericles in ancient Athens, to Rousseau in eighteenth-century France, to Americans in the 1960s who hoped that poor people would overcome their problems by participating in Community Action Councils or the National Welfare Rights Organization, great expectations for human development have long been linked to partici-

---

[5] See Robert A. Dahl and Edward R. Tufte, *Size and Democracy* (Palo Alto, Calif.: Stanford University Press, 1973), for a good if pessimistic discussion of size and population factors.

[6] J. S. Mill, "Representative Government," in *Utilitarianism, Liberty and Representative Government* (New York: Dutton, 1951), p. 238.

patory democracy. One of the most recent instances of this idea was the black power movement, whose proponents have held that only when blacks ran their own institutions would they grow as people.

Having asserted that participating in politics will develop us as individuals, what do advocates see as the specific ways we will develop? And what is the evidence that people do in fact develop in those ways? The evidence is mixed, but some of it suggests that people grow in self-esteem and happiness if they become involved in determining the key dimensions of their life. The authors draw on all kinds of experiences — from local politics to industrial experiments in worker participation — to suggest that the active, involved, respected participant is likely to feel good about him- or herself and to be a better person as a result.[7]

Third, some supporters of participatory democracy say that it can provide a responsive, enduring government. They argue that it is preferable to other forms because it is more open to change and is therefore a superior instrument for decision making. A participatory polity can consider more options more quickly, they believe, because it is unlikely to be encumbered by conservative bureaucracies and slow-moving traditional political institutions. The assembly of classical Athens and the town meeting of New England did act very quickly when necessary. In addition, the closeness of this form of government to the citizenry guarantees that it will be remarkably adaptable, ready to respond to different conditions and shifting popular sentiments. Participatory democrats insist that this flexibility and responsiveness will enable a participatory government to endure, for it will not become brittle as do political orders that are cut off from citizens and change.

Fourth, supporters of participatory democracy stress that it would accomplish another valuable goal besides promoting genuine democracy, better citizens, and a responsive and enduring government. They insist that participatory politics will encourage the growth of community. They contend that maximizing an individual's control over his or her life encourages voluntary rather than forced cooperation; it allows people to deal with each other as individuals instead of with remote government institutions. Advocates are confident that, in a truly participatory democracy, citizens would care about their local communities as much as, or even more than, their selfish personal desires. They complain that citizenship as we practice it in the United States is remote and alienating. Individuals are taught to pursue their private interests, but not to value community or the public interest. Participatory democrats look to the day when shared participation in government changes these attitudes.

The renewed interest in participatory politics in recent decades has three

---

[7] C. Pateman, *Participation and Democratic Theory* (Cambridge: Cambridge University Press, 1970); A. Kaufman, "Human Nature and Participatory Democracy," in W. Connolly, ed., *The Bias of Pluralism* (New York: Atherton, 1969); P. Bachrach, *The Theory of Democratic Elitism: A Critique* (Boston: Little, Brown, 1967); T. Cook and P. Morgan, *Participatory Democracy* (San Francisco: Canfield Press, 1971).

sources. One of these is contemporary Marxist theory and practice. Many American and European Marxists insist that workers should have control of their working environment through direct decision making on the job. They believe that self-government in the vital economic sphere of life is at least as essential as in formal government institutions, because they hold that economic relations determine most other relationships in politics.

No one doubts that increasing workers' control in local places of employment could reduce efficiency and make coordination of national economic life difficult. Many enthusiasts for workers' control thus hesitate to advocate complete self-management for decentralized office workers or factory employees. But they are often willing to take substantial risks to achieve as much participation as possible. Pointing to the widespread Yugoslavian experiments that have given workers some role in factory and general economic management on the local level, they claim that although the results so far are flawed, they nevertheless hold great promise.

A second source of renewed interest in participatory democracy has been found among many local neighborhood and activist groups. This interest derives from the New Left and civil rights movements of the 1960s. As veterans of these upheavals worked their way through many American communities in the 1970s, they had a large impact. Numerous local groups have organized, some formally and some informally. These include neighborhood associations and cooperatives concerned with everything from buying food together to living together. In every case they show concern with participatory self-government, sometimes arguing about its reality in their organization with great intensity.

One side of this movement has been the community-control movement, which partly originated in the "war on poverty" in the 1960s, filled with citizens who insist that the people ought to determine, at the local level, policies that affect them. But such enthusiasts for community power as antibusing or black power activists need to ask themselves right from the beginning one hard crucial question: If they believe blacks in New York City have a democratic right to manage the schools in their neighborhoods, are they prepared to grant the same right to opponents of busing in the white suburbs of Baltimore, Maryland? Or, if they favor local control of schools in white South Boston, are they willing to grant the same right to the black Roxbury section? If they are not, then they are not really advocating a more participatory policy but, rather, seeking some particular policy ends by a handy but inconsistent means.

Radical proponents of community power usually want to shift power to local neighborhood assemblies. These assemblies would give neighborhood residents control of education, police and fire protection, welfare, and other basic government activities within the neighborhood. The extent of decentralization suggested differs from thinker to thinker, as does the amount of outside (city, state, or national) coordination to be permitted, but the goal is always to ensure a good deal of both local participation and local control.

Usually the radicals also argue that local control means nothing unless it includes control over the raising and spending of public money. Many go on to argue that even this objective will be meaningless unless wealth is redistributed among areas and neighborhoods. The affluent businesses and suburbs of the United States must be made to support poorer areas. Whether or not one agrees with this idea in theory, in practice it would be hard to achieve. Wealth and income are very unevenly distributed among individuals, neighborhoods, regions, and states in the United States. Yet radicals often insist there is no other route to genuine local control. [8]

Less radical advocates of a more participatory government favor experimenting with neighborhood city halls or creating elected, advisory neighborhood councils. These measures are not designed to turn over full policymaking control to neighborhoods. Rather, their purpose is to find a realistic compromise between American democracy as it is presently constituted and the goal of greater citizen participation — or at least greater citizen-government contact — at the community level. The hope is that, whatever forms the new institutions take, they will promote a greater role in decision making for local citizens, while the city or regional government continues to coordinate their activities with those of other neighborhoods.

The greatest obstacle participatory democrats face at present is that they usually are not taken seriously. Participatory ideas often are brushed aside as an outdated fad of the 1960s, to be disregarded today by sensible people. Other skeptics acknowledge the long history of participatory ideals but assert that attempts to implement them have proved impractical. Athens of the classical age is gone, as are many New England town meetings; and most hippie communes did not survive the 1960s.

The Case against Participatory Democracy Critics of participatory democracy often do not dispute that *as an abstract ideal* it best exemplifies democratic self-government. But they pepper its supporters with practical questions: Who will provide the self-governing but poor ghetto neighborhood or commune with the money for basic government services, such as police or fire protection? What will happen to dissenters in participatory communities? Can small communities really be efficient or open to change? In short, many informed skeptics do not deny that in principle the participatory model of democracy is attractive, but critics charge that it cannot (1) compete with the existing system in efficiency or (2) even work at all. There are widespread and grave fears that in participatory politics power fragmentation would reach a height that would render governing a total impossibility.

Few small areas and no urban neighborhoods are self-sufficient economically or socially. They almost always depend heavily on other neighborhoods, cities, states, and regions. If such basic problems as pollution management or labor relations were given to local, participatory communities to handle, coor-

---

[8] M. Kotler, *Neighborhood Government* (New York: Bobbs-Merrill, 1969); Robert Dahl, *After the Revolution?* (New Haven: Yale University Press, 1970), pp. 132, 133.

Participatory Democracy

Participatory democracy is still very much alive in many places in the United States. The two photos, top and center, show town meetings in two parts of the country, one in Hanover, New Hampshire and another in Lacey, Washington. Such meetings usually consider local issues, including the appropriate hair length for Lacey's high school students. Probably the most important subjects on the agenda are financial, relating to expenditures and taxes. Decisions in this area affect local residents directly. For them the town meeting provides the opportunity to participate in these decisions. They are governing themselves.

The bottom photo is from another world, one in which most Americans live today. It is a world of heavily populated urban and suburban areas where forms of direct participatory democracy are not common. Yet many proponents of participatory politics insist that direct citizen control can be increased even in densely populated areas. This woman, involved in a rat control program, illustrates local participation that can exist when neighborhoods are organized, sometimes block by block, to deal with local problems. Such participation sometimes leads to victories showing citizens that they can fight City Hall; at the least, it reveals to citizens how government actually works.

dination among units would be difficult. The possibilities for fragmented, inefficient action (or inaction) among adjoining communities would be high. Each community would be able to go its own way, whatever the costs to the entire region or nation. (One town could pollute a river many towns depend on, just as one area's antiunion policies could depress the wage scale in an entire region.) Citizen frustration might quickly soar. Few citizens think that the only important thing about democratic government is how much it lets them *participate in* policymaking. They also want government to *produce* policies that will surmount common problems.

How important to us is increased political participation? How much efficiency would we be willing to sacrifice to get a more participatory government? Participatory democrats concede that at first there might well be a loss of efficiency and coordination in the creation of a participatory polity. But they would be willing to pay this price in return for the benefits they expect — achievement of genuine democracy, authentic community, and more humane citizens. They distrust a civilization that they think values efficiency above all else.

Another major objection to participatory democracy focuses on what skeptics consider its ludicrous assumptions about the citizen. Participatory politics, they charge, demands far more time and commitment from citizens than they are willing to spend on politics. The limited evidence available from actual participatory experiments suggests that the doubters are right. This conclusion is strengthened by the often discouraging efforts of many community organizers, especially in recent years. It is certainly not hurt by the mixed successes of local participatory groups in maintaining broad interest and support. Finally, even the Yugoslav experiments, which give factory workers control of some management functions, suggest that critics are right. Interest in participation has remained low. Workers are occasionally spurred to action when their job conditions, pay, or production rates are at issue; but broader questions attract little active interest. Moreover, many workers resent the cost involved in the time spent on participation.[9] Candid participatory democrats recognize the problem and admit that it will take time and training before citizens learn to alter their attitudes. They realize that no single communal or other participatory experiment can easily accomplish the almost spiritual transformation they hope for. They do not expect the transformation to be sudden or miraculous, but they do believe it is possible.

Opponents of participatory politics often doubt whether most citizens are competent to make the crucial day-to-day policy decisions that governing involves. They cite the considerable evidence that the average voter lacks the information and the coherent set of beliefs needed to function effectively as a regular decision maker. In the light of these findings, critics question how

---

[9] Adizis, *Industrial Democracy: Yugoslav Style*, New York: Free Press, 1971), pp. 185, 224; J. Kolaja, *Worker's Councils* (New York: Praeger, 1966), pp. 45–50; David Turnquist, "On The Job," in T. Cook and P. Morgan, eds., *Participatory Democracy* (San Francisco: Canfield Press, 1971), p. 10.

giving more power to the electorate could be anything but the grossest of errors. They assert that the electorate's record is dubious enough when it comes to candidate selection, and that to ask it to act on complex issues would be to court disaster.

Although some participatory democrats dispute the evidence that casts doubt on the average voter's political competence, more ask whether there is anything necessary or permanent about this state of affairs. Some feel that reports of voter apathy are self-fulfilling prophecies that discourage efforts to educate citizens to higher levels of political information and consciousness. The trouble with many social scientists, Alvin Gouldner has remarked, is that instead of "assuming responsibilities as realistic clinicians, striving to further democratic potentialities wherever they can, many social scientists have become morticians, all too eager to bury men's hopes."[10]

Informed participatory democrats know that even the more optimistic voting studies present a picture that falls far short of the participatory ideal, and that all of them report the decline of popular voting in the 1960s and 1970s. But few participatory democrats are much interested in these studies. They do not feel that how citizens *do* behave in a political system that they consider hostile to such citizen activity should be the gauge of how they *could* behave. In short, they claim that we cannot assume that the future must be patterned on the present.

Skeptics realize that no argument is dearer to participatory democrats than the claim that the system they espouse has a potential for beneficial human development. But the skeptics feel there is scant evidence of exactly what effects more participation might have on the individual. There are modest data suggesting that decentralized power coupled with increased participation can cause citizens to feel they are more politically effective. There is no assurance, however, that this feeling will develop people's trust in government, much less lead to participatory politics. After all, decentralization and direct self-government increase citizens' responsibilities for policies that fail — and increase their frustrations over such failures.

Studies of Israeli kibbutzim (cooperatively owned settlements), the Yugoslav experiments, and American communal experiments of the past cast doubt on the likelihood of a desirable, "new" individual emerging from participatory experiences. Clearly, the high rate of failure of these undertakings suggests that old attitudes die very hard. Even studies of participatory communities that manage to survive (such as the Israeli kibbutzim), do not support the participatory democrats' contention that they produce individuals who experience great growth as creative, freedom-loving persons. Instead, what appears to happen in such communities is that citizens become more community-oriented and community-dependent.[11]

[10] A. Gouldner, "The Denial of Options," in H. Kariel, ed., *Frontiers of Democratic Theory* (New York: Random House, 1970), p. 126.

[11] R. Kanter, *Commitment and Community* (Cambridge, Mass.: Harvard University Press, 1972); Murray Weingarten, "The Individual and the Community," in E. Josephson and M. Jo-

Too Much "Community"? There is much less controversy over the participatory democrats' conviction that a successful participatory community would encourage a deeper commitment to human community than exists in the United States. This is likely. But would such a development be entirely beneficial? Participatory government, whether in some national form or in decentralized control of local schools by South Boston whites or Harlem blacks, may create so much "community" that individual rights, especially those of dissenters, would be sacrificed. Critics note that currently the United States offers political and social counterpressures and escape routes to protect dissenters. What protection, they ask, would dissenters have in a participatory community, which lacks such escape routes from the often powerful, often unspoken, and sometimes not even consciously recognized pressures to conform that the group can exert on the individual?

In many a small town, consensus rather than protection for the dissenter dominates public morality and public behavior. Even when rights to dissent are formally protected, as in small legislative assemblies in many American localities or in the Israeli kibbutzim, community pressures for agreement tend to eliminate dissent. Critics also understand that when local communities are torn apart by painful conflict, they have fewer mechanisms to diffuse such conflict than does a larger, more pluralistic society.[12]

Local majority tyranny poses especially dangerous threats to racial minorities. Although many black power advocates have demanded community control of schools and police in black areas, skeptics warn that more participatory democracy could seriously damage the aspirations of blacks (or other easily identifiable minority groups). For every black ghetto, there are many southern counties where even now local control gives much power to white majorities insensitive to black minorities. More community control would only afford racists more power to oppress blacks.

It is undeniable that many self-governing communities, from medieval monasteries to modern Chinese villages, have sacrificed individual rights in the name of community goals. However, supporters of participatory politics maintain that this is not inevitable. Dissenters exist in many American small towns; they may not be loved, but they survive. Supporters also question the relevance of such examples as life in monastic communities, insisting that proposals for participatory democracy must not be judged by the record of communities with no pretense of commitment to individual rights. Furthermore, they insist, the chance that a community will damage individual political liberty is a risk that must be taken, not least because participatory politics may actually produce a great flowering of all kinds of liberty.

sephson, eds., *Man Alone* (New York: Dell, 1962), pp. 516–32; Y. Talmon, *Family and Community in the Kibbutz* (Cambridge, Mass.: Harvard University Press, 1972); Bruno Bettelheim, *The Children of the Dream* (London: Collier, 1969).

[12] R. Kanter, *Commitment and Community;* Arthur Vidich and J. Bensman, *Small Town in Mass Society* (New York: Anchor Books, 1960); A. H. Birch, *Small Town Politics* (Oxford: Oxford University Press, 1959).

They always conclude by declaring that the ultimate tests of their idea of democracy must be: what role for the people? and how little elitism? Here, they insist, they are unbeatable. They love self-government and hate leaders. Their critics suggest, however, that their demanding yet hopelessly fragmented forms of government are really an invitation to elitism. People will soon turn to leaders to escape this unrealistic mess, and there will be nothing to halt the tyranny of these leaders except participatory pieties.

POPULISM Populists believe that we need to increase popular influence and control over governments while also providing the centralized, coordinated leadership participatory democrats spurn. Populists see citizen dissastisfaction as the inevitable consequence of our political situation — of an American government that is both insufficiently democratic and fragmented without capable leadership. They consider citizen discontent a positive sign both because it shows the good sense of many people and because it may facilitate changes populists seek.

As far as most populists are concerned, the current popular charge that American government is not democratic enough is simply overdue recognition of what populists have been saying for years. In the late nineteenth century a great populist movement swept farm-belt and western mining states. Its most powerful and most repeated argument was that the people, rather than small but well-entrenched rich special interests, should rule. This theme continues to be sounded today, as populists worry about elitism in our government and claim that special interests, such as the oil corporations or the liberal media, manipulate the United States to their own advantage and profit while the people have only the rhetoric of democracy to sustain them.

Over the years, then, populist democracy has championed the will of the people and insisted that this popular will be realized in government. For almost a century, populists have supported measures they believed would facilitate popular control while maintaining an effective central government. Sometimes these include electoral instruments, especially the initative, recall, and the referendum. The *initiative*, which some states and localities use, permits the people to propose laws directly. If a certain percentage of voters favors a proposal, it is placed on the election ballot; if it is approved by a majority on election day, it becomes law. The intiative provides the people with a weapon against elected legislatures or city councils that are unresponsive to the popular will.

Recall, which is less frequently employed, provides that if a certain percentage of the voters demands it, elected officials must stand for reelection before their terms are up. The objective here is to control leaders who may feel that between regular elections they can do as they please. Impeachment proceedings provided for federal officers in our national Constitution are a kind of recall procedure. Populists favor the vigorous and unhesitating use of recall, including impeachment, whenever necessary.

The *referendum* has been the best-known and the favorite instrument of populists since the late nineteenth century. It is much used at the state and local levels of government, but populists want it to be used even more widely. Referendum laws provide that some types of legislation may not become law without the approval of the electorate in direct vote. The kinds of measures that must receive popular consent vary from place to place; often they include constitutional amendments and certain types of expenditures, such as school bond spending proposals. Many populists would like to subject all major policies to popular vote.

The populist argument is twofold. Adherents of populism believe it is the only form of government that can provide both a maximum of democracy and responsive leadership. They believe that participatory democracy is impossible in our complex and populous society and that representative government is the only practical possibility (though where there can be effective and democratic decentralization, they favor it). Populists contend that popular control can be greatly increased if devices like the referendum are combined with representative bodies. They insist that referenda force elected representatives to be much more sensitive to the voice of the people. A populist government would require leaders to ask what the people want rather than merely responding to one interest group or another.

Faith in People The force of the populists' argument depends on their belief that the American people do have considerable political judgment and wisdom. Populists point out that faith in the average citizen has always been the core of the genuinely democratic persuasion. They share this confidence with participatory democrats and, like them, never cease to wonder at what they consider the cynicism of most defenders of our present political system. Some go so far as to ask why many cynics favor any popular input at all, if they are so convinced of the electorate's incompetence and lack of interest.

Populists reject pessimistic conclusions about citizens' political behavior. They cite recent evidence that they think suggests that the electorate is a good deal more competent than many election studies in the 1940s and 1950s purported to show.[13] They note that voters, beginning with the 1964 presidential election and continuing through the presidential elections of the 1970s, showed considerably more sensitivity to issues than most earlier voting studies had suggested they ordinarily would. About two-thirds of the voters referred to issue positions in explaining their presidential choices. This was a far greater fraction of the electorate than that which referred to party loyalties, though a smaller one than the three-quarters or four-fifths who referred to personality characteristics of the candidates.[14]

However, there has been no parallel evidence of a similar rise in voter in-

[13] G. Pomper, *Voters' Choice* (New York: Dodd, Mead, 1975); Richard Boyd, "Electoral Trends in Postwar Politics," in James Barber, ed., *Choosing the President* (Englewood Cliffs, N.J.: Prentice-Hall, 1974); Norman Nie, Sidney Verba, and John Petrocik, *The Changing American Voter* (Cambridge, Mass.: Harvard University Press, 1976).

[14] Nie, Verba, and Petrocik, *The Changing American Voter*, pp. 167, 297.

Populist Democracy

The populist strain in American democracy sometimes looks back to the Populist movement of the 1880s and 1890s. This populism was a protest movement of small farmers and miners against what they perceived to be a government that acted in the interests of the big banks, railroads, and corporations. In 1892 a Populist party was formed and ran a presidential candidate who captured twenty-two electoral votes; voters also elected ten representatives, five senators, and about fifteen hundred state legislators. In 1896 they joined with the Democrats in support of "The Great Commoner" William Jennings Bryan's unsuccessful presidential campaign. This drawing of an altercation between Populist and anti-Populist Kansas legislators in 1893 illustrates the turbulence that sometimes accompanied this movement.

In our own time, certain politicians' styles have been described as "populist," a term often used imprecisely to convey an identification with the "common man." Former President Carter was occasionally seen in this light because of his expressed interest in the views of average citizens and his willingness to meet with them; here he is seen visiting with a family in Clinton, Massachusetts after attending the Clinton town meeting in 1977. Former Oklahoma Senator Fred Harris, who made an unsuccessful bid for the 1976 Democratic presidential nomination, claimed to be a populist in substance more than style. He often used the rhetoric of the early populists, promising to take government out of the hands of the big interests and return power as much as possible to citizens at the local level.

formation about issues or about the operations of government. There is also no evidence that a jump in issue voting is occurring at levels of voting other than the presidential. It may well be that the sensitivity expressed in presidential voting in the 1960s and earlier 1970s was a fluke. The 1976 and 1980 elections did not go back to the old pattern but were less reassuring than those of 1964–72. Finally, the fact that fewer people have voted in presidential elections even as issue voting has gained is hardly a good sign for populists. In 1960 some 63 percent of the adult population voted; by 1980 it was down to 53 percent.

Yet none of this discourages populists. They read all these signs in two ways. First, they say, these are indicators that citizens *can* be issue-oriented; they have that capacity. That they do not always act this way even at the presidential level and that voting is declining leads to their second point. It suggests, populists contend, that people are rejecting the current democratic system in the United States. People know it is not for them and are voting on it with their feet. This, populists say, is simply more evidence of the soundness of the American people, who know they could have a far better system than they do have.

The Value of Leadership The second populist tenet is that their form of democracy can translate popular desires into action by providing strong elected leaders. Populists contend that much of the present gap between citizen and state originates in many people's accurate perception that our government just cannot seem to act — at least in response to popular demands. Populists are acutely aware that the fragmentation of power in our political system benefits well-protected "special interests." They propose to end this fragmented situation and to break the logjam.

Populists are convinced that if government is to act today and plan effectively for tomorrow, it needs centralized power — power to define its values and policies, power to control special interests when necessary, power to get bureaucracy moving, power to act. Yet the power they seek for action-oriented leaders would not be unchecked. On the contrary, procedures like the initiative, the referendum, and recall would force leaders to be aware of and responsive to the people's wishes. And where possible there would be decentralization. Populists contend that populist government, which would lead at the behest of the popular will, would be far more responsible and controlled than our present form of government, in which power is often less responsible to the people. They point out, for example, that even after approval of Jimmy Carter's plan for a cabinet-level Department of Energy in 1977, power over energy policy was diffused among dozens of agencies, making it difficult for citizens to monitor or influence policy and much easier for wealthy and resourceful special interests (in this case the energy companies) to pursue their own selfish interests.

Populism today has a host of critics. On the level of principle, all sides attack populism. Some skeptics believe that populists celebrate popular participation and popular wisdom uncritically. They argue that populists do not seem to take seriously the mixed evidence about citizens' levels of political information, the coherence of their position on issues, and their commitment to issue voting. They wonder whether populism might lead to majority tyranny, enforced by an often incoherent, uninformed, and irrational majority. Participatory democrats doubt that a direct role for the citizenry would survive the transition from populist theory to practice. They suspect that leaders seeking power often will express populist sentiments and then abandon them when safely in office. Participatory democrats also raise these questions: Could greater popular participation and expanded leadership really remain in harness together for long? Or would the populist affinity for action overwhelm the expanded popular participation promoted by populist rhetoric?

The Problems of Popular Participation

Besides such theoretical questions, there is the practical issue: Does populism work? Because we have no genuinely populist societies to evalute, much of the practical critique focuses on the referendum as an instrument for popular self-government. Social scientists have made many studies of referenda in various American states and localities. Some note the discouraging finding that a candidate's or proposition's fate is affected by its location on the ballot: For example, the farther down the ballot an item is, the greater the number of "no" votes it is likely to receive.

Other observers seriously question the assumption that majority opinions exist for referenda to tap. In fact, there is good reason to believe that citizen views on many issues are unformed, nonexistent, or composed of a great variety of positions. This complexity cannot possibly be reflected in a referendum that asks for a simple yea or nay. Thus referenda may not be as democratic as populists assert. They may produce a majority for one side or another, but it will be a majority composed of many uninformed and widely disparate views, which the simple vote totals do not accurately reflect.

It is also conceivable that even on an issue on which opinions are clear and strong, the results of a referendum may not reflect the actual position most people prefer. This is the so-called paradox of voting. For example, imagine that the issue is how much money a government should spend on welfare, and that three distinct views are held by groups of about equal strength: (1) increase welfare support; (2) decrease support; and (3) maintain the current level of support. No matter how the question was phrased on the ballot, the result would not reflect the wishes of a majority. If the question were "Should more money be given?" the majority would vote no, and the current level would be maintained, even though half of those voting no did not favor current levels. If the question were "Should the current level be maintained?" the vote again would be no, but half the majority would want to increase the level and half would want it lowered. The natural inference from such a negative vote —that a majority favors lower supports — would not in fact be the position of a majority of the electorate. How often would the electorate be divided so that the majority vote would misrepresent the majority view? No one knows for sure. Perhaps the populists are right in saying this would not happen often. The critics' main point, however, remains valid: The belief that there are "issue majorities" just waiting to be heard is often an illusion.

Other evidence also indicates to critics that populists give citizens too much credit for interest in issues. Studies show that people usually do not vote on referenda as often as they do on candidates, although as more controversial issues such as gun control or nuclear power plants appear on the ballot, referendum voting may go up. Some interpreters suggest that the common tendency to vote no automatically on all referenda (apparently on the assumption that they are all requests for money) is another sign of voter uncertainty and disinterest.[15] Populists do not agree. They often read such negative voting as a sign of the electorate's well-founded distrust in politicians and their schemes. To say that people vote against a proposition because they are not interested in it seems to populists to be an attempt to discredit an electorate that does not always behave as "sophisticated" critics want it to do. Populists further contend that even if people do lack interest in many ballot propositions, it cannot be concluded that they are uninterested in major issues. The populists suggest, rather, that really crucial questions such as issues of war or peace or fundamental questions of economic policy rarely appear on the ballot. More often, they say, the voter is presented with seemingly minor questions about debt limits or constitutional revision that are expressed in almost willfully indecipherable language.

Critics of the populist position also raise the problem of so-called intense minorities. Why, these critics ask, should the majority rule when the majority may not care much about its position, whereas a defeated minority may care passionately? If a minority of 49 percent is seriously affected by an issue, surely its sentiments should weigh more heavily in the scales of democratic representation than the judgment of an apathetic 51 percent. Defenders of our present form of government insist that the aim of democracy is the representation of people's deepest needs, not mechanical majority rule. They declare that our system's openness to group competition and influence makes it more responsive to concerned minorities than populism would be, because it takes intensity into account.

Populists do not agree that this is a serious problem. They doubt that intense minorities are frequently overwhelmed by apathetic majorities. They also note what they consider the unmistakably elitist tone of the objections to populism that are made in the name of intensity. They consider it ironic that there is so much anxiety over the possibility that populism may occasionally neglect intense minorities' wishes. For example, they point out that we have done very well by the intense minority of doctors, but very poorly by the large

---

[15] R. Niemi, "Majority Decision Making," *American Political Science Review* 63 (June 1969); John Mueller, "Voting on the Prospositions: Ballot Patterns and Historical Trends in California," *American Political Science Review* 63 (December 1969): 1197–1212; Duane Lockhard, *The Politics of State and Local Government* (New York: Macmillan, 1969), p. 251.

majority of citizens who for the past thirty years have favored comprehensive state-financed medical care.

Socialist democrats feel that any "democratization" of the American political system that does not attack economic inequalities and economic control will not be democracy no matter who ostensibly rules. All that will be certain is that behind the façade of any democratic system, including populism, will be elite control. Economic elites will continue to govern through their power and position. To think differently is to engage in the pleasant populist assumption that an abstraction called "the people" can overcome the reality called economic power.

Populists respond by denying that the people would be helpless to govern themselves under populism. They challenge the view that the people would allow any elite, open or secret, to rule for long. They consider this a cynical opinion, just as they consider it cynical to suggest that citizens are unlikely to agree with the policy ideas many populists hold. Populism involves gambling on the good sense of the citizenry, yet they see it as a worthwhile gamble, especially if citizens are better informed. They insist that people are not the problem in the United States or elsewhere and that to make a fetish of doubts is to deny the entire idea of democracy. They urge us to concentrate on educating the electorate, not on self-fulfilling pessimism.

The Problems of Strong Leadership

Some have also criticized populism's call for strong leadership. Participatory democrats question the reliability of any elite, even a supposedly responsive one. Others point out that having strong leadership does not guarantee that things will get done. Moreover, although centralized decison making by strong leaders often works when policy aims are obvious, it is less successful when the tasks to be performed are diverse and change from day to day. Here a decentralized, highly flexible arrangement for governing may be more appropriate. It may be sensible to run a driver's license renewal office in a centralized fashion, for instance; but would it be as wise to operate a welfare office — or perhaps the national government as a whole — in this fashion? After all, many decisions must be based on specific situations and substantial complexities; good judgment as well as strong leadership is often crucial. Depending on "leaders" or on a "majority will" would not go far toward solving most day-to-day problems.

Nor are powerful leaders necessarily responsible decision makers. As President Nixon showed in his last years in the White House, strong leaders may choose to listen only to a small, uncritical group of admiring advisors who are themselves isolated from vital sources of information and consequently out of touch with the world around them. Although Nixon could have been removed by Congress, the House impeachment hearings showed (as we saw in Chapter 5 on Congress) that people are usually reluctant to take such drastic action without long deliberation. A strong leader thus could conceivably do a great deal of damage before being recalled.

Populists do not believe that leadership is a cure-all. They do not need to be reminded of the dangers of leadership and centralized bureaucrats; they are naturally suspicious of politicians and bureaucrats. They propose to guard against the dangers of runaway leadership by providing for as much decentralization as possible and by electing leaders who are closely in touch with popular sentiments, instead of accepting leaders who are little more than errand boys for special interests. Populists invariably return to what they consider the essential need both for more popular input and for more leadership, centralized rather than fragmented. They remain convinced that an action-oriented government, led by dynamic leaders who seek to obtain realization of the popular will, is what democracy is all about.

DEMOCRATIC SOCIALISM Within the United States there is no doubt that the debate over alternative forms of democracy takes place largely within the confines of reform pluralism, participatory democracy, and populism. But in the larger world, another alternative, what we may term *socialist democracy*, receives much attention. The range of democratic socialism's appeal is great. But despite such imperfect examples as Sweden and Nicaragua, it has proved more popular as a rallying cry than in actual governments.

Most democratic socialists identify four features in democracy, although how much they emphasize one or another can vary a good deal. First, they stress the importance of approximate economic equality among all citizens. Second, they argue that the entire community must own the major means of production or, at least, have effective control over them. Third, they favor a good deal of participation by workers in key economic decisions — worker democracy. Last, they insist that there can be no democracy unless citizens are roughly equal politically.

The Case for Socialist Democracy Three arguments socialist democrats make for their viewpoint are especially central. They always contend that democracy must be a way of life among people who respect each other as persons. From this angle only a democracy that creates and maintains citizens of approximately equal station in life (very much including economic life) can possibly instill such respect. According to this view, when equality does not exist, respect inevitably goes to the powerful and the monied, even if it is the respect of hate. Socialist democrats vigorously challenge other democrats: Isn't democracy about equal respect for the voice and wisdom of everyone? If it is, then we have to create an economic system that ensures equal respect in practice rather than as a piety that people ignore in practice.

Second, socialist democrats argue that democracy must be about a just life and a just society. It is not simply a method of decision making. It is, again, a just way of life — that must never be forgotten. For socialist democrats this means that there is another reason for concern with rough economic equality for all citizens. This is what social justice demands. Although not all are Marxists, they usually follow Marx's definition of justice: to each according to his or her similar needs. Not to follow this goal, they think, is to deny respect for each human being.

Third, socialist democrats are convinced that such a democratic society — such a socialist democracy — is also valuable for a practical political reason. It will free citizens to participate as near equals in the decision-making processes of government. Socialist democrats find it absurd that the American political system — indeed, almost all political systems — claims to support democratic political equality while actually allowing enormous economic inequalities, apparently on the assumption that one can separate the economic and political spheres. Socialist democrats deny this vigorously, declaring that the two realms are deeply and permanently intertwined. They believe that there can be considerable political equality only when there is substantial economic equality. Only when people see behind the fact that everyone has the vote in the United States, only when they note that it is the few who have and employ money in politics who really count in election campaigns —or, even more, in the interest-group process — will they abandon the illusion that pluralism is democracy. Then citizens will come to their senses and insist on much more economic equality as an essential prerequisite to democratic politics among equals.

The strong link between economic and political equality makes socialist democracy unique among democratic theories today. Except for an occasional participatory democrat or populist democrat who is also firmly committed to this kind of linkage, socialist democrats stand alone. This is also true of socialist democrats' contention that considerable public ownership and/or control of the economy is essential for democracy. In fact, this is what makes these democrats *socialist* democrats. The declining enthusiasm among some socialist democrats for public ownership of most of the economy (as opposed to control of it) is really peripheral to the essential point. Ownership or control, they expect the result to be the same: the economy will serve the general community and not act as the major single source of human inequality.

It should be noted, finally, that socialist democrats do not have in mind a single *form* that democratic socialism might take. Usually they argue that this is an important, but secondary, question. Some favor a strong national government, elected by citizens in competitive free elections, while insisting that government must be bound by the goal of rough equality and considerable worker participation on levels below the national government. Others favor a sharply decentralized political system in which the ideals of participatory democracy come true, but in a socialist setting that emphasizes worker participation.

The Case against Socialist Democracy Critics of socialist democracy abound. Pluralists and reform pluralists lead the way. Pluralists say it is one thing to favor equality of opportunity in political or economic life and quite another to force substantive equality. They do not think people will tolerate the latter, given a choice. But pluralists are not sure people will continue to have a choice under such a system. The truth about socialist democrats, these critics suggest, is that they have a low commitment to liberty. Despite socialist democrats' disclaimers that they want to protect the political freedom to speak out, to petition, to run for office, pluralists are skeptical. They doubt that a society that is no longer very pluralistic in economic terms can provide enough independent groups with clout to block the excesses and errors of those in power.

Moreover, they suspect that most democratic socialists are so engaged by their hatred for capitalism and the rich and by their desire for economic equality that to achieve this goal they might sacrifice democratic liberties in the name of "economic democracy" or "the public good" or "temporary necessity." They cite a long list of revolutions made in the modern world under the broad rubric of democratic socialism. And they note that almost all soon enough abandoned democratic liberties and thus democracy. Pluralists fear there would be too much elite rule and far, far too little fragmented power — or pluralism.

The second argument pluralists make is that socialist democracy will not work in yet another way. They assert that its demands for political and economic equality run directly against human nature, or at least human experience. This is not merely a matter of repeating contentions about the inevitable inequalities caused in politics by differences in interest, luck, or skills. It is also a question of the possibility of achieving anything like economic equality — and then maintaining it — as the basis for significant political equality. Pluralists look at the economic life of nations from the United States to the Soviet Union. Official goals may differ, but the reality is sharp income differentials and a striving by a major part of both populations to get more than others economically. There is little behavioral commitment to strict economic equality.

Populists and participatory democrats also make two main objections. They contend that the matter of the form of government is much more important than most socialist democrats think. Each understands that there is a stream of socialism closer to their view of the appropriate form — some socialists are more participatory, some more populist. Both insist that the direction socialist democracy goes when it sets up its political system will always have an enormous impact on whether it is democratic. Participatory democrats assert that any democratic socialism that does not concentrate largely on participation will be more socialism than democracy, something they say is true of most socialist states today. Populists assert that ignoring the importance of leadership as well as participation will doom any socialist democracy to impotence in accomplishing what people want. On the other hand, they criticize existent socialist regimes for failing to provide for participation and for seeing it as a threat to leadership.

Populists and participatory democrats are, second, predictably uncomfortable with the socialist aspect of democratic socialism. Most participatory enthusiasts, like many populists, are hardly eager devotees of giant corporations — or giant unions. They also usually recognize the gap in influence that sharp income differentials ensure. Since both theories of democracy are efforts to increase popular influence and to reduce the role of special interests whose roots are often in economic selfishness, there is a natural sympathy with socialist democracy.

Yet populists and participatory democrats usually think it is unnecessary to go to the "extreme" of socialism or socialist control of the economy. In part this is a dispute about how great the social changes need to be to expand democracy. In part it is a dispute over whether or not the economic factor is as overwhelming in human motivation as democratic socialists assert. There is a third element, too. For populists and many participatory democrats, there is considerable suspicion that socialists are more in love with economic equality and socialist control than with democracy. Participatory democrats and populists agree that if people in their political systems choose these goals, then they should be implemented. But they often doubt whether, on the other hand, a socialist democracy would let a modified capitalism back in if the people wanted it. Often the socialist democrat is confident people would never take such a "reactionary" path — but who knows? Socialist democrats insist that they have a strong commitment to civil liberties and political freedom, and they argue that it is not fair to prejudge them on the basis of other, nondemocratic socialist regimes.

CONCLUSION This chapter has explored four alternatives to pluralist democracy in the United States. Socialist democrats insist that democracy must be about equality as well as participation in the economic and political realms. Participatory democrats believe that direct self-government by citizens in decentralized units is the only kind of genuine democracy. They see our government as far too remote from the people. Populists agree. They argue for a greater role for citizen participation in selecting leaders and in adopting government policies. They also want a government with strong leaders who can act decisively when the people want them to do so. They insist that our government is not only far too undemocratic, but that it also fails to act in too many cases. On the other hand, participatory democracy seems to populists to be utopian and irrelevant. Finally, reform pluralists seek to create a democratic government without drastically changing our present system. They hope to get more groups organized to participate and to make the competition among groups a good deal more fair.

Our examination of alternative ideas and systems of democracy has tried to focus on their response to three main complaints posed to the American political system: it is too elitist, it is too divided to get anything done, and citizens are just not up to its demands. There is not, nor can there be, any single answer to whether or not one or more of these alternatives addresses these problems more successfully than the others. Given different values, concerns, and emphases, all of us will offer our own answers. What we should all understand, however, is that by no means is our system of democracy the only possible form in either theory or practice. It has no inherent claim to be de-

mocracy in its most logical or perfect expression. It must prove in competition with other versions that it really is not too elitist; that it can act decisively; and that it is in line with a realistic view of people as citizens. Above all, it must confront the gap between citizen and state and convince a considerable body of skeptics that it not only does not cause the current gap but that it is also the best means to narrow it. The challenge is formidable. On its success will turn the direction — and perhaps the fate — of democracy in the United States.

SUGGESTIONS FOR FURTHER READING

Dahl, Robert. *After the Revolution?* New Haven: Yale University Press, 1970. A skeptical look at radical democratic theories.

Harris, Fred. *The New Populism.* New York: Saturday Review Press, 1976. The interesting manifesto of a practicing populist.

Kotler, M. *Neighborhood Government.* New York: Bobbs-Merrill, 1969. Important work by one of the current advocates of local control and decentralization in our cities.

Margolis, Michael. *Viable Democracy.* New York: Penguin Books, 1979. Interesting discussion of alternatives and the case for a combination of populism and pluralism.

Pateman, Carole. *Participation and Democratic Theory.* Cambridge: Cambridge University Press, 1970. A vigorous argument for participatory democracy and workers' control.

Thompson, Dennis. *The Democratic Citizen.* Cambridge: Cambridge University Press, 1970. An informed and thoughtful discussion of democratic theory literature.

THE DECLARATION OF INDEPENDENCE

When in the Course of human events, it becomes necessary for one people to dissolve the political bands which have connected them with another, and to assume among the Powers of the earth, the separate and equal station to which the Laws of Nature and of Nature's God entitle them, a decent respect to the opinions of mankind requires that they should declare the causes which impel them to the separation.

We hold these truths to be self-evident, that all men are created equal, that they are endowed by their Creator with certain unalienable Rights, that among these are Life, Liberty and the pursuit of Happiness. That to secure these rights, Governments are instituted among Men, deriving their just powers from the consent of the governed, That whenever any Form of Government becomes destructive of these ends, it is the Right of the People to alter or to abolish it, and to institute new Government, laying its foundation on such principles and organizing its powers in such form, as to them shall seem most likely to effect their Safety and Happiness. Prudence, indeed, will dictate that Governments long established should not be changed for light and transient causes; and accordingly all experience hath shown, that mankind are more disposed to suffer, while evils are sufferable, than to right themselves by abolishing the forms to which they are accustomed. But when a long train of abuses and usurpations, pursuing invariably the same Object evinces a design to reduce them under absolute Despotism, it is their right, it is their duty, to throw off such Government, and to provide new Guards for their future security.—Such has been the patient sufferance of these Colonies; and such is now the necessity which constrains them to alter their former Systems of Government. The history of the present King of Great Britain is a history of repeated injuries and usurpations, all having in direct object the establishment of an absolute Tyranny over these States. To prove this, let Facts be submitted to a candid world.

He has refused his Assent to Laws, the most wholesome and necessary for the public good.

He has forbidden his Governors to pass Laws of immediate and pressing importance, unless suspended in their operation till his Assent should be obtained; and when so suspended, he has utterly neglected to attend to them.

He has refused to pass other Laws for the accommodation of large districts of people, unless those people would relinquish the right of Representation in the Legislature, a right inestimable to them and formidable to tyrants only.

He has called together legislative bodies at places unusual, uncomfortable, and distant from the depository of their public Records, for the sole purpose of fatiguing them into compliance with his measures.

He has dissolved Representative Houses repeatedly, for opposing with manly firmness his invasions on the rights of the people.

He has refused for a long time, after such dissolutions, to cause others to be elected; whereby the Legislative Powers, incapable of Annihilation, have returned to the People at large for their exercise; the State remaining in the mean time exposed to all the dangers of invasion from without, and convulsions within.

He has endeavoured to prevent the population of these States; for that purpose obstructing the Laws of Naturalization of Foreigners; refusing to pass others to encourage their migration hither, and raising the conditions of new Appropriations of Lands.

He has obstructed the Administration of Justice, by refusing his Assent to Laws for establishing Judiciary powers.

He has made Judges dependent on his Will alone, for the tenure of their offices, and the amount and payment of their salaries.

He has erected a multitude of New Offices, and sent hither swarms of Officers to harass our People, and eat out their substance.

He has kept among us in times of peace, Standing Armies without the Consent of our legislature.

He has affected to render the Military independent of and superior to the Civil power.

He has combined with others to subject us to a jurisdiction foreign to our constitution, and unacknowledged by our laws; giving his Assent to their acts of pretended Legislation:

For quartering large bodies of armed troops among us:

For protecting them, by a mock Trial, from punishment for any Murders which they should commit on the Inhabitants of these States:

For cutting off our Trade with all parts of the world.

For imposing taxes on us without our Consent:

For depriving us in many cases, of the benefits of Trial by Jury:

For transporting us beyond Seas to be tried for pretended offences:

For abolishing the free System of English Laws in a neighbouring Province, establishing therein an Arbitrary government, and englarging its Boundaries so as to render it at once an example and fit instrument for introducing the same absolute rule into these Colonies.

For taking away our Charters, abolishing our most valuable Laws, and altering fundamentally the Forms of our Governments:

For suspending our own Legislature, and declaring themselves invested with Power to legislate for us in all cases whatsoever.

He has abdicated Government here, by declaring us out of his Protection and waging War against us.

He has plundered our seas, ravaged our Coasts, burnt our towns, and destroyed the lives of our people.

He is at this time transporting large Armies of foreign Mercenaries to compleat the works of death, desolation and tyranny, already begun with circumstances of Cruelty & perfidy scarcely paralleled in the most barbarous ages, and totally unworthy the Head of a civilized nation.

He has constrained our fellow Citizens taken Captive on the high Seas to bear Arms against their Country, to become the executioners of their friends and Brethren, or to fall themselves by their Hands.

He has excited domestic insurrections amongst us, and has endeavoured to bring on the inhabitants of our frontiers, the merciless Indian Savages, whose known rule of warfare, is an undistinguished destruction of all ages, sexes and conditions.

In every stage of these Oppressions We have Petitioned for Redress in the most humble terms: Our repeated Petitions have been answered only by repeated injury. A Prince, whose character is thus marked by every act which may define a Tyrant, is unfit to be the ruler of a free People.

Nor have We been wanting in attention to our British brethren. We have warned them from time to time of attempts by their legislature to extend an unwarrantable jurisdiction over us. We have reminded them of the circumstances of our emigration and settlement here. We have appealed to their native justice and magnanimity, and we have conjured them by the ties of our common kindred to disavow these usurpations, which, would inevitably interrupt our connections and correspondence. They too have been deaf to the voice of justice and of consanguinity. We must, therefore, acquiesce in the necessity, which denounces our Separation, and hold them, as we hold the rest of mankind, Enemies in War, in Peace Friends.

We, therefore, the Representatives of the United States of America, in General Congress, Assembled, appealing to the Supreme Judge of the world for the rectitude of our intentions, do, in the Name, and by Authority of the good People of these Colonies, solemnly publish and declare, That these United Colonies are, and of Right ought to be Free and Independent States; that they are Absolved from all Allegiance to the British Crown, and that all political connection between them and the State of Great Britain, is and ought to be totally dissolved; and that as Free and Independent States, they have full Power to levy War, conclude Peace, contract Alliances, establish Commerce, and to do all other Acts and Things which Independent States may of right do. And for the support of this Declaration, with a firm reliance on the protection of divine Providence, we mutually pledge to each other our Lives, our Fortunes and our sacred Honor.

THE CONSTITUTION
OF THE UNITED STATES
OF AMERICA

We the People of the United States, in Order to form a more perfect Union, establish Justice, insure domestic Tranquility, provide for the common defence, promote the general Welfare, and secure the Blessings of Liberty to ourselves and our Posterity, do ordain and establish this Constitution for the United States of America.

Article I

Section. 1. All legislative Powers herein granted shall be vested in a Congress of the United States, which shall consist of a Senate and House of Representatives.

Section. 2. The House of Representatives shall be composed of Members chosen every second Year by the People of the several States, and the Electors in each State shall have the Qualifications requisite for Electors of the most numerous Branch of the State Legislature.

No Person shall be a Representative who shall not have attained to the age of twenty five Years, and been seven Years a Citizen of the United States, and who shall not, when elected, be an Inhabitant of that State in which he shall be chosen.

Representatives and direct Taxes shall be apportioned among the several States which may be included within this Union, according to their respective Numbers, *which shall be determined by adding to the whole Number of free Persons, including those bound to Service for a Term of Years,* and excluding Indians not taxed, *three fifths of all other persons.* [1] The actual Enumeration shall be made within three Years after the first Meeting of the Congress of the United States, and within every subsequent Term of ten Years, in such Manner as they shall by Law direct. The Number of Representatives shall not exceed one for every thirty Thousand, but each State shall have at Least one Representative; and until such enumeration shall be made, the State of New Hampshire shall be entitled to chuse three, Massachusetts eight, Rhode-Island and Providence Plantations one, Connecticut five, New-York six, New Jersey four, Pennsylvania eight, Delaware one, Maryland six, Virginia ten, North Carolina five, South Carolina five, and Georgia three.

When vacancies happen in the Representation from any State, the Executive Authority thereof shall issue Writs of Election to fill such Vacancies.

The House of Representatives shall chuse their Speaker and other Officers; and shall have the sole Power of Impeachment.

Section. 3. The Senate of the United States shall be composed of two Senators from each State, *chosen by the Legislature thereof,* [2] for six Years; and each Senator shall have one Vote.

Immediately after they shall be assembled in Consequence of the first Election, they shall be divided as equally as may be into three Classes. The Seats of the Senators of the first Class shall be vacated at the Expiration of the second Year, of the second Class at the Expiration of the fourth Year, and of the third Class at the Expiration of the sixth Year, so

---

[1] Italics are used throughout to indicate passages that have been altered by subsequent amendments. In this case see Amendment XIV.

[2] See Amendment XVII.

that one third may be chosen every second Year; *and if Vacancies happen by Resignation, or otherwise, during the Recess of the Legislature of any State, the Executive thereof may make temporary Appointments until the next Meeting of the Legislature, which shall then fill such Vancancies.*[3]

No Person shall be a Senator who shall not have attained to the Age of thirty Years, and been nine Years a Citizen of the United States, and who shall not, when elected, be an Inhabitant of that State for which he shall be chosen.

The Vice President of the United States shall be President of the Senate, but shall have no Vote, unless they be equally divided.

The Senate shall choose their other Officers, and also a President pro tempore, in the Absence of the Vice President, or when he shall exercise the Office of President of the United States.

The Senate shall have the sole Power to try all Impeachments. When sitting for that Purpose, they shall be on Oath or Affirmation. When the President of the United States is tried, the Chief Justice shall preside: And no Person shall be convicted without the Concurrence of two thirds of the Members present.

Judgment in Cases of Impeachment shall not extend further than to removal from Office, and disqualification to hold and enjoy any Office of honor, Trust or Profit under the United States: but the Party convicted shall nevertheless be liable and subject to Indictment, Trial, Judgment and Punishment, according to Law.

Section. 4. The Times, Places and Manner of holding Elections for Senators and Representatives, shall be prescribed in each State by the Legislature thereof; but the Congress may at any time by Law make or alter such Regulations, except as to the Places of chusing Senators.

The Congress shall assemble at least once in a Year, and such Meeting shall be on the first Monday in December, unless they shall by Law appoint a different Day.[4]

Section. 5. Each House shall be the Judge of the Elections, Returns and Qualifications of its own Members, and a Majority of each shall constitute a Quorum to do Business; but a smaller Number may adjourn from day to day, and may be authorized to compel the Attendance of absent Members, in such Manner, and under such Penalties as each House may provide.

Each House may determine the Rules of its Proceedings, punish its Members for disorderly Behavior, and, with the Concurrence of two thirds, expel a Member.

Each House shall keep a Journal of its Proceedings, and from time to time publish the same, excepting such Parts as may in their Judgment require Secrecy; and the Yeas and Nays of the Members of either House on any question shall, at the Desire of one fifth of those Present, be entered on the Journal.

Neither House, during the Session of Congress, shall, without the Consent of the other, adjourn for more than three days, nor to any other Place than that in which the two Houses shall be sitting.

Section. 6. The Senators and Representatives shall receive a Compensation for their Services, to be ascertained by Law, and paid out of the Treasury of the United States. They shall in all Cases, except Treason, Felony and Breach of the Peace, be privileged from Arrest during their Attendance at the Session of their respective Houses, and in going to

[3]*Ibid.*
[4]See Amendment XX.

and returning from the same; and for any Speech or Debate in either House, they shall not be questioned in any other Place.

No Senator or Represenative shall, during the Time for which he was elected, be appointed to any civil Office under the Authority of the United States, which shall have been created, or the Emoluments whereof shall have been encreased during such time; and no Person holding any Office under the United States, shall be a Member of either House during his Continuance in Office.

Section. 7. All Bills for raising Revenue shall originate in the House of Represenatives; but the Senate may propose or concur with Amendments as on other Bills.

Every Bill which shall have passed the House of Representatives and the Senate, shall, before it become a Law, be presented to the President of the United States; if he approve he shall sign it, but if not he shall return it, with his Objections to that House in which it shall have originated, who shall enter the Objections at large on their Journal, and proceed to reconsider it. If after such Reconsideration two thirds of that House shall agree to pass the Bill, it shall be sent, together with the Objections, to the other House, by which it shall likewise be reconsidered, and if approved by two thirds of that House, it shall become a Law. But in all such Cases the Votes of both Houses shall be determined by Yeas and Nays, and the Names of the Persons voting for and against the Bill shall be entered on the Journal of each House respectively. If any Bill shall not be returned by the President within ten Days (Sundays excepted) after it shall have been presented to him, the Same shall be a Law, in like Manner as if he had signed it, unless Congress by their Adjournment prevent its Return, in which Case it shall not be a Law.

Every Order, Resolution, or Vote to which the Concurrence of the Senate and House of Representatives may be necessary (except on a question of Adjournment) shall be presented to the President of the United States; and before the Same shall take Effect, shall be approved by him, or being disapproved by him, shall be repassed by two thirds of the Senate and House of Representatives, according to the Rules and Limitations prescribed in the Case of a Bill.

Section. 8. The Congress shall have Power to lay and collect Taxes, Duties, Imposts and Excises, to pay the Debts and provide for the common Defence and general Welfare of the United States; but all Duties, Imports and Excises shall be uniform throughout the United States;

To borrow Money on the credit of the United States;

To regulate Commerce with foreign Nations, and among the several States, and with the Indian Tribes;

To establish an uniform Rule of Naturalization, and uniform Laws on the subject of Bankruptcies throughout the United States;

To coin Money, regulate the Value thereof, and of foreign Coin, and fix the Standard of Weights and Measures;

To provide for the Punishment of counterfeiting the Securities and Current Coin of the United States;

To establish Post Offices and post Roads;

To promote the Progress of Science and useful Arts, by securing for limited Times to Authors and Inventors the exclusive Right to their respective Writings and Discoveries;

To constitute Tribunals inferior to the Supreme Court;

To define and punish Piracies and Felonies committed on the high Seas and Offences against the Law of Nations;

To declare War, grant Letters of Marque and Reprisal, and make Rules concerning Captures on Land and Water;

To raise and support Armies, but no Appropriation of Money to that Use shall be for a longer Term than two Years;

To provide and maintain a Navy;

To make Rules for the Government and Regulation of the land and naval Forces;

To provide for calling forth the Militia to execute the Laws of the Union, suppress Insurrections and repel Invasions;

To provide for organizing, arming, and disciplining, the Militia, and for governing such Part of them as may be employed in the Service of the United States, reserving to the States respectively, the Appointment of the Officers, and the Authority of training the Militia according to the discipline prescribed by Congress;

To exercise exclusive Legislation in all Cases whatsoever, over such District (not exceeding ten Miles square) as may, by Cession of particular States, and the Acceptance of Congress, become the Seat of the Government of the United States, and to exercise like Authority over all Places purchased by the Consent of the Legislature of the State in which the Same shall be, for the Erection of Forts, Magazines, Arsenals, dock-Yards, and other needful Buildings;—And

To make all Laws which shall be necessary and proper for carrying into Execution the foregoing Powers, and all other Powers vested by this Constitution in the Government of the United States, or in any Department or Officer thereof.

Section. 9. The Migration or Importation of such Persons as any of the States now existing shall think proper to admit, shall not be prohibited by the Congress prior to the Year one thousand eight hundred and eight, but a Tax or duty may be imposed on such Importation, not exceeding ten dollars for each Person.

The Privilege of the Writ of Habeas Corpus shall not be suspended, unless when in Cases of Rebellion or Invasion the public Safety may require it.

No Bill of Attainder or ex post facto Law shall be passed.

No Capitation, or other direct, Tax shall be laid, unless in Proportion to the Census or Enumeration herein before directed to be taken.

No Tax or Duty shall be laid on Articles exported from any State.

No Preference shall be given by any Regulation of Commerce or Revenue to the Ports of one State over those of another: nor shall Vessels bound to, or from, one State, be obliged to enter, clear, or pay Duties in another.

No Money shall be drawn from the Treasury, but in Consequence of Appropriations made by Law; and a regular Statement and Account of the Receipts and Expenditures of all public Money shall be published from time to time.

No title of Nobility shall be granted by the United States: And no Person holding any Office of Profit or Trust under them, shall, without the Consent of the Congress, accept of any present, Emolument, Office, or Title, of any kind whatever, from any King, Prince, or foreign State.

Section. 10. No State shall enter into any Treaty, Alliance, or Confederation; grant Letters of Marque and Reprisal; coin Money; emit Bills of Credit; make any Thing but gold and silver Coin a Tender in Payment of Debts; pass any Bill of Attainder, ex post facto Law, or Law impairing the Obligation of Contracts, or Grant any Title of Nobility.

No State shall, without the Consent of the Congress, lay any Imposts or Duties on Imports or Exports, except what may be absolutely necessary for executing its inspection Laws: and the net Produce of all Duties and Imposts, laid by any State on Imports or Exports, shall be for the Use of the Treasury of the United States; and all such Laws be subject to the Revision and Control of the Congress.

No State shall, without the Consent of Congress, lay any Duty of Tonnage, keep

Troops, or Ships of War in time of Peace, enter into any Agreement or Compact with another State, or with a foreign Power, or engage in War, unless actually invaded, or in such imminent Danger as will not admit of delay.

Article II

Section. 1. The executive Power shall be vested in a President of the United States of America. He shall hold his Office during the Term of four Years, and, together with the Vice President, chosen for the same Term be elected as follows:

Each State shall appoint, in such Manner as the Legislature thereof may direct, a Number of Electors, equal to the whole Number of Senators and Representatives to which the State may be entitled in the Congress: but no Senator or Representative, or Person holding an Office of Trust or Profit under the United States, shall be appointed an Elector.

The Electors shall meet in their respective States, and vote by Ballot for two Persons, of whom one at least shall not be an Inhabitant of the same State with themselves. And they shall make a List of all the Persons voted for, and of the Number of Votes for each; which List they shall sign and certify, and transmit sealed to the Seat of the Government of the United States, directed to the President of the Senate. The President of the Senate shall, in the Presence of the Senate and House of Representatives, open all the Certificates, and the Votes shall then be counted. The Person having the greatest Number of Votes shall be the President, if such Number be a Majority of the whole Number of Electors appointed; and if there be more than one who have such Majority, and have an equal Number of Votes, then the House of Representatives shall immediately chuse by Ballot one of them for President; and if no Person have a Majority, then from the five highest on the List the said House shall in like Manner chuse the President. But in chusing the President, the votes shall be taken by States, the Representation from each State having one Vote; A quorum for this purpose shall consist of a Member or Members from two thirds of the States, and a Majority of all the States shall be necessary to a Choice. In every Case, after the Choice of the President, the Person having the Greatest Number of Votes of the Electors shall be the Vice President. But if there should remain two or more who have equal Votes, the Senate shall chuse from them by Ballot the Vice President. [5]

The Congress may determine the Time of chusing the Electors, and the Day on which they shall give their Votes; which Day shall be the same throughout the United States.

No Person except a natural born Citizen, or a Citizen of the United States, at the time of the Adoption of this Constitution, shall be eligible to the Office of President; neither shall any Person be eligible to that Office who shall not have attained to the Age of thirty five Years, and been fourteen Years a Resident within the United States.

The Case of the Removal of the President from Office, or of his Death, Resignation, or Inability to discharge the Powers and Duties of the said Office, the Same shall devolve on the Vice President, and the Congress may by Law provide for the Case of Removal, Death, Resignation or Inability, both of the President and Vice President, declaring what Officer shall then act as President, and such Officer shall act accordingly, until the Disability be removed, or a President shall be elected.

The President shall, at stated Times, receive for his Services, a Compensation which shall neither be encreased nor diminished during the Period for which he shall have been elected, and he shall not receive within that Period any other Emolument from the United States, or any of them.

Before he enter on the Execution of his Office, he shall take the following Oath or Affirmation: — "I do solemnly swear (or affirm) that I will faithfully execute the Office of

[5]See Amendment XII.

President of the United States, and will to the best of my Ability, preserve, protect, and defend the Constitution of the United States."

Section. 2. The President shall be Commander in Chief of the Army and Navy of the United States, and of the Militia of the several States, when called into the actual service of the United States; he may require the Opinion, in writing, of the principal Officer in each of the executive Departments, upon any Subject relating to the Duties of their respective Offices, and he shall have Power to grant Reprieves and Pardons for Offences against the United States, except in Case of Impeachment.

He shall have Power, by and with the Advice and Consent of the Senate, to make Treaties, provided two thirds of the Senators present concur; and he shall nominate, and by and with the Advice and Consent of the Senate, shall appoint Ambassadors, and other public Ministers and Consuls, Judges of the supreme Court, and all other Officers of the United States, whose Appointments are not herein otherwise provided for, and which shall be established by Law; but the Congress may by Law vest the Appointment of such inferior Officers, as they think proper, in the President alone, in the Courts of Law, or in the Heads of Departments.

The President shall have Power to fill up all Vacancies that may happen during the Recess of the Senate, by granting Commissions which shall expire at the End of their next Session.

Section. 3. He shall from time to time give to the Congress Information of the State of the Union, and recommend to their Consideration such Measures as he shall judge necessary and expedient; he may, on extraordinary Occasions, convene both Houses, or either of them, and in Case of Disagreement between them, with Respect to the Time of Adjournment, he may adjourn them to such Time as he shall think proper; he shall receive Ambassadors and other public Ministers, he shall take Care that the Laws be faithfully executed, and shall Commission all the Officers of the United States.

Section. 4. The President, Vice President, and all civil Officers of the United States, shall be removed from Office on Impeachment for, and Conviction of, Treason, Bribery, or other Crimes and Misdemeanors.

Article III

Section. 1. The judicial Power of the United States, shall be vested in one supreme Court and in such inferior Courts as the Congress may from time to time ordain and establish. The Judges, both of the supreme and inferior Courts, shall hold their Offices during good Behavior, and shall, at stated Times, receive for their Services, a Compensation, which shall not be diminished during their Continuance in Office.

Section. 2. The Judicial Power shall extend to all Cases, in Law and Equity, arising under this Constitution, the Laws of the United States, and Treaties made, or which shall be made, under their Authority;—to all Cases affecting Ambassadors, other public Ministers and Consuls;—to all Cases of admiralty and maritime Jurisdiction;—to Controversies to which the United States shall be a Party;—to Controversies between two or more States;—*between a State and Citizens of another State;*[6]—between Citizens of different States;—between Citizens of the same State claiming Lands under Grants of different states, *and between a State, or the Citizens thereof, and foreign States, Citizens, or Subjects.*[7]

In all cases affecting Ambassadors, other public Ministers and Consuls, and those in

[6]See Amendment XI.
[7]*Ibid.*

which a State shall be Party, the supreme Court shall have original Jurisdiction. In all the other Cases before mentioned, the supreme Court shall have appellate Jurisdiction, both as to Law and Fact, with such Exceptions, and under such Regulations as the Congress shall make.

The Trial of all Crimes, except in Cases of Impeachment, shall be by Jury; and such Trial shall be held in the State where the said Crimes shall have been committed; but when not committed within any State, the Trial shall be at such Place or Places as the Congress may by Law have directed.

Section. 3. Treason against the United States, shall consist only in levying War against them, or in adhering to their Enemies, giving them Aid and Comfort. No person shall be convicted of Treason unless on the Testimony of two Witnesses to the same overt Act, or on Confession in open Court.

The Congress shall have Power to declare the Punishment of Treason, but no Attainder of Treason shall work Corruption of Blood, or Forfeiture except during the Life of the Person attainted.

Article IV

Section. 1. Full Faith and Credit shall be given in each State to the public Acts, Records, and judicial Proceedings of every other State. And the Congress may by general Laws prescribe the Manner in which such Acts, Records, and Proceedings shall be proved, and the Effect thereof.

Section. 2. The Citizens of each State shall be entitled to all Privileges and Immunities of Citizens in the several States.

A Person charged in any State with Treason, Felony, or other Crime, who shall flee from Justice, and be found in another State, shall on Demand of the executive Authority of the State from which he fled, be delivered up, to be removed to the State having Jurisdiction of the Crime.

No Person held to Service or Labour in one State, under the Laws thereof, escaping into another, shall, in Consequence of any Law or Regulation therein, be discharged from such Service or Labour, but shall be delivered up on Claim of the Party to whom such Service or Labour may be due. [8]

Section. 3. New States may be admitted by the Congress into this Union; but no new State shall be formed or erected within the Jurisdiction of any other State; nor any State be formed by the Junction of two or more States, or Parts of States, without the Consent of the Legislatures of the States concerned as well as of the Congress.

The Congress shall have Power to dispose of and make all needful Rules and Regulations respecting the Territory or other Property belonging to the United States; and nothing in this Constitution shall be so construed as to Prejudice any claims of the United States, or of any particular State.

Section. 4. The United States shall guarantee to every State in this Union a Republican Form of Government, and shall protect each of them against Invasion; and on Application of the Legislature, or of the Executive (when the Legislature cannot be convened) against domestic Violence.

Article V

The Congress, whenever two thirds of both Houses shall deem it necessary, shall

[8]See Amendment XIII.

propose Amendments to this Constitution, or, on the Application of the Legislatures of two thirds of the several States, shall call a Convention for proposing Amendments, which, in either Case, shall be valid to all Intents and Purposes, as Part of this Constitution, when ratified by the Legislatures of three fourths of the several States, or by Conventions in three fourths thereof, as the one or the other Mode of Ratification may be proposed by the Congress; Provided that no Amendment which may be made prior to the Year One thousand eight hundred and eight shall in any Manner affect the first and fourth Clauses in the Ninth Section of the first Article; and that no State, without its Consent, shall be deprived of its equal Suffrage in the Senate.

Article VI

All Debts contracted and Engagements entered into, before the Adoption of this Constitution shall be as valid against the United States under this Constitution, as under the Confederation.

This Constitution, and the Laws of the United States which shall be made in Pursuance thereof; and all Treaties made, or which shall be made, under the Authority of the United States, shall be the supreme Law of the Land; and the Judges in every State shall be bound thereby, any Thing in the Constitution or Laws of any State to the Contrary notwithstanding.

The Senators and Representatives before mentioned, and the Members of the several State Legislatures, and all executive and judicial Officers, both of the United States and of the several States, shall be bound by Oath or Affirmation, to support this Constitution; but no religious Test shall ever be required as a Qualification to any Office or public Trust under the United States.

Article VII

The Ratification of the Conventions of nine States, shall be sufficient for the Establishment of this Constitution between the States so ratifying the Same.

Done in Convention by the Unanimous Consent of the States present the Seventeenth Day of September in the Year of our Lord one thousand seven hundred and eighty seven and of the Independence of the United States of America the twelfth. In witness whereof We have hereunto subscribed our Names.

*   *   *

Articles in addition to, and amendment of, the Constitution of the United States of America, proposed by Congress, and ratified by the several States, pursuant to the Fifth Article of the original Constitution.

Amendment I

[Ratification of the first ten amendments was completed December 15, 1791]

Congress shall make no law respecting an establishment of religion, or prohibiting the free exercise thereof; or abridging the freedom of speech, or of the press; or the right of the people peaceably to assemble, and to petition the Government for a redress of grievances.

Amendment II

A well regulated Militia, being necessary to the security of a free State, the right of the people to keep and bear Arms, shall not be infringed.

Amendment III

No Soldier shall, in time of peace be quartered in any house, without the consent of the Owner, nor in time of war, but in a manner to be prescribed by law.

Amendment IV

The right of the people to be secure in their persons, houses, papers, and effects, against unreasonable searches and seizures, shall not be violated, and no Warrants shall issue, but upon probable cause, supported by Oath or affirmation, and particularly describing the place to be searched, and the persons or things to be seized.

Amendment V

No person shall be held to answer for a capital, or otherwise infamous crime, unless on a presentment or indictment of a Grand Jury, except in cases arising in the land or naval forces, or in the Militia, when an actual service in time of War or public danger; nor shall any person be subject for the same offence to be twice put in jeopardy of life or limb; nor shall be compelled in any criminal case to be a witness against himself, nor be deprived of life, liberty, or property, without due process of law; nor shall private property be taken for public use, without just compensation.

Amendment VI

In all criminal prosecutions, the accused shall enjoy the right to a speedy and public trial, by an impartial jury of the State and district wherein the crime shall have been committed, which district shall have been previously ascertained by law, and to be informed of the nature and cause of the accusation; to be confronted with the witness against him; to have compulsory process for obtaining witness in his favor, and to have the Assistance of Counsel for his defence.

Amendment VII

In Suits at common law, where the value in controversy shall exceed twenty dollars, the right of trial by jury shall be preserved, and no fact tried by a jury, shall be otherwise re-examined in any Court of the United States, than according to the rules of the common law.

Amendment VIII

Excessive bail shall not be required, nor excessive fines imposed, nor cruel and unusual punishments inflicted.

Amendment IX

The enumeration in the Constitution, of certain rights, shall not be construed to deny or disparage others retained by the people.

Amendment X

The powers not delegated to the United States by the Constitution, nor prohibited by it to the States, are reserved to the States respectively, or to the people.

Amendment XI

[January 8, 1798]

The Judicial power of the United States shall not be construed to extend to any suit in law or equity, commenced or prosecuted against one of the United States by Citizens of another State, or by Citizens or Subjects of any Foreign State.

Amendment XII

[September 25, 1804]

The Electors shall meet in their respective states and vote by ballot for President and Vice President, one of whom, at least, shall not be an inhabitant of the same state with themselves; they shall name in their ballots the person voted for as President, and in distinct ballots the person voted for as Vice President, and they shall make distinct lists of all persons voted for as President, and of all persons voted for as Vice President, and of the number of votes for each, which lists they shall sign and certify, and transmit sealed to the seat of the government of the United States, directed to the President of the Senate: — The President of the Senate shall, in the presence of the Senate and House of Representatives, open all the certificates and the votes shall then be counted; — The person having the greatest number of votes for President, shall be the President, if such number be a majority of the whole number of Electors appointed; and if no person have such majority, then from the persons having the highest numbers not exceeding three on the list of those voted for as President, the House of Representatives shall choose immediately, by ballot, the President. But in choosing the President, the votes shall be taken by states, the representation from each state having one vote; a quorum for this purpose shall consist of a member or members from two thirds of the states, and a majority of all the states shall be necessary to a choice. And if the House of Representatives shall not choose a President whenever the right of choice shall devolve upon them, *before the fourth day of March next following,*[9] then the Vice President shall act as President as in the case of the death or other constitutional disability of the President.—The person having the greatest number of votes as Vice President, shall be the Vice President, if such number be a majority of the whole number of Electors appointed, and if no person have a majority, then from the two highest numbers on the list, the Senate shall choose the Vice President; a quorum for the purpose shall consist of two-thirds of the whole number of Senators, and a majority of the whole number shall be necessary to a choice. But no person constitutionally ineligible to the office of President shall be eligible to that of Vice President of the United States.

Amendment XIII

[December 18, 1865]

Section 1. Neither slavery nor involuntary servitude, except as a punishment for crime whereof the party shall have been duly convicted, shall exist within the United States, or any place subject to their jurisdiction.

Section 2. Congress shall have power to enforce this article by appropriate legislation.

Amendment XIV

[July 28, 1868]

Section 1. All persons born or naturalized in the United States, and subject to the jurisdiction thereof, are citizens of the United States and of the State wherein they reside. No State shall make or enforce any law which shall abridge the privileges or immunities of citizens of the United States; nor shall any state deprive any person of life, liberty, or

[9]See Amendment XX.

property, without due process of law; nor deny to any person within its jurisdiction the equal protection of the laws.

Section 2. Representatives shall be apportioned among the several States according to their respective numbers, counting the whole number of persons in each State, excluding Indians not taxed. But when the right to vote at any election for the choice of electors for President and Vice President of the United States, Representatives in Congress, the Executive and Judicial officers of a State, or the members of the Legislature thereof, is denied to any of the male inhabitants of such State, being twenty one years of age, and citizens of the United States, or in any way abridged, except for participation in rebellion, or other crime, the basis of representation therein shall be reduced in the proportion which the number of such male citizens shall bear to the whole number of male citizens twenty one years of age in such State.

Section 3. No person shall be a Senator or Representative in Congress, or elector of President and Vice President, or hold any office, civil or military, under the United States, or under any State who having previously taken an oath, as a member of Congress, or as an officer of the United States, or as a member of any State legislature, or as an executive or judicial officer of any State, to support the Constitution of the United States, shall have engaged in insurrection or rebellion against the same, or given aid or comfort to the enemies thereof. But Congress may by a vote of two thirds of each House remove such disability.

Section 4. The validity of the public debt of the United States authorized by law, including debts incurred for payment of pensions and bounties for services in suppressing insurrection or rebellion shall not be questioned. But neither the United States nor any State shall assume or pay any debt or obligation incurred in aid of insurrection or rebellion against the United States, or any claim for the loss or emancipation of any slave; but all such debts, obligations, and claims shall be held illegal and void.

Section 5. The Congress shall have power to enforce, by appropriate legislation, the provisions of this article.

Amendment XV

[*March 30, 1870*]

Section 1. The right of citizens of the United States to vote shall not be denied or abridged by the United States or by any State on account of race, color, or previous condition of servitude.

Section 2. The Congress shall have power to enforce this article by appropriate legislation.

Amendment XVI

[*February 25, 1913*]

The Congress shall have power to lay and collect taxes on incomes, from whatever source derived, without apportionment among the several States, and without regard to any census or enumeration.

Amendment XVII

[*May 31, 1913*]

The Senate of the United States shall be composed of two Senators from each State, elected by the people thereof, for six years; and each Senator shall have one vote. The electors in each State shall have the qualifications requisite for electors of the most numerous branch of the State legislatures.

When vacancies happen in the representation of any State in the Senate, the executive authority of such State shall issue writs of election to fill such vacancies: *Provided*, That the legislature of any State may empower the executive thereof to make temporary appointments until the people fill the vacancies by election as the legislature may direct.

This amendment shall not be so construed as to affect the election or term of any Senator chosen before it becomes valid as part of the Constitution.

Amendment XVIII

[*January 29, 1919*]

Section 1. *After one year from the ratification of this article the manufacture, sale, or transportation of intoxicating liquors within, the importation thereof into, or the exportation thereof from the United States and all territory subject to the jurisdiction thereof for beverage purposes is hereby prohibited.*

Section 2. *The Congress and the several States shall have concurrent power to enforce this article by appropriate legislation.*

Section 3. *This article shall be inoperative unless it shall have been ratified as an amendment to the Constitution by the legislatures of the several States, as provided in the Constitution, within seven years from the date of submission hereof to the States by the Congress.* [10]

Amendment XIX

[*August 26, 1920*]

The right of citizens of the United States to vote shall not be denied or abridged by the United States or by any State on account of sex.

Congress shall have power to enforce this article by appropriate legislation.

Amendment XX

[*February 6, 1933*]

Section 1. The terms of the President and Vice President shall end at noon on the 20th day of January, and the terms of Senators and Representatives at noon on the 3rd day of January, of the years in which such terms would have ended if this article had not been ratified; and the terms of their successors shall then begin.

Section 2. The Congress shall assemble at least once in every year, and such meeting shall begin at noon on the 3rd day of January unless they shall by law appoint a different day.

Section 3. If, at the time fixed for the beginning of the term of the President, the President elect shall have died, the Vice President elect shall become President. If a President shall not have been chosen before the time fixed for the beginning of his term, or if the President elect shall have failed to qualify, then the Vice President elect shall act as President until a President shall have qualified; and the Congress may by law provide for the case wherein neither a President elect nor a Vice President elect shall have qualified, declaring who shall then act as President, or the manner in which one who is to act shall be selected, and such person shall act accordingly until a President or Vice President shall have qualified.

Section 4. The Congress may by law provide for the case of the death of any of the persons from whom the House of Representatives may choose a President whenever the right of choice shall have devolved upon them, and for the case of the death of any of

[10]Repealed by Amendment XXI.

the persons from whom the Senate may choose a Vice President whenever the right of choice shall have devolved upon them.

Section 5. Sections 1 and 2 shall take effect on the 15th day of October following the ratification of this article.

Section 6. This article shall be inoperative unless it shall have been ratified as an amendment to the Constitution by the legislatures of three fourths of the several States within seven years from the date of its submission.

Amendment XXI

[December 5, 1933]

Section 1. The eighteenth article of amendment to the Constitution of the United States is hereby repealed.

Section 2. The transportation or importation into any State, Territory, or possession of the United States for delivery or use therein of intoxicating liquors, in violation of the laws thereof, is hereby prohibited.

Section 3. This article shall be inoperative unless it shall have been ratified as an amendment to the Constitution by conventions in the several States, as provided in the Constitution, within seven years from the date of the submission hereof to the States by the Congress.

Amendment XXII

[February 26, 1951]

Section 1. No person shall be elected to the office of the President more than twice, and no person who has held the office of President, or acted as President, for more than two years of a term to which some other person was elected President shall be elected to the office of President more than once. But this Article shall not apply to any person holding the office of President when this Article was proposed by the Congress, and shall not prevent any person who may be holding the office of President, or acting as President, during the term within which this Article becomes operative from holding the office of President or acting as President during the remainder of such term.

Section 2. This article shall be inoperative unless it shall have been ratified as an amendment to the Constitution by the legislatures of three fourths of the several States within seven years from the date of its submission to the States by the Congress.

Amendment XXIII

[March 29, 1961]

Section 1. The District constituting the seat of Government of the United States shall appoint in such manner as the Congress may direct:

A number of electors of President and Vice President equal to the whole number of Senators and Representatives in Congress to which the District would be entitled if it were a State, but in no event more than the least populous State; they shall be in addition to those appointed by the States, but they shall be considered, for the purposes of the election of President and Vice President, to be electors appointed by a State; and they shall meet in the District and perform such duties as provided by the twelfth article of amendment.

Section 2. The Congress shall have power to enforce this article by appropriate legislation.

Amendment XXIV

[January 23, 1964]

Section 1. The right of citizens of the United States to vote in any primary or other election for President or Vice President, for electors for President or Vice President, or for Senator or Representative in Congress, shall not be denied or abridged by the United States or any state by reason of failure to pay any poll tax or other tax.

Section 2. The Congress shall have power to enforce this article by appropriate legislation.

Amendment XXV
[February 10, 1967]

Section 1. In case of the removal of the President from office or of his death or resignation, the Vice President shall become President.

Section 2. Whenever there is a vacancy in the office of the Vice President, the President shall nominate a Vice President who shall take office upon confirmation by a majority vote of both Houses of Congress.

Section 3. Whenever the President transmits to the President pro tempore of the Senate and the Speaker of the House of Representatives his written declaration that he is unable to discharge the powers and duties of his office, and until he transmits to them a written declaration to the contrary, such powers and duties shall be discharged by the Vice President as Acting President.

Section 4. Whenever the Vice President and a majority of either the principal officers of the executive departments or of such other body as Congress may by law provide, transmit to the President pro tempore of the Senate and the Speaker of the House of Representatives their written declaration that the President is unable to discharge the powers and duties of his office, the Vice President shall immediately assume the powers and duties of the office as Acting President.

Thereafter, when the President transmits to the President pro tempore of the Senate and the Speaker of the House of Representatives his written declaration that no inability exists, he shall resume the powers and duties of his office unless the Vice President and a majority of either the principal officers of the executive department[s] or of such other body as Congress may by law provide, transmit within four days to the President pro tempore of the Senate and the Speaker of the House of Representatives their written declaration that the President is unable to discharge the powers and duties of his office. Thereupon Congress shall decide the issue, assembling within forty-eight hours for that purpose if not in session. If the Congress, within twenty-one days after receipt of the latter written declaration, or, if Congress is not in session, within twenty-one days after Congress is required to assemble, determines by two-thirds vote of both Houses that the President is unable to discharge the powers and duties of his office, the Vice President shall continue to discharge the same as Acting President; otherwise, the President shall resume the powers and duties of his office.

Amendment XXVI
[June 30, 1971]

Section 1. The right of citizens of the United States, who are 18 years of age or older, to vote shall not be denied or abridged by the United States or by any state on account of age.

Section 2. The Congress shall have power to enforce this article by appropriate legislation.

Amendment XXVII

Which prohibits discrimination based on sex by any law or action of any government—federal, state, or local—went to the states for ratification in March 1972.

INDEX